Born in China, NORMAN ENDICOTT was educated in Canada and England. He has degrees in History and English from the University of Toronto and the University of Oxford. He is presently Professor of English Literature in University College, the University of Toronto, and has written articles and reviews on seventeenth- and twentieth-century English literature in literary and learned journals.

THOMAS AND DOROTHY BROWNE, c. 1641
By courtesy of National Portrait Gallery, London.

10/27/81

THE PROSE OF
SIR THOMAS BROWNE

Religio Medici, Hydriotaphia,
The Garden of Cyrus,
A Letter to a Friend,
Christian Morals,
WITH SELECTIONS FROM
Pseudodoxia Epidemica, Miscellany Tracts,
AND FROM MS NOTEBOOKS AND LETTERS

EDITED, WITH AN INTRODUCTION,
NOTES, AND VARIANTS, BY
NORMAN ENDICOTT

The Norton Library
W · W · NORTON & COMPANY · INC ·
NEW YORK

W. W. Norton & Company, Inc. also publishes *The Norton
Anthology of English Literature,* edited by M. H. Abrams et al; *The
Norton Anthology of Poetry,* edited by Arthur M. Eastman et al; *World
Masterpieces,* edited by Maynard Mack et al; *The Norton Reader,* edited
by Arthur M. Eastman et al; *The Norton Facsimile of the First Folio of
Shakespeare,* prepared by Charlton Hinman; and the Norton Critical
Editions.

Library of Congress Cataloging in Publication Data

Browne, Sir Thomas, 1605–1682.
  The prose of Sir Thomas Browne.

  (The Norton library seventeenth-century series)
  Original ed. issued in series: The Anchor seventeenth-century
series, ACO-9.
  Bibliography: p.
  I. Endicott, Norman J., ed. II. Title.
[PR3327.A6 1972]   828'.4'09   72-4339
ISBN 0-393-00619-0

ACKNOWLEDGMENTS

I am indebted to previous editors of Browne and also to the librarians and the collections of the British Museum, the Bodleian Library, the National Portrait Gallery, London, the Norwich Public Library, St. John's College, Cambridge, Pembroke College, Oxford, The Osler Library (McGill University), Yale University, Lehigh University, Columbia University, and the University of Toronto for courtesies, books, and permission to use photographic reproductions.

CONTENTS

PREFATORY NOTE

For the Norton Library edition of *The Prose of Sir Thomas Browne* a number of errors and misprints have been corrected, and two recent books have been added to the Selected Bibliography.

INTRODUCTION

Religio Medici[1] was written about 1635 as an intimate and private expression of Browne's religious beliefs and temper, and was intended only for himself and one or two friends. At about the same time, according to his own statement, he wrote some other pieces "of affinitie thereto" which we should like to have, but which he never published and probably destroyed in consequence of what he seems to have felt was the notoriety of *Religio Medici*. Although not quite thirty, Browne could risk "calling him selfe a scholler." This unexhilarating phrase throws little light on the quality of a book that still interests its readers most strongly as the clouded revelation of an unusual and enigmatic personality. But it may remind us that the author was a young man of bookish and scholarly interests who, though now a doctor probably waiting for patients, had not long before gone through the still largely scholastic training of Oxford, followed by three years of further study in Europe.

According to Browne's own statement, which there is no reason to disbelieve, the piece was "communicated" to a friend, who obviously liked it enough to pass it on, so that "it became common to many." By the time it was printed, piratically, in 1642, seven years after its composition, it had been often transcribed. No autograph version is known, but there are eight surviving manuscript copies, one very incomplete, and none textually satisfactory. Browne himself spoke of successive corruption, as the text was copied and circulated, until a "most depraved" copy was used for the pirated printed texts. He may or must have known that his book was privately circulating, but was very emphatic that any reader could see that it had never been intended for the press. Again we should believe him. Once it had been printed in a bad text, and publicly

[1] Full titles of books or articles cited briefly will be found in the Selected Bibliography, and further comments on individual works in the Notes and Commentary.

commented on in print by Sir Kenelm Digby,[2] it was proper and
necessary for the author to provide a correct version. This was
printed in 1643 by the same printer who had brought out the pirated
text, with the engraved title changed to emphasize the authority
of the new text.

By 1642 the politico-religious storm of Puritanism and civil war
was about to break out. The address to the reader in the authorized
edition of 1643 has some strong sentences about "the name of his
Majesty defamed" and the "honour of Parliament depraved" by the
press. The first paragraph of the book itself shows strong dislike of
"ardour" and "contention" as an approach to religious differences,
special distaste for those who usurp the gates of Heaven and turn
the keys on others, and an almost unreal civility in such phrases as
"the honorable stile" or "happy stile" of being a Christian. Browne
was very clear, however, in stating that his Protestantism was the
result not of baptism, clime, parents and early education, but of
knowledge, thought, and choice.

The almost immediate translation into Latin made Browne's "private exercise" a European book—perhaps the first *literary* (as distinct from learned) English book to reach a wide continental audience since More's *Utopia*. Some of its European readers suspected
it of being covertly much more sceptical and questioning than it
was, but it was certainly a book relevant to Europe as well as to
England. It is English as well as Anglican, but there is nothing in-
sular in its subject matter, its tolerance, its whole intellectual character. And although Browne's earliest annotators were less than half
right in comparing him to Montaigne (a comparison Browne did
not like), it was inevitable that they should do so, in view of his
tentativeness, the constant personal references, and such statements
as the much-quoted "I could never divide my selfe from any man
upon the difference of an opinion, or be angry with his judgement
for not agreeing with mee in that, from which perhaps within a
few dayes I should dissent my selfe." Of the inwardness of each self
Browne had the strongest sense. As he wrote many years later in
A Letter to a Friend, "so intrinsecall is euery man vnto himself,
that some doubt may bee made whether any one would exchange
his being, or substantially become another man."

----

[2] *Observations Upon . . . Religio Medici,* by Sir Kenelm Digby (1643).

By and large *Religio Medici* is a digressive but not too disorderly exploration of Browne's religious experience and views on certain aspects of religion and thought. He is not a theologian, though he has read a respectable amount of theology. He is thoughtful, curious, and discursive, not closely analytical. He meditates on the great "staire or scale [i.e. ladder] of creatures" and the duty of a devout and learned admiration of nature as the art of God. As a complement to this, he emphasizes the nothingness of the world when seen in the perspective of eternity. Few of the various minor or secondary questions he considers—the cessation of oracles, the nature of angels, the soul of the world, witches, Fortune and Providence, the soul immediately after death, the age of the world, problems of creation as described in Genesis—are as esoteric or unusual as they have sometimes been thought by readers not very familiar with the reading and inquiries of Browne's time. But they are sometimes treated in a very personal way, and Browne himself sometimes encourages us to think of him as having "an extravagant and irregular head," as, later, he shows, perhaps, a certain vanity in the expression of his liking to be off the high road, and in his ability to draw interesting matter even from "bye and barren themes."

The central theme in the first and much longer part of *Religio* is the relation between Reason and Faith, and this is largely centered on problems of biblical interpretation. Browne is so little tormented by either doubts or dogma, he is so disarmingly (or, to the more severe, so shockingly) frank about not being frightened of Hell, and not believing that people can be "scared into Heaven," that it may require an effort to take him as seriously as the words require when he speaks of the internal "Battle of Lepanto"[3] between Reason and Faith. It would seem rather that mortal conflict can be avoided on almost all issues by the practice of "moderate and peacable discretion." But no one could doubt the sincerity and pervasive character of his belief, or suspect that his tolerance came from indifference. His best-known phrase on Man in the scale of creatures is that he is "that great and true *Amphibium*" able to live in the divided and distinguished worlds of sense and reason, and his agreement with Tertullian about believing certain things because they are impossible to human understanding is pushed further to a defense of belief

[3] By which in 1571 Christian Europe was saved from the Turkish power.

"not only above but contrary to Reason and against the Arguments of our proper senses." This needs to be read in the context of theological history, and shows at least an honest refusal to take the easy way so prevalent in his times, that is, resolution of all difficulties either by allegorical interpretation, or the explanation that any difficult passages in Scripture are expressed in a way accommodated to human capacities. Not only is Browne no theologian, however; he has obviously a temperamental preference for "Platonick" or "allegorical description" (he first wrote "rhetorical definition") as against Aristotelian-scholastic definition. But this preference is supported by a conviction (as in *Religio Medici* 1.10) that some definitions do not define, and that therefore phrases like "the soul is man's angel" or "light is the shadow of God" satisfy the imagination ("humour the fancy") in a symbolic image or representation of something that must remain a mystery.

In letters written shortly after reading *Religio Medici,* in Latin, in 1644 or 1645, Gui Patin, the French scholar and doctor, described the book as full of strange and ravishing thoughts and as the kind of writing in which the subtlety of the human spirit reveals itself (*Lettres,* 1846, I, 340 and 354). A century later Dr. Johnson noted its quick succession of images, subtlety of disquisition, and strength of language. In almost the same words with which—in an historically influential pronouncement—Dr. Johnson condemned Donne as a poet, though not as a wit, he more than excused Browne for his "mixture of heterogeneous words brought together from distant regions" by saying that these *verba ardentia,* "forcible expressions," are often the happy or pleasing achievement of one who would not have reached them had he been much afraid of "the shame of falling" (*Christian Morals,* 1756, viii and liv).

Religio Medici is in fact a book of remarkable verbal texture, in which the complexity of overtones, and the correspondences between passages in different parts of the book, are again and again such that, though Browne is often memorable enough in phrase or sentence, it is only from the whole effect of the circling movement of his thought, as we follow and participate in the changes of tone, in the rhetorical bravado, in the turns of ironic humor, in the self-dramatization, that we appreciate the kind of book it is. And the paradoxes, usually, make up in subtlety for what they lack in boldness. One thing we must remember, however—indeed it is a part of our exploratory pleasure in reading the book—and that is that as a self-portrait *Religio* hides as well as reveals. It presents its author in a way that allows for direct expressions of temperament and opinion, and also for some stylization, as in passages about his "melancholy and contemplative" character. His praise of friendship, in its time not as unusual in intensity of style as it may now appear, seems related at once to remarks about his "solitary and retired imagination" and to later evidence of his capacity for friendship.

In her book on Browne Mrs. Bennett opens her discussion of *Pseudodoxia Epidemica* (commonly *Vulgar Errors*, from the running title) with the comment that we no longer read it "to find out the facts about phenomena, but to enjoy the company of the author and 'the climate of opinion' in which he wrote." But whereas up to relatively recent times this statement might have led into easy illustrations of the "quaintness" of some of the material in *Pseudodoxia* (the antipathy of toads and spiders, the basilisk, the jointlessness of elephants, etc.) and a general assumption that Browne's approach was hardly worth considering seriously in its basic positions or method, Mrs. Bennett, like Professor Huntley and other recent writers, describes and attempts to evaluate his approaches, and the way in which he used his knowledge and intelligence to dispel ignorance. It would be very enlightening to most readers of *Pseudodoxia* to look at the kind of stuff found in some of the books on errors to which Browne himself rather non-committally refers.

For the first edition (1646) of his book Browne chose an epigraph from the great literary scholar, Julius Caesar Scaliger: a statement that to collect from books what writers have produced, is laborious and most dangerous, and that true knowledge of things must be got from things themselves. To the second edition, published four years later, he added another quotation, again not from a scientist but this time from a church father (Tertullian) modestly justifying what he was attempting on the ground that "the first step to knowledge is to know what is false." The knowledge of things may have to be learned from things themselves, but since Browne was himself more scholar than experimentalist, since *Pseudodoxia* is in any event concerned with published accumulations of error passed on from one writer to another for centuries (and is itself in large part an accumulation from notebooks) the text contains references to a very great number of major and minor classical and modern writers of every kind. Browne owned most of the books to which he referred. They cannot be described or annotated for a modern reader of *Pseudodoxia,* yet to appreciate the degree or way in which Browne was old-fashioned or gullible or "superstitious," even the literary reader—perhaps especially the literary reader—should ideally have some notion of the parallels in other respectable sixteenth- and seventeenth-century scientists and learned men.

About twenty years ago Lord Keynes, having examined a mass of Isaac Newton's MSS (much concerned with alchemy and theology) referred to Newton as at times "the last of the magicians" (Royal Society of London, *Newton Tercentenary Celebrations, 15–19 July, 1946,* Macmillan, New York, and Cambridge University Press, 1947, p. 28). In the last volume of his monumental *History of Magic and Experimental Science* (1958, VIII, 589 ff.), Professor Lynn Thorndike takes up the comment with warm agreement, having already made the same kind of point on various occasions, as for instance in the statement that for all his pioneering greatness Robert Boyle "shared most of the follies of 17th century medicine" and hoped for experimental proof of witchcraft and transmutation (VIII, 195). Similarly (VI, 292) Fallopio was a first-rate anatomist, yet recommended the wearing of an umbilicus in a silver ring as an amulet against colic. There is not much to be said for any general comparison of Browne and Bacon,[4] but however impressive Bacon's clarity and power of generalization, it is certainly unhistorical to know only Bacon's pronouncements without looking at his book of "experiments," *Sylva Sylvarum,* where there is so little real experiment, and so large an amount of traditional credulity. When William Gilbert (whom Browne rightly praises for his important work on magnetism) leaves off describing scientific magnetic experiments and begins to "philosophize freely," he quotes Hermes Trismegistus and says the heavenly bodies have souls. John Napier, "inventor of logarithms" (1614) also wrote a work on Revelations which the all-out astrologer William Lilly could praise extravagantly. With all his emphasis on "things themselves" and induction, Bacon was ignorant of or opposed to many of the experiments of his time, merely arro-

---

[4] E. S. Merton has an interesting comparison of Browne's types of error and Bacon's "idols," in "Sir Thomas Browne's Scientific Quest."

gant in his references to Hippocrates and Galen (whom he should have praised),[5] and cold to fruitful hypothesis. His direct influence in the seventeenth century has been much exaggerated, though his social eminence gave his general approach great prestige.

As an experimental scientist Browne is not of importance, but the first book of *Pseudodoxia* (almost all included in this volume) demonstrates the sobriety and intelligence with which he approached his "three inducements of belief"—authority, reason or probable truth, experiment—even if it is also true that Satan is unexpectedly busy in the background, and that Browne is sometimes too anxious to reconcile opposite opinions, as well as put them all down. Chapters 5–9 provide good evidence that he had anything but undiscriminating respect for authorities; the additions and variants included in this text (and one or two letters) illustrate clearly, I hope, the way in which Browne kept up with the publications in the fields in which he was interested. Although now primarily read as part of English literature, he himself seems to have read very little of the literature of his own time. But English and European books of medicine, science (especially astronomy and biology), and general learning he read as they appeared. He had most of the older standard texts; the auction *Sale Catalogue* of his library (sold in 1711 with additions made by his son Edward), shows how many of the important new books in science and learning he bought. In the sixteen-fifties he was impressed by Jan Hevelius' very important book on the geography of the moon, and even more impressed by Harvey's *On the Generation of Animals*—Harvey's earlier discovery of the circulation of the blood, Browne had called more important than the discovery of America. In the sixteen-sixties he revised sections of *Pseudodoxia* as the result of reading the microscopical observations of Henry Power (the first English microscopist) and Hooke. In the sixteen-seventies we find him reading the latest works in medicine and the extremely significant microscopical discoveries of Leeuwenhoek, as reported by the Royal Society, and writing to his son Edward to tell him to read them.

Passages from other books of *Pseudodoxia* than the first have been chosen for their interest and their relevance to Browne's habits of

5 "But when we come to Bacon's own medicine, I feel sure that the reader will prefer that of Galen and Hippocrates" (Thorndike, VII. 65).

mind, reading, and actual experiments. Whether Adam had a navel
(having been created by God) and a few other similar items have
been included, but the quaintness or oddity of some of the more
vulgar or more ancient errors has not weighed heavily in the choice
of selections. Perhaps not heavily enough, since one of the pleasures
of modern exploration of seventeenth-century learning comes from
a happy awareness of our effortless superiority in simply being modern. It is also true that much unpatronizing pleasure may be got
from some of the items of folklore, such as lights burning blue in
the presence of spirits (with which we may be familiar from a
famous scene in *Richard III*), breaking eggshells to keep the witches
from using them (a habit still knowingly practiced even today),
and so on. When, in 1650, Browne himself added some examples of
this kind of folklore to his book (in 5.22), he also added, as a final
comment on the chapter, two lines from the *Satires* of Persius:

> *Disce, sed ira cadat naso rugosaque sanna,*
> *Dum veteres avias tibi de pulmone revello.*

> Listen, but first your brows from anger clear,
> And bid your nose dismiss that rising sneer.
> Listen, while I the genuine truth impart,
> And root those old wives' fables from your heart.
>   (GIFFORD)

But a selection must be a selection.

Up to a point, though not up to the real point of its long-
appreciated eloquence and beauty in the final chapters, we owe
Hydriotaphia to erudite ignorance, that is, to Browne's mistaken
idea that the urns he was discussing were Roman, whereas they
were in fact Saxon. In the first sentence of the second chapter
Browne says he will not "disparage" the reader's learning by re-
peating accounts of "Solemnities, Ceremonies, Rites of Cremation
or enterrment so solemnly delivered by Authours." "Disparage" may
seem a little unreal (to say nothing of the unkind suggestion that
Browne was disguising his own borrowings) and a good deal of
attention has been paid by editors to some of the borrowings, especially those from J. Kirchmann's *De Funeribus Romanorum*,
1625. The general subject had attracted a good deal of scholarly

attention.[6] No doubt it was a great convenience for Browne, leading a busy doctor's life, to have much of his historical material gathered together, especially as Kirchmann has indices of places, rites, monuments, memorable speeches, epitaphs, authors cited, etc. A much earlier book, Claude Guichard's *Funerailles et diverses manières d'ensevelir des Rommains, Grecs et autres nations* . . . (1581), not, as far as I know, referred to by editors or critics of Browne, extends to over five hundred quarto pages, plus tables, etc. with so much literary and historical quotation and reference that the list of authors cited takes three triple-columned pages. Is it being altogether too partial to say that Browne knew his classical writers and antiquities as well as the others who quote so plentifully the same passages from major and minor writers? Writing of Conrad Gesner's *History of Animals*, Professor Thorndike makes the simple but fundamental observation that even it is primarily concerned with names and words and with information and allusions for the use and enjoyment of the scholar and literary reader rather than with the collection and presentation of facts for scientific purposes. This is also true, I think, of *Hydriotaphia* (as it is not of *Pseudodoxia*) and Browne emphasizes the fact when he speaks of it and its companion discourse as intended for friends and not to be disapproved for excursions and "collateral truths though at some distance from their principals."

The basic theme in the final chapters of *Hydriotaphia*, and also in the other books on pagan burials, is the contrast between the pious hopelessness (at best) of pagan rites, and Christian faith. But it may be noted that whereas the fourth chapter of *Hydriotaphia* opens with "Christians have handsomely glossed the deformity of death . . ." we see the original reflection in one of Browne's notebooks (MS Sloane 1862, folio 48^v) in "Men have somewhat glosed the deformity of death . . .". Browne had the kind of mind and curiosity that made him interested in the facts themselves and also in the "ground of reason" (in Plutarch's phrase) behind rites and ceremonies. He had also the humanity and the historical and poetic imagination to relive those moments "When the Funerall Pyre was out and the last Valediction over," those "sober obsequies in which

---

[6] Browne refers also to F. Perucci's *Pompe Funebri*, 1639, which was in part derived from T. Porcacchi's *Funerali Antichi di diversi Popoli e Nationi*, 1574.

few could be so mean as not to provide wood, pitch, a mourner, and an Urne." *Hydriotaphia* opens (in the dedicatory letter) with poignant sentences about friendship and death and closes with eloquent Christian reflections about returning to God. It brings into our consciousness not merely the drums and tramplings of three conquests in England, but the vaster expanses of time imaged in "the iniquity of oblivion blindely scattereth her poppy." And beyond time is eternity. Being born into and out of time is symbolized in the unifying metaphor of the urn and the womb, a metaphor which, Browne himself suggests, is particularly appropriate to one whose profession is medicine.

If in *Hydriotaphia* the underlying theme is the contrast between Pagan and Christian attitudes to death, in *The Garden of Cyrus* Browne is concerned with correspondences: intricate order in the world of nature. In *Hydriotaphia* we have "ceremonies of bravery"; in *The Garden of Cyrus* "botanical bravery." But there is no opposition between ashes and spirits, between this world and the next. God is the ordainer of order and mystical mathematics of the City of Heaven as of mathematical arrangements of vegetable forms. E. S. Merton ("The Botany of Sir Thomas Browne") remarks that *The Garden of Cyrus* is, among other things, the notebook of a careful and imaginative botanist, one who combines a scientist's love for plants with an artist's appreciation of the higher geometry of nature, and again, "a generation later he would have had the first modern answers to many of the questions which were baffling him." (One might instance a notebook entry, "noe man hath yet determined the true use of a flower.") For the "other things" (certainly in places for a modern reader well into the "inexcusable Pythagorisme" or number mysticism rhetorically warned against) Browne was in part inspired by Plato's *Timaeus,* and in the first chapters guided by two sixteenth-century books on gardens and agriculture.[7] In the third chapter ("natural" considerations) there is a great deal of personal observation, largely in digressions. In the two final ("mystical") chapters Browne supported his queries by a range of usual and unusual learning needing very learned annotation to be

---

[7] *Hortorum Libri Triginta* by Bênoit Court (B. Curtius) 1560, and *Villae Libri XII* by G. B. della Porta, 1592. On Browne's use of them see J. S. Finch, "Sir Thomas Browne and the Quincunx," and the elaborate notes in Martin's edition of Browne.

understood. A good deal of this part of *The Garden of Cyrus* seems to be, seriously enough, a kind of human shadow-structure of the real mystical mathematics of God in nature. But parts of the fifth chapter may give the impression of being written in a slightly amused (not bemused) condition of learned showing-off to friends. It need not be assumed, I think, that the "arithmetical divinity" of the "Cabalistic Doctors" is taken very seriously.

Toward the end of the *Religio* Browne called his life "a miracle of thirty years." This was because it had been providentially guided, not because he had done such wonderful things or had apocalyptic visions. He was not, in any precise contemporary sense, a mystic, and rather emphatically exempted himself as a personal witness in the phrase "if any" with which he introduced the comments on ecstatic experiences in the final sentences of *Christian Morals*, a repetition, slightly revised, from *Hydriotaphia*. "If any," he wrote, "have been so happy as personally to understand Christian Annihilation, Extasy, Exolution, Transformation, The Kiss of the Spouse, and Ingression into the Divine Shadow, according to Mystical Theology, they have already had an handsome Anticipation of Heaven."

His own ordinary approach to God was through nature as the art of God, like others of his time sucking divinity, as well as medicine, from the flowers. As an ironic observer of humanity he was not unaware of how fearfully as well as wonderfully we are made—"there is all *Africa* and her prodigies in us," prodigies meaning also monstrosities. His observation of nature was not troubled by problems of monsters, depravity, redness of tooth and claw. Toads and savage bears "express the actions of their inward forms." Browne did not so much see the world in a grain of sand (which we may all contemplate if we have the power of contemplation) as see and transform things which it takes a peculiar kind of observing curiosity to see at all. In *The Garden of Cyrus* he describes the teazle, but not as most of us have seen its ragged head:

> The *Arbustetum* or Thicket on the head of the Teasel may be observed in this order: And he that considereth that fabrick so regularly palisadoed, and stemm'd with flowers of the royall colour; in the house of the solitary maggot,* may finde the Seraglio of *Solomon*.

* There being a single Maggot found in almost every head (Browne).

This sentence, like the unmistakably identifiable phrase of a particular composer, like certain lines of poetry which, we feel, could have only one source, is recognizable as quintessential Browne. Its origin is close botanical observation of the insignificant and a great interest in facts; its coloring is biblical, and for this kind of natural philosophy Solomon is the proper presiding genius; in its (almost absurd) ironic overtones and its whole witty surprise it is a part of seventeenth-century metaphysical poetry.

CHRONOLOGY OF BROWNE'S LIFE AND WORKS

1605   Born October 19 (?) in Cheapside, London, the son of a successful mercer who had come to London from Cheshire, where his family were of the minor gentry.

1613   Death of his father, leaving a considerable estate, but with substantial and doubtful debts owing to him.

1614   Within about seven months, his mother married a robustious Low Countries captain and courtier, Sir Thomas Dutton. Quarrels about estate and guardianship. Edward Browne, Thomas Browne's uncle, a grocer, made sole executor and guardian of the children's part of the estate. (Browne had three sisters, one born after his father's death.) Further disputes about estate in years following.

1616–1623   At Winchester College, a great public school. Just failed to get scholarship to New College, Oxford.

1623–1629   Pembroke College, Oxford (still Broadgates Hall when Browne entered it, as a commoner, in 1623); B.A., June 1626, M.A., June 1629. The Master of Pembroke, Dr. Thomas Clayton, Regius Professor of Physic (and previously Professor of Music, Gresham College, 1607–1611) "the one distinguished teacher of medicine at Oxford" (J. S. Finch) at that time. While in his first year Browne chosen to make the undergraduate Latin oration when Broadgates Hall became Pembroke College in honor of the Earl of Pembroke. His first published piece was a Latin poem (in *Camdeni Insignia,* 1624) in honor of William Camden, scholar and antiquarian, of whom Ben Jonson wrote "to whom I owe / All that I am in arts, all that I know."

1629   Visited a good part of Ireland with his stepfather, Sir Thomas Dutton, who had been made Scoutmaster General of the Army in Ireland in 1610 (then and for many years practically a sinecure) but who in 1627 took up Irish lands granted years before, built a house in Longford, and was in command of an important chain of forts.

1629–1633   In November 1629 received remaining share of father's estate and pursued medical studies at the most highly regarded medical centers in Europe, that is, at Montpellier, Padua, and Leiden. Probably spent most time at Montpellier, received M.D. at Leiden, December, 1633.

1634 Stepfather died (of a blow in a quarrel); mother remained in Ireland.

1634–1635 Before he was thirty had written *Religio Medici* and other pieces "of affinitie thereto," not extant. *Religio Medici* was written, he said, in such a place that from first setting pen to paper he was without "any good booke" for reference or stimulus.

1634–1637 Practiced medicine in Oxfordshire (?) and Yorkshire.

1637 Incorporated M.D. Oxford; 1637 or 1638 moved to Norwich (a city with a population of only fifteen to twenty thousand people, but after London probably the largest city[1] in England in the seventeenth century) to establish practice; lived there until death, with a wide English (and to some extent European) reputation as scholar and doctor.

1641 Married Dorothy Mileham, of Norfolk family of minor gentry; they had twelve children of whom four died in infancy and one, Edward, a physician, practiced in London, and became President of the College of Physicians and Fellow of the Royal Society.

1642 *Religio Medici* published in two pirated editions. Authorized text published in following year; republished again and again in English and also in Latin (several editions), Dutch, and French.

1646 *Pseudodoxia Epidemica* (*Vulgar Errors*) published; republished, with revisions, many times in the 17th century; 17th or 18th century translations into Dutch, French, Italian.

1642–1658 Took no active part in Civil War or politics, but outspokenly Royalist in sympathies. Norwich was Parliamentarian and Puritan.

1658 *Hydriotaphia* (*Urne Buriall*) and *The Garden of Cyrus* published.

1671 Knighted by Charles II on a visit to Norwich (as a very distinguished citizen, the mayor having declined the honor.)

1682 Died on October 19.

1683 *Certain Miscellany Tracts* published (most copies dated 1684); translated into Dutch in 1688.

---

[1] From information and statistics provided by the present Librarian of the Norwich Public Libraries, Mr. Philip Hepworth. Norwich, Bristol, and York were about the same size.

1686   *Collected Works* published; translated into Dutch in 1688.
1690   *A Letter to a Friend* published.
1712   *Posthumous Works* published with a brief Life and Minutes for a life by the Rev. John Whitefoot of Norwich, a friend of many years.
1716   *Christian Morals* published; in 1756 republished with a Life and critical introduction by Dr. Johnson.

EXPLANATION OF THE NOTES

There are three sets of notes for the text in this edition:

(a) Browne's original notes. These are given in full in *Religio Medici, Pseudodoxia, Christian Morals,* and the material from MS. They are indicated in the text by asterisks, for example *, and are to be found on the bottom of the page on which the relevant text appears;

(b) variants, or alternate manuscript versions, designated in the right-hand margin opposite the line of text where they occur, by a dagger, for example †, and are to be found at the back of the book, under chapter and section headings and in the section *Textual Notes;*

(c) explanatory notes, or more extended commentary, including some selections or excerpts from Browne's original notes, are designated in the right-hand margin by a superscript number opposite the line of text to which they refer, for example 1, and are to be found in the back of the book in the section *Notes and Commentary;*

(d) there is also a Glossary of words and persons to be found at the back of the book.

RELIGIO MEDICI

Religio, Medici.

Printed for Andrew Crooke. 1642. Will: Marshall Sqs:

In the authorized edition of 1643, printed by the
same printer, Andrew Crooke, the title is removed
from the engraving and incorporated into a description of the book as "A true and full coppy of
that which was most unperfectly and Surreptitiously printed before under the name of Religio
Medici."

TO THE READER†

Certainly that man were greedy of life, who should desire [1]
to live when all the world were at an end; and he must needs
be very impatient, who would repine at death in the societie
of all things that suffer under it. Had not almost every man
suffered by the presse; or were not the tyranny thereof become universall; I had not wanted reason for complaint: but
in times wherein I have lived to behold the highest perversion
of that excellent invention; the name of his Majesty defamed,
the honour of Parliament depraved, the writings of both de-
pravedly, anticipatively, counterfeitly imprinted; complaints
may seeme ridiculous in private persons, and men of my condition may be as incapable of affronts, as hopelesse of their [2]
reparations. And truly had not the duty I owe unto the im-
portunitie of friends, and the allegeance I must ever acknowledge unto truth prevayled with me; the inactivitie of my
disposition might have made these sufferings continuall, and
time that brings other things to light, should have satisfied me
in the remedy of its oblivion. But because things evidently
false are not onely printed, but many things of truth most
falsly set forth; in this latter I could not but thinke my selfe
engaged: for though we have no power to redresse the former, yet in the other the reparation being within our selves,
I have at present represented unto the world a full and intended copy of that Peece which was most imperfectly and
surreptitiously published before.

This I confesse about seven yeares past, with some others
of affinitie thereto, for my private exercise and satisfaction, I
had at leisurable houres composed; which being communicated unto one, it became common unto many, and was by
transcription successively corrupted untill it arrived in a most
depraved copy at the presse. He that shall peruse that worke,
and shall take notice of sundry particularities and personall

expressions therein, will easily discerne the intention was not
publik: and being a private exercise directed to my selfe,   3
what is delivered therein was rather a memoriall unto me
then an example or rule unto any other: and therefore if there
bee any singularitie therein correspondent unto the private
conceptions of any man, it doth not advantage them; or if dissentaneous thereunto, it no way overthrowes them. It was
penned in such a place and with such disadvantage, that (I   4
protest) from the first setting of pen unto paper, I had not the
assistance of any good booke, whereby to promote my invention or relieve my memory; and therefore there might be
many reall lapses therein, which others might take notice of,
and more that I suspected my selfe. It was set downe many
yeares past, and was the sense of my conceptions at that time,
not an immutable law unto my advancing judgement at all
times, and therefore there might be many things therein
plausible unto my passed apprehension, which are not agreeable unto my present selfe. There are many things delivered
Rhetorically, many expressions therein meerely Tropicall, and
as they best illustrate my intention; and therefore also there
are many things to be taken in a soft and flexible sense, and
not to be called unto the rigid test of reason. Lastly all that is
contained therein is in submission unto maturer discernments,
and as I have declared shall no further father them then the
best and learned judgements shall authorize them; under favour of which considerations I have made its secrecie publike and committed the truth thereof to every ingenuous
Reader.

                                              Thomas Browne.

RELIGIO MEDICI

The First Part

SECT. 1. For my Religion, though there be severall circumstances that might perswade the world I have none at all, as the generall scandall of my profession, the naturall course   5,6 of my studies, the indifferency of my behaviour, and discourse in matters of Religion, neither violently defending one, nor with that common ardour and contention opposing   † another; yet in despight hereof I dare, without usurpation, assume the honorable stile of a Christian: not that I meerely owe this title to the Font, my education, or Clime wherein I was borne, as being bred up either to confirme those principles my Parents instilled into my unwary understanding; or by a generall consent proceed in the Religion of my Countrey: But having, in my riper yeares, and confirmed judgement, seene and examined all, I finde my selfe obliged by the principles of Grace, and the law of mine owne reason, to embrace no other name but this; neither doth herein my zeale so farre make me forget the generall charitie I owe unto humanity, as rather to hate then pity Turkes, Infidels, and (what is worse) Jewes, rather contenting my selfe to enjoy that happy stile, then maligning those who refuse so glorious a title.

SECT. 2. But because the name of a Christian is become too generall to expresse our faith, there being a Geography of Religions as well as Lands, and every Clime distinguished not onely by their lawes and limits, but circumscribed by their doctrines and rules of Faith; To be particular, I am of that reformed new-cast Religion, wherein I mislike nothing but the name; of the same beliefe our Saviour taught, the   7 Apostles disseminated, the Fathers authorised, and the Mar-

tyrs confirmed; but by the sinister ends of Princes, the ambition and avarice of Prelates, and the fatall corruption of   †,8
times, so decaied, impaired, and fallen from its native
beauty, that it required the carefull and charitable hand of
these times to restore it to its primitive integrity: Now the
accidentall occasion whereon, the slender meanes whereby,
the low and abject condition of the person by whom so good   9
a worke was set on foot, which in our adversaries begets   †
contempt and scorn, fills me with wonder, and is the very
same objection the insolent Pagans first cast at Christ and his
Disciples.

SECT. 3. Yet have I not so shaken hands with those desperate   10,11
Resolutions, who had rather venture at large their decaied
bottome, then bring her in to be new trim'd in the dock; who
had rather promiscuously retaine all, then abridge any, and
obstinately be what they are, then what they have beene, as
to stand in diameter and swords point with them: we have
reformed from them, not against them; for omitting those
improperations and termes of scurrility betwixt us, which
onely difference our affections, and not our cause, there is
between us one common name and appellation, one faith,
and necessary body of principles common to us both; and
therefore I am not scrupulous to converse and live with
them, to enter their Churches in defect of ours, and either
pray with them, or for them: I could never perceive any rationall consequence from those many texts which prohibite
the children of Israel to pollute themselves with the Temples
of the Heathens; we being all Christians, and not divided
by such detested impieties as might prophane our prayers,
or the place wherein we make them; or that a resolved conscience may not adore her Maker any where, especially in
places devoted to his service; where if their devotions offend
him, mine may please him, if theirs prophane it, mine may
hallow it; Holy water and Crucifix (dangerous to the common people) deceive not my judgement, nor abuse my devotion at all: I am, I confesse, naturally inclined to that,
which misguided zeale termes superstition; my common conversation I do acknowledge austere, my behaviour full of

rigour, sometimes not without morosity; yet at my devotion
I love to use the civility of my knee, my hat, and hand, with
all those outward and sensible motions, which may expresse,
or promote my invisible devotion. I should violate my owne
arme rather then a Church, nor willingly deface the memory   †
of Saint or Martyr. At the sight of a Crosse or Crucifix I can
dispence with my hat, but scarce with the thought and memory of my Saviour; I cannot laugh at but rather pity the fruit-   †
lesse journeys of Pilgrims, or contemne the miserable
condition of Friers; for though misplaced in circumstance,
there is something in it of devotion: I could never heare the
*Ave Marie Bell without an elevation, or thinke it a suffi-
cient warrant, because they erred in one circumstance, for me
to erre in all, that is in silence and dumbe contempt; whilst
therefore they directed their devotions to her, I offered mine
to God, and rectified the errours of their prayers by rightly
ordering mine owne. At a solemne Procession I have wept   12
abundantly, while my consorts, blinde with opposition and
prejudice, have fallen into an accesse of scorne and laughter: †
There are questionlesse both in Greek, Roman, and African
Churches, solemnities, and ceremonies, whereof the wiser
zeales doe make a Christian use, and stand condemned by
us; not as evill in themselves, but as allurements and baits of
superstition to those vulgar heads that looke asquint on the
face of truth, and those unstable judgements that cannot
consist in the narrow point and centre of vertue without a
reele or stagger to the circumference.

SECT. 4. As there were many Reformers, so likewise many
reformations; every Countrey proceeding in a particular way
and Method, according as their nationall interest together
with their constitution and clime inclined them, some angrily
and with extremitie, others calmely, and with mediocrity,
not rending, but easily dividing the community, and leaving
an honest possibility of a reconciliation, which though peaceable Spirits doe desire, and may conceive that revolution of

----

* A Church Bell that tolls every day at 6 and 12 of the Clocke, at the hearing
whereof every one in what place soever either of house or street betakes him to
his prayer, which is commonly directed to the *Virgin.*

time, and the mercies of God may effect; yet that judgement
that shall consider the present antipathies between the two
extreames, their contrarieties in condition, affection and
opinion, may with the same hopes expect an union in the
poles of Heaven.

SECT. 5. But to difference my self neerer, and draw into a
lesser circle: There is no Church whose every part so squares
unto my conscience, whose articles, constitutions, and customes seeme so consonant unto reason, and as it were framed
to my particular devotion, as this whereof I hold my beliefe,
the Church of *England,* to whose faith I am a sworne subject, and therefore in a double obligation subscribe unto her
Articles, and endeavour to observe her Constitutions; [no
man shall reach my faith unto another Article, or command   †,13
my obedience to a Canon more]: whatsoever is beyond,
as points indifferent, I observe according to the rules of
my private reason, or the humor and fashion of my devotion, neither believing this, because *Luther* affirmed it, nor   †
disapproving that, because *Calvin* hath disavouched it. I
condemne not all things in the Councell of *Trent,* nor ap-   14
prove all in the Synod of *Dort.* In briefe, where the Scripture   15
is silent, the Church is my Text; where that speakes, 'tis but
my Comment; where there is a joynt silence of both, I borrow
not the rules of my Religion from *Rome* or *Geneva,* but the
dictates of my owne reason. It is an unjust scandall of our
adversaries, and a grosse error in our selves, to compute the
Nativity of our Religion from *Henry* the eight, who though
he rejected the Pope, refus'd not the faith of *Rome,* and effected no more then what his owne Predecessors desired and
assayed in ages past, and was conceived the State of *Venice*   16
would have attempted in our dayes. It is as uncharitable a
point in us to fall upon those popular scurrilities and opprobrious scoffes of the Bishop of *Rome,* to whom as a tem-   †
porall Prince, we owe the duty of good language: I confesse
there is cause of passion betweene us; by his sentence I stand
excommunicated, Heretick is the best language he affords
me; yet can no eare witnesse I ever returned to him the
name of Antichrist, Man of Sin, or whore of *Babylon;* It is the

method of charity to suffer without reaction; those usuall
Satyrs, and invectives of the Pulpit may perchance produce
a good effect on the vulgar, whose eares are opener to
Rhetorick then Logick, yet doe they in no wise confirme the
faith of wiser beleevers, who know that a good cause needs
not to be patron'd by a passion, but can sustaine it selfe upon
a temperate dispute.

SECT. 6. I could never divide my selfe from any man upon the
difference of an opinion, or be angry with his judgement for
not agreeing with mee in that, from which perhaps within a
few dayes I should dissent my selfe: I have no Genius to disputes in Religion, and have often thought it wisedome to
decline them, especially upon a disadvantage, or when the
cause of truth might suffer in the weakenesse of my patron-
age: where we desire to be informed, 'tis good to contest
with men above our selves; but to confirme and establish
our opinions, 'tis best to argue with judgements below our
own, that the frequent spoyles and victories over their reasons may settle in our selves an esteeme, and confirmed opinion of our owne. Every man is not a proper Champion for
Truth, nor fit to take up the Gantlet in the cause of Veritie:
Many from the ignorance of these Maximes, and an inconsiderate zeale unto Truth, have too rashly charged the
troopes of error, and remaine as Trophees unto the enemies
of Truth: A man may be in as just possession of Truth as of a
City, and yet bee forced to surrender; 'tis therefore farre better to enjoy her with peace, then to hazzard her on a battell:
If therefore there rise any doubts in my way, I doe forget
them, or at least defer them, till my better setled judgement,
and more manly reason be able to resolve them; for I perceive every mans owne reason is his best *Oedipus,* and will   17
upon a reasonable truce, find a way to loose those bonds
wherewith the subtilties of errour have enchained our more
flexible and tender judgements. In Philosophy where truth
seemes double-faced, there is no man more paradoxicall then
my self; but in Divinity I love to keepe the road, and though   †
not in an implicite, yet an humble faith, follow the great
wheele of the Church, by which I move, not reserving any

proper poles or motion from the epicycle of my own braine;
by this meanes I leave no gap for Heresies, Schismes, or Errors, of which at present I hope I shall not injure Truth to   †
say, I have no taint or tincture. I must confesse my greener
studies have beene polluted with two or three, not any begotten in the latter Centuries, but old and obsolete, such
as could never have been revived, but by such extravagant
and irregular heads as mine; for indeed Heresies perish not
with their Authors, but like the river *Arethusa,* though they
lose their currents in one place, they rise up againe in another: one generall Councell is not able to extirpate one
singular Heresie; it may be canceld for the present, but revolution of time and the like aspects from Heaven, will restore
it, when it will flourish till it be condemned againe; for as
though there were a *Metempsuchosis,* and the soule of one
man passed into another, opinions doe find after certain revolutions, men and mindes like those that first begat them. To
see our selves againe, we need not looke for *Platoes*° yeare;
every man is not onely himselfe; there have beene many
Diogenes, and as many *Timons,* though but few of that
name; men are lived over againe, the world is now as it was
in ages past; there was none then, but there hath been some
one since that parallels him, and is as it were his revived
selfe.

SECT. 7. Now the first of mine was that of the Arabians, that
the soules of men perished with their bodies, but should yet
bee raised againe at the last day; not that I did absolutely
conceive a mortality of the soule; but if that were, which
faith, not Philosophy, hath yet throughly disproved, and that
both entred the grave together, yet I held the same conceit thereof that wee all doe of the body, that it should rise
againe. Surely it is but the merits of our unworthy natures, if
wee sleepe in darkenesse, untill the last alarum: A serious
reflex upon my own unworthinesse did make me backward

° A revolution of certaine thousand yeares when all things should returne
unto their former estate, and he be teaching againe in his schoole as when he
delivered this opinion.

from challenging this prerogative of my soule; so I might enjoy my Saviour at the last, I could with patience be nothing
almost unto eternity. The second was that of *Origen*, that   †
God would not persist in his vengeance for ever, but after a
definite time of his wrath hee would release the damned
soules from torture; Which error I fell into upon a serious
contemplation of the great attribute of God, his mercy; and
did a little cherish it in my selfe, because I found therein no
malice, and a ready weight to sway me from the other extream of despaire, whereunto melancholy and contemplative
natures are too easily disposed. A third there is which I did
never positively maintaine or practise, but have often wished
it had been consonant to Truth, and not offensive to my Religion, and that is the prayer for the dead; whereunto I was   18
inclined from some charitable inducements, whereby I could   †
scarce containe my prayers for a friend at the ringing of a
Bell, or behold his corpse without an oraison for his soule:
'Twas a good way me thought to be remembered by Posterity, and farre more noble then an History. These opinions
I never maintained with pertinacity, or endeavoured to
enveagle any mans beliefe unto mine, nor so much as ever
revealed or disputed them with my dearest friends; by which
means I neither propagated them in others, nor confirmed
them in my selfe, but suffering them to flame upon their
owne substance, without addition of new fuell, they went
out insensibly of themselves; therefore these opinions,
though condemned by lawfull Councels, were not Heresies
in me, but bare Errors, and single Lapses of my understanding, without a joynt depravity of my will: Those have
not only depraved understandings but diseased affections,
which cannot enjoy a singularity without a Heresie, or be
the author of an opinion without they be of a Sect also; this
was the villany of the first Schisme of *Lucifer,* who was not
content to erre alone, but drew into his faction many Legions of Spirits; and upon this experience hee tempted only
Eve, as well understanding the communicable nature of sin,
and that to deceive but one, was tacitely and upon consequence to delude them both.

SECT. 8. That Heresies should arise we have the prophecy of   †,19
Christ, but that old ones should be abolished wee hold no
prediction. That there must be heresies, is true, not onely
in our Church, but also in any other: even in Doctrines
hereticall there will be super-heresies, and Arians not onely
divided from their Church, but also among themselves: for
heads that are disposed unto Schisme and complexionally
propense to innovation, are naturally indisposed for a community, nor will ever be confined unto the order or oeconomy
of one body; and therefore when they separate from others
they knit but loosely among themselves; nor contented with
a generall breach or dichotomie with their Church, do subdivide and mince themselves almost into Atomes. 'Tis true,
that men of singular parts and humors have not beene free
from singular opinions and conceits in all ages; retaining
something not onely beside the opinion of his own Church
or any other, but also any particular Author: which notwithstanding a sober judgement may doe without offence or
heresie; for there is yet after all the decrees of counsells and
the niceties of the Schooles, many things untouch'd, un-
imagin'd, wherein the libertie of an honest reason may play
and expatiate with security and farre without the circle of an
heresie.

SECT. 9. As for those wingy mysteries in Divinity, and ayery
subtilties in Religion, which have unhindg'd the braines of
better heads, they never stretched the *Pia Mater* of mine;
me thinkes there be not impossibilities enough in Religion
for an active faith; the deepest mysteries ours containes,
have not only been illustrated, but maintained by syllogisme,
and the rule of reason: I love to lose my selfe in a mystery,
to pursue my Reason to an *o altitudo*. 'Tis my solitary rec-   †,20
reation to pose my apprehension with those involved aenig-
ma's and riddles of the Trinity, with Incarnation, and
Resurrection. I can answer all the objections of Satan, and
my rebellious reason, with that odde resolution I learned
of *Tertullian, Certum est quia impossibile est.* I desire to   21
exercise my faith in the difficultest points, for to credit ordi-   †
nary and visible objects is not faith, but perswasion. Some

beleeve the better for seeing Christ his Sepulchre, and when they have seene the Red Sea, doubt not of the miracle. Now contrarily I blesse my selfe, and am thankefull that I lived not in the dayes of miracles, that I never saw Christ nor his Disciples; I would not have beene one of those Israelites that passed the Red Sea, nor one of Christs Patients, on whom he wrought his wonders; then had my faith beene thrust upon me, nor should I enjoy that greater blessing pronounced to all that believe and saw not. 'Tis an easie and necessary beliefe to credit what our eye and sense hath examined: I believe he was dead, buried, and rose againe; and desire to see him in his glory, rather then to contemplate him in his Cenotaphe, or Sepulchre. Nor is this much to beleeve; as we have reason, we owe this faith unto History: they only had the advantage of a bold and noble faith, who lived before his comming, who upon obscure prophesies and mysticall Types could raise a beliefe, and expect apparent impossibilities.

SECT. 10. 'Tis true, there is an edge in all firme beliefe, and with an easie Metaphor wee may say the sword of faith; but in these obscurities I rather use it in the adjunct the Apostle 22 gives it, a Buckler; under which I perceive a wary combatant may lie invulnerable. Since I was of understanding to know † we know nothing, my reason hath beene more pliable to the will of faith; I am now content to understand a mystery without a rigid definition, in an easie and Platonick description. That allegorical description of *Hermes** pleaseth mee be- †,23 yond all the Metaphysicall definitions of Divines; where I cannot satisfie my reason, I love to humour my fancy: I had as leive you tell me that *anima est angelus hominis, est Corpus Dei*, as *Entelechia; Lux est umbra Dei*, as *actus perspicui:* where there is an obscurity too deepe for our rea- son, 'tis good to sit downe with a description, periphrasis, or † adumbration; for by acquainting our reason how unable it is to display the visible and obvious effects of nature, it be- † comes more humble and submissive unto the subtilties of

* [*Deus est*] *Sphaera, cujus centrum ubique, circumferentia nullibi.* †

faith; and thus I teach my haggard and unreclaimed reason
to stoope unto the lure of faith. I believe there was already a
tree whose fruit our unhappy parents tasted, though in the
same Chapter, where God forbids it, 'tis positively said, the †
plants of the field were not yet growne; for God had not ²⁴
caused it to raine upon the earth. I beleeve that the Serpent
(if we shall literally understand it) from his proper forme
and figure, made his motion on his belly before the curse. I
find the triall of the Pucellage and Virginity of women, which
God ordained the Jewes, is very fallible. Experience, and ²⁵
History informes me, that not onely many particular women,
but likewise whole Nations have escaped the curse of childbirth, which God seemes to pronounce upon the whole Sex;
yet doe I beleeve that all this is true, which indeed my reason would perswade me to be false; and this I think is no
vulgar part of faith, to believe a thing not only above, but
contrary to reason, and against the arguments of our proper
senses.

SECT. 11. In my solitary and retired imagination (*Neque* ²⁶
enim cum porticus aut me lectulus accepit, desum mihi) I
remember I am not alone, and therefore forget not to contemplate him and his attributes who is ever with mee, especially those two mighty ones, his wisedome and eternitie;
with the one I recreate, with the other I confound my
understanding; for who can speake of eternitie without a
solœcisme, or thinke thereof without an extasie? Time we
may comprehend, 'tis but five days elder then our selves,
and hath the same Horoscope with the world; but to retire
so farre backe as to apprehend a beginning, to give such
an infinite start forward, as to conceive an end in an essence that wee affirme hath neither the one nor the other; it
puts my Reason to Saint *Pauls* Sanctuary; my Philosophy ²⁷
dares not say the Angells can doe it; God hath not made a
creature that can comprehend him, 'tis the priviledge of his
owne nature; *I am that I am*, was his owne definition unto
Moses; and 'twas a short one, to confound mortalitie, that
durst question God, or aske him what hee was; indeed he
onely is, all others have [beene] and shall be, but in eternity

there is no distinction of Tenses; and therefore that terrible
terme *Predestination,* which hath troubled so many weake
heads to conceive, and the wisest to explaine, is in respect to
God no prescious determination of our estates to come, but
a definitive blast of his will already fulfilled, and at the in-   †
stant that he first decreed it; for to his eternitie, which is
indivisible, and altogether, the last Trumpe is already
sounded, the reprobates in the flame, and the blessed in
Abrahams bosome. Saint *Peter* spake modestly when hee   †,†
said, a thousand yeares to God are but as one day; for, to
speake like a Philosopher, those continued instants of time   †
which flow into a thousand yeares, make not to him one mo-   †
ment; what to us is to come, to his Eternitie is present, his
whole duration being but one permanent point without succession, parts, flux, or division.

SECT. 12. There is no Attribute that adds more difficulty to
the mystery of the Trinity, where though in a relative way
of Father and Son, we must deny a priority. I wonder how
Aristotle could conceive the world eternall, or how hee could   28
make good two Eternities: his similitude of a Triangle, comprehended in a square, doth somewhat illustrate the Trinitie
of our soules, and that the Triple Unity of God; for there is
in us not three, but a Trinity of soules, because there is
within us, if not three distinct soules, yet differing faculties,
that can, and doe subsist apart in different subjects, and
yet in us are so united as to make but one soule and substance; if one soule were so perfect as to informe three distinct bodies, that were a petty Trinity: conceive the distinct
number of three, not divided nor separated by the intellect,
but actually comprehended in its Unity, and that is a perfect Trinity. I have often admired the mysticall way of
Pythagoras, and the secret Magicke of numbers; Beware of   29,30
Philosophy, is a precept not to be received in too large a
sense; for in this masse of nature there is a set of things which
carry in their front, though not in capitall letters, yet in
stenography, and short Characters, something of Divinitie,
which to wiser reasons serve as Luminaries in the abysse of
knowledge, and to judicious beliefes as scales and roundles

to mount the pinnacles and highest pieces of Divinity. The
severe Schooles shall never laugh me out of the Philosophy   31
of *Hermes*, that this visible World is but a picture of the invisible, wherein, as in a pourtract, things are not truely, but
in equivocall shapes, and as they counterfeit some more reall
substance in that invisible fabrick.

SECT. 13. That other attribute wherewith I recreate my devotion, is his wisdome, in which I am happy; and for the contemplation of this onely, do not repent me that I was bred
in the way of study: The advantage I have of the vulgar,
with the content and happinesse I conceive therein, is an
ample recompence for all my endeavours, in what part of
knowledg soever. Wisedome is his most beauteous attribute,   †
no man can attaine unto it, yet *Solomon* pleased God when
hee desired it. Hee is wise, because hee knowes all things;
and hee knoweth all things because he made them all; but
his greatest knowledg is in comprehending that he made
not, that is himselfe. And this is also the greatest knowledge
in man. For this do I honour my own profession and embrace
the counsell even of the Devill himselfe: had he read such a   32
Lecture in Paradise as hee did at *Delphos*, we had better
knowne our selves, nor had we stood in feare to know him.
I know he is wise in all, wonderfull in what we conceive,
but far more in what we comprehend not; for we behold
him but asquint upon reflex or shadow; our understanding
is dimmer than *Moses* Eye; we are ignorant of the back parts,   33
or lower side of his Divinity; therefore to pry into the maze
of his Counsels, is not onely folly in Man, but presumption
even in Angels; like us, they are his servants, not his Sena-   †
tors; he holds no Councell, but that mysticall one of the
Trinity, wherein though there be three persons, there is but
one minde that decrees, without contradiction; nor needs
he any, his actions are not begot with deliberation, his wisedome naturally knowes what's best; his intellect stands ready
fraught with the superlative and purest Idea's of goodnesse;
consultation and election, which are two motions in us, make

* γνῶθι σεαυτόν, *nosce teipsum.*

but one in him, his actions springing from his power, at the
first touch of his will. These are Contemplations Metaphysi-
call; my humble speculations have another Method, and are
content to trace and discover those impressions hee hath left †
on his creatures, and the obvious effects of nature; there is
no danger to profound these mysteries, no *Sanctum sanc-*
torum in Philosophy: The world was made to be inhabited
by beasts, but studied and contemplated by man: 'tis the
debt of our reason wee owe unto God, and the homage we
pay for not being beasts; without this, the world is still as
though it had not been, or as it was before the sixt day when
as yet there was not a creature that could conceive or say
there was a world. The wisedome of God receives small hon- †
our from those vulgar heads that rudely stare about, and
with a grosse rusticity admire his workes; those highly mag- †
nifie him, whose judicious enquiry into his acts, and deliberate research into his creatures, returne the duty of a
devout and learned admiration. Therefore, †

> Search while thou wilt, and let thy reason goe
> To ransome truth even to the Abysse below.
> Rally the scattered causes, and that line
> Which nature twists be able to untwine.
> It is thy Makers will, for unto none
> But unto reason can he ere be knowne.
> The Devills doe know thee, but those damned meteours
> Build not thy glory, but confound thy creatures.
> Teach my endeavours so thy workes to read,
> That learning them, in thee I may proceed.
> Give thou my reason that instructive flight,
> Whose weary wings may on thy hands still light.
> Teach me to soare aloft, yet ever so,
> When neare the Sunne, to stoope againe below.
> Thus shall my humble feathers safely hover,
> And though neere earth, more then the heavens discover.
> And then at last, when homeward I shall drive
> Rich with the spoyles of nature to my hive,
> There will I sit, like that industrious flye,
> Buzzing thy prayses, which shall never die
> Till death abrupts them, and succeeding glory
> Bid me goe on in a more lasting story.

And this is almost all wherein an humble creature may endeavour to requite, and someway to retribute unto his Creator; for if not he that sayeth, *Lord, Lord, but he that doth
the will of the Father* shall be saved; certainely our wills
must bee our performances, and our intents make out our
actions; otherwise our pious labours shall finde anxiety in
their graves, and our best endeavours not hope, but feare a
resurrection.

SECT. 14. There is but one first cause, and foure second causes   34
of all things; some are without efficient, as God, others without matter, as Angels, some without forme, as the first matter; but every Essence, created or uncreated, hath its finall
cause, and some positive end both of its Essence and operation; This is the cause I grope after in the workes of nature,
on this hangs the providence of God; to raise so beauteous a
structure as the world and the creatures thereof, was but his
Art, but their sundry and divided operations, with their predestinated ends, are from the treasury of his wisedome. In
the causes, nature, and affections of the Eclipse of the Sunne   †
and Moone, there is most excellent speculation; but to
profound farther, and to contemplate a reason why his provi-   †
dence hath so disposed and ordered their motions in that
vast circle, as to conjoyne and obscure each other, is a
sweeter piece of reason, and a diviner point of Philosophy;
therefore sometimes, and in some things, there appears to   †
mee as much divinity in *Galen* his Books *De usu partium,*   35
as in *Suarez* Metaphysicks: Had *Aristotle* beene as curious
in the enquiry of this cause as he was of the other, hee had
not left behinde him an imperfect piece of Philosophy, but
an absolute tract of Divinity.

SECT. 15. *Natura nihil agit frustra,* is the only indisputable   36
axiome in Philosophy; there are no *Grotesques* in nature; nor
any thing framed to fill up empty cantons, and unnecessary
spaces; in the most imperfect creatures, and such as were   37
not preserved in the Arke, but having their seeds and principles in the wombe of nature, are every-where where the
power of the Sun is; in these is the wisedome of his hand

discovered: Out of this ranke *Solomon* chose the object of
his admiration, indeed what reason may not goe to Schoole
to the wisedome of Bees, Ants, and Spiders? what wise hand
teacheth them to doe what reason cannot teach us? ruder
heads stand amazed at those prodigious pieces of nature,
Whales, Elephants, Dromidaries, and Camels; these I confesse, are the Colossus and Majestick pieces of her hand;
but in these narrow Engines there is more curious Mathematicks, and the civilitie of these little Citizens more neatly
sets forth the wisedome of their Maker; Who admires not   †
Regio-Montanus his Fly beyond his Eagle, or wonders not
more at the operation of two soules in those little bodies,   38
than but one in the trunck of a Cedar? I could never content
my contemplation with those generall pieces of wonder, the   †,39
flux and reflux of the Sea, the encrease of Nile, the conversion of the Needle to the North, and have studied to match
and parallel those in the more obvious and neglected pieces
of Nature, which without further travell I can doe in the
Cosmography of my selfe; wee carry with us the wonders we
seeke without us: There is all *Africa* and her prodigies in us;
we are that bold and adventurous piece of nature, which he
that studies wisely learnes in a *compendium,* what others
labour at in a divided piece and endlesse volume.

SECT. 16. Thus are there two bookes from whence I collect
my Divinity; besides that written one of God, another of his
servant Nature, that universall and publik Manuscript, that
lies expans'd unto the eyes of all: those that never saw him
in the one, have discovered him in the other: This was the
Scripture and Theology of the Heathens: the naturall motion
of the Sun made them more admire him, than its supernaturall station did the Children of Israel; the ordinary
effects of nature wrought more admiration in them, than in   †
the other all his miracles; surely the Heathens knew better
how to joyne and reade these mysticall letters, than wee
Christians, who cast a more carelesse eye on these common
Hieroglyphicks, and disdain to suck Divinity from the flowers
of nature. Nor do I so forget God, as to adore the name of
Nature; which I define not with the Schooles, the principle   40

of motion and rest, but that streight and regular line, that
setled and constant course the wisedome of God hath ordained the actions of his creatures, according to their severall kinds. To make a revolution every day is the nature of
the Sun, because that necessary course which God hath ordained it, from which it cannot swerve, but by a faculty from
that voyce which first did give it motion. Now this course of
Nature God seldome alters or perverts, but like an excellent
Artist hath so contrived his worke, that with the selfe same
instrument, without a new creation he may effect his
obscurest designes. Thus he sweetned the water with a   †,41
wood, preserved the creatures in the Arke, which the blast
of his mouth might have as easily created: for God is like a   42
skilfull Geometrician, who when more easily and with one
stroke of his Compasse, he might describe, or divide a right
line, had yet rather doe this in a circle or longer way, according to the constituted and forelaid principles of his art:
yet this rule of his hee doth sometimes pervert, to acquaint
the world with his prerogative, lest the arrogancy of our reason should question his power, and conclude he could not;
and thus I call the effects of nature the works of God, whose
hand and instrument she only is; and therefore to ascribe
his actions unto her, is to devolve the honor of the principall
agent upon the instrument; which if with reason we may
doe, then let our hammers rise up and boast they have built
our houses, and our pens receive the honour of our writings.
I hold there is a generall beauty in the works of God, and
therefore no deformity in any kind or species of creature
whatsoever: I cannot tell by what Logick we call a Toad, a
Beare, or an Elephant, ugly, they being created in those outward shapes and figures which best expresse the actions of
their inward formes; and having past that generall visitation
of God, who saw that all that he had made was good, that is,
conformable to his will, which abhors deformity, and is the
rule of order and beauty; there is no deformity but in a
monstrosity, wherein notwithstanding there is a kind of
beauty, Nature so ingeniously contriving the irregular parts,
as they become sometimes more remarkable than the principall Fabrick. To speake yet more narrowly, there was never

any thing ugly, or misshapen, but the Chaos; wherein notwithstanding, to speake strictly, there was no deformity, because no forme, nor was it yet impregnate by the voyce of
God: Now nature is not at variance with art, nor art with
nature; they both being the servants of his providence: Art
is the perfection of Nature: Were the world now as it was
the sixt day, there were yet a Chaos: Nature hath made one
world, and Art another. In briefe, all things are artificiall, for
nature is the Art of God.

SECT. 17. This is the ordinary and open way of his providence,
which art and industry have in a good part discovered, whose
effects wee may foretell without an Oracle; To foreshew these
is not Prophesie, but Prognostication. There is another way
full of Meanders and Labyrinths, whereof the Devill and
Spirits have no exact Ephemerides; and that is a more particular and obscure method of his providence, directing the
operations of individualls and single Essences: this we call   43
Fortune, that serpentine and crooked line, whereby he
drawes those actions his wisedome intends in a more unknowne and secret way; This cryptick and involved method
of his providence have I ever admired, nor can I relate the
history of my life, the occurrences of my dayes, the escapes of
dangers, and hits of chance, with a *Bezo las Manos* to Fortune, or a bare Gramercy to my good starres: *Abraham* might
have thought the Ram in the thicket came thither by accident; humane reason would have said that meere chance conveyed *Moses* in the Arke to the sight of *Pharaohs* daughter;
what a Labyrinth is there in the story of *Joseph*, able to convert a Stoick? Surely there are in every mans life certaine
rubs, doublings, and wrenches which passe a while under the
effects of chance, but at the last, well examined, prove the
meere hand of God: 'Twas not dumbe chance that, to discover the Fougade or Powder-plot, contrived a miscarriage
in the letter. I like the victory of 88 the better for that one   44,45
occurrence which our enemies imputed to our dishonour, and
the partiality of Fortune, to wit, the tempests and contrarietie
of winds. King *Philip* did not detract from the Nation, when
he said, he sent his Armado to fight with men, and not to com-

bate with the winds. Where there is a manifest disproportion
between the powers and forces of two severall agents, upon a
maxime of reason wee may promise the victory to the superiour; but when unexpected accidents slip in, and unthought
of occurrences intervene, these must proceed from a power
that owes no obedience to those axioms: where, as in the writing upon the wall, we behold the hand, but see not the spring
that moves it. The successe of that pety Province of Holland
(of which the Grand Seignieur proudly said, That if they   46
should trouble him as they did the Spaniard, hee would send
his men with shovels and pick-axes, and throw it into the sea)
I cannot altogether ascribe to the ingenuity and industry of
the people, but to the mercy of God, that hath disposed them
to such a thriving *Genius;* and to the will of providence, that
dispenseth her favour to each Countrey in their preordinate   †
season. All cannot be happy at once, for because the glory of
one State depends upon the ruine of another, there is a revolution and vicissitude of their greatnesse, which must obey   †
the swing of that wheele, not moved by Intelligences, but by
the hand of God, whereby all Estates arise to their Zenith and
verticall points, according to their predestinated periods. For
the lives not onely of men, but of Commonweales, and the
whole World, run not upon an Helix that still enlargeth, but
on a Circle where arriving to their Meridian, they decline in
obscurity, and fall under the Horizon againe.

SECT. 18. These must not therefore bee named the effects of
fortune, but in a relative way, and as we terme the workes of
nature. It was the ignorance of mans reason that begat this
very name, and by a carelesse terme miscalled the providence
of God: for there is no liberty for causes to operate in a loose
and stragling way, nor any effect whatsoever, but hath its
warrant from some universall or superiour cause. 'Tis not a
ridiculous devotion, to say a Prayer before a game at Tables;
for even in *sortilegies* and matters of greatest uncertainty,
there is a setled and preordered course of effects; 'tis we that
are blind, not fortune: because our eye is too dim to discover
the mystery of her effects, we foolishly paint her blind, and
hoodwink the providence of the Almighty. I cannot justifie

that contemptible Proverb, *That fooles onely are fortunate,*
or that insolent Paradox, *That a wise man is out of the reach
of fortune;* much lesse those opprobrious Epithets of Poets,   47
Whore, Baud, and *Strumpet:* 'Tis I confesse the common fate
of men of singular gifts of mind, to be destitute of those of
fortune; which doth not any way deject the spirit of wiser
judgements, who throughly understand the justice of this proceeding; and being enriched with higher donatives, cast a
more carelesse eye on these vulgar parts of felicity. 'Tis a
most unjust ambition, to desire to engrosse the mercies of the
Almighty, nor to be content with the goods of mind, without
a possession of those of body or fortune: and 'tis an errour
worse than heresie, to adore these complementall and circum-
stanciall pieces of felicity, and undervalue those perfections
and essentiall points of happinesse, wherein we resemble our
Maker. To wiser desires 'tis satisfaction enough to deserve,
though not to enjoy the favours of Fortune; let providence
provide for fooles: 'tis not partiality, but equity in God, who
deales with us but as our naturall parents; those that are able
of body and mind, he leaves to their deserts; to those of
weaker merits hee imparts a larger portion, and pieces out
the defect of one by the excesse of the other. Thus have wee
no just quarrell with Nature, for leaving us naked, or to envie
the hornes, hoofs, skins, and furs of other creatures, being provided with reason, that can supply them all. Wee need not
labour with so many arguments to confute judiciall Astrology;   48
for if there be a truth therein, it doth not injure Divinity; if
to be born under *Mercury* disposeth us to be witty, under
Jupiter to be wealthy, I doe not owe a knee unto these, but
unto that mercifull hand that hath ordered my indifferent
and uncertaine nativity unto such benevolous aspects. Those   †
that held that all things were governed by fortune, had not
erred, had they not persisted there: The Romans, that erected
a Temple to Fortune, acknowledged therein, though in a
blinder way, somewhat of Divinity; for in a wise supputation
all things begin and end in the Almighty. There is a neerer
way to heaven than *Homers* chaine; an easie Logick may   49
conjoyne heaven and earth in one argument, and with lesse
than a Sorites resolve all things into God. For though wee

Christen effects by their most sensible and nearest causes, yet
is God the true and infallible cause of all, whose concourse
though it be generall, yet doth it subdivide it selfe into the
particular actions of every thing, and is that spirit, by which
each singular essence not onely subsists, but performes its
operations.   †

SECT. 19. The bad construction and perverse comment on
these paire of second causes, or visible hands of God, have
perverted the devotion of many into Atheisme; who forgetting the honest advisoes of faith, have listened unto the con-
spiracie of Passion and Reason. I have therefore alwayes
endeavoured to compose those fewds and angry dissentions
between affection, faith, and reason: For there is in our soule
a kind of Triumvirate, or Triple government of three competitors, which distract the peace of this our Commonwealth, not
lesse than did that other the State of Rome.

As Reason is a rebell unto Faith, so passion unto Reason: As
the propositions of Faith seeme absurd unto Reason, so the
Theorems of Reason unto passion, and both unto Faith; yet a   †
moderate and peaceable discretion may so state and order
the matter, that they may bee all Kings, and yet make but one
Monarchy, every one exercising his Soveraignty and Prerogative in a due time and place, according to the restraint and
limit of circumstance. There are, as in Philosophy, so in Di-   †
vinity, sturdy doubts and boysterous objections, wherewith
the unhappinesse of our knowledge too neerely acquainteth
us. More of these no man hath knowne than my selfe, which
I confesse I conquered, not in a martiall posture, but on my
knees. For our endeavours are not onely to combate with   †
doubts, but alwayes to dispute with the Devill; the villany of
that spirit takes a hint of infidelity from our Studies, and by
demonstrating a naturality in one way, makes us mistrust a
miracle in another. Thus having perus'd the Archidoxis and   50
read the secret Sympathies of things, he would disswade my
beliefe from the miracle of the Brazen Serpent, make me con-   51
ceit that image worked by Sympathie, and was but an Ægyp-
tian tricke to cure their diseases without a miracle. Againe,
having seene some experiments of *Bitumen,* and having read

farre more of *Naptha,* he whispered to my curiositie the fire
of the Altar might be naturall, and bid me mistrust a miracle [52]
in *Elias,* when he entrench'd the Altar round with water; for
that inflamable substance yeelds not easily unto water, but
flames in the armes of its Antagonist: and thus would hee in-
veagle my beliefe to thinke the combustion of *Sodom* might
be naturall, and that there was an Asphaltick and Bituminous
nature in that Lake before the fire of *Gomorrha:* I know that
Manna is now plentifully gathered in *Calabria,* and *Josephus*
tels me in his dayes 'twas as plentifull in *Arabia;* the Devill
therefore made the *quere,* Where was then the miracle in the
dayes of *Moses?* the *Israelites* saw but that in his time, the natives of those Countries behold in ours. Thus the Devill
played at Chesse with mee, and yeelding a pawne, thought
to gaine a Queen of me, taking advantage of my honest endeavours; and whilst I laboured to raise the structure of my
reason, hee striv'd to undermine the edifice of my faith.

SECT. 20. Neither had these or any other ever such advantage †
of me, as to encline me to any point of infidelity or desperate
positions of Atheisme; for I have beene these many yeares of
opinion there was never any. Those that held Religion was
the difference of man from beasts, have spoken probably, and
proceed upon a principle as inductive as the other: That doctrine of *Epicurus,* that denied the providence of God, was no
Atheism, but a magnificent and high-strained conceit of his
Majesty, which hee deemed too sublime to minde the triviall
actions of those inferiour creatures: That fatall necessitie of
the Stoickes, is nothing but the immutable Law of his will.
Those that heretofore denied the Divinitie of the holy Ghost,
have been condemned but as Heretickes; and those that now
deny our Saviour, (though more than Hereticks) are not so
much as Atheists: for though they deny two persons in the
Trinity, they hold as we do, there is but one God.

That villain and Secretary of Hell, that composed that miscreant piece of the three Impostors, though divided from all [53]
Religions, and was neither Jew, Turk, nor Christian, was not a
positive Atheist. I confesse every Countrey hath its *Machia-
vell,* every age its *Lucian,* whereof common heads must not

heare, nor more advanced judgements too rashly venture on:
'tis the Rhetorick of Satan, and may pervert a loose or prejudicate beleefe.

SECT. 21. I confesse I have perused them all, and can discover
nothing that may startle a discreet beliefe: yet are there
heads carried off with the wind and breath of such motives. I
remember a Doctor in Physick of Italy, who could not perfectly believe the immortality of the soule, because *Galen*
seemed to make a doubt thereof. With another I was familiarly acquainted in France, a Divine, and man of singular
parts, that on the same point was so plunged and gravelled
with three lines of *Seneca*,* that all our Antidotes, drawne   54
from both Scripture and Philosophy, could not expel the poy-
son of his errour. There are a set of heads, that can credit the
relations of Mariners, yet question the testimony of Saint   †
Paul; and peremptorily maintaine the traditions of *Aelian* or
Pliny, yet in Histories of Scripture raise Quere's and objections, beleeving no more than they can parallel in humane
Authors. I confesse there are in Scripture stories that doe exceed the fables of Poets, and to a captious Reader sound like   †
Garagantua or *Bevis:* Search all the Legends of times past,
and the fabulous conceits of these present, and 'twill bee
hard to find one that deserves to carry the buckler unto
Sampson, yet is all this of an easie possibility, if we conceive
a divine concourse or an influence but from the little finger of
the Almighty. It is impossible that either in the discourse of
man, or in the infallible voyce of God, to the weaknesse of our
apprehensions, there should not appeare irregularities, contradictions, and antinomies: my selfe could shew a catalogue of doubts, never yet imagined nor questioned, as I
know, which are not resolved at the first hearing; not fantas-
tick Quere's or objections of ayre: for I cannot heare of Atoms
in Divinity. I can read the story of the Pigeon that was sent
out of the Ark, and returned no more, yet not question how
shee found out her mate that was left behind: That *Lazarus*
was raised from the dead, yet not demand where in the in-

---

* *Post mortem nihil est, ipsaque mors nihil.* / *Mors individua est noxia corpori,*
Nec patiens animae— / *Toti morimur, nullaque pars manet Nostri.*

terim his soule awaited; or raise a Law-case, whether his heire might lawfully detaine his inheritance, bequeathed unto him by his death; and he, though restored to life, have no Plea or title unto his former possessions. Whether *Eve* was framed out of the left side of *Adam,* I dispute not; because I stand not yet assured which is the right side of a man, or whether there be any such distinction in Nature: that she † was edified out of the ribbe of *Adam* I believe, yet raise no question who shall arise with that ribbe at the Resurrection. Whether *Adam* was an Hermaphrodite, as the Rabbines contend upon the Letter of the Text; because it is contrary to reason there should bee an Hermaphrodite before there was a woman, or a composition of two natures before there was a second composed. Likewise, whether the world was created 55 in Autumne, Summer, or the Spring, because it was created in them all; for whatsoever Signe the Sun possesseth, those foure seasons are actually existent: It is the nature of this Luminary to distinguish the severall seasons of the yeare, all which it makes at one time in the whole earth, and successively in any part thereof. There are a bundle of curiosi- † ties, not onely in Philosophy but in Divinity, proposed and discussed by men of most supposed abilities, which indeed are not worthy our vacant houres, much lesse our serious studies; Pieces onely fit to be placed in *Pantagruels Library, or 56 bound up with *Tartaretus de modo Cacandi.*

SECT. 22. These are niceties that become not those that peruse so serious a Mystery. There are others more generally questioned and called to the Barre, yet methinkes of an easie, and possible truth. 'Tis ridiculous to put off or drowne the generall Flood of *Noah* in that particular inundation of *Deucalion:* that there was a Deluge once, seemes not to mee so great a miracle, as that there is not one alwayes. How all the kinds of Creatures, not only in their owne bulks, but with a competency of food and sustenance, might be preserved in one Arke, and within the extent of three hundred cubits, to a reason that rightly examines it, will appeare very foesible. †

* In Rabelais.

There is another secret, not contained in the Scripture, which
is more hard to comprehend, and put the honest Father to   57
the refuge of a Miracle; and that is, not onely how the distinct
pieces of the world, and divided Ilands should bee first
planted by men, but inhabited by Tygers, Panthers, and
Beares. How *America* abounded with beasts of prey and nox-
ious Animals, yet contained not in it that necessary creature,
a Horse. By what passage those, not onely Birds, but dan-   †
gerous and unwelcome Beasts came over: How there bee
creatures there, which are not found in this triple Continent;
all which must needs bee strange unto us, that hold but one
Arke, and that the creatures began their progress from the
mountaines of *Ararat.* They who to salve this, would make the
Deluge particular, proceed upon a Principle that I can no
way grant; not onely upon the negative of holy Scriptures, but
of mine owne reason, whereby I can make it probable, that
the world was as well peopled in the time of *Noah* as in ours,
and fifteene hundred yeares to people the world, as full a
time for them as foure thousand yeares since have beene to
us. There are other assertions and common tenents drawn
from Scripture, and generally beleeved as Scripture; whereunto, notwithstanding, I would never betray the libertie of my
reason. 'Tis a Postulate to me, that *Methusalem* was the longest liv'd of all the Children of *Adam,* and no man will bee
able to prove it; when from the processe of the Text I can
manifest it may be otherwise. That *Judas* perished by hang-   †,58
ing himself, there is no certainety in Scripture, though in one
place it seemes to affirme it, and by a doubtfull word hath
given occasion so to translate it; yet in another place, in a
more punctuall description, it makes it improbable, and
seemes to overthrow it. That our Fathers, after the Flood,
erected the Tower of *Babell,* to preserve themselves against a
second Deluge, is generally opinioned and beleeved; yet is
there another intention of theirs expressed in Scripture: Besides, it is improbable from the circumstance of the place,
that is, a plain in the land of *Shinar.* These are no points of
Faith, and therefore may admit a free dispute. There are yet
others, and those familiarly concluded from the Text, wherein
(under favour) I see no consequence. [To instance in one or   †

two, as to proove the Trinity from that speech of God in the plurall number, *faciamus hominem,* Lett us make man, which is but the common style of princes and men of eminency; hee that shall read one of his Majesties proclamations may with the same Logicke conclude there bee two Kings in England.] The Church of *Rome* confidently proves the opinion of Tutelary Angels, from that answer when *Peter* knockt at the doore, *'Tis not he but his Angel;* that is, might some say, his Messenger, or some body from him; for so the Originall signifies, and is as likely to be the doubtfull Families meaning. This exposition I once suggested to a young Divine, that answered upon this point, to which I remember the *Franciscan* Opponent replyed no more, but, That it was a new and no authentick interpretation.

SECT. 23. These are but the conclusions and fallible discourses of man upon the word of God, for such I doe beleeve the holy Scriptures; yet, were it of man, I could not choose but say, it was the singularest and superlative Piece that hath been extant since the Creation; were I a Pagan, I should not refraine the Lecture of it; and cannot but commend the judgement of *Ptolomy,* that thought not his Library compleate without it: the Alcoran of the Turks (I speake without prejudice) is an ill composed Piece, containing in it vaine and ridiculous errours in Philosophy, impossibilities, fictions, and vanities beyond laughter, maintained by evident and open Sophismes, the policy of Ignorance, deposition of Universities, and banishment of Learning. That hath gotten foot by armes and violence; This without a blow hath disseminated it selfe through the whole earth. It is not unremarkable what *Philo* first observed, that the Law of Moses continued two thousand yeares without the least alteration; whereas, we see, the Lawes of other Commonweales doe alter with occasions; and even those that pretended their originall from some Divinity, to have vanished without trace or memory. I beleeve, besides *Zoroaster,* there were divers that wrote before *Moses,* who notwithstanding have suffered the common fate of time. Mens Workes have an age like themselves; and though they outlive their Authors, yet have they a stint and period to their

59,†

†,60

61

02

†,63

duration: This onely is a Worke too hard for the teeth of time,
and cannot perish but in the generall flames, when all things
shall confesse their ashes.

SECT. 24. I have heard some with deepe sighs lament the lost
lines of *Cicero;* others with as many groanes deplore the
combustion of the Library of *Alexandria;* for my owne part,   64
I thinke there be too many in the world, and could with
patience behold the urne and ashes of the *Vatican,* could I   65
with a few others recover the perished leaves of *Solomon.*   66
I would not omit a Copy of *Enochs* Pillars, had they many   67
neerer Authors than *Josephus,* or did not relish somewhat of
the Fable. Some men have written more than others have
spoken; *Pineda* quotes more Authors in one worke, than are
necessary in a whole world. Of those three great inventions   68,†
of *Germany,* there are two which are not without their incommodities, and 'tis disputable whether they exceed not
their use and commodities. 'Tis not a melancholy *Utinam* of
mine owne, but the desire of better heads, that there were a   †
generall Synod; not to unite the incompatible differences of   †
Religion, but for the benefit of learning, to reduce it as it lay
at first in a few and solid Authours; and to condemne to the
fire those swarms and millions of *Rhapsodies,* begotten onely
to distract and abuse the weaker judgements of Scholars, and
to maintaine the Trade and Mystery of Typographers.

SECT. 25. I cannot but wonder with what exceptions the *Sa-
maritanes* could confine their beliefe to the *Pentateuch,* or
five books of *Moses.* I am amazed at the Rabbinicall Inter-   †,†
pretations of the Jews, upon the Old Testament, as much as
their defection from the New: and truely it is beyond wonder,
how that contemptible and degenerate issue of *Jacob,* once so
devoted to Ethnick Superstition, and so easily seduced to the
Idolatry of their Neighbours, should now in such an obstinate
and peremptory beliefe adhere unto their owne Doctrine, expect impossibilities, and in the face and eye of the Church

* *Pineda* in his *Monarchia Ecclesiastica* quotes one thousand and fortie
Authors.

persist without the least hope of conversion: This is a vice in
them, that were a vertue in us; for obstinacy in a bad cause,
is but constancy in a good. And herein I must accuse those of
my own Religion; for there is not any of such a fugitive faith,
such an unstable belief, as a Christian; none that do so oft
transforme themselves, not unto severall shapes of Christianity and of the same Species, but unto more unnaturall and
contrary formes of Jew and Mahometan; that from the name
of Saviour, can descend to the bare terme of Prophet; and   †
from an old belicfc that he is come, fall to a new expectation
of his comming: It is the promise of Christ to make us all one
flock; but how and when this union shall be, is as obscure to
me as the last day. Of those foure members of Religion wee   69
hold a slender proportion; there are I confesse some new
additions, yet small to those which accrew to our Adversaries,
and those onely drawne from the revolt of Pagans, men but of
negative impieties, and such as deny Christ, but because they
never heard of him: But the Religion of the Jew is expresly
against the Christian, and the Mahometan against both; for
the Turke, in the bulke hee now stands, he is beyond all hope
of conversion; if hee fall asunder there may be conceived
hopes, but not without strong improbabilities. The Jew is obstinate in all fortunes; the persecution of fifteene hundred
yeares hath but confirmed them in their errour: they have already endured whatsoever may be inflicted, and have suffered, in a bad cause, even to the commendation of their   †,70
enemies. Persecution is a bad and indirect way to plant Religion; It hath beene the unhappy method of angry devotions,
not onely to confirme honest Religion, but wicked Heresies,
and extravagant opinions. It was the first stone and Basis of
our Faith, none can more justly boast of persecutions, and
glory in the number and valour of Martyrs; For, to speake
properly, those are true and almost onely examples of fortitude: Those that are fetch'd from the field, or drawne from
the actions of the Campe, are not oft-times so truely prece-
dents of valour as audacity, and at the best attaine but to
some bastard piece of fortitude: If wee shall strictly examine
the circumstances and requisites which *Aristotle* requires to   71

true and perfect valour, we shall finde the name onely in his
Master *Alexander,* and as little in that Romane Worthy, *Julius
Caesar;* and if any, in that easie and active way, have done
so nobly as to deserve that name, yet in the passive and more
terrible piece these have surpassed, and in a more heroical
way may claime the honour of that Title. 'Tis not in the
power of every honest faith to proceed thus farre, or passe to
Heaven through the flames; every one hath it not in that full
measure, nor in so audacious and resolute a temper, as to endure those terrible tests and trialls, who notwithstanding in a
peaceable way doe truely adore their Saviour, and have (no
doubt) a faith acceptable in the eyes of God.

SECT. 26. Now as all that die in warre are not termed Souldiers, so neither can I properly terme all those that suffer in
matters of Religion, Martyrs. The Councell of *Constance* con-   72
demnes *John Husse* for an Heretick, the Stories of his owne
party stile him a Martyr: He must needs offend the Divinity   †
of both, that sayes hee was neither the one nor the other:
There are many (questionlesse) canonized on earth, that
shall never be Saints in Heaven; and have their names in
Histories and Martyrologies, who in the eyes of God are not
so perfect Martyrs as was that wise Heathen, *Socrates,* that
suffered on a fundamentall point of Religion, the Unity of   73
God. I have often pitied the miserable Bishop that suffered   †,74
in the cause of *Antipodes,* yet cannot choose but accuse him
of as much madnesse, for exposing his living on such a trifle,   †
as those of ignorance and folly that condemned him. I think
my conscience will not give me the lie, if I say, there are   †
not many extant that in a noble way feare the face of death
lesse than my selfe, yet from the morall duty I owe to the
Commandement of God, and the natural respect that I ten-   †
der unto the conservation of my essence and being, I would
not perish upon a Ceremony, Politick point, or indifferency: †
nor is my beleefe of that untractable temper, as not to bow at
their obstacles, or connive at matters wherein there are not
manifest impieties. The leaven therefore and ferment of all,
not onely Civill, but Religious actions, is wisedome; without

which, to commit our selves to the flame is Homicide, and (I feare) but to passe through one fire into another.

SECT. 27. That Miracles are ceased, I can neither prove, nor absolutely deny, much less define the time and period of their cessation; that they survived Christ, is manifest upon record of Scripture; that they out-lived the Apostles also, and were revived at the conversion of Nations, many yeares after, we cannot deny, if wee shall not question those Writers whose testimonies wee doe not controvert, in points that make for our owne opinions; therefore that may have some truth in it that is reported by the Jesuites of their Miracles in the In- 75 dies; I could wish it were true, or had any other testimony then their owne Pennes: they may easily beleeve those Miracles abroad, who daily conceive a greater at home; the transmutation of those visible elements into the body and blood of our Saviour: for the conversion of water into wine, which he wrought in *Cana*, or, what the Devill would have had him done in the wildernesse, of stones into Bread, compared to this, will scarce deserve the name of a Miracle: Though indeed, to speake properly, there is not one Miracle greater than another, they being the extraordinary effects of the † hand of God, to which all things are of an equall facility; and to create the world as easie as one single creature. For this is also a miracle, not onely to produce effects against or above Nature, but before Nature; and to create Nature as great a miracle, as to contradict or transcend her. Wee doe too narrowly define the power of God, restraining it to our capacities. I hold that God can doe all things; how he should work contradictions, I do not understand, yet dare not therefore deny. I cannot see why the Angel of God should question *Esdras* 76 to recall the time past, if it were beyond his owne power; or that God should pose mortalitie in that, which hee was not able to performe himselfe. I will not say God cannot, but hee will not performe many things, which wee plainely affirme he cannot: this I am sure is the mannerliest proposition, wherein notwithstanding I hold no Paradox. For strictly his power is the same with his will, and they both with all the rest doe make but one God.

SECT. 28. Therefore that Miracles have beene I doe beleeve,   †
that they may yet bee wrought by the living I doe not deny:
but have no confidence in those which are fathered on the
dead; and this hath ever made me suspect the efficacy of reliques, to examine the bones, question the habits and apper-
tinencies of Saints, and even of Christ himselfe: I cannot conceive why the Crosse that *Helena* found and whereon Christ   77
himself died should have power to restore others unto life; I
excuse not *Constantine* from a fall off his horse, or a mischiefe
from his enemies, upon the wearing those nayles on his bri-
dle, which our Saviour bore upon the Crosse in his hands: I
compute among your *Piae Fraudes,* nor many degrees before
consecrated swords and roses, that which *Baldwin* King of
Jerusalem returned the *Genovese* for their cost and paines in
his warre, to wit the ashes of *John* the Baptist. Those that hold
the sanctitie of their soules doth leave behind a tincture and
sacred facultie on their bodies, speake naturally of Miracles,
and doe not salve the doubt. Now one reason I tender so little
devotion unto reliques, is, I think, the slender and doubtfull
respect I have alwayes held unto Antiquities: for that indeed
which I admire is farre before antiquity, that is, Eternity,
and that is God himselfe; who though hee be stiled the Antient of dayes, cannot receive the adjunct of antiquity, who
was before the world, and shall be after it, yet is not older
then it; for in his yeares there is no Climacter; his duration is
eternity, and farre more venerable then antiquitie.

SECT. 29. But above all things, I wonder how the curiositie
of wiser heads could passe that great and indisputable miracle, the cessation of Oracles: and in what swoun their reasons   78
lay, to content themselves and sit downe with such far-fetch't
and ridiculous reasons as *Plutarch* alleadgeth for it. The
Jewes that can beleeve that supernaturall solstice of the
Sunne in the dayes of *Joshua,* have yet the impudence to   79
deny the Eclipse, which even Pagans confessed at his death: †,80
but for this, it is evident beyond contradiction, *the Devill
himselfe confessed it. Certainly it is not a warrantable curi-

* In his Oracle to *Augustus.*   81

osity, to examine the verity of Scripture by the concordance
of humane history, or seek to confirme the Chronicle of *Hester*
or *Daniel,* by the authority of *Megasthenes* or *Herodotus.*   †
I confesse I have had an unhappy curiosity this way, till I
laughed my selfe out of it with a piece of *Justine,* where hee   82
delivers that the children of *Israel* for being scabbed were
banished out of Egypt. And truely since I have understood
the occurrences of the world, and know in what counterfeit
shapes and deceitfull vizzards times present represent on the
stage things past; I doe beleeve them little more than things
to come. Some have beene of my opinion, and endevoured
to write the history of their own lives; wherein *Moses* hath
outgone them all, and left not onely the story of his life, but
as some will have it of his death also.   †

SECT. 30. It is a riddle to me, how this story of Oracles hath
not worm'd out of the world that doubtfull conceit of Spirits   83
and Witches; how so many learned heads should so farre forget their Metaphysicks, and destroy the Ladder and scale of
creatures, as to question the existence of Spirits: for my part,
I have ever beleeved, and doe now know, that there are
Witches; they that doubt of these, doe not onely deny them,
but Spirits; and are obliquely and upon consequence a sort,
not of Infidels, but Atheists. Those that to confute their incredulity desire to see apparitions, shall questionlesse never
behold any, nor have the power to be so much as Witches;
the Devill hath them already in a heresie as capitall as Witchcraft, and to appeare to them, were but to convert them: Of
all the delusions wherewith he deceives mortalitie, there is
not any that puzleth mee more than the Legerdemain of
Changelings; I doe not credit those transformations of reasonable creatures into beasts, or that the Devill hath a power
to transpeciate a man into a horse, who tempted Christ (as
a triall of his Divinitie) to convert but stones into bread. I
could beleeve that Spirits use with man the act of carnality,
and that in both sexes; I conceive they may assume, steale,
or contrive a body, wherein there may be action enough to
content decrepit lust, or passion to satisfie more active ven-
eries; yet in both, without a possibility of generation: and

therefore that opinion, that Antichrist should be borne of the
Tribe of *Dan* by conjunction with the Devill, is ridiculous,
and a conceit fitter for a Rabbin than a Christian. I hold that
the Devill doth really possesse some men, the spirit of melancholy others, the spirit of delusion others; that as the Devill
is concealed and denyed by some, so God and good Angels
are pretended by others, whereof the late detection of the   †
Maid of Germany hath left a pregnant example.   †,84

SECT. 31. Againe, I beleeve that all that use sorceries, incantations, and spells, are not Witches, or, as we terme them,
Magicians; I conceive there is a traditionall Magicke, not
learned immediately from the Devill, but at second hand from
his Schollers; who having once the secret betrayed, are able,
and doe emperically practice without his advice, they both
proceeding upon the principles of nature: where actives,
aptly conjoyned to disposed passives, will under any Master
produce their effects. Thus I thinke at first a great part of
Philosophy was Witchcraft, which being afterward derived   †
from one to another, proved but Philosophy, and was indeed †
no more then the honest effects of Nature: What invented by
us is Philosophy, learned from him is Magicke. Wee doe
surely owe the honour of many secrets to the discovery of   †
good and bad Angels. I could never passe that sentence of
Paracelsus without an asterisk or annotation: *Ascendens   85,86
constellatum multa revelat, quaerentibus magnalia naturae,
i.e. opera Dei.* I doe thinke that many mysteries ascribed to
our owne inventions have beene the courteous revelations of
Spirits; for those noble essences in heaven beare a friendly regard unto their fellow natures on earth; and therefore [I] beleeve that those many prodigies and ominous prognostickes,
which fore-run the ruines of States, Princes, and private persons, are the charitable premonitions of good Angels, which
more carelesse enquiries terme but the effects of chance and
nature.

SECT. 32. Now, besides these particular and divided Spirits,
there may be (for ought I know) an universall and common   87

* Thereby is meant our good Angel appointed us from our nativity.

Spirit to the whole world. It was the opinion of *Plato*, and it is yet of the *Hermeticall* Philosophers; if there be a common nature that unites and tyes the scattered and divided individuals into one species, why may there not bee one that unites them all? However, I am sure there is a common Spirit that playes within us, yet makes no part of us; and that is the Spirit of God, the fire and scintillation of that noble and mighty Essence, which is the life and radicall heat of spirits, † and those essences that know not the vertue of the Sunne; a fire quite contrary to the fire of Hell: This is that gentle heate that brooded on the waters, and in six dayes hatched the world; this is that irradiation that dispells the mists of Hell, the clouds of horrour, feare, sorrow, despaire; and preserves the region of the mind in serenity: whosoever feels not the warme gale and gentle ventilation of this Spirit, (though I feele his pulse) I dare not say he lives; for truely without this, to mee there is no heat under the Tropick; nor any light, though I dwelt in the body of the Sunne.

> As when the labouring Sun hath wrought his track
> Up to the top of lofty *Cancers* back,
> The ycie Ocean cracks, the frozen pole
> Thawes with the heat of the Celestiall coale;
> So when thy absent beames begin t'impart
> Again a Solstice on my frozen heart,
> My winter's ov'r, my drooping spirits sing,
> And every part revives into a Spring.
> But if thy quickning beames a while decline,
> And with their light blesse not this Orbe of mine,
> A chilly frost surpriseth every member,
> And in the midst of June I feele December.
> O how this earthly temper doth debase   †
> The noble Soule, in this her humble place!
> Whose wingy nature ever doth aspire
> To reach that place whence first it tooke its fire.
> These flames I feele, which in my heart doe dwell,
> Are not thy beames, but take their fire from hell:
> O quench them all, and let thy light divine
> Be as the Sunne to this poore Orbe of mine;
> And to thy sacred Spirit convert those fires,
> Whose earthly fumes choake my devout aspires.

SECT. 33. Therefore for Spirits I am so farre from denying their existence, that I could easily beleeve, that not onely whole Countries, but particular persons have their Tutelary, and Guardian Angels: It is not a new opinion of the Church of *Rome,* but an old one of *Pythagoras* and *Plato;* there is no   †
heresie in it, and if not manifestly defin'd in Scripture, yet is it an opinion of a good and wholesome use in the course and actions of a mans life, and would serve as an *Hypothesis* to salve many doubts, whereof common Philosophy affordeth no solution. Now if you demand my opinion and Metaphysicks of their natures, I confesse them very shallow, most of them in a negative way, like that of God; or in a comparative,   88,89
between our selves and fellow creatures; for there is in this Universe a Staire, or manifest Scale of creatures, rising not disorderly, or in confusion, but with a comely method and proportion: betweene creatures of meere existence and things of life, there is a large disproportion of nature; betweene plants and animals or creatures of sense, a wider difference; between them and man, a farre greater: and if the proportion hold on, betweene man and Angels there should bee yet a greater. We doe not comprehend their natures, who retaine the first definition of *Porphyry,* and distinguish them from   †,90
our selves by immortality; for before his fall, man also was immortall; yet must wee needs affirme that he had a different essence from the Angels: having therefore no certaine knowledge of their natures, 'tis no bad method of the Schooles, whatsoever perfection we finde obscurely in our selves, in a more compleate and absolute way to ascribe unto them. I beleeve they have an extemporary knowledge, and upon the first motion of their reason doe what we cannot without study or deliberation; that they know things by their formes, and define by specificall differences what we describe by acci-   †
dents and properties; and therefore probabilities to us may bee demonstrations unto them: that they have knowledge not onely of the specificall, but numericall formes of individualls, and understand by what reserved difference each single *Hy-postasis* (besides the relation to its species) becomes its nu-mericall selfe. That as the Soule hath a power to move the body it informes, so there's a Faculty to move any, though

informe none; ours upon restraint of time, place and distance; but that invisible hand that conveyed *Habakkuk* to the Lions den, or *Philip* to *Azotus*, infringeth this rule, and hath a secret conveyance, wherewith mortality is not acquainted; if they have that intuitive knowledge, whereby as in reflexion they behold the thoughts of one another, I cannot peremptorily deny but they know a great part of ours. They that to refute the Invocation of Saints, have denied that they have any knowledge of our affaires below, have proceeded too farre, and must pardon my opinion, till I can thoroughly answer that piece of Scripture, *At the conversion of a sinner, the Angels of heaven rejoyce.* I cannot with those in that great Father, securely interpret the worke of the first day, *Fiat Lux*, to the creation of Angels; though (I confesse) there is not any creature that hath so neare a glympse of their nature, as light in the Sunne and Elements; we stile it a bare accident, but where it subsists alone, 'tis a spirituall Substance, and may bee an Angel: in briefe, conceive light invisible, and that is a Spirit.

SECT. 34. These are certainly the Magisteriall and master pieces of the Creator, the Flower (or as we may say) the best part of nothing; actually existing, what we are but in hopes, and probabilitie; we are onely that amphibious piece betweene a corporall and spirituall essence, that middle forme that linkes those two together, and makes good the method of God and nature, that jumps not from extreames, but unites the incompatible distances by some middle and participating natures. That wee are the breath and similitude of God, it is indisputable, and upon record of holy Scripture, but to call our selves a Microcosme, or little world, I thought it onely a pleasant trope of Rhetorick, till my neare judgement and second thoughts told me there was a reall truth therein: for first wee are a rude masse, and in the ranke of creatures which only are, and have a dull kinde of being not yet priviledged with life, or preferred to sense or reason; next we live the life of plants, the life of animals, the life of men, and at last the life of spirits, running on in one mysterious nature those five kinds of existences, which comprehend the crea-

tures not onely of the world, but of the Universe; thus is man
that great and true *Amphibium,* whose nature is disposed to
live not onely like other creatures in divers elements, but in
divided and distinguished worlds; for though there bee but
one world to sense, there are two to reason; the one visible,   †
the other invisible, whereof *Moses* seemes to have left noe   94
description, and of the other so obscurely, that some parts   †,95
thereof are yet in controversie; and truely for the first chap-   †
ters of *Genesis,* I must confesse a great deale of obscurity;
though Divines have to the power of humane reason endeavoured to make all goe in a literall meaning, yet those allegoricall interpretations are also probable, and perhaps the
mysticall method of *Moses* bred up in the Hieroglyphicall
Schooles of the Egyptians.

SECT. 35. Now for that immateriall world, me thinkes wee
need not wander so farre as the first moveable, for even in this
materiall fabricke the spirits walke as freely exempt from the
affections of time, place, and motion, as beyond the extream-   †
est circumference: doe but extract from the corpulency of
bodies, or resolve things beyond their first matter, and you   96
discover the habitation of Angels, which if I call the ubiqui-
tary and omnipresent essence of God, I hope I shall not offend Divinity; for before the Creation of the world God was
really all things. For the Angels hee created no new world,
or determinate mansion, and therefore they are every where
where is his essence, and doe live at a distance even in himselfe: that God made all things for man, is in some sense true,
yet not so farre as to subordinate the creation of those purer
creatures unto ours, though as ministring spirits they doe,
and are willing to fulfill the will of God in these lower and
sublunary affaires of man; God made all things for himself,
and it is impossible hee should make them for any other end
than his owne glory; it is all he can receive, and all that is
without himselfe; for honour being an externall adjunct, and
in the honourer rather than in the person honoured, it was
necessary to make a creature, from whom hee might receive
this homage; and that is in the other world Angels, in this,
man; which when we neglect, we forget the very end of our

creation, and may justly provoke God, not onely to repent
that hee hath made the world, but that hee hath sworne he   97
would not destroy it. That there is but one world, is a conclusion of faith. *Aristotle* with all his Philosophy hath not beene
able to prove it, and as weakely that the world was eternall;   98
that dispute much troubled the pennes of the antient Philosophers, but *Moses* decided that question, and all is salved with
the new terme of a creation, that is, a production of something out of nothing; and what is that? Whatsoever is opposite
to something, or more exactly, that which is truely contrary
unto God: for he onely is, all others have an existence with
dependency, and are something but by a distinction; and
herein is Divinity conformant unto Philosophy, and genera-   †
tion not onely founded on contrarieties, but also creation;
God being all things is contrary unto nothing, out of which
were made all things, and so nothing became something, and
Omneity informed *Nullity* into an essence.

SECT. 36. The whole Creation is a mystery, and particularly
that of man; at the blast of his mouth were the rest of the   99
creatures made, and at his bare word they started out of nothing: but in the frame of man (as the text describes it) he   100
played the sensible operator, and seemed not so much to
create, as make him; when hee had separated the materials   101
of other creatures, there consequently resulted a forme and
soule, but having raised the wals of man, he was driven to a
second and harder creation of a substance like himselfe, an
incorruptible and immortall soule. For these two affections we
have the Philosophy and opinion of the Heathens, the flat
affirmative of *Plato*, and not a negative from *Aristotle*: there   102,103
is another scruple cast in by Divinity (concerning its production) much disputed in the *Germane* auditories, and with
that indifferency and equality of arguments, as leave the controversie undetermined. I am not of *Paracelsus* minde that
boldly delivers a receipt to make a man without conjunction,   104
yet cannot but wonder at the multitude of heads that doe
deny traduction, having no other argument to confirme their
beliefe, then that Rhetoricall sentence, and *Antimetathesis* of   †
Augustine, Creando infunditur, infundendo creatur: either   105

opinion will consist well enough with religion, yet I should
rather incline to this, did not one objection haunt mee, not
wrung from speculations and subtilties, but from common
sense, and observation; not pickt from the leaves of any author, but bred amongst the weeds and tares of mine owne
braine. And this is a conclusion from the equivocall and monstrous productions in the copulation of man with beast; for if
the soule of man bee not transmitted and transfused in the
seed of the parents, why are not those productions meerely
beasts, but have also a tincture and impression of reason in
as high a measure as it can evidence it selfe in those improper
organs? Nor truely can I peremptorily deny that the soule, in
this her sublunary estate, is wholly and in all acceptions inor-   †
ganicall, but that for the performance of her ordinary actions,
is required not onely a symmetry and proper disposition of
Organs, but a Crasis and temper correspondent to its operations; yet is not this masse of flesh and visible structure the instrument and proper corps of the soule, but rather of sense,
and that the hand of reason. In our study of Anatomy there   106
is a masse of mysterious Philosophy, and such as reduced the
very Heathens to Divinitie; yet amongst all those rare discoveries and curious pieces I finde in the fabricke of man, I doe
not so much content my selfe as in that I finde not, that is, no
Organe or proper instrument for the rationall soule; for in the
braine, which wee tearme the seate of reason, there is not any
thing of moment more than I can discover in the cranie of a
beast: and this is a sensible and no inconsiderable argument   †
of the inorganity of the soule, at least in that sense we usually
so receive it. Thus we are men, and we know not how; there
is something in us, that can be without us, and will be after
us; though it is strange that it hath no history, what it was before us, nor cannot tell how it entred in us.

SECT. 37. Now for these wals of flesh, wherein the soule doth
seeme to be immured before the Resurrection, it is nothing
but an elementall composition, and a fabricke that must fall
to ashes; *All flesh is grasse,* is not onely metaphorically, but
literally true, for all those creatures we behold, are but the
hearbs of the field, digested into flesh in them, or more re-

motely carnified in our selves. Nay further, we are what we all
abhorre, *Anthropophagi* and Cannibals, devourers not onely
of men, but of our selves; and that not in an allegory, but a
positive truth; for all this masse of flesh which wee behold,
came in at our mouths: this frame wee looke upon, hath beene
upon our trenchers; In briefe, we have devoured our selves. I
cannot beleeve the wisedome of *Pythagoras* did ever positively, and in a literall sense, affirme his *Metempsychosis,* or
impossible transmigration of the soules of men into beasts: of
all Metamorphoses or transmigrations, I beleeve onely one,
that is of *Lots* wife, for that of *Nabuchodonosor* proceeded 107,108
not so farre; In all others I conceive no further verity then is
contained in their implicite sense and morality: I beleeve that
the whole frame of a beast doth perish, and is left in the same
estate after death as before it was materialled into life; that
the soules of men know neither contrary nor corruption; that
they subsist beyond the body, and outlive death by the priviledge of their proper natures, and without a miracle; that the
soules of the faithfull, as they leave earth, take possession of
Heaven: that those apparitions and ghosts of departed persons are not the wandring soules of men, but the unquiet
walkes of Devils, prompting and suggesting us unto mischiefe, bloud and villany, instilling, and stealing into our
hearts that the blessed spirits are not at rest in their graves,
but wander solicitous of the affaires of the world. That those
phantasmes appeare often, and doe frequent Cemiteries, 109
charnall houses, and Churches, it is because those are the
dormitories of the dead, where the Devill like an insolent
Champion beholds with pride the spoyles and Trophies of his
victory in *Adam*.

SECT. 38. This is that dismall conquest we all deplore, that
makes us so often cry, (O) *Adam, quid fecisti?* I thanke God 110
I have not those strait ligaments, or narrow obligations to the
world, as to dote on life, or be convulst and tremble at the
name of death: Not that I am insensible of the dread and horrour thereof, or by raking into the bowels of the deceased,
continuall sight of Anatomies, Skeletons, or Cadaverous reliques, like Vespilloes, or Grave-makers, I am become stupid,

or have forgot the apprehension of mortality; but that mar-
shalling all the horrours, and contemplating the extremities
thereof, I finde not any thing therein able to daunt the courage of a man, much lesse a well resolved Christian. And therefore am not angry at the errour of our first parents, or unwilling to beare a part of this common fate, and like the best of
them to dye, that is, to cease to breathe, to take a farewell of
the elements, to be a kinde of nothing for a moment, to be
within one instant of a spirit. When I take a full view and   †
circle of my selfe, without this reasonable moderator, and
equall piece of justice, Death, I doe conceive my selfe the
miserablest person extant; were there not another life that I
hope for, all the vanities of this world should not intreat a moments breath from me; could the Devill worke my beliefe to
imagine I could never dye, I would not out-live that very   †
thought; I have so abject a conceit of this common way of
existence, this retaining to the Sunne and Elements, I cannot
thinke this is to be a man, or to live according to the dignitie
of humanity; in expectation of a better, I can with patience
embrace this life, yet in my best meditations doe often desire   †
death; [It is a symptom of melancholy to be afraid of death,
and yet sometimes to desire it; this latter I have often discovered in my selfe, and thinke no man ever desired life, as
I have sometimes death.] I honour any man that contemnes   †
it, nor can I highly love any that is afraid of it; this makes me   †
naturally love a Souldier, and honour those tattered and contemptible Regiments that will die at the command of a Ser-
geant. For a Pagan there may bee some motives to bee in love
with life; but for a Christian to be amazed at death, I see not
how hee can escape this Dilemma, that he is too sensible of
this life, or hopelesse of the life to come.

SECT. 39. Some Divines count *Adam* 30 yeares old at his creation, because they suppose him created in the perfect age and
stature of man; and surely wee are all out of the computation
of our age, and every man is some moneths elder than hee
bethinkes him; for we live, move, have a being, and are subject to the actions of the elements, and the malice of diseases
in that other world, the truest Microcosme, the wombe of our

mother; for besides that generall and common existence wee
are conceived to hold in our Chaos, and whilst wee sleepe
within the bosome of our causes, wee enjoy a being and life in
three distinct worlds, wherein we receive most manifest grad-
uations: In that obscure world and wombe of our mother, our
time is short, computed by the Moone; yet longer than the
dayes of many creatures that behold the Sunne, our selves
being not yet without life, sense, and reason, though for the   111
manifestation of its actions, it awaits the opportunity of objects, and seemes to live there but in its roote and soule of
vegetation: entring afterwards upon the scene of the world,
wee arise up and become another creature, performing the
reasonable actions of man, and obscurely manifesting that
part of Divinity in us, but not in complement and perfection,
till we have once more cast our secondine, that is, this slough
of flesh, and are delivered into the last world, that is, that ineffable place of *Paul*, that proper *ubi* of spirits. The smattering   112
I have of the Philosophers stone, (which is something more   113
then the perfect exaltation of gold) hath taught me a great
deale of Divinity, and instructed my beliefe, how that immortall spirit and incorruptible substance of my soule may lye
obscure, and sleepe a while within this house of flesh. Those
strange and mysticall transmigrations that I have observed in   114
Silkewormes, turn'd my Philosophy into Divinity. There is in
these workes of nature, which seeme to puzle reason, something Divine, and hath more in it then the eye of a common
spectator doth discover.*

SECT. 40. I am naturally bashful, nor hath conversation, age, or
travell, beene able to effront, or enharden me, yet I have one
part of modesty which I have seldome discovered in another,
that is (to speake truly) I am not so much afraid of death, as

* [I have therefore forsaken those strict definitions of death, by priva-   †,115
tion of life, extinction of naturall heate, separation etc. of soule and
body, and have fram'd one in an hermeticall way unto mine owne
fancie; *est mutatio ultima, quâ perficitur nobile illud extractum Microcosmi*, for to mee that consider things in a naturall and experimentall
way, man seemes to bee but a digestion or a preparative way unto that
last and glorious Elixar which lies imprison'd in the chaines of flesh &c.]
Pembroke MS only.

ashamed thereof; 'tis the very disgrace and ignominy of our
natures, that in a moment can so disfigure us that our nearest
friends, Wife, and Children stand afraid and start at us. The
Birds and Beasts of the field that before in a naturall feare
obeyed us, forgetting all allegiance, begin to prey upon us.
This very conceite hath in a tempest disposed and left me   116
willing to be swallowed up in the abysse of waters; wherein
I had perished unseene, unpityed, without wondring eyes,
teares of pity, Lectures of mortality, and none had said, *quan-*
tum mutatus ab illo! Not that I am ashamed of the Anatomy   117
of my parts, or can accuse nature for playing the bungler in
any part of me, or my owne vitious life for contracting any
shamefull disease upon me, whereby I might not call my selfe
as wholesome a morsell for the wormes as any.

SECT. 41. Some upon the courage of a fruitful issue, wherein,   118
as in the truest Chronicle, they seem to outlive themselves,
can with greater patience away with death. This conceit and
counterfeit subsisting in our progenies seemes to mee a meere
fallacy, unworthy the desires of a man, that can but conceive
a thought of the next world; who, in a nobler ambition, should
desire to live in his substance in Heaven rather than in his   †
name and shadow on earth. And therefore at my death I   †
meane to take a totall adieu of the world, not caring for a
Monument, History, or Epitaph, not so much as the bare
memory of my name to be found any where but in the universall Register of God: I am not yet so Cynicall as to approve
the *Testament of *Diogenes;* nor doe I altogether allow that
Rodomontado of *Lucan;*   119

> —*Coelo tegitur, qui non habet urnam.*

> He that unburied lies wants not his Herse,
> For unto him a tombe's the Universe.

But commend in my calmer judgement those ingenuous intentions that desire to sleepe by the urnes of their Fathers,
and strive to goe the nearest way unto corruption. I doe not   †

* Who willed his friend not to bury him, but to hang him up with a staffe
in his hand to fright away the Crowes.

envy the temper of Crowes and Dawes, nor the numerous [120]
and weary dayes of our Fathers before the Flood. If there bee
any truth in Astrology, I may outlive a Jubilee; as yet I have
not seene one revolution of *Saturne*, nor hath my pulse beate [121]
thirty yeares, and yet, excepting one, have seene the Ashes, [122]
and left under ground, all the kings of *Europe*, have beene [123]
contemporary to three Emperours, four Grand Signiours, and
as many Popes; mee thinkes I have outlived my selfe, and begin to bee weary of the Sunne; I have shaken hands with [†]
delight in my warme blood and Canicular dayes; I perceive
I doe Anticipate the vices of age, the world to mee is but a
dreame, or mock show, and wee all therein but Pantalones
and Antickes to my severer contemplations.

SECT. 42. It is not, I confesse, an unlawfull Prayer to desire to [†]
surpasse the dayes of our Saviour, or wish to out-live that age
wherein he thought fittest to dye, yet if (as Divinity affirmes)
there shall be no gray hayres in Heaven, but all shall rise in
the perfect state of men, we doe but out-live those perfections
in this world, to be recalled unto them by a greater miracle
in the next, and run on here but to be retrograde hereafter.
Were there any hopes to out-live vice, or a point to be superannuated from sin, it were worthy our knees to implore the
dayes of *Methuselah*. But age doth not rectifie, but incurvate
our natures, turning bad dispositions into worser habits, and
(like diseases) brings on incurable vices; for every day as we
grow weaker in age, we grow stronger in sinne, and the number of our dayes doth but make our sinnes innumerable. The
same vice committed at sixteene, is not the same, though it
agree in all other circumstances, at forty, but swels and dou-
bles from the circumstances of our ages, wherein besides the
constant and inexcusable habit of transgressing, the maturity
of our Judgement cuts off pretence unto excuse or pardon:
every sin, the oftner it is committed, the more it acquireth in
the quality of evill; as it succeeds in time, so it precedes in de- [†]
grees of badnesse, for as they proceed they ever multiply, and
like figures in Arithmeticke, the last stands for more than all
that went before it: And though I thinke no man can live well [†]
once, but hee that could live twice, yet for my owne part, I

would not live over my houres past, or beginne againe the
thred of my dayes; not upon *Cicero's* ground, because I have   124
lived them well, but for feare I should live them worse: I find
my growing Judgement dayly instruct me how to be better,
but my untamed affections and confirmed vitiosity makes mee
dayly doe worse; I finde in my confirmed age the same sinnes
I discovered in my youth; I committed many then because I
was a child, and because I commit them still, I am yet an Infant. Therefore I perceive a man may be twice a child before
the dayes of dotage, and stand in need of *Aesons* bath before
threescore.

SECT. 43. And truely there goes a great deale of providence to   †
produce a mans life unto threescore: there is more required
than an able temper for those yeeres; though the radicall humour containe in it sufficient oyle for seventie, yet I perceive
in some it gives no light past thirtie; men assigne not all the
causes of long life that write whole bookes thereof. They that
found themselves on the radicall balsome or vitall sulphur of
the parts, determine not why *Abel* liv'd not so long as *Adam*.
There is therefore a secret glome or bottome of our dayes;
'twas his wisedome to determine them, but his perpetuall
and waking providence that fulfils and accomplisheth them,
wherein the spirits, our selves, and all the creatures of God in
a secret and disputed way doe execute his will. Let them not
therefore complaine of immaturitie that die about thirty; they
fall but like the whole world, whose solid and well composed
substance must not expect the duration and period of its constitution; when all things are compleated in it, its age is accomplished, and the last and generall fever may as naturally
destroy it before six thousand, as me before forty. There is   125
therfore some other hand that twines the thread of life than
that of nature; wee are not onely ignorant in Antipathies and
occult qualities, our ends are as obscure as our beginnings; the
line of our dayes is drawne by night, and the various effects
therein by a pencill that is invisible; wherein though wee confesse our ignorance, I am sure wee doe not erre, if wee say, it
is the hand of God.

SECT. 44. I am much taken with two verses of *Lucan,* since I [126]
have beene able not onely, as we doe at Schoole, to construe,
but understand:

> *Victurosque Dei celant, ut vivere durent,*
> *Felix esse mori.*

> We're all deluded, vainely searching wayes
> To make us happy by the length of dayes;
> For cunningly to make's protract this breath,
> The Gods conceale the happines of Death.

There be many excellent straines in that Poet, wherewith his
Stoicall Genius hath liberally supplyed him; and truely there
are singular pieces in the Philosophy of *Zeno,* and doctrine of
the Stoickes, which I perceive, delivered in a Pulpit, pass for
currant Divinity: yet herein are they in extreames, that can
allow a man to be his own *Assassine,* and so highly extol the
end and suicide of *Cato;* this is indeed not to feare death, but
yet to bee afraid of life. It is a brave act of valour to contemne
death, but where life is more terrible than death, it is then the
truest valour to dare to live, and herein Religion hath taught [127]
us a noble example: For all the valiant acts of *Curtius,*
Scevola, or *Codrus,* do not parallel or match that one of *Job;*
and sure there is no torture to the racke of a disease, nor any
Poynyards in death it selfe like those in the way and prologue
unto it. *Emori nolo, sed me esse mortuum nihil curo,* I would [128]
not die, but care not to be dead. Were I of *Caesars* Religion,
I should be of his desires, and wish rather to goe off at one
blow, then to be sawed in peeces by the grating torture of a
disease. Men that looke no further than their outsides thinke †
health an appertinance unto life, and quarrell with their constitutions for being sick; but I that have examined the parts
of man, and know upon what tender filaments that Fabrick
hangs, doe wonder that we are not always so; and considering the thousand dores that lead to death doe thanke my God
that we can die but once. 'Tis not onely the mischiefe of diseases, and the villanie of poysons that make an end of us, we
vainly accuse the fury of Gunnes, and the new inventions of
death; 'tis in the power of every hand to destroy us, and wee
are beholding unto every one wee meete hee doth not kill

us. There is therefore but one comfort left, that though it be
in the power of the weakest arme to take away life, it is not in
the strongest to deprive us of death: God would not exempt
himselfe from that; the misery of immortality in the flesh he
undertooke not, that was in it immortall. Certainly there is no
happinesse within this circle of flesh, nor is it in the Opticks
of these eyes to behold felicity; the first day of our Jubilee is
death; the devill hath therefore fail'd of his desires; wee are
happier with death than we should have beene without it:
there is no misery but in himselfe where there is no end of
misery; and so indeed in his own sense, the Stoick is in the
right. Hee forgets that hee can die who complaines of misery;
wee are in the power of no calamitie while death is in our
owne.

SECT. 45. Now besides this literall and positive kinde of death,
there are others whereof Divines make mention, and those, I
thinke, not meerely Metaphoricall, as Mortification, dying
unto sin and the world; therefore, I say, every man hath a
double Horoscope, one of his humanity, his birth; another of
his Christianity, his baptisme, and from this doe I compute or
calculate my Nativitie, not reckoning those *Horae combustae,*
and odde dayes, or esteeming my selfe any thing, before I
was my Saviours, and inrolled in the Register of Christ: Whosoever enjoyes not this life, I count him but an apparition,
though he weare about him the sensible affections of flesh. In
these morall acceptions, the way to be immortall is to die
daily, nor can I thinke I have the true Theory of death, when
I contemplate a skull, or behold a Skeleton with those vulgar
imaginations it casts upon us; I have therefore enlarged that
common *Memento mori,* into a more Christian memorandum,   129
Memento quatuor novissima, those foure inevitable points of   130
us all, Death, Judgement, Heaven, and Hell. Neither did the
contemplations of the Heathens rest in their graves, without
a further thought of *Rhadamanth,* or some judiciall proceeding after death, though in another way, and upon suggestion
of their naturall reasons. I cannot but marvaile from what
Sybill or Oracle they stole the prophesy of the worlds destruction by fire, or whence *Lucan* learned to say,   131

Communis mundo superest rogus, ossibus astra Misturus.

There yet remaines to th' world one common fire,
Wherein our bones with stars shall make one pyre.

I beleeve the world growes neare its end, yet is neither old [132]
nor decayed, nor will ever perish upon the ruines of its owne
principles. As Creation was a work above nature, so is its ad- [†]
versary, annihilation; without which the world hath not its
end, but its mutation. Now what fire should bee able to con- [†]
sume it thus farre, without the breath of God, which is the
truest consuming flame, my Philosophy cannot informe me.
Some beleeve there went not a minute to the worlds creation, [†,133]
nor shal there go to its destruction; those six dayes so punctually described, make not to them one moment, but rather
seem to manifest the method and Idea of that great worke in [†,†]
the intellect of God, than the manner how hee proceeded in
its operation. I cannot dreame there should be at the last day
any such Judiciall proceeding, or calling to the Barre, as indeed the Scripture seemes to imply, and the literall commentators doe conceive: for unspeakable mysteries in the
Scriptures are often delivered in a vulgar and illustrative way,
and being written unto man, are delivered, not as they truely
are, but as they may bee understood; wherein notwithstanding the different interpretations according to different capacities may stand firme with our devotion, nor bee any way
prejudiciall to each single edification.

SECT. 46. Now to determine the day and yeare of this inevitable time, is not onely convincible and statute madnesse, but
also manifest impiety; How shall we interpret *Elias* 6000
yeares, or imagine the secret communicated to a Rabbi, [134]
which God hath denyed unto his Angels? It had beene an [135]
excellent quaere, to have posed the devill of *Delphos,* and
must needs have forced him to some strange amphibology; it
hath not onely mocked the predictions of sundry Astrologers
in ages past, but the prophecies of many melancholy heads in
these present, who, neither understanding reasonably things
past or present, pretend a knowledge of things to come; heads
ordained onely to manifest the incredible effects of melan-

choly, and to fulfill °old prophesies rather than be the authors of new. In those dayes there shall come warres and   †,†,136
rumours of warres, to me seemes no prophesie, but a constant truth, in all times verified since it was pronounced.
There shall bee signes in the Moone and Starres, how comes
he then like a theefe in the night, when he gives an item of
his comming? That common signe drawne from the revelation of Antichrist, is as obscure as any; in our common compute he hath beene come these many yeares, but for my owne
part to speake freely, I am halfe of opinion that Antichrist is   †,†,137
the Philosophers stone in Divinity, for the discovery and invention whereof, though there be prescribed rules, and probable inductions, yet hath hardly any man attained the perfect   †
discovery thereof. That generall opinion that the world
growes neere its end, hath possessed all ages past as neerely
as ours; I am afraid that the Soules that now depart, cannot
escape that lingring expostulation of the Saints under the Altar, *Quousque, Domine? How long, O Lord?* and groane in   138
the expectation of the great Jubilee.

SECT. 47. This is the day that must make good that great
attribute of God, his Justice; that must reconcile those unan-
swerable doubts that torment the wisest understandings, and
reduce those seeming inequalities and respective distributions in this world, to an equality and recompensive Justice
in the next. This is that one day, that shall include and comprehend all that went before it, wherein as in the last scene,
all the Actors must enter to compleate and make up the Catastrophe of this great peece. This is the day whose memory
hath onely power to make us honest in the darke, and to bee
vertuous without a witnesse. *Ipsa sui pretium virtus sibi,* that   †,139
vertue is her owne reward, is but a cold principle, and not
able to maintaine our variable resolutions in a constant and
setled way of goodnesse. I have practised that honest artifice   140
of *Seneca,* and in my retired and solitary imaginations, to detaine me from the foulenesse of vice, have fancyed to my selfe
the presence of my deare and worthiest friends, before
whom I should lose my head, rather than be vitious; yet

° In those dayes there shall come lyers and false prophets.

herein I found that there was nought but morall honesty, and
this was not to be vertuous for his sake that must reward us
at the last. I have tryed if I could reach that great resolution of   141
his, and be honest without a thought of Heaven or Hell; and
indeed I found upon a naturall inclination, and inbred loyalty   †
unto vertue, that I could serve her without a livery, yet not in
that resolved and venerable way, but that the frailty of my
nature, upon an easie temptation, might be induced to forget
her. The life therefore and spirit of all our actions is the resurrection, and stable apprehension that our ashes shall enjoy
the fruits of our pious endeavours; without this, all Religion is   †
a Fallacy, and those impieties of *Lucian, Euripides,* and *Ju-*   142
lian are no blasphemies, but subtile verities, and Atheists
have beene the onely Philosophers.

SECT. 48. How shall the dead arise, is no question of my
faith; to beleeve onely possibilities, is not faith, but meere
Philosophy; many things are true in Divinity, which are
neither inducible by reason, nor confirmable by sense, and
many things in Philosophy confirmable by sense, yet not inducible by reason. Thus it is impossible by any solid or
demonstrative reasons to perswade a man to beleeve the
conversion of the Needle to the North; though this be possible, and true, and easily credible, upon a single experiment
unto the sense. I beleeve that our estranged and divided
ashes shall unite againe; that our separated dust after so
many pilgrimages and transformations into the parts of mineralls, Plants, Animals, Elements, shall at the voyce of God
returne into their primitive shapes; and joyne againe to
make up their primary and predestinate formes. As at the
Creation there was a separation of that confused masse into
its species, so at the destruction thereof there shall bee a
separation into its distinct individuals. As at the Creation of
the world, all the distinct species that wee behold lay involved in one masse, till the fruitfull voyce of God separated
this united multitude into its severall species: so at the last
day, when these corrupted reliques shall be scattered in the
wildernesse of formes, and seeme to have forgot their proper
habits, God by a powerfull voyce shall command them

backe into their proper shapes, and call them out by their single individuals: Then shall appeare the fertilitie of *Adam,* and the magicke of that sperme that hath dilated into so many millions. [What is made to be immortall, Nature can- †
not, nor will the voyce of God, destroy. These bodies that wee behold to perish, were in their created natures immor-tall, and liable unto death but accidentally and upon forfeit; and therefore they owe not that naturall homage unto death as other bodies, but may be restored to immortality with a lesser miracle, and by a bare and easie revocation of the curse returne immortall.] I have often beheld as a miracle, that artificiall resurrection and revivification of *Mercury,* how being mortified into a thousand shapes, it assumes †
again its owne, and returns to its numericall selfe. Let us †
speake naturally, and like Philosophers: the formes of altera-ble bodies in these sensible corruptions perish not; nor, as wee imagine, wholly quit their mansions, but retire and con-tract themselves into their secret and unaccessible parts, where they may best protect themselves from the action of their Antagonist. A plant or vegetable consumed to ashes, to a contemplative and schoole Philosopher seemes utterly destroyed, and the forme to have taken his leave for ever: But to a sensible Artist the formes are not perished, but with- †
drawne into their incombustible part, where they lie secure from the action of that devouring element. This is made †
good by experience, which can from the ashes of a plant   143
revivifie the plant, and from its cinders recall it into its stalk   †
and leaves againe. What the Art of man can doe in these in-feriour pieces, what blasphemy is it to affirme the finger of God cannot doe in these more perfect and sensible struc-   144
tures? This is that mysticall Philosophy, from whence no true Scholler becomes an Atheist, but from the visible effects of nature growes up a reall Divine, and beholds not in a dreame, as *Ezekiel,* but in an ocular and visible object the   145
types of his resurrection.

SECT. 49. Now, the necessary Mansions of our restored selves are those two contrary and incompatible places wee call Heaven and Hell; to define them, or strictly to determine

what and where these are, surpasseth my Divinity. That
elegant Apostle which seemed to have a glimpse of Heaven,   146
hath left but a negative description thereof; Which neither
eye hath seen, nor earc hath heard, nor can it enter into the
heart of man: he was translated out of himself to behold it,
but being returned into himselfe could not expresse it. Saint   147
Johns description by Emeralds, Chrysolites, and pretious
stones, is too weake to expresse the materiall Heaven we behold. Briefely therefore, where the soule hath the full measure and complement of happinesse, where the boundlesse
appetite of that spirit remaines compleately satisfied, that it
can neither desire addition nor alteration; that I thinke is
truely Heaven: and this can onely be in the enjoyment of
that essence, whose infinite goodnesse is able to terminate
the desires of it selfe, and the insatiable wishes of ours;   †
wherever God will thus manifest himselfe, there is Heaven,
though within the circle of this sensible world. Thus the
soule of man may bee in Heaven any where, even within the
limits of his owne proper body, and when it ceaseth to live
in the body, it may remaine in its owne soule, that is its Creator. And thus wee may say that Saint *Paul,* whether in the
body, or out of the body, was yet in Heaven. To place it in
the Empyreall, or beyond the tenth Spheare, is to forget the
worlds destruction; for when this sensible world shall be
destroyed, all shall then bee here as it is now there, an
Empyreall Heaven, a *quasi* vacuitie, when to aske where
Heaven is, is to demand where the Presence of God is, or
where wee have the glory of that happy vision. *Moses,* that
was bred up in all the learning of the *Egyptians,* committed
a grosse absurdity in Philosophy, when with these eyes of
flesh he desired to see God, and petitioned his Maker, that is
truth it selfe, to a contradiction. Those that imagine
Heaven and Hell neighbours, and conceive a vicinity between those two extreames, upon consequence of the Parable, where *Dives* discoursed with *Lazarus* in *Abrahams*   148
bosome, do too grossely conceive of those glorified creatures,
whose eyes shall easily out-see the Sunne, and behold without a Perspective the extremest distances: for if there shall
be in our glorified eyes, the faculty of sight and reception of

objects, I could thinke the visible species there to be in as
unlimitable a way as now the intellectuall. I grant that two
bodies placed beyond the tenth Spheare, or in a vacuity,
according to *Aristotles* Philosophy, could not behold each   149
other, because there wants a body or Medium to hand and
transport the visible rayes of the object unto the sense; but
when there shall be a generall defect of either Medium to
convey, or light to prepare and dispose that Medium, and
yet a perfect vision, wee must suspend the rules of our Philosophy, and make all good by a more absolute piece of
Opticks.

SECT. 50. I cannot tell how to say that fire is the essence of
hell; I know not what to make of Purgatory, or conceive a
flame that can either prey upon, or purifie the substance of   †
a soule; those flames of sulphure mentioned in the Scrip-   150
tures, I take not to be understood of this present Hell, but
of that to come, where fire shall make up the complement of
our tortures, and have a body or subject whereon to manifest
its tyranny: some who have had the honour to be textuarie
in Divinity, are of opinion it shall be the same specificall fire
with ours. This is hard to conceive; yet can I make good how
even that may prey upon our bodies, and yet not consume
us: for in this materiall world, there are bodies that persist
invincible in the powerfullest flames, and though by the action of fire they fall into ignition and liquation, yet will they
never suffer a destruction: I would gladly know how *Moses*
with an actuall fire calcin'd or burnt the golden Calfe into
powder: for that mysticall mettle of gold, whose solary and
celestiall nature I admire, exposed unto the violence of fire, †
grows onely hot, and liquifies, but consumeth not: so when
the consumable and volatile pieces of our bodies shall be refined into a more impregnable and fixed temper like gold,
though they suffer from the action of flames, they shall never
perish, but lye immortall in the armes of fire. And surely if
this frame must suffer onely by the action of this element,
there will many bodies escape, and not onely Heaven, but
earth will not bee at an end, but rather a beginning; For at
present it is not earth, but a composition of fire, water, earth,

and aire: but at that time, spoyled of these ingredients, it
shall appeare in a substance more like it selfe, its ashes.
Philosophers that opinioned the worlds destruction by fire,
did never dreame of annihilation, which is beyond the power
of sublunary causes; for the last and powerfullest action of
that element is but vitrification or a reduction of a body into
Glasse; and therefore some of our Chymicks facetiously affirm, [yea, and urge Scripture for it] that at the last fire all
shall be chrystallized and reverberated into glasse, which
is the utmost action of that element. Nor need we fear this
term "annihilation", or wonder that God will destroy the †
workes of his Creation: for man subsisting, who is, and will
then truely appeare a Microcosme, the world cannot bee
said to be destroyed. For the eyes of God, and perhaps also
of our glorified selves, shall as really behold and contemplate
the world in its Epitome or contracted essence, as now they †
doe at large and in its dilated substance. In the seed of a
Plant to the eyes of God, and to the understanding of man,
there exists, though in an invisible way, the perfect leaves,
flowers, and fruit thereof: (for things that are in *posse* to the
sense, are actually existent to the understanding). Thus God
beholds all things, who contemplates as fully his workes in
their Epitome, as in their full volume, and beheld as amply
the whole world in that little compendium of the sixth day,
as in the scattered and dilated pieces of those five before.

SECT. 51. Men commonly set forth the torments of Hell by
fire, and the extremity of corporall afflictions, and describe
Hell in the same method that *Mahomet* doth Heaven. This
indeed makes a noyse, and drums in popular eares: but if
this be the terrible piece thereof, it is not worthy to stand in
diameter with Heaven, whose happinesse consists in that
part that is best able to comprehend it, that immortall essence, that translated divinity and colony of God, the soule.
Surely though wee place Hell under earth, the Devils walke †
and purlue is about it: men speake too popularly who place
it in those flaming mountaines, which to grosser apprehensions represent Hell. The heart of man is the place the devill
dwels in; I feele somtimes a hell within my selfe, *Lucifer*

keeps his court in my brest, *Legion* is revived in me. There   151
are as many hels as *Anaxagoras* conceited worlds; there was   152
more than one hell in *Magdalen,* when there were seven   153
devils, for every devill is an hell unto himselfe: hee holds
enough of torture in his owne *ubi,* and needs not the misery
of circumference to afflict him, and thus a distracted conscience here is a shadow or introduction unto hell hereafter;
Who can but pity the mercifull intention of those hands that
doe destroy themselves? the devill, were it in his power,
would doe the like; which being impossible, his miseries are
endlesse, and he suffers most in that attribute wherein he is
impassible, his immortality.

SECT. 52. I thanke God, and with joy I mention it, I was never
afraid of Hell, nor never grew pale at the description of that
place; I have so fixed my contemplations on Heaven, that I
have almost forgot the Idea of Hell, and I am afraid rather to
lose the joyes of the one than endure the misery of the other;
to be deprived of them is a perfect hell, and needs me
thinkes no addition to compleate our afflictions; that terrible
terme hath never detained me from sin, nor do I owe any
good action to the name thereof: I feare God, yet am not
afraid of him, his mercies make me ashamed of my sins, before his judgements afraid thereof: these are the forced and
secondary method of his wisedome, which he useth but as
the last remedy, and upon provocation, a course rather to
deterre the wicked, than incite the vertuous to his worship.   †
I can hardly thinke there was ever any scared into Heaven;   †
they go the fairest way to Heaven that would serve God without a Hell; other Mercenaries that crouch unto him in feare
of Hell, though they terme themselves the servants, are indeed but the slaves of the Almighty.

SECT. 53. And to be true, and speake my soule, when I survey the occurrences of my life, and call into account the
finger of God, I can perceive nothing but an abysse and
masse of mercies, either in generall to mankind, or in particular to my selfe; and whether out of the prejudice of my
affection, or an inverting and partiall conceit of his mercies,

I know not, but those which others terme crosses, afflictions, judgements, misfortunes, to me who enquire farther into them than their visible effects, they both appeare, and in event have ever proved the secret and dissembled favours of his affection. It is a singular piece of wisedome to apprehend truly, and without passion, the workes of God, and so well to distinguish his justice from his mercy, as not to miscall those noble attributes; yet it is likewise an honest piece of Logick so to dispute and argue the proceedings of God, as to distinguish even his judgements into mercies. For God is mercifull unto all, because better to the worst, than the best deserve; and to say he punisheth none in this world, though it be a Paradox, is no absurdity. To one that hath committed murther, if the judge should onely ordaine a Fine it were a madnesse to call this a punishment, and to repine at the sentence, rather than admire the clemency of the Judge. Thus our offences being mortall, and deserving not onely death, but damnation, if the goodnesse of God be content to traverse and passe them over with a losse, misfortune, or disease; what frensie were it to terme this a punishment, rather than an extremity of mercy, and to groane under the rod of his judgements, rather than admire the Scepter of his mercies? Therefore to adore, honour, and admire him, is a debt of gratitude due from the obligation of our nature, states, and conditions; and with these thoughts, he that knowes them best, will not deny that I adore him; that I obtaine Heaven, or the blisse thereof, is accidentall, and not the intended worke of my devotion, it being a felicitie I can neither thinke to deserve, nor scarse in modesty to expect. For these two ends of us all, either as rewards or punishments, are mercifully ordained and disproportionally disposed unto our actions, the one being so far beyond our deserts, the other so infinitely below our demerits.

SECT. 54. There is no salvation to those that beleeve not in Christ, that is, say some, since his Nativity, and as Divinity affirmeth, before also; which makes me much apprehend the end of those honest Worthies and Philosophers which dyed before his Incarnation. It is hard to place those soules in Hell [154]

whose worthy lives doe teach us vertue on earth; methinks,
amongst those many subdivisions of hell, there might have
bin one Limbo left for these: What a strange vision will it   155
be to see their poeticall fictions converted into verities, and
their imagined and fancied Furies, into reall Devils? How
strange to them will sound the History of *Adam,* when they
shall suffer for him they never heard of? when they that de-   †
rive their Genealogy from the Gods, shall know they are the
unhappy issue of sinfull man? It is an insolent part of reason
to controvert the works of God, or question the justice of his
proceedings; Could humility teach others, as it hath instructed me, to contemplate the infinite and incomprehensible distance betwixt the Creator and the creature, or did wee
seriously perpend that one Simile of Saint *Paul, Shall the
vessell say to the Potter, Why hast thou made me thus?* it
would prevent these arrogant disputes of reason; nor would
wee argue the definitive sentence of God, either to Heaven
or Hell. Men that live according to the right rule and law of
reason, live but in their owne kinde, as beasts doe in theirs;
who justly obey the prescript of their natures, and therefore
cannot reasonably demand a reward of their actions, as onely
obeying the naturall dictates of their reason. It will therefore, and must at last appeare, that all salvation is through
Christ; which verity I feare these great examples of vertue
must confirme, and make it good, how the perfectest actions
of earth have no title or claime unto Heaven.

SECT. 55. Nor truely doe I thinke the lives of these or any
other were ever correspondent, or in all points conformable
unto their doctrines; it is evident that *Aristotle* transgressed
the rule of his owne Ethicks; the Stoicks that condemne passion, and command a man to laugh in *Phalaris* his Bull, could
not endure without a groane a fit of the stone or collick. The
Scepticks that affirmed they knew nothing, even in that
opinion confuted themselves, and thought they knew more   †
than all the world beside. *Diogenes* I hold to bee the most
vaineglorious man of his time, and more ambitious in re-
fusing all Honours, than *Alexander* in rejecting none. Vice
and the Devill put a fallacie upon our reasons, and pro-

voking us too hastily to run from it, entangle and profound us deeper in it. The Duke of *Venice*, that weds himselfe unto the Sea by casting therein a ring of Gold, I will not argue of   †
prodigality, because it is a solemnity of good use and conse-
quence in the State. But the Philosopher that threw his   156
money into the Sea to avoyd avarice, was a notorious prodi-
gal. There is no road or ready way to vertue, it is not an easie point of art to untangle our selves from this riddle, or web of sin: To perfect vertue, as to Religion, there is required a Panoplia, or compleat armour, that, whilst we lye at close ward   †
against one Vice, we lye not open to the vennie of another: †
And indeed wiser discretions that have the thred of reason to conduct them, offend without a pardon; whereas under heads may stumble without dishonour. There goe so many circum-
stances to piece up one good action, that it is a lesson to be good, and wee are forced to be vertuous by the booke. Againe, the practice of men holds not an equall pace, yea, and often runnes counter to their Theory; we naturally know what is good, but naturally pursue what is evill: the Rhetoricke wherewith I perswade another cannot perswade my selfe: there is a depraved appetite in us, that will with patience heare the learned instructions of Reason; but yet performe no farther than agrees to its owne irregular Humour. In briefe, we all are monsters, that is, a composition of man and beast, wherein we must endeavour to be as the Poets fancy that wise man *Chiron*, that is, to have the Region of Man above that of Beast, and sense to sit but at the feete of reason. Lastly, I doe desire with God that all, but yet affirme with men that few shall know salvation, that the bridge is narrow, the passage   157
straite unto life; yet those who doe confine the Church of God, either to particular Nations, Churches, or Families, have made it farre narrower than our Saviour ever meant it.

SECT. 56. The vulgarity of those judgements that wrap the   †
Church of God in *Strabo's* cloake and restrain it unto Eu-
rope, seeme to mee as bad Geographers as *Alexander*, who thought hee had conquer'd all the world, when hee had not subdued the halfe of any part thereof: For we cannot deny the Church of God both in Asia and Africa, if we doe not

forget the peregrinations of the Apostles, the death of their
Martyrs, the sessions of many, and even in our reformed
judgement, lawfull councells held in those parts in the mi-
noritie and nonage of ours: nor must a few differences, more
remarkable in the eyes of man than perhaps in the judgement of God, excommunicate from heaven one another,
much lesse those Christians who are in a manner all Martyrs,
maintaining their faith in the noble way of persecution, and
serving God in the fire, whereas we honour him but in the
Sunshine. 'Tis true we all hold there is a number of Elect,
and many to be saved, yet take our opinions together, and
from the confusion thereof there will be no such thing as salvation, nor shall any one be saved; for first the Church of
Rome condemneth us, wee likewise them, the Sub-reformists
and Sectaries sentence the Doctrine of our Church as damna-
ble, the Atomist, or Familist reprobates all these, and all   158
these them againe. Thus whilst the mercies of God doth
promise us heaven, our conceits and opinions exclude us from
that place. There must be therefore more than one Saint
Peter; particular Churches and Sects usurpe the gates of
heaven, and turne the key against each other, and thus we
goe to heaven against each others wills, conceits and opinions,
and with as much uncharity as ignorance, doe erre I feare
in points not onely of our own, but on anothers salvation.

SECT. 57. I beleeve many are saved who to man seeme reprobated, and many are reprobated, who in the opinion and
sentence of man, stand elected; there will appeare at the last
day strange and unexpected examples both of his justice and
his mercy, and therefore to define either is folly in man, and
insolency even in the devils; those acute and subtill spirits,
in all their sagacity, can hardly divine who shall be saved;   †
which if they could prognostick, their labour were at an end;
nor need they compasse the earth, seeking whom they may
devoure. Those who upon a rigid application of the Law,
sentence *Solomon* unto damnation, condemne not onely him,
but themselves, and the whole world; for by the letter and
written Word of God, we are without exception in the state
of death, but there is a prerogative of God, and an arbitrary

pleasure above the letter of his owne Law, by which alone wee can pretend unto salvation, and through which *Solomon* might be as easily saved as those who condemne him.

SECT. 58. The number of those who pretend unto salvation, and those infinite swarmes who thinke to passe through the eye of this Needle, hath much amazed me. That name and †
compellation of *little Flocke,* doth not comfort but deject 159
my devotion, especially when I reflect upon mine owne un-worthinesse, wherein, according to my humble apprehensions, I am below them all. I beleeve there shall never be an Anarchy in Heaven, but as there are Hierarchies amongst the 160
Angels, so shall there be degrees of priority amongst the Saints. Yet is it (I protest) beyond my ambition to aspire unto the first rankes; my desires onely are, and I shall be happy therein, to be but the last man, and bring up the Rere in Heaven.

SECT. 59. Againe, I am confident, and fully perswaded, yet dare not take my oath of my salvation; I am as it were sure, and do beleeve, without all doubt, that there is such a City as *Constantinople,* yet for me to take my Oath thereon were a kinde of perjury, because I hold no infallible warrant from my owne sense to confirme me in the certainty thereof. And truely, though many pretend an absolute certainty of their salvation, yet when an humble soule shall contemplate her owne unworthinesse, she shall meete with many doubts and suddainely finde how little wee stand in need of the precept †
of Saint *Paul, Worke out your salvation with feare and trembling.* That which is the cause of my election, I hold to be the cause of my salvation, which was the mercy and bene-placit of God, before I was, or the foundation of the world. *Before Abraham was, I am,* is the saying of Christ, yet is it true in some sense if I say it of my selfe, for I was not onely before my selfe, but *Adam,* that is, in the Idea of God, and the decree of that Synod held from all Eternity. And in this sense, I say, the world was before the Creation, and at an end before it had a beginning; and thus was I dead before I †

was alive; though my grave be *England,* my dying place was
Paradise, and *Eve* miscarried of mee before she conceiv'd of
Cain.

SECT. 60. Insolent zeales that doe decry good workes and rely   †,161
onely upon faith, take not away merit: for depending upon   †
the efficacy of their faith, they enforce the condition of God,
and in a more sophisticall way doe seeme to challenge
Heaven. It was decreed by God, that onely those that lapt   162
in the waters like dogges, should have the honour to destroy
the *Midianites,* yet could none of those justly challenge, or
imagine hee deserved that honour thereupon. I doe not deny,
but that true faith, and such as God requires, is not onely a
marke or token, but also a meanes of our Salvation, but
where to finde this, is as obscure to me, as my last end. And
if our Saviour could object unto his owne Disciples, and fa-
vourites, a faith, that to the quantity of a graine of Mustard
seed, is able to remove mountaines; surely, that which wee
boast of, is not any thing, or at the most, but a remove from
nothing. This is the Tenor of my beleefe, wherein, though
there be many things singular, and to the humour of my irregular selfe, yet, if they square not with maturer Judgements, I disclaime them, and doe no further father them,
than the learned and best Judgements shall authorize them.

THE SECOND PART

SECT. 1. Now for that other Vertue of Charity, without which
Faith is a meer notion, and of no existence, I have ever endeavoured to nourish the mercifull disposition and humane
inclination I borrowed from my Parents, and regulate it to
the written and prescribed Lawes of Charity; and if I hold
the true Anatomy of my selfe, I am delineated and naturally
framed to such a piece of vertue: for I am of a constitution
so generall, that it consorts and sympathizeth with all things;
I have no antipathy, or rather Idio-syncrasie, in dyet, humour, ayre, any thing; I wonder not at the *French,* for their
dishes of frogges, snailes, and toadstooles, nor at the Jewes

for Locusts and Grasse-hoppers, but being amongst them, make them my common viands; and I finde they agree with my stomach as well as theirs; I could digest a Sallad gathered in a Church-yard, as well as in a Garden. I cannot start at the presence of a Serpent, Scorpion, Lizard, or Salamander; at the sight of a Toad, or Viper, I finde in me no desire to take up a stone to destroy them. I feele not in my selfe those common antipathies that I can discover in others: Those national repugnances doe not touch me, nor do I behold with prejudice the *French, Italian, Spaniard,* or *Dutch;* †
but where I find their actions in ballance with my Countreymens, I honour, love, and embrace them in the same degree; I was borne in the eighth Climate, but seeme to bee framed †
and constellated unto all; I am no Plant that will not prosper out of a Garden. All places, all ayres make unto me one Country; I am in *England* every where, and under any meridian; I have beene shipwrackt, yet am not enemy with the sea or winds; I can study, play, or sleepe in a tempest. In briefe, I am averse from nothing, [neither Plant, Animall, nor Spirit]; my conscience would give mee the lie if I should say I absolutely detest or hate any essence but the Devill, †
or so at least abhorre any thing but that wee might come to composition. If there be any among those common objects of hatred I doe contemne and laugh at, it is that great enemy of reason, vertue, and religion, the multitude; that numerous piece of monstrosity, which taken asunder seeme men, and the reasonable creatures of God; but confused together, make but one great beast, and a monstrosity more prodigious than Hydra; it is no breach of Charity to call these fooles, it is the stile all holy Writers have afforded them, set downe by *Solomon* in canonicall Scripture, and a point of our faith to beleeve so. Neither in the name of multitude doe I onely include the base and minor sort of people; there is a rabble even amongst the Gentry, a sort of Plebeian heads, whose fancy moves with the same wheele as these; men in the same Levell with Mechanickes, though their fortunes doe somewhat guild their infirmities, and their purses compound for their follies. But as in casting account, three or foure men together come short in account of one man placed 1

by himself below them: So neither are a troope of these
ignorant Doradoes of that true esteeme and value, as many
a forlorne person, whose condition doth place him below   †
their feet. Let us speake like Politicians; there is a Nobility
without Heraldry, a naturall dignity whereby one man is
ranked with another, another filed before him, according to
the quality of his desert, and preheminence of his good parts.
Though the corruption of these times, and the byas of present
practise wheele another way, thus it was in the first and
primitive Common-wealths, and is yet in the integrity and
Cradle of well-order'd polities, till corruption getteth
ground, ruder desires labouring after that which wiser considerations contemn, every one having a liberty to amasse
and heape up riches, and they a licence or faculty to doe
or purchase any thing.

SECT. 2. This generall and indifferent temper of mine doth
more neerely dispose mee to this noble vertue. It is a happinesse to be borne and framed unto vertue, and to grow
up from the seeds of nature, rather than the inoculation and
forced graffes of education; yet if we are directed only by our
particular Natures, and regulate our inclinations by no
higher rule than that of our reasons, we are but Moralists;
Divinity will still call us Heathens. Therefore this great
worke of charity must have other motives, ends, and im-
pulsives; I give no almes to satisfie the hunger of my Brother,   †
but to fulfill and accomplish the Will and Command of my
God; I draw not my purse for his sake that demands it, but
his that enjoyned it; I relieve no man upon the Rhetorick of
his miseries, nor to content mine own commiserating disposition, for this is still but morall charity, and an act that oweth
more to passion than reason. Hee that relieves another upon
the bare suggestion and bowels of pity, doth not this so much
for his sake as for his own: for by compassion we make anothers misery our own, and so by relieving them, we relieve our selves also. It is as erroneous a conceite to redresse
other mens misfortunes upon that common consideration of
merciful natures, that it may bee one day our own case; for
this is a sinister and politick kind of charity, wherby we   †

seem to bespeak the pities of men, in the like occasions; and truly I have observed that these professed Eleemosynaries, though in a croud or multitude, doe yet direct and place their petitions on a few and selected persons; there is surely a Physiogonomy, which those experienced and Master Mendicants observe, whereby they instantly discover a mercifull aspect, and will single out a face wherein they spy the signatures and markes of mercy: for there are mystically in our faces certaine characters which carry in them the motto of our Soules, wherein he that cannot read A.B.C. may read our natures. I hold moreover that there is a Phytognomy, or Physiognomy, not onely of men, but of Plants, and Vegetables; and in every one of them, some outward figures which hang as signes and bushes of their inward formes. The finger of God hath left an inscription upon all his workes, not graphicall or composed of Letters, but of their severall formes, constitutions, parts, and operations, which aptly joyned together doe make one word that doth expresse their natures. By these Letters God cals the Starres by their names, and by this Alphabet *Adam* assigned to every creature a name peculiar to its Nature. Now there are besides these Characters in our faces, certaine mysticall figures in our hands, which I dare not call meere dashes, strokes *à la volée*, or at randome, because delineated by a pencill that never workes in vaine; and hereof I take more particular notice, because I carry that in mine owne hand, which I could never read of, nor discover in another. *Aristotle*, I confesse, in his acute and singular booke of Physiognomy, hath made no mention of Chiromancy, yet I beleeve the *Egyptians*, who were neerer addicted to those abstruse and mysticall sciences, had a knowledge therein, to which those vagabond and counterfeit *Egyptians* did after pretend, and [2] perhaps retained a few corrupted principles, which sometimes might verifie their prognostickes.

It is the common wonder of all men, how among so many millions of faces, there should be none alike; Now contrary, I wonder as much how there should be any; he that shall consider how many thousand severall words have been carelesly and without study composed out of 24 Letters; withall how [3]

many hundred lines there are to be drawn in the fabrick of
one man; shall easily finde that this variety is necessary: And
it will bee very hard that they shall so concur as to make one
portract like another. Let a Painter carelesly limn out a Million of faces, and you shall finde them all different; yea let
him have his copy before him, yet after all his art there will
remaine a sensible distinction; for the patterne or example of
every thing is the perfectest in that kind, whereof wee still
come short, though wee transcend or goe beyond it, because
herein it is wide and agrees not in all points unto its Copy. Nor
doth the similitude of creatures disparage the variety of nature, nor any way confound the workes of God. For even in
things alike, there is diversitie, and those that doe seeme to
accord, doe manifestly disagree. And thus is Man like God,
for in the same things that wee resemble him, wee are utterly
different from him. There was never any thing so like another,
as in all points to concurre; there will ever some reserved difference slip in, to prevent the Identity, without which, two
severall things would not be alike, but the same, which is impossible.

SECT. 3. But to returne from Philosophy to Charity, I hold not
so narrow a conceit of this vertue, as to conceive that to give
alms is onely to be Charitable, or thinke a piece of Liberality
can comprehend the Totall of Charity; Divinity hath wisely
divided the acts thereof into many branches, and hath taught   †
us in this narrow way, many pathes unto goodnesse; as many
wayes as we may doe good, so many wayes we may bee
Charitable; there are infirmities, not onely of body, but of
soule, and fortunes, which doe require the mercifull hand of
our abilities. I cannot contemn a man for ignorance, but behold him with as much pity as I doe *Lazarus*. It is no greater
Charity to cloath his body, than apparell the nakednesse of
his Soule. It is an honourable object to see the reasons of other
men weare our Liveries, and their borrowed understandings
doe homage to the bounty of ours. It is the cheapest way of
beneficence, and like the naturall charity of the Sunne illumi-
nates another without obscuring it selfe. To be reserved and
caitif in this part of goodnesse, is the sordidest part of covet-

ousnesse, and more contemptible than pecuniary avarice. To †
this (as calling my selfe a Scholler) I am obliged by the duty
of my condition; I make not therefore my head a grave, but a
treasure of knowledge; I intend no Monopoly, but a Communi-
nity in learning; I study not for my owne sake onely, but for
theirs that study not for themselves. I envy no man that
knowes more than my selfe; but pity them that know lesse. I
instruct no man as an exercise of my knowledge, or with an
intent rather to nourish and keepe it alive in mine owne head,
than beget and propagate it in his; and in the midst of all my
endeavours there is but one thought that dejects me, that my
acquired parts must perish with my selfe, nor can bee Lega-
cyed among my honoured Friends. I cannot fall out or contemne a man for an errour, or conceive why a difference in
opinion should divide an affection: for controversies, disputes, and argumentations, both in Philosophy, and in Divinity, if they meete with discreet and peaceable natures, doe
not infringe the Lawes of Charity. In all disputes, so much as
there is of passion, so much there is of nothing to the purpose,
for then reason like a bad hound spends upon a false sent,
and forsakes the question first started. And this is one reason
why controversies are never determined, for, though they be
amply proposed, they are scarse at all handled, they doe so
swell with unnecessary Digressions, and the Parenthesis on 4
the party is often as large as the maine discourse upon the
Subject. The Foundations of Religion are already established,
and the principles of Salvation subscribed unto by all; there
remaine not many controversies worth a passion, and yet †
never any disputed without, not onely in Divinity, but in inferiour Arts. What a βατραχομυομαχία and hot skirmish is be- 5
twixt S. and T. in *Lucian?* How doe Grammarians hack and 6
slash for the Genitive case in **Jupiter?* [How many Synods †
have been assembled and angerly broke up againe about a
line in *Propria quae maribus?*] How doe they breake their 7
owne pates to salve that of *Priscian? Si foret in terris, rideret* 8,9
Democritus. Yea, even amongst wiser militants, how many
wounds have beene given, and credits slaine, for the poore

* Whether *Jovis* or *Jupiteris.*

victory of an opinion or beggerly conquest of a distinction?
Schollers are men of peace, they beare no armes, but their
tongues are sharper then *Actius* his razor, their pens carry far-   10
ther, and give a lowder report than thunder; I had rather
stand the shock of a Basilisco, than the fury of a mercilesse   †
Pen. It is not meere zeale to Learning, or devotion to the
Muses, that wiser Princes Patron the Arts, and carry an indul-
gent aspect unto Schollers, but a desire to have their names
eternized by the memory of their writings, and a feare of the
revengefull pen of succeeding ages: for these are the men,
that when they have played their parts, and had their *exits*,
must step out and give the morall of their Scenes, and deliver
unto posterity an Inventory of their vertues and vices. And
surely there goes a great deale of conscience to the compiling   11
of an History, there is no reproach to the scandall of a Story;   12
It is such an Authenticke kinde of falsehood that with authority belies our good names to all Nations and Posteritie.

SECT. 4. There is another offence unto Charity, which no Author hath ever written of, and few take notice of, and that's
the reproach, not of whole professions, mysteries, and conditions, but of whole nations, wherein by opprobrious Epithets
wee miscall each other, and by an uncharitable Logicke from
a disposition in a few conclude a habit in all.

> *Le mutin Anglois, et le bravache Escossois;*   13
> *Le bougre Italien, et le fol François;*
> *Le poultron Romain, le larron de Gascongne,*
> *L'Espagnol superbe, et l'Aleman yvrongne.*

Saint *Paul*, that cals the *Cretians* lyers, doth it but indirectly,   14
and upon quotation of their owne Poet. It is as bloody a
thought in one way as *Neroes* was in another. For by a word   15
wee wound a thousand, and at one blow assassine the honour
of a Nation. It is as compleate a piece of madnesse to miscall
and rave against the times, or thinke to recall men to reason,
by a fit of passion: *Democritus* that thought to laugh the
times into goodnesse, seemes to mee as deepely Hypochon-
driack, as *Heraclitus* that bewailed them; it moves not my
spleene to behold the multitude in their proper humours, that

is, in their fits of folly and madnesse, as well understanding
that Wisedome is not prophan'd unto the World, and 'tis the
priviledge of a few to be vertuous. They that endeavour to
abolish vice destroy also vertue, for contraries, though they
destroy one another, are yet the life of one another. Thus vertue (abolish vice) is an Idea; againe, the communitie of sinne
doth not disparage goodnesse; for when vice gaines upon the
major part, vertue, in whom it remaines, becomes more excellent, and being lost in some, multiplies its goodnesse in others
which remaine untouched, and persists intire in the generall
inundation. I can therefore behold vice without a Satyre, content onely with an admonition, or instructive reprehension;
for Noble natures, and such as are capable of goodnesse, are
railed into vice, that might as easily bee admonished into vertue; and we should be all so farre the Orators of goodnesse,
as to protect her from the power of vice, and maintaine the
cause of injured truth. No man can justly censure or condemne another, because indeed no man truely knowes another. This I perceive in my selfe, for I am in the darke to all
the world, and my nearest friends behold mee but in a cloud;
those that know mee but superficially, thinke lesse of me than
I doe of my selfe; those of my neere acquaintance thinke
more; God, who trucly knowes mee, knowes that I am nothing, for hee onely beholds me, and all the world, who lookes
not on us through a derived ray, or a trajection of a sensible   16
species, but beholds the substance without the helpes of accidents, and the formes of things, as wee their operations. Further, no man can judge another, because no man knowes
himselfe; for we censure others but as they disagree from
that humour which wee fancy laudable in our selves, and
commend others but for that wherein they seeme to quadrate
and consent with us. So that in conclusion, all is but that we
all condemne, selfe-love. 'Tis the generall complaint of these
times, and perhaps of those past, that charity growes cold;
which I perceive most verified in those which most doe manifest the fires and flames of zeale; for it is a vertue that best
agrees with coldest natures, and such as are complexioned for
humility: But how shall we expect charity towards others,
when we are uncharitable to our selves? Charity begins at

home, is the voyce of the world, yet is every man his owne   †
greatest enemy, and as it were, his owne executioner. *Non*   17
occides, is the Commandement of God, yet scarse observed by
any man; for I perceive every man is his owne *Atropos*, and
lends a hand to cut the thred of his own dayes. *Cain* was not
therefore the first murtherer, but *Adam*, who brought in
death; whereof hee beheld the practise and example in his
owne sonne *Abel*, and saw that verified in the experience of
another, which faith could not perswade him in the Theory of
himselfe.

SECT. 5. There is I thinke no man that apprehends his owne   †,18
miseries lesse than my selfe, and no man that so neerely apprehends anothers. I could lose an arme without a teare, and
with a few groans, mee thinkes, be quartered into pieces; yet
can I weepe most seriously at a Play, and receive with a true
passion, the counterfeit griefes of those knowne and professed
Impostors. It is a barbarous part of inhumanity to adde unto   †
any afflicted parties misery, or endeavour to multiply in any
man a passion, whose single nature is already above his patience; this was the greatest affliction of *Job*, and those oblique expostulations of his friends a deeper injury than the
downe-right blowes of the Devill. It is not the teares of our
owne eyes onely, but of our friends also, that doe exhaust the
current of our sorrowes, which, falling into many streames,
runnes more peaceably, and is contented with a narrower   †
channel. It is an act within the power of charity, to translate
a passion out of one breast into another, and to divide a sorrow almost out of it selfe; for an affliction, like a dimension,
may be so divided, as if not indivisible, at least to become insensible. Now with my friend I desire not to share or participate, but to engrosse his sorrowes, that by making them mine
owne, I may more easily discusse them; for in mine owne
reason, and within my selfe I can command that which I
cannot entreate without my selfe, and within the circle of another. I have often thought those Noble paires and examples
of friendship not so truely Histories of what had beene, as
fictions of what should be, but I now perceive nothing in
them but possibilities, nor any thing in the Heroick examples   19

of *Damon* and *Pythias, Achilles* and *Patroclus,* which mee †
thinkes upon some grounds I could not performe within the †
narrow compasse of my selfe. That a man should lay down his
life for his friend, seemes strange to vulgar affections, and
such as confine themselves within that worldly principle,
Charity beginnes at home. For mine owne part I could never
remember the relations that I hold unto my selfe, nor the re- †
spect I owe unto mine owne nature, in the cause of God, my
Country, and my Friends. Next to these three, I doe embrace
my selfe; I confesse I doe not observe that order that the
Schooles ordaine our affections, to love our Parents, Wives,
Children, and then our friends; for excepting the injunctions
of Religion, I doe not finde in my selfe such a necessary and 20
indissoluble Sympathy to all those of my bloud. I hope I doe
not breake the fifth Commandement, if I conceive I may love †
my friend before the nearest of my bloud, even those to
whom I owe the principles of life; I never yet cast a true 21
affection on a Woman, but I have loved my Friend as I do
vertue, my soule, my God. From hence me thinkes I doe con- †
ceive how God loves man, what happinesse there is in the
love of God. Omitting all other, there are three most mysticall
unions: Two natures in one person; three persons in one nature; one soule in two bodies. For though indeed they bee
really divided, yet are they so united, as they seeme but one,
and make rather a duality then two distinct soules.

SECT. 6. There are wonders in true affection, it is a body of
Ænigmaes, mysteries, and riddles, wherein two so become
one, as they both become two; I love my friend before my
selfe, and yet me thinkes I do not love him enough; some few
months hence my multiplyed affection will make me beleeve
I have not loved him at all; when I am from him, I am dead
till I bee with him, when I am with him, I am not satisfied,
but would still be nearer him; united soules are not satisfied
with embraces, but desire to be truely each other, which being impossible, their desires are infinite, and must proceed
without a possibility of satisfaction. Another misery there is in
affection, that whom we truely love like our owne selves, wee †
forget their lookes, nor can our memory retaine the Idea of

their faces; and it is no wonder, for they are our selves, and
our affection makes their lookes our owne. This noble affec-   †
tion fals not on vulgar and common constitutions, but on such
as are mark'd for vertue; he that can love his friend with this
noble ardour, will in a competent degree affect all. Now, if
wee can bring our affections to looke beyond the body, and
cast an eye upon the soule, wee have found out the true object, not onely of friendship but charity; and the greatest
happinesse that wee can bequeath the soule, is that wherein
we all doe place our last felicity, Salvation, which though it
bee not in our power to bestow, it is in our charity and pious
invocations to desire, if not to procure. And further, I cannot   †,22
contentedly frame a Prayer for my selfe in particular, with-   †
out a catalogue of my friends, nor request a happinesse
wherein my sociable disposition doth not desire the fellow-
ship of my neighbour. I never heare the Toll of a passing
Bell, though in my mirth [and at a Taverne] without my
prayers and best wishes for the departing spirit; I cannot goe
to cure the body of my Patient, but I forget my profession,
and call unto God for his soule; I cannot see one say his
Prayers, but in stead of imitating him, I fall into a supplication for him, who perhaps is no more to mee than a common
nature: and if God hath vouchsafed an eare to my supplications, there are surely many happy that never saw me, and
enjoy the blessing of mine unknowne devotions. To pray for
enemies, that is, for their salvation, is no harsh precept, but
the practise of our daily and ordinary devotions. I cannot beleeve the story of the Italian; our bad wishes and uncharita-   23
ble desires proceed no further than this life; it is the Devill,
and the uncharitable votes of Hell, that desire our misery in
the world to come.

SECT. 7. To doe no injury, nor take none, was a principle,
which to my former yeares, and impatient affections, seemed
to containe enough of morality, but my more setled yeares
and Christian constitution have fallen upon severer resolutions. I can hold there is no such thing as injury; that if there   †
be, there is no such injury as revenge, and no such revenge as
the contempt of an injury; that to hate another, is to maligne

himselfe; that the truest way to love another, is to despise our
selves. I were unjust unto mine owne conscience, if I should
say I am at variance with any thing like my selfe; I finde
there are many pieces in this one fabricke of man; this frame
is raised upon a masse of Antipathies: I am one mee thinkes,
but as the world; wherein notwithstanding there are a
swarme of distinct essences, and in them another world of
contrarieties; wee carry private and domesticke enemies
within, publike and more hostile adversaries without. The
Devill, that did but buffet Saint *Paul,* playes mee thinkes at
sharpe with me: Let mee be nothing if within the compasse
of my selfe, I doe not find the battell of *Lepanto,* passion
against reason, reason against faith, faith against the Devill,
and my conscience against all. There is another man within
mee that's angry with mee, rebukes, commands, and dastards
mee. I have no conscience of Marble to resist the hammer of
more heavie offences, nor yet so soft and waxen, as to take the
impression of each single peccadillo or scape of infirmity. I
am of a strange beliefe, that it is as easie to be forgiven some
sinnes, as to commit some others. For my originall sinne, I
hold it to be washed away in my Baptisme; for my actuall
transgressions, I compute and reckon with God but from my
last repentance, Sacrament or generall absolution: And there- †
fore am not terrified with the sinnes or madnesse of my
youth. I thanke the goodnesse of God I have no sinnes that
want a name; I am not singular in offences, my transgressions
are Epidemicall, and from the common breath of our corruption. For there are certaine tempers of body, which matcht †
with an humorous depravity of mind, doe hatch and produce
viciosities, whose newnesse and monstrosity of nature admits
no name: this was the temper of that Lecher that carnald 24
with a Statua, and the constitution of *Nero* in his Spintrian 25
recreations. For the heavens are not onely fruitfull in new
and unheard of starres, the earth in plants and animals, but
mens minds also in villany and vices; now the dulnesse of my
reason, and the vulgarity of my disposition, never prompted
my invention, nor sollicited my affection unto any of these;
yet even those common and *quotidian* infirmities that so necessarily attend me, and doe seeme to bee my very nature,

have so dejected me, so broken the estimation that I should
have otherwise of my selfe, that I repute my selfe the abject-
est piece of mortality; [that I detest mine owne nature, and   †
in my retired imaginations cannot withhold my hands from
violence on my selfe;] Divines prescribe a fit of sorrow to repentance; there goes indignation, anger, contempt and ha-   †
tred, into mine, passions of a contrary nature, which neither
seeme to sute with this action, nor my proper constitution. It
is no breach of charity to our selves to be at variance with
our vices, nor to abhorre that part of us which is an enemy to
the ground of charity, our God; wherein wee doe but imitate
our great selves, the world, whose divided Antipathies and
contrary faces doe yet carry a charitable regard unto the
whole, by their particular discords preserving the common
harmony, and keeping in fetters those powers, whose rebel-
lions once Masters, might bee the ruine of all.

SECT. 8. I thanke God, amongst those millions of vices I doe
inherit and hold from *Adam*, I have escaped one, and that a
mortall enemy to Charity, the first and father sin, not onely
of man, but of the devil, Pride, a vice whose name is com-   26
prehended in a Monosyllable, but in its nature not circumscribed with a world; I have escaped it in a condition that
can hardly avoid it: those petty acquisitions and reputed perfections that advance and elevate the conceits of other men,
adde no feathers unto mine; I have seene a Grammarian
towre and plume himselfe over a single line in *Horace*, and
shew more pride in the construction of one Ode, than the   27
Author in the composure of the whole book. For my owne
part, besides the *Jargon* and *Patois* of severall Provinces, I
understand no lesse then six Languages, yet I protest I have
no higher conceit of my selfe, than had our Fathers before
the confusion of *Babel*, when there was but one Language in   28
the world, and none to boast himselfe either Linguist or Cri-
ticke. I have not onely seene severall Countries, beheld the
nature of their climes, the Chorography of their Provinces,
Topography of their Cities, but understood their severall
Lawes, Customes and Policies; yet cannot all this perswade
the dulnesse of my spirit unto such an opinion of my self, as

I behold in nimbler and conceited heads, that never looked a
degree beyond their nests. I know the names, and somewhat
more, of all the constellations in my Horizon, yet I have seene   †
a prating Mariner, that could onely name the Poynters and   20
the North Starre, out-talke mee, and conceit himselfe a whole
Spheare above mee. I know most of the Plants of my Country,   †
and of those about mee; yet methinkes I do not know so
many as when I did but know an hundred, and had scarcely
ever Simpled further than Cheapside: for indeed heads of   30
capacity, and such as are not full with a handfull, or easie
measure of knowledg, thinke they know nothing, till they
know all; which being impossible, they fall upon the opinion
of *Socrates,* and onely know they know not any thing. I cannot thinke that *Homer* pin'd away upon the riddle of the   31
Fisherman, or that *Aristotle,* who understood the uncertainty
of knowledge, and confessed so often the reason of man too
weake for the workes of nature, did ever drowne himselfe
upon the flux and reflux of *Euripus:* wee doe but learne to-day   32
what our better advanced judgements will unteach us to   †
morrow: and *Aristotle* doth but instruct us, as *Plato* did him;
that is, to confute himselfe. I have runne through all sects,   †
yet finde no rest in any; though our first studies and *junior*
endeavors may stile us Peripateticks, Stoicks, or Academicks,   33
yet I perceive the wisest heads prove at last almost all Scepticks, and stand like *Janus* in the field of knowledge. I have
therefore one common and authentick Philosophy I learned
in the Schooles, whereby I discourse and satisfie the reason
of other men; another more reserved and drawne from experience, whereby I content mine owne. *Solomon* that com-
plained of ignorance in the height of knowledge, hath not
onely humbled my conceits, but discouraged my endeavours.
There is yet another conceit that hath sometimes made me
shut my bookes; which tels mee it is a vanity to waste our
dayes in the blind pursuit of knowledge; it is but attending a
little longer, and wee shall enjoy that by instinct and infusion
which we endeavour at here by labour and inquisition: it is
better to sit downe in a modest ignorance, and rest contented
with the naturall blessing of our owne reasons, then buy the
uncertaine knowledge of this life with sweat and vexation,

which death gives every foole gratis, and is an accessory of   34
our glorification.

SECT. 9. I was never yet once, and commend their resolutions   †,35
who never marry twice; not that I disallow of second marriage, as neither in all cases of Polygamy, which, considering
some times and the unequall number of both sexes, may bee   †
also necessary. The whole woman was made for man, but the   †
twelfth part of man for woman: man is the whole world and
the breath of God, woman the rib and crooked piece of man.   †
I could be content that we might procreate like trees, without   †
conjunction, or that there were any way to perpetuate the   ,
world without this triviall and vulgar way of coition; It is the
foolishest act a wise man commits in all his life, nor is there
any thing that will more deject his coold imagination, when
hee shall consider what an odde and unworthy piece of folly   36
hee hath committed; I speake not in prejudice, nor am averse
from that sweet sexe, but naturally amorous of all that is
beautifull; I can looke a whole day with delight upon a handsome Picture, though it be but of an Horse. It is my temper,
and I like it the better, to affect all harmony, and sure there is
musicke even in the beauty, and the silent note which *Cupid*
strikes, farre sweeter than the sound of an instrument. For
there is a musicke where-ever there is a harmony, order, or
proportion; and thus farre we may maintain the musick of
the spheares; for those well ordered motions, and regular
paces, though they give no sound unto the eare, yet to the understanding they strike a note most full of harmony. Whosoever is harmonically composed delights in harmony; which   †
makes me much mistrust the symmetry of those heads which
declaime against all Church musicke. For my selfe, not only   †,37
from my obedience, but my particular genius, I doe embrace   †,†
it; for even that vulgar and Taverne Musicke, which makes
one man merry, another mad, strikes mee into a deepe fit of   †
devotion, and a profound contemplation of the first Composer;   †
there is something in it of Divinity more than the eare discovers. It is an Hieroglyphicall and shadowed lesson of the
whole world, and the Creatures of God; such a melody to the
eare, as the whole world well understood, would afford the

understanding. In briefe, it is a sensible fit of that Harmony, which intellectually sounds in the eares of God. [It unties the †
ligaments of my frame, takes me to pieces, dilates me out of my self, and by degrees, me thinkes, resolves me into Heaven.] I will not say with *Plato*, the Soule is an Harmony, 38
but harmonicall, and hath its neerest sympathy unto musicke: thus, some whose temper of body agrees, and humours the constitution of their soules, are borne Poets, though indeed all are naturally inclined unto Rhythme. This made *Tacitus*, in 39
the very first line of his Story, fall upon a verse; and *Cicero*, the worst of Poets, but *declayming for a Poet, fall in the very first sentence upon a perfect *Hexameter. I feele not in me those sordid, and unchristian desires of my profession; I doe not secretly implore and wish for Plagues, rejoyce at Famines, revolve Ephemerides, and Almanacks, in expectation of malignant Aspects, fatal conjunctions, and Eclipses: I rejoyce not at unwholsome Springs, nor unseasonable Winters; my Prayer goes with the Husbandmans; I desire every thing in its proper season, that neither men nor the times bee out of temper. Let mee bee sicke my selfe, if sometimes the malady of my patient be not a disease unto me; I desire rather to cure his infirmities than my owne necessities; where I do him no good me thinkes it is scarce honest gaine, though I confesse 'tis but the worthy salary of our well-intended endeavours: I am not onely ashamed, but heartily sorry, that besides death, there are diseases incurable, yet not for my own sake, or that they be beyond my art, but for the generall cause and sake of humanity, whose common cause I apprehend as mine own: And to speak more generally, those three Noble 40
professions which all civil Common wealths doe honour, are raised upon the fall of *Adam*, and are not any way exempt from their infirmities; there are not onely diseases incurable in Physicke, but cases indissoluble in Lawe, Vices incorrigible †
in Divinity: if general Councells may erre, I doe not see why particular Courts should be infallible; their perfectest rules are raised upon the erroneous reason of Man, and the Lawes †

* *Urbem Romam in principio Reges habuere.*
* *Pro Archia Poeta.*
* *In qua me non inficior mediocriter esse.*

of one, doe but condemn the rules of another; as *Aristotle* oft-
times the opinions of his predecessours, because, though   †
agreeable to reason, yet were not consonant to his owne rules,
and the Logicke of his proper principles. Againe, to speake
nothing of the sinne against the Holy Ghost, whose cure not   41
onely, but whose nature is unknowne, I can cure the gout or
stone in some, sooner than Divinity, Pride or Avarice in others. I can cure vices by Physicke, when they remaine incurable by Divinity, and shall obey my pils, when they contemne
their precepts. I boast nothing, but plainely say, we all labour
against our owne cure, for death is the cure of all diseases.
There is no Catholicon or universall remedy I know but this,
which though nauseous to queasie stomachs, yet to prepared
appetites is Nectar, and a pleasant potion of immortality.

SECT. 10. For my conversation, it is like the Sunne's with all
men, and with a friendly aspect to good and bad. Me thinkes
there is no man bad, and the worst, best; that is, while they
are kept within the circle of those qualities wherein they are
good: there is no mans minde of such discordant and jarring
a temper, to which a tuneable disposition may not strike a
harmony. *Magnae virtutes nec minora vitia* is the poesie of   †,42
the best natures, and may bee inverted on the worst; there
are in the most depraved and venomous dispositions, certaine
pieces that remaine untoucht; which by an Antiperistasis become more excellent, or by the excellency of their antipathies
are able to preserve themselves from the contagion of their
enemy vices, and persist entire beyond the generall corruption. For it is also thus in nature. The greatest Balsames doe   †,43
lie enveloped in the bodies of the most powerfull Corrosives;
I say moreover, and I ground upon experience, that poysons
containe within themselves their owne Antidote, and that
which preserves them from the venom of themselves; without which they were not deleterious to others onely, but to
themselves also. But it is the corruption that I feare within
me, not the contagion of commerce without me. 'Tis that unruly regiment within me, that will destroy me, 'tis I that doe
infect my selfe, the man without a Navell yet lives in me; I   44
feele that originall canker corrode and devour me, and there-

fore *Defenda me Dios de me,* Lord deliver me from my selfe, is a part of my Letany, and the first voyce of my retired imaginations. There is no man alone, because every man is a *Microcosme,* and carries the whole world about him; *Nunquam minus solus quam cum solus,* though it bee the Apothegme of a wise man, is yet true in the mouth of a foole; for indeed, though in a Wildernesse, a man is never alone, not onely because hee is with himselfe, and his owne thoughts, but because he is with the devill, who ever consorts with our solitude, and is that unruly rebell that musters up those disordered motions, which accompany our sequestred imaginations: And to speake more narrowly, there is no such thing as solitude, nor any thing that can be said to be alone, and by it selfe, but God, who is his owne circle, and can subsist by himselfe; all others besides their dissimilary and Heterogeneous parts, which in a manner multiply their natures, cannot subsist without the concourse of God, and the society of that hand which doth uphold their natures. In briefe, there can be nothing truely alone, and by its self, which is not truely one, and such is onely God: All others doe transcend an unity, and so by consequence are many.

SECT. 11. Now for my life, it is a miracle of thirty yeares, which to relate, were not an History, but a peece of Poetry, and would sound to common eares like a fable; for the world, I count it not an Inne, but an Hospitall, and a place, not to live, but to die in. The world that I regard is my selfe; it is the Microcosme of mine owne frame that I cast mine eye on; for the other, I use it but like my Globe, and turne it round sometimes for my recreation. Men that look upon my outside, perusing onely my condition, and fortunes, do erre in my altitude; for I am above *Atlas* his shoulders. The earth is a point not onely in respect of the heavens above us, but of that heavenly and celestiall part within us: that masse of flesh that circumscribes me, limits not my mind: that surface that tells the heavens it hath an end, cannot perswade me I have any; I take my circle to be above three hundred and sixty; though the number of the Arke do measure my body, it comprehendeth not my minde: whilst I study to finde how I am a Micro-

cosme or little world, I finde my selfe something more than
the great. There is surely a peece of Divinity in us, something
that was before the Elements, and owes no homage unto the
Sun. Nature tels me I am the Image of God, as well as Scripture; he that understands not thus much, hath not his introduction or first lesson, and is yet to begin the Alphabet of
man. Let me not injure the felicity of others, if I say I am as   †
happy as any, [I have that in me can convert poverty into
riches, adversity into prosperity: I am more invulnerable then   46
Achilles, fortune hath not one place to hit me;] *Ruat coelum,*   47
Fiat voluntas tua, salveth all; so that whatsoever happens, it
is but what our daily prayers desire. In briefe, I am content,
and what should providence adde more? Surely this is it wee
call Happinesse, and this doe I enjoy; with this I am happy
in a dreame, and as content to enjoy a happinesse in a fancie
as others in a more apparent truth and reality. There is
surely a neerer apprehension of any thing that delights us in
our dreames, than in our awaked senses; [with this I can bee
a King without a Crowne, rich without a stiver, in heaven   †
though on earth, enjoy my friend and embrace him at a distance when I cannot behold him;] without this I were unhappy; for my awaked judgement discontents me, ever whispering unto me, that I am from my friend; but my friendly
dreames in the night requite me, and make me thinke I am
within his armes. I thanke God for my happy dreames, as I
doe for my good rest, for there is a satisfaction in them unto
reasonable desires, and such as can be content with a fit of
happinesse; and surely it is not a melancholy conceite to
thinke we are all asleepe in this world, and that the conceits
of this life are as meare dreames to those of the next, as the
Phantasmes of the night, to the conceits of the day. There is   †
an equall delusion in both, and the one doth but seeme to
bee the embleme or picture of the other; we are somewhat
more than our selves in our sleepes, and the slumber of the
body seemes to bee but the waking of the soule. It is the
ligation of sense, but the liberty of reason, and our awaking
conceptions doe not match the fancies of our sleepes. At my
Nativity, my ascendant was the watery signe of *Scorpius;* I   †
was borne in the Planetary hour of *Saturne,* and I think I   48

have a peece of that Leaden Planet in me. I am no way facetious, nor disposed for the mirth and galliardize of company, yet in one dreame I can compose a whole Comedy,
behold the action, apprehend the jests, and laugh my selfe
awake at the conceits thereof; were my memory as faithfull
as my reason is then fruitfull, I would never study but in
my dreames, and this time also would I chuse for my devotions; but our grosser memories have then so little hold of our
abstracted understandings, that they forget the story, and
can only relate to our awaked soules, a confused and broken
tale of that that hath passed. *Aristotle,* who hath written a
singular tract of sleepe, hath not me thinkes throughly defined   †
it, nor yet Galen, though hee seeme to have corrected it; for
those *Noctambuloes* and night-walkers, though in their
sleepe, doe yet enjoy the action of their senses: we must
therefore say that there is something in us that is not in the
jurisdiction of *Morpheus;* and that those abstracted and
ecstaticke soules doe walke about in their owne corps, as spirits with the bodies they assume, wherein they seeme to
heare, see, and feele, though indeed the organs are destitute
of sense, and their natures of those faculties that should informe them. Thus it is observed that men sometimes upon   †
the houre of their departure, doe speake and reason above
themselves. For then the soule begins to bee freed from the
ligaments of the body, begins to reason like her selfe, and to
discourse in a straine above mortality.

SECT. 12. We tearme sleepe a death, and yet it is waking that
kils us, and destroyes those spirits that are the house of life.
'Tis indeed a part of life that best expresseth death, for every   †
man truely lives so long as hee acts his nature, or some way
makes good the faculties of himselfe. *Themistocles* therefore   49
that slew his Souldier in his sleepe, was a mercifull executioner; 'tis a kinde of punishment the mildnesse of no lawes
hath invented: I wonder the fancy of *Lucan* and *Seneca* did   50
not discover it. It is that death by which we may be literally
said to die daily, a death which *Adam* died before his mortality; a death whereby we live a middle and moderating
point betweene life and death; in fine, so like death, I dare

not trust it without my prayers, and an halfe adiew unto the
world, [and truly 'tis a fit time for our devotion, and therefore   †
I cannot laie downe my head without an Orizon] and take my
farewell in a Colloquy with God.

> The night is come like to the day,
> Depart not thou great God away.
> Let not my sinnes, blacke as the night,
> Eclipse the lustre of thy light.
> Keepe still in my Horizon, for to me,
> The Sunne makes not the day, but thee.
> Thou whose nature cannot sleepe,
> On my temples centry keepe;
> Guard me 'gainst those watchfull foes,
> Whose eyes are open while mine close.
> Let no dreames my head infest,
> But such as *Jacobs* temples blest.
> While I doe rest, my soule advance,
> Make my sleepe a holy trance:
> That I may, my rest being wrought,
> Awake into some holy thought.
> And with as active vigour runne
> My course, as doth the nimble Sunne.
> Sleepe is a death, O make me try,
> By sleeping, what it is to die.
> And as gently lay my head
> On my Grave, as now my bed.
> How ere I rest, great God, let me
> Awake againe at last with thee.
> And thus assur'd, behold I lie
> Securely, or to wake or die.
> These are my drowsie dayes, in vaine
> I now doe wake to sleepe againe.
> O come that houre, when I shall never
> Sleepe againe, but wake for ever!

This is the dormitive I take to bedward, I need no other
Laudanum than this to make me sleepe; after which I close
mine eyes in security, content to take my leave of the Sunne,
and sleepe unto the resurrection.

SECT. 13. The method I should use in distributive justice, I
often observe in commutative, and keepe a Geometricall

proportion in both, whereby becomming equable to others,
I become unjust to my selfe, and supererogate in that common principle, Doe unto others as thou wouldest be done
unto thy selfe. I was not borne unto riches, neither is it I   †
thinke my Starre to be wealthy; or if it were, the freedome
of my minde, and franknesse of my disposition, were able to
contradict and crosse my fates: for to me, avarice seemes not
so much a vice, as a deplorable piece of madnesse; to conceive our selves Urinals, or bee perswaded that wee are
dead, is not so ridiculous, nor so many degrees beyond the
power of Hellebore, as this. The opinions of theory and   51
positions of men are not so voyd of reason as their practised
conclusions: some have held that Snow is blacke, that the   †,52
earth moves, that the soule is fire, ayre, water; but all this is   53
Philosophy, and there is no *delirium,* if we doe but speculate   †
the folly and indisputable dotage of avarice. To that subterraneous Idoll, and God of the earth, I doe confesse I am an   54
Atheist; I cannot perswade my selfe to honour that which   †
the world adores; whatsoever vertue its prepared substance
may have within my body, it hath no influence nor operation
without; I would not entertaine a base designe, or an action
that should call mee villaine, for the Indies; and for this onely
doe I love and honour my owne soule, and have mee thinkes,
two armes too few to embrace my selfe. *Aristotle* is too se-   55
vere, that will not allow us to bee truely liberall without
wealth, and the bountifull hand of fortune; if this be true,
I must confesse I am charitable onely in my liberall intentions, and bountifull well-wishes. But if the example of the
Mite bee not onely an act of wonder, but an example of the
noblest charity, surely poore men may also build Hospitals,   †
and the rich alone have not erected Cathedralls. I have a
private method which others observe not; I take the opportunity of my selfe to do good, I borrow occasion of charity
from mine owne necessities, and supply the wants of others,
when I am in most neede my selfe; [when I am reduc'd to   †
the last tester, I love to divide it to the poore;] for it is an
honest stratagem to take advantage of our selves, and so to
husband the acts of vertue that where they are defective in   †
one circumstance, they may repay their want and multiply

their goodnesse in another. I have not *Peru* in my desires, but a competence, and abilitie to performe those good workes to which hee hath inclined my nature. Hee is rich, who hath enough to bee charitable; and it is hard to bee so poore, that a noble minde may not finde a way to this piece of goodnesse. *He that giveth to the poore lendeth to the* [56] *Lord;* there is more Rhetorick in that one sentence than in a Library of Sermons, and indeed if those sentences were understood by the Reader, with the same Emphasis as they are delivered by the Author, wee needed not those Volumes of instructions, but might bee honest by an Epitome. Upon this motive onely I cannot behold a Begger without relieving his Necessities with my purse, or his soule with my prayers; these scenicall and accidentall differences betweene us cannot make mee forget that common and untoucht part of us both: there is under these *Centoes* and miserable outsides, these mutilate and semi-bodies, a soule of the same alloy with our owne, whose Genealogy is God as well as ours, and in as faire a way to Salvation as our selves. Statists that labour to contrive a Common-wealth without poverty, take away the object of charity, not understanding only the Common-wealth of a Christian, but forgetting the prophecy [57] of Christ.

SECT. 14. Now there is another part of charity, which is the Basis and Pillar of this, and that is the love of God, for whom wee love our neighbour: for this I thinke charity, to love God for himselfe, and our neighbour for God. All that is truely amiable is God, or as it were a divided piece of him, that retaines a reflex or shadow of himselfe. Nor is it strange that wee should place affection on that which is invisible; all that wee truely love is thus; what wee adore under affection of our senses, deserves not the honour of so pure a title. Thus wee adore vertue, though to the eyes of sense shee bee invisible. Thus that part of our noble friends that [†] wee love, is not that part that we embrace, but that insensible part that our armes cannot embrace. God being all goodnesse, can love nothing but himselfe; hee loves us but for that part which is as it were himselfe, and the traduction of

his holy Spirit. Let us call to assize the love of our parents, †
the affection of our wives and children, and they are all
dumbe showes, and dreames, without reality, truth, or constancy; for first there is a strong bond of affection betweene
us and our parents, yet how easily dissolved? We betake
our selves to a woman, forgetting our mothers in a wife, and
the wombe that bare us in that that shall beare our image.
This woman blessing us with children, our affection leaves †
the levell it held before, and sinkes from our bed unto our
issue and picture of posterity, where affection holds no
steady mansion. They growing up in yeares desire our ends,
or applying themselves to a woman, take a lawfull way to
love another better than our selves. Thus I perceive a man
may bee buried alive, and behold his grave in his owne issue.

SECT. 15. I conclude therefore and say, there is no happinesse
under (or as *Copernicus* will have it, above) the Sunne, nor
any Crambe in that repeated veritie and burthen of all the
wisedom of *Solomon, All is vanitie and vexation of spirit;*
there is no felicity in that the world adores. *Aristotle* whilst
hee labours to refute the Idea's of *Plato,* fals upon one himselfe: for his *summum bonum* is a *Chimæra,* and there is no ⁵⁸
such thing as his Felicity. That wherein God himselfe is
happy, the holy Angels are happy, in whose defect the
Devils are unhappy; that dare I call happinesse: whatsoever
conduceth unto this, may with an easie Metaphor deserve
that name; whatsoever else the world termes happines, is to
me a story out of *Pliny,* an apparition, or neat delusion, †,⁵⁹
wherein there is no more of happinesse than the name.
Blesse mee in this life with but the peace of my conscience,
command of my affections, the love of thy selfe and my †,⁶⁰
dearest friends, and I shall be happy enough to pity *Caesar.*
These are O Lord the humble desires of my most reasonable
ambition and all I dare call happinesse on earth: wherein I
set no rule or limit to thy hand or providence. Dispose of
me according to the wisedome of thy pleasure. Thy will †
bee done, though in my owne undoing. †,⁶¹

FINIS.

PSEUDODOXIA EPIDEMICA

PSEUDODOXIA EPIDEMICA

The chapters included in this selection are:

Pseudodoxia Epidemica:

OR,

ENQUIRIES

INTO

Very many Received

TENENTS,

And commonly Presumed

TRUTHS.

By Thomas Browne Dr of Physick.

The Second Edition,

Corrected and much Enlarged by the Author.

TOGETHER

With some Marginall Observations, and a Table
Alphabeticall at the end.

Jul. Scalig.

*Ex Libris colligere quæ prodiderunt Authores longè est periculosissimum;
Rerum ipsarum cognitio vera, è rebus ipsis est.*

LONDON,

Printed by *A. Miller*, for *Edw. Dod* and *Nath.
Ekins*, at the Gunne in Ivie Lane. 1650.

TO THE
READER

Would Truth dispense, we could be content, with Plato, that knowledge were but Remembrance; that Intellectuall acquisition were but Reminiscentiall evocation, and new impressions but the colourishing of old stamps which stood pale in the soul before. For, what is worse, knowledge is made by oblivion; and to purchase a clear and warrantable body of Truth, we must forget and part with much we know. Our tender Enquiries taking up Learning at large, and together with true and assured notions, receiving many, wherein our reviewing judgements doe finde no satisfaction; † and therefore in this Encyclopaedie and round of knowledge, like the great and exemplary wheeles of heaven, we must observe two Circles: that while we are daily carried about, and whirled on by the swinge and rapt of the one, † we may maintain a naturall and proper course, in the slow and sober wheele of the other. And this we shall more readily perform, if we timely survey our knowledge; impartially singling out those encroachments, which junior compliance and popular credulity hath admitted. Whereof at present we have endeavoured a long and serious *Adviso;* proposing not only a large and copious List, but from experience and reason attempting their decisions.

And first we crave exceeding pardon in the audacity of the Attempt; humbly acknowledging a work of such concernment unto Truth, and difficulty in it self, did well deserve the conjunction of many heads: And surely more advantageous had it been unto Truth, to have fallen into the endeavours of some cooperating advancers, that might have 1 performed it to the life, and added authority thereto: which the privacie of our condition, and unequall abilities cannot expect. Whereby notwithstanding we have not been diverted, nor have our solitary attempts been so discouraged, as to despair the favourable look of Learning upon our single and unsupported endeavours.

Nor have we let fall our Penne, upon discouragement of contradiction, unbelief, and difficulty of disswasion from radicated beliefs, and points of high prescription; although we are very sensible how hardly teaching years doe learn, what roots old age contracteth into errors, and how such as are but Acorns in our younger brows, grow Oaks in our elder †
heads, and become inflexible unto the powerfullest arm of reason. Although we have also beheld, what cold requitals others have found in their severall redemptions of Truth; and how their ingenuous enquiries have been dismissed with censure, and obloquie of singularities.

Some consideration we hope from the course of our Profession; which though it leadeth us into many Truths that passe undiscerned by others, yet doth it disturb their communications, and much interrupt the office of our Pens in their well intended transmissions: and therefore surely in this work attempts will exceed performances: it being composed by snatches of time, as medicall vacations, and the fruitlesse importunity of Uroscopy* would permit us. And therefore also perhaps it hath not found that regular and constant stile, those infallible experiments, and those assured determinations, which the subject sometime requireth, and might be expected from others, whose quiet doors and unmolested hours afford no such distractions. Although who shall indifferently perpend the exceeding difficulty, which either the obscurity of the subject, or unavoidable paradoxologie must often put upon the Attemptor, will easily discern, a work of this nature is not to be performed upon one legge, and   2
should smell of oyle if duly and deservedly handled.   3

Our first intentions considering the common interest of Truth, resolved to propose it unto the Latine republike and equall judges of Europe; but owing in the first place this service unto our Countrey, and therein especially unto its ingenuous Gentry, we have declared our self in a Language

---

* Inspection of Urines.

best conceived. Although I confesse, the quality of the Subject will sometimes carry us into expressions beyond meer English apprehensions; and indeed if elegancie still proceedeth, and English Pens maintain that stream we have of late observed to flow from many, we shall within few years be fain to learn Latine to understand English, and a work will prove of equall facility in either. Nor have we addressed our Penne or stile unto the people, (whom Books doe not redresse, and are this way incapable of reduction) but unto the knowing and leading part of Learning; as well understanding (at least probably hoping) except they be watered from higher regions, and fructifying meteors of knowledge, these weeds must lose their alimentall sappe and wither of themselves; whose conserving influence, could our endeavours prevent, we should trust the rest unto the sythe of Time, and hopefull dominion of Truth.

We hope it will not be unconsidered, that we finde no open tract, or constant manuduction in this Labyrinth; but are oft-times fain to wander in the America and untravelled parts of Truth: For though not many years past, Dr. Primrose hath made a learned and full Discourse of vulgar Errors in Physick, yet have we discussed but two or three thereof. Scipio Mercurii hath also left an excellent Tract in Italian concerning popular Errors; but confining himself only unto those in Physick, he hath little conduced unto the generality of our Doctrine. Laurentius Joubertus, by the same Title led our expectation into thoughts of great relief; whereby notwithstanding we reaped no advantage; it answering scarce at all the promise of the inscription. Nor perhaps (if it were yet extant) should we finde any farther Assistance from that ancient piece of Andreas,* pretending the same Title. And therefore we are often constrained to stand alone against the strength of opinion; and to meet the Goliah and Giant of Authority, with contemptible pibbles, and feeble arguments, drawn from the scrip and slender stock of our selves. Nor have we indeed scarce named any Author whose Name we doe not honour; and if detraction

4

†,5

6

7

* περὶ τῶν ψευδῶς πεπιστευμένων Athenaei *lib.* 7.

†

could invite us, discretion surely would contain us from any
derogatory intention, where highest Pens and friendliest elo- †
quence must fail in commendation.

And therefore also we cannot but hope the equitable considerations and candour of reasonable mindes. We cannot expect the frown of *Theologie* herein; nor can they which
behold the present state of things, and controversie of points
so long received in Divinity, condemn our sober enquiries
in the doubtfull appertinancies of Arts, and Receptaries of
Philosophy. Surely Philologers and Criticall Discoursers, who
look beyond the shell and obvious exteriours of things, will
not be angry with our narrower explorations. And we cannot doubt, our brothers in Physick (whose knowledge in
Naturals will lead them into a nearer apprehension of many
things delivered) will friendly accept, if not countenance
our endeavours. Nor can we conceive, it may be unwelcome
unto those honoured Worthies, who endeavour the advancement of Learning: as being likely to finde a clearer progression, when so many rubbes are levelled, and many untruths
taken off, which passing as principles with common beliefs,
disturb the tranquillity of Axiomes, which otherwise might
be raised. And wise men cannot but know, that Arts and
Learning want this expurgation: and if the course of truth
be permitted unto its self, like that of Time and uncorrected
computations, it cannot escape many errours, which duration
still enlargeth.

Lastly, We are not Magisteriall in opinions, nor have we
Dictator-like obtruded our conceptions; but in the humility
of Enquiries or disquisitions, have only proposed them unto
more ocular discerners. And therefore opinions are free, and
open it is for any to think or declare the contrary. And we
shall so farre encourage contradiction, as to promise no dis-
turbance, or reoppose any Penne, that shall Fallaciously re- †
fute us; that shall only lay hold of our lapses, single out
Digressions, Corollaries, or Ornamentall conceptions, to evidence his own in as indifferent truths. And shall only take
notice of such, whose experimentall and judicious knowledge
shall solemnly look upon it; not only to destroy of ours, but
to establish of his own, not to traduce or extenuate, but to

explain and dilucidate, to adde and ampliate, according to the laudable custome of the Ancients in their sober promotions of Learning. Unto whom notwithstanding, we shall not contentiously rejoin, or only to justifie our own, but to applaud or confirm his maturer assertions; and shall conferre what is in us unto his name and honour; Ready to be swallowed in any worthy enlarger: as having acquired our end, if any way, or under any name we may obtain a worke, so much desired, and yet desiderated of Truth. 8,†

Thomas Browne. †

THE FIRST BOOK:
OR,
GENERALL PART

Chap. 1.
Of the Causes of Common Errors.

The first and father cause of common Error, is the common infirmity of humane nature; of whose deceptible condition, although perhaps there should not need any other eviction, then the frequent errors we shall our selves commit, even in the expresse declarement hereof: Yet shall we illustrate the same from more infallible constitutions, and persons presumed as farre from us in condition, as time, that is our first and ingenerated forefathers. From whom as we derive our being, and the severall wounds of constitution; so may we in some manner excuse our infirmities in the depravity of those parts, whose traductions were pure in them, and their originals but once removed from God. Who notwithstanding (if posterity may take leave to judge of the fact, as they are assured to suffer in the punishment) were grossely deceived in their perfection; and so weakly deluded in the clarity of their understanding, that it hath left no small obscurity in ours, how error should gain upon them.

For first, They were deceived by Satan; and that not in an invisible insinuation, but an open and discoverable apparition, that is, in the form of a Serpent; whereby although there were many occasions of suspition, and such as could not easily escape a weaker circumspection, yet did the unwary apprehension of Eve take no advantage thereof. It hath therefore seemed strange unto some, she should be deluded by a Serpent, or subject her reason to a beast, which God had subjected unto hers. It hath empuzzeled the enquiries of others to apprehend, and enforced them unto strange conceptions, to make out how without fear or doubt she could discourse with such a creature, or hear a Serpent speak, without suspition of imposture. The wits of others, have been so bold as to accuse her simplicity in receiving his temptation so coldly; and when such specious effects of the fruit were promised, as to make them like gods, not to desire, at least not to wonder, he pursued not that benefit himself. And had it been their own case would perhaps have replied, If the taste of this fruit maketh the eaters like gods, why remainest thou a beast? If it maketh us but like gods, we are so already. If thereby our eyes shall be opened hereafter, they are at present quick enough to discover thy deceit, and we desire them no opener to behold our own shame. If to know good and evil be our advantage, although we have free will unto both, we desire to perform but one; we know 'tis good to obey the Commandment of God, but evil if we transgresse it.

They were deceived by one another, and in the greatest disadvantage of delusion, that is the stronger by the weaker: For Eve presented the fruit, and Adam received it from her. Thus the Serpent was cunning enough to begin the deceit in the weaker; and the weaker of strength sufficient to consummate the fraud in the stronger. Art and fallacy was used unto her, a naked offer proved sufficient unto him: so his superstructure was his ruine, and the fertility of his sleep, an issue of death unto him. And although the condition of sex and posteriority of creation might somewhat extenuate the error of the woman: Yet was it very strange and inexcusable in the man; especially if as some affirm, he was the wisest of all men since; or if as others have conceived, he was not ignorant of the fall of the Angels, and had thereby example and punishment to deterre him.

They were deceived from themselves, and their own apprehensions; for Eve either mistook or traduced the Commandment of God. Of every tree of the garden thou maiest freely eat, but of the tree of knowledge of good and evil thou shalt not eat, for in the day thou eatest thereof, thou shalt surely die. Now Eve upon the question of the Serpent returned the precept in different tearms, You shall not eat of it, neither shall you touch it lest perhaps you die. In which

of life before that of good and evil, they had yet suffered the
curse of mortality; or whether the efficacie of the one had
not overpowered the penalty of the other, we leave it unto
God. For he alone can truly determine these and all things
else; who as he hath proposed the world unto our disputation, so hath he reserved many things unto his own resolution; whose determinations we cannot hope from flesh, but
must with reverence suspend unto that great day, whose
justice shall either condemn our curiosities, or resolve our
disquisitions.

Lastly, Man was not only deceivable in his integrity, but   14
the Angels of light in all their clarity. He that said he would
be like the highest did erre if in some way he conceived not
himself so already; but in attempting so high an effect from
himself, he mis-understood the nature of God, and held a
false apprehension of his own; whereby vainly attempting
not only insolencies, but impossibilities, he deceived himself
as low as hell. In brief, there is nothing infallible but God,
who cannot possibly erre. For things are really true as they
correspond unto his conception; and have so much of verity,
as they hold of conformity unto that intellect, in whose Idea
they had their first determinations. And therefore being the
rule, he cannot be irregular; nor being truth it self, conceivea-
bly admit the impossible society of error.

[Chap. 2, "A further illustration of the same," omitted.]

CHAP. 3.
OF THE SECOND CAUSE OF POPULAR ERRORS;
THE ERRONEOUS DISPOSITION OF THE PEOPLE.

Having thus declared the fallible nature of man even from
his first production, we have beheld the generall cause of
error. But as for popular errors, they are more neerly founded
upon an erroneous inclination of the people; as being the
most deceptible part of mankinde, and ready with open arms
to receive the encroachments of error. Which condition of
theirs although deduceable from many grounds, yet shall we

evidence it but from a few, and such as most neerly and undeniably declare their natures.

How unequall discerners of truth they are, and openly exposed unto error, will first appear from their unquallified intellectuals, unable to umpire the difficulty of its dissentions. For error, to speak strictly, is a firm assent unto falsity. Now whether the object whereunto they deliver up their assent be true or false, they are incompetent judges.

For the assured truth of things is derived from the principles of knowledge, and causes which determine their verities. Whereof their uncultivated understandings scarce holding any theory, they are but bad discerners of verity; and in the numerous track of error, but casually do hit the point and unity of truth.

Their understanding is so feeble in the discernment of falsities, and averting the errors of reason, that it submitteth unto the fallacies of sense, and is unable to rectifie the error of its sensations. Thus the greater part of mankinde having but one eye of sence and reason, conceive the earth farre bigger then the Sun, the fixed Stars lesser then the Moon, their figures plain, and their spaces equidistant. For thus their sence informeth them, and herein their reason cannot rectifie them; and therefore hopelesly continuing in their mistakes, they live and die in their absurdities; passing their daies in perverted apprehensions and conceptions of the world, derogatory unto God, and the wisdome of the creation.

Again, Being so illiterate in point of intellect, and their sense so incorrected, they are farther indisposed ever to attain unto truth, as commonly proceeding in those waies, which have most reference unto sense, and wherein there lieth most notable and popular delusion.

For being unable to weild the intellectuall arms of reason, they are fain to betake themselves unto wasters and the blunter weapons of truth; affecting the grosse and sensible waies of doctrine, and such as will not consist with strict and subtile reason. Thus unto them a piece of Rhetorick is a sufficient argument of Logick, an Apologue* of Aesope, beyond

* Fable.   †

a Syllogisme in Barbara; parables then propositions, and
proverbs more powerfull then demonstrations. And therefore
are they led rather by example, then precept; receiving per-
swasions from visible inducements, before intellectuall instructions. And therefore also they judge of humane actions
by the event; for being uncapable of operable circumstances,
or rightly to judge the prudentiality of affairs, they only gaze
upon the visible successe, and thereafter condemn or cry up
the whole progression. And so from this ground in the Lecture of holy Scripture, their apprehensions are commonly confined unto the literall sense of the text; from whence have
ensued the grosse and duller fort of heresies. For not attain-
ing the deuteroscopy, and second intention of the words,
they are fain to omit their superconsequencies, coherencies,
figures, or tropologies, and are not sometime perswaded by   15
fire beyond their literalities. And therefore also things invisible but unto intellectuall discernments, to humour the grosse-
nesse of their comprehensions, have been degraded from
their proper forms, and God himself dishonoured into
manuall expressions. And so likewise being unprovided, or   16
unsufficient for higher speculations, they will alwaies betake themselves unto sensible representations, and can
hardly be restrained the dulnesse of Idolatry. A sinne or folly
not only derogatory unto God, but men; overthrowing their
reason, as well as his divinity. In brief, a reciprocation, or
rather an Inversion of the creation; making God one way, as   †
he made us another; that is, after our Image, as he made us
after his.

Moreover, their understanding thus weak in it self, and
perverted by sensible delusions, is yet farther impaired by
the dominion of their appetite; that is, the irrationall and
brutall part of the soul, which lording it over the sovereign
faculty, interrupts the actions of that noble part, and choaks
those tender sparks, which Adam hath left them of reason.
And therefore they do not only swarm with errors, but vices
depending thereon. Thus they commonly affect no man any
farther then he deserts his reason, or complies with their
aberrancies. Hence they embrace not vertue for it self, but its
reward; and the argument from pleasure or utility is farre

more powerfull, then that from vertuous honesty; which
Mahomet and his contrivers well understood, when he set   17
out the felicity of his heaven, by the contentments of flesh,
and the delights of sense: slightly passing over the accomplishment of the soul, and the beatitude of that part which
earth and visibilities too weakly affect. But the wisdom of
our Saviour, and the simplicity of his truth proceeded another way; defying the popular provisions of happinesse from
sensible expectations; placing his felicity in things removed
from sense, and the intellectuall enjoyment of God. And
thereforo the doctrine of the one was never afraid of Universities, or endeavoured the banishment of learning like
the other. And though Galen doth sometime nibble at Moses,   18
and beside the Apostate Christian,* some Heathens have
questioned his Philosophicall part or treaty of the Creation:
Yet is there surely no reasonable Pagan, that will not admire
the rationall and well grounded precepts of Christ; whose
life as it was conformable unto his doctrine, so was that unto
the highest rules of reason; and must therefore flourish in
the advancement of learning, and the perfection of parts best
able to comprehend it.

Again, Their individuall imperfections being great, they
are moreover enlarged by their aggregation; and being erroneous in their single numbers once hudled together, they
will be error it self. For being a confusion of knaves and fools,
and a farraginous concurrence of all conditions, tempers, sex,
and ages; it is but naturall if their determinations be monstrous, and many waies inconsistent with truth. And therefore
wise men have alwaies applauded their own judgement, in
the contradiction of that of the people; and their soberest adversaries, have ever afforded them the stile of fools and mad
men; and to speak impartially, their actions have often made
good these Epithites. Had Orestes been Judge, he would not   †,19
have acquitted that Lystrian rabble of madnesse,* who upon   20
a visible miracle, falling into so high a conceit of Paul and
Barnabas, that they termed the one Jupiter, the other Mercurius; that they brought oxen and garlands, and were hardly

---

* *Julian.*   †
* *Non sani esse hominis, non sanus jurat Orestes.*

restrained from sacrificing unto them; did notwithstanding
suddenly after fall upon Paul, and having stoned him, drew
him for dead out of the city. It might have hazarded the sides
of Democritus, had he been present at that tumult of De-   21
metrius; when the people flocking together in great numbers,
some cried one thing, and some another, and the assembly
was confused, and the most part knew not wherefore they
were come together; notwithstanding, all with one voice for
the space of two hours cried out, Great is Diana of the Ephe-
sians. It had overcome the patience of Job, as it did the meek-
nesse of Moses, and would surely have mastered any, but
the longanimity and lasting sufferance of God, had they
beheld the mutiny in the wildernesse; when after ten great
miracles in Egypt, and some in the same place, they melted
down their stolen ear-rings into a calf, and monstrously cried   22
out, These are thy gods O Israel, that brought thee out of the
land of Egypt. It much accuseth the impatiencie of Peter,   23
who could not endure the staves of the multitude, and is the
greatest example of lenity in our Saviour, when he desired of
God forgivenesse unto those, who having one day brought
him into the City in triumph, did presently after act all dishonour upon him, and nothing could be heard but *Crucifige*
in their courts. Certainly he that considereth these things in
Gods peculiar people, will easily discern how little of truth
there is in the waies of the multitude; and though sometimes
they are flattered with that Aphorisme, will hardly beleeve   24
the voice of the people to be the voice of God.

Lastly, Being thus divided from truth in themselves, they
are yet farther removed by advenient deception. For true it
is (and I hope shall not offend their vulgarities) if I say they
are daily mocked into error by subtler devisors, and have
been expresly deluded, by all professions and ages. Thus the   †
Priests of Elder time, have put upon them many incredible
conceits, not only deluding their apprehensions with Ariolation, South-saying, and such oblique Idolatries; but winning
their credulities unto the literall and down-right adorement
of Cats, Lizards and Beetles. And thus also in some Christian   25
Churches, wherein is presumed an irreprovable truth, if all be
true that is suspected, or half what is related, there have not

wanted many strange deceptions, and some thereof are still
confessed by the name of Pious fraudes. Thus Theudas an †,26
Impostor was able to lead away four thousand into the wildernesse, and the delusions of Mahomet almost the fourth
part of mankinde. Thus all heresies how grosse soever, have
found a welcome with the people. For thus, many of the Jews †
were wrought into belief, that Herod was the Messias; and
David George of Leyden, and Arden, were not without a 27,28
party amongst the people, who maintained the same opinion
of themselves almost in our daies.

Physitians (many at least that make profession thereof) be- †
side divers lesse discoverable waies of fraud, have made them
beleeve, there is the book of fate, or the power of Aarons 29
brest-plate in Urines. And therefore hereunto they have recourse as unto the Oracle of life, the great determinator of
virginity, conception, fertility, and the inscrutable infirmities
of the whole body. For as though there were a seminality in
Urine, or that like the seed it carried with it the Idea of every
part, they foolishly conceive we visibly behold therein the
Anatomy of every particle, and can thereby indigitate their
affections; and running into any demands expect from us a †
sudden resolution in things wherein the devil of Delphos 30
would demurre, and we know hath taken respite of some
daies to answer easier questions.

Saltimbancoes, Quacksalvers and Charlatans, deceive them
in lower degrees. Were Aesop alive, the Piazza and Pont 31,†
Neuf* could not but speak their fallacies; mean while there
are too many, whose cries cannot conceale their mischiefs.
For their Impostures are full of cruelty, and worse then any
other; deluding not only unto pecuniary defraudations, but
the irreparable deceit of death.

Astrologers, which pretend to be of Cabala with the starres
(such I mean as abuse that worthy enquiry;) have not been
wanting in their deceptions. Who having wonne their belief
unto principles whereof they make great doubt themselves,
have made them beleeve that arbitrary events below, have
necessary causes above; whereupon their credulities assent

* Places in Venice and Paris, where Mountebanks play their pranks.

unto any prognosticks, and daily swallow the predictions of
men, which considering the independencie of their causes,   †
and contingencie in their events, are only in the prescience of
God.

Fortune tellers, Juglers, Geomancers, and the like incantatory impostors, though commonly men of inferiour rank, and
from whom without illumination they can expect no more then   †
from themselves, do daily and professedly delude them. Unto
whom (what is deplorable in men and Christians) too many
applying themselves, betwixt jest and earnest, betray the
cause of truth, and insensibly make up the legionary body of
error.

Statistes and Politicians, unto whom *Ragione di Stato* is the
first considerable, as though it were their businesse to deceive
the people, as a Maxime do hold, that truth is to be concealed
from them; unto whom although they reveale the visible design, yet do they commonly conceale the capitall intention.
And therefore have they alway been the instruments of great
designes, yet seldome understood the true intention of any;
accomplishing the drifts of wiser heads, as inanimate and ignorant Agents the generall designe of the world; who though
in some latitude of sense, and in a naturall cognition perform
their proper actions, yet do they unknowingly concurre unto
higher ends, and blindely advance the great intention of nature. Now how farre they may be kept in ignorance, a great
example there is in the people of Rome, who never knew the
true and proper name of their own City. For beside that common appellation received by the Citizens, it had a proper
and secret name concealed from them: *Cujus alterum nomen*   32
dicere secretis Ceremoniarum nefas habetur, saith Plinie;
lest the name thereof being discovered unto their enemies,   †
their Penates and Patronall gods might be called forth by
charms and incantations. For according unto the tradition of
Magitians, the tutelary spirits will not remove at common appellations, but at the proper names of things whereunto they
are protectors.

Thus having been deceived by themselves, and continually
deluded by others, they must needs be stuffed with errors,
and even over-runne with these inferiour falsities; whereunto

whosoever shall resigne their reasons, either from the root of
deceit in themselves, or inability to resist such triviall ingan-
nations* from others; although their condition and fortunes
may place them many Spheres above the multitude, yet are
they still within the line of vulgarity, and Democraticall enemies of truth.

CHAP. 4.

OF THE NEARER AND MORE IMMEDIATE CAUSES OF POPULAR ERROURS,
BOTH IN THE WISER AND COMMON SORT, MISAPPREHENSION,
FALLACY, OR FALSE DIDUCTION, CREDULITY, SUPINITY,
ADHERENCE UNTO ANTIQUITIE, TRADITION AND AUTHORITIE.

The first is a mistake, or a conception of things, either in
their first apprehensions, or secondary relations. So Eve mistook the Commandment, either from the immediate injunction of God, or from the secondary narration of her husband.
So might the Disciples mistake our Saviour, in his answer
unto Peter, concerning the death of John, as is delivered,
John 21. Peter seeing John, saith unto Jesus, Lord, and what
shall this man doe? Jesus saith, If I will, that he tarry till I
come, what is that unto thee? Then went this saying abroad
among the brethren, that that Disciple should not die. Thus
began the conceit and opinion of the Centaures, that is, in
the mistake of the first beholders, as is declared by Servius;
when some young Thessalians on horseback were beheld
afarre off, while their horses watered, that is, while their
heads were depressed, they were conceived by the first spectators to be but one animall; and answerable hereunto have
their pictures been drawn ever since.

And as simple mistakes commonly beget fallacies, so men
rest not in false apprehensions, without absurd and inconsequent diductions; from fallacious foundations, and misapprehended mediums, erecting conclusions no way inferrible from
their premises. Now the fallacies whereby men deceive others, and are deceived themselves, the Ancients have divided

* Deceptions.   †

into Verball and Reall. Of the Verball, and such as conclude
from mistakes of the word, although there be no lesse then
six, yet are there but two thereof worthy our notation; and
unto which the rest may be referred: that is the fallacie of
Aequivocation and Amphibologie; which conclude from the
ambiguity of some one word, or the ambiguous syntaxis of
many put together. From this fallacy arose that calamitous error of the Jews, misapprehending the Prophesies of their Messias, and expounding them alwaies unto literall and temporall
expectations. By this way many errors crept in and perverted
the doctrine of Pythagoras, whilest men received his precepts
in a different sense from his intention; converting Metaphors
into proprieties, and receiving as litterall expressions, obscure
and involved truths. Thus when he enjoined his Disciples an
abstinence from beans, many conceived they were with severity debarred the use of that pulse, which notwithstanding
could not be his meaning; for as Aristoxenus who wrote his
life, averreth, he delighted much in that kinde of food himself. But herein as Plutarch observeth, he had no other intention, then to disswade men from Magistracy, or undertaking
the publike offices of state; for by beans were the Magistrates
elected in some parts of Greece; and after his daies, we reade
in Thucydides, of the Councell of the bean in Athens. The   33
same word also in Greek doth signifie a testicle, and hath
been thought by some an injunction only of continencie, as
Aul. Gellius hath expounded, and as Empedocles may also be   34
interpreted, πᾶν δεῖλοι κυαμῶν ἀπὸ χεῖρας ἔχεσθε that is,   †
Testiculis miseri dextras subducite. Again his injunction is,
not to harbour Swallows in our houses: Whose advice notwithstanding we doe not contemn, who daily admit and
cherish them. For herein a caution is only implied not to entertain ungratefull and thanklesse persons, which like the
swallow are no way commodious unto us; but having made
use of our habitations, and served their own turns, forsake
us. So he commands to deface the print of a cauldron in the
ashes, after it hath boyled. Which strictly to observe were
condemnable superstition: For hereby he covertly adviseth
us not to persevere in anger, but after our choler hath boyled,
to retain no impression thereof. In the like sense are to be

received, or they will else be misapprehended, when he adviseth his Disciples to give the right hand but to few, to put
no viands in a chamberpot, not to passe over a balance, not
to rake up fire with a sword, or pisse against the Sunne.
Which enigmaticall deliveries comprehend usefull verities,
but being mistaken by literall Expositors at the first, they
have been misunderstood by most since, and may be occasion
of error to verball capacities for ever.

This fallacy in the first delusion Satan put upon Eve, and
his whole tentation might be the same Elench continued; so †
when he said, Ye shall not die, that was in his equivocation,
ye shall not incurre a present death, or a destruction imme- †
diately ensuing your transgression. Your eyes shall be opened;
that is, not to the enlargement of your knowledge, but discovery of your shame and proper confusion. You shall know
good and evil; that is, you shall have knowledge of good by
its privation, but cognisance of evil by sense and visible experience. And the same fallacy or way of deceit so well succeeding in Paradise, he continued in his Oracles through all
the world. Which had not men more warily understood, they
might have performed many acts inconsistent with his intention. Brutus might have made haste with Tarquine to 35
have kissed his own mother. The Athenians might have built 36
them wooden walls, or doubled the Altar at Delphos. 37

The circle of this fallacy is very large, and herein may be
comprised all Ironicall mistakes; for intended expressions
receiving inverted significations; all deductions from metaphors, parables, allegories, unto reall and rigid interpretations. Whereby have risen not only popular errors in
Philosophy, but vulgar and senselesse heresies in Divinity; as
will be evident unto any that shall examine their foundations,
as they stand related by Epiphanius, Austin,° or Prateolus. 38

Other waies there are of deceit, which consist not in false
apprehension of words, that is, verball expressions or senten-
tiall significations, but fraudulent deductions, or inconsequent
illations, from a false conception of things. Of these extradictionary and reall fallacies, Aristotle and Logicians make in

---

° *De Haeresibus.* †

number six, but we observe that men are most commonly deceived by four thereof: those are, *Petitio principii. A dicto
secundum quid ad dictum simpliciter. A non causa pro causa.*
And *fallacia consequentis.*

The first is *petitio principii.* Which fallacie is committed,
when a question is made a medium, or we assume a medium
as granted, whereof we remain as unsatisfied as of the question. Briefly, where that is assumed as a principle, to prove
another thing, which is not conceded as true it self. By this
fallacie was Eve deceived, when she took for granted, the
false assertion of the devil; Ye shall not surely die; for God
doth know that in the day ye shall eat thereof, your eyes   †
shall be opened, and you shall be as gods. Which was but a
bare affirmation of Satan without any proof or probable in-
ducement; contrary unto the command of God and former
belief of her self. And this was the Logick of the Jews, when
they accused our Saviour unto Pilate; who demanding a reasonable impeachment, or the allegation of some crime worthy
of condemnation; they only replied, if he had not been
worthy of death, we would not have brought him before thee.
Wherein there was neither accusation of the person, nor satisfaction of the Judge, who well understood a bare accusation
was no presumption of guilt, and the clamors of the people
no accusation at all. The same fallacie is sometime used in
the dispute between Job and his friends; they often taking
that for granted which afterward he disproveth.   †

The second is *à dicto secundum quid ad dictum simpliciter,*
when from that which is but true in a qualified sense, an in-
conditionall and absolute verity is inferred; transferring the
speciall consideration of things unto their generall acceptions,
or concluding from their strict acception, unto that without
all limitation. This fallacie men commit when they argue
from a particular to a generall; as when we conclude the vices
or qualities of a few upon a whole Nation, or from a part
unto the whole. Thus the devil argued with our Saviour, and
by this he would perswade him he might be secure if he cast
himself from the pinacle: for said he, it is written, He shall
give his Angels charge concerning thee, and in their hands
they shall bear thee up, lest at any time thou dash thy foot

against a stone. But this illation was fallacious, leaving out part of the text, Psalm 91. He shall keep thee in all thy waies; that is, in the waies of righteousnesse, and not of rash attempts: so he urged a part for the whole, and inferred more in the conclusion, then was contained in the premises. By the same fallacie we proceed, when we conclude from the signe unto the thing signified. By this incroachment Idolatry first crept in, men converting the symbolicall use of Idols into their proper worship, and receiving the representation of things as the substance and thing it self. So the statue of Belus 39 at first erected in his memory, was in after times adored as a Divinity. And so also in the Sacrament of the Eucharist, the bread and wine which were but the signalls or visible signes, were made the things signified, and worshipped as the body † of Christ. And hereby generally men are deceived that take things spoken in some latitude without any at all. Hereby the Jews were deceived concerning the commandment of the Sabbath, accusing our Saviour for healing the sick, and his disciples for plucking the ears of corn, upon that day. And by this deplorable mistake they were deceived unto destruction, upon the assault of Pompey the great made upon that day, by 40 whose superstitious observation they could not defend themselves, or perform any labour whatsoever.

The third is *a non causa pro causa*, when that is pretended for a cause which is not, or not in that sense which is inferred. Upon this consequence the law of Mahomet forbids the use of wine, and his successors abolished Universities: by this also many Christians have condemned literature, misunderstanding the counsel of Saint Paul, who adviseth no further then 41 to beware of Philosophy. On this foundation were built the conclusions of Southsayers in their Auguriall, and Tripudiary divinations; collecting presages from voice or food of birds, and conjoyning events unto causes of no connexion. Hereupon also are grounded the grosse mistakes in the cure of many diseases; not only from the last medicine, and sympa- 42 theticall receits, but amulets, charms, and all incantatory applications; deriving effects not only from inconcurring causes, but things devoid of all efficiencie whatever.

The fourth is the fallacie of the consequent; which if strictly taken, may be a fallacious illation in reference unto antecedencie, or consequencie; as to conclude from the position of the antecedent, unto the position of the consequent, or from the remotion of the consequent to the remotion of the antecedent. This is usually committed, when in connexed propositions the termes adhere contingently. This is frequent in Oratorie illations; and thus the Pharisees, because he conversed with Publicans and sinners, accused the holinesse of Christ. But if this fallacie be largely taken, it is committed in any vicious illation, offending the rules of good consequence; and so it may be very large, and comprehend all false illations against the setled laws of Logick. But the most usuall inconsequencies are from particulars, from negatives, and from affirmative conclusions in the second figure, wherein indeed offences are most frequent, and their discoveries not difficult.

Chap. 5.
Of Credulity and Supinity.

A Third cause of common Errors is the Credulity of men, that is, an easie assent to what is obtruded, or a beleeving at first ear what is delivered by others. This is a weaknesse in the understanding, without examination assenting unto things which from their natures and causes doe carry no perswasion; whereby men often swallow falsities for truths, dubiosities for certainties, fesibilities for possibilities, and things impossible as possibilities themselves. Which, though a weaknesse of the Intellect, and most discoverable in vulgar heads, yet hath it sometime fallen upon wiser brains, and great advancers of truth. Thus many wise Athenians so far forgot their Philosophy, and the nature of humane production, that they descended unto beliefs the originall of their Nation was from the Earth, and had no other beginning then from the seminality and womb of their great Mother. Thus is it not without wonder, how those learned Arabicks so tamely delivered up their belief unto the absurdities of the Alcoran. How the noble Geber, Avicenna and Almanzor, should rest satisfied in   43

the nature and causes of earthquakes, delivered from the doctrine of their Prophet; that is, from the motion of a great Bull, upon whose hornes all the earth is poised. How their faiths could decline so low, as to concede their generations in heaven, to be made by the smell of a citron, or that the felicity of their Paradise should consist in a Jubilee of copulation, †
that is a coition of one act prolonged unto fifty years. Thus is it almost beyond wonder, how the belief of reasonable creatures, should ever submit unto Idolatry: and the credulity of those men scarce credible (without presumption of a second fall) who could beleeve a Deity in the work of their own hands. For although in that ancient and diffused adoration of Idols, unto the Priests and subtiler heads the worship perhaps might be symbolicall, and as those Images some way related unto their deities; yet was the Idolatry direct and down-right in the people; whose credulity is illimitable; who may be made beleeve that any thing is God; and may be made beleeve there is no God at all.

And as Credulity is the cause of Error, so incredulity oftentimes of not enjoying truth; and that not only an obstinate incredulity, whereby we will not acknowledge assent unto what is reasonably inferred, but any Academicall reservation in matters of easie truth, or rather scepticall infidelity against the evidence of reason and sense. For these are conceptions befalling wise men, as absurd as the apprehensions of fools, and the credulity of the people which promiscuously swallow any thing. For this is not only derogatory unto the wisdom of God, who hath proposed the world unto our knowledge, and thereby the notion of himself, but also detractory unto the intellect and sense of man expressedly disposed for that inquisition. And therefore *hoc tantum scio quod nihil scio,* is not to ⁴⁴
be received in an absolute sense, but is comparatively expressed unto the number of things whereof our knowledge is ignorant, nor will it acquit the insatisfaction of those which quarrell with all things, or dispute of matters concerning whose verities we have conviction from reason, or decision from the inerrable and requisite conditions of sense. And therefore if any affirm the earth doth move, and will not beleeve with us, it standeth still; because he hath probable rea-

sons for it, and I no infallible sense nor reason against it, I
will not quarrell with his assertion. But if like Zeno he shall   45
walk about, and yet deny there is any motion in nature,
surely that man was constituted for Anticyra, and were a fit   †,†
companion for those, who having a conceit they are dead,
cannot be convicted into the society of the living.

The fourth is a supinity or neglect of enquiry, even in matters whereof we doubt; rather beleeving, then going to see, or   †
doubting with ease and gratis, then beleeving with difficulty
or purchase; whereby, either from a temperamentall inactiv-
ity we are unready to put in execution the suggestions or
dictates of reason; or by a content and acquiescence in every
species of truth, we embrace the shadow thereof, or so much
as may palliate its just and substantiall acquirements. Had
our forefathers sat down in these resolutions, or had their
curiosities been sedentary, who pursued the knowledge of
things through all the corners of nature, the face of truth had
been obscure unto us, whose lustre in some part their indus-
tries have revealed.

Certainly the sweat of their labours was not salt unto them,
and they took delight in the dust of their endeavours. For
questionlesse in knowledge there is no slender difficulty, and
truth which wise men say doth lye in a well, is not recover-
able but by exantlation. It were some extenuation of the
curse, if *in sudore vultus tui,* were confinable unto corporall   46
exercitations, and there still remained a Paradise or unthorny
place of knowledge. But now our understandings being
eclipsed, as well as our tempers infirmed, we must betake our
selves to waies of reparation, and depend upon the illumination of our endeavours. For thus we may in some measure
repair our primary ruines, and build our selves men again.
And though the attempts of some have been precipitous, and
their enquiries so audacious as to come within command of
the flaming swords, and lost themselves in attempts above
humanity; yet have the enquiries of most defected by the
way, and tyred within the sober circumference of knowledge.

And this is the reason why some have transcribed any
thing; and although they cannot but doubt thereof, yet nei-

ther make experiment by sense or enquiry by reason, but live
in doubts of things whose satisfaction is in their own power;
which is indeed the inexcusable part of our ignorance, and
may perhaps fill up the charge of the last day. For not obeying the dictates of reason, and neglecting the cries of truth,
we fail not only in the trust of our undertakings, but in the
intention of man it self. Which although more veniall unto ordinary constitutions, and such as are not framed beyond the
capacity of beaten notions, yet will it inexcusably condemn
some men, who having received excellent endowments, have   †
yet sat down by the way, and frustrated the intention of their
habilities. For certainly as some men have sinned in the principles of humanity, and must answer, for not being men, so
others offend if they be not more; *Magis extra vitia quam*   47
cum virtutibus, would commend those, these are not excusable without an Excellency. For great constitutions, and such
as are constellated unto knowledge, do nothing till they out-
doe all; they come short of themselves if they go not beyond
others, and must not sit down under the degree of worthies.
God expects no lustre from the minor stars, but if the Sun
should not illuminate all, it were a sin in Nature. *Ultimus*   48
bonorum, will not excuse every man, nor is it sufficient for all
to hold the common levell; Mens names should not only distinguish them: A man should be something that men are not,
and individuall in somewhat beside his proper nature. Thus
while it exceeds not the bounds of reason and modesty, we
cannot condemn singularity. *Nos numerus sumus,* is the motto   49
of the multitude, and for that reason are they fools. For things
as they recede from unity, the more they approach to imperfection, and deformity; for they hold their perfection in their
simplicities, and as they nearest approach unto God.

Now as there are many great wits to be condemned, who
have neglected the increment of Arts, and the sedulous pursuit of knowledge; so are there not a few very much to be
pittied, whose industry being not attended with naturall
parts, they have sweat to little purpose, and rolled the stone
in vain. Which chiefly proceedeth from naturall incapacity,
and geniall indisposition, at least to those particulars whereunto they apply their endeavours. And this is one reason why

though Universities be full of men, they are oftentimes empty
of learning. Why as there are some which do much without
learning, so others but little with it, and few that attain to any   †
measure of it. For many heads that undertake it, were never
squared nor timbred for it. There are not only particular men,
but whole nations indisposed for learning; whereunto is required not only education, but a pregnant Minerva and teem-
ing constitution. For the wisdome of God hath divided the
Genius of men according to the different affairs of the world,
and varied their inclinations according to the variety of Actions to be performed therein. Which they who consider not,
rudely rushing upon professions and waies of life unequall to
their natures, dishonour not only themselves and their func-
tions, but pervert the harmony of the whole world. For if the
world went on as God hath ordained it, and were every one
implied in points concordant to their Natures; Professions,
Arts and Common-wealths would rise up of themselves; nor
needed we a Lanthorn to finde a man in Athens.   50

Chap. 6.
Of adherence unto Antiquity.

But the mortallest enemy unto knowledge, and that which
hath done the greatest execution upon truth, hath been a
peremptory adhesion unto Authority, and more especially
the establishing of our belief upon the dictates of Antiquity.   †
For (as every capacity may observe) most men of Ages present, so superstitiously do look on Ages past, that the authorities of the one, exceed the reasons of the other. Whose
persons indeed being farre removed from our times, their
works, which seldome with us passe uncontrouled, either by
contemporaries or immediate successors, are now become out
of the distance of envies: And the farther removed from present times, are conceived to approach the nearer unto truth
it self. Now hereby methinks we manifestly delude our selves,
and widely walk out of the track of truth.

For first, men hereby impose a thraldome on their times,
which the ingenuity of no age should endure, or indeed the

presumption of any did ever yet enjoin. Thus Hippocrates about 2000 years agoe, conceived it no injustice, either to examine or refute the doctrines of his predecessors: Galen the like, and Aristotle most of any. Yet did not any of these conceive themselves infallible, or set down their dictates as verities irrefragable; but when they either deliver their own inventions, or reject other mens opinions, they proceed with Judgement and Ingenuity, establishing their assertions, not only with great solidity, but submitting them also unto the correction of future discovery.

Secondly, Men that adore times past, consider not that those times were once present, that is, as our own are at this instant, and we our selves unto those to come, as they unto us at present; as we relye on them, even so will those on us, and magnifie us hereafter, who at present condemn our selves. Which very absurdity is daily committed amongst us even in the esteem and censure of our own times. And to speak impartially, old men from whom we should expect the greatest example of wisdome, do most exceed in this point of folly; commending the daies of their youth they scarce remember, at least well understood not; extolling those times their younger years have heard their fathers condemn, and condemning those times the gray heads of their posterity shall commend. And thus is it the humour of many heads to extoll the daies of their forefathers, and declaim against the wickednesse of times present. Which notwithstanding they cannot handsomely doe, without the borrowed help and satyres of times past; condemning the vices of their times, by the expressions of vices in times which they commend, which cannot but argue the community of vice in both. Horace therefore, Juvenall and Perseus were no prophets, although their lines did seem to indigitate and point at our times. There is a certain list of vices committed in all ages, and declaimed against by all Authors, which will last as long as humane nature; or digested into common places may serve for any theme, and never be out of date untill Dooms day.

Thirdly, The testimonies of Antiquity and such as passe oraculously amongst us, were not if we consider them alwaies so exact, as to examine the doctrine they delivered. For some,

and those the acutest of them, have left unto us many things
of falsity, controulable, not only by criticall and collective
reason, but common and countrey observation. Hereof there
want not many examples in Aristotle, through all his book of   52
animals; we shall instance only in three of his Problemes,
and all contained under one Section. The first enquireth why
a Man doth cough, but not an Oxe or Cow? whereas notwithstanding the contrary is often observed by husbandmen, and
stands confirmed by those who have expresly treated *de re
Rustica,* and have also delivered divers remedies for it. Why
Juments, as Horses, Oxen and Asses, have no eructation or   †
belching, whereas indeed the contrary is often observed, and
also delivered by Columella. And thirdly, why man alone   †
hath gray haires? whereas it cannot escape the eies, and ordinary observation of all men, that horses, dogs, and foxes, wax
gray with age in our Countries, and in the colder regions many
other animals without it. And though favourable construc-   †
tions may somewhat extenuate the rigour of these conces-
sions, yet will scarce any palliate that in the fourth of his
meteors, That salt is easiest dissolvible in cold water: Nor that
of Dioscorides, That Quicksilver is best preserved in Tinne
and Lead.

Other Authors write often dubiously, even in matters
wherein is expected a strict and definitive truth; extenuating
their affirmations with *aiunt, ferunt, fortasse,* as Dioscorides,   53
Galen, Aristotle, and many more. Others by hear say, taking
upon trust most they have delivered; whose volumes are
meer collections, drawn from the mouthes or leaves of other
Authors; as may be observed in Plinie, Aelian, Athenaeus,
and many more. Not a few transcriptively; subscribing their
names unto other mens endeavours, and meerly transcribing
almost all they have written. The Latines transcribing the
Greeks, the Greeks and Latines each other. Thus hath Justine   54,†
borrowed all from Trogus Pompeius, and Julius Solinus in a
manner transcribed Plinie. Thus have Lucian and Apuleius
served Lucius Pratensis; men both living in the same time,
and both transcribing the same Authour, in those famous
Books, Entituled *Lucius* by the one, and *Aureus Asinus* by   55
the other. In the same measure hath Simocrates in his Tract

de Nilo, dealt with Diodorus Siculus, as may be observed in
that work annexed unto Herodotus, and translated by Junger-
mannus. Thus Eratosthenes wholly translated Timotheus *de
Insulis,* not reserving the very Preface. The very same doth
Strabo report of Eudorus and Ariston in a Treatise entituled †
de Nilo. Clemens Alexandrinus hath observed many examples †
hereof among the Greeks; and Plinie speaketh very plainly
in his Preface, that conferring his Authors, and comparing
their works together, he generally found those that went before *verbatim* transcribed, by those that followed after, and
their originals never so much as mentioned. To omit how †
much the wittiest peece of Ovid is beholding unto Parthenius 56
Chius; even the magnified Virgil hath borrowed almost all his
works: his Eclogues from Theocritus, his Georgicks from
Hesiod and Aratus, his Aeneads from Homer; the second
Book whereof containing the exploit of Sinon and the Trojan †
horse (as Macrobius observeth) he hath *verbatim* derived
from Pisander. Our own profession is not excusable herein.
Thus Oribasius, Aetius, and Aegineta have in a manner trans-
scribed Galen. But Marcellus Empericus who hath left a famous work *de medicamentis,* hath word for word, transcribed
all Scribonius Largus, *de compositione medicamentorum,* and †
not left out his very peroration. Thus may we perceive the
Ancients were but men, even like our selves. The practice of
transcription in our daies was no monster in theirs: Plagiarie
had not its nativity with printing; but began in times when
thefts were difficult, and the paucity of books scarce wanted
that invention.

[Nor did they only make large use of other Authors, but †
often without mention of their names. *Aristotle,* who seems to
have borrowed many things from *Hippocrates,* in the most
favourable construction, makes mention but once° of him,
and that by the by, and without reference unto his present
Doctrine. *Virgil,* so much beholding unto *Homer,* hath not his
name in all his Works; and *Plinie,* who seems to borrow many
Authors out of *Dioscorides,* hath taken no notice of him. I
wish men were not still content to plume themselves with

° In his Politicks.

others Feathers. Fear of discovery, not single ingenuity affords
Quotations rather then Transcriptions; wherein not withstanding the Plagiarisme of many makes little consideration,
whereof though great Authors may complain, small ones cannot but take notice.]

Fourthly, While we so eagerly adhear unto Antiquity, and
the accounts of elder times, we are to consider the fabulous
condition thereof; and that we shall not deny if we call to
minde the mendacity of Greece, from whom we have re-   57
ceived most relations, and that a considerable part of Ancient
times, was by the Greeks themselves termed μύθικον that is,
made up or stuffed out with fables. And surely the fabulous
inclination of those daies, was greater then any since; which
swarmed so with fables, and from such slender grounds took
hintes for fictions, poysoning the world ever after; wherein,
how far they exceeded, may be exemplified from Palaepha-   58
tus,* in his book of fabulous narrations. That fable of Orpheus, who by the melody of his musick, made woods and
trees to follow him, was raised upon a slender foundation;
for there were a crew of mad women, retired unto a mountain, from whence being pacified by his Musick, they
descended with boughs in their hands, which unto the fabu-
losity of those times, proved a sufficient ground to celebrate
unto all posterity the Magick of Orpheus harp, and its power
to attract the senselesse trees about it. That Medea the famous Sorceresse could renue youth, and make old men young
again, was nothing else, but that from the knowledge of simples she had a receit to make white hair black, and reduce old
heads into the tincture of youth again. The fable of Gerion   59
and Cerberus with three heads was this: Gerion was of the   60
City Tricarinia, that is, of three heads, and Cerberus of the   †,61
same place was one of his dogs, which running into a cave
upon pursuit of his masters oxen, Hercules perforce drew him
out of that place; from whence the conceits of those daies affirmed no lesse, then that Hercules descended into hell, and
brought up Cerberus into the habitation of the living. Upon
the like grounds was raised the figment of Briareus, who

---

* An ancient Author who writ περὶ ἀπίστων, *sive de incredibilibus,* whereof
some part is yet extant.

dwelling in a City called Hecatonchiria, the fancies of those
times assigned him an hundred hands. Twas ground enough   62
to fancy wings unto Daedalus, in that he stole out of a window from Minos, and sailed away with his son Icarus; who
steering his course wisely, escaped; but his son carrying too
high a saile was drowned. That Niobe weeping over her children was turned into a stone, was nothing else but that during her life, she erected over their sepultures, a marble tombe
of her own. When Acteon had undone himself with dogs, and
the prodigall attendance of hunting, they made a solemn
story how he was devoured by his hounds. And upon the like
grounds was raised the Anthropophagie* of Diomedes his   63
horses. Upon as slender foundation was built the fable of the
Minotaure; for one Taurus a servant of Minos gat his mis-   64
tresse Pasiphae with childe; from whence the infant was
named Minotaurus. Now this unto the fabulosities of those
times was thought sufficient to accuse Pasiphae of Beastiality,
or admitting conjunction with a Bull; and in succeeding ages
gave a hint of depravity unto Domitian to act the fable into   65
reality. In like manner, as Diodorus plainly delivereth, the   †
famous fable of Charon had its nativity, who being no other
but the common Ferryman of Ægypt, that wafted over the
dead bodies from Memphis; was made by the Greeks to be
the Ferryman of hell, and solemn stories raised after him.
Lastly, We shall not need to enlarge, if that be true which
grounded the generation of Castor and Helena out of an egge,
because they were born and brought up in an upper room,
according unto the word ᾠον, which with the Lacedaemonians
had also that signification.

Fiftly, We applaud many things delivered by the Ancients,
which are in themselves but ordinary, and come short of our
own conceptions. Thus we usually extoll, and our Orations
cannot escape the sayings of the wise men of Greece. *Nosce*   66
teipsum of Thales: *Nosce tempus* of Pittacus: *Nihil nimis* of
Cleobulus; which notwithstanding to speak indifferently, are
but vulgar precepts in Morality, carrying with them nothing
above the line, or beyond the extemporary sententiosity of

* Eating of mans Flesh.

common conceits with us. Thus we magnifie the Apothegmes,
or reputed replies of wisdom, whereof many are to be seen
in Laertius, more in Lycosthenes, not a few in the second book   67
of Macrobius, in the salts of Cicero, Augustus, and the Comi-   68,69
call wits of those times: in most whereof there is not much to
admire, and are me thinks exceeded, not only in the replies
of wise men, but the passages of society and urbanities of
our times. And thus we extoll their adages or proverbs, and
Erasmus hath taken great pains to make collections of them;   70
whereof notwithstanding the greater part will, I beleeve, unto
indifferent judges be esteemed no extraordinaries; and may   †
be paralleled, if not exceeded, by those of more unlearned
nations, and many of our own.

Sixtly, We urge authorities, in points that need not, and
introduce the testimony of ancient writers, to confirm things
evidently beleeved, and whereto no reasonable hearer but
would assent without them; such as are; *Nemo mortalium*   71
omnibus horis sapit. Virtute nil praestantius, nil pulchrius.
Omnia vincit amor. Praeclarum quiddam veritas. All which,
although things known and vulgar, are frequently urged by
many men, and though triviall verities in our mouthes, yet
noted from Plato, Ovid, or Cicero, they become reputed elegancies. For many hundred, to instance but in one we meet
with while we are writing. Antonius Guevara that elegant
Spaniard, in his book intituled, *The Diall of Princes*, beginneth his Epistle thus. Apolonius Thyaneus disputing with the
Scholars of Hiarchus, said, that among all the affections of nature, nothing was more naturall, then the desire all have to
preserve life; which being a confessed truth, and a verity
acknowledged by all, it was a superfluous affectation to derive
its authority from Apolonius, or seek a confirmation thereof
as farre as India, and the learned Scholers of Hiarchus.
Which, whether it be not all one to strengthen common dignities and principles known by themselves, with the authority
of Mathematicians; or think a man should beleeve the whole
is greater then its parts, rather upon the authority of Euclide,
then if it were propounded alone; I leave unto the second
and wiser cogitations of all men. Tis sure a practice that sa-
vours much of Pedantery; a reserve of Puerility we have not

shaken off from School; where being seasoned with Minor sentences, by a neglect of higher enquiries, they prescribe upon our riper ears, and are never worn out but with our memories.

Lastly, While we so devoutly adhere unto Antiquity in some things, we doe not consider we have deserted them in severall others. For they indeed have not only been imper- †
fect in the conceit of some things, but either ignorant or erro-
neous in many more. They understood not the motion of the †
eight sphear from West to East, and so conceived the longitude of the starres invariable. They conceived the torrid Zone
unhabitable, and so made frustrate the goodliest part of the
earth. But we now know 'tis very well empeopled, and the
habitation thereof esteemed so happy, that some have made
it the proper seat of Paradise; and been so farre from judg-
ing it unhabitable, that they have made it the first habitation
of all. Many of the Ancients denied the Antipodes, and some
unto the penality of contrary affirmations; but the experience
of our enlarged navigations, can now assert them beyond all
dubitation. Having thus totally relinquisht them in some
things, it may not be presumptuous to examine them in
others; but surely most unreasonable to adhere to them in all,
as though they were infallible or could not erre in any.

Chap. 7.
Of Authority.

Nor is only a resolved prostration unto Antiquity a powerfull enemy unto knowledge, but any confident adherence
unto Authority, or resignation of our judgements upon the
testimony of Age or Author whatsoever.

For first, To speak generally, an argument from Authority †
to wiser examinations, is but a weaker kinde of proof, it being
but a topicall probation, and as we term it, an inartificiall
argument, depending upon a naked asseveration: wherein
neither declaring the causes, affections or adjuncts of what
we beleeve, it carrieth not with it the reasonable inducements of knowledge; and therefore *Contra negantem prin-* 72

cipia, Ipse dixit, or *Oportet discentem credere,* although postulates very accommodable unto Junior indoctrinations, yet are their authorities but temporary, and not to be imbraced beyond the minority of our intellectuals. For our advanced beliefs are not to be built upon dictates, but having received the probable inducements of truth, we become emancipated from testimoniall ingagements, and are to erect upon the surer base of reason.

Secondly, Unto reasonable perpensions it hath no place in some Sciences, small in others, and suffereth many restrictions, even where it is most admitted. It is of no validity in the Mathematicks, especially the mother part thereof Arithmetick and Geometry. For these Sciences concluding from dignities and principles known by themselves, receive not satisfaction from probable reasons, much lesse from bare and peremptory asseverations. And therefore if all Athens should decree, that in every triangle, two sides, which soever be taken, are greater then the side remaining; or that in rectangle triangles the square which is made of the side that subtendeth the right angle, is equall to the squares which are made of the sides containing the right angle: Although there be a certain truth therein, Geometritians notwithstanding would not receive satisfaction without demonstration thereof. 'Tis true, by the vulgarity of Philosophers there are many points beleeved without probation; nor if a man affirme from Ptolomy, that the Sun is bigger then the Earth, shall he probably meet with any contradiction; whereunto notwithstanding Astronomers will not assent without some convincing argument or demonstrative proof thereof. And therefore certainly of all men a Philosopher should be no swearer: for an oath which is the end of controversies in Law, cannot determine any here; nor are the deepest sacraments or desperate imprecations of any force to perswade, where reason only, and necessary mediums must induce.

In naturall Philosophy more generally pursued amongst us, it carrieth but slender consideration; for that also proceeding from setled principles, therein is expected a satisfaction from scientificall progressions, and such as beget a sure or rationall belief. For if Authority might have made out

the assertions of Philosophy, we might have held, that snow [73]
was black, that the sea was but the sweat of the earth, and [74]
many of the like absurdities. Then was Aristotle injurious to [75]
fall upon Melissus, to reject the assertions of Anaxagoras,
Anaximander, and Empedocles; then were we also ungratefull unto himself; from whom our Junior endeavours embracing many things on his authority, our mature and secondary
enquiries are forced to quit those receptions, and to adhere
unto the nearer accounts of reason. And although it be not
unusuall, even in Philosophicall tractates to make enumeration of Authors, yet are there reasons usually introduced, and
to ingenuous readers do carry the stroak in the perswasion.
And surely if we account it reasonable among our selves, and
not injurious unto rationall Authors, no farther to abet their
opinions then as they are supported by solid reasons: cer- †
tainly with more excusable reservation may we shrink at their
bare testimonies, whose argument is but precarious, and subsists upon the charity of our assentments.

In Morality, Rhetorick, Law and History, there is I confesse †
a frequent and allowable use of testimony; and yet herein I
perceive, it is not unlimitable, but admitteth many restrictions. Thus in law both Civill and Divine, that is only esteemed a legall testimony, which receives comprobation †
from the mouths of at least two witnesses; and that not only
for prevention of calumny, but assurance against mistake;
whereas notwithstanding the solid reason of one man, is as
sufficient as the clamor of a whole Nation; and with impre-
judicate apprehensions begets as firm a belief as the authority
or aggregated testimony of many hundreds. For reason being
the very root of our natures, and the principles thereof common unto all; what is against the laws of true reason, or the
unerring understanding of any one, if rightly apprehended,
must be disclaimed by all Nations, and rejected even by
mankinde.

Again, A testimony is of small validity if deduced from men
out of their own profession; so if Lactantius affirm the figure
of the earth is plain, or Austin himself deny there are Antipodes; though venerable Fathers of the Church, and ever to
be honoured, will their Authorities prove sufficient to ground

a belief thereon? whereas notwithstanding the solid reason or confirmed experience of any man, is very approvable in what profession soever. So Raymund Sebund, a Physitian of Tholouze, besides his learned Dialogues, *de natura humana*, hath written a naturall Theologie, demonstrating therein the Attributes of God, and attempting the like in most points of Religion. So Hugo Grocius a Civilian, did write an excellent Tract of the verity of Christian Religion. Wherein most ra- †,†
tionally delivering themselves, their works will be embraced by most that understand them, and their reasons enforce belief even from prejudicate Readers. Neither indeed have the authorities of men been ever so awfull, but that by some they have been rejected, even in their own professions: Thus Aristotle affirming the birth of the Infant or time of its gestation 76
extended sometimes unto the eleventh moneth, but Hippocrates averring that it exceedeth not the tenth, Adrian the †
Emperour in a solemn processe, determined for Aristotle; but Justinian many years after, took in with Hippocrates and reversed the Decree of the other. Thus have Councels not only condemned private men, but the Decrees and Acts of one another. So Galen after all his veneration of Hippocrates, in some things hath fallen from him; Avicen in many from Galen; and others succeeding from him. And although the singularity of Paracelsus be intolerable, who sparing only Hippocrates, hath reviled not only the Authors, but almost all the learning that went before him; yet is it not much lesse injurious unto knowledge obstinately and inconvincibly to side with any one. Which humour unhappily possessing many, they have by prejudice withdrawn themselves into parties, and contemning the soveraignty of truth, seditiously abetted the private divisions of error.

Moreover a Testimony in points historicall, and where it is of unavoidable use, is of no illation in the negative; nor is it of consequence that Herodotus writing nothing of Rome, there was therefore no such city in his time; or because Dioscorides hath made no mention of Unicorns horn, there is therefore no such thing in Nature. Indeed, intending an accurate enumeration of Medicall materials, the omission hereof affords some probability it was not used by the Ancients, but will not conclude the nonexistence thereof. For so may we annihilate many simples unknown to his enquiries, as Senna, Rhabarbe, Bezoar, Ambregris, and divers others. Whereas indeed the reason of man hath no such restraint, concluding not only affirmatively but negatively; not only affirming there is no magnitude beyond the last heavens, but also denying there is any vacuity within them. Although it be confessed, the affirmative hath the prerogative illation, and Barbara engrosseth the powerfull demonstration.

Lastly, The strange relations made by Authors, may sufficiently discourage our adherence unto Authority, and which if we beleeve we must be apt to swallow any thing. Thus Basil will tell us, the Serpent went erect like man, and that that beast could speak before the fall. Tostatus would make us beleeve that Nilus encreaseth every new Moon. Leonardo Fioravanti an Italian Physitian, beside many other secrets assumeth unto himself the discovery of one concerning Pellitory of the wall; that is, that it never groweth in the sight of the North starre. *Dove si possa vedere la stella Tramontana,* [77] wherein how wide he is from truth is easily discoverable unto every one who hath but Astronomy enough to know that starre. Franciscus Sanctius in a laudable Comment upon Alciats Emblems, affirmeth and that from experience, a Nightin- [78] gale hath no tongue. *Avem Philomelam lingua carere pro certo affirmare possum, nisi me oculi fallunt.* Which if any man for a while shall beleeve upon his experience, he may at his leasure refute it by his own. What fool almost would beleeve, at least, what wise man would relye upon that Antidote delivered by Pierius in his Hieroglyphicks against the sting of a Scorpion? that is, to sit upon an Asse with ones face toward his taile; for so the pain leaveth the man, and passeth into the beast. It were me thinks but an uncomfortable receit for a Quartane Ague (and yet as good perhaps as many others used) to have recourse unto the remedy of Sammoni- [79] cus; that is, to lay the fourth book of Homers Iliads under ones head, according to the precept of that Physitian and Poet, *Maeoniae Iliados quartum suppone trementi.* There are surely few that have belief to swallow, or hope enough to ex-

periment the Collyrium* of Albertus, which promiseth a
strange effect, and such as Theeves would count inestimable;
that is, to make one see in the dark: yet thus much, according
unto his receit, will the right eye of an Hedge-hog boyled in
oyle and preserved in a brasen vessell effect. As strange it is,
and unto vicious inclinations were worth a nights lodging*
with Lais, what is delivered in *Kiranides;* that the left stone   80
of a Weesell, wrapt up in the skin of a she Mule, is able to
secure incontinency from conception.

These with swarms of others have men delivered in their
writings, whose verities are only supported by their Authorities: but being neither consonant unto reason, nor correspondent unto experiment, their affirmations are unto us no
Axiomes; we esteem thereof as things unsaid, and account
them but in the list of nothing. I wish herein the Chymistes   81
had been more sparing; who over-magnifying their preparations, inveigle the curiosity of many, and delude the
security of most. For if experiments would answer their enco-
miums, the Stone and Quartane Agues, were not opprobrious
unto Physitians; we might contemn that first and most uncomfortable Aphorisme* of Hippocrates; For surely that Art
were soon attained, that hath so generall remedies; and life
could not be short, were there such to prolong it.

Chap. 8.
A brief enumeration of Authors.

Now for as much as we have discoursed of Authority, and
there is scarce any tradition or popular error but stands also
delivered by some good Author; we shall endeavour a short
discovery of such as for the major part have given authority
hereto: who though excellent and usefull Authors, yet being
either transcriptive, or following common relations, their accounts are not to be swallowed at large, or entertained without a prudent circumspection. In whom the *ipse dixit,*

* An eye medecine.
* Ten thousand drachmes.
* *Ars longa, vita brevis.*   †

although it be no powerfull argument in any, is yet lesse authentick then in many other, because they deliver not their own experiences, but others affirmations, and write from others as we our selves from them.

1. The first in order as also in time, shall be Herodotus of Halicarnassus, an excellent and very elegant Historian, whose books of history were so well received in his own daies, that at their rehearsall in the Olympick games, they obtained the names of the nine Muses, and continued in such esteem unto descending Ages, that Cicero termed him *Historiarum parens.* And Dionysius his Countreyman, in an Epistle to Pompey, after an expresse comparison, affords him the better of Thucydides; all which notwithstanding, he hath received from some, the stile of *Mendaciorum pater;* his authority was much infringed by Plutarch, who being offended with him, as Polybius had been with Philarcus, for speaking too coldly of his Countreymen, hath left a particular Tract, *de Malignitate Herodoti.* But in this latter Century, Camerarius and Stephanus have stepped in, and by their witty Apologies, effectually endeavoured to frustrate the Arguments of Plutarch or any other. Now in this Author, as may be observed in our ensuing Discourse, and is better discernable in the perusall of himself, there are many things fabulously delivered, and not to be accepted as truths: whereby neverthelesse if any man be deceived, the Author is not so culpable as the believer. For he indeed imitating the father Poet, whose life he hath also written, and as Thucydides observeth, as well intending the delight as benefit of his Reader, hath besprinkled his work with many fabulosities, whereby if any man be led into error, he mistaketh the intention of the Author, who plainly confesseth he writeth many things by hearsay, and forgetteth a very considerable caution of his, that is, *Ego quae fando cognovi, exponere narratione mea debeo omnia; credere autem esse vera omnia, non debeo.*

2. In the second place is Ctesias the Cnidian, Physician unto Artaxerxes King of Persia; his books are often cited by ancient Writers; and by the industry of Stephanus and Rodomanus, there are extant some fragments thereof in our daies; he wrote the History of Persia, and many narrations of India.

In the first as having a fair opportunity to know the truth, and as Diodorus affirmeth the perusall of Persian Records, his testimony is acceptable. In his Indian relations, wherein are †contained strange and incredible accounts, he is surely to be read with suspension; these were they which weakned his authority with former ages; for as we may observe, he is sel- †dome mentioned, without a derogatory parenthesis in any Author. Aristotle besides the frequent undervaluing of his authority, in his books of Animals gives him the lie no lesse then twice, concerning the seed of Elephants. Strabo in his eleventh Book hath left a harder censure of him. *Equidem* 84 *facilius Hesiodo et Homero, aliquis fidem adhibuerit, itemque Tragicis Poetis, quam Ctesiae, Herodoto, Hellanico et eorum similibus.* But Lucian hath spoken more plainly then any. *Scripsit Ctesias de Indorum regione, deque iis quae apud* 84 *illos sunt, ea quae nec ipse vidit, neque ex ullius sermone audivit.* Yet were his relations taken up by some succeeding †Writers, and many thereof revived by our Countryman, Sir John Mandevell, Knight and Doctor in Physick, who after thirty years peregrination died at Liège, and was there hon- †ourably interred. He left a book of his travells, which hath been honoured with the translation of many languages, and now continued above three hundred years; herein he often attesteth the fabulous relations of Ctesias, and seems to confirm the refuted accounts of Antiquity. All which may still be received in some acceptions of morality, and to a pregnant invention, may afford commendable mythologie; but in a naturall and proper exposition, it containeth impossibilities and things inconsistent with truth.

3. There is a Book *de mirandis auditionibus,* ascribed unto Aristotle; another *de mirabilibus narrationibus,* written long after by Antigonus; another also of the same title by Phlegon †Trallianus, translated by Xilander, and with the Annotations of Meursius; all whereof make good the promise of their titles and may be read with caution. Which if any man shall likewise observe in the Lecture of Philostratus, concerning the life of Apollonius; or not only in ancient Writers, but shall carry a wary eye on Paulus Venetus, Jovius, Olaus Magnus,

Nierembergius, and many other, I think his circumspection is
laudable, and he may thereby decline occasion of Error.

4. Dioscorides Anazarbeus; he wrote many books in Physick, but six thereof *de Materia Medica,* have found the greatest esteem; he is an Author of good Antiquity and use;   †
preferred by Galen before Cratevas, Pamphilus, and all that
attempted the like description before him; yet all he delivereth therein is not to be conceived Oraculous. For beside that,
following the warres under Anthony, the course of his life
would not permit a punctuall examen in all; There are many
things concerning the nature of simples, traditionally delivered, and to which I beleeve he gave no assent himself. It
had been an excellent receit, and in his time when Sadles
were scarce in fashion of very great use, if that were true,
which he delivers, that Vitex, or Agnus Castus held only in
the hand, preserveth the rider from galling. It were a strange
effect, and whores would forsake the experiment of Savine, if
that were a truth which he delivereth of Brake or femall
fearn, that only treading over it it causeth a sudden abortion.
It were to be wished true, and women would Idolize him,
could that be made out which he recordeth of Phyllon, Mercury, and other vegetables, that the juice of the masle plant
drunk, or the leaves but applied unto the genitals, determines
their conceptions unto males. In these relations although he
be more sparing, his predecessours were very numerous; and
Galen hereof most sharply accuseth Pamphilus. Many of the
like nature we meet sometimes in Oribasius, Aetius, Trallia-   †
nus, Serapion, Evax and Marcellus; whereof some containing
no colour of verity, we may at first sight reject them; others
which seem to carry some face of truth, we may reduce unto
experiment. And herein we shall rather perform good offices
unto truth, then any disservice unto their relators, who have
well deserved of succeeding ages, from whom having received the conceptions of former times, we have the readier
hint of their conformity with ours, and may accordingly ex-
plore and sift their verities.

5. *Plinius Secundus* of Verona; a man of great eloquence,
and industry indefatigable, as may appear by his writings,   †
especially those now extant, and which are never like to

perish, but even with learning it self; that is, his naturall His-   †
tory. He was the greatest Collector or Rhapsodist of all the
Latines, and as Suetonius *de viris Illustribus* observeth, he
collected this piece out of two thousand Latine and Greek
Authors. Now, what is very strange, there is scarce a popular
error passant in our daies, which is not either directly expressed, or diductively contained in this work; which being in
the hands of most men, hath proved a powerfull occasion of
their propogation. Wherein notwithstanding, the credulity of
the Reader is more condemnable then the curiosity of the
Author. For commonly he nameth the Authors, from whom he
received those accounts; and writes but as he reades, as in his   †
Preface to Vespasian he acknowledgeth.

6. Claudius Aelianus; who flourished not long after in the
reign of Trajan, unto whom he dedicated his Tacticks; an
elegant and miscellaneous Author, he hath left two books
which are in the hands of every one, his History of Animals,
and his *Varia historia*. Wherein are contained many things
suspicious, not a few false, some impossible; he is much beholding unto Ctesias, and in many subjects writes more confidently than Plinie.

7. Julius Solinus, who lived also about his time: He left a
work entituled *Polyhistor*, containing great variety of matter,
and is with most in good request at this day. But to speak
freely what cannot be concealed, it is but Plinie varied, or a
transcription of his naturall history; nor is it without all wonder it hath continued so long, but is now likely, and deserves
indeed to live for ever; not so much for the elegancy of the
text, as the excellency of the comment, lately performed by   85
Salmasius, under the name of Plinian exercitations.

8. Athenaeus a delectable Author and very various, and as
Casaubone in his Epistle stiles him *Graecorum Plinius*. There   †
is extant of his, a famous piece under the name of *Deipnosophista*, or *caena sapientum*, containing the discourse of   86
many learned men, at a feast provided by Laurentius. It is a
laborious collection out of many Authors, and some whereof
are mentioned no where else. It containeth strange and singular relations, not without some spice or sprinkling of all learning. The Author was probably a better Grammarian then

Philosopher, dealing but hardly with Aristotle and Plato, and
betraieth himself much in his Chapter *de curiositate Aristote-*
lis. In brief, he is an Author of excellent use, and may with
discretion be read unto great advantage: and hath therefore
well deserved the Comments of Casaubon and Dalecampius.
But being miscellaneous in many things, he is to be received
with suspition; for such as amasse all relations, must erre in
some, and may without offence be unbeleeved in many.

9. We will not omit the works of Nicander, a Poet of good [87]
Antiquity, that is, his *Theriaca,* and *Alexipharmaca,* translated and commented by Gorraeus: for therein are contained
severall traditions, and popular conceits, of venemous beasts;
which only deducted, the work is to be embraced, as containing the first description of poysons and their Antidotes,
whereof Dioscorides, Pliny and Galen, have made especiall
use in elder times; and Ardoynus, Grevinus and others, in
times more near our own. We might perhaps let passe Oppianus, that famous Cilician Poet. There are extant of his in
Greek, four books of Cynegeticks or venation, five of Halieuticks or piscation, commented and published by Ritterhusius;
wherein describing beasts of venery and fishes, he hath indeed but sparingly inserted the vulgar conceptions thereof.
So that abating the annuall mutation of Sexes in the Hyaena, [88]
the single Sex of the Rhinoceros, the antipathy between two
drummes of a Lamb and a Wolfes skinne, the informity of
Cubbes, the venation of Centaures, the copulation of the
Murena and the Viper, with some few others, he may be read
with great delight and profit. It is not without some wonder
his elegant lines are so neglected. Surely hereby we reject
one of the best Epick Poets,[*] and much condemn the judgement of Antoninus, whose apprehensions so honoured his [89]
Poems, that as some report, for every verse, he assigned him
a Stater of gold.

10. More warily are we to receive the relations of Philes,
who in Greek Iambicks delivered the proprieties of Animals,
for herein he hath amassed the vulgar accounts recorded by
the Ancients, and hath therein especially followed Aelian.

---

[*] That write Hexameters or long Verses. [†]

And likewise Johannes Tzetzes, a Grammarian, who besides
a Comment upon Hesiod and Homer, hath left us *Chiliads de*   90
Varia Historia; wherein delivering the accounts of Ctesias,
Herodotus, and most of the Ancients, he is to be embraced
with caution, and as a transcriptive relator.

11. We cannot without partiality omit all caution even of
holy Writers, and such whose names are venerable unto all
posterity; not to meddle at all with miraculous Authors, or
any Legendary relators. We are not without circumspection
to receive some books even of Authentick and renowned Fathers. So are we to read the leaves of Basil and Ambrose, in
their books entituled *Hexameron,* or *The description of the
Creation;* Wherein delivering particular accounts of all the
Creatures, they have left us relations sutable to those of
Aelian, Plinie and other naturall Writers; whose authorities
herein they followed, and from whom most probably they
desumed their Narrations. And the like hath been committed
by Epiphanius, in his Physiologie, that is, a book he hath left
concerning the nature of Animals. With no lesse caution must
we look on Isidor, Bishop of Sevil, who having left in twenty   †
books, an accurate work *de Originibus,* hath to the Etymologie of words, superadded their received natures; wherein
most generally he consents with common opinions and Authors which have delivered them.

12. Albertus Bishop of Ratisbone; for his great learning
and latitude of knowledge sirnamed Magnus; besides divinity, he hath written many Tracts in Philosophy; what we are
chiefly to receive with caution, are his naturall tractates, more
especially those of Mineralls, Vegetables and Animals, which
are indeed chiefly Collections out of Aristotle, Aelian and
Plinie, and respectively contain many of our popular errors.
A man who hath much advanced these opinions by the authority of his name, and delivered most conceits, with strict
enquiry into few. In the same classis, may well be placed Vincentius Bellvacensis; or rather he from whom he collected his
Speculum naturale, that is, *Gulielmus de Conchis;* as also
Hortus Sanitatis; and *Bartholomeus Glanvill,* sirnamed *Anglicus,* who writ *de Proprietatibus rerum.* Hither also may be
referred *Kiranides;* which is a collection out of Harpocration   †

the Greek, and sundry Arabick writers; delivering not only the Naturall but Magicall propriety of things; a work as full of vanity as variety; containing many relations, whose invention is as difficult as their beliefs, and their experiments sometime as hard as either.

13. We had almost forgot *Jeronimus Cardanus* that famous [91] Physician of Milan, a great enquirer of truth, but too greedy a receiver of it; he hath left many excellent discourses, Medicall, Naturall and Astrologicall; the most suspicious are those two he wrote by admonition in a dream, that is, *de subtilitate et varietate rerum.* Assuredly this learned man hath taken many things upon trust, and although examined some, hath let slip many others. He is of singular use unto a prudent Reader, but unto him that only desireth Hoties, or to replenish his head with varities; like many others before related, either in the Originall or confirmation, he may become no small occasion of error.

14. Lastly, Authors are also suspicious, nor greedily to be swallowed, who pretend to write of secrets, to deliver Antipathies, Sympathies, and the occult abstrusities of things; in the list whereof may be accounted, Alexis Pedimontanus: Antonius Mizaldus, Trinum Magicum, and many others; not omitting that famous Philosopher of Naples, Baptista Porta, in whose works, although there be contained many excellent things, and verified upon his own experience, yet are there many also receptary, and such as will not endure the test. Who although he hath delivered many strange relations in his † *Phytognomonica,* and his *Villa;* yet hath he more remarkably expressed himself in his Naturall Magick, and the miraculous effects of Nature. Which containing various and delectable subjects, withall promising wondrous and easie effects, they are entertained by Readers at all hands; whereof the major part sit down in his authority, and thereby omit not only the certainty of truth, but the pleasure of its experiment.

Thus have we made a brief enumeration of these learned men; not willing any to decline their Works (without which it is not easie to attain any measure of generall knowledge) but to apply themselves with caution thereunto. And seeing the lapses of these worthy pens, to cast a wary eye on those

diminutive, and pamphlet Treaties daily published amongst
us; pieces maintaining rather Typography then verity; Authors presumably writing by common places, wherein for
many years promiscuously amassing all that makes for their
subject, they break forth at last in trite and fruitlesse Rapso-
dies; doing thereby not only open injury unto learning, but
committing a secret treachery upon truth. For their relations
falling upon credulous Readers, they meet with prepared beliefs; whose supinities had rather assent unto all, then adventure the triall of any.

Thus, I say, must these Authors be read, and thus must we
be read our selves; for discoursing of matters dubious, and
many controvertible truths; we cannot without arrogancy entreat a credulity, or implore any farther assent, then the
probability of our reasons, and verity of experiments induce.

CHAP. 9.
OF THE SAME.

There are beside these Authors and such as have positively
promoted errors, divers other which are in some way accessory; whose verities although they doe not directly assert, yet
doe they obliquely concurre unto their beliefs. In which account are many holy Writers, Preachers, Moralists, Rhetoricians, Orators and Poets; for they depending upon invention,
deduce their mediums from all things whatsoever; and playing much upon the simile, or illustrative argumentation, to   †
induce their Enthymemes unto the people, they take up
popular conceits, and from traditions unjustifiable or really
false, illustrate matters of undeniable truth. Wherein al-   †
though their intention be sincere, and that course not much
condemnable; yet doth it notoriously strengthen common er-   †
rors, and authorise opinions injurious unto truth.

Thus have some Divines drawn into argument the fable of
the Phoenix, made use of that of the Salamander, Pelican,   †,92
Basilisk, and divers relations of Pliny; deducing from thence
most worthy morals, and even upon our Saviour. Now although this be not prejudiciall unto wiser judgements, who

are but weakly moved with such argument, yet is it oftentimes occasion of error unto vulgar heads, who expect in the
fable as equall a truth as in the morall, and conceive that infallible Philosophy, which is in any sense delivered by Divinity. But wiser discerners do well understand, that every Art
hath its own circle; that the effects of things are best examined by sciences wherein are delivered their causes; that
strict and definitive expressions are alway required in Philosophy, but a loose and popular delivery will serve oftentimes in Divinity. As may be observed even in holy Scripture;
which often omitteth the exact account of things; describing
them rather to our apprehensions, then leaving doubts in vulgar mindes, upon their unknown and Philosophicall descriptions. Thus it termeth the Sun and the Moon, the two great
lights of heaven. Now if any shall from hence conclude, the
Moon is second in magnitude unto the Sunne, he must excuse
my belief; and I think it cannot be taken for heresie, if herein
I rather adhere unto the demonstration of Ptolomy, then the
popular description of Moses. Thus is it said, Chron. 2.4. That
Solomon made a molten sea of ten cubits, from brim to brim
round in compasse, and five cubits the height thereof, and a
line of thirty cubits did compasse it round about. Now in this
description, the circumference is made just treble unto the
diameter, that is, as 10 to 30 or 7 to 21. But Archimedes demonstrates in his *Cyclometria,* that the proportion of the diameter, unto the circumference, is as 7 unto almost 22, which
will occasion a sensible difference, that is almost a cubit. Now
if herein I adhere unto Archimedes who speaketh exactly,
rather then the sacred Text which speaketh largely, I hope I
shall not offend Divinity: I am sure I shall have reason and
experience of every circle to support me.

Thus Morall Writers, Rhetoricians and Orators make use of
severall relations which will not consist with verity. Aristotle
in his Ethicks takes up the conceit of the Bever, and the
divulsion of his Testicles. The tradition of the Bear, the Viper,
and divers others are frequent amongst Orators. All which
although unto the illiterate and undiscerning hearers may
seem a confirmation of their realities; yet is this no reasonable
establishment unto others, who will not depend hereon other-

wise then common Apologues; which being of impossible falsities, do notwithstanding include wholesome moralities, and
such as expiate the trespasse of their absurdities.

The Hieroglyphicall doctrine of the Egyptians (which in
their four hundred years cohabition some conjecture they
learned from the Hebrews) hath much advanced many popular conceits; for using an Alphabet of things, and not of
words, through the Image and pictures thereof, they endeavoured to speak their hidden conceits, in the letters and language of nature. In pursuit whereof, although in many things
they exceeded not their true and reall apprehensions; yet in
some other they either framing the story, or taking up the
tradition, conduceable unto their intentions, obliquely confirmed many falsities; which as authentick and conceded
truths did after passe unto the Greeks; from them unto other
nations, are still retained by symbolical writers, Emblemat-
istes, Heraldes and others. Whereof some are strictly maintained for truths, as naturally making good their artificiall
representations; others symbollically intended are literally
received, and swallowed in the first sense, without all gust of
the second. Famous in this doctrine in former ages were
Heraiscus, Cheremon and Epius, especially Orus Apollo Nilia-
cus; who lived in the reign of Theodosius and in Aegyptian
language left two books of Hieroglyphicks, translated into
Greek by Philippus, in Latine published by Hoschelius, and a   †
full collection of all made lately by Pierius. [But no man is   93,†
likely to profound the ocean of that Doctrine beyond that
eminent example of industrious learning, Kircherus.]   94

Painters who are the visible representers of things, and such
as by the learned sense of the eye endeavour to inform the
understanding, are not inculpable herein; who either describing naturals as they are, or actions as they have been, have
oftentimes erred in their delineations; which being the books
that all can reade, are fruitfull advancers of these conceptions; especially in common and popular apprehensions; who
being unable for farther enquiry, must rest in the text, and
letter of their descriptions.

Lastly, Poets and Poeticall Writers have in this point exceeded others, leaving unto us the notions of Harpies, Cen-   †

taurs, Gryphins, and many more. Now how ever to make use
of fictions, Apologues and fables be not unwarrantable, and
the intent of these inventions might point at laudable ends;
Yet doe they afford our junior capacities a frequent occasion
of error; setling impressions in our tender memories, which
our advanced judgements doe generally neglect to expunge.
This way the vain and idle fictions of the Gentiles did first
insinuate into the heads of Christians; and thus are they continued even unto our daies: Our first and literary apprehensions being commonly instructed in Authors which handle
nothing else; wherewith our memories being stuffed, our inventions become Pedantick, and cannot avoid their allusions;
driving at these as at the highest elegancies, which are but
the frigidities of wit, and become not the genius of manly ingenuities. It were therefore no losse like that of Galens study [95]
if these had found the same fate; and would in some way
requite the neglect of solid Authors, if they were lesse pursued. For were a pregnant wit educated in ignorance hereof,
receiving only impressions from realities; upon such solid
foundations, it must surely raise more substantiall superstructions, and fall upon very many excellent strains, which have
been jusled off by their intrusions.

Chap. 10.
Of the last and common promoter of false Opinions, the endeavours of Satan.

But beside the infirmities of humane nature, the seed of
error within our selves, and the severall waies of delusion
from each other, there is an invisible Agent, and secret pro-
moter without us, whose activity is undiscerned, and plaies
in the dark upon us; and that is the first contriver of Error,
and professed opposer of Truth, the devil. For though permitted unto his proper principles, Adam perhaps would have
sinned without the suggestion of Satan, and from the trans-
gressive infirmities of himself might have erred alone, as well
as the Angels before him. And although also there were no
devil at all, yet is there now in our natures a confessed suffi-

ciency unto corruption; and the frailty of our own Oeconomie
were able to betray us out of truth; yet wants there not another Agent, who taking advantage hereof, proceedeth to
obscure the diviner part, and efface all tract of its traduction:
To attempt a particular of all his wiles, is too bold an Arithmetick for man: what most considerably concerneth his
popular and practised waies of delusion, he first deceiveth
mankinde in five main points concerning God and himself.

And first his endeavours have ever been, and they cease
not yet, to instill a belief in the minde of man, There is no
God at all. And this he specially labours to establish in a
direct and literall apprehension; that is, that there is no such
reality existent, that the necessity of his entity dependeth
upon ours, and is but a Politicall Chymera; That the naturall
truth of God is an artificiall erection of man, and the Creator
himself but a subtile invention of the creature. Where he succeeds not thus high, he labours to introduce a secondary and
deductive Atheisme; that although men concede there is a
God, yet should they deny his providence; and therefore assertions have flown about, that he intendeth only the care of
the species or common natures, but letteth loose the guard of
individuals, and single existencies therein: That he looks not
below the Moon, but hath designed the regiment of sublunary affairs unto inferiour deputations. To promote which
apprehensions or empuzzell their due conceptions, he cast-
eth in the notions of fate, destiny, fortune, chance and necessity; tearms commonly misconceived by vulgar heads, and
their propriety sometime perverted by the wisest. Whereby
extinguishing in mindes the compensation of vertue and
vice, the hope and fear of heaven or hell; they comply in
their actions unto the drift of his delusions, and live like creatures below the capacity of either.

Now hereby he not only undermineth the Base of religion,
and destroieth the principle preambulous unto all belief, but
puts upon us the remotest error from truth. For Atheisme is
the greatest falsity, and to affirm there is no God, the highest
lie in Nature. And therefore strictly taken, some men will say
his labour is in vain; For many there are, who cannot conceive there was ever any absolute Atheist, or such as could

determine there was no God, without all check from himself, or contradiction from his other opinions; and therefore those few so called by elder times, might be the best of Pagans; suffering that name rather, in relation to the gods of the Gentiles, then the true Creatour of all. A conceit that cannot befall his greatest enemy, or him that would induce the same in us; who hath a sensible apprehension hereof, for he beleeveth with trembling. To speak yet more strictly and conformably unto some opinions, no creature can wish thus much; nor can the will which hath a power to runne into velleities, and wishes of impossibilities, have any *utinam* of this. For to desire there were no God, were plainly to unwish their own being; which must needs be annihilated in the substraction of that essence, which substantially supporteth them, and restrains them from regression into nothing. And if as some contend, no creature can desire his own annihilation, that Nothing is not appetible, and not to be at all, is worse then to be in the miserablest condition of something; the devil himself could not embrace that motion, nor would the enemy of God be freed by such a Redemption.

But coldly thriving in this designe, as being repulsed by the principles of humanity, and the Dictates of that production which cannot deny its originall, he fetcheth a wider circle; and when he cannot make men conceive there is no God at all, he endeavours to make them beleeve, there is not one but many; wherein he hath been so successfull with common heads, that he hath led their belief thorow all the works of Nature.

Now in this latter attempt, the subtilty of his circumvension hath indirectly obtained the former. For although to opinion there be many gods, may seem an accesse in Religion, and † such as cannot at all consist with Atheisme, yet doth it diductively and upon inference include the same: for unity is the inseparable and essentiall attribute of Deity; And if there be more then one God, it is no Atheisme to say there is no God at all. And herein though Socrates only suffered, yet ⁹⁶ were Plato and Aristotle guilty of the same truth; who demonstratively understanding the simplicity of perfection, and the indivisible condition of the first causator, it was not in

the power of earth, or Areopagy° of hell to work them from
it. For holding an Apodicticall° knowledge, and assured science of its verity, to perswade their apprehensions unto a
plurality of gods in the world, were to make Euclide beleeve
there were more then one Center in a Circle, or one right
Angle in a Triangle; which were indeed a fruitlesse attempt,
and inferreth absurdities beyond the evasion of hell. For
though Mechanick and vulgar heads ascend not unto such
comprehensions, who live not commonly unto half the advantage of their principles; yet did they not escape the eye
of wiser Minervas, and such as made good the genealogie of   97
Jupiters brains; who although they had divers styles for God,
yet under many appellations acknowledged one divinity:
rather conceiving thereby the evidence or acts of his power
in severall waies and places, then a multiplication of Essence,
or reall distraction of unity in any one.

Again, To render our errours more monstrous (and what
unto miracle sets forth the patience of God,) he hath endeavoured to make the world beleeve, that he was God himself; and failing of his first attempt to be but like the highest
in heaven, he hath obtained with men to be the same on
earth; and hath accordingly assumed the annexes of divinity, and the prerogatives of the Creator, drawing into
practice the operation of miracles, and the prescience of
things to come. Thus hath he in a specious way wrought cures
upon the sick: plaied over the wondrous acts of Prophets, and
counterfeited many miracles of Christ and his Apostles. Thus
hath he openly contended with God; And to this effect his
insolency was not ashamed to play a solemne prize with   98
Moses; wherein although his performance were very
specious, and beyond the common apprehension of any
power below a Deity, yet was it not such as could make good
his Omnipotency. For he was wholly confounded in the conversion of dust into lice. An act Philosophy can scarce deny to
be above the power of Nature, nor upon a requisite predis-
position beyond the efficacy of the Sun. Wherein notwith-

° Areopagus the severe Court of Athens.
° Demonstrative.   †

99

standing the head of the old Serpent was confessedly too weak for Moses hand, and the arm of his magicians too short for the finger of God.

Thus hath he also made men beleeve that he can raise the dead; that he hath the key of life and death, and a prerogative above that principle which makes no regression from privations. The Stoicks that opinioned the souls of wise men dwelt about the Moon, and those of fools wandred about the earth, advantaged the conceit of this effect; wherein the Epicureans, who held that death was nothing, nor nothing after death, must contradict their principles to be deceived. Nor could the Pythagorian or such as maintained the transmigration of souls give easie admittance hereto: for holding that separated souls successively supplied other bodies; they could hardly allow the raising of souls from other worlds, which at the same time, they conceived conjoined unto bodies in this. More inconsistent with these opinions is the error of Christians, who holding the dead doe rest in the Lord, doe yet beleeve they are at the lure of the devil; that he who is in bonds himself commandeth the fetters of the dead, and dwelling in the bottomlesse lake, the blessed from Abrahams bosome; that can beleeve the reall resurrection of †
Samuel; or that there is any thing but delusion in the practice of Necromancy* and popular conception of Ghosts.

He hath moreover endeavoured the opinion of Deity, by the delusion of Dreams, and the discovery of things to come in sleep, above the prescience of our waked senses. In this expectation he perswaded the credulity of elder times to take up their lodging before his temple, in skinnes of their own sacrifices, till his reservednesse had contrived answers, whose accomplishments were in his power, or not beyond his presagement. Which way, although it hath pleased Almighty God sometimes to reveale himself, yet was the proceeding very different. For the revelations of heaven are conveied by new impressions, and the immediate illumination of the soul; ◀
whereas the deceiving spirit, by concitation of humors, produceth his conceited phantasmes; or by compounding the

* Divination by the dead. †

species already residing, doth make up words which mentally speak his intentions.

But above all other he most advanced his Deity in the solemn practice of Oracles, wherein in severall parts of the world, he publikely professed his divinity; but how short they flew of that spirit, whose omniscience they would resemble, their weaknesse sufficiently declared. What jugling there was therein, the Oratour* plainly confessed, who being good at the same game himself, could say that Pythia   100 Philippised. Who can but laugh at the carriage of Ammon unto Alexander, who addressing unto him as God, was made to beleeve, he was a god himself? How openly did he betray his Indivinity unto Crœsus, who being ruined by his Amphi-   †,101 bology, and expostulating with him for so ungratefull a deceit, received no higher answer, then the excuse of his impotency upon the contradiction of fate, and the setled law of powers beyond his power to controle! What more then sublunary directions, or such as might proceed from the oracle of humane reason, was in his advice unto the Spartans in the time of a great plague; when for the cessation thereof, he wisht them to have recourse unto a Fawn, that is in open tearms unto one Nebrus,* a good Physitian of those daies? From no diviner a spirit came his reply unto Caracalla, who requiring a remedy for his gout, received no other counsell then to refrain cold drink; which was but a dieteticall caution, and such as without a journey unto Aesculapius, cu-   . linary prescription and kitchin Aphorismes might have afforded at home. Nor surely if any truth there were therein of more then naturall activity was his counsell unto Democritus, when for the falling sicknesse he commended the Maggot in a Goats head. For many things secret are true; sympathies and antipathies are safely authentick unto us, who ignorant of their causes may yet acknowledge their effects. Beside being a naturall Magician he may perform many acts in waies above our knowledge, though not transcending our naturall power, when our knowledge shall direct it; part hereof hath been discovered by himself, and some

* Demosthenes.
* Nebros in Greek, a Fawn.

by humane indagation: which though magnified as fresh inventions unto us, are stale unto his cognition. I hardly beleeve he hath from elder times unknown the verticity of the loadstone; surely his perspicacity discerned it to respect the North, when ours beheld it indeterminately. Many secrets there are in nature of difficult discovery unto man, of easie knowledge unto Satan; whereof some his vain-glory cannot conceale, others his envy will never discover.

Again, Such is the mystery of his delusion, that although he labour to make us beleeve that he is God, and supremest nature whatsoever, yet would he also perswade our beliefs, that he is lesse then Angels or men; and his condition not only subjected unto rationall powers, but the action of things which have no efficacy on our selves. Thus hath he inveigled no small part of the world into a credulity of artificiall Magick: That there is an Art, which without compact commandeth the powers of hell; whence some have delivered the polity of spirits, and left an account even to their Provinciall dominions; that they stand in awe of charmes, spells and conjurations; that he is afraid of letters and characters, of notes and dashes, which set together doe signifie nothing; and not only in the dictionary of man, but the subtiler vocabulary of Satan. That there is any power in Bitumen, pitch or brimstone, to purifie the air from his uncleannesse; that any vertue there is in Hipericon° to make good the   †
name of *fuga Daemonis;* any such magick as is ascribed unto   102
the root Baaras by Josephus, or Cynospastus by Aelianus, it is not easie to beleeve; nor is it naturally made out what is delivered of Tobias, that by the fume of a fishes liver, he put   103
to flight Asmodeus. That they are afraid of the pentangle° of Solomon, though so set forth with the body of man, as to touch and point out the five places wherein our Saviour was wounded, I know not how to assent. If perhaps he hath fled from holy water, if he cares not to hear the sound of Tetragrammaton,° if his eye delight not in the sign of the Crosse, and that sometimes he will seem to be charmed with words of

---

° S. Johns wort.
° So called by Magicians; 3 triangles intersected and made of five lines.
° Implying Jehovah which in Hebrew consisteth of four letters.

holy Scripture, and to flye from the letter and dead verbal-
ity, who must only start at the life and animated interiors
thereof: It may be feared they are but Parthian flights, Am-   104
buscado retreats, and elusory tergiversations, whereby to
confirm our credulities, he will comply with the opinion of
such powers, which in themselves have no activities. Whereof
having once begot in our mindes an assured dependence, he
makes us rely on powers which he but precariously obeies;
and to desert those true and only charmes which hell cannot withstand.

Lastly, To lead us farther into darknesse, and quite to lose
us in this maze of error, he would make men beleeve there
is no such creature as himself, and that he is not only subject
unto inferiour creatures but in the rank of nothing. Insinuating into mens mindes there is no devill at all, and contriveth accordingly many waies to conceale or indubitate his existency. Wherein beside that he anihilates the blessed Angels
and spirits in the rank of his creation, he begets a security of
himself and a carelesse eye unto the last remunerations. And
therefore hereto he inveigleth, not only Sadduces and such
as retain unto the Church of God, but is also content that
Epicurus, Democritus or any heathen should hold the same.
And to this effect he maketh men beleeve that apparitions,
and such as confirm his existence are either deceptions of
sight, or melancholy depravements of phancy: Thus when
he had not only appeared but spake unto Brutus, Cassius the   105
Epicurian was ready at hand to perswade him, it was but a
mistake in his weary imagination, and that indeed there were
no such realities in nature. Thus he endeavours to propagate
the unbelief of witches, whose concession infers his coexist-   106
ency; by this means also he advanceth the opinion of totall
death, and staggereth the immortality of the soul: for such as
deny there are spirits subsistent without bodies, will with
more difficulty affirm the separated existence of their own.

Now to induce and bring about these falsities, he hath
laboured to destroy the evidence of truth, that is the revealed
verity and written word of God. To which intent he hath obtained with some to repudiate the books of Moses, others
those of the Prophets, and some both to deny the Gospell

and authentick histories of Christ; to reject that of John, and
receive that of Judas; to disallow all, and erect another of
Thomas. And when neither their corruption by Valentinus   107
and Arrius, their mutilation by Marcion, Manes and Ebion
could satisfie his design, he attempted the ruine and totall
destruction thereof; as he sedulously endeavoured, by the
power and subtilty of Julian, Maximinus and Dioclesian.   108

But the longevity of that piece, which hath so long escaped the common fate, and the providence of that Spirit
which ever waketh over it, may at last discourage such attempts; and if not make doubtfull its mortality, at least
indubitably declare this is a stone too bigge for Saturns   †,109
mouth, and a bit indeed Oblivion cannot swallow.

And thus how strangely he possesseth us with errors may
clearly be observed; deluding us into contradictory and inconsistent falsities; whilest he would make us beleeve, That
there is no God. That there are many. That he himself is
God. That he is lesse then Angels or Men. That he is nothing at all.

Nor hath he only by these wiles depraved the conception   †
of the Creator, but with such riddles hath also entangled the
Nature of our Redeemer. Some denying his humanity, and
that he was one of the Angels, as Ebion; that the Father
and Sonne were but one person, as Sabellius; that his body
was phantasticall, as Manes, Basilides, Priscillian, Jovinianus;
that he only passed through Mary, as Eutyches and Valen-   †
tinus. Some denying his Divinity; that he was begotten of
humane principles, and the seminall sonne of Joseph; as
Carpocras, Symmachus, Photinus. That he was Seth the son
of Adam, as the Sethians. That he was lesse then Angels, as
Cherinthus. That he was inferiour unto Melchisedech, as   110
Theodotus. That he was not God, but God dwelt in him, as
Nicolaus. And some embroiling them both. So did they
which converted the Trinity into a quaternity, and affirmed
two persons in Christ, as Paulus Samosatenus; that held he
was man without a soul, and that the word performed that
office in him, as Apollinaris. That he was both Son and Father, as Montanus. That Jesus suffered, but Christ remained
impatible, as Cherinthus. Thus he endeavours to entangle

truths: And when he cannot possibly destroy its substance he cunningly confounds its apprehensions; that from the inconsistent and contrary determinations thereof, consectary impieties, and hopefull conclusions may arise, there's no such thing at all.

[Chap. 11, "A further Illustration" of the devil's deceits, concludes Book One.]

THE SECOND BOOK:
OF SUNDRY POPULAR TENENTS CONCERNING MINERALL AND VEGETABLE BODIES . . .

CHAP. 2.
CONCERNING THE LOADSTONE.   1

OF THINGS PARTICULARLY SPOKEN THEREOF EVIDENTLY OR PROBABLY TRUE. OF THINGS GENERALLY BELEEVED, OR PARTICULARLY DELIVERED, MANIFESTLY OR PROBABLY FALSE. IN THE FIRST OF THE MAGNETICALL VERTUE OF THE EARTH, OF THE FOUR MOTIONS OF THE STONE, THAT IS, ITS VERTICITY OR DIRECTION, ITS ATTRACTION OR COITION, ITS DECLINATION, ITS VARIATION, AND ALSO OF ITS ANTIQUITY. IN THE SECOND A REJECTION OF SUNDRY OPINIONS AND RELATIONS THEREOF, NATURALL, MEDICALL, HISTORICALL, MAGICALL.

And first we conceive the earth to be a Magneticall body.   2
A Magneticall body, we term not only that which hath a power attractive; but that which seated in a convenient medium naturally disposeth it self to one invariable and fixed situation. And such a Magneticall vertue we conceive to be in the Globe of the earth; whereby as unto its naturall points and proper terms it disposeth it self unto the poles; being so framed, constituted and ordered unto these points, that those parts which are now at the poles, would not naturally abide under the Aequator; nor Green-land remain in the place of Magellanica. And if the whole earth were violently removed, yet would it not forgoe its primitive points; nor

pitch in the East or West, but return unto its polary position again. For though by compactnesse or gravity it may acquire the lowest place, and become the center of the universe, yet that it makes good that point, not varying at all by the accession of bodies upon, or secession thereof, from its surface, perturbing the equilibration of either Hemisphear (whereby the altitude of the starres might vary) or that it strictly maintains the north and southern points; that neither upon the motions of the heavens, ayre and windes without, large eruptions and division of parts within, its polary parts should never incline or veere unto the Aequator (whereby the latitude of places should also vary) it cannot so well be salved from gravity as a Magneticall verticity. This is probably that foundation the wisdome of the Creator hath laid unto the earth; in this sense we may more nearly apprehend, and sensibly make out the expressions of holy Scripture, as that of Psal. 93.1. *Firmavit orbem terrae qui non commovebitur,* he [3] hath made the round world so sure that it cannot be moved: as when it is said by Job, *Extendit Aquilonem super vacuo,* &c. He stretcheth forth the North upon the empty place, and hangeth the earth upon nothing. And this is the most probable answer unto that great question, Job 38. Whereupon are the foundations of the earth fastened, or who laid the corner stone thereof? Had they been acquainted with this principle, Anaxagoras, Socrates and Democritus had better made out the ground of this stability: Xenophanes had not been fain to say the earth had no bottome; and Thales Milesius to make it swim in water. [Now whether the earth [t,4] stand still, or moveth circularly, we may concede this Magneticall stability: For although it move, in that conversion the poles and center may still remaine the same, as is conceived in the Magneticall bodies of heaven, especially Jupiter and the Sunne; which according to Galileus, Kepler, and Fabricius, are observed to have Dineticall motions and certaine revolutions about the proper centers; and though the one in about the space of ten dayes, the other in less then one, accomplish this revolution, yet do they observe a constant habitude unto their poles and firme themselves thereon in their gyration.]

Nor is the vigour of this great body included only in its self, or circumferenced by its surface, but diffused at indeterminate distances through the ayre, water and all bodies circumjacent; exciting and impregnating Magneticall bodies within its surface or without it, and performing in a secret and invisible way what we evidently behold effected by the Loadstone. For these effluxions penetrate all bodies, and [5] like the species of visible objects are ever ready in the me-[6] dium, and lay hold on all bodies proportionate or capable of their action; those bodies likewise being of a congenerous nature doe readily receive the impressions of their motor; and if not fettered by their gravity, conform themselves to situations, wherein they best unite unto their Animator. And this will sufficiently appear from the observations that are to follow, which can no better way be made out then this we speak of, the Magneticall vigour of the earth. Now whether these effluviums do flye by striated Atomes and winding particles as *Renatus des Cartes* conceiveth, or glide by [7] streams attracted from either pole and Hemisphere of the earth unto the Aequator, as Sir Kenelme Digby excellently [8] declareth, it takes not away this vertue of the earth; but more distinctly sets down the gests and progresse thereof; and are conceits of eminent use to salve Magneticall phenomena's. And as in Astronomy those hypotheses though never so strange are best esteemed which best doe salve apparencies*; so surely in Philosophy those principles (though seeming monstrous) may with advantage be embraced, which best confirm experiment, and afford the readiest reason of observation. And truly the doctrine of effluxions, their penetrating natures, their invisible paths, and insuspected effects, are very considerable; for besides this Magneticall one of the earth, severall effusions there may be from divers other bodies, which invisibly act their parts at any time, and perhaps through any medium; a part of Philosophy but yet in discovery, and will I fear prove the last leaf to be turned over in the book of Nature.

First, Therefore true it is, and confirmable by every ex-

* Apparencies, observations.   †

periment, that Steel and good Iron never excited by the Loadstone, discover in themselves a verticity; that is, a directive or polary faculty; whereby, conveniently placed, they doe septentrionate at one extream, and Australize at another; this is manifestible in long and thin plates of Steel perforated in the middle and equilibrated; or by an easier way in long wires equiponderate with untwisted Silk and soft wax; for in this manner pendulous, they will conform themselves Meridionally; directing one extream unto the North, another to the South. The same is also manifest in Steel wires thrust through little sphears or globes of Cork and floated on the water; or in naked needles gently let fall thereon; for so disposed they will not rest untill they have found out the Meridian, and as near as they can lye parallel unto the axis of the earth: Sometimes the eye, sometimes the point Northward in divers needles, but the same point alwaies in most; Conforming themselves unto the whole earth, in the same manner as they doe unto every Loadstone; For if a needle untoucht be hanged above a Loadstone, it will convert into a parallel position thereto; for in this situation it can best receive its verticity and be excited proportionably at both extreams. Now this direction proceeds not primitively from themselves, but is derivative and contracted from the Magneticall effluxions of the earth; which they have winded in their hammering and formation, or else by long continuance in one position, as we shall declare hereafter.

It is likewise true what is delivered of Irons heated in the fire, that they contract a verticity in their refrigeration; for heated red hot and cooled in the meridian from North to South, they presently contract a polary power, and being poysed in ayre or water convert that part unto the North which respected that point in its refrigeration; so that if they had no sensible verticity before, it may be acquired by this way; or if they had any, it might be exchanged by contrary position in the cooling. For by the fire they omit not only many drossie and scorious parts, but whatsoever they had received either from the earth or Loadstone; and so being naked and despoiled of all verticity, the Magneticall Atomes invade their bodies with more effect and agility.

Neither is it only true what Gilbertus first observed, that Irons refrigerated North and South acquire a Directive faculty; but if they be cooled upright and perpendicularly they will also obtain the same. That part which is cooled toward the North on this side the Aequator, converting it self unto the North, and attracting the South point of the needle: the other and highest extream respecting the South, and attracting the Northern, according unto the laws Magneticall: For (what must be observed) contrary poles or faces attract each other, as the North the South; and the like decline each other, as the North the North. Now on this side of the Aequator, that extream which is next the earth is animated unto the North, and the contrary unto the South; so that in Coition it applies it self quite oppositely, the Coition or attraction being contrary to the Verticity or Direction. Contrary, if we speak according unto common use, yet alike if we conceive the vertue of the North pole to diffuse it self and open at the South, and the South at the North again.

This polarity from refrigeration upon extremity and in defect of a Loadstone might serve to invigorate and touch a needle any where; and this, allowing variation, is also the readiest way at any season to discover the North or South; and surely farre more certain then what is affirmed of the grains and circles in trees, or the figure in the root of Fern.[*] For if we erect a red hot wire untill it coole, then hang it up with wax and untwisted Silk, where the lower end and that which cooled next the earth doth rest, that is the Northern point; and this we affirm will still be true, whether it be cooled in the ayre or extinguished in water, oyle of vitrioll, *Aqua fortis,* or Quicksilver. And this is also evidenced in culinary utensils and Irons that often feel the force of fire, as tongs, fireshovels, prongs and Andirons; all which acquire a Magneticall and polary condition, and being suspended, convert their lower extreams unto the North; with the same attracting the Southern point of the needle. For easier experiment if we place a needle touched at the foot of tongs or

[*] Some conceive that the figure of the tree or spread-eagle in the root of Brake or Fern stands North and South; but not truly.

andirons, it will obvert or turn aside its lillie or North point, and conform its cuspis or South extream unto the andiron. The like verticity though more obscurely is also contracted by bricks and tiles, as we have made triall in some taken out of the backs of chimneys. Now to contract this Direction, there needs not a totall ignition, nor is it necessary the Irons should be red hot all over. For if a wire be heated only at one end, according as that end is cooled upward or downward, it respectively acquires a verticity; as we have declared in wires totally candent. Nor is it absolutely requisite they should be cooled perpendicularly, or strictly lye in the meridian; for whether they be refrigerated inclinatorily or somewhat Aequinoxially, that is toward the Eastern or Western points; though in a lesser degree, they discover some verticity.

Nor is this only true in Irons but in the Loadstone it self. For if a Loadstone be made red hot, it amits the magneticall vigour it had before in it self, and acquires another from the earth in its refrigeration, for that part which cooleth toward the earth will acquire the respect of the North, and attract the Southern point or cuspis of the Needle. The experiment hereof we made in a Loadstone of a parallelogram or long square figure; wherein only inverting the extremes as it came out of the fire, we altered the poles or faces thereof at pleasure.

It is also true what is delivered of the Direction and coition of Irons, that they contract a verticity by long and continued position, that is, not onely being placed from North to South, and lying in the meridian, but respecting the Zenith and perpendicular unto the center of the earth; as is most manifest in barres of windowes, casements, hinges and the like. For if we present the Needle unto their lower extremes, it wheels about and turns its Southern point unto them. The same condition in long time doe bricks contract which are placed in walls; and therefore it may be a fallible way to finde out the meridian by placing the Needle on a wall; for some bricks therein, by a long and continued position, are often magnetically enabled to distract the polarity of the Needle. And therefore those Irons, which are said to have †

been converted into Loadstones; whether they were reall
conversions, or only attractive augmentations, might be much
promoted by this position: as the Iron crosse of an hundred
weight upon the Church of St. John in Ariminum, or that
Loadston'd Iron of Caesar Moderatus, set down by *Aldrovandus.

Lastly, Irons doe manifest a verticity not only upon refrigeration and constant situation, but (what is wonderfull
and advanceth the magneticall hypothesis) they evidence
the same by meer position according as they are inverted,
and their extreams disposed respectively unto the earth. For
if an Iron or Steele not firmly excited, be held perpendicularly or inclinatorily unto the Needle; the lower end thereof
will attract the *cuspis* or Southern point; but if the same extream be inverted and held under the Needle, it will then
attract the lilly or northern point; for by inversion it chang-
eth its direction acquired before, and receiveth a new and
southern polarity from the earth, as being the upper extream.
Now if an iron be touched before, it varieth not in this manner; for then it admits not this magneticall impression, as
being already informed by the Loadstone, and polarily determined by its preaction.

And from these grounds may we best determine why the
Northern pole of the Loadstone attracteth a greater weight
then the Southern on this side the Aequator; why the stone
is best preserved in a naturall and polary situation; and why
as Gilbertus observeth, it respecteth that pole out of the
earth, which it regarded in its minerall bed and subterraneous position.

It is likewise true and wonderfull what is delivered of the
Inclination or Declination of the Loadstone; that is, the descent of the needle below the plain of the Horizon. For
long needles which stood before upon their *axis* parallell
unto the Horizon, being vigorously excited, incline and bend
downward, depressing the North extream below the Horizon. That is the North on this, the South on the other side of
the Aequator; and at the very Line or middle circle stand   †

* *De miner lib 1.*   9

without deflection. And this is evidenced not only from observations of the needle in severall parts of the earth, but
sundry experiments in any part thereof; as in a long Steel †
wire, equilibrated or evenly hallanced in the ayre; for excited
by a vigorous Loadstone it will somewhat depresse its animated extream, and intersect the horizontall circumference. †
It is also manifest in a needle pierced through a globe of
Cork so cut away and pared by degrees that it will swim
under water, yet sink not unto the bottome; which may be
well effected; for if the Cork be a thought too light to sink
under the surface, the body of the water may be attenu-
ated with spirits of wine; if too heavy, it may be incrassated
with salt; and if by chance too much be added, it may again
be thinned by a proportionable addition of fresh water. If
then the needle be taken out, actively touched and put in
again, it will depresse and bow down its northern head toward the bottome, and advance its southern extremity toward the brim. This way invented by Gilbertus may seem of
difficulty; the same with lesse labour may be observed in a
needled sphere of Cork equally contiguous unto the surface
of the water; for if the needle be not exactly equiponderant,
that end which is a thought too light, if touched becometh
even; that needle also which will but just swim under water,
if forcibly touched will sink deeper, and sometime unto the
bottome. If likewise that inclinatory vertue be destroyed by
a touch from the contrary pole, that end which before was
elevated will then decline; and this perhaps might be observed in some scales exactly ballanced, and in such needles
which for their bulk can hardly be supported by the water.
For if they be powerfully excited and equally let fall, they
commonly sink down and break the water at that extream
whereat they were septentrionally excited; and by this way
it is conceived there may be some fraud in the weighing of
precious commodities, and such as carry a value in quarter
grains, by placing a powerfull Loadstone above or below, according as we intend to depresse or elevate one extream.

  Now if these Magneticall emissions be only qualities, and
the gravity of bodies incline them only unto the earth; surely
that which moveth other bodies to descent carrieth not the

stroak in this, but rather the Magneticall alliciency of the
earth; unto which with alacrity it applieth it self, and in the   †
very same way unto the whole earth, as it doth unto a single
Loadstone: for if an untouched needle be at a distance suspended over a Loadstone, it will not hang parallel, but decline at the north extream, and at that part will first salute its
Director. Again, what is also wonderfull, this inclination is
not invariable; for just under the line the needle lieth parallel
with the Horizon, but sailing North or South it beginneth to
incline, and increaseth according as it approacheth unto
either pole; and would at last endeavour to erect it self; and
this is no more then what it doth upon the Loadstone, and
that more plainly upon the Terrella or sphericall magnet Cos-
mographically set out with circles of the Globe. For at the   †
Aequator thereof the needle will stand rectangularly; but approaching northward toward the tropick it will regard the
stone obliquely; and when it attaineth the pole, directly; and
if its bulk be no impediment, erect it self and stand perpendicularly thereon. And therefore upon strict observation of
this inclination in severall latitudes and due records preserved, instruments are made whereby without the help of
Sunne or Star, the latitude of the place may be discovered;
and yet it appears the observations of men have not as yet
been so just and equall as is desirable, for of those tables of
declination which I have perused, there are not any two that
punctually agree, though some have been thought exactly
calculated, especially that which *Ridley* received from M^r   10
Brigs in our time Geometry Professor in *Oxford*.   11
It is also probable what is delivered concerning the variation of the compasse that is the cause and ground thereof;
for the manner, as being confirmed by observation, we shall
not at all dispute. The variation of the compasse is an Arch
of the Horizon intercepted between the true and Magneticall
meridian; or more plainly, a deflexion and siding East and
West from the true meridian. The true meridian is a major
circle passing through the poles of the world, and the Zenith
or Vertex of any place, exactly dividing the East from the
West. Now on this line the needle exactly lieth not, but di-
verts and varieth its point, that is, the North point on this side

the Aequator, the South on the other; sometimes unto the East, sometime toward the West, and in some few places varieth not at all. First, therefore it is observed that betwixt the shore of Ircland, France, Spain, Guiny and the Azores, the North point varieth toward the East, and that in some variety; at London it varieth eleven degrees, at Antwerp nine, at Rome but five; at some parts of the Azores it deflecteth not, but lieth in the true meridian; on the other side of the Azores, and this side of the Aequator, the North point of the needle wheeleth to the West; so that in the latitude of 36 near the shore, the variation is about eleven degrees; but on the other side the Aequator, it is quite otherwise: for about Capo Frio in Brasilia, the South point varieth twelve degrees unto the West, and about the mouth of the Straits of Magellan five or six; but elongating from the coast of Brasilia toward the shore of Africa it varieth Eastward, and ariving at Capo de las Agullas, it resteth in the Meridian, and looketh neither way.

Now the cause of this variation may be the inequality of the earth, variously disposed, and differently intermixed with the Sea: withall the different disposure of its Magneticall vigor in the eminencies and stronger parts thereof; for the needle naturally endeavours to conform unto the Meridian, but being distracted, driveth that way where the greater and powerfuller part of the earth is placed. Which may be illustrated from what hath been delivered before, and may be conceived by any that understands the generalities of Geography. For whereas on this side the Meridian, or the Isles of Azores, where the first Meridian is placed, the needle varieth Eastward, it may be occasioned by that vast Tract of earth, that is, of Europe, Asia and Africa, seated toward the East, and disposing the needle that way. For arriving at some part of the Azores, or Islands of Saint Michael, which have a middle situation between these continents, and that vast and almost answerable Tract of America, it seemeth equally distracted by both; and diverting unto neither, doth parallel and place it self upon the true Meridian. But sayling farther it veers its Lilly to the West, and regardeth that quarter wherein the land is nearer or greater; and in the same latitude as it approacheth the shoar augmenteth its variation. And †

therefore as some observe, if Columbus or whosoever first discovered America, had apprehended the cause of this variation, having passed more then half the way, he might have
been confirmed in the discovery; and assuredly foretold there
lay a vast and mighty continent toward the West. The reason
I confesse and inference is good, but the instance perhaps not
so. For Columbus knew not the variation of the compasse,
whereof Sebastian Cabot first took notice, who after made
discovery in the Northern parts of that continent. And it happened indeed that part of America was first discovered,
which was on this side farthest distant, that is, Jamaica, Cuba,
and the Isles in the Bay of Mexico. And from this variation
doe some new discoverers deduce a probability in the attempts of the Northern passage toward the Indies.

Now because where the greater continents are joined, the
action and effluence is also greater, therefore those needles
doe suffer the greatest variation which are in countries which
most doe feel that action. And therefore hath Rome far lesse
variation then London; for on the West side of Rome, are
seated the great continents of France, Spain, Germany,
which take off the exuperance and in some way balance the
vigour of the Eastern parts. But unto England there is almost
no earth West, but the whole extent of Europe and Asia
lieth Eastward; and therefore at London it varieth eleven
degrees, that is, almost one *Rhomb.* Thus also by reason of
the great continent of Brasilia, Peru and Chili, the needle deflecteth toward the land twelve degrees; but at the straits of
Magellan where the land is narrowed, and the sea on the
other side, it varieth but five or six. And so likewise, because
the Cape *de las Agullas* hath sea on both sides near it, and
other land remote and as it were æquidistant from it;
therefore at that point the needle conforms unto the true
Meridian, and is not distracted by the vicinity of Adjacencies.
This is the generall and great cause of variation. But if in
certain creeks and valleys the needle prove irregular, and
vary beyond expectance, it may be imputed unto some vigorous part of the earth, or Magneticall eminence not far distant. And this was the invention of Dr. Gilbert not many
years past, a Physitian in London. And therefore although

some assume the invention of its direction, and others have had the glory of the Card; yet in the experiments, grounds, and causes thereof, England produced the Father Philosopher, and discovered more in it, then Columbus or Americus did ever by it.

Unto this in great part true the reason of Kircherus may [†,12] be added: that this variation proceedeth not only from terrestrious eminencies, and magneticall veins of earth, laterally respecting the needle, but the different coagmentation of the earth disposed unto the poles, lying under the sea and waters; which affect the needle with great or lesser variation, according to the vigour or imbecillity of these subterraneous lines: or the entire or broken compagination of the magneticall fabrick under it: as is observeable from severall Loadstones placed at the bottome of any water: for a Loadstone or needle upon the surface, will variously conform it self, according to the vigour or faintnesse of the Loadstones under it.

Thus also a reason may be alledged for the variation of the variation, and why, according to observation, the variation of the needle hath after some years been found to vary in some places, for this may proceed from mutations of the earth, by subterraneous fires, fumes, minerall spirits, or otherwise; which altering the constitution of the magneticall parts, in processe of time, doth vary the variation over the place.

It is also probable what is conceived of its Antiquity, that the knowledge of its polary power and direction unto the North was unknown unto the Ancients; and though Levinus Lemnius, and Caelius Calcagninus, are of another belief, is justly placed with new inventions by Pancirollus. For their Achilles and strongest argument is an expression in Plautus, a very ancient Authour, and contemporary unto Ennius. *Hic* [13] *ventus jam secundus est, cape modè versoriam.* Now this *versoriam* they construe to be the compasse, which notwithstanding according unto Pineda, who hath discussed the point, Turnebus, Cabeus and divers others, is better interpreted the rope that helps to turn the ship; or as we say, doth make it tack about; the Compasse declaring rather the ship is turned, then conferring unto its conversion. As for the long expeditions and sundry voiages of elder times, which might confirm

the Antiquity of this invention, it is not improbable they were
performed by the help of stars; and so might the Phoenicean   †
navigators, and also Ulysses sail about the Mediterranean by
the flight of birds, or keeping near the shore, and so might
Hanno coast about Africa, or by the help of oars, as is expressed in the voyage of Jonah. And whereas it is contended
that this verticity was not unknown unto Salomon, in whom   14
is presumed a universality of knowledge; it will as forceably
follow he knew the Art of Typography, powder and guns, or
had the Philosophers stone, yet sent unto Ophir for gold. It
is not to be denied, that beside his politicall wisdom, his
knowledge in Philosophy was very large; and perhaps from
his works therein, the ancient Philosophers, especially Aristotle, who had the assistance of Alexanders acquirements,
collected great observables; yet if he knew the use of the
Compasse, his ships were surely very slow, that made a three
years voyage from Eziongeber in the red Sea unto Ophir,
which is supposed to be Taprobana or Malaca in the Indies,
not many moneths sayl; and since in the same or lesser time,
Drake and Candish performed their voyage about the earth.   15

And as the knowledge of its verticity is not so old as some
conceive, so is it more ancient then most beleeve; nor had its
discovery with guns, printing, or as many think, some years
before the discovery of America. For it was not unknown
unto Petrus Peregrinus a Frenchman, who two hundred years
since left a Tract of the Magnet, and a perpetuall motion to
be made thereby, preserved by Gasserus. Paulus Venetus,
and about five hundred years past, Albertus Magnus make
mention hereof, and quote for it a book of Aristotle *de lapide,*
which book although we finde in the Catalogue of Laertius,   16
yet with Cabeus I rather judge it to be the work of some
Arabick writer, not many years before the daies of Albertus.

Lastly, It is likewise true what some have delivered of   ⌁
Crocus Martis, that is, steel corroded with vinegar, sulphur
or otherwise, and after reverberated by fire. For the Loadstone will not at all attract it, nor will it adhere, but lie
therein like sand. This is to be understood of *Crocus martis*
well reverberated, and into a violet colour: for common
chalybs praeparatus, or corroded and powdered steel, the

Loadstone attracts like ordinary filings of iron; and many times most of that which passeth for *Crocus martis*. So that this way may serve as a test of its preparation; after which it becometh a very good medecine in fluxes. The like may be affirmed of Flakes of iron that are rusty and begin to tend unto earth; for their cognation then expireth, and the Loadstone will not regard them.

And therefore this may serve as a tryall of good Steel; the Loadstone taking up a greater masse of that which is most pure, it may also decide the conversion of wood into Iron, as is pretended from some waters: and the common conversion of Iron into Copper by the mediation of blew Coperose: for the Loadstone will not attract it, although it may be questioned, whether in this operation the Iron or Coperose be transmuted; as may be doubted from the cognation of Coperose with Copper; and the quantity of Iron remaining after the conversion. And the same may be usefull to some discovery concerning Vitrioll or Coperose of Mars, by some called Salt of Steel, made by the spirits of Vitrioll or Sulphur. For the corroded powder of Steel will after ablution be actively attracted by the Loadstone; and also remaineth in little diminished quantity. And therefore whether those shooting Salts partake but little of steel, and be not rather the vitriolous spirits fixed into Salt by the effluvium or odor of Steel, is not without good question.

CHAP. 3.

CONCERNING THE LOADSTONE, THEREIN OF SUNDRY COMMON OPINIONS, AND RECEIVED RELATIONS, NATURALL, HISTORICALL, MEDICALL, MAGICALL.

And first not only a simple Heterodox, but a very hard Parodox, it will seem, and of great absurdity unto obstinate ears, if we say attraction is unjustly appropriated unto the Loadstone, and that perhaps we speak not properly, when we say vulgarly the Loadstone draweth Iron; and yet herein we should not want experiment and great authority. The words of Renatus *des Cartes* in his principles of Philosophy

are very plain. *Praeterea magnes trahet ferrum, sive potius* [17]
*magnes et ferrum ad invicem accedunt, neque enim ulla ibi
tractio est.* The same is solemnly determined by Cabeus. *Nec* [18]
*magnes trahit proprie ferrum, nec ferrum ad se magnetum
provocat, sed ambo pari conatu ad invicem confluunt.* Concordant hereto is the assertion of Doctor Ridley, Physitian
unto the Emperour of Russia, in his Tract of Magneticall bodies; defining Magneticall attraction to be a naturall incitation
and disposition conforming unto contiguity; an union of one
Magneticall body with another, and no violent haling of the
weak unto the stronger. And this is also the doctrine of Gil- [19]
bertus; by whom this motion is termed coition, and that not
made by any faculty attractive of one, but a Syndrome and
concourse of each; a coition alway of their vigours, and also
of their bodies, if bulk or impediment prevent not; and therefore those contrary actions which flow from opposite poles or
faces, are not so properly explusion and attraction, as Sequela
and Fuga, a mutuall flight and following. Consonant whereto [†]
are also the determinations of °Helmontus and Kircherus.

The same is also confirmed by experiment; for if a piece of
Iron be fastened in the side of a bowl or bason of water, a
Loadstone swimming freely in a boat of cork, will presently
make unto it. And so if a Steel or knife untouched be offered
toward the needle that is touched, the needle nimbly moveth
toward it; and conformeth unto union with the Steel that
moveth not. Again, If a Loadstone be finely filed, the atomes
or dust thereof will adhere unto Iron that was never touched,
even as the powder of Iron doth also unto the Loadstone.
And lastly, If in two skiffs of cork, a Loadstone and Steel be
placed within the orb of their activities, the one doth not
move, the other standing still, but both hoise sayle and steer
unto each other; so that if the Loadstone attract, the Steel
hath also its attraction; for in this action the Alliciency is re-
ciprocall; which jointly felt, they mutually approach and run
into each others armes.

And therefore surely more moderate expressions become
this action, then what the Ancients have used; which some

° [Helmontus, Kircherus, and Licetus. 58]   [20]

have delivered in the most violent termes of their language; [21]
so Austine cals it, *Mirabilem ferri raptorem: Hippocrates,*
λίθος ὅ τι τὸν σίδηρον ἁρπάζει, *Lapis, qui ferrum rapit.* Galen disputing against Epicurus useth the term ἕλκειν, but this is
also too violent: among the Ancients Aristotle spake most
warily, λίθος ὅστις τὸν σίδηρον κινεῖ, *Lapis qui ferrum movet:*
and in some tollerable acception doe run the expressions of
Aquinas, Scaliger and Cusanus.

Many relations are made, and great expectations are raised
from the *Magnes Carneus,* or a Loadstone, that hath a faculty [22]
to attract not only Iron but flesh; but this upon enquiry, and
as Cabeus hath also observed, is nothing else but a weak and
inanimate kinde of Loadstone, veined here and there with a
few magneticall and ferreous lines; but chiefly consisting of
a bolary and clammy substance, whereby it adheres like
Hæmatites, or *Terra Lemnia,* unto the Lipps; and this is that
stone which is to be understood, when Physitians join it with
Aetites or the Eagle stone, and promise therein a vertue
against abortion.

There is sometime a mistake concerning the variation of
the compasse, and therein one point is taken for another. For
beyond the Aequator some men account its variation by the
diversion of the Northern point, whereas beyond that circle
the Southern point is sovereign, and the North submits his
preheminency. For in the Southern coast either of America
or Africa, the Southern point deflects and varieth toward the
land, as being disposed and spirited that way by the meridionall and proper Hemisphere. And therefore on that side
of the earth the varying point is best accounted by the South.
And therefore also the writings of some, and Maps of others,
are to be enquired, that make the needle decline unto the
East twelve degrees at Capo Frio, and six at the straits of
Magellan; accounting hereby one point for another, and preferring the North in the liberties and province of the South.

But certainly false it is what is commonly affirmed and
beleeved, that Garlick doth hinder the attraction of the Loadstone; which is notwithstanding delivered by grave and
worthy Writers; by Pliny, Solinus, Ptolomy, Plutarch, Albertus, Mathiolus, Rueus, Langius, and many more. An effect as [23]

strange as that of Homers Moly, and the Garlick the gods   24
bestowed upon Ulysses. But that it is evidently false, many
experiments declare. For an Iron wire heated red hot and
quenched in the juyce of Garlick, doth notwithstanding contract a verticity from the earth, and attracteth the Southern
point of the Needle. If also the tooth of a Loadstone be covered or stuck in Garlick, it will notwithstanding attract; and
Needles excited and fixed in Garlick untill they begin to rust,
doe yet retain their attractive and polary respects.

Of the same stamp is that which is obtruded upon us by
Authors ancient and modern, that an Adamant or Diamond
prevents or suspends the attraction of the Loadstone; as is
in open termes delivered by Pliny. *Adamas dissidet cum*   25
Magnete Lapide, ut juxta positus ferrum non patiatur ab-
strahi, aut si admotus magnes apprehenderit, rapiat atque
auferat. For if a Diamond be placed between a needle and a
Loadstone, there will neverthelesse ensue a Coition even
over the body of the Diamond: and an easie matter it is to
touch or excite a needle through a Diamond, by placing it at
the tooth of a Loadstone; and therefore the relation is false
or our estimation of these gems untrue; nor are they Diamonds which carry that name amongst us.

It is not suddenly to be received what Paracelsus in his
book *De generatione rerum* affirmeth, that if a Loadstone be
anointed with Mercuriall oyle, or only put into Quicksilver, it
omitteth its attraction for ever. For we have found that Loadstones and touched needles which have laid long time in
Quicksilver have not amitted their attraction; and we also
finde that red hot needles or wires extinguished in Quicksilver, doe yet acquire a verticity according to the Laws of
position in extinction. Of greater repugnancy unto reason is
that which he delivers concerning its graduation, that heated
in fire and often extinguished in oyle of Mars or Iron, it acquires an ability to extract or draw forth a naile fastened in a
wall; for, as we have declared before, the vigor of the Loadstone is destroyed by fire, nor will it be reimpregnated by
any other Magnete then the earth.

Nor is it to be made out what seemeth very plausible, and   †
formerly hath deceived us, that a Loadstone will not attract

an Iron or Steel red hot. The falsity hereof discovered first by Kircherus, we can confirm by iterated experiment; very sensibly in armed Loadstones, and obscurely in any other.

True it is, that besides fire some other waies there are of its destruction, as Age, Rust, and what is least dreamt on, an unnaturall or contrary situation. For being impolarily adjoined unto a more vigorous Loadstone, it will in a short time exchange its poles; or being kept in undue position, that is, not lying on the meridian or with its poles inverted, it receives in longer time impair in activity, exchange of faces, and is more powerfully preserved by site then by the dust of Steel. But the sudden and surest way is fire; that is, fire not only actuall but potentiall; the one surely and suddenly, the other slowly and imperfectly; the one changing, the other destroying the figure. For if distilled Vinegar or Aqua fortis be powred upon the powder of Loadstone, the subsiding powder dried, retains some magneticall vertue, and will be attracted by the Loadstone: but if the menstruum or dissolvent be evaporated to a consistence, and afterward doth shoot into Icycles or Crystals, the Loadstone hath no power upon them; and if in a full dissolution of Steel a separation of parts be made by precipitation or exhalation, the exsiccated powder hath lost its wings and ascends not unto the Loadstone. And though a Loadstone fired doe presently omit its proper vertue, and according to the position in cooling contracts a new verticity from the earth, yet if the same be laid a while in Aqua fortis or other corrosive water, and taken out before a considerable corrosion; it still reserves its attraction, and will convert the Needle according to former polarity. And [†] that duly preserved from violent corrosion, or the naturall disease of rust, it may long conserve its vertue. Beside the Magneticall vertue of the earth, which hath lasted since the creation, a great example we have from the observation of our learned friend M[r] *Graves**, in an Aegyptian Idoll cut out of Loadstone, and found among the Mummies; which still retains its attraction, though probably taken out of the mine about two thousand years agoe.

* In his learned *Pyramidographia*.   [†,26]

It is improbable what Pliny affirmeth concerning the object
of its attraction, that it attracts not only ferreous bodies, but
also *liquorem vitri;* for in the body of glasse there is no ferreous or Magneticall nature which might occasion attraction.
For of the glasse we use, the purest is made of the finest
sand and the ashes of Chali or Glassewort, and the courser
or green sort of the ashes of brake or other plants. True it is   †
that in the making of glasse, it hath been an ancient practice
to cast in pieces of Loadstone [or perhaps manganes]; con-   †,†
ceiving it carried away all ferreous and earthy parts from the
pure and running portion of glasse, which the Loadstone
would not respect; and therefore if that attraction were not
rather electricall then Magneticall, it was a wondrous effect
what Helmont delivereth concerning a glasse wherein the
magistery of Loadstone was prepared; which after retained
an attractive quality.

But that the Magnete attracteth more then common Iron,   †
we can affirm. It attracteth the Smyris or Emery in powder;   †
It draweth the shining or glassie powder brought from the Indies, and usually implied in writing dust. There is also in
Smiths cinders by some adhesion of Iron whereby they appear as it were glazed, sometime to be found a Magneticall
operation; for some thereof applied have power to move the
Needle. But whether the ashes of vegetables which grow over
Iron mines contract a Magneticall quality; as containing some
minerall particles, which by sublimation ascend unto their
roots, and are attracted together with their nourishment; according as some affirm from the like observations upon the
mines of Silver, Quicksilver and Gold; we must refer unto
further experiment.

It is also improbable and something singular what some
conceive, and Eusebius Nierembergius a late writer and
Jesuit of Spain delivers, that the body of man is Magneticall,
and being placed in a boat, the vessell will never rest untill
the head respecteth the North. If this be true, the bodies of
Christians doe lye unnaturally in their graves; King Cheops   †,27
in his tomb, and the Jews in their beds have fallen upon the
naturall position: who reverentially declining the situation of
their temple, nor willing to lye as that stood; doe place their

beds from North to South, and delight to sleep meridionally. †
This opinion confirmed would much advance the microcosmi-
call conceit, and commend the Geography of Paracelsus; who
according to the cardinall points of the world divideth the
body of man; and therefore working upon humane ordure
and by long preparation rendring it odiferous, he terms it
Zibeta Occidentalis, Western Civet; making the face the
East, but the posteriors the America or Western part of his
microcosme. The verity [or rather falsity] hereof, might eas- †,28
ily be tried in Wales, where there are portable boats, and
made of leather, which would convert upon the impulsion of
any verticity; and seem to be the same whereof in his description of Brittain Caesar hath left some mention.

Another kinde of verticity, is that which Angelus *doce mihi
jus, alias* Michael Sundevogis°, in a Tract *de sulphure,* dis- 29
covereth in Vegetables, from sticks let fall or depressed
under water; which equally framed and permitted unto
themselves, will ascend at the upper end, or that which was
verticall in its vegetation; wherein notwithstanding, as yet,
we have not found satisfaction. Although perhaps too greedy
of magnalities, we are apt to make but favourable experiments concerning welcome truths, and such desired verities.

It is also wondrous strange [and untrue] what Laelius †
Bisciola reporteth, that if unto ten ounces of Loadstone one
of Iron be added, it encreaseth not unto eleven, but weighs
ten ounces still. A relation inexcusable in a work of leasura- †
ble howres:° the examination being as ready as the relation,
and the falsity tried as easily as delivered. Nor is it to be
omitted what is taken up by Caesius Bernardus a late min-
eralogist, and originally confirmed by Porta, that needles
touched with a Diamond contract a verticity, even as they
doe with a Loadstone; which will not consist with experiment. And therefore, as Gilbertus observeth, he might be
deceived, in touching such needles with Diamonds, which
had a verticity before, as we have declared most needles to
have; and so had he touched them with gold or silver, he
might have concluded a magneticall vertue therein.

° Anagrammatically.
° *Horae subsecivae.*

In the same form may we place Fracastorius his attraction
of silver, Philostratus his *Pantarbes;* Apollodorus, and Beda   †,30
his relation of the Loadstone that attracted only in the night.
But most inexcusable is Franciscus Rueus, a man of our own   31
profession; who in his Discourse of gemmes mentioned in the
Apocalyps, undertakes a Chapter of the Loadstone; wherein
substantially and upon experiment he scarce delivereth any
thing, making enumeration of its traditionall qualities;
whereof he seemeth to beleeve many, and some above convicted by experience, he is fain to salve as impostures of the
devil. But Boetius de Boot, Physician unto Rodulphus the second, hath recompenced this defect; and in his Tract, *de La-
pidibus et Gemmis,* speaks very materially hereof, and his
discourse is consonant unto experience and reason.

As for relations Historicall, though many there be of lesse
account, yet two alone deserve consideration; The first concerneth magneticall rocks, and attractive mountains in severall parts of the earth. The other the tombe of Mahomet and
bodies suspended in the aire. Of rocks magneticall there are
likewise two relations; for some are delivered to be in the Indies, and some in the extremity of the North, and about the
very pole. The Northern account is commonly ascribed unto
Olaus Magnus Archbishop of Upsale, who out of his predeces-
sour Joannes, Saxo and others, compiled a history of some
Northern Nations; but this assertion we have not discovered
in that work of his which passeth among us, and should beleeve his Geography herein no more then that in the first
line of his book; when he affirmeth that Biarmia (which is
not seventy degrees in latitude) hath the pole for its Zenith,
and Equinoctiall for the Horizon.

Now upon this foundation, how uncertain soever, men
have erected mighty illations; ascribing thereto the cause of
the Needles direction, and conceiving the effluxions from
these mountains and rocks invite the lilly toward the North;
which conceit though countenanced by learned men, is not
made out either by experience or reason; for no man hath yet
attained or given a sensible account of the pole by some degrees. It is also observed the Needle doth very much vary
as it approacheth the pole; whereas were there such direction

from the rocks, upon a nearer approachment it would more directly respect them. Beside, were there such magneticall rocks under the pole, yet being so far removed they would produce no such effect; for they that saile by the Isle of Ilva now called Elba in the Thuscan sea which abounds in veins of Loadstone, observe no variation or inclination of the Needle; much lesse may they expect a direction from rocks at the end of the earth. And lastly, men that ascribe thus much unto rocks of the North, must presume or discover the like magneticals at the South: For in the Southern seas and far beyond the Aequator, variations are large, and declinations as constant as in the Northern Ocean.

The other relation of Loadstone mines and rocks, in the shore of India, is delivered of old by Pliny; wherein saith he, they are so placed both in abundance and vigor, that it proves an adventure of hazard to passe those coasts in a ship with Iron nailes. Serapion the Moor, an Author of good esteem and reasonable antiquity, confirmeth the same, whose expression in the word *magnes* is this. The mine of this stone is in the sea coast of India; whereto when Ships approach, there is no Iron in them which flies not like a bird unto these mountains; and therefore their Ships are fastened not with Iron but wood, for otherwise they would be torn to peeces. But this assertion, how positive soever, is contradicted by all Navigators that passe that way; which are now many and of our own Nation; and might surely have been controuled by Nearchus the Admirall of Alexander; who not knowing the compasse, was fain to coast that shore.

For the relation concerning Mahomet, it is generally beleeved his tomb at Medina Talnabi, in Arabia, without any visible supporters hangeth in the ayre between two Loadstones artificially contrived both above and below. Which conceit is very fabulous, and evidently false from the testimony of ocular Testators; who affirm his tomb is made of stone and lyeth upon the ground; as besides others the learned Vossius observeth from Gabriel Sionita, and Joannes Hesronita, two Maronites, in their relations hereof. Of such intentions and attempt by Mahometans we read in some re-

lators; and that might be the occasion of the fable, which by
tradition of time and distance of place enlarged into the story
of being accomplished. And this hath been promoted by attempts of the like nature; for we reade in Pliny that one Di-
nocrates began to Arch the Temple of Arsinoe in Alexandria
with Loadstone, that so her statue might be suspended in
the ayre to the amazement of the beholders. And to lead on
our credulity herein, confirmation may be drawn from History and Writers of good authority: so is it reported by Ruf-
finus, that in the Temple of Serapis there was an Iron Chariot
suspended by Loadstones in the ayre, which stones removed,
the Chariot fell and dashed into pieces. The like doth Beda
report of Bellerophons horse, which framed of Iron, and
placed between two Loadstones with wings expansed, hung
pendulous in the ayre.

The verity of these stories we shall not further dispute,
their possibility we may in some way determine; if we conceive, what no man will deny, that bodies suspended in the
ayre have this suspension from one or many Loadstones
placed both above and below it; or else by one or many
placed only above it. Likewise the body to be suspended in
respect of the Loadstone above, is either placed first at a
pendulous distance in the medium, or else attracted unto
that site by the vigor of the Loadstone; and so we first affirm
that possible it is a body may be suspended between two
Loadstones; that is, it being so equally attracted unto both
that it determineth it self unto neither. But surely this position will be of no duration; for if the ayre be agitated or the
body waved either way, it omits the equilibration and disposeth it self unto the nearest attractor. Again, it is not impossible (though hardly feisible) by a single Loadstone to
suspend an Iron in the ayre, the Iron being artificially
placed, and at a distance guided toward the stone, untill it
finde the neutrall point, wherein its gravity just equals the
magneticall quality; the one exactly extolling as much as the
other depresseth [and thus must be interpreted Fracas-
torius]. And lastly, impossible it is that if an Iron rest upon   †
the ground, and a Loadstone be placed over it, it should ever

so arise as to hang in the way or medium; for that vigor
which at a distance is able to overcome the resistance of its
gravity and to lift it up from the earth, will as it approacheth
nearer be still more able to attract it; and it will never remain
in the middle that could not abide in the extreams: [and thus †
is to be understood Gilbertus]. Now the way of *Baptista* 33
Porta that by a thred fasteneth a Needle to a table, and then
so guides and orders the same, that by the attraction of the
Loadstone it abideth in the ayre, infringeth not this reason;
for this is a violent retention; and if the thred be loosened, the
Needle ascends and adheres unto the Attractor.

The third consideration concerneth Medicall relations;
wherein what ever effects are delivered, they are either derived from its minerall and ferreous condition, or else magneticall operation. Unto the ferreous and minerall quality
pertaineth what Dioscorides an ancient Writer and Souldier
under Anthony and Cleopatra, affirmeth, that half a dram of
Loadstone given with honey and water, proves a purgative
medicine, and evacuateth grosse humors. But this is a quality
of great incertainty; for omitting the vehicle of water and
honey, which is of a laxative power it self, the powder of
some Loadstones in this dose doth rather constipate and
binde, then purge and loosen the belly. And if sometimes it
cause any laxity, it is probably in the same way with Iron and
Steel unprepared; which will disturb some bodies, and work
by purge and vomit. And therefore, whereas it is delivered
in a book ascribed unto Galen that it is a good medicine in
dropsies, and evacuates the waters of persons so affected: It
may I confesse by siccity and astriction afford a confirmation unto parts relaxed, and such as be hydropically disposed; and by these qualities it may be usefull in Hernias
or Ruptures, and for these it is commended by Aetius,
Aegineta and Oribasius; who only affirm that it contains the
vertue of Haematites, and being burnt was sometimes
vended for it. Wherein notwithstanding there is an higher †
vertue: and in the same prepared, or in rich veins thereof,
though crude, we have observed the effects of Chalybeat
medicines; and the benefits of Iron and Steel in strong ob-

structions. And therefore that was probably a different vein
of Loadstone, or infected with other minerall mixture, which
the ancients commended for a purgative medicine, and
ranked the same with the violentest kindes thereof: with
Hippophae, Cneoron and Thymelaea, as we finde it in Hippocrates*; and might be somewhat doubtfull, whether by
the Magnesian stone, he understood the Loadstone; did not
Achilles Statius define the same, the stone that loveth Iron.

To this minerall condition belongeth what is delivered by   †
some, that wounds which are made with weapons excited by
the Loadstone, contract a malignity, and become of more
difficult cure; which neverthelesse is not to be found in the
incision of Chyrurgions with knives and lancets touched;
which leave no such effect behinde them. Hither must we
also referre that affirmative which saies the Loadstone is
poison; and therefore in the lists of poisons we finde it in
many Authors. But this our experience cannot confirm, and
the practice of the King of Zeilan clearly contradicteth; who
as *Garcias ab Horto,* Physician unto the Spanish Viceroy de-   34
livereth, hath all his meat served up in dishes of Loadstone,
and conceives thereby he preserveth the vigour of youth.

But surely from a magneticall activity must be made out
what is let fall by Aetius, that a Loadstone held in the hand
of one that is podagricall, doth either cure or give great ease
in the Gout. Or what Marcellus Empericus affirmeth, that
as an amulet it also cureth the head-ach; which are but additions unto its proper nature, and hopefull enlargements of
its allowed attraction; for perceiving its secret power to
draw magneticall bodies, men have invented a new attraction to draw out the dolour and pain of any part. And from
such grounds it surely became a philter, and was conceived a
medicine of some venereall attraction; and therefore upon
this stone they graved the Image of Venus, according unto
that of Claudian, *Venerem magnetica gemma figurat.* Hither
must we also referre what is delivered concerning its power
to draw out of the body bullets and heads of arrows, and for
the like intention is mixed up in plaisters: which course al-

* *De morbis internis.*

though as vain and ineffectuall it be rejected by many good
Authors, yet is it not me thinks so readily to be denied, nor
the practice of many Physicians which have thus com- †
pounded plaisters, thus suddenly to be condemned, as may
be observed in the *Emplastrum divinum Nicolai,* the *Emplastrum nigrum* of Augspurge, the Opodeldoch and *At-
tractivum* of Paracelsus, with severall more in the Dispen-
satory of Wecker, and practice of Sennertus; the cure
also of Hernias, or Ruptures in Pareus, and the method also
of curation lately delivered by Daniel Beckherus, and approved by the Professors of Leyden, in the Tract *de
Cultrivoro Prussiaco,* 1636; that is, of a young man of Spruce- †
land that casually swallowed down a knife about ten inches
long, which was cut out of his stomach and the wound
healed up. In which cure to attract the knife to a convenient
situation, there was applied a plaister made up with the
powder of Loadstone. Now this kinde of practice Libavius,
Gilbertus, and lately Swickardus in his *Ars Magnetica,* condemn, as vain, and altogether unusefull; because a Loadstone in powder hath no attractive power; for in that form
it omits his polary respects, and loseth those parts which are
the rule of attraction.

Wherein to speak compendiously, if experiment hath not †
deceived us, we first affirm, that a Loadstone in powder
omits not all attraction. For if the powder of a rich vein be in
a reasonable quantity presented toward the Needle freely
placed, it will not appear to be void of all activity, but will
be able to stir it. Nor hath it only a power to move the Needle
in powder and by it self, but this will it also doe, if incorporated and mixed with plaisters; as we have made triall in
the *Emplastrum de Minio,* with half an ounce of the masse,
mixing a dram of Loadstone. For applying the magdaleon or
roale unto the Needle it would both stir and attract it; not
equally in all parts, but more vigorously in some, according
unto the mine of the stone more plentifully dispersed in the
masse. And lastly, in the Loadstone powdered, the polary
respects are not wholly destroyed. For those diminutive particles are not atomicall or meerly indivisible, but consist of

dimensions sufficient for their operations, though in obscurer   †
effects. Thus if unto the powder of Loadstone or Iron we
admove the North pole of the Loadstone, the powders or small
divisions will erect and conform themselves thereto: but if
the South pole approach, they will subside, and inverting
their bodies respect the Loadstone with the other extream.
And this will happen not only in a body of powder together,
but in any particle or dust divided from it.

Now though we disavow not these plaisters, yet shall we   †
not omit two cautions in their use; that therein the stone be
not too subtilly powdered; for it will better manifest its attraction in a more sensible dimension. That where is desired
a speedy effect, it may be considered whether it were not
better to relinquish the powdered plaisters, and to apply an
entire Loadstone unto the part: And though the other be not
wholly ineffectuall, whether this way be not more powerfull, and so might have been in the cure of the young man
delivered by Beckerus.

The last consideration concerneth Magicall relations; in
which account we comprehend effects derived and fathered
upon hidden qualities, specificall forms, Antipathies and
Sympathies, whereof from received grounds of Art, no reasons are derived. Herein relations are strange and numerous,
men being apt in all ages to multiply wonders, and Philosophers dealing with admirable bodies as Historians have done
with excellent men; upon the strength of their great atchieve-
ments, ascribing acts unto them not only false, but impossible; and exceeding truth as much in their relations, as they
have others in their actions. Hereof we shall briefly mention
some delivered by Authors of good esteem; whereby we
may discover the fabulous inventions of some, the credulous
supinity of others, and the great disservice unto truth by
both; multiplying obscurities in nature, and authorising hidden qualities that are false; whereas wise men are ashamed
there are so many true.

And first, Dioscorides puts a shrewd quality upon it, and
such as men are apt enough to experiment, and therewith
discovers the incontinency of a wife, by placing the Load-

stone under her pillow; whereupon she will not be able to remain in bed with her husband. The same he also makes a help unto theevery. For theeves saith he, having a designe upon a house, doe make a fire at the four corners thereof, and cast therein the fragments of Loadstone; whence ariseth a fume that so disturbeth the inhabitants, that they forsake the house and leave it to the spoil of the robbers. This relation how ridiculous soever, hath Albertus taken up above a thousand years after, and Marbodeus the Frenchman hath continued it the same in Latine verse; which with the notes of Pictorius is currant unto our daies. As strange must be the Lithomancy or divination from this stone, whereby as Tzetzes delivers, Helenus the Prophet foretold the destruction of Troy; and the Magick thereof, not safely to be beleeved, which was delivered by Orpheus, that sprinkled with water it will upon a question emit a voice not much unlike an Infant. But surely the Loadstone of Laurentius Guascus the Physician is never to be matched; wherewith as Cardan delivereth, whatsoever needles or bodies were touched, the wounds and punctures made thereby, were never felt at all. And yet as strange a vertue is that which is delivered by some, that a Loadstone preserved in the salt of a Remora, acquires a power to attract gold out of the deepest wells. Certainly a studied absurdity, not casually cast out, but plotted for perpetuity: for the strangenesse of the effect ever to be admired, and the difficulty of the triall never to convicted.

These conceits are of that monstrosity that they refute themselves in their recitements. There is another of better notice, and whispered thorow the world with some attention; credulous and vulgar auditors readily beleeving it, and more judicious and distinctive heads not altogether rejecting it. The conceit is excellent, and if the effect would follow, somewhat divine; whereby we might communicate like spirits, and conferre on earth with Menippus in the Moon; which is pretended from the sympathy of two needles touched with the same Loadstone, and placed in the center of two Abecedary circles, or rings with letters described round about them; one friend keeping one, and another the other, and agreeing upon an hour wherein they will communicate: For then, saith tradition, at what distance of place soever, when one needle shall be removed unto any letter; the other by a wonderfull sympathy will move unto the same. But herein I confesse my experience can finde no truth; for having expresly framed two circles of wood, and according to the number of the Latine letters divided each into twenty three parts; placing therein two stiles or needles composed of the same steel, touched with the same Loadstone, and at the same point: of these two, whensoever I removed the one, although but at the distance of half a spanne, the other would stand like Hercules pillars, and if the earth stand still, have surely no motion at all. Now as it is not possible that any body should have no boundaries, or Sphere of its activity, so is it improbable it should effect that at distance, which nearer hand it cannot at all perform.

Again, The conceit is ill contrived, and one effect inferred, whereas the contrary will ensue. For if the removing of one of the needles from A to B should have any action or influence on the other; it would not intice it from A to B, but repell it from A to Z: for needles excited by the same point of the stone, doe not attract, but avoid each other, even as these also doe, when their invigorated extreams approach unto one another.

Lastly, Were this conceit assuredly true, yet were it not a conclusion at every distance to be tried by every head: it being no ordinary or Almanack businesse, but a probleme Mathematicall, to finde out the difference of hours in different places; nor doe the wisest exactly satisfie themselves in all. For the hours of severall places anticipate each other, according unto their Longitudes; which are not exactly discovered of every place; and therefore the triall hereof at a considerable intervall, is best performed at the distance of the Antæci; that is, such habitations as have the same Meridian and equall parallel, on different sides of the Aequator; or more plainly the same Longitude, and the same Latitude unto the South, which we have in the North.

For unto such Situations it is noon and midnight at the very same time.

And therefore the Sympathy of these Needles is much of the same mould, with that intelligence which is pretended from the flesh of one body transmuted by insision into another. For if by the Art of Taliacotius,* a permutation of flesh, or transmutation be made from one mans body into another, as if a piece of flesh be exchanged from the bicipitall muscle of either parties arme, and about them both, an Alphabet circumscribed; upon a time appointed, as some conceptions affirm, they may communicate at what distance soever. For if the one shall prick himself in *A,* the other at the same time will have a sense thereof in the same part; and upon inspection of his arme, perceive what letters the other points out in his. Which is a way of intelligence very strange, and would requite the Art of Pythagoras, who could reade a reverse in the Moon.

Now this Magneticall conceit how strange soever, might have some originall in reason; for men observing no solid body whatsoever did interrupt its action, might be induced to beleeve no distance would terminate the same; and most conceiving it pointed unto the pole of heaven, might also opinion that nothing between could restrain it. Whosoever was the Author, the Aeolus that blew it about was Famianus Strada, that elegant Jesuit in his Rhetoricall prolusions, who chose out this subject to expresse the stile of Lucretius. But neither Baptista Porta, *de furtivis literarum notis,* Trithemius in his Steganography, Selenus in his Cryptography, or *Nuncius inanimatus** make any consideration hereof: although they deliver many waies to communicate thoughts at a distance. And this we will not deny may in some manner be effected by the Loadstone; that is, from one room into another; by placing a table in the wall common unto both, and writing thereon the same letters one against another: for upon the approach of a vigorous Loadstone unto a letter on this side, the Needle will move unto the same on the

* *De curtorum chyrurgia.*
* *Nunc. inanim:* by D. Godwin Bish. of Hereford.

other: But this is a very different way from ours at present;
and hereof there are many waies delivered, and more may
be discovered which contradict not the rule of its operations.

As for *unguentum Armarium,* called also *Magneticum,* it   36
belongs not to this discourse, it neither having the Loadstone for its ingredient, nor any one of its actions: but supposeth other principles, as common and universall spirits,
which convey the action of the remedy unto the part, and
conjoins the vertue of bodies far disjoined. But perhaps the
cures it doth, are not worth so mighty principles; it commonly healing but simple wounds, and such as mundified
and kept clean, doe need no other hand then that of Nature,
and the Balsam of the proper part. Unto which effect, there
being fields of Medicines, it may be a hazardous curiosity to   †,37
rely on this; and because men say the effect doth generally follow, it might be worth the experiment to try, whether
the same will not ensue upon the same method of cure, by
ordinary Balsams, or common vulnerary plasters.

Many other Magnetismes may be pretended, and the like   †
attractions through all the creatures of nature. Whether the
same be verified in the action of the Sun upon inferiour
bodies, whether there by Aeolian magnets, whether the
flux and reflux of the sea be caused by any Magnetisme from   38
the Moon; whether the like be really made out, or rather
metaphorically verified in the sympathies of plants and animals, might afford a large dispute; and Kircherus in his
Catena Magnetica hath excellently discussed the same;
which work came late unto our hand, but might have much
advantaged this discourse.

Other Discourses there might be made of the Loadstone,
as Morall, Mysticall, Theologicall; and some have handsomly done them, as Ambrose, Austine, Gulielmus Parisiensis,
and many more; but these fall under no rule, and are as
boundlesse as mens inventions; and though honest mindes
doe glorifie God hereby; yet doe they most powerfully magnifie him, and are to be looked on with another eye, who
demonstratively set forth its Magnalities; who not from pos-

tulated or precarious inferences, entreat a courteous assent, but from experiments and undeniable effects enforce the wonder of its Maker.

THE THIRD BOOK:

OF DIVERS POPULAR AND RECEIVED TENETS CONCERNING ANIMALS, WHICH EXAMINED, PROVE EITHER FALSE OR DUBIOUS.

CHAP. 1.
OF THE ELEPHANT.

The first shall be of the Elephant; whereof there generally passeth an opinion it hath no joints; and this absurdity is seconded with another, that being unable to lie down, it sleepeth against a tree; which the Hunters observing doe saw almost asunder; whereon the beast relying, by the fall of the tree falls also down it self, and is able to rise no more. Which conceit is not the daughter of latter times, but an old and gray-headed error, even in the daies of Aristotle, as he delivereth in his book, *de incessu animalium;* and stands successively related by severall other Authors; by Diodorus Siculus, Strabo, Ambrose, Cassiodore, Solinus and many more. Now herein me thinks men much forget themselves, not well considering the absurdity of such assertions.

For first, they affirm it hath no joints, and yet concede it walks and moves about; whereby they conceive there may be a progression or advancement made in motion without inflexion of parts. Now all progression or animall locomotion being (as Aristotle teacheth) performed *tractu et pulsu;* that is, by drawing on, or impelling forward some part which was before in station, or at quiet; where there are no joints or flexures, neither can there be these actions; and this is true, not only in Quadrupedes, Volatils and Fishes, which have distinct and prominent organs of motion, legs, wings and fins; but in such also as perform their progression by the trunck, as Serpents, Wormes and Leeches; whereof though

some want bones, and all extended articulations, yet have
they arthriticall analogies*; and by the motion of fibrous
and musculous parts, are able to make progression. Which
to conceive in bodies inflexible, and without all protrusion
of parts, were to expect a race from Hercules his pillars;
or hope to behold the effects of Orpheus his harp; when
Trees found joints, and danced after his musick.   †

Again, While men conceive they never lie down, and enjoy not the position of rest, ordained unto all pedestrious ani-   †
mals, hereby they imagin (what reason cannot conceive)
that an animall of the vastest dimension and longest duration, should live in a continuall motion, without that alternity
and vicissitude of rest whereby all others continue; and yet
must thus much come to passe, if we opinion they lie not
down and enjoy no decumbence at all. For station is properly no rest, but one kinde of motion, relating unto that
which Physitians (from Galen) doe name extensive or ton-
icall; that is, an extension of the muscles and organs of motion maintaining the body at length or in its proper figure;
wherein although it seem to be unmoved, it is neverthelesse   †
not without all motion; for in this position the muscles are
sensibly extended, and labour to support the body; which
permitted unto its proper gravity, would suddenly subside
and fall unto the earth, as it happeneth in sleep, diseases
and death. From which occult action and invisible motion
of the muscles in station (as Galen declareth) proceed more
offensive lassitudes then from ambulation. And therefore
the Tyranny of some have tormented men with long and enforced station; and though Ixion and Sisiphus which alwaies   1
moved, doe seem to have the hardest measure, yet was not
Titius favoured, that lay extended upon Caucasus; and
Tantalus suffered somewhat more then thirst, that stood perpetually in hell. Thus Mercurialis in his Gymnasticks justly
makes standing one kinde of exercise; and Galen when we
lye down, commends unto us middle figures; that is, not to
lye directly, or at length, but somewhat inflected, that the
muscles may be at rest; for such as he termeth *Hypobole-*

* Jointlike parts.   †

maioi or figures of excesse, either shrinking up or stretching
out, are wearisome positions, and such as perturb the quiet
of those parts. Now various parts doe variously discover   †
these indolent and quiet positions: some in right lines, as
the wrists, some at right angles, as the cubit; others at
oblique angles, as the fingers and the knees: all resting satisfied in postures of moderation, and none enduring the extremity of flexure or extension.

Moreover men herein doe strangely forget the obvious relations of history, affirming they have no joints, whereas they
daily reade of severall actions which are not performable
without them. They forget what is delivered by Xiphilinus,
and also by Suetonius in the lives of Nero and Galba, that
Elephants have been instructed to walk on ropes, in publike
shews before the people; which is not easily performed by
man, and requireth not only a broad foot, but a pliable
flexure of joints, and commandible disposure of all parts of
progression. They passe by that memorable place in Curtius,
concerning the Elephant of King Porus, *Indus qui Ele-*   2
phantem regebat, descendere eum ratus, more solito
procumbere jussit in genua, caeteri quoque (ita enim insti-
tuti erant) demisere corpora in terram. They remember not
the expression of Osorius *de rebus gestis Emanuelis,* when
he speaks of the Elephant presented to Leo the tenth,
Pontificem ter genibus flexis, et demisso corporis habitu   3
venerabundus salutavit. But above all, they call not to minde
that memorable shew of Germanicus, wherein twelve Ele-   4
phants danced unto the sound of musick, and after laid them
down in the Tricliniums, or places of festivall Recumbency.

They forget the Etymologie of the Knee, approved by   †
some Grammarians.* They disturb the position of the young
ones in the wombe: which upon extension of leggs is not easily conceiveable, and contrary unto the generall contrivance
of nature. Nor doe they consider the impossible exclusion
thereof, upon extension and rigour of the leggs.

Lastly, They forget or consult not experience; whereof
not many years past, we have had the advantage in England,

* γόνυ from γωνία   5

by an Elephant shewn in many parts thereof; not only in the
posture of standing, but kneeling and lying down. Whereby
although the opinion at present be well suppressed, yet from   †
some strings of tradition, and fruitfull recurrence of error,   †
it is not improbable it may revive in the next generation
again; this being not the first that hath been seen in England; for (besides some other since) as Polydore Virgil relateth, Lewis the French King sent one to Henry the third;
and Emanuel of Portugall another to Leo the tenth into
Italy; where notwithstanding the error is still alive and epidemicall, as with us.

The hint and ground of this opinion might be the grosse
and somewhat Cylindricall composure of the legs, the equality and lesse perceptible disposure of the joints, especially
in the fore legs of this Animall; they appearing when he   †
standeth, like pillars of flesh, without any evidence of articulation. The different flexure and order of the joints might
also countenance the same; being not disposed in the Elephant as they are in other quadrupedes, but carry a nearer
conformity into those of man; that is, the bought of the fore-
legs not directly backward, but laterally and somewhat
inward; but the hough or suffraginous flexure behinde rather
outward. Contrary unto many other quadrupedes, and such
as can scratch the ear with the hinder foot, as Horses,
Camels, Deer, Sheep and Dogges; for their fore legs bend
like our legs, and their hinder legs like our arms, when we
move them to our shoulders. But quadrupedes oviparous, as
Frogs, Lizards, Crocodiles, have their joints and motive
flexures more analogously framed unto ours; and some
among viviparous; that is, such thereof as can bring their
fore-feet and meat therein into their mouthes, as most can
doe that have the clavicles or collarbones; whereby their
breasts are broader, and their shoulders more asunder, as the
Ape, the Monkey, the Squirrell and some others. If therefore any shall affirm the joints of Elephants are differently
framed from most of other quadrupedes, and more obscurely
and grossely almost then any; he doth herein no injury unto
truth. But if *à dicto secundum quid ad dictum simpliciter,*   ⁶
he affirmeth also they have no articulations at all; he incurs

the controllment of reason, and cannot avoid the contradiction also of sense.

As for the manner of their venation, if we consult historicall experience, we shall finde it to be otherwise then as is commonly presumed, by sawing away of trees; the accounts whereof are to be seen at large in *Johannes Hugo, Edwardus Lopez, Garcias ab Horto, Cadamustus* and many more.

Other concernments there are of the Elephant, which † might admit of discourse; and if we should question the teeth of Elephants, that is, whether they be properly so termed, or might not rather be called horns; it were no new enquiry of mine, but a paradox as old as Oppianus.[*] Whether as Pliny and divers since affirm, that Elephants are terrified, and make away upon the grunting of Swine, *Garcias ab Horto* may decide, who affirmeth upon experience they enter their stalls, and live promiscuously in the woods of Malavar. That the situation of the genitalls is averse, and their copulation like that of Camels, as Pliny hath also delivered, is not to be received; for we have beheld that part in a different position; and their coition is made by supersaliency like that of Horses, as we are informed by some who have beheld them in that act. That some Elephants have not only written whole sentences, as Aelian ocularly testifieth, but have also spoken, as Oppianus delivereth, and Christophorus a Costa particularly relateth; although it sound like that of Achilles Horse in Homer, we doe not conceive impossible: nor beside the affinity of reason in this Animall any such intollerable incapacity in the organs of divers quadrupedes, whereby they might not be taught to speak, or become imitators of speech like birds. Strange it is how the curiosity of men that have been active in the instruction of beasts, have never fallen upon this artifice; and among those many paradoxicall and unheard of imitations, should not attempt to make one speak. The Serpent that spake unto Eve, the Dogs and Cats that usually speak unto Witches, might afford some encouragement. And since broad and thick chops are required in birds that speak, since lips and

[*] *Cyneget. lib. 2.* †

teeth are also organs of speech; from these there is also an
advantage in quadrupedes, and a proximity of reason in
Elephants and Apes above them all. Since also an Echo will   †
speak without any mouth at all, articulately returning the
voice of man, by only ordering the vocall spirit in concave
and hollow places; whether the musculous and motive parts
about the hollow mouthes of beasts, may not dispose the
passing spirit into some articulate notes, seems a querie of
no great doubt.

CHAP. 5.
OF THE BADGER.

That a Brock or Badger hath the legs of one side shorter
then of the other, though an opinion perhaps not very ancient, is yet very generall; received not only by theorists and
unexperienced beleevers, but assented unto by most who   7
have the opportunity to behold and hunt them daily. Which
notwithstanding upon enquiry I finde repugnant unto the
three determinators of truth, Authority, Sense and Reason.
For first, Albertus *Magnus* speaks dubiously, confessing he
could not confirm the verity hereof; but Aldrovand affirmeth
plainly, there can be no such inequality observed. And for
my own part, upon indifferent enquiry, I cannot discover this
difference, although the regardible side be defined, and the
brevity by most imputed unto the left.

Again, It seems no easie affront unto reason, and generally
repugnant unto the course of nature; for if we survey the
totall set of animals, we may in their legs, or organs of
progression, observe an equality of length, and parity of numeration; that is, not any to have an odde leg, or the supporters and movers of one side not exactly answered by the
other. Although the hinder may be unequall unto the fore
and middle legs, as in Frogs, Locusts and Grashoppers; or
both unto the middle, as in some beetles, and spiders, as is
determined by Aristotle *de incessu animalium.* Perfect and
viviparous quadrupeds, so standing in their position of
pronenesse, that the opposite joints of neighbour legs consist

in the same plane; and a line descending from their navell intersects at right angles the axis of the earth. It happeneth often I confesse that a Lobster hath the chely or great claw of one side longer then the other; but this is not properly their leg, but a part of apprehension, and whereby they hold or seize upon their prey; for the legs and proper parts of progression are inverted backward, and stand in a position opposite unto these.

Lastly, The monstrosity is ill contrived, and with some dis-advantage; the shortnesse being affixed unto the legs of one side, which might have been more tolerably placed upon the thwart or Diagoniall* movers; for the progression of quad-rupeds being performed *per Diametrum,* that is the crosse legs moving or resting together, so that two are alwaies in motion, and two in station at the same time; the brevity had been more tolerable in the crosse legs. For then the motion and station had been performed by equall legs; whereas herein they are both performed by unequall organs, and the imperfection becomes discoverable at every hand.

CHAP. 18.
OF MOLLS. †

That Molls are blinde and have no eyes, though a common opinion, is received with much variety; some affirming only they have no sight, as Oppianus, the Proverb *Talpa Caecior,* 8 and the word σπαλαχία, or Talpitas, which in Hesychius is made the same with *caecitas:* some that they have eies, but no sight, as the text of Aristotle seems to imply; some neither eies nor sight, as Albertus, Pliny, and the vulgar opinion; some both eies and sight, as Scaliger, Aldrovandus, and some others. Of which opinions the last with some restriction, is most consonant unto truth: for that they have eyes in their head is manifest unto any that wants them not in his own; and are discoverable, not only in old ones, but as we have observed in young and naked conceptions, taken out of the

---

* Diagonion, a line drawn from the crosse angles. †

belly of the Dam. And he that exactly enquires into the
cavity of their cranies, may discover some propagation of
nerves communicated unto these parts; but that the humors
together with their coats are also distinct (though Galen seem
to affirm it) transcendeth our discovery; for separating these
little Orbes, and including them in magnifying glasses, we
discerned no more then Aristotle mentions, τῶν ὀφθαλμῶν
μέλαινα, that is, *humorem nigrum,* nor any more if they be   9
broken. That therefore they have eies we must of necessity
affirm, but that they be comparatively incomplete we need
not to denie: So Galen affirmes the parts of generation in
women are imperfect, in respect of those of men, as the eies
of Molls in regard of other animals; So Aristotle termes them
πηρουμένους, which Gaza translates *oblaesos,* and Scaliger by   10
a word of Imperfection, *inchoatos.*

Now as that they have eies is manifest unto sense, so that
they have sight not incongruous unto reason, if we call not in
question the providence of this provision, that is, to assign the
organs, and yet deny the office, to grant them eies and
withold all manner of vision. For as the inference is fair,
affirmatively deduced from the action to the organ, that they
have eies because they see; so is it also from the organ to
the action, that they have eies, therefore some sight designed;
if we take the intention of Nature in every species, and except the casuall impediments, or morbosities in individuals.
But as their eies are more imperfect then others, so doe we
conceive of their sight, or act of vision; for they will runne
against things, and hudling forwards fall from high places.
So that they are not blinde, nor yet distinctly see; there is
in them no cecity, yet more then a cecutiency; they have
sight enough to discern the light, though not perhaps to distinguish of objects or colours; so are they not exactly blinde,
for light is one object of vision. And this (as Scaliger observeth) might be as full a sight as Nature first intended;
for living in darknesse under the earth, they had no further
need of eies then to avoid the light; and to be sensible when
ever they lost that darknesse of earth, which was their naturall confinement. And therefore however Translators doe
render the word of Aristotle or Galen, that is, *imperfectos,*

oblaesos or *inchoatos,* it is not much considerable; for their eies are sufficiently begun to finish this action, and competently perfect for this imperfect Vision.

And lastly, although they had neither eies nor sight, yet could they not be termed blinde. For blindnesse being a privative term unto sight, this appellation is not admittible in propriety of speech, and will overthrow the doctrine of privations; which presuppose positive formes or habits, and are not indefinite negations, denying in all subjects, but such alone wherein the positive habits are in their proper nature, and placed without repugnancy. So doe we improperly say a Moll is blinde, if we deny it the organs or a capacity of vision from its created nature; so when the text of John had said, that person was blinde from his nativity, whose cecity our Saviour cured, it was not warrantable in Nonnus to say he had no eies at all, as in the judgement of Heinsius, as he de- †
scribeth in his paraphrase; and as some ancient Fathers affirm, that by this miracle they were created in him. And so though the sense may be accepted, that proverb must be candidly interpreted, which maketh fishes mute; and calls them silent which have no voice in Nature.

Now this conceit is erected upon a misapprehension or mistake in the symptomes of vision; men confounding abolishment, diminution and depravement, and naming that an abolition of sight, which indeed is but an abatement. For if vision be abolished, it is called *caecitas,* or blindnesse; if depraved and receive its objects erroneously, Hallucination; if diminished, *hebetudo visus, caligatio,* or dimnesse. Now instead of a diminution or imperfect vision in the Moll, we affirm an abolition or totall privation; in stead of caligation or dimnesse, we conclude a cecity or blindnesse, which hath been frequently inferred concerning other animals; so some affirm the water Rat is blinde, so Sammonicus and Nicander doe call the *Mus-Araneus,* the shrew or Ranny, blinde; And because darknesse was before light, the Aegyptians worshipped the same: So are slow-Wormes accounted blinde, †
and the like we affirm proverbially of the Beetle; although their eies be evident, and they will flye against lights, like many other insects; and though also Aristotle determines,

that the eies are apparent in all flying insects, though other
senses be obscure, and not perceptible at all. And if from a
diminution we may inferre a totall privation, or affirm that
other Animals are blinde which doe not acutely see, or comparatively unto others, we shall condemn unto blindnesse
many not so esteemed; for such as have corneous or horney
eies, as Lobsters and crustaceous animals, are generally dim-
sighted; all insects that have *antennae,* or long hornes to feel
out their way, as Butter-flies and Locusts; or their fore-legs so
disposed, that they much advance before their heads, as may
be observed in Spiders; and if the Eagle were judge, we
might be blinde our selves; the expression therefore of Scripture in the story of Jacob is surely with circumspection; And
it came to passe when Jacob was old, and his eies were dim,
quando caligarunt oculi, saith Jerom and Tremellius, which
are expressions of diminution, and not of absolute privation.

[Other concerns there are of Molls, which though not com-   †
monly opinioned are not commonly enough considered: As
the peculiar formation of their feet, the slender *ossa Jugalia,*   †
and Dogteeth, and how hard it is to keep them alive out of
the Earth: As also the ferility and voracity of these animals;
for though they be contented with Roots, and stringy parts of
Plants, or Wormes under ground, yet when they are above it
will sometimes tear and eat on another, and in a large glass
wherein a Moll, a Toad, and a Viper were inclosed, we have
known the Moll to dispatch them and to devour a good part
of them both.]

CHAP. 20.
OF SNAYLES.

That Snailes have two eyes, and at the end of their Horns,   †
beside the assertion of the people, is the opinion of some
Learned men. Which notwithstanding Scaliger tearms but
imitation of eyes; which Pliny contradicts, and Aristotle upon
consequence denies, when he affirms that testaceous animals
have no eyes at all. And for my own part after much inquiry,
I am not satisfied that these are eyes, or that those black and   11

atramentous spots which seem to represent them are any
ocular realities. For if any object be presented unto them,
they will sometime seem to decline it, and sometime run
against it. If also these black extremities, or presumed eyes
be clipped off, they will notwithstanding make use of their
protrusions or horns, and poke out their way as before. Again,
if they were eyes or instruments of vision, they would have
their originals in the head, and from thence derive their motive and optick organs; but their roots and first extremities
are seated low upon the sides of the back, as may be perceived in the whiter sort of Snayles when they retract them.
And lastly, if we concede they have two eyes, we must also
grant, they have no lesse then four; for not only the two
greater extensions above have these imitations of eyes, but
also the two lesser below: and if they be dextrously dis-   †
sected, there will be found on either side two black filaments
or membranous strings, which extend into the long and
shorter cornicle upon protrusion. And therefore if they have
two eyes, they have also four, which will be monstrous, and
beyond the affirmation of any.

Now the reason why we name these black strings eyes, is,
because we know not what to call them else, and understand
not the proper use of that part; which indeed is very obscure,
and not delivered by any; but may probably be said to assist
the protrusion and retraction of their horns; which being a
weak and hollow body, require some inward establishment, to
confirm the length of their advancement; which we observe
they cannot extend without the concurrence hereof. For if
with your finger you apprehend the top of the horn, and draw
out this black and membranous emission, the horn will be
excluded no more; but if you clip off the extremity, or only
singe the top thereof with *Aqua fortis,* or other corrosive water, leaving a considerable part behinde; they will neverthelesse exclude their horns, and therewith explorate their way
as before. And indeed the exact sense of these extremities is
very remarkable; for if you dip a pen in *Aqua fortis,* oyl of
vitriol, or Turpentine, and present it towards these points,
they will at a reasonable distance decline the acrimony
thereof, retiring or distorting them to avoid it; and this they

will nimbly perform if objected to the extremes, but slowly
or not at all, if approached unto their roots.

What hath been therefore delivered concerning the plurality, paucity or anomalous situation of eyes, is either monstrous, fabulous, or under things never seen includes good
sense or meaning. And so may we receive the figment of Argus, who was an Hieroglyphick of heaven, in those centuries
of eyes expressing the stars, and their alternate wakings, the
vicissitude of day and night; which strictly taken cannot be
admitted; for the subject of sleep is not the eye, but the common sense, which once asleep, all eyes must be at rest. And
therefore what is delivered as an Embleme of vigilancy, that
the Hare and Lion doe sleep with one eye open, doth not
evince they are any more awake then if they were both
closed. For the open eye beholds in sleep no more then that
which is closed; and no more one eye in them then two in
other animals that sleep with both open; as some by disease,
and others naturally which have no eye-lids at all.

As for Polyphemus, although the story be fabulous, the
monstrosity is not impossible. For the act of Vision may be
performed with one eye; and in the deception and fallacy of
sight, hath this advantage of two, that it beholds not objects
double, or sees two things for one. For this doth happen
when the axis of the visive cones, diffused from the object,
fall not upon the same plane; but that which is conveyed into
one eye, is more depressed or elevated then that which enters
the other. So if beholding a Candle, we protrude either upward or downward the pupill of one eye, the object will appear double; but if we shut the other eye, and behold it with
one, it will then appear but single; and if we abduce the eye
unto either corner, the object will not duplicate; for in that
position the axis of the cones remain in the same plane, as is
demonstrated in the opticks, and delivered by Galen, in his
tenth *De usu partium.*

Relations also there are of men that could make themselves
invisible, which belongs not to this discourse; but may serve
as notable expressions of wise and prudent men, who so contrive their affairs, that although their actions be manifest,
their designes are not discoverable. In this acception there is

nothing left of doubt, and Giges ring remaineth still amongst us; for vulgar eyes behold no more of wise men then doth the Sun; they may discover their exteriour and outward waies, but their interiour and inward pieces he only sees, that sees into their beings.   †

CHAP. 21.

OF THE CAMELEON.

Concerning the Cameleon there generally passeth an opinion that it liveth only upon ayre, and is sustained by no other aliment; Thus much is in plain termes affirmed by Solinus, Pliny and others, and by this periphrasis is the same described by Ovid. All which notwithstanding, upon enquiry I finde the assertion mainly controvertible, and very much to fail in the three inducements of belief.

And first for its verity, although asserted by some, and traditionally delivered by others, yet is it very questionable. For beside Aelian, who is seldome defective in these accounts, Aristotle distinctly treating hereof, hath made no mention of this remarkeable propriety; which either suspecting its verity, or presuming its falsity he surely omitted; for that he remained ignorant of this account it is not easily conceivable, it being the common opinion, and generally received by all men. Some have positively denied it, as Augustinus, Niphus, Stobaeus, Dalechampius, Fortunius Licetus, with many more; others have experimentally refuted it, as namely *Johannes Landius,* who in the relation of Scaliger, observed a Cameleon to lick up a fly from his breast; But *Bellonius*° hath been more satisfactorily experimentall, not only affirming they feed on Flyes, Caterpillars, Beetles and other insects, but upon exenteration he found these animals in their bellies; [whereto we might also add the experimen-   † tal decisions of the worthy *Peireschius* and learned *Emanuel Vizzianus,* in that Chameleon which had been often observed to drink water, and delight to feed on Meal-worms.] And al-

° *Comment. in Ocell. Lucan.*   †,12

though we have not had the advantage of our own observation, yet have we received the like confirmation from many
ocular spectators.

As touching the verisimility or probable truth of this relation, severall reasons there are which seem to overthrow it.
For first, there are found in this animall, the guts, the stomack, and other parts officiall unto nutrition; which were its
aliment the empty reception of air, their provisions had been
superfluous. Now the wisdom of nature abhorring superfluities, and effecting nothing in vain, unto the intention of these
operations respectively contriveth the Organs; and therefore
where we finde such Instruments, we may with strictnesse
expect their actions, and where we discover them not, we
may with safety conclude the non-intention of their operations. So when we observe that oviperous animals, as Lizards,   †
Frogs, Birds, and most Fishes have neither bladder nor kid-
neys, we may with reason inferre they do not urine at all: †
But whereas in the same kinde we discover these parts in the
Tortoys, we cannot deny he exerciseth that excretion; Nor   †
was there any absurdity in Pliny, when for medicinall uses he
commended the urine of a Tortoise. So when we perceive
that Bats have teats, it is not unreasonable to inferre they
suckle their younglings with milk; but whereas no other flying animall hath these parts, we cannot from them expect a
viviparous exclusion; but either a generation of eggs, or some
vermiparous separation, whose navell is within it self at first,
and its nutrition after not inwardly dependant of its originall.

Again, Nature is so far from leaving any one part without
its proper action, that she oft times imposeth two or three
labours upon one, so the pizell in animals is both officiall unto
urine and to generation, but the first and primary use is generation; for many creatures enjoy that part which urine not,
as fishes, birds, and quadrupeds oviparous. But not on the   †
contrary, for the secundary action subsisteth not alone, but
in concomitancy with the other; so the nostrils are usefull
both for respiration and smelling, but the principall use is
smelling; for many have nostrils which have no lungs, as
fishes, but none have lungs or respiration, which have not
some shew, or some analogy of nostrils. Thus we perceive

the providence of nature, that is, the wisdome of God, which disposeth of no part in vain, and some parts unto two or three uses, will not provide any without the execution of its proper office, nor where there is no digestion to be made, make any parts inservient to that intention.

Beside the teeth, the tongue of this animall is a second argument to overthrow this airie nutrication: and that not only in its proper nature, but also its peculiar figure. For of this part properly taken there are two ends; that is, the formation of the voice, and the execution of taste: for the voice, it can have no office in Camelions, for they are mute animals; as beside fishes, are most other sorts of Lizards. As for their taste, if their nutriment be air, neither can it be an instrument thereof; for the body of that element is ingustible, void of all sapidity, and without any action of the tongue is by the rough artery or wezon conducted into the lungs. And therefore Pliny much forgets the strictnesse of his assertion, when he alloweth excrements unto that animall, that feedeth only upon air; which notwithstanding with the urine of an Asse, he commends as a magicall medicine upon our enemies.

The figure of the tongue seems also to overthrow the presumption of this aliment, which according to exact delineation, is in this animall peculiar, and seemeth contrived for prey. For in so little a creature it is at the least half a palm long, and being it self very slow in motion, hath in this part a very great agility; withall its food being flies and such as suddenly escape, it hath in the tongue a mucous and slymy extremity, whereby upon a sudden emission it inviscates and tangleth those insects. And therefore some have thought its name not unsuitable unto its nature; the nomination in Greek is a little Lion*; not so much for the resemblance of shape, as affinity of condition; that is for vigilancy in its prey, and sudden rapacity thereof, which it performeth not like the Lion with its teeth, but a sudden and unexpected ejaculation of the tongue. This exposition is favoured by some, especially the old glosse upon Leviticus, whereby in the Translation of Jerome and the Septuagint, this animall is forbidden; what-

* Χαμαιλέων

ever it be, it seems more reasonable then that of Isidore, who
derives this name *a Camelo et Leone,* as presuming herein
resemblance with a Camell.   †

As for the possibility hereof, it is not also unquestionable;
and wise men are of opinion, the bodies of animals cannot
receive a proper aliment from air: for beside that taste being
(as Aristotle terms it) a kinde of touch; it is required the
aliment should be tangible, and fall under the palpable affections of touch; beside also that there is some sapor in all
aliments, as being to be distinguished and judged by the gust,
which cannot be admitted in air: Beside these, I say, if we
consider the nature of aliment, and the proper use of air in
respiration, it will very hardly fall under the name hereof, or
properly attain the act of nutrication.

And first concerning its nature, to make a perfect nutrition
into the body nourished, there is required a transmutation
of the nutriment; now where this conversion or aggeneration
is made, there is also required in the aliment a familiarity
of matter, and such a community or vicinity unto a living nature, as by one act of the soul may be converted into the
body of the living, and enjoy one common soul. Which cannot be effected by air, it concurring only with our flesh in
common principles, which are at the largest distance from
life, and common also unto inanimated constitutions. And
therefore when it is said by Fernelius, and asserted by divers
others, that we are only nourished by living bodies, and such
as are some way proceeding from them, that is, the fruits,
effects, parts, or seeds thereof, they have laid out an object
very agreeable unto assimulation; for these indeed are fit to
receive a quick and immediate conversion, as holding some
community with our selves, and containing approximate dispositions unto animation.

Secondly (as is argued by Aristotle against the Pythago-
reans) whatsoever properly nourisheth before its assimulation, by the action of naturall heat it receiveth a corpulency   †
or incrassation progressionall unto its conversion; which notwithstanding cannot be effected upon the air; for the action
of heat doth not condense but rarifie that body, and by at-
tenuation rather then for nutrition, disposeth it for expulsion.

Thirdly (which is the argument of Hippocrates) all aliment received into the body, must be therein a considerable space retained, and not immediatly expelled. Now air but momentally remaining in our bodies, it hath no proportionable space for its conversion; only of length enough to refrigerate the heart; which having once performed, lest being it self heated again, it should suffocate that part, it maketh no stay, but hasteth back the same way it passed in.

Fourthly, The proper use of ayre attracted by the lungs, and without which there is no durable continuation in life, is not the nutrition of parts, but the contemperation of that fervour in the heart, and the ventilation of that fire alwaies maintained in the forge of life; whereby although in some manner it concurreth unto nutrition, yet can it not receive the proper name of nutriment; and therefore by Hippocrates *de alimento*, it is termed *Alimentum non Alimentum*, a nourishment and no nourishment. That is, in a large acception, but not in propriety of language; conserving the body, not nourishing the same, not repairing it by assimulation, but preserving it by ventilation; for thereby the naturall flame is preserved from extinction, and so the individuum supported in some way like nutrition. And so when it is said by the same Author, *Pulmo contrarium corpori alimentum trahit, reliqua omnia idem,* it is not to be taken in a strict and proper sense; but the quality in the one, the substance is meant in the other. For air in regard of our naturall heat is cold, and in that quality contrary unto it; but what is properly aliment, of what quality soever, is potentially the same, and in a substantiall identity unto it. †

13

Again, Some are so farre from affirming the air to afford † any nutriment, that they plainly deny it to be any element, or that it entreth into mixt bodies as any principle in their compositions, but performeth other offices in the universe, as to fill all vacuities about the earth or beneath it, to convey the heat of the sun, to maintain fires and flames, to serve for the flight of volatils, respiration of breathing animals, and refrigeration of others. And although we receive it as an element, yet since the transmutation of elements and simple bodies is not beyond great question, since also it is no easie

matter to demonstrate that air is so much as convertible into
water; how transmutable it is into flesh, may be of deeper
doubt.

And although the air attracted may be conceived to nourish the invisible flame of life, in as much as common and
culinary flames are nourished by the air about them; I confesse we doubt that air is the pabulous supply of fire, much   †
lesse that flame is properly air kindled. And the same before
us, hath been denied by the Lord of Verulam, in his Tract
of life and death, and also by Dr Jorden in his book of Minerall waters. For that which substantially maintaineth the
fire, is the combustible matter in the kindled body, and not
the ambient air, which affordeth exhalation to its fuliginous
atomes; nor that which causeth the flame properly to be
termed air, but rather as he expresseth it, the accension of
fuliginous exhalations, which contain an unctuosity in them,
and arise from the matter of fuell; which opinion is very probable, and will salve many doubts, whereof the common conceit affordeth no solution.

As first, How fire is stricken out of flints? that is not by
kindling the air from the collision of two hard bodies; for   †
then Diamonds should doe the like better then flints; but   †
rather from the sulphur and inflamable effluviums contained
in them. The like saith Jorden we observe in canes and
woods, that are unctuous and full of oyle, which will yeeld
fire by frication, or collision, not by kindling the air about
them, but the inflamable oyle within them. Why the fire goes
out without air? that is, because the fuliginous exhalations
wanting evaporation recoyle upon the flame and choak it, as
is evident in cupping-glasses; and the artifice of charcoals,
where if the air be altogether excluded, the fire goes out.
Why some lamps included in close bodies have burned many   14
hundred years, as that discovered in the sepulchre of Tullia
the sister of Cicero, and that of Olibius many years after, near
Padua? because whatever was their matter, either a preparation of gold, or Naptha, the duration proceeded from the purity of their oyle which yeelded no fuliginous exhalations to
suffocate the fire; For if air had nourished the flame, it had
not continued many minutes, for it would have been spent

and wasted by the fire. Why a piece of flax will kindle, although it touch not the flame? because the fire extendeth further, then indeed it is visible, being at some distance from the wick, a pellucide and transparent body, and thinner then the air it self. Why mettals in their liquation, although they intensly heat the air above their surface, arise not yet into a flame, nor kindle the air about them? because their sulphur is more fixed, and they emit not inflamable exhalations. And lastly, why a lamp or candle burneth only in the air about it, and inflameth not the air at a distance from it? because the flame extendeth not beyond the inflamable effluence, but closely adheres unto the originall of its inflamation; and therefore it only warmeth, not kindleth the air about it. Which notwithstanding it will doe, if the ambient air be impregnate with subtile inflamabilities, and such as are of quick accension; as experiment is made in a close room, upon an evaparation of spirits of wine and Camphire; as subterraneous fires doe sometimes happen; and as Creusa and Alexanders boy in the bath were set on fire by Naptha. 15

Lastly, The Element of air is so far from nourishing the body, that some have questioned the power of water; many conceiving it enters not the body in the power of aliment, or that from thence there proceeds a substantiall supply. For beside that some creatures drink not at all, unto others it performes the common office of air, and serves for refrigeration of the heart, as unto fishes, who receive it, and expell it by the gils; even unto our selves, and more perfect animals, though many waies assistent thereto, it performs no substantiall nutrition, serving for refrigeration, dilution of solid aliment, and its elixation in the stomack; which from thence as a vehicle it conveys through lesse accessible cavities into the liver, from thence into the veines, and so in a rorid substance through the capillary cavities into every part; which having performed, it is afterward excluded by urine, sweat and ferous separations. And this opinion surely possessed the Ancients; for when they so highly commended that water which is suddenly hot and cold, which is without all savour, the lightest, the thinnest, and which will soonest boile Beans or

Pease, they had no consideration of nutrition; whereunto had
they had respect, they would have surely commended grosse
and turbid streames, in whose confusion at least, there might
be contained some nutriment; and not jejune or limpid water,
nearer the simplicity of its Element. Although, I confess, our   †
clearest waters and such as seem simple unto sense, are much
compounded unto reason, as may be observed in the evaporation of large quantities of water; wherein beside a terreous
residence some salt is also found, as is also observable in rain
water; which appearing pure and empty, is full of seminall
principles, and carrieth vitall atomes of plants and animals in
it, which have not perished in the great circulation of nature,
as may be discovered from severall insects generated in raine
water, from the prevalent fructification of plants thereby; and
(beside the reall plant of Cornerius*) from vegetable figu-   16
rations, upon the sides of glasses, so rarely delineated in
frosts.

All which considered, severer heads will be apt enough to
conceive the opinion of this animall, not much unlike unto
that of the Astomi, or men without mouthes in Pliny; sutable
unto the relation of the Mares in Spain, and their subventa-   18
neous conceptions, from the Western winde; and in some way
more unreasonable then the figment of Rabican the famous
horse in Ariosto, which being conceived by flame and winde,
never tasted grasse, or fed on any grosser provender then air;
for this way of nutrition was answerable unto the principles
of his generation; which being not airy, but grosse and seminall in the Chameleon, unto its conservation there is required
a solid pasture, and a food congenerous unto the principles
of its nature.

The grounds of this opinion are many; the first observed
by Theophrastus, was the inflation or swelling of the body,
made in this animall upon inspiration or drawing in its
breath; which people observing, have thought it to feed upon
air. But this effect is rather occasioned upon the greatnesse
of its lungs, which in this animall are very large, and by their
backward situation afford a more observable dilatation; and

* *Libavius tom. 4 chym.*   †,17

though their lungs be lesse, the like inflation is also observable in Toads [but especially in Sentortoises]. †

A second is the continuall hiation or holding open its
mouth, which men observing conceive the intention thereof
to receive the aliment of air; but this is also occasioned by
the greatnesse of its lungs; for repletion whereof not having
a sufficient or ready supply by its nostrils, it is enforced to
dilate and hold open the jawes.

The third is the paucity of bloud observed in this animall,
scarce at all to be found but in the eye, and about the heart;
which defect being observed, inclined some into thoughts,
that the air was a sufficient maintenance for these exanguious
parts. But this defect or rather paucity of bloud, is also agreeable unto many other animals, whose solid nutriment we doe
not controvert; as may be observed in other sorts of Lizards,
in Frogs and divers Fishes; and therefore an Horse-leech
will hardly be made to fasten upon a fish; and we doe not
reade of much bloud that was drawn from Frogs by Mice, in
that famous battell of Homer. 19

The last and most common ground which begat or promoted this opinion, is the long continuation hereof without
any visible food, which some observing, precipitously conclude they eat not any at all. It cannot be denied it is (if not
the most of any) a very abstemious animall, and such as by
reason of its frigidity, paucity of bloud, and latitancy in the
winter (about which time the observations are often made)
will long subsist without a visible sustentation. But a like condition may be also observed in many other animals; for Lizards and Leeches, as we have made triall, will live some
moneths without sustenance, and we have included Snailes
in glasses all winter, which have returned to feed again in
the spring. Now these notwithstanding, are not conceived to
passe all their lives without food; for so to argue is fallacious, †
and is moreover sufficiently convicted by experience. And
therefore probably other relations are of the same verity,
which are of the like affinity; as is the conceit of the *Rhintace* 20
in Persia, the *Canis Levis* of America, and the *Manucodiata*
or bird of Paradise in India.

To assign a reason of this abstinence in animals, or declare how without a supply there ensueth no destructive exhaustion, exceedeth the limits and intention of my discourse. Fortunius Licetus in his excellent Tract, *De his qui diu vivunt*   21 *sine alimento,* hath very ingeniously attempted it; deducing the cause hereof from an equall conformity of naturall heat and moisture, at least no considerable exuperancy in either; which concurring in an unactive proportion, the naturall heat consumeth not the moisture (whereby ensueth no exhaustion) and the condition of naturall moisture is able to resist the slender action of heat (whereby it needeth no reparation) and this is evident in Snakes, Lizards, Snailes, and divers other insects latitant many moneths in the year; which being cold creatures, containing a weak heat in a crasse or copious humidity, doe long subsist without nutrition: For the activity of the agent, being not able to overmaster the resistance of the patient, there will ensue no deperdition. And upon the like grounds it is, that cold and phlegmatick bodies, and (as Hippocrates determineth) that old men will best endure fasting. Now the same harmony and stationary constitution, as it happeneth in many species, so doth it fall out sometime in Individuals. For we reade of many who have lived long time without aliment; and beside deceits and impostures, there may be veritable Relations of some, who without a miracle, and by peculiarity of temper, have far outfasted Elias. Which notwithstanding doth not take off the   22,† miracle, for that may be miraculously effected in one, which is naturally causable in another. Some naturally living unto an hundred, unto which age, others notwithstanding could not attain without a miracle.

Chap. 22.

Of the Oestridge.

The common opinion of the Oestridge, Struthiocamelus   † or Sparrow-Camell, conceives that it digesteth Iron; and this is confirmed by the affirmations of many; beside swarmes of others, Rhodiginus in his prelections taketh it for granted, Johannes Langius in his Epistles pleadeth experiment for it;

the common picture also confirmeth it, which usually describeth this animall with an horshoe in its mouth. Notwith- [23]
standing upon enquiry we finde it very questionable, and the
negative seems most reasonably entertained; whose verity
indeed we doe the rather desire, because hereby we shall relieve our ignorance of one occult quality; for in the list
thereof it is accounted, and in that notion imperiously obtruded upon us. For my own part, although I have had the
sight of this animall, I have not had the opportunity of its [24]
experiment, but have received great occasions of doubt,
from learned discoursers thereon.

For Aristotle and Oppianus who have particularly treated
hereof are silent in this singularity; either omitting it as dubious, or as the Comment saith, rejecting it as fabulous. Pliny
speaketh generally, affirming only, the digestion is wonderfull in this animall; Aelian delivereth, that it digesteth stones,
without any mention of Iron; Leo Africanus, who lived in
those Countries wherein they most abound, speaketh dimin-
utively, and but half way into this assertion; *Surdum ac sim-* [25]
plex animal est, quicquid invenit, absque delectu, usque ad
ferrum devorat: Fernelius in his second book *De abditis* [26]
rerum causis, extenuates it, and Riolanus in his Comment
thereof positively denies it. Some have experimentally refuted it, as Albertus Magnus; and most plainly Ulysses
Aldrovandus, whose words are these; *Ego ferri frusta de-*
vorare, dum Tridenti essem, observavi, sed quae incocta
rursus excerneret, that is, at my being at Trent, I observed
the Oestridge to swallow Iron, but yet to exclude it undi-
gested again.

Now beside experiment, it is in vain to attempt against it
by Philosophicall argument, it being an occult quality, which
contemns the law of Reason, and defends it self by admitting
no reason at all. As for its possibility we shall not at present
dispute; nor will we affirm that Iron ingested, receiveth in
the stomack of the Oestridge no alteration at all; but if any
such there be, we suspect this effect rather from some way
of corrosion, then any of digestion; not any liquid reduction
or tendance to chilification by the power of naturall heat, but
rather some attrition from an acide and vitriolous humidity

in the stomack, which may absterse and shave the scorious
parts thereof. So rusty Iron crammed down the throat of a
Cock, will become terse and clear again in its gizard: So the
Counter which according to the relation of *Amatus*, remained a whole year in the body of a youth, and came out
much consumed at last, might suffer this diminution, rather
from sharp and acide humours, then the strength of naturall
heat, as he supposeth. So silver swallowed and retained some
time in the body, will turn black, as if it had been dipped in
Aqua fortis, or some corrosive water; but Lead will remain
unaltered; for that mettall containeth in it a sweet salt or
sugar, whereby it resisteth ordinary corrosion, and will not
easily dissolve even in *Aqua fortis*. So when for medicall
uses, we take down the filings of Iron or Steel, we must not
conceive it passeth unaltered from us; for though the grosser
parts be excluded again, yet are the dissoluble parts ex-
tracted, whereby it becomes effectuall in deopilations; and
therefore for speedier operation we make extinctions, in-
fusions, and the like, whereby we extract the salt and active
parts of the medicine; which being in solution, more easily
enter the veins. And this is that the Chymists mainly drive at
in the attempt of their *Aurum Potabile;* that is, to reduce that
indigestible substance into such a form as may not be ejected
by siege, but enter the cavities, and lesse accessible parts of
the body, without corrosion.

The ground of this conceit is its swallowing down fragments of Iron, which men observing, by a froward illation,
have therefore conceived it digesteth them; which is an inference not to be admitted, as being a fallacy of the consequent, that is, concluding a position of the consequent, from
the position of the antecedent. For many things are swallowed by animals, rather for condiment, gust or medica-
ment, then any substantiall nutriment. So Poultrey, and
especially the Turkey, doe of themselves take down stones;
and we have found at one time in the gizard of a Turkey no
lesse then seven hundred. Now these rather concurre unto   27
digestion, then are themselves digested; for we have found
them also in the guts and excrements; but their descent is
very slow, for we have given them stones and small pieces   †

of iron, which eighteen daies after we have found remaining in the gizard. And therefore the experiment of Langius
and others might be mistaken, whilst after the taking they
expected it should come down within a day or two after.
Thus also we swallow cherry-stones, but void them uncon-
cocted, and we usually say they preserve us from surfet; for
being hard bodies they conceive a strong and durable heat in
the stomack, and so prevent the crudities of their fruit; And
upon the like reason do culinary operators observe, that flesh
boils best, when the bones are boiled with it. Thus dogs
will eat grasse, which they digest not: Thus Camels to make
the water sapid, doe raise the mud with their feet: thus
horses will knabble at wals, Pigeons delight in salt stones,
Rats will gnaw Iron, and Aristotle saith the Elephant swal-
loweth stones. And thus may also the Oestridge swallow
Iron; not as his proper aliment, but for the ends above expressed, and even as we observe the like in other animals.

[And whether these fragments of iron and hard substances †
swallowed by the Oestridge, have not also that use in their
stomacks, which they have in other birds; that is, in some
way to supply the use of teeth, by commolition, grinding
and compression of their proper aliment, upon the action of
the strongly conformed muscles of the stomack; as the
honor'd Dr. *Harvey* discourseth, may also be considered.]

What effect therefore may be expected from the stomack
of an Oestridge by application alone to further digestion in
ours, beside the experimentall refute of Galen, we referre it
unto considerations above alledged; Or whether there be
any more credit to be given unto the medicine of Aelian,
who affirms the stones they swallow have a peculiar vertue
for the eyes, then that of Hermolaus and Pliny drawn from
the urine of this animall; let them determine who can swallow so strange a transmission of qualities, or beleeve that any
Bird or flying animall doth urine beside the Bat.

That therefore an Oestridge will swallow or take down †
iron, is easily to be granted: that oftentimes they passe entire
away, if we admit of ocular testimony, not to be denied; and
though some experiment may also plead, that sometimes
they are so altered, as not to be found or excluded in any

discernable parcels: yet whether this be not effected by some way of corrosion, from sharp and dissolving humidities, rather then any proper digestion, chilifactive mutation, or alimentall conversion, is with good reason doubted.

CHAP. 27.   †
OF SOME OTHERS.

That a Chicken is formed out of the yelk of the egge, with   28,†
some ancient Philosophers the people still opinion. Whether it be not rather the nutriment of the Pullet, may also be considered: Since umbilicall vessels are carried unto it: Since much of the yelk remaineth after the Chicken is formed: Since in a Chicken newly hatched, the stomack is tincted yellow, and the belly full of yelk, which is drawn in at the navell or umbilicall vessels toward the vent, as may be discerned in Chickens, within a day or two before exclusion.

Whether the Chicken be made out of the white, or that be not also its aliment, is likewise very questionable: Since an umbilicall vessell is derived unto it: Since after the for-   †
mation and perfect shape of the Chicken, much of the white remaineth.

Whether it be not made out of the grando, gallature, germe or tredde of the egge, as Aquapendente and stricter   †
enquiry informeth us, doth seem of lesser doubt: for at the   †
blunter end it is not discovered after the Chicken is formed; by this also the yelk and white are continued, whereby it may conveniently receive its nutriment from them both.

Now that from such slender materials, nature should effect this production, it is no more then is observed in other animals, and even in grains and kernels, the greatest part is but the nutriment of that generative particle, so disproportionable unto it.

A greater difficulty in the doctrine of egges, is, how the sperm of the Cock improlificates and makes the ovall conception fruitfull, or how it attaineth unto every egge, since the vitellary or place of the yelk is very high: Since the ovary or part where the white involveth it, is in the second region of the matrix, which is somewhat long and inverted: Since also a Cock will in one day fertilitate the whole racemation or cluster of egges, which are not excluded in many weeks after.

[But these at last, and how in the *Cicatricula* or little pale † circle formation first beginning, how the *Grando* or tredle are but the poles and establishing particles of the tender membrans, firmly conserving the floating parts in their proper places, with many other observables, that occular Philosopher, and singular discloser of truth, Dr. Harvey, hath discov- 29 ered, in that excellent discourse of Generation; so strongly erected upon the two great pillars of truth, experience and solid reason.]

That the sex is discernable from the figure of egges, or that Cocks or Hens proceed from long or round ones, as many contend, experiment will easily frustrate.

The Aegyptians observed a better way to hatch their egges in ovens, then the Babylonians to roast them at the bottom of a sling, by swinging them round about, till heat from motion had concocted them; for that confuseth all parts without any such effect.

Though slight distinction be made between boiled and roasted egges, yet is there no slender difference, for the one is much drier then the other: the egge expiring lesse in the elixation or boiling; whereas in the assation or roasting, it will sometimes abate a dragme, that is threescore grains in weight. So a new laid egge will not so easily be boiled hard, because it contains a greater stock of humid parts; which must be evaporated, before the heat can bring the inexhalable parts into consistence.

Why the Hen hatcheth not the egge in her belly, or maketh not at least some rudiment thereof within her self, by the naturall heat of inward parts, since the same is performed by incubation from an outward warmth after? Why the egge is thinner at one extream? Why there is some cavity or emptinesse at the blunter end? Why we open them at that part? Why there is also a little grando or tred at the lesser † end? Why the greater end is first excluded? [Why some

egges are all red, as the Kestrils; some only red at one end,   †
as those of the Kites and Buzzards?] Why some egges are
not ovall but round, as those of fishes &c. are problemes,
whose decisions would too much enlarge this discourse.

[Remainder of chapter on various subjects.]

THE FOURTH BOOK:

OF MANY POPULAR AND RECEIVED TENENTS CONCERNING MAN,
WHICH EXAMINED, PROVE EITHER FALSE OR DUBIOUS.

CHAP. 1.
OF THE ERECTNESSE OF MAN.

That onely Man hath an erect figure, and for to behold
and look up toward heaven, according to that of the Poet,   1

> *Pronaque cum spectant animalia caetera terram,*
> *Os homini sublime dedit, caelumque tueri*
> *Jussit, et erectos ad sydera tollere vultus,*

is a double assertion, whose first part may be true; if we
take erectnesse strictly, and so as Galen hath defined it; for
they only, saith he, have an erect figure, whose spine and
thighbone are carried in right lines; and so indeed of any we
yet know, Man only is erect. For the thighes of other animals doe stand at angles with their spine, and have rectangular positions in birds, and perfect Quadrupeds; nor doth the
Frog, though stretched out, or swimming, attain the rectitude
of man, or carry its thigh without all angularity. And thus is
it also true that man only sitteth, if we define sitting to be a
firmation of the body upon the Ischias: wherein if the position be just and naturall, the thigh-bone lieth at right angles
to the spine, and the leg bone or tibia to the thigh. For others
when they seem to sit, as Dogs, Cats, or Lions, doe make
unto their spine acute angles with their thigh, and acute to
the thigh with their shank. Thus is it likewise true, what

Aristotle alledgeth in that Problem*; why man alone suffereth pollutions in the night? because man only lieth upon
his back; if we define not the same by every supine position, but when the spine is in rectitude with the thigh, and
both with the armes lie parallell to the Horizon; so that a line
through their navel will passe through the Zenith and centre
of the earth; and so cannot other animals lie upon their
backs; for though the spine lie parallell with the Horizon,
yet will their legs incline, and lie at angles unto it. And upon
these three divers positions in man, wherein the spine can
only be at right lines with the thigh, arise those remarkable
postures, prone, supine and erect; which are but differenced
in situation or in angular postures upon the back, the belly
and the feet.

But if erectnesse be popularly taken, and as it is largely
opposed unto pronenesse, or the posture of animals looking
downwards, carrying their venters or opposite part to the
spine directly towards the earth, it may admit of question. †
For though in Serpents and Lizards we may truly allow a
pronenesse, yet Galen acknowledgeth that perfect Quadrupeds, as Horses, Oxen and Camels, are but partly prone,
and have some part of erectnesse. And birds or flying animals are so farre from this kinde of pronenesse, that they
are almost erect; advancing the head and breast in their progression, and only prone in the act of volitation. And if
that be true which is delivered of the Penguin or *Anser
Magellanicus*,* often described in Maps about those Straits,
that they go erect like men, and with their breast and belly
doe make one line perpendicular unto the axis of the earth;
it will make up the exact erectnesse of man. Nor will that
insect come very short which we have often beheld, that is,
one kinde of Locust which stands not prone, or a little inclining upward, but in a large erectnesse; elevating alwaies
the two fore legs, and sustaining it self in the middle of the
other four; by Zoographers* called *mantis,* and by the common people of Provence, *Prega Dio,* the Prophet and praying †

---

* ἐξονειρωκτικός
* Observe also the *Urias Bellonii* and *Mergus major.*   †
* Describers of Animals.   †

Locust; as being generally found in the posture of supplication, or such as resembleth ours, when we lift up our hands to heaven.

As for the end of this erection, to look up toward heaven; though confirmed by severall testimonies, and the Greek Etymology of man, it is not so readily to be admitted; and as a popular and vain conceit was anciently rejected by Galen; who in his third *De usu partium*, determines, that man is erect because he was made with hands, and was therewith to exercise all Arts, which in any other figure he could not have performed; as he excellently declareth in that place, where he also proves that man could have been made neither Quadruped nor Centaur.

And for the accomplishment of this intention, that is, to †
look up and behold the heavens, man hath a notable disadvantage in the eyelid; whereof the upper is farre greater then the lower, which abridgeth the sight upwards; contrary to those of birds, who herein have the advantage of man: Insomuch that the learned Plempius* is bold to affirm that if he had had the formation of the eyelids, he would have contrived them quite otherwise.

The ground and occasion of this conceit was a literall apprehension of a figurative expression in Plato, as Galen thus †
delivers; To opinion that man is erect to look up and behold the heavens, is a conceit only fit for those that never saw the fish Uranoscopus, that is, the Beholder of heaven; which hath its eyes so placed, that it lookes up directly to heaven; which man doth not, except he recline, or bend his head backward: and thus to look up to heaven, agreeth not only unto Men, but Asses; to omit birds with long necks, which look not only upwards, but round about at pleasure; and therefore men of this opinion understood not Plato when he said that man doth *Sursum aspicere;* for thereby was not meant to gape or look upward with the eye, but to have his thoughts sublime; and not only to behold, but speculate their nature, with the eye of the understanding.

Now although Galen in this place makes instance but in

* Plemp. *Ophthalmographia.*

one, yet are there other fishes, whose eies regard the heavens, as Plane, and cartilagineous fishes, as pectinals, or such as have their bones made laterally like a comb; for † when they apply themselves to sleep or rest upon the white side, their eies on the other side look upward toward heaven. For birds, they generally carry their heads erectly like man, and have advantage in their upper eyelid; and † many that have long necks, and bear their heads somewhat backward, behold farre more of the heavens, and seem to look above the aequinoxiall circle; and so also in many Quadrupeds, although their progression be partly prone, yet is the sight of their eye direct, not respecting the earth but heaven; and makes an higher arch of altitude then our own. The position of a Frogge with his head above water exceedeth these; for therein he seemes to behold a large part of the heavens, and the acies of his eye to ascend as high as the Tropick; but he that hath beheld the posture of a Bittor, will not deny that it beholds almost the very Zenith.

THE FIFTH BOOK:

OF MANY THINGS QUESTIONABLE AS THEY ARE COMMONLY DESCRIBED IN PICTURES.

CHAP. 1.
OF THE PICTURE OF THE PELECAN.

And first in every place we meet with the picture of the Pelecan, opening her breast with her bill, and feeding her young ones with the bloud distilling from her. Thus is it set forth not only in common signes, but in the Crest and Schucheon of many Noble families; hath been asserted by many holy Writers, and was an Hieroglyphick of piety and pity among the Aegyptians; on which consideration, they spared them at their tables.

Notwithstanding upon enquiry we finde no mention hereof in Ancient Zoographers, and such as have particularly dis- †

coursed upon Animals, as Aristotle, Aelian, Pliny, Solinus and many more; who seldome forget proprieties of such a nature, and have been very punctuall in lesse considerable Records. Some ground hereof I confesse we may allow, nor need we deny a remarkable affection in Pelecans toward their young; for Aelian discoursing of Storks, and their affection toward their brood, whom they instruct to fly, and unto whom they re-deliver up the provision of their bellies, concludeth at last, that Herons and Pelecans doe the like.

As for the testimonies of Ancient Fathers, and Ecclesiasticall writers, we may more safely conceive therein some Emblematicall then any reall Story: so doth Eucherius confesse it to be the Embleme of Christ; and we are unwilling literally to receive that account of Jerome, that perceiving her young ones destroied by Serpents, she openeth her side with her bill, by the bloud whereof they revive and return unto life again. By which relation they might indeed illustrate the destruction of man by the old Serpent, and his restorement by the bloud of Christ; and in this sense we shall not dispute the like relations of Austine, Isidore, Albertus, and many more; and under an Emblematicall intention, we accept it in coat-armour.

As for the Hieroglyphick of the Aegyptians, they erected the same upon another consideration, which was parentall †
affection; manifested in the protection of her young ones, when her nest was set on fire. For as for letting out her bloud, it was not the assertion of the Egyptians, but seems translated unto the Pelecan from the Vulture, as Pierius hath most plainly delivered. *Sed quod Pelicanum (ut etiam aliis ple-* 1
risque persuasum est) rostro pectus dissecantem pingunt, ita
ut suo sanguine filios alat, ab Aegyptiorum historia valde
alienum est, illi enim vulturem tantum id facere tradiderunt.

And lastly, As concerning the picture, if naturally examined, and not Hieroglyphically conceived, it containeth many improprieties, disagreeing almost in all things from the true and proper description. For first, whereas it is commonly set forth green or yellow, in its proper colour it is inclining to white; excepting the extremities or tops of the wing feathers, which are black. It is described in the bignesse of a Hen, † whereas it approacheth and sometimes exceedeth the magnitude of a Swan. It is commonly painted with a short bill; whereas that of the Pelecan attaineth sometimes the length of two spans. The bill is made acute or pointed at the end; whereas it is flat and broad, and somewhat inverted at the extream. It is described like fissipedes, or birds which have their feet or claws divided; whereas it is palmipedous, or fin-footed like Swans and Geese; according to the Method of nature in latirostrous or flat-bild birds; which being generally swimmers, the organ is wisely contriv'd unto the action, and they are framed with fins or oares upon their feet; and therefore they neither light, nor build on trees, if we except Cormorants, who make their nests like Herons. Lastly, There is one part omitted more remarkable then any other, that is the chowle or crop adhering unto the lower side of the bill, and so descending by the throat; a bagge or sachell very observable, and of capacity almost beyond credit; which notwithstanding, this animall could not want; for therein it receiveth † Oysters, Cochles, Scollops, and other testaceous animals, which being not able to break, it retains them untill they open, and vomiting them up, takes out the meat contained. This is that part preserved for a rarity, and wherein (as Sanctius delivers) in one dissected, a Negro childe was found. 2

[A possibility there may be of opening and bleeding their † breast; for this may be done by the uncous and pointed extremity of their bill; and some probability also that they sometimes do it, for their own relief, though not for their young ones; that is by nibling and biting themselves on the itching part of their breast, upon fullness or acrimony of blood. And the same may be better made out, if (as some relate) their feathers on that part are sometimes observed to be red and tincted with blood.]

CHAP. 5.
OF THE PICTURE OF ADAM AND EVE WITH NAVELS.

Another mistake there may be in the Picture of our first Parents, who after the manner of their posterity are both de-

lineated with a Navell. And this is observable not only in ordinary and stained peeces, but in the Authentick draughts of
Urbin, Angelo and others. Which notwithstanding cannot be   3
allowed, except we impute that unto the first cause, which
we impose not on the second; or what we deny unto nature,
we impute unto Naturity it self; that is, that in the first and
most accomplished peece, the Creator affected superfluities,
or ordained parts without all use or office.

For the use of the Navell is to continue the infant unto the
Mother, and by the vessels thereof to convey its aliment and
sustentation. The vessels whereof it consisteth, are the umbilicall vein, which is a branch of the Porta, and implanted in
the liver of the Infant; two Arteries likewise arising from the
Iliacall branches, by which the Infant receiveth the purer portion of bloud and spirits from the mother; and lastly, the
Urachos or ligamentall passage derived from the bottome of
the bladder, whereby it dischargeth the waterish and urinary
part of its aliment. Now upon the birth, when the Infant for-
saketh the wombe, although it dilacerate, and break the involving membranes, yet doe these vessels hold, and by the
mediation thereof the Infant is connected unto the wombe,
not only before, but a while also after the birth. These therefore the midwife cutteth off, contriving them into a knot close
unto the body of the Infant; from whence ensueth that tor-
tuosity or complicated nodosity we usually call the Navell;
occasioned by the colligation of vessels before mentioned.
Now the Navell being a part, not precedent, but subsequent   †
unto generation, nativity or parturition, it cannot be well
imagined at the creation or extraordinary formation of Adam,
who immediately issued from the Artifice of God; nor also
that of Eve; who was not solemnly begotten, but suddenly   4
framed, and anomalously proceeded from Adam.

And if we be led into conclusions that Adam had also this
part, because we behold the same in our selves, the inference
is not reasonable; for if we conceive the way of his formation,
or of the first animals, did carry in all points a strict conformity unto succeeding productions, we might fall into imaginations that Adam was made without Teeth; or that he ran
through those notable alterations in the vessels of the heart,

which the Infant suffereth after birth: we need not dispute whether the egge or Bird were first; and might conceive that Dogges were created blinde, because we observe they are littered so with us. Which to affirm, is to confound, at least to regulate creation unto generation, the first Acts of God unto the second of Nature, which were determined in that generall indulgence, Encrease and multiply, produce or propagate each other; that is, not answerably in all points, but in a prolonged method according to seminall progression. For the formation of things at first was different from their generation after; and although it had nothing to precede it, was aptly contrived for that which should succeed it. And therefore though Adam were framed without this part, as having no other wombe then that of his proper principles, yet was not his posterity without the same: for the seminality of his fabrick contained the power thereof; and was endued with the science of those parts whose predestinations upon succession it did accomplish.

All the Navell therefore and conjunctive part we can suppose in Adam, was his dependency on his Maker, and the connexion he must needs have unto heaven, who was the Sonne of God. For holding no dependence on any preceding efficient but God; in the act of his production there may be conceived some connexion, and Adam to have been in a momentall Navell with his Maker. And although from his carnality and corporall existence, the conjunction seemeth no nearer then of causality and effect; yet in his immortall and diviner part he seemed to hold a nearer coherence, and an umbilicality even with God himself. And so indeed although the propriety of this part be found but in some animals, and many species there are which have no Navell at all; yet is there one link and common connexion, one generall ligament, and necessary obligation of all whatever unto God. Whereby although they act themselves at distance, and seem to be at loose, yet doe they hold a continuity with their Maker. Which catenation or conserving union when ever his pleasure shall divide, let goe, or separate, they shall fall from their existence, essence, and operations; in brief, they must retire unto their primitive nothing, and shrink into their Chaos again.

They who hold the egge was before the Bird, prevent this †,⁵
doubt in many other animals, which also extendeth unto
them; for Birds are nourished by umbilicall vessels, and the
Navell is manifest sometimes a day or two after exclusion;
the same is probable in all oviparous exclusions, if the lesser
part of egges must serve for the formation, the greater part
for nutriment. The same is made out in the egges of Snakes;
and is not improbable in the generation of Porwiggles or Tadpoles; and may be also true in some vermiparous exclusions;
although (as we have observed the daily progresse thereof)
the whole Maggot is little enough to make a Flye, without
any part remaining.

CHAP. 22.   †

OF SOME OTHERS.

1. That temperamentall dignotions, and conjecture of prevalent humours, may be collected from spots in our nails, we
are not averse to concede. But yet not ready to admit sundry
divinations, vulgarly raised upon them. Nor doe we observe it
verified in others, what Cardan° discovered as a property in
himself: to have found therein some signes of most events
that ever happened unto him. Or that there is much considerable in that doctrine of Cheiromancy, that spots in the top of °
the nailes doe signifie things past; in the middle, things present; and at the bottome, events to come. That white specks
presage our felicity, blew ones our misfortunes. That those in
the nail of the thumb have significations of honour, those in
the forefinger of riches, and so respectively in other fingers,
(according to Planeticall relations, from whence they receive
their names) as Tricassus hath taken up, and Picciolus° well
rejecteth.

We shall not proceed to querie, what truth there is in Palmistrie, or divination from those lines in our hands, of high
denomination. Although if any thing be therein, it seems not
confinable unto man; but other creatures are also consider-

° *De varietate rerum.*
° *De inspectione manus.* [72]

able: as is the forefoot of the Moll, and especially of the Monkey; wherein we have observed the table line, that of life, and of the liver.

2. That Children committed unto the school of Nature, without institution would naturally speak the primitive language of the world, was the opinion of ancient heathens, and continued since by Christians; who will have it our Hebrew tongue, as being the language of Adam. That this were true were much to be desired, not only for the easie attainment of that usefull tongue, but to determine the true and primitive Hebrew. For whether the present Hebrew be the unconfounded language of Babel, and that which remaining in Heber was continued by Abraham and his posterity; or rather the language of Phaenicia and Canaan, wherein he lived, some learned men I perceive doe yet remain unsatisfied. Although I confesse probability stands fairest for the former; nor are they without all reason, who think that at the confusion of tongues, there was no constitution of a new speech in every family, but a variation and permutation of the old; out of one common language raising severall dialects; the primitive tongue remaining still entire. Which they who retained might make a shift to understand most of the rest. By vertue whereof in those primitive times and greener confusions, Abraham of the family of Heber was able to converse with the Chaldeans, to understand Mesopotamians, Chananites, Philistins and Aegyptians; whose severall dialects he could reduce unto the originall and primitive tongue, and so be able to understand them.

3. Though uselesse unto us and rather of molestation, we commonly refrain from killing Swallows, and esteem it unlucky to destroy them: whether herein there be not a pagan relique, we have some reason to doubt. For we reade in Aelian,* that these birds were sacred unto the Penates or houshold gods of the ancients, and therefore were preserved. The same they also honoured as the nuncio's of the spring; and we finde [in Athenaeus] the Rhodians had a solemn song to welcome in the Swallow.

* The same is extant in the 8th of Athenaeus.

4. That Candles and lights burn dimme and blew at the apparition of spirits, may be true, if the ambient ayre be full of sulphurious spirits, as it happeneth oft times in mines; where damps and acide exhalations are able to extinguish them. And may be also verified, when spirits doe make themselves visible by bodies of such effluviums. But of lower consideration is the common foretelling of strangers, from the fungous parcells about the wicks of Candles: which only sig-   †
nifieth a moist and pluvious ayre about them, hindering the avolation of the light and favillous particles: whereupon they are forced to settle upon the snast.

5. Though Corall doth properly preserve and fasten the Teeth in men, yet is it used in children to make an easier passage for them: and for that intent is worn about their necks. But whether this custome were not superstitiously founded, as presumed an amulet or defensative against fascination, is not beyond all doubt. For the same is delivered by Pliny.*
Aruspices religiosum Coralli gestamen amoliendis periculis   8
arbitrantur; et surculi infantiae alligati, tutelam habere creduntur.

6. A strange kinde of exploration and peculiar way of Rhabdomancy is that which is used in minerall discoveries; that is, with a forked hazell, commonly called Moses his rod, which freely held forth, will stirre and play if any mine be under it. And though many there are who have attempted to make it good, yet untill better information, we are of opinion with Agricola,* that in it self it is a fruitlesse exploration, strongly senting of Pagan derivation, and the *virgula Divina,* proverbially magnified of old. The ground whereof were the Magicall rods in Poets; that of Pallas in Homer, that of Mercury that charmed Argus, and that of Circe which transformed the followers of Ulysses; too boldly usurping the name of Moses rod;   9
from which notwithstanding, and that of Aaron, were probably occasioned the fables of all the rest. For that of Moses must needs be famous unto the Aegyptians; and that of Aaron unto many other nations, as being preserved in the Arke, untill the destruction of the Temple built by Solomon.

* *Lib.* 32.
* *De re metallica. lib.* 2.

7. A practise there is among us to determine doubtfull matters, by the opening of a book, and letting fall a staff; which notwithstanding are ancient fragments of Pagan divinations. The first an imitation of *Sortes Homericae,* or *Virgilianae,* drawing determinations from verses casually occurring. The same was practised by Severus, who entertained ominous hopes of the Empire, from that verse in Virgil, *Tu regere imperio populos Romane memento;* and Gordianus who reigned but few daies was discouraged by another, that is, *Ostendunt terris hunc tantum fata nec ultra esse sinunt.* Nor was this only performed in Heathen Authours, but upon the sacred text of Scripture, as Gregorius Turonensis hath left some account; and as the practise of the Emperor Heraclius, before his Expedition into Asia minor, is delivered by Cedrenus.

As for the Divination or decision from the staffe, it is an Auguriall relique, and the practise thereof is accused by God himself;* My people ask counsel of their stocks, and their staffe declareth unto them. Of this kinde of Rhabdomancy was that practised by Nabuchadonosor in that Caldean miscellany, delivered by Ezekiel;* The King of Babylon stood at the parting of the way, at the head of the two waies to use divination, he made his arrowes bright, he consulted with Images, he looked in the Liver; at the right hand were the divinations of Jerusalem. That is, as Estius expoundeth it, the left way leading unto Rabbah the chief city of the Ammonites, and the right unto Jerusalem, he consulted Idols and entrails, he threw up a bundle of Arrows to see which way they would light; and falling on the right hand he marched towards Jerusalem. A like way of Belomancy or Divination by Arrowes hath been in request with Scythians, Alanes, Germans, with the Africans and Turks of Algier. But of another nature was that which was practised by Elisha,* when by an Arrow shot from an Eastern window, he presignified the destruction of Syria; or when according unto the three stroaks of Joash, with an Arrow upon the ground, he foretold the number of his victories. For thereby the Spirit of God particu-

10

11

* Hosea 4.
* Exekiel 24.
* 2 King. 13–15.

lar'd the same, and determined the stroaks of the King unto
three, which the hopes of the Prophet expected in twice that
number.

We are unwilling to enlarge concerning many other; only   †
referring unto Christian considerations, what naturall effects
can reasonably be expected, when to prevent the Ephialtes
or night-Mare we hang up an hollow stone in our stables;
when for amulets against Agues we use the chips of Gallowes
and places of Execution. When for Warts we rub our hands
before the Moon, or commit any maculated part unto the
touch of the dead. Swarms hereof our learned Selden and   12
criticall Philologers might illustrate, whose abler performances our adventures doe but sollicite; mean while I hope
they will plausibly receive our attempts, or candidly correct
our misconjectures.

8. We cannot omit to observe, the tenacity of ancient customes, in the nominall observation of the severall daies of the
week, according to Gentile and Pagan appellations*: for the
Originall is very high, and as old as the ancient Aegyptians,
who named the same according to the seven Planets, the admired Starres of heaven, and reputed deities among them.
Unto every one assigning a severall day; not according to
their celestiall order, or as they are disposed in heaven; but
after a diatesseron or musicall fourth. For beginning Saturday
with Saturn the supremest Planet, they accounted by Jupiter
and Mars unto Sol, making Sunday. From Sol in like manner
by Venus and Mercurie unto Luna, making Munday; and so
through all the rest. And the same order they confirmed by
numbring the houres of the day unto twenty four, according
to the naturall order of the Planets. For beginning to account
from Saturn, Jupiter, Mars, and so about unto twenty four,
the next day will fall unto Sōl; whence accounting twenty
four, the next will happen unto Luna, making Munday. And
so with the rest, according to the account and order observed
still among us.

The Jews themselves in their Astrologicall considerations
concerning Nativities and Planetary hours, observe the same
order, upon as witty foundations. Because by an equall inter-

* *Dion Cassii. lib.* 37.

vall they make seven triangles, the bases whereof are the seven sides of a septilaterall figure, described within a circle. That is, If a figure of seven sides be described in a circle, and at the angles thereof the names of the Planets be placed, in their naturall order on it: if we begin with Saturn, and successively draw lines from angle to angle untill seven equicrurall triangles be described, whose bases are the seven sides of the septilaterall figure; the triangles will be made by this 13 order*. The first being made by Saturn, Sol and Luna, that is Saturday, Sunday and Munday; and so the rest in the order still retained.

But thus much is observable, that however in celestiall considerations they embraced the received order of the Planets, yet did they not retain either characters or names in common use amongst us; but declining humane denominations, they assigned them names from some remarkable qualities, as is very observable in their red and splendent Planets, that is of Mars and Venus.* But the change of their names disparaged not the consideration of their natures; nor did they thereby reject all memory of these remarkable Starres which God himself admitted in his Tabernacle, if conjecture will hold concerning the golden Candlestick; whose shaft resembled the Sunne, and six branches the Planets about it.

> *Disce, sed ira cadat naso, rugosaque sanna,*
> *Dum veteres avias tibi de pulmone revello.*   14

THE SIXTH BOOK

Chap. 5.

A Digression of the wisdome of God in the site and motion of the Sunne.

Having thus beheld the ignorance of man in some things, his errour and blindenesse in others, that is, in the measure of duration both of years and seasons, let us a while admire

* *Cujus icon apud doct. Gaffarel. cap. 11. Et Fabrit. Paduanium.*   †
* *Maadim. Nogab.*

the Wisdome of God in this distinguisher of times, and visible
Deity (as some have termed it) the Sunne; which though
some from its glory adore, and all for its benefits admire, we
shall advance from other considerations; and such as illustrate the artifice of its Maker. Nor do we think we can excuse
the duty of our knowledge, if we only bestow the flourish of
Poetry hereon, or those commendatory conceits which popularly set forth the eminency of this creature; except we
ascend unto subtiler considerations, and such as rightly understood, convincingly declare the wisedom of the Creator.   †
Which since a Spanish Physitian* hath begun, we will enlarge
with our deductions; and this we shall endeavour from two
considerations; its proper situation, and wisely ordered motion.

And first, we cannot passe over his providence in that it
moveth at all; for had it stood still, and were it fixed like the
earth, there had been then no distinction of times, either of
day or year, of Spring, of Autumn, of Summer, or of Winter;
for these seasons are defined by the motions of the Sunne;
when that approacheth nearest our Zenith or verticall point,   †
we call it Summer, when furthest off, Winter, when in the
middle spaces, Spring or Autumn; whereas remaining in one
place these distinctions had ceased, and consequently the
generation of all things depending on their vicissitudes; making in one hemisphere a perpetuall Summer, in the other a
deplorable and comfortlesse Winter. And thus had it also
been continuall day unto some, and perpetuall night unto
others; for the day is defined by the abode of the Sun above
the Horizon, and the night by its continuance below; so
should we have needed another Sunne, one to illustrate our
Hemisphere, a second to enlighten the other; which incon-   †
venience will ensue, in what site soever we place it, whether
in the poles, or the Aequator, or between them both; no
sphericall body of what bignesse soever illuminating the
whole sphere of another, although it illuminate something
more then half of a lesser, according unto the doctrine of the
Opticks.

* Valesius *de Philos. Sacr.*   †

His wisedom is again discernable, not only in that it moveth at all, and in its bare motion, but wonderfull in contriving the line of revolution; which from his artifice is so effected, that by a vicissitude in one body and light, it sufficeth the whole earth, affording thereby a possible or pleasurable habitation in every part thereof; and that is the line Ecliptick; all which to effect by any other circle it had been impossible. For first, if we imagine the Sunne to make his course out of the Ecliptick, and upon a line without any obliquity, let it be conceived within that Circle, that is, either on the Aequator, or else on either side (for if we should place it either in the Meridian or Colures, beside the subversion of its course from East to West, there would ensue the like incommodities.) Now if we conceive the Sun to move between the obliquity of this Ecliptick in a line upon one side of the Aequator, then would the Sunne be visible but unto one pole, that is, the same which was nearest unto it. So that unto the one it would be perpetuall day, unto the other perpetuall night; the one would be oppressed with constant heat, the other with insufferable cold; and so the defect of alternation would utterly impugn the generation of all things, which naturally require a vicissitude of heat to their production, and no lesse to their encrease and conservation.

But if we concaive it to move in the Aequator; first, unto a parallel sphere, or such as have the pole for their Zenith, it would have made neither perfect day nor night. For being in the Aequator it would intersect their Horizon, and be half above and half beneath it, or rather it would have made perpetuall night to both: for though in regard of the rationall Horizon, which bissecteth the Globe into equall parts, the Sunne in the Aequator would intersect the Horizon: yet in respect of the sensible Horizon (which is defined by the eye) the Sunne would be visible unto neither, For if as ocular witnesses report, and some do also write, by reason of the convexity of the Earth the eye of man under the Aequator cannot discover both the poles, neither would the eye under the poles discover the Sunne in the Aequator. Thus would there nothing fructifie either near or under them, the Sun being Horizontall to the poles, and of no considerable altitude unto parts a reasonable distance from them. Again, unto a right sphere, or such as dwell under the Aequator, although it made a difference in day and night, yet would it not make any distinction of seasons: for unto them it would be constant Summer, it being alwaies verticall, and never deflecting from them: So had there been no fructification at all, and the Countries subjected would be as unhabitable, as indeed antiquity conceived them.

Lastly, It moving thus upon the Aequator, unto what position soever, although it had made a day, yet could it have made no year; for it could not have had those two motions now ascribed unto it, that is, from East to West, whereby it makes the day, and likewise from West to East, whereby the year is computed. For according to [received] Astronomy,   †
the poles of the Aequator are the same with those of the *Primum Mobile*. Now it is impossible that on the same circle, having the same poles, both these motions from opposite terms, should be at the same time performed; all which is salved, if we allow the Sunne an obliquity in his annuall motion, and conceive him to move upon the poles of the Zodiack, distant from these of the world 23 degrees and a half. Thus may we discern the necessity of its obliquity, and how inconvenient its motion had been upon a circle parallell to the Aequator, or upon the Aequator it self.

Now with what providence this obliquity is determined, we shall perceive upon the ensuing inconveniences from any deviation. For first, if its obliquity had been lesse (as in stead of twenty three degrees, twelve or the half thereof) the vicissitude of seasons appointed for the generation of all things would surely have been too short; for different seasons would have hudled upon each other, and unto some it had not been much better then if it had moved on the Aequator. But had the obliquity been greater then now it is, as double or of 40 degrees; severall parts of the earth had not been able to endure the disproportionable differences of seasons, occasioned by the great recesse and distance of the Sunne; for unto some habitations the Summer would have been extream hot, and the Winter extream cold; likewise the Summer temperate unto some, but excessive and in extremity unto others, as unto those who should dwell under the Tropick of Cancer, as then would do some part of Spain, or ten degrees beyond, as Germany, and some part of England; who would have Summers as now the Moors of Africa; for the Sun would sometime be verticall unto them: but they would have Winters like those beyond the Artick Circle, for in that season the Sun would be removed above 80 degrees from them. Again, it would be temperate to some habitations in the Summer, but very extream in the Winter: temperate to those in two or three degrees beyond the Artick Circle, as now it is unto us; for they would be equidistant from that Tropick, even as we are from this at present; but the Winter would be extreme, the Sunne being removed above an hundred degrees, and so consequently would not be visible in their Horizon; no position of sphere discovering any Starre distant above 90 degrees, which is the distance of every Zenith from the Horizon. And thus if the obliquity of this Circle had been lesse, the vicissitude of seasons had been so small as not to be distinguished; if greater, so large and disproportionable as not to be endured.

Now for its situation, although it held this Eclyptick line, yet had it been seated in any other Orbe, inconveniences would ensue of condition like the former; for had it been placed in the lowest sphere, and where is now the Moon, the year would have consisted but of one moneth; for in that space of time it would have passed through every part of the Ecliptick; so would there have been no reasonable distinction of seasons required for the generation and fructifying of all things, contrary seasons which destroy the effects of one another so suddenly succeeding. Besides by this vicinity unto the earth its heat had been intollerable: for if (as many affirm) there is a different sense of heat from the different points of its proper orbe, and that in the Apogeum or highest point (which happeneth in Cancer) it is not so hot under that Tropick, on this side the Aequator, as unto the other side in the Perigeum or lowest part of the eccentric (which happeneth in Capricornus) surely being placed in an orbe farre lower, its heat would be unsufferable; nor needed we a fable to set the world on fire.

But had it been placed in the highest Orbe or that of the eight sphere, there had been none but Platoes year, and a farre lesse distinction of seasons; for one year had then been many; and according unto the slow revolution of that orbe which absolveth not his course in many thousand years, no man had lived to attain the account thereof. These are the inconveniences ensuing upon its situation in the extreme orbs, and had it been placed in the middle orbs of the Planets, there would have ensued absurdities of a middle nature unto them.

Now whether we adhere unto the hypothesis of Copernicus, affirming the Earth to move, and the Sunne to stand still; or whether we hold as some of late have concluded from the spots in the Sunne, which appear and disappear again; that besides the revolution it maketh with its Orbs, it hath also a dineticall motion and rowles upon its own Poles; whether I say we affirm these or no, the illations before mentioned are not thereby infringed. We therefore conclude this contemplation, and are not afraid to beleeve, it may be literally said of the wisdom of God, what men will have figuratively spoken of the works of Christ; that if the wonders thereof were duly described, the whole world, that is, all within the last circumference, would not contain them. For as his wisedom is infinite, so cannot the due expressions thereof be finite; and if the world comprise him not, neither can it comprehend the story of him.

Chap. 10.
Of the Blacknesse of Negroes.

It is evident not only in the generall frame of Nature, that things most manifest unto sense, have proved obscure unto the understanding: But even in proper and appropriate objects, wherein we affirm the sense cannot erre, the faculties of reason most often fail us. Thus of colours in generall, under whose glosse and vernish all things are seen, no man hath yet beheld the true nature; or positively set down their incontroulable causes. Which while some ascribe unto the mixture of the Elements, others to the graduality of opacity and light; they have left our endeavours to grope them out by twilight, and by darknesse almost to discover that whose existence is evidenced by light. The Chymists have attempted laudably, reducing their causes unto Sal, Sulphur, and Mercury; and had they made it out so well in this, as in the objects of smell and taste, their endeavours had been more acceptable: For whereas they refer Sapor unto Salt, and Odor unto Sulphur, they vary much concerning colour; some reducing it unto Mercury, some to Sulphur, others unto Salt. Wherein indeed the last conceit doth not oppresse the former; and though Sulphur seem to carry the master stroak, yet Salt may have a strong cooperation. For beside the fixed and terrestrious Salt, there is in naturall bodies a *Sal niter* referring unto Sulphur; there is also a volatile or Armoniac Salt, retaining unto Mercury; by which Salts the colours of bodies are sensibly qualified, and receive degrees of lustre or obscurity, superficiality or profundity, fixation or volatility.

Their generall or first natures being thus obscure, there will be greater difficulties in their particular discoveries; for being farther removed from their simplicities they fall into more complexed considerations; and so require a subtiler act of reason to distinguish and call forth their natures. Thus although a man understood the generall nature of colours, yet were it no easie probleme to resolve, Why Grasse is green? Why Garlick, Molyes, and Porrets have white roots, deep green leaves, and black seeds? Why severall docks, and sorts of Rhubarb with yellow roots, send forth purple flowers? Why also from Lactary or milky plants which have a white and lacteous juice dispersed through every part, there arise flowers blue and yellow? Moreover beside the specificall and first digressions ordained from the Creation, which might be urged to salve the variety in every species; Why shall the Marvaile of Peru produce its flowers of different colours, and that not once, or constantly, but every day and variously? Why Tulips of one colour produce some of another, and running through almost all, should still escape a blue? And lastly, Why some men, yea and they a mighty and considerable part of mankinde, should first acquire and still retain the glosse and tincture of blacknesse? which whoever strictly enquires, shall finde no lesse of darknesse in the cause, then blacknesse in the effect it self; there arising unto examination no such satisfactory and unquarrellable reasons, as may confirm the causes generally received; which are but two in number. The heat and scorch of the Sunne; or the curse of God on Cham and his posterity.

The first was generally received by the Ancients, who in obscurities had no higher recourse then unto Nature, as may appear by a Discourse concerning this point in Strabo. By Aristotle it seems to be implied, in those Problems which enquire why the Sunne makes men black, and not the fire? why it whitens wax, yet blacks the skin? By the word Aethiops it self, applied to the memorablest Nations of Negroes, that is of a burnt and torrid countenance. The fancie of the fable infers also the Antiquity of the opinion; which deriveth the complexion from the deviation of the Sunne, and the conflagration of all things under Phaeton. But this opinion though generally embraced, was I perceive rejected by Aristobulus a very ancient Geographer; as is discovered by Strabo. It hath been doubted by severall modern Writers, particularly by Ortelius; but amply and satisfactorily discussed as we know by no man. We shall therefore endeavour a full delivery hereof, declaring the grounds of doubt, and reasons of deniall; which rightly understood, may if not overthrow, yet shrewdly shake the security of this assertion.

[A long discussion of various difficulties and opinions.]

CHAP. 11.
OF THE SAME.

A second opinion there is, that this complexion was first a curse of God derived unto them from Cham, upon whom it was inflicted for discovering the nakednesse of Noah. Which notwithstanding is sooner affirmed then proved, and carrieth with it sundry improbabilities. For first, if we derive the curse on Cham, or in generall upon his posterity, we shall Benegroe   †

a greater part of the earth then ever was so conceived; and not only paint the Aethiopians, and reputed sonnes of Cush, but the people also of Aegypt, Arabia, Assyria, and Chaldea; for by his race were these Countries also peopled. And if con- †
cordantly unto Berosus, the fragment of Cato *de Originibus,* some things of Halicarnasseus, Macrobius, and out of them of Leandro and Annius, we shall conceive of the travels of Camese or Cham; we may introduce a generation of Negroes as high as Italy; which part was never culpable of deformity, but hath produced the magnified examples of beauty.

Secondly, The curse mentioned in Scripture was not denounced upon Cham, but Canaan his youngest son; and the reasons thereof are divers. The first, from the Jewish Tradition, whereby it is conceived, that Canaan made the discovery of the nakednesse of Noah, and notified it unto Cham. Secondly, to have cursed Cham had been to curse all his posterity, whereof but one was guilty of the fact. And lastly, he spared Cham, because he had blessed him before, cap. 9. Now if we confine this curse unto Canaan, and think the same fulfilled in his posterity; then doe we induce this complexion on the Sidonians; then was the promised land a tract of Negroes; For from Canaan were descended the Canaanites, Jebusites, Amorites, Gergezites, and Hivites, which were †
possessed of that Land.

Thirdly, Although we should place the originall of this curse upon one of the sonnes of Cham, yet were it not known from which of them to derive it. For the particularity of their descents is imperfectly set down by accountants, nor is it distinctly determinable from whom thereof the Aethiopians are proceeded. For whereas these of Africa are generally esteemed to be the Issue of Chus, the elder sonne of Cham, it is not so easily made out. For the land of Chus, which the Septuagint translates Aethiopia, makes no part of Africa; nor is it the habitation of Blackmores, but the Country of Arabia, especially the Happy, and Stony; possessions and †,3
Colonies of all the sonnes of Chus, excepting Nimrod, and Havilah; possessed and planted wholly by the children of Chus, that is, by Sabtah and Raamah, Sabtacha, and the sonnes of Raamah, Dedan and Sheba, according unto whose

names the Nations of those parts have received their denominations, as may be collected from Pliny and Ptolomy; and as we are informed by credible Authors, they hold a fair Analogy in their names, even unto our daies. So the wife of Moses translated in Scripture an Aethiopian, and so confirmed by the fabulous relation of Josephus, was none of the daughters of Africa, nor any Negroe of Aethiopia, but the daughter of Jethro, Prince and Priest of Madian; which was a part of Arabia the Stony, bordering upon the Red Sea. So the Queen of Sheba came not unto Solomon out of Aethiopia, but from Arabia, and that part thereof which bore the name of the first planter, the sonne of Chus. So whether the Eunuch which Philip the Deacon baptised, were servant unto Candace Queen of the African Aethiopia (although Damianus *à* Goes, Codignus and the Aethiopick relations averre) is yet by many, and with strong suspitions doubted. So that Army of a million, which Zerah King of Aethiopia is said to bring against Asa, was drawn out of Arabia, and the plantations of Chus; not out of Aethiopia, and the remote habitations of the Moors. For it is said that Asa pursuing his victory, took from him the City Gerar; now Gerar was no city in or near Aethiopia, but a place between Cadesh and Zur, where Abraham formerly sojourned. Since therefore these African Aethiopians are not convinced by the common acception to be the sons of Chus, whether they be not the posterity of Phut, or Mizraim, or both, it is not assuredly determined. For Mizraim, he possessed Aegypt, and the East parts of Africa. From Lubym his son came the Lybians, and perhaps from them the Aethiopians: Phut possessed Mauritania, and the Western parts of Africa, and from these perhaps descended the Moors of the West, of Mandinga, Meleguette and Guinie. But from Canaan, upon whom the curse was pronounced, none of these had their originall, for he was restrained unto Canaan and Syria; although in after Ages many Colonies dispersed, and some thereof upon the coasts of Africa, and prepossessions of his elder brothers.

Fourthly, To take away all doubt or any probable divarication, the curse is plainly specified in the Text, nor need we [4] dispute it, like the mark of Cain; *Servus servorum erit fra-*

tribus suis, Cursed be Canaan, a servant of servants shall he
be unto his brethren; which was after fulfilled in the conquest
of Canaan, subdued by the Israelites, the posterity of Sem.
Which Prophecy Abraham well understanding, took an oath
of his servant not to take a wife for his son Isaac out of the
daughters of the Canaanites; And the like was performed by
Isaac in the behalf of his son Jacob. As for Cham and his other
sons, this curse attained them not; for Nimrod the son of Chus
set up his kingdom in Babylon, and erected the first great
Empire, Mizraim and his posterity grew mighty Monarchs in
Egypt; and the Empire of the Aethiopians hath been as large
as either. Nor did the curse descend in generall upon the †
posterity of Canaan: for the Sidonians, Arkites, Hamathites,
Sinites, Arvadites, and Zemarites seem exempted. But why
there being eleven sonnes, five only were condemned, and
six escaped the malediction, is a secret beyond discovery.

Lastly, Whereas men affirm this colour as a Curse, I cannot
make out the propriety of that name, it neither seeming so
to them, nor reasonably unto us; for they take so much content therein, that they esteem deformity by other colours, describing the Devil, and terrible objects, White. And if we
seriously consult the definitions of beauty, and exactly perpend what wise men determine thereof, we shall not apprehend a curse, or any deformity therein. For first, some place
the essence thereof in the proportion of parts; conceiving it
to consist in a comely commensurability of the whole unto the
parts, and the parts between themselves; which is the determination of the best and learned Writers. Now hereby the
Moors are not excluded from beauty; there being in this description no consideration of colours, but an apt connexion
and frame of parts and the whole. Others there be, and those
most in number, which place it not only in proportion of parts,
but also in grace of colour. But to make Colour essentiall
unto Beauty, there will arise no slender difficulty; For Aristotle in two definitions of pulchritude, and Galen in one, have
made no mention of colour. Neither will it agree unto the
Beauty of Animals; wherein notwithstanding there is an approved pulchritude. Thus horses are handsome under any
colour, and the symmetry of parts obscures the consideration

of complexions. Thus in concolour animals and such as are
confined unto one colour, we measure not their Beauty
thereby; for if a Crow or Black-bird grow white, we generally
account it more pretty; And even in monstrosity descend not
to opinion of deformity. By this way likewise the Moores escape the curse of deformity; there concurring no stationary
colour, and sometimes not any unto Beauty.

The Platonick contemplators reject both these descriptions
founded upon parts and colours, or either; as M. Leo the
Jew hath excellently discoursed in his Genealogy of Love:
defining Beauty a formall grace, which delights and moves
them to love which comprehend it. This grace say they, discoverable outwardly, is the resplendor and Raye of some interiour and invisible Beauty, and proceedeth from the forms
of compositions amiable. Whose faculties if they can aptly
contrive their matter, they beget in the subject an agreeable
and pleasing beauty; if over-ruled thereby, they evidence
not their perfections, but runne into deformity. For seeing
that out of the same materials Thersites and Paris, Beauty   5
and monstrosity, may be contrived; the forms and operative
faculties introduce and determine their perfections. Which in
naturall bodies receive exactnesse in every kinde, according
to the first Idea of the Creator, and in contrived bodies the
phancy of the Artificer. And by this consideration of Beauty,
the Moores also are not excluded, but hold a common share
therein with all mankinde.

Lastly, In whatsoever its Theory consisteth, or if in the
generall, we allow the common conceit of symmetry and of
colour, yet to descend unto singularities, or determine in what
symmetry or colour it consisted, were a slippery designation.   †
For Beauty is determined by opinion, and seems to have no
essence that holds one notion with all; that seeming beaute-   †
ous unto one, which hath no favour with another; and that
unto every one, according as custome hath made it naturall,
or sympathy and conformity of mindes shall make it seem
agreeable. Thus flat noses seem comely unto the Moore, an
Aquiline or hawked one unto the Persian, a large and prominent nose unto the Romane; but none of all these are acceptable in our opinion. Thus some think it most ornamentall

to wear their Bracelets on their Wrests, others say it is better to have them about their Ancles; some think it most comely to wear their Rings and Jewels in the Ear, others will have them about their Privities; a third will not think they are compleat except they hang them in their lips, cheeks or noses. Thus Homer to set off Minerva calleth her γλαυκῶπις, that is, gray or light-blue eyed: now this unto us seems farre lesse amiable then the black. Thus we that are of contrary complexions accuse the blacknesse of the Mores as ugly: But the Spouse in the Canticles excuseth this conceit, in that description of hers, I am black, but comely. And howsoever Cerberus and the furies of hell be described by the Poets under this complexion, yet in the beauty of our Saviour blacknesse is commended, when it is said, his locks are bushie and black as a Raven. So that to inferre this as a curse, or to reason it as a deformity, is no way reasonable; the two foundations of beauty, Symmetry and Complexion, receiving such various apprehensions; that no deviation will be expounded so high as a curse or undeniable deformity, without a manifest and confessed degree of monstrosity.

Lastly, It is a very injurious method unto Philosophy, and a perpetuall promotion of ignorance in points of obscurity not open unto easie considerations, to fall upon a present refuge unto Miracles; or recurre unto immediate contrivance from the insearchable hands of God. Thus in the conceit of the evil odor of the Jews, Christians without a farther research into the verity of the thing, or enquiry into the cause, draw up a judgement upon them from the passion of their Saviour. Thus in the wondrous effects of the clime of Ireland, and the freedom from all venemous creatures, the credulity of common conceit imputes this immunity unto the benediction of St. Patrick, as Beda and Gyraldus have left recorded. Thus the Asse having a peculiar mark of a crosse made by a black list down his back, and another athwart, or at right angles down his shoulders; common opinion ascribes this figure unto a peculiar signation; since that beast had the honour to bear our Saviour on his back. Certainly this is a course more desperate then Antipathies, Sympathies or occult qualities; wherein by a finall and satisfactive discernment of faith, we lay the last

and particular effects upon the first and generall cause of all
things; whereas in the other, we doe but palliate our determi-   9
nations, untill our advanced endeavours doe totally reject or
partially salve their evasions.

THE SEVENTH BOOK

CHAP. 18.
MORE BRIEFLY OF SOME OTHERS.

Other relations there are, and those in very good Authors,
which though we doe not positively deny, yet have they not
been unquestioned by some, and at least as improbable truths   †
have been received by others. Unto some it hath seemed Incredible what Herodotus reporteth of the great Army of
Xerxes, that drank whole Rivers dry. And unto the Author
himself it appeared wondrous strange, that they exhausted
not the provision of the Countrey, rather then the waters
thereof. For as he maketh the account, and Budeus *de Asse*
correcting the miscompute of Valla, delivereth it; if every
man of the Army had had a chenix of Corne a day, that is a
sextary and half, or about two pints and a quarter, the Army
had daily expended ten hundred thousand and fourty me-
dimna's, or measures containing six Bushels. Which rightly
considered, the Abderites had reason to blesse the heavens,
that Xerxes eat but one meale a day; and Pythius his noble
host might with lesse charge and possible provision entertain
both him and his Army. And yet may all be salved, if we
take it hyperbolically, as wise men receive that expression in
Job, concerning Behemoth or the Elephant; Behold, he drink-   1
eth up a River and hasteth not, he trusteth that he can draw
up Jordane into his mouth.

2. That Anniball eat or brake through the Alpes with Vinegar, may be too grossely taken, and the Author of his life annexed unto Plutarch affirmeth only, he used this artifice upon
the tops of some of the highest mountains. For as it is vulgarly

understood, that he cut a passage for his Army through those mighty mountains, it may seem incredible, not only in the greatnesse of the effect, but the quantity of the efficient: and such as behold them, may think an Ocean of Vinegar too little for that effect. 'Twas a work indeed rather to be expected from earthquakes and inundations, then any corrosive waters, and much condemneth the judgement of Xerxes, that wrought through Mount Athos with Mattocks.

3. That Archimedes burnt the ships of Marcellus, with † specculums of parabolicall figures, at three furlongs, or as some will have it at the distance of three miles, sounds hard unto reason, and artificiall experience: and therefore justly questioned by Kircherus,* who after long enquiry could finde but one made by Manfredus Septalius that fired at fifteen paces. And therefore more probable it is, that the ships were neerer the shoar, or about some thirty paces: at which distance notwithstanding the effect was very great. But whereas men conceive the ships were more easily set on flame, by reason of the pitch about them, it seemeth no advantage. Since burning glasses will melt pitch or make it boyle, not easily set it on fire.

4. The story of the Fabii, whereof three hundred and six marching against the Veientes, were all slain, and one childe alone to support the family remained, is surely not to be parallcld, nor easie to be conceived; except we can imagine, that of three hundred and six, but one had children below the service of warre; that the rest were all unmaried; or the wife but of one impregnated.

5. The received story of Milo, who by daily lifting a Calf, attained an ability to carry it being a Bull, is a witty conceit, and handsomely sets forth the efficacy of Assuefaction. But surely the account had been more reasonably placed upon some person not much exceeding in strength, and such a one as without the assistance of custome could never have performed that act; which some may presume that Milo without precedent artifice or any other preparative, had strength enough to perform. For, as relations declare, he was the most

* *De luce et umbra.*

pancraticall man of Greece, and as Galen reporteth, and
Mercurialis in his Gymnasticks representeth, he was able to   2
persist erect upon an oyled plank, and not to be removed by
the force or protrusion of three men. And if that be true
which Athenaeus reporteth, he was little beholding to custome for this ability. For in the Olympick games, for the space
of a furlong, he carried an Oxe of four years upon his shoulders; and the same day he carried it in his belly; for as it is
there delivered he eat it up himself. Surely he had been a
proper guest at Grandgousiers feast,* and might have matcht   3
his throat that eat six pilgrims for a salad.

6. It much disadvantageth the Panegyrick of Synesius,*
and is no small disparagement unto baldnesse, if it be true
what is related by Aelian concerning Aeschilus, whose balde
pate was mistaken for a rock, and so was brained by a Tortoise which an Eagle let fall upon it. Certainly it was a very
great mistake in the perspicacity of that Animall, and some   4
men critically disposed, would from hence confute the opin-   †
ion of Copernicus; never conceiving how the motion of the
earth below, should not wave him from a knock perpendicularly directed from a body in the ayre above.

* *In Rabelais.*
* Who writ in the praise of baldnesse.

[As a concluding epigraph to *Pseudodoxia,* Browne added
in 50 a quotation from Lactantius: *Primus sapientiae gradus
est, falsa intellegere.*]   5

HYDRIOTAPHIA

OR

URNE BURIALL

HYDRIOTAPHIA,

URNE-BURIALL,

OR,

A Difcourfe of the Sepulchrall
Urnes lately found in
NORFOLK.

Together with
The Garden of *CYRUS,*
OR THE
Quincunciall, Lozenge, or
Net-work Plantations of the An-
cients, Artificially, Naturally,.
Myftically Confidered.
With Sundry Obfervations.

By *Thomas Browne* D. of Phyfick,

LONDON,
Printed for *Hen. Brome* at the Signe of the
Gun in *Ivy-lane.* 1658.

Worthy and Honoured Friend
THOMAS Le GROS   **1**
of *Crostwick* Esquire.

When the Funerall pyre was out, and the last valediction
over, men took a lasting adieu of their interred Friends, little
expecting the curiosity of future ages should comment upon
their ashes, and having no old experience of the duration of
their Reliques, held no opinion of such after-considerations.

But who knows the fate of his bones, or how often he is to
be buried? who hath the Oracle of his ashes, or whether they
are to be scattered? The Reliques of many lie like the ruines **2**
of *Pompeys,* in all parts of the earth; And when they arrive
at your hands, these may seem to have wandred far, who
in a direct and *Meridian* Travell, have but few miles of
known Earth between your self and the Pole.   **3**

That the bones of *Theseus* should be seen again in *Athens,* **4**
was not beyond conjecture, and hopeful expectation; but that
these should arise so opportunely to serve your self, was an
hit of fate and honour beyond prediction.

We cannot but wish these Urnes might have the effect of
Theatrical vessels, and great *Hippodrome* Urnes in *Rome;* **5**
to resound the acclamations and honour due unto you. But
these are sad and sepulchral Pitchers, which have no joyful
voices; silently expressing old mortality, the ruines of forgotten times, and can only speak with life, how long in this
corruptible frame, some parts may be uncorrupted; yet able
to out-last bones long unborn, and noblest pyle among us. **6**

We present not these as any strange sight or spectacle unknown to your eyes, who have beheld the best of Urnes, and
noblest variety of Ashes; Who are your self no slender master
of Antiquities, and can daily command the view of so many
Imperiall faces; Which raiseth your thoughts unto old things, **7**

and consideration of times before you, when even living men
were Antiquities; when the living might exceed the dead, and
to depart this world, could not be properly said, to go unto
the greater number. And so run up your thoughts upon the   8
ancient of dayes, the Antiquaries truest object, unto whom
the eldest parcels are young, and earth it self an Infant;
and without Aegyptian account makes but small noise in   9
thousands.

We were hinted by the occasion, not catched the opportunity to write of old things, or intrude upon the Antiquary.
We are coldly drawn unto discourses of Antiquities, who have
scarce time before us to comprehend new things, or make out
learned Novelties. But seeing they arose as they lay, almost
in silence among us, at least in short account suddenly passed
over; we were very unwilling they should die again, and be
buried twice among us.

Beside, to preserve the living, and make the dead to live,
to keep men out of their Urnes, and discourse of humane
fragments in them, is not impertinent unto our profession;
whose study is life and death, who daily behold examples of
mortality, and of all men least need artificial *memento's,* or
coffins by our bed side, to minde us of our graves.

'Tis time to observe Occurrences, and let nothing remarkable escape us; The Supinity of elder dayes hath left so much
in silence, or time hath so martyred the Records, that the
most industrious heads do finde no easie work to erect a new   10
Britannia.

'Tis opportune to look back upon old times, and contemplate our Forefathers. Great examples grow thin, and to be
fetched from the passed world. Simplicity flies away, and
iniquity comes at long strides upon us. We have enough to
do to make up our selves from present and passed times, and
the whole stage of things scarce serveth for our instruction.
A compleat peece of vertue must be made up from the *Centos*
of all ages, as all the beauties of *Greece* could make but one 11
handsome *Venus.*

When the bones of King *Arthur* were digged up, the old   12
Race might think, they beheld therein some Originals of
themselves; Unto these of our Urnes none here can pretend   13

relation, and can only behold the Reliques of those persons, who in their life giving the Law unto their predecessors, † after long obscurity, now lye at their mercies. But remembring the early civility they brought upon these Countreys, and forgetting long passed mischiefs; We mercifully preserve their bones, and pisse not upon their ashes. 14

In the offer of these Antiquities we drive not at ancient Families, so long out-lasted by them; We are farre from erecting your worth upon the pillars of your Fore-fathers, whose merits you illustrate. We honour your old Virtues, conformable unto times before you, which are the Noblest Armoury. And having long experience of your friendly conversation, void of empty Formality, full of freedome, constant and Generous Honesty, I look upon you as a Gemme of the 15 Old Rock, and must professe my self even to Urne and Ashes,

Your ever faithfull Friend,

and Servant,

Norwich　　　　　　　　　　　*Thomas Browne.*

May 1.

En sum quòd digitis Quinque Levatur onus. ꝑropert:

"See, I am now what can be lifted with five fingers."
(Propertius, *Elegies* 4.11.14.)
[*Et sum . . . legatur* is the now accepted reading, but Browne took his
reading from the 1604 edition of Catullus, Tibullus, and Propertius (SC).]

HYDRIOTAPHIA
Urne-Buriall

OR,

A Brief Discourse of the Sepulchrall Urnes
lately found in N O R F O L K.

CHAPTER 1.

In the deep discovery of the Subterranean world, a shallow part would satisfie some enquirers; who, if two or three
yards were open about the surface, would not care to rake
the bowels of *Potosi,* and regions towards the Centre. Nature [16]
hath furnished one part of the Earth, and man another. The
treasures of time lie high, in Urnes, Coynes, and Monuments,
scarce below the roots of some vegetables. Time hath endlesse rarities, and shows of all varieties; which reveals old
things in heaven, makes new discoveries in earth, and even
earth it self a discovery. That great Antiquity *America* lay
buried for thousands of years; and a large part of the earth
is still in the Urne unto us.

Though if *Adam* were made out of an extract of the Earth, [17]
all parts might challenge a restitution, yet few have returned
their bones farre lower then they might receive them; not affecting the graves of Giants, under hilly and heavy coverings,
but content with lesse then their owne depth, have wished
their bones might lie soft, and the earth be light upon them;
Even such as hope to rise again, would not be content with
centrall interrment, or so desperately to place their reliques
as to lie beyond discovery, and in no way to be seen again;
which happy contrivance hath made communication with our
forefathers, and left unto our view some parts, which they
never beheld themselves.

Though earth hath engrossed the name, yet water hath

proved the smartest grave; which in forty dayes swallowed almost mankinde, and the living creation; Fishes not wholly escaping, except the Salt Ocean were handsomely contempered by a mixture of the fresh Element.

Many have taken voluminous pains to determine the state of the soul upon disunion; but men have been most phantasticall in the singular contrivances of their corporall dissolution: whilest the sobrest Nations have rested in two wayes, of simple inhumation and burning.

That carnall interment or burying, was of the elder date, the old examples of *Abraham* and the Patriarchs are sufficient to illustrate; And were without competition, if it could be made out, that *Adam* was buried near *Damascus,* or Mount *Calvary,* according to some Tradition. God himself, that buried but one, was pleased to make choice of this way, collectible from Scripture-expression, and the hot contest between Satan and the Arch-Angel, about discovering the body of *Moses.* But the practice of Burning was also of great Antiquity, and of no slender extent. For (not to derive the same from *Hercules*) noble descriptions there are hereof in the Grecian Funerals of *Homer,* In the formall Obsequies of *Patroclus,* and *Achilles;* and somewhat elder in the *Theban* warre, and solemn combustion of *Meneceus,* and *Archemorus,* contemporary unto *Jair* the Eighth Judge of *Israel.* Confirmable also among the *Trojans,* from the Funerall Pyre of *Hector,* burnt before the gates of *Troy,* And the burning of *Penthisilea* the *Amazonean Queen:* and long continuance of that practice, in the inward Countries of *Asia;* while as low as the Reign of *Julian,* we finde that the King of *Chionia* burnt the body of his Son, and interred the ashes in a silver Urne.

The same practice extended also farre West, and besides *Herulians, Getes,* and *Thracians,* was in use with most of the *Celtae, Sarmatians, Germans, Gauls, Danes, Swedes, Norwegians;* not to omit some use thereof among *Carthaginians* and *Americans:* Of greater Antiquity among the *Romans* then most opinion, or *Pliny* seems to allow. For (beside the old Table Laws of burning or burying within the City, of making the Funerall fire with plained wood, or quenching the

18

19

20

21

fire with wine.) *Manlius* the Consul burnt the body of his Son: *Numa* by speciall clause of his Will, was not burnt but buried; And *Remus* was solemnly burned, according to the description of *Ovid*.

Cornelius Sylla was not the first whose body was burned in *Rome*, but of the *Cornelian* Family, which being indifferently, not frequently used before; from that time spread, and became the prevalent practice. Not totally pursued in the highest runne of Cremation; For when even Crows were [22] funerally burnt, *Poppaea* the Wife of *Nero* found a peculiar [23] grave enterment. Now as all customes were founded upon some bottome of Reason, so there wanted not grounds for this; according to severall apprehensions of the most rationall dissolution. Some being of the opinion of *Thales*, that water was the originall of all things, thought it most equall to submit unto the principle of putrefaction, and conclude in a moist relentment. Others conceived it most natural to end in fire, as due unto the master principle in the composition, according to the doctrine of *Heraclitus*. And therefore heaped up large piles, more actively to waft them toward that Element, whereby they also declined a visible degeneration into worms, and left a lasting parcell of their composition.

Some apprehended a purifying virtue in fire, refining the grosser commixture, and firing out the Aethereall particles so deeply immersed in it. And such as by tradition or rationall conjecture held any hint of the finall pyre of all things; or that this Element at last must be too hard for all the rest; might conceive most naturally of the fiery dissolution. Others pretending no natural grounds, politickly declined the malice of enemies upon their buried bodies. Which consideration led *Sylla* unto this practise; who having thus served the body of [24] *Marius*, could not but fear a retaliation upon his own; entertained after in the Civill wars, and revengeful contentions of *Rome*.

But as many Nations embraced, and many left it indifferent, so others too much affected, or strictly declined this practice. The *Indian Brachmans* seemed too great friends unto fire, who burnt themselves alive, and thought it the noblest

way to end their dayes in fire; according to the expression
of the Indian, burning himself at *Athens,* in his last words
upon the pyre unto the amazed spectators, *Thus I make my
selfe Immortall.*

But the *Chaldeans* the great Idolaters of fire, abhorred the
burning of their carcasses, as a pollution of that Deity. The
Persian Magi declined it upon the like scruple, and being
only sollicitous about their bones, exposed their flesh to the
prey of Birds and Dogges. And the *Persees* now in *India,*
which expose their bodies unto Vultures, and endure not so
much as *feretra* or Biers of Wood, the proper Fuell of fire,
are led on with such niceties. But whether the ancient *Germans* who burned their dead, held any such fear to pollute
their Deity of *Herthus,* or the earth, we have no Authentick
conjecture.

The Aegyptians were afraid of fire, not as a Deity, but a
devouring Element, mercilesly consuming their bodies, and
leaving too little of them; and therefore by precious Embalments, depositure in dry earths, or handsome inclosure in
glasses, contrived the notablest wayes of integrall conservation. And from such Aegyptian scruples imbibed by *Pythagoras,* it may be conjectured that *Numa* and the Pythagoricall
Sect first waved the fiery solution.

The *Scythians* who swore by winde and sword, that is, by
life and death, were so farre from burning their bodies, that
they declined all interrment, and made their graves in the
ayr: And the *Ichthyophagi* or fish-eating Nations about
Aegypt, affected the Sea for their grave: Thereby declining
visible corruption, and restoring the debt of their bodies.
Whereas the old Heroes in *Homer* dreaded nothing more
than water or drowning; probably upon the old opinion of the
fiery substance of the soul, only extinguishable by that Element; And therefore the Poet emphatically implieth the totall
destruction in this kinde of death, which happened to *Ajax
Oileus.*   25

The old *Balearians* had a peculiar mode, for they used
great Urnes and much wood, but no fire in their burials, while
they bruised the flesh and bones of the dead, crowded them

into Urnes, and laid heapes of wood upon them. And the
Chinois without cremation or urnall interrment of their bodies, make use of trees and much burning, while they plant a
Pine-tree by their grave, and burn great numbers of printed
draughts of slaves and horses over it, civilly content with their
companies in effigie, which barbarous Nations exact unto
reality.

Christians abhorred this way of obsequies, and though they
stickt not to give their bodies to be burnt in their lives, detested that mode after death; affecting rather a depositure
than absumption, and properly submitting unto the sentence
of God, to return not unto ashes but unto dust againe, conformable unto the practice of the Patriarchs, the interrment
of our Saviour, of *Peter, Paul,* and the ancient Martyrs. And
so farre at last declining promiscuous enterrment with Pagans, that some have suffered Ecclesiastical censures, for   [26]
making no scruple thereof.

The *Musselman* beleevers will never admit this fiery resolution. For they hold a present trial from their black and white   [27]
Angels in the grave; which they must have made so hollow,
that they may rise upon their knees.

The Jewish Nation, though they entertained the old way
of inhumation, yet sometimes admitted this practice. For
the men of *Jabesh* burnt the body of *Saul.* And by no pro-   [28]
hibited practice to avoid contagion or pollution, in time of
pestilence, burnt the bodies of their friends. And when they   [29]
burnt not their dead bodies, yet sometimes used great burnings neare and about them, deducible from the expressions
concerning *Jehoram, Sedechias,* and the sumptuous pyre of   [30,31]
Asa: And were so little averse from Pagan burning, that the   [32]
Jews lamenting the death of *Caesar* their friend, and revenger   [33]
on *Pompey,* frequented the place where his body was burnt
for many nights together. And as they raised noble Monuments and *Mausolaeums* for their own Nation, so they were   [34]
not scrupulous in erecting some for others, according to the
practice of *Daniel,* who left that lasting sepulchrall pyle in
Echbatana, for the *Medean* and *Persian* Kings.

But even in times of subjection and hottest use, they con-

formed not unto the *Romane* practice of burning; whereby
the Prophecy was secured concerning the body of Christ,   35
that it should not see corruption, or a bone should not be
broken; which we beleeve was also providentially prevented,
from the Souldiers spear and nails that past by the little bones
both in his hands and feet: Nor of ordinary contrivance, that   †
it should not corrupt on the Crosse, according to the Laws
of *Romane* Crucifixion, or an hair of his head perish, though
observable in Jewish customes, to cut the hairs of Malefactors.

Nor in their long co-habitation with Aegyptians, crept into
a custome of their exact embalming, wherein deeply slashing
the muscles, and taking out the brains and entrails, they had
broken the subject of so entire a Resurrection, nor fully answered the types of *Enoch, Eliah,* or *Jonah,* which yet to   36
prevent or restore, was of equall facility unto that rising
power, able to break the fasciations and bands of death, to
get clear out of the Cere-cloth, and an hundred pounds of
oyntment, and out of the Sepulchre before the stone was
rolled from it.

But though they embraced not this practice of burning, yet
entertained they many ceremonies agreeable unto *Greeke*
and *Romane* obsequies. And he that observeth their funerall
Feasts, their Lamentations at the grave, their musick, and
weeping mourners; how they closed the eyes of their friends,
how they washed, anointed, and kissed the dead; may easily
conclude these were not meere Pagan-Civilities. But whether
that mournfull burthen, and treble calling out after Absalom,   37
had any reference unto the last conclamation, and triple vale-   38
diction, used by other Nations, we hold but a wavering conjecture.

Civilians make sepulture but of the Law of Nations, others
doe naturally found it and discover it also in animals. They
that are so thick skinned as still to credit the story of the
Phoenix, may say something for animall burning: More serious conjectures finde some examples of sepulture in Ele-   39
phants, Cranes, the Sepulchrall Cells of Pismires and practice
of Bees; which civill society carrieth out their dead, and hath
exequies, if not interrments.

CHAPTER 2.

The Solemnities, Ceremonies, Rites of their Cremation or enterrment, so solemnly delivered by Authours, we shall not disparage our Reader to repeat. Only the last and lasting part in their Urns, collected bones and Ashes, we cannot wholly omit, or decline that Subject, which occasion lately presented, in some discovered among us. [1]

In a Field of old *Walsingham,* not many moneths past, were digged up between fourty and fifty Urnes, deposited in a dry and sandy soile, not a yard deep, nor farre from one another: Not all strictly of one figure, but most answering these described: Some containing two pounds of bones, distinguishable in skulls, ribs, jawes, thigh-bones, and teeth, with fresh impressions of their combustion. Besides the extraneous substances, like peeces of small boxes, or combes handsomely wrought, handles of small brasse instruments, brazen nippers, and in one some kinde of *Opale.* [2]

Near the same plot of ground, for about six yards compasse were digged up coals and incinerated substances, which begat conjecture that this was the *Ustrina* or place of burning their bodies, or some sacrificing place unto the *Manes,* which was properly below the surface of the ground, as the *Arae* and Altars unto the gods and *Heroes* above it. [3]

That these were the Urnes of *Romanes* from the common custome and place where they were found, is no obscure conjecture, not farre from a *Romane* Garrison, and but five Miles from *Brancaster,* set down by ancient Record under the name of *Brannodunum.* And where the adjoyning Towne, containing seven Parishes, in no very different sound, but Saxon Termination, still retains the Name of *Burnham,* which being an early station, it is not improbable the neighbour parts were filled with habitations, either of *Romanes* themselves, or *Brittains Romanised,* which observed the *Romane* customes. [4]

Nor is it improbable that the *Romanes* early possessed this Countrey; for though we meet not with such strict particulars of these parts, before the new Institution of *Constantine,* and [5]

military charge of the Count of the *Saxon* shore, and that   6
about the *Saxon* Invasions, the *Dalmatian* Horsemen were in
the Garrison of *Brancaster:* Yet in the time of *Claudius, Ves-
pasian,* and *Severus,* we finde no lesse then three Legions dispersed through the Province of *Brittain.* And as high as the
Reign of *Claudius* a great overthrow was given unto the *Iceni,*
by the *Romane* Lieutenant *Ostorius.* Not long after, the
Countrey was so molested, that in hope of a better state,
Prasutagus bequeathed his Kingdome unto *Nero* and his
Daughters; and *Boadicea* his Queen fought the last decisive
Battle with *Paulinus.* After which time and Conquest of
Agricola the Lieutenant of *Vespasian,* probable it is they
wholly possessed this Countrey, ordering it into Garrisons or
Habitations, best suitable with their securities. And so some
Romane Habitations, not improbable in these parts, as high
as the time of *Vespasian,* where the *Saxons* after seated, in
whose thin-fill'd Mappes we yet finde the Name of *Walsing-*   7
ham. Now if the *Iceni* were but *Gammadims, Anconians,* or
men that lived in an Angle wedge or Elbow of *Brittain,* according to the Originall Etymologie, this countrey will challenge the Emphaticall appellation, as most properly making
the Elbow or Iken of *Icenia.*

   That *Britain* was notably populous is undeniable, from that
expression of *Caesar.* That the *Romans* themselves were early   8
in no small Numbers, Seventy Thousand with their associats   9
slain by *Boadicea,* affords a sure account. And though many
Roman habitations are now unknowne, yet some by old
works, Rampiers, Coynes, and Urnes doe testifie their Possessions. Some Urnes have been found at *Castor,* some also
about *Southcreake,* and not many years past, no lesse then
ten in a Field at *Buxton,* not near any recorded Garison. Nor   10
is it strange to finde *Romane* Coynes of Copper and Silver
among us; of *Vespasian, Trajan, Adrian, Commodus, Antoninus, Severus,* &c. But the greater number of *Dioclesian,
Constantine, Constans, Valens,* with many of *Victorinus, Post-
humius, Tetricus,* and the thirty Tyrants in the Reigne of
Gallienus; and some as high as *Adrianus* have been found
about *Thetford,* or *Sitomagus,* mentioned in the itinerary of
Antoninus, as the way from *Venta* or *Caster* unto *London.* But

the most frequent discovery is made at the two *Casters* by [11]
Norwich and *Yarmouth*, at *Burghcastle* and *Brancaster.* [12]

Besides the *Norman, Saxon* and *Danish* peeces of *Cuthred,
Canutus, William, Matilda,* and others, som Brittish Coynes of
gold have been dispersedly found; And no small number of
silver peeces near *Norwich;* with a rude head upon the ob- [13]
verse, and an ill formed horse on the reverse, with Inscriptions *Ic. Duro.T.* whether implying *Iceni, Durotriges, Tas-
cia,* or *Trinobantes,* we leave to higher conjecture. Vulgar
Chronology will have *Norwich* Castle as old as *Julius Caesar;*
but his distance from these parts, and its *Gothick* form of
structure, abridgeth such Antiquity. The *British* Coyns afford
conjecture of early habitation in these parts, though the City
of *Norwich* arose from the ruines of *Venta,* and though perhaps not without some habitation before, was enlarged,
builded, and nominated by the *Saxons.* In what bulk or popu-
losity it stood in the old East-angle Monarchy, tradition and
history are silent. Considerable it was in the *Danish* Eruptions, when *Sueno* burnt *Thetford* and *Norwich,* and *Ulfketel*
the Governour thereof, was able to make some resistance, and
after endeavoured to burn the *Danish* Navy.

How the *Romanes* left so many Coynes in Countreys of
their Conquests, seems of hard resolution, except we consider
how they buried them under ground, when upon barbarous
invasions they were fain to desert their habitations in most
part of their Empire; and the strictnesse of their laws forbid-
ding to transfer them to any other uses; Wherein the *Spartans* [14]
were singular, who to make their Copper money uselesse,
contempered it with vinegar. That the *Brittains* left any, some
wonder; since their money was iron, and Iron rings before
Caesar; and those of after stamp by permission, and but small
in bulk and bignesse. That so few of the *Saxons* remain, because overcome by succeeding Conquerours upon the place,
their Coynes by degrees passed into other stamps, and the
marks of after ages.

Then the time of these Urnes deposited, or precise Antiquity of these Reliques, nothing of more uncertainty. For since
the Lieutenant of *Claudius* seems to have made the first progresse into these parts, since *Boadicea* was overthrown by the

Forces of *Nero*, and *Agricola* put a full end to these Conquests; it is not probable the Countrey was fully garrison'd or
planted before; and therefore however these Urnes might be
of later date, not likely of higher Antiquity.

And the succeeding Emperours desisted not from their
Conquests in these and other parts: as testified by history and
medall inscription yet extant. The Province of *Brittain* in so
divided a distance from *Rome*, beholding the faces of many
Imperiall persons, and in large account no fewer then *Caesar*,
Claudius, *Britannicus*, *Vespasian*, *Titus*, *Adrian*, *Severus*,
Commodus, *Geta*, and *Caracalla*.

A great obscurity herein, because no medall or Emperours   15
Coyne enclosed, which might denote the date of their enterr-
ments. Observable in many Urnes, and found in those of
Spittle Fields by *London*, which contained the Coynes of   16
Claudius, *Vespasian*, *Commodus*, *Antoninus*, attended with
Lacrymatories, Lamps, Bottles of Liquor, and other appurte-
nances of affectionate superstition, which in these rurall in-
terrements were wanting.

Some uncertainty there is from the period or term of burning, or the cessation of that practise. *Macrobius* affirmeth it
was disused in his dayes. But most agree, though without au-   17
thentick record, that it ceased with the *Antonini*. Most safely
to be understood after the Reigne of those Emperours, which
assumed the name of *Antoninus*, extending unto *Heliogabalus*. Not strictly after *Marcus;* For about fifty years later we
finde the magnificent burning, and consecration of *Severus;*   18
and if we so fix this period or cessation, these Urnes will challenge above thirteen hundred years.

But whether this practise was onely then left by Emperours
and great persons, or generally about *Rome*, and not in other
Provinces, we hold no authentick account. For after *Tertullian*, in the dayes of *Minucius* it was obviously objected upon
Christians, that they condemned the practise of burning. And
we finde a passage in *Sidonius*, which asserteth that practise
in *France* unto a lower account. And perhaps not fully disused till Christianity fully established, which gave the finall
extinction to these sepulchrall Bonefires.

Whether they were the bones of men or women or chil-

dren, no authentick decision from ancient custome in distinct
places of buriall. Although not improbably conjectured, that
the double Sepulture or burying place of *Abraham,* had in it [19]
such intension. But from exility of bones, thinnesse of skulls,
smallnesse of teeth, ribbes, and thigh-bones; not improbable
that many thereof were persons of *minor* age, or women. Confirmable also from things contained in them: In most were
found substances resembling Combes, Plates like Boxes, fastened with Iron pins, and handsomely overwrought like the
necks or Bridges of Musicall Instruments, long brasse plates
overwrought like the handles of neat implements, brazen nippers to pull away hair, and in one a kinde of *Opale* yet maintaining a blewish colour.

Now that they accustomed to burn or bury with them,
things wherein they excelled, delighted, or which were dear
unto them, either as farewells unto all pleasure, or vain apprehension that they might use them in the other world, is
testified by all Antiquity. Observable from the Gemme or [20]
Berill Ring upon the finger of *Cynthia,* the Mistresse of *Propertius,* when after her Funerall Pyre her Ghost appeared
unto him. And notably illustrated from the Contents of that
Romane Urne preserved by Cardinall *Farnese,* wherein [21]
besides great number of Gemmes with heads of Gods and
Goddesses, were found an Ape of *Agath,* a Grashopper, an
Elephant of Ambre, a Crystall Ball, three glasses, two
Spoones, and six Nuts of Crystall. And beyond the content
of Urnes, in the Monument of *Childerick* the first, and fourth [22]
King from *Pharamond,* casually discovered three years past at
Tournay, restoring unto the world much gold richly adorning
his Sword, two hundred Rubies, many hundred Imperial
Coyns, three hundred golden Bees, the bones and horseshoe
of his horse enterred with him, according to the barbarous
magnificence of those dayes in their sepulchrall Obsequies.
Although if we steer by the conjecture of many and Septua- [23]
gint expression; some trace thereof may be found even with
the ancient Hebrews, not only from the Sepulcrall treasure
of *David,* but the circumcision knives which *Josuah* also
buried.

Some men considering the contents of these Urnes, lasting

peeces and toyes included in them, and the custome of burning with many other Nations, might somewhat doubt whether all Urnes found among us, were properly *Romane* Reliques, or some not belonging unto our *Brittish, Saxon,* or *Danish* Forefathers.

In the form of Buriall among the ancient *Brittains,* the large Discourses of *Caesar, Tacitus,* and *Strabo* are silent: For the discovery whereof, with other particulars, we much deplore the losse of that Letter which *Cicero* expected or received   24 from his Brother *Quintus,* as a resolution of *Brittish* customes; or the account which might have been made by *Scribonius Largus* the Physician, accompanying the Emperour *Claudius,* who might have also discovered that frugall Bit of the Old   25 *Brittains,* which in the bignesse of a Bean could satisfie their thirst and hunger.

But that the *Druids* and ruling Priests used to burn and bury, is expressed by *Pomponius;* That *Bellinus* the Brother of *Brennus,* and King of *Brittains* was burnt, is acknowledged by *Polydorus.* That they held that practise in *Gallia, Caesar* expresly delivereth. Whether the *Brittains* (probably descended from them, of like Religion, Language and Manners) did not sometimes make use of burning; or whether at least such as were after civilized unto the *Romane* life and manners, conformed not unto this practise, we have no historicall assertion or deniall. But since from the account of *Tacitus* the *Romanes* early wrought so much civility upon the Brittish stock, that they brought them to build Temples, to wear the Gowne, and study the *Romane* Laws and language; that they conformed also unto their religious rites and customes in burials, seems no improbable conjecture.

That burning the dead was used in *Sarmatia,* is affirmed by *Gaguinus,* that the *Sueons* and *Gothlanders* used to burne their Princes and great persons, is delivered by *Saxo* and   26 *Olaus;* that this was the old *Germane* practise, is also asserted by *Tacitus.* And though we are bare in historicall particulars of such obsequies in this Island, or that the *Saxons, Jutes,* and *Angles* burnt their dead, yet came they from parts where 'twas of ancient practise; the *Germanes* using it, from whom they were descended. And even in *Jutland* and *Sleswick* in

Anglia Cymbrica, Urnes with bones were found not many years before us.

But the *Danish* and Northern Nations have raised an *Aera* or point of compute from their Custome of burning their dead: Some deriving it from *Unguinus,* some from *Frotho* the great; who ordained by Law, that Princes and Chief Commanders should be committed unto the fire, though the common sort had the common grave enterrment. So *Starkatterus* that old *Heroe* was burnt, and *Ringo* royally burnt the body of *Harald* the King slain by him.

What time this custome generally expired in that Nation, we discern no assured period; whether it ceased before Christianity, or upon their Conversion, by *Ansgarius* the Gaul in the time of *Ludovicus Pius* the Sonne of *Charles* the great, according to good computes; or whether it might not be used by some persons, while for a hundred and eighty years Paganisme and Christianity were promiscuously embraced among them, there is no assured conclusion. About which times the *Danes* were busie in *England,* and particularly infested this Countrey: Where many Castles and strong holds were built by them, or against them, and great number of names and Families still derived from them. But since this custome was probably disused before their Invasion or Conquest, and the *Romanes* confessedly practised the same, since their possession of this Island, the most assured account will fall upon the *Romanes,* or *Brittains Romanized.*

However certain it is, that Urnes conceived of no *Romane* Originall, are often digged up both in *Norway,* and *Denmark,* handsomely described, and graphically represented by the Learned Physician *Wormius.* And in some parts of *Denmark* in no ordinary number, as stands delivered by Authours exactly describing those Countreys. And they contained not only bones, but many other substances in them, as Knives, peeces of Iron, Brasse and Wood, and one of *Norwaye* a brasse guilded Jewes-harp.

Nor were they confused or carelesse in disposing the noblest sort, while they placed large stones in circle about the Urnes, or bodies which they interred: Somewhat answerable unto the Monument of *Rollrich* stones in *England,* or 27

sepulcrall Monument probably erected by *Rollo*, who after
conquered *Normandy*. Where 'tis not improbable somewhat
might be discovered. Mean while to what Nation or person
belonged that large Urne found at *Ashburie*, containing   28
mighty bones, and a Buckler; What those large Urnes found
at little *Massingham*, or why the *Anglesea* Urnes are placed
with their mouths downward, remains yet undiscovered.

CHAPTER 3.

Playstered and whited Sepulchres were anciently affected
in cadaverous, and corruptive Burials; And the rigid Jews
were wont to garnish the Sepulchres of the righteous; *Ulysses*   1
in *Hecuba* cared not how meanly he lived, so he might finde   2
a noble Tomb after death. Great Persons affected great Monuments, and the fair and larger Urnes contained no vulgar
ashes, which makes that disparity in those which time dis-
covereth among us. The present Urnes were not of one capacity, the largest containing above a gallon, some not much
above half that measure; nor all of one figure, wherein there
is no strict conformity, in the same or different Countreys;
Observable from those represented by *Casalius, Bosio,* and
others, though all found in *Italy*. While many have handles,
ears, and long necks, but most imitate a circular figure, in a
sphericall and round composure; whether from any mystery,
best duration, or capacity, were but a conjecture. But the
common form with necks was a proper figure, making our
last bed like our first; nor much unlike the Urnes of our Nativity, while we lay in the nether part of the Earth, and in-   3
ward vault of our Microcosme. Many Urnes are red, these but
of a black colour, somewhat smooth, and dully sounding,
which begat some doubt, whether they were burnt, or only
baked in Oven or Sunne: According to the ancient way in
many bricks, tiles, pots, and testaceous works; and as the
word *testa* is properly to be taken, when occurring without
addition: And chiefly intended by *Pliny*, when he commend-   4
eth bricks and tiles of two years old, and to make them in
the spring. Nor only these concealed peeces, but the open

magnificence of Antiquity, ran much in the Artifice of Clay. Hereof the house of *Mausolus* was built, thus old *Jupiter* stood in the Capitoll, and the *Statua* of *Hercules* made in the Reign of *Tarquinius Priscus,* was extant in *Plinies* dayes. And such as declined burning or Funerall Urnes, affected Coffins of Clay, according to the mode of *Pythagoras,* and way pre- 5 ferred by *Varro.* But the spirit of great ones was above these circumscriptions, affecting copper, silver, gold, and porphyrie Urnes, wherein *Severus* lay, after a serious view and sentence on that which should contain him. Some of these Urnes were thought to have been silvered over, from sparklings in several pots, with small Tinsell parcels; uncertain whether from the earth, or the first mixture in them.

Among these Urnes we could obtain no good account of their coverings; Only one seemed arched over with some kinde of brickwork. Of those found at *Buxton* some were covered with flints, some in other parts with tiles, those at *Yarmouth Caster,* were closed with *Romane* bricks. And some have proper earthen covers adapted and fitted to them. But in the *Homerical* Urne of *Patroclus,* whatever was the solid 6 Tegument, we finde the immediate covering to be a purple peece of silk: And such as had no covers might have the earth closely pressed into them, after which disposure were probably some of these, wherein we found the bones and ashes half mortered unto the sand and sides of the Urne; and some long roots of Quich, or Dogs-grass wreathed about the bones.

No Lamps, included Liquors, Lachrymatories, or Tearbottles attended these rurall Urnes, either as sacred unto the *Manes,* or passionate expressions of their surviving friends. While with rich flames, and hired tears they solemnized their Obsequies, and in the most lamented Monuments made one part of their Inscriptions. Some finde sepulchrall Vessels containing liquors, which time hath incrassated into gellies. For beside these Lachrymatories, notable Lamps, with Vessels of Oyles and Aromaticall Liquors attended noble Ossuaries. And some yet retaining a Vinosity and spirit in them, which 7 if any have tasted they have farre exceeded the Palats of Antiquity. Liquors not to be computed by years of annuall Magistrates, but by great conjunctions and the fatall periods 8 of Kingdomes. The draughts of Consulary date, were but crude unto these, and *Opimian* Wine but in the must unto them. ⁹

In sundry Graves and Sepulchres, we meet with Rings, Coynes, and Chalices; Ancient frugality was so severe, that they allowed no gold to attend the Corps, but only that which ¹⁰ served to fasten their teeth. Whether the *Opaline* stone in this Urne were burnt upon the finger of the dead, or cast into the fire by some affectionate friend, it will consist with either custome. But other incinerable substances were found so fresh, that they could feel no sindge from fire. These upon view were judged to be wood, but sinking in water and tried by the fire, we found them to be bone or Ivory. In their hardnesse and yellow colour they most resembled Box, which in old expressions found the Epithete of Eternall, and perhaps in ¹¹ such conservatories might have passed uncorrupted.

That Bay-leaves were found green in the Tomb of S. *Humbert,* after an hundred and fifty years, was looked upon as miraculous. Remarkable it was unto old Spectators, that the Cypresse of the Temple of *Diana* lasted so many hundred ¹² years: The wood of the Ark and Olive Rod of *Aaron* were older at the Captivity. But the Cypresse of the Ark of *Noah,* was the greatest vegetable Antiquity, if *Josephus* were not deceived, by some fragments of it in his dayes. To omit the Moore-logs, and Firre-trees found under-ground in many parts of *England;* the undated ruines of windes, flouds or earthquakes; and which in *Flanders* still shew from what quarter they fell, as generally lying in a North-East position. ¹³

But though we found not these peeces to be Wood, according to first apprehension, yet we missed not altogether of some woody substance; For the bones were not so clearly pickt, but some coals were found amongst them; A way to make wood perpetuall, and a fit associat for metall, whereon was laid the foundation of the great *Ephesian* Temple, and which were made the lasting tests of old boundaries and Landmarks; Whilest we look on these, we admire not Observations of Coals found fresh, after four hundred years. In a ¹⁴ long deserted habitation, even Egge-shels have been found fresh, not tending to corruption.

In the Monument of King *Childerick,* the Iron Reliques
were found all rusty and crumbling into peeces. But our little
Iron pins which fastened the Ivory works, held well together,
and lost not their Magneticall quality, though wanting a tenacious moisture for the firmer union of parts; although it be
hardly drawn into fusion, yet that metall soon submitteth
unto rust and dissolution. In the brazen peeces we admired
not the duration but the freedome from rust, and ill savour,
upon the hardest attrition; but now exposed unto the piercing
Atomes of ayre, in the space of a few moneths, they begin to
spot and betray their green entrals. We conceive not these
Urnes to have descended thus naked as they appear, or to
have entred their graves without the old habit of flowers. The
Urne of *Philopaemen* was so laden with flowers and ribbons,   15
that it afforded no sight of it self. The rigid *Lycurgus* allowed
Olive and Myrtle. The *Athenians* might fairly except against
the practise of *Democritus* to be buried up in honey; as fear-   16
ing to embezzle a great commodity of their Countrey, and the
best of that kinde in *Europe.* But *Plato* seemed too frugally   17
politick, who allowed no larger Monument then would contain four Heroick Verses, and designed the most barren
ground for sepulture: Though we cannot commend the goodnesse of that sepulchrall ground, which was set at no higher
rate then the mean salary of *Judas.* Though the earth had   18
confounded the ashes of these Ossuaries, yet the bones were
so smartly burnt, that some thin plates of brasse were found
half melted among them: whereby we apprehend they were
not of the meanest carcasses, perfunctorily fired as sometimes
in military, and commonly in pestilence, burnings; or after
the manner of abject corps, hudled forth and carelesly burnt,
without the Esquiline Port at *Rome;* which was an affront
contrived upon *Tiberius,* while they but half burnt his body,   19
and in the Amphitheatre, according to the custome in notable Malefactors; whereas *Nero* seemed not so much to feare   20
his death, as that his head should be cut off, and his body
not burnt entire.

Some finding many fragments of sculs in these Urnes, suspected a mixture of bones; In none we searched was there
cause of such conjecture, though sometimes they declined not

that practise; The ashes of *Domitian* were mingled with those   21
of *Julia*, of *Achilles* with those of *Patroclus:* All Urnes con-   22
tained not single ashes; Without confused burnings they af-
fectionately compounded their bones; passionately endeav-
ouring to continue their living Unions. And when distance of
death denied such conjunctions, unsatisfied affections conceived some satisfaction to be neighbours in the grave, to lye
Urne by Urne, and touch but in their names. And many were
so curious to continue their living relations, that they contrived large, and family Urnes, wherein the Ashes of their   †,23
nearest friends and kindred might successively be received,
at least some parcels thereof, while their collaterall memorials
lay in *minor* vessels about them.

Antiquity held too light thoughts from Objects of mortality,
while some drew provocatives of mirth from Anatomies, and   24
Juglers shewed tricks with Skeletons. When Fidlers made not
so pleasant mirth as Fencers, and men could sit with quiet
stomacks while hanging was plaied before them. Old consid-   25
erations made few *memento's* by sculs and bones upon their
monuments. In the Aegyptian Obelisks and Hieroglyphicall
figures, it is not easie to meet with bones. The sepulchrall
Lamps speak nothing lesse then sepulture; and in their literall
draughts prove often obscene and antick peeces: Where we
finde D.M. it is obvious to meet with sacrificing *patera's*, and   26
vessels of libation, upon old sepulchrall Monuments. In the
Jewish *Hypogaeum* and subterranean Cell at *Rome*, was little   27
observable beside the variety of Lamps, and frequent
draughts of the holy Candlestick. In authentick draughts of
Anthony and *Jerome*, we meet with thigh-bones and deaths
heads; but the cemiteriall Cels of ancient Christians and
Martyrs, were filled with draughts of Scripture Stories; not
declining the flourishes of Cypresse, Palmes, and Olive; and
the mysticall Figures of Peacocks, Doves and Cocks. But
iterately affecting the pourtraits of *Enoch, Lazarus, Jonas,*
and the Vision of *Ezechiel*, as hopefull draughts, and hinting
imagery of the Resurrection; which is the life of the grave,
and sweetens our habitations in the Land of Moles and
Pismires.

Gentile Inscriptions precisely delivered the extent of mens lives, seldome the manner of their deaths, which history it self so often leaves obscure in the records of memorable persons. There is scarce any Philosopher but dies twice or thrice in *Laertius;* Nor almost any life without two or three deaths in *Plutarch;* which makes the tragicall ends of noble persons more favourably resented by compassionate Readers, who finde some relief in the Election of such differences.

The certainty of death is attended with uncertainties, in time, manner, places. The variety of Monuments hath often obscured true graves: and *Cenotaphs* confounded Sepulchres. For beside their reall Tombs, many have found honorary and empty Sepulchres. The variety of *Homers* Monuments made him of various Countreys. *Euripides* had his Tomb in *Attica,* †
but his sepulture in *Macedonia.* And *Severus* found his real Sepulchre in *Rome,* but his empty grave in *Gallia.* 28

He that lay in a golden Urne eminently above the Earth, 29
was not like to finde the quiet of these bones. Many of these Urnes were broke by a vulgar discoverer in hope of inclosed treasure. The ashes of *Marcellus* were lost above ground, upon the like account. Where profit hath prompted, no age hath wanted such miners. For which the most barbarous Expilators found the most civill Rhetorick. Gold once out of the 30
earth is no more due unto it; What was unreasonably committed to the ground is reasonably resumed from it: Let Monuments and rich Fabricks, not Riches adorn mens ashes. The commerce of the living is not to be transferred unto the dead: It is no injustice to take that which none complains to †
lose, and no man is wronged where no man is possessor.

What virtue yet sleeps in this *terra damnata* and aged cinders, were petty magick to experiment; These crumbling reliques and long-fired particles superannate such expectations: Bones, hairs, nails, and teeth of the dead, were the treasures of old Sorcerers. In vain we revive such practices; Present superstition too visibly perpetuates the folly of our Fore-fathers, wherein unto old Observation this Island was 31
so compleat, that it might have instructed *Persia.*

Plato's historian of the other world lies twelve dayes incor- 32
rupted, while his soul was viewing the large stations of the

dead. How to keep the corps seven dayes from corruption by anointing and washing, without exenteration, were an hazardable peece of art, in our choisest practice. How they made distinct separation of bones and ashes from fiery admixture, hath found no historicall solution. Though they seemed to make a distinct collection, and overlooked not *Pyrrhus* his   33 toe. Some provision they might make by fictile Vessels, Coverings, Tiles, or flat stones, upon and about the body. And in the same Field, not farre from these Urnes, many stones were found under ground, as also by carefull separation of extraneous matter, composing and raking up the burnt bones with forks, observable in that notable lamp of *Galvanus*. *Marlia-*   34 *nus*, who had the sight of the *Vas Ustrinum*, or vessell wherein they burnt the dead, found in the Esquiline Field at *Rome*, might have afforded clearer solution. But their insatisfaction herein begat that remarkable invention in the Funerall Pyres of some Princes, by incombustible sheets made with a texture of *Asbestos*, incremable flax, or Salamanders wool, which preserved their bones and ashes incommixed.

How the bulk of a man should sink into so few pounds of bones and ashes, may seem strange unto any who considers not its constitution, and how slender a masse will remain upon an open and urging fire of the carnall composition. Even bones themselves reduced into ashes, do abate a notable proportion. And consisting much of a volatile salt, when that is fired out, make a light kind of cinders. Although their bulk be disproportionable to their weight, when the heavy principle of Salt is fired out and the Earth almost only remaineth; Observable in sallow, which makes more Ashes then Oake; and discovers the common fraud of selling Ashes by measure, and not by ponderation.

Some bones make best Skeletons, some bodies quick and speediest ashes: Who would expect a quick flame from Hydropicall *Heraclitus?* The poysoned Souldier when his Belly brake, put out two pyres in *Plutarch*. But in the plague of *Athens*, one private pyre served two or three Intruders; and the *Saracens*, burnt in large heaps by the King of *Castile*, shewed how little Fuell sufficeth. Though the Funerall pyre of *Patroclus* took up an hundred foot, a peece of an old boat burnt *Pompey;* And if the burthen of *Isaac* were sufficient for an holocaust, a man may carry his owne pyre.

From animals are drawn good burning lights, and good medicines against burning; Though the seminall humour seems of a contrary nature to fire, yet the body compleated proves a combustible lump, wherein fire findes flame even from bones, and some fuell almost from all parts. Though the Metropolis of humidity seems least disposed unto it, which [35] might render the sculls of these Urnes lesse burned then other bones. But all flies or sinks before fire almost in all bodies: When the common ligament is dissolved, the attenuable parts ascend, the rest subside in coal, calx or ashes.

To burn the bones of the King of *Edom* for Lyme, seems [36] no irrationall ferity; But to drink of the ashes of dead rela- [37] tions, a passionate prodigality. He that hath the ashes of his friend, hath an everlasting treasure: where fire taketh leave, corruption slowly enters; In bones well burnt, fire makes a wall against it self; experimented in copels, and tests of metals, which consist of such ingredients. What the Sun compoundeth, fire analyseth, not transmuteth. That devouring agent leaves almost allwayes a morsell for the Earth, whereof all things are but a colonie; and which, if time permits, the mother Element will have in their primitive masse again.

He that looks for Urnes and old sepulchrall reliques, must not seek them in the ruines of Temples; where no Religion anciently placed them. These were found in a Field, according to ancient custome, in noble or private buriall; the old practise of the *Canaanites,* the Family of *Abraham,* and the burying place of *Josua,* in the borders of his possessions; and also agreeable unto *Roman* practice to bury by high-wayes, whereby their Monuments were under eye: Memorials of themselves, and *memento's* of mortality into living passengers; whom the Epitaphs of great ones were fain to beg to stay and look upon them. A language though sometimes used, [38] not so proper in Church-Inscriptions. The sensible Rhetorick of the dead, to exemplarity of good life, first admitted the bones of pious men, and Martyrs within Church-wals; which in succeeding ages crept into promiscuous practise. While *Constantine* was peculiarly favoured to be admitted unto the

Church Porch; and the first thus buried in *England* was in the   [39]
dayes of *Cuthred.*

Christians dispute how their bodies should lye in the grave.
In urnall enterrment they clearly escaped this Controversie:
Though we decline the Religious consideration, yet in cemiteriall and narrower burying places, to avoid confusion and
crosse position, a certain posture were to be admitted; Which
even Pagan civility observed. The *Persians* lay North and
South, The *Megarians* and *Phoenicians* placed their heads to
the East: The *Athenians*, some think, towards the West,
which Christians still retain. And *Beda* will have it to be the
posture of our Saviour. That he was crucified with his face
towards the West, we will not contend with tradition and
probable account; But we applaud not the hand of the
Painter, in exalting his Crosse so high above those on either
side; since hereof we finde no authentick account in history,
and even the crosses found by *Helena* pretend no such dis-   [40]
tinction from longitude or dimension.

To be gnaw'd out of our graves, to have our sculs made   [41]
drinking-bowls, and our bones turned into Pipes, to delight
and sport our Enemies, are Tragicall abominations, escaped
in burning Burials.

Urnall enterrments, and burnt Reliques lye not in fear of
worms, or to be an heritage for Serpents; In carnall sepulture,
corruptions seem peculiar unto parts, and some speak of
snakes out of the spinall marrow. But while we suppose common wormes in graves, 'tis not easie to finde any there; few
in Churchyards above a foot deep, fewer or none in Churches,
though in fresh decayed bodies. Teeth, bones, and hair, give
the most lasting defiance to corruption. In an Hydropicall
body ten years buried in a Church-yard, we met with a fat
concretion, where the nitre of the Earth, and the salt and
lixivious liquor of the body, had coagulated large lumps of   [42]
fat, into the consistence of the hardest castle-soap; whereof
part remaineth with us. After a battle with the *Persians* the
Roman Corps decayed in few dayes, while the *Persian* bodies
remained dry and uncorrupted. Bodies in the same ground do
not uniformly dissolve, nor bones equally moulder; whereof
in the opprobrious disease we expect no long duration. The

body of the Marquesse of *Dorset* seemed sound and handsomely cereclothed, that after seventy eight years was found 43
uncorrupted. Common Tombs preserve not beyond powder:
A firmer consistence and compage of parts might be expected
from Arefaction, deep buriall or charcoal. The greatest Antiquities of mortall bodies may remain in petrified bones,
whereof, though we take not in the pillar of *Lots* wife, or
Metamorphosis of *Ortelius,* some may be older then Pyra- 44
mids, in the petrified Reliques of the generall inundation.
When *Alexander* opened the Tomb of *Cyrus,* the remaining
bones discovered his proportion, whereof urnall fragments
afford but a bad conjecture, and have this disadvantage of
grave enterrments, that they leave us ignorant of most personall discoveries. For since bones afford not only rectitude †
and stability, but figure unto the body; It is no impossible
Physiognomy to conjecture at fleshy appendencies; and after
what shape the muscles and carnous parts might hang in their
full consistences. A full spread *Cariola* shews a well-shaped 45
horse behinde, handsome formed sculls give some analogie
of fleshy resemblance. A criticall view of bones makes a good
distinction of sexes. Even colour is not beyond conjecture;
since it is hard to be deceived in the distinction of *Negro's* 46
sculls. *Dantes* Characters are to be found in sculls as well as 47
faces. *Hercules* is not onely known by his foot. Other parts
make out their comproportions, and inferences upon whole or
parts. And since the dimensions of the head measure the
whole body, and the figure thereof gives conjecture of the
principall faculties; Physiognomy outlives our selves, and
ends not in our graves.

Severe contemplators observing these lasting reliques, may
think them good monuments of persons past, little advantage
to future beings. And considering that power which subdueth
all things unto it self, that can resume the scattered Atomes,
or identifie out of any thing, conceive it superfluous to expect
a resurrection out of Reliques. But the soul subsisting, other
matter clothed with due accidents, may salve the individual-
ity: Yet the Saints we observe arose from graves and monuments, about the holy City. Some think the ancient Patriarchs
so earnestly desired to lay their bones in *Canaan,* as hoping

to make a part of that Resurrection, and though thirty miles
from Mount *Calvary*, at least to lie in that Region, which
should produce the first-fruits of the dead. And if according
to learned conjecture, the bodies of men shall rise where
their greatest Reliques remain, many are not like to erre in
the Topography of their Resurrection, though their bones or
bodies be after translated by Angels into the field of *Ezechiels*   48
vision, or as some will order it, into the Valley of Judgement,
or *Jehosaphat*.

Chapter 4.

Christians have handsomely glossed the deformity of
death, by careful consideration of the body, and civil rites
which take off brutall terminations. And though they conceived all reparable by a resurrection, cast not off all care of
enterrment. And since the ashes of Sacrifices burnt upon the
Altar of God, were carefully carried out by the Priests, and
deposed in a clean field; since they acknowledged their
bodies to be the lodging of Christ, and temples of the holy
Ghost, they devolved not all upon the sufficiency of soul existence; and therefore with long services and full solemnities
concluded their last Exequies, wherein to all distinctions the   1
Greek devotion seems most pathetically ceremonious.   2
Christian invention hath chiefly driven at Rites which
speak hopes of another life, and hints of a Resurrection. And
if the ancient Gentiles held not the immortality of their better part, and some subsistence after death; in severall rites,
customes, actions and expressions, they contradicted their
own opinions: wherein *Democritus* went high, even to the
thought of a resurrection, as scoffingly recorded by *Pliny*.   3
What can be more expresse than the expression of *Phocyl-
lides?* Or who would expect from Lucretius a sentence of   4
Ecclesiastes? Before *Plato* could speak, the soul had wings in   5
Homer, which fell not, but flew out of the body into the mansions of the dead; who also observed that handsome distinction of *Demas* and *Soma*, for the body conjoyned to the soul
and body separated from it. *Lucian* spoke much truth in jest,

when he said, that part of *Hercules* which proceeded from
Alchmena perished, that from *Jupiter* remained immortall.
Thus *Socrates* was content that his friends should bury his [6]
body, so they would not think they buried *Socrates,* and re-
garding only his immortall part, was indifferent to be burnt
or buried. From such Considerations *Diogenes* might con- [7]
temn Sepulture. And being satisfied that the soul could not
perish, grow carelesse of corporall enterrment. The *Stoicks*
who thought the souls of wise men had their habitation about
the *moon,* might make slight account of subterraneous deposition; whereas the *Pythagorians* and transcorporating Philosophers, who were to be often buried, held great care of
their enterrment. And the Platonicks rejected not a due care
of the grave, though they put their ashes to unreasonable expectations, in their tedious term of return and long set revo- [8]
lution.

Men have lost their reason in nothing so much as their religion, wherein stones and clouts make Martyrs; and since
the religion of one seems madnesse unto another, to afford an
account or rationall of old Rites, requires no rigid Reader;
That they kindled the pyre aversly, or turning their face from
it, was an handsome Symbole of unwilling ministration; That
they washed their bones with wine and milk, that the mother
wrapt them in Linnen, and dryed them in her bosome, the
first fostering part, and place of their nourishment; That they
opened their eyes towards heaven, before they kindled the
fire, as the place of their hopes or originall, were no improper
Ceremonies. Their last valediction thrice uttered by the at- [9]
tendants was also very solemn, and somewhat answered by
Christians, who thought it too little, if they threw not the
earth thrice upon the enterred body. That in strewing their
Tombs the *Romans* affected the Rose, the Greeks *Amaranthus*
and myrtle; that the Funerall pyre consisted of sweet fuell,
Cypresse, Firre, Larix, Yewe, and Trees perpetually verdant,
lay silent expressions of their surviving hopes: Wherein
Christians which deck their Coffins with Bays have found a
more elegant Embleme. For that tree seeming dead, will restore it self from the root, and its dry and exuccous leaves
resume their verdure again; which if we mistake not, we have

also observed in furze. Whether the planting of yewe in
Churchyards, hold not its originall from ancient Funerall
rites, or as an Embleme of Resurrection from its perpetual
verdure, may also admit conjecture.

They made use of Musick to excite or quiet the affections
of their friends, according to different harmonies. But the
secret and symbolicall hint was the harmonical nature of the
soul; which delivered from the body, went again to enjoy the
primitive harmony of heaven, from whence it first descended;
which according to its progresse traced by antiquity, came   10
down by *Cancer,* and ascended by *Capricornus.*

They burnt not children before their teeth appeared, as
apprehending their bodies too tender a morsell for fire, and
that their gristly bones would scarce leave separable reliques
after the pyrall combustion. That they kindled not fire in their
houses for some dayes after, was a strict memoriall of the late
afflicting fire. And mourning without hope, they had an
happy fraud against excessive lamentation, by a common
opinion that deep sorrows disturbed their ghosts.   11

That they buried their dead on their backs, or in a supine
position, seems agreeable unto profound sleep, and common
posture of dying; contrary to the most naturall way of birth;
And unlike our pendulous posture, in the doubtfull state of   †,12
the womb. *Diogenes* was singular, who preferred a prone
situation in the grave, and some Christians like neither, who 13
decline the figure of rest, and make choice of an erect posture.

That they carried them out of the world with their feet
forward, is not inconsonant unto reason: As contrary unto   14
the native posture of man, and his production first into it.
And also agreeable unto their opinions, while they bid adieu
unto the world, not to look again upon it; whereas *Mahometans,* who think to return to a delightfull life again, are carried forth with their heads forward, and looking toward their
houses.

They closed their eyes as parts which first die or first discover the sad effects of death. But their iterated clamations
to excitate their dying or dead friends, or revoke them unto
life again, was a vanity of affection; as not presumably ignorant of the criticall tests of death, by apposition of feathers,

glasses, and reflexion of figures, which dead eyes represent not; which, however not strictly verifiable in fresh and warm *cadavers,* could hardly elude the test, in corps of four of five dayes.

That they suck'd in the last breath of their expiring friends, was surely a practice of no medicall institution, but a loose opinion that the soul passed out that way, and a fondnesse of affection from some *Pythagoricall* foundation, that the spirit of one body passed into another; which they wished might be their own.

That they powred oyle upon the pyre, was a tolerable practice, while the intention rested in facilitating the accension; But to place good *Omens* in the quick and speedy burning, to sacrifice unto the windes for a dispatch in this office, was a low form of superstition.

The *Archimime* or *Jester* attending the Funerall train, and [15] imitating the speeches, gesture, and manners of the deceased, was too light for such solemnities, contradicting their Funerall Orations, and dolefull rites of the grave.

That they buried a peece of money with them as a Fee of the *Elysian Ferriman,* was a practise full of folly. But the an [16] cient custome of placing coynes in considerable Urnes, and the present practise of burying medals in the Noble Foundations of *Europe,* are laudable wayes of historicall discoveries, in actions, persons, Chronologies; and posterity will applaud them.

We examine not the old Laws of Sepulture, exempting certain persons from buriall or burning. But hereby we apprehend that these were not the bones of persons Planet-struck or burnt with fire from Heaven: No Reliques of Traitors to their Countrey, Self-killers, or Sacrilegious Malefactors; Persons in old apprehension unworthy of the *earth;* condemned unto the *Tartara's* of Hell, and bottomlesse pit of [17] *Pluto,* from whence there was no redemption. [†]

Nor were only many customes questionable in order to their Obsequies, but also sundry practises, fictions, and conceptions, discordant or obscure, of their state and future beings; whether unto eight or ten bodies of men to adde one of a woman, as being more inflammable, and unctuously con-

stituted for the better pyrall combustion, were any rationall
practise: Or whether the complaint of *Perianders* Wife be   18
tolerable, that wanting her Funerall burning she suffered intolerable cold in Hell, according to the constitution of the
infernall house of *Pluto*, wherein cold makes a great part of
their tortures; it cannot passe without some question.

Why the Female Ghosts appear unto *Ulysses*, before the   19
Heroes and masculine spirits? Why the *Psyche* or soul of
Tiresias is of the masculine gender; who being blinde on
earth sees more then all the rest in hell; Why the Funerall
Suppers consisted of Egges, Beans, Smallage, and Lettuce,
since the dead are made to eat *Asphodels* about the *Elyzian*
medows? Why since there is no Sacrifice acceptable, nor any
propitiation for the Covenant of the grave; men set up the
Deity of *Morta*, and fruitlesly adored Divinities without ears?
it cannot escape some doubt.

The dead seem all alive in the humane *Hades* of *Homer*,
yet cannot well speak, prophesie, or know the living, except
they drink bloud, wherein is the life of man. And therefore
the souls of *Penelope's* Paramours conducted by *Mercury*
chirped like bats, and those which followed *Hercules* made a
noise but like a flock of birds.

The departed spirits know things past and to come, yet are
ignorant of things present. *Agamemnon* foretels what should
happen unto *Ulysses*, yet ignorantly enquires what is become
of his own Son. The Ghosts are afraid of swords in *Homer*,
yet *Sybilla* tels *Aeneas* in *Virgil*, the thin habit of spirits was
beyond the force of weapons. The spirits put off their malice
with their bodies, and *Caesar* and *Pompey* accord in Latine
Hell, yet *Ajax* in *Homer* endures not a conference with *Ulysses*: And *Deiphobus* appears all mangled in *Virgils* Ghosts,
yet we meet with perfect shadows among the wounded ghosts
of *Homer*.

Since *Charon* in *Lucian* applauds his condition among the
dead, whether it be handsomely said of *Achilles*, that living
contemner of death, that he had rather be a Plowmans servant then Emperour of the dead? How *Hercules* his soul is in   20
hell, and yet in heaven, and *Julius* his soul in a Starre, yet
seen by *Aeneas* in hell, except the Ghosts were but Images

and shadows of the soul, received in higher mansions, according to the ancient division of body, soul, and image or *simulachrum* of them both. The particulars of future beings must needs be dark unto ancient Theories, which Christian Philosophy yet determines but in a Cloud of opinions. A Dialogue between two Infants in the womb concerning the state of this world, might handsomely illustrate our ignorance of the next, whereof methinks we yet discourse in *Platoes* denne, and are but *Embryon* Philosophers. [21]

Pythagoras escapes in the fabulous hell of *Dante,* among that swarm of Philosophers, wherein whilest we meet with *Plato* and *Socrates, Cato* is to be found in no lower place then Purgatory. Among all the set, *Epicurus* is most considerable, whom men make honest without an *Elyzium,* who contemned life without encouragement of immortality, and making nothing after death, yet made nothing of the King of terrours. [22]

Were the happinesse of the next world as closely apprehended as the felicities of this, it were a martyrdome to live; and unto such as consider none hereafter, it must be more then death to dye, which makes us amazed at those audacities, that durst be nothing, and return into their *Chaos* again. Certainly such spirits as could contemn death, when they expected no better being after, would have scorned to live had they known any. And therefore we applaud not the judgment of *Machiavel,* that Christianity makes men cowards, or that with the confidence of but half dying, the despised virtues of patience and humility, have abased the spirits of men, which Pagan principles exalted, but rather regulated the wildenesse of audacities, in the attempts, grounds, and eternall sequels of death; wherein men of the boldest spirits are often prodigiously temerarious. Nor can we extenuate the valour of ancient Martyrs, who contemned death in the uncomfortable scene of their lives, and in their decrepit Martyrdomes did probably lose not many moneths of their dayes, or parted with life when it was scarce worth the living. For (beside that long time past holds no consideration unto a slender time to come) they had no small disadvantage from the constitution of old age, which naturally makes men fearfull; complexionally superannuated from the bold and couragious [23] [24] thoughts of youth and fervent years. But the contempt of death from corporall animosity, promoteth not our felicity. They may sit in the *Orchestra,* and noblest Seats of Heaven, who have held up shaking hands in the fire, and humanely contended for glory.

Mean while *Epicurus* lyes deep in *Dante's* hell, wherein we meet with Tombs enclosing souls which denied their immortalities. But whether the virtuous heathen, who lived better then he spake, or erring in the principles of himself, yet lived above Philosophers of more specious Maximes, lye so deep as he is placed; at least so low as not to rise against Christians, who beleeving or knowing that truth, have lastingly denied it in their practise and conversation, were a quaery too sad to insist on.

But all or most apprehensions rested in Opinions of some future being, which ignorantly or coldly beleeved, begat those perverted conceptions, Ceremonies, Sayings, which Christians pity or laugh at. Happy are they, which live not in that disadvantage of time, when men could say little for futurity, but from reason. Whereby the noblest mindes fell often upon doubtfull deaths, and melancholly Dissolutions; With these hopes *Socrates* warmed his doubtfull spirits   25 against that cold potion, and *Cato* before he durst give the fatall stroak spent part of the night in reading the immortality of *Plato,* thereby confirming his wavering hand unto the animosity of that attempt.

It is the heaviest stone that melancholy can throw at a man, to tell him he is at the end of his nature; or that there is no further state to come, unto which this seemes progressionall, and otherwise made in vaine; Without this accomplishment the naturall expectation and desire of such a state, were but a fallacy in nature; unsatisfied Considerators would quarrell the justice of their constitutions, and rest content that *Adam* had fallen lower, whereby by knowing no other Originall, and deeper ignorance of themselves, they might have enjoyed the happinesse of inferiour Creatures; who in tranquility possesse their Constitutions, as having not the apprehension to deplore their own natures. And being framed below the circumference of these hopes, or cognition of better being, the

wisedom of God hath necessitated their Contentment: But
the superiour ingredient and obscured part of our selves,
whereto all present felicities afford no resting contentment,
will be able at last to tell us we are more then our present
selves; and evacuate such hopes in the fruition of their own
accomplishments.

Chapter 5.

Now since these dead bones have already out-lasted the
living ones of *Methuselah,* and in a yard under ground, and
thin walls of clay, out-worn all the strong and specious buildings above it; and quietly rested under the drums and tramplings of three conquests; What Prince can promise such   1
diuturnity unto his Reliques, or might not gladly say,

Sic ego componi versus in ossa velim.

Time which antiquates Antiquities, and hath an art to make
dust of all things, hath yet spared these *minor* Monuments.
In vain we hope to be known by open and visible conservatories, when to be unknown was the means of their continuation and obscurity their protection: If they dyed by violent
hands, and were thrust into their Urnes, these bones become
considerable, and some old Philosophers would honour them,   8
whose souls they conceived most pure, which were thus
snatched from their bodies; and to retain a stronger propen-
sion unto them: whereas they weariedly left a languishing
corps, and with faint desires of re-union. If they fell by long
and aged decay, yet wrapt up in the bundle of time, they
fall into indistinction, and make but one blot with Infants. If
we begin to die when we live, and long life be but a prolonga-
tion of death; our life is a sad composition; We live with
death, and die not in a moment. How many pulses made up
the life of *Methuselah,* were work for *Archimedes:* Common
Counters summe up the life of *Moses* his man. Our dayes be-   4
come considerable like petty sums by minute accumulations;
where numerous fractions make up but small round numbers;
and our dayes of a span long make not one little finger.   5

If the nearnesse of our last necessity brought a nearer conformity unto it, there were a happinesse in hoary hairs, and
no calamity in half senses. But the long habit of living indis-
poseth us for dying; When Avarice makes us the sport of   6
death; When even *David* grew politickly cruell; and *Solomon*   7
could hardly be said to be the wisest of men. But many are
too early old, and before the date of age. Adversity stretcheth
our dayes, misery makes *Alcmenas* nights, and time hath no   8
wings unto it. But the most tedious being is that which can
unwish it self, content to be nothing, or never to have been,
which was beyond the *male*-content of *Job*, who cursed not
the day of his life, but his Nativity: Content to have so farre
been, as to have a Title to future being; Although he had
lived here but in an hidden state of life, and as it were an
abortion.

What Song the *Syrens* sang, or what name *Achilles* as-   9
sumed when he hid himself among women, though puzling
Questions are not beyond all conjecture. What time the persons of these Ossuaries entred the famous Nations of the   10
dead, and slept with Princes and Counsellours, might admit   11
a wide solution. But who were the proprietaries of these
bones, or what bodies these ashes made up, were a question
above Antiquarism; Not to be resolved by man, nor easily
perhaps by spirits, except we consult the Provinciall Guard- 12
ians, or tutellary Observators. Had they made as good provision for their names, as they have done for their Reliques,
they had not so grosly erred in the art of perpetuation. But to
subsist in bones, and be but Pyramidally extant, is a fallacy
in duration. Vain ashes, which in the oblivion of names,
persons, times, and sexes, have found unto themselves a fruitlesse continuation, and only arise unto late posterity, as Emblemes of mortall vanities; Antidotes against pride, vainglory,
and madding vices. Pagan vainglories which thought the
world might last for ever, had encouragement for ambition,
and finding no *Atropos* unto the immortality of their Names,
were never dampt with the necessity of oblivion. Even old
ambitions had the advantage of ours, in the attempts of their
vain-glories, who acting early, and before the probable Meridian of time, have by this time found great accomplishment

of their designes, whereby the ancient *Heroes* have already
out-lasted their Monuments, and Mechanicall preservations.
But in this latter Scene of time we cannot expect such Mummies unto our memories, when ambition may fear the Prophecy of *Elias,* and *Charles* the fifth can never hope to live [13]
within two *Methusela's* of *Hector.* [14]

And therefore restlesse inquietude for the diuturnity of our
memories unto present considerations, seems a vanity almost
out of date, and superanuated peece of folly. We cannot hope
to live so long in our names, as some have done in their persons, one face of *Janus* holds no proportion unto the other.
'Tis too late to be ambitious. The great mutations of the world
are acted, or time may be too short for our designes. To extend our memories by Monuments, whose death we dayly
pray for, and whose duration we cannot hope, without injury
to our expectations, in the advent of the last day, were a contradiction to our beliefs. We whose generations are ordained
in this setting part of time, are providentially taken off from
such imaginations. And being necessitated to eye the remaining particle of futurity, are naturally constituted unto
thoughts of the next world, and cannot excusably decline the
consideration of that duration, which maketh Pyramids pillars of snow, and all that's past a moment.

Circles and right lines limit and close all bodies, and the
mortall right-lined circle, must conclude and shut up all. [15]
There is no antidote against the *Opium* of time, which tem-
porally considereth all things; Our Fathers finde their graves
in our short memories, and sadly tell us how we may be
buried in our Survivors. Grave-stones tell truth scarce fourty [16]
years. Generations passe while some trees stand, and old
Families last not three Oaks. To be read by bare Inscriptions
like many in *Gruter,* to hope for Eternity by Aenigmaticall
Epithetes, or first letters of our names, to be studied by Antiquaries, who we were, and have new Names given us like
many of the Mummies, are cold consolations unto the Stu- [17]
dents of perpetuity, even by everlasting Languages.

To be content that times to come should only know there
was such a man, not caring whether they knew more of him,
was a frigid ambition in *Cardan:* disparaging his horoscopal [18]

inclination and judgement of himself. Who cares to subsist
like *Hippocrates* Patients, or *Achilles* horses in *Homer,* under   19,20
naked nominations, without deserts and noble acts, which are
the balsame of our memories, the *Entelechia* and soul of our
subsistences. To be namelesse in worthy deeds exceeds an
infamous history. The *Canaanitish* woman lives more happily   21
without a name, then *Herodias* with one. And who had not
rather have been the good theef, then *Pilate?*

But the iniquity of oblivion blindely scattereth her poppy,
and deals with the memory of men without distinction to
merit of perpetuity. Who can but pity the founder of the
Pyramids? *Herostratus* lives that burnt the Temple of *Diana,*
he is almost lost that built it; Time hath spared the Epitaph   22
of *Adrians* horse, confounded that of himself. In vain we   23
compute our felicities by the advantage of our good names,
since bad have equall durations; and *Thersites* is like to live
as long as *Agamemnon.* Who knows whether the best of men
be known? or whether there be not more remarkable persons
forgot, then any that stand remembred in the known account
of time? Without the favor of the everlasting Register the first
man had been as unknown as the last, and *Methuselahs* long
life had been his only Chronicle.

Oblivion is not to be hired: The greater part must be content to be as though they had not been, to be found in the
Register of God, not in the record of man. Twenty seven   24
Names make up the first story, and the recorded names ever
since contain not one living Century. The number of the dead   25
long exceedeth all that shall live. The night of time far surpasseth the day, and who knows when was the Aequinox?
Every houre addes unto that current Arithmetique, which
scarce stands one moment. And since death must be the
Lucina of life, and even Pagans could doubt whether thus to   26
live, were to dye. Since our longest Sunne sets at right de-   27
scensions, and makes but winter arches, and therefore it cannot be long before we lie down in darknesse, and have our
light in ashes. Since the brother of death daily haunts us with   28
dying *memento's,* and time that grows old it self, bids us hope
no long duration: Diuturnity is a dream and folly of expectation.

Darknesse and light divide the course of time, and oblivion shares with memory a great part even of our living beings; we slightly remember our felicities, and the smartest stroaks of affliction leave but short smart upon us. Sense endureth no extremities, and sorrows destroy us or themselves. To weep [29] into stones are fables. Afflictions induce callosities, miseries are slippery, or fall like snow upon us, which notwithstanding is no unhappy stupidity. To be ignorant of evils to come, and forgetfull of evils past, is a mercifull provision in nature, whereby we digest the mixture of our few and evil dayes, and our delivered senses not relapsing into cutting remembrances, our sorrows are not kept raw by the edge of repetitions. A great part of Antiquity contented their hopes of subsistency with a transmigration of their souls. A good way to continue their memories, while having the advantage of plurall successions, they could not but act something remarkable in such variety of beings, and enjoying the fame of their passed selves, make accumulation of glory unto their last durations. Others rather then be lost in the uncomfortable night of nothing, were content to recede into the common being, and make one particle of the publick soul of all things, which was no more then to return into their unknown and divine Originall again. Aegyptian ingenuity was more unsatisfied, contriving their bodies in sweet consistences, to attend the return of their souls. But all was vanity, feeding the winde, and [30] folly. The Aegyptian Mummies, which *Cambyses* or time hath spared, avarice now consumeth. Mummie is become [31] Merchandise, *Mizraim* cures wounds, and *Pharaoh* is sold for balsoms. [32]

In vain do individuals hope for Immortality, or any patent from oblivion, in preservations below the Moon: Men have been deceived even in their flatteries above the Sun, and studied conceits to perpetuate their names in heaven. The various Cosmography of that part hath already varied the names of contrived constellations; *Nimrod* is lost in *Orion*, [33] and *Osyris* in the Dogge-starre. While we look for incorrup- [34] tion in the heavens, we finde they are but like the Earth; Durable in their main bodies, alterable in their parts: whereof **beside Comets and new** Stars, perspectives begin to tell tales.

And the spots that wander about the Sun, with *Phaetons* favour, would make clear conviction.

There is nothing strictly immortall, but immortality; whatever hath no beginning may be confident of no end. All
others have a dependent being, and within the reach of destruction, which is the peculiar of that necessary essence that   35
cannot destroy it self; And the highest strain of omnipotency
to be so powerfully constituted, as not to suffer even from the
power of it self. But the sufficiency of Christian Immortality
frustrates all earthly glory, and the quality of either state   36
after death, makes a folly of posthumous memory. God who
can only destroy our souls, and hath assured our resurrection, either of our bodies or names hath directly promised no
duration. Wherein there is so much of chance that the boldest
Expectants have found unhappy frustrations; and to hold
long subsistence, seems but a scape in oblivion. But man is a
Noble Animal, splendid in ashes, and pompous in the grave,
solemnizing Nativities and Deaths with equall lustre, nor
omitting Ceremonies of bravery, in the infamy of his nature.

Life is a pure flame, and we live by an invisible Sun within
us. A small fire sufficeth for life, great flames seemed too little
after death, while men vainly affected precious pyres, and to
burn like *Sardanapalus;* but the wisedom of funerall Laws   37,38
found the folly of prodigall blazes, and reduced undoing fires
unto the rule of sober obsequies, wherein few could be so
mean as not to provide wood, pitch, a mourner, and an Urne.   39

Five Languages secured not the Epitaph of *Gordianus;*   40
The man of God lives longer without a Tomb then any by   41
one, invisibly interred by Angels; and adjudged to obscurity,
though not without some marks directing humane discovery.
Enoch and *Elias* without either tomb or buriall, in an anoma-   42,43
lous state of being, are the great Examples of perpetuity, in
their long and living memory, in strict account being still on
this side death, and having a late part yet to act upon this
stage of earth. If in the decretory term of the world we shall
not all dye but be changed, according to received translation;   44
the last day will make but few graves; at least quick Resur-
rections will anticipate lasting Sepultures; Some Graves will
be opened before they be quite closed, and *Lazarus* be no

wonder. When many that feared to dye shall groane that they can dye but once, the dismall state is the second and living death, when life puts despair on the damned; when men shall wish the coverings of Mountaines, not of Monuments, [45] and annihilation shall be courted.

While some have studied Monuments, others have studiously declined them: and some have been so vainly boisterous, that they durst not acknowledge their Graves; wherein *Alaricus* seems most subtle, who had a River turned to hide [46] his bones at the bottome. Even *Sylla* that thought himself safe in his Urne, could not prevent revenging tongues, and stones thrown at his Monument. Happy are they whom privacy makes innocent, who deal so with men in this world, that they are not afraid to meet them in the next, who when they dye, make no commotion among the dead, and are not toucht with that poeticall taunt of *Isaiah*. [47]

Pyramids, Arches, Obelisks, were but the irregularities of vain-glory, and wilde enormities of ancient magnanimity. But the most magnanimous resolution rests in the Christian Religion, which trampleth upon pride, and sits on the neck of ambition, humbly pursuing that infallible perpetuity unto which all others must diminish their diameters, and be poorly seen in Angles of contingency. [48]

Pious spirits who passed their dayes in raptures of futurity, made little more of this world, then the world that was before it, while they lay obscure in the Chaos of pre-ordination, and [49] night of their fore-beings. And if any have been so happy as truly to understand Christian annihilation, extasis, exolution, [50] liquefaction, transformation, the kisse of the Spouse, gustation of God, and ingression into the divine shadow, they have already had an handsome anticipation of heaven; the glory of the world is surely over, and the earth in ashes unto them.

To subsist in lasting Monuments, to live in their productions, to exist in their names, and praedicament of *Chymera's*, [51] was large satisfaction unto old expectations, and made one part of their *Elyziums.* But all this is nothing in the Metaphysicks of true belief. To live indeed is to be again our selves, which being not only an hope but an evidence in noble beleevers, 'Tis all one to lye in St *Innocents* Church-yard, [52]

as in the Sands of *Aegypt:* Ready to be any thing, in the
extasie of being ever, and as content with six foot as the
Moles of *Adrianus.*   53

Lucan

Tabesne cadavera solvat
An rogus haud refert.   54

THE GARDEN OF CYRUS

THE
GARDEN
OF
CYRUS.

OR,

The Quincunciall, Lozenge,
or Net-work Plantations
of the Ancients, Artificially
Naturally, Mystically
Considered.

BY

Thomas Brown D. of Physick

Printed in the Year, 1658.

TO MY
Worthy and Honored Friend
NICHOLAS BACON
of *Gillingham* Esquire.

1

Had I not observed that Purblinde men have discoursed
well of sight, and some without issue, excellently of Generation; I that was never master of any considerable garden, had
not attempted this Subject. But the Earth is the Garden of
Nature, and each fruitfull Countrey a Paradise. *Dioscorides*
made most of his Observations in his march about with *Antonius;* and *Theophrastus* raised his generalities chiefly from
the field.

Beside we write no Herball, nor can this Volume deceive
you, who have handled the massiest thereof: who know that
three Folio's are yet too little, and how New Herbals fly from
America upon us; from persevering Enquirers, and old in
those singularities, we expect such Descriptions. Wherein
England is now so exact, that it yeelds not to other Countreys.

We pretend not to multiply vegetable divisions by Quincuncial and Reticulate plants; or erect a new Phytology. The
Field of knowledge hath been so traced, it is hard to spring
any thing new. Of old things we write something new, if truth
may receive addition, or envy will have any thing new; since
the Ancients knew the late Anatomicall discoveries, and *Hippocrates* the Circulation.

You have been so long out of trite learning, that 'tis hard
to finde a subject proper for you; and if you have met with
a Sheet upon this, we have missed our intention. In this multiplicity of writing, bye and barren Themes are best fitted for
invention; Subjects so often discoursed confine the Imagination, and fix our conceptions unto the notions of fore-writers.
Beside, such Discourses allow excursions, and venially admit

of collaterall truths, though at some distance from their principals. Wherein if we sometimes take wide liberty, we are not
single, but erre by great example.   9

He that will illustrate the excellency of this order, may
easily fail upon so spruce a Subject, wherein we have not
affrighted the common Reader with any other Diagramms,
then of it self; and have industriously declined illustrations
from rare and unknown plants.

Your discerning judgement so well acquainted with that
study, will expect herein no mathematicall truths, as well
understanding how few generalities and *U finita's* there are
in nature. How *Scaliger* hath found exceptions in most Uni-   10
versals of *Aristotle* and *Theophrastus*. How Botanicall Maximes must have fair allowance, and are tolerably currant, if
not intolerably over-ballanced by exceptions.

You have wisely ordered your vegetable delights, beyond
the reach of exception. The Turks who passt their dayes in
Gardens here, will have Gardens also hereafter, and delight-
ing in Flowers on earth, must have Lillies and Roses in
Heaven. In Garden Delights 'tis not easie to hold a Mediocrity; that insinuating pleasure is seldome without some extremity. The Antients venially delighted in flourishing
Gardens; Many were Florists that knew not the true use of a   11
Flower; And in *Plinies* dayes none had directly treated of that
Subject. Some commendably affected Plantations of venemous Vegetables, some confined their delights unto single   12
plants, and *Cato* seemed to dote upon Cabbadge; While the   13
Ingenuous delight of Tulipists stands saluted with hard lan-   14
guage, even by their own Professors.

That in this Garden Discourse we range into extraneous
things, and many parts of Art and Nature, we follow herein
the example of old and new Plantations, wherein noble spirits
contented not themselves with Trees, but by the attendance
of Aviaries, Fish Ponds, and all variety of Animals, they made
their gardens the Epitome of the earth, and some resemblance of the secular shows of old.

That we conjoyn these parts of different Subjects, or that
this should succeed the other; Your judgement will admit
without impute of incongruity; Since the delightfull world

comes after death, and Paradise succeeds the Grave. Since the verdant state of things is the Symbole of the Resurrection, and to flourish in the state of Glory, we must first be sown in 15 corruption. Beside the ancient practise of Noble Persons, to conclude in Garden-Graves, and Urnes themselves of old, to be wrapt up in flowers and garlands.

Nullum sine venia placuisse eloquium, is more sensibly un- 16 derstood by Writers, then by Readers; nor well apprehended by either, till works have hanged out like *Apelles* his Pictures; 17 wherein even common eyes will finde something for emendation.

To wish all Readers of your abilities, were unreasonably to multiply the number of Scholars beyond the temper of these times. But unto this ill-judging age, we charitably desire a portion of your equity, judgement, candour, and ingenuity; wherein you are so rich, as not to lose by diffusion. And be- 18 ing a flourishing branch of that Noble Family, unto which we owe so much observance, you are not new set, but long rooted in such perfection, whereof having had so lasting confirmation in your worthy conversation, constant amity, and expression; and knowing you a serious Student in the highest *arcana's* of Nature; with much excuse we bring these low delights, and poor maniples to your Treasure.

> Your affectionate Friend
> and Servant,
> *Thomas Browne.*

Norwich *May* 1.

The Garden of Cyrus.

The Quincunciall, Lozenge, or Net-work Plantations of the Ancients, Artificially, Naturally, Mystically considered.

CHAPTER I

That *Vulcan* gave arrows unto *Apollo* and *Diana* the fourth [19]
day after their Nativities, according to Gentile Theology, may
passe for no blinde apprehension of the Creation of the Sunne
and Moon, in the work of the fourth day; When the diffused
light contracted into Orbes, and shooting rayes, of those Luminaries. Plainer Descriptions there are from Pagan pens, of
the creatures of the fourth day; While the divine Philosopher [20]
unhappily omitteth the noblest part of the third; And *Ovid*
(whom many conceive to have borrowed his description from
Moses) coldly deserting the remarkable account of the text,
in three words, describeth this work of the third day; the vege- [21]
table creation, and first ornamentall Scene of nature; the
primitive food of animals, and first story of Physick, in Dieteti-
cal conservation.

For though Physick may pleade high, from that medicall
act of God, in casting so deep a sleep upon our first Parent;
And Chirurgery finde its whole art, in that one passage con- [22]
cerning the Rib of *Adam*, yet is there no rivality with Garden
contrivance and Herbery. For if Paradise were planted the
third day of the Creation, as wiser Divinity concludeth, the
Nativity thereof was too early for Horoscopie; Gardens were
before Gardiners, and but some hours after the earth.

Of deeper doubt is its Topography, and locall designation;
yet being the primitive garden, and without much controver- [23]
sie seated in the East; it is more then probable the first cu-

riosity, and cultivation of plants, most flourished in those quarters. And since the Ark of *Noah* first toucht upon some mountains of *Armenia,* the planting art arose again in the East, and found its revolution not far from the place of its Nativity, about the Plains of those Regions. And if *Zoroaster* 24 were either *Cham, Chus,* or *Mizraim,* they were early proficients therein, who left (as *Pliny* delivereth) a work of Agriculture.

However the account of the Pensill or hanging gardens of 25 *Babylon,* if made by *Semiramis,* the third or fourth from *Nimrod,* is of no slender antiquity; which being not framed upon ordinary levell of ground, but raised upon pillars, admitting under-passages, we cannot accept as the first *Babylonian* Gardens; But a more eminent progress and advancement in that art, then any that went before it: Somewhat answering or hinting the old Opinion concerning Paradise it self, with many conceptions elevated above the plane of the Earth.

Nebuchodonosor, whom some will have to be the famous *Syrian* King of *Diodorus,* beautifully repaired that City; and so magnificently built his hanging gardens; that from succeeding Writers he had the honour of the first. From whence overlooking *Babylon,* and all the Region about it, he found no circumscription to the eye of his ambition, till over-delighted with the bravery of this Paradise, in his melancholy metamor- 26 phosis, he found the folly of that delight, and a proper punishment, in the contrary habitation, in wilde plantations and wandrings of the fields.

The *Persian* Gallants who destroyed this Monarchy, maintained their Botanicall bravery. Unto whom we owe the very name of Paradise: wherewith we meet not in Scripture before the time of *Solomon,* and conceived originally *Persian.* The word for that disputed Garden expressing in the Hebrew no more then a Field enclosed, which from the same Root is content to derive a garden and a Buckler.

Cyrus the elder, brought up in Woods and Mountains, when time and power enabled, pursued the dictate of his education, and brought the treasures of the field into rule and circum-scription. So nobly beautifying the hanging Gar-

dens of *Babylon,* that he was also thought to be the authour
thereof.

Ahasuerus (whom many conceive to have been *Artaxerxes
Longi-manus*) in the Countrey and City of Flowers, and in   27
an open Garden, entertained his Princes and people, while
Vasthi more modestly treated the Ladies within the Palace
thereof.

But if (as some opinion) King *Ahasuerus* were *Artaxerxes
Mnemon,* that found a life and reign answerable unto his
great memory, our magnified *Cyrus* was his second Brother:
who gave the occasion of that memorable work, and almost
miraculous retrait of *Xenophon.* A person of high spirit and   28
honour, naturally a King, though fatally prevented by the
harmlesse chance of *post*-geniture: Not only a Lord of Gardens, but a manuall planter thereof: disposing his trees like
his armies in regular ordination. So that while old *Laertes*   †,29
hath found a name in *Homer* for pruning hedges, and clear-
ing away thorns and bryars; while King *Attalus* lives for his
poysonous plantations of *Aconites,* Henbane, Hellebore, and
plants hardly admitted within the walls of Paradise; While
many of the Ancients do poorly live in the single names of   30
Vegetables; All stories do look upon *Cyrus,* as the splendid
and regular planter.

According whereto *Xenophon* describeth his gallant plan-   31
tation at *Sardis,* thus rendred by *Strebaeus: Arbores pari
intervallo sitas, rectos ordines, & omnia perpulchrè in Quin-
cuncem directa.* Which we shall take for granted as being accordingly rendred by the most elegant of the *Latines;* and by   32
no made term, but in use before by *Varro.* That is the rows
and orders so handsomly disposed; or five trees so set together, that a regular angularity, and through prospect, was
left on every side, Owing this name not only unto the Quin-

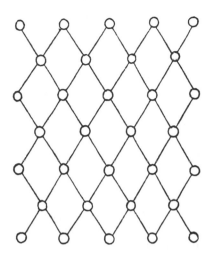

Quid Quincunce ſpecioſius, qui, in quamcunqʒ partem ſpectaueris, rectus eſt. Quintilian :∥

tuple number of Trees, but the figure declaring that number; which being doubled at the angle, makes up the Letter X, that is the Emphaticall decussation, or fundamentall figure. 33

Now though in some ancient and modern practice the *area* or decussated plot, might be a perfect square, answerable to a *Tuscan Pedestall,* and the *Quinquernio* or Cinque-point of a dye; wherein by Diagonall lines the intersection was rectangular; accomodable unto Plantations of large growing Trees; and we 34

must not deny our selves the advantage of this order; yet shall we chiefly insist upon that of *Curtius* and *Porta,* in their brief description hereof. Wherein the *decussis* is made within a longilaterall square, with opposite angles, acute and obtuse at the intersection; and so upon progression making a *Rhombus* or Lozenge figuration, which seemeth very agreeable unto the Originall figure; Answerable whereunto we observe the decussated characters in many consulary Coynes, and even in those of *Constantine* and his Sons, which pretend their pattern in the Sky; the crucigerous Ensigne carried this figure, not transversly or rectangularly intersected, but in a 35 decussation, after the form of an *Andrean* or *Burgundian* cross, which answereth this description.

Where by the way we shall decline the old Theme, so traced by antiquity, of crosses and crucifixion: Whereof some being right, and of one single peece without traversion or transome, do little advantage our subject. Nor shall we take in the mysticall *Tau,* or the Crosse of our blessed Saviour, which having in some descriptions an *Empedon* or crossing foot-stay, made not one single transversion. And since the Learned *Lipsius* hath made some doubt even of the Crosse of Sᵗ *Andrew;* since some Martyrologicall Histories deliver his death by the generall Name of a crosse, and *Hippolitus* will have him suffer by the sword; we should have enough to make out the received Crosse of that Martyr. Nor shall we urge the *labarum*, and famous Standard of *Constantine*, or make further use thereof, then as the first Letters in the Name of our Saviour Christ, in use among Christians, before the dayes of *Constantine,* to be observed in Sepulchral Monuments of Martyrs, in the Reign of *Adrian,* and *Antoninus;* and to be found in the Antiquities of the Gentiles, before the advent of Christ, as in the Medall of King *Ptolomy,* signed with the same characters; and might be the beginning of some word or name, which Antiquaries have not hit on.

We will not revive the mysterious crosses of *Aegypt*, with circles on their heads, in the breast of *Serapis,* and the hands of their Geniall spirits, not unlike the character of *Venus,* and looked on by ancient Christians, with relation unto Christ. Since however they first began, the Aegyptians thereby expressed the processe and motion of the spirit of the world, and the diffusion thereof upon the Celestiall and Elementall nature; implyed by a circle and right-lined intersection. A secret in their Telesmes and magicall Characters among them. Though he that considereth the plain crosse upon the head of the Owl in the Laterane Obelisk, or the crosse erected upon a picher diffusing streams of water into two basins, with sprinkling branches in them, and all described upon a two-footed Altar, as in the Hieroglyphicks of the brasen Table of *Bembus;* will hardly decline all thought of Christian signality in them.

We shall not call in the Hebrew *Tenupha,* or ceremony of their Oblations, waved by the Priest unto the four quarters of the world, after the form of a cross, as in the peace-offerings. And if it were clearly made out what is remarkably delivered from the Traditions of the Rabbins, that as the Oyle was powred coronally or circularly upon the head of Kings, so the High-Priest was anointed decussatively or in the form of a X; though it could not escape a typical thought of Christ, from mysticall considerators; yet being the conceit is Hebrew, we should rather expect its verification from Analogy in that language, then to confine the same unto the unconcerned Letters of *Greece*, or make it out by the characters of *Cadmus* or *Palamedes*.

Of this Quincunciall Ordination the Ancients practised much, discoursed little; and the Moderns have nothing enlarged; which he that more nearly considereth, in the form of its square *Rhombus*, and decussation, with the severall commodities, mysteries, parallelismes, and resemblances, both in Art and Nature, shall easily discern the elegancy of this order.

That this was in some wayes of practice in diverse and distant Nations, hints or deliveries there are from no slender Antiquity. In the hanging Gardens of *Babylon*, from *Abydenus*, *Eusebius*, and others, *Curtius* describeth this Rule of decussation. In the memorable Garden of *Alcinous*, anciently conceived an originall phancy, from Paradise, mention there is of well contrived order; For so hath *Didymus* and *Eustathius* expounded the emphatical word. *Diomedes* describing the Rurall possessions of his father, gives account in the same Language of Trees orderly planted. And *Ulysses* being a boy was promised by his Father fourty Figge-trees, and fifty rows of Vines producing all kinde of grapes. [36]

That the Eastern Inhabitants of *India* made use of such order, even in open Plantations, is deducible from *Theophrastus;* who describing the trees whereof they made their garments, plainly delivereth that they were planted κατ' ὄρχους and in such order that at a distance men would mistake them for Vineyards. The same seems confirmed in *Greece* from a singular expression in *Aristotle* concerning the order of Vines, [37] delivered by a military term representing the orders of Souldiers, which also confirmeth the antiquity of this form yet used in vineall plantations.

That the same was used in Latine plantations is plainly confirmed from the commending penne of *Varro, Quintilian,* and handsome Description of *Virgil*. [38]

That the first Plantations not long after the Floud were disposed after this manner, the generality and antiquity of this

order observed in Vineyards, and Wine plantations, affordeth
some conjecture. And since from judicious enquiry *Saturn,*   [39]
who divided the world between his three Sonnes, who beareth a Sickle in his hand, who taught the plantations of Vines,
the setting, grafting of trees, and the best part of Agriculture,
is discovered to be *Noah;* whether this early dispersed Husbandry in Vineyards had not its Originall in that Patriarch, is
no such Paralogicall doubt.

And if it were clear that this was used by *Noah* after the
Floud, I could easily beleeve it was in use before it; Not willing to fix to such ancient inventions no higher originall then   [†]
Noah; Nor readily conceiving those aged *Heroes,* whose diet
was vegetable, and only or chiefly consisted in the fruits of
the earth, were much deficient in their splendid cultivations;
or after the experience of fifteen hundred years, left much
for future discovery in Botanicall Agriculture. Nor fully perswaded that Wine was the invention of *Noah,* that fermented
Liquors, which often make themselves, so long escaped their
Luxury or experience; that the first sinne of the new world   [40]
was no sin of the old. That *Cain* and *Abel* were the first that
offered Sacrifice; or because the Scripture is silent, that *Adam*
or *Isaac* offered none at all.

Whether *Abraham,* brought up in the first planting Countrey, observed not some rule hereof, when he planted a grove
at *Beer-sheba;* or whether at least a like ordination were not
in the Garden of *Solomon,* probability may contest, Answerably unto the wisedom of that eminent Botanologer, and
orderly disposer of all his other works. Especially since this
was one peece of Gallantry, wherein he pursued the specious
part of felicity, according to his own description. I made me   [41]
Gardens and Orchards, and planted Trees in them of all
kindes of fruit. I made me Pools of water, to water therewith
the wood that bringeth forth Trees; which was no ordinary
plantation, if according to the *Targum,* or *Chaldee Para-*
phrase, it contained all kindes of Plants, and some fetched
as far as *India;* And the extent thereof were from the wall of
Jerusalem unto the water of *Siloah.*

And if *Jordan* were but *Jaar Eden,* that is, the River of
Eden, Genesar but *Gansar* or the Prince of Gardens; and it

could be made out, that the Plain of *Jordan* were watered not comparatively, but causally, and because it was the Paradise of God, as the Learned *Abramas* hinteth, he was not far from the Prototype and originall of Plantations. And since even in Paradise it self, the tree of knowledge was placed in the middle of the Garden, whatever was the ambient figure, there wanted not a centre and rule of decussation. Whether the groves and sacred Plantations of Antiquity, were not thus orderly placed, either by *quaternio's*, or quintuple ordinations, may favourably be doubted. For since they were so methodicall in the constitutions of their temples as to observe the due scituation, aspect, manner, form, and order in Architectonicall relations, whether they were not as distinct in their groves and Plantations about them, in form and *species* respectively unto their Deities, is not without probability of conjecture. And in their groves of the Sunne this was a fit number, by multiplication to denote the dayes of the year; and might Hieroglyphically speak as much, as the mysticall *Statua* of *Janus* in the Language of his fingers. And since they were so criticall in the number of his horses, the strings of his Harp, and rayes about his head, denoting the orbes of heaven, the Seasons and Moneths of the Yeare; witty Idolatry would hardly be flat in other appropriations.

42

43

Chapter II

Nor was this only a form of practise in Plantations, but found imitation from high Antiquity, in sundry artificiall contrivances and manuall operations. For to omit the position of squared stones, *cuneatim* or *wedgwise* in the Walls of *Roman* and *Gothick* buildings; and the *lithostrata* or figured pavements of the ancients, which consisted not all of square stones, but were divided into triquetrous segments, honeycombs, and sexangular figures, according to *Vitruvius;* The squared stones and bricks in ancient fabricks, were placed after this order. And two above or below conjoyned by a middle stone or *Plinthus*, observable in the ruines of *Forum Nervae*, the *Mausoleum* of *Augustus*, the Pyramid of *Cestius*,

and the sculpture draughts of the larger Pyramids of Aegypt.   ¹
And therefore in the draughts of eminent fabricks, Painters
do commonly imitate this order in the lines of their description.

In the Laureat draughts of sculpture and picture, the
leaves and foliate works are commonly thus contrived, which
is but in imitation of the *Pulvinaria,* and ancient pillow-work,
observable in *Ionick* peeces, about columns, temples and altars. To omit many other analogies, in Architectonicall
draughts, which art it self is founded upon fives, as having its   ²
subject and most gracefull peeces divided by this number.

The Triumphal Oval, and Civicall Crowns of Laurel, Oake,
and Myrtle, when fully made, were pleated after this order.
And to omit the crossed Crowns of Christian Princes; what
figure that was which *Anastatius* described upon the head of
Leo the third; or who first brought in the Arched Crown?
That of Charles the great, (which seems the first remarkably   ³
closed Crown,) was framed after this manner; with an intersection in the middle from the main crossing barres, and the
interspaces unto the frontal circle continued by handsome
network-plates, much after this order. Whereon we shall not
insist, because from greater Antiquity, and practice of consecration, we meet with the radiated and starry Crown, upon
the head of *Augustus,* and many succeeding Emperors. Since
the Armenians and Parthians had a peculiar royall Capp;
And the Grecians from *Alexander* another kinde of diadem.
And even Diadems themselves were but fasciations, and
handsome ligatures, about the heads of Princes; nor wholly
omitted in the mitrall Crown, which common picture seems   ⁴
to set too upright and forward upon the head of *Aaron:*
Worne sometimes singly, or doubly by Princes, according to
their Kingdomes; and no more to be expected from two   ⁵
Crowns at once, upon the head of *Ptolomy.* And so easily
made out when historians tell us, some bound up wounds,
some hanged themselves with diadems.

The beds of the antients were corded somewhat after this
fashion: That is not directly, as ours at present, but obliquely,
from side to side, and after the manner of network; whereby

they strengthened the spondae or bedsides, and spent less
cord in the work: as is demonstrated by *Blancanus*.   6

And as they lay in crossed beds, so they sat upon seeming
crosselegg'd seats: in which form the noblest thereof were
framed: Observable in the triumphall seats, the *sella curulis,*
or *Aedyle Chayres,* in the coyns of *Cestius, Sylla,* and *Julius.*
That they sat also crosse legg'd many noble draughts declare;
and in this figure the sitting gods and goddesses are drawn in
medalls and medallions. And beside this kinde of work in   7
Retiarie and hanging textures, in embroderies, and eminent
needle-works; the like is obvious unto every eye in glass-
windows. Nor only in Glassie contrivances, but also in Lattice
and Stone-work, conceived in the Temple of *Solomon;*
wherein the windows are termed *fenestrae reticulatae,* or
lights framed like nets. And agreeable unto the Greek expression concerning Christ in the Canticles, looking through the   8
nets, which ours hath rendered, he looketh forth at the windows, shewing himselfe through the lattesse; that is, partly
seen and unseen, according to the visible and invisible side
of his nature. To omit the noble reticulate work, in the chapi-
ters of the pillars of *Solomon,* with Lillies, and Pomegranats
upon a network ground; and the *Craticula* or grate through   9
which the ashes fell in the altar of burnt offerings.

That the networks and nets of antiquity were little different in the form from ours at present, is confirmable from the
nets in the hands of the Retiarie gladiators, the proper combatants with the secutores. To omit the ancient Conopeion or
gnatnet, of the Aegyptians, the inventors of that Artifice: the
rushey labyrinths of *Theocritus;* the nosegaynets, which hung
from the head under the nostrils of Princes; and that uneasie
metaphor of *Reticulum Jecoris,* which some expound the   10
lobe, we the caule above the liver. As for that famous net-
work of *Vulcan,* which inclosed *Mars* and *Venus,* and caused
that unextinguishable laugh in heaven; since the gods them-   11
selves could not discern it, we shall not prie into it; Although
why *Vulcan* bound them, *Neptune* loosed them, and *Apollo*
should first discover them, might afford no vulgar mythologie.   12
Heralds have not omitted this order or imitation thereof,
whiles they Symbollically adorn their Scuchions with Mascles

Fusils and Saltyrs, and while they disposed the figures of
Ermins, and vaired coats in this Quincuncial method.

The same is not forgot by Lapidaries while they cut their
gemms pyramidally, or by aequicrural triangles. Perspective
picturers, in their Base, Horison, and lines of distances, can-   †
not escape these Rhomboidall decussations. Sculptors in their
strongest shadows, after this order do draw their double
Hatches. And the very *Americans* do naturally fall upon it, in
their neat and curious textures, which is also observed in the
elegant artifices of *Europe*. But this is no law unto the woof
of the neat *Retiarie* Spider, which seems to weave without
transversion, and by the union of right lines to make out a
continued surface, which is beyond the common art of Tex-
tury, and may still nettle *Minerva* the Goddesse of that mys-   13
tery. And he that shall hatch the little seeds, either found in
small webs, or white round Egges, carried under the bellies
of some Spiders, and behold how at their first production in
boxes, they will presently fill the same with their webbs, may
observe the early and untaught finger of nature, and how
they are natively provided with a stock sufficient for such
Texture.

The Rurall charm against *Dodder, Tetter,* and strangling
weeds, was contrived after this order, while they placed a
chalked Tile at the four corners, and one in the middle of
their fields, which though ridiculous in the intention, was rationall in the contrivance, and a good way to diffuse the
magick through all parts of the *Area.*

Somewhat after this manner they ordered the little stones
in the old game of *Pentalithismus,* or casting up five stones to
catch them on the back of their hand, And with some resemblance hereof, the *Proci* or Prodigall Paramours disposed their
men, when they played at *Penelope.* For being themselves an   14
hundred and eight, they set fifty four stones on either side,
and one in the middle, which they called *Penelope,* which he
that hit was master of the game.

In Chesse-boards and Tables we yet finde Pyramids and
Squares, I wish we had their true and ancient description,
farre different from ours, or the *Chet mat* of the *Persians,*
which might continue some elegant remarkables, as being an

invention as High as *Hermes* the Secretary of *Osyris,* figuring [15] the whole world, the motion of the Planets, with Eclipses of Sunne and Moon.

Physicians are not without the use of this decussation in severall operations, in ligatures and union of dissolved continuities. Mechanicks make use hereof in forcipall Organs, and Instruments of Incision; wherein who can but magnifie the power of decussation, inservient to contrary ends, solution and consolidation, union, and division, illustrable from *Aristotle* in the old *Nucifragium* or Nutcracker, and the Instruments of Evulsion, compression or incision; which consisting of two *Vectes* or armes, converted towards each other, the innitency and stresse being made upon the *hypomochlion* or fulciment in the decussation, the greater compression is made by the union of two impulsors.

The *Roman Batalia* was ordered after this manner, whereof [16] as sufficiently known *Virgil* hath left but an hint, and obscure intimation. For thus were the maniples and cohorts of the *Hastati, Principes* and *Triarii* placed in their bodies, wherein consisted the strength of the *Roman* battle.

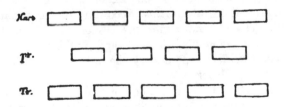

By this Ordination they readily fell into each other; the *Hastati* being pressed, handsomely retired into the intervalls of the *principes,* these into that of the *Triarii,* which making as it were a new body, might joyntly renew the battle, wherein consisted the secret of their successes. And therefore it was remarkably singular in the battle of *Africa,* that *Scipio* fearing a rout from the Elephants of the Enemy, left not the *Principes* in their alternate distances, whereby the Elephants passing the vacuities of the *Hastati,* might have run upon them, but drew his battle into right order, and leaving the passages bare, defeated the mischief intended by the Ele-

phants. Out of this figure were made two remarkable forms of
Battle, the *Cuneus* and *Forceps,* or the sheare and wedge bat-
tles, each made of half a *Rhombus,* and but differenced by
position. The wedge invented to break or work into a body,
the *forceps* to environ and defeat the power thereof, composed out of the selectest Souldiery and disposed into the
form of an V, wherein receiving the wedge, it inclosed it on
both sides. After this form the famous *Narses* ordered his bat-   †
tle against the *Franks,* and by this figure the *Almans* were
enclosed, and cut in peeces.

The *Rhombus* or Lozenge figure so visible in this order, was
also a remarkable form of battle in the *Grecian* Cavalry, observed by the *Thessalians,* and *Philip* King of *Macedon,* and
frequently by the *Parthians,* as being most ready to turn
every way, and best to be commanded, as having its ductors,
or Commanders at each Angle.

The *Macedonian Phalanx* (a long time thought invincible)
consisted of a long square. For though they might be sixteen
in Rank and file, yet when they shut close, so that the sixt
pike advanced before the first ranck, though the number
might be square, the figure was oblong, answerable unto the
Quincunciall quadrate of *Curtius.* According to this square,
Thucydides delivers, the *Athenians* disposed their battle
against the *Lacedemonians* brickwise, and by the same word
the Learned *Guellius* expoundeth the quadrate of *Virgil,*   17
after the form of a brick or tile.

And as the first station and position of trees, so was the first
habitation of men, not in round Cities, as of later foundation;
For the form of *Babylon* the first City was square, and so
shall also be the last, according to the description of the holy
City in the Apocalyps. The famous pillars of *Seth* before the   18,19
floud had also the like foundation, if they were but *antidilu-
vian* Obelisks, and such as *Cham* and his *Aegyptian* race
imitated after the Floud.

But *Nineveh* which Authours acknowledge to have exceeded *Babylon,* was of a longilaterall figure, ninety five Furlongs broad, and an hundred and fifty long, and so making
about sixty miles in circuit, which is the measure of three
dayes journey, according unto military marches, or castren-

siall mansions. So that if *Jonas* entred at the narrower side, he found enough for one dayes walk to attain the heart of the City, to make his Proclamation. And if we imagine a City extending from *Ware* to *London*, the expression will be moderate of six score thousand Infants, although we allow vacuities, fields, and intervals of habitation, as there needs must be when the monument of *Ninus* took up no lesse then ten furlongs. [20] [21]

And though none of the seven wonders, yet a noble peece of Antiquity, and made by a Copy exceeding all the rest, had its principall parts disposed after this manner, that is, the Labyrinth of *Crete*, built upon a long quadrate, containing five large squares, communicating by right inflections, terminating in the centre of the middle square, and lodging of the *Minotaur*, if we conform unto the description of the elegant medall thereof in *Agostino*. And though in many accounts we reckon grosly by the square, yet is that very often to be accepted as a long-sided quadrate, which was the figure of the Ark of the Covenant, the table of the Shew-bread, and the stone wherein the names of the twelve Tribes were engraved, that is, three in a row, naturally making a longilaterall Figure, the perfect quadrate being made by nine. [22] [23]

What figure the stones themselves maintained, tradition and Scripture are silent, yet Lapidaries in precious stones affect a Table or long square, and in such proportion, that the two laterall, and also the three inferiour Tables are equall unto the superiour, and the angles of the laterall Tables contain and constitute the *hypothenusae*, or broader sides subtending.

That the Tables of the Law were of this figure, general imitation and tradition hath confirmed; yet are we unwilling to load the shoulders of *Moses* with such massie stones as some pictures lay upon them, since 'tis plainly delivered that he came down with them in his hand; since the word strictly taken implies no such massie hewing, but cutting, and fashioning of them into shape and surface; since some will have them Emeralds, and if they were made of the materials of Mount *Sina*, not improbable that they were marble: Since the words were not many, the letters short of seven hundred, [24] and the Tables written on both sides required no such capacity.

The beds of the Ancients were different from ours at present, which are almost square, being framed ob-long, and about a double unto their breadth; not much unlike the *area*, or bed of this Quincuncial quadrate. The single beds of *Greece* were six foot, and a little more in length, three in breadth; the Giant-like bed of *Og*, which had four cubits of   25 bredth, nine and a half in length, varied not much from this proportion. The Funeral bed of King *Cheops*, in the greater Pyramid, which holds seven in length, and four foot in bredth, had no great difformity from this measure; And whatsoever were the bredth, the length could hardly be lesse of the tyrannical bed of *Procrustes*, since in a shorter measure he had not been fitted with persons for his cruelty of extension. But the old sepulchral bed, or *Amazonian* Tomb in the market-place of *Megara*, was in the form of a Lozenge; readily made out by the composure of the body. For the arms not lying fasciated or wrapt up after the *Grecian* manner, but in a middle distention, the including Lines will strictly make out that figure.

CHAPTER III

Now although this elegant ordination of vegetables hath found coincidence or imitation in sundry works of Art, yet is it not also destitute of naturall examples, and though overlooked by all, was elegantly observable, in severall works of nature.

Could we satisfie our selves in the position of the lights above, or discover the wisedom of that order so invariably maintained in the fixed Stars of heaven; Could we have any light, why the stellary part of the first masse, separated into this order, that the Girdle of *Orion* should ever maintain its line, and the two Starres in *Charles's* Wain never leave pointing at the Pole-Starre; we might abate the *Pythagoricall* Musick of the Spheres, the sevenfold Pipe of *Pan*, and the strange Cryptography of *Gaffarell* in his Starrie Booke of Heaven.   1

But not to look so high as Heaven or the single Quincunx of the *Hyades* upon the head of *Taurus,* the Triangle, and remarkable *Crusero* about the foot of the *Centaur;* observable rudiments there are hereof in subterraneous concretions, and bodies in the Earth; in the *Gypsum* or *Talcum Rhomboides,* in the Favaginites or honey-comb-stone, in the *Asteria* and *Astroites,* and in the crucigerous stone of S. *Iago* of *Gallicia.*

The same is observably effected in the *Julus, Catkins,* or pendulous excrescencies of severall Trees, of Wallnuts, Alders, and Hazels, which hanging all the Winter, and maintaining their Net-worke close, by the expansion thereof are the early foretellers of the Spring, discoverable also in long Pepper, and elegantly in the *Julus* of *Calamus Aromaticus,* so plentifully growing with us in the first palmes of Willowes, and in the Flowers of Sycamore, Petasites, Asphodelus, and *Blattaria,* before explication. After such order stand the flowery Branches in our best spread *Verbascum,* and the seeds about the spicous head or torch of *Tapsas Barbatus,* in as fair a regularity as the circular and wreathed order will admit, which advanceth one side of the square, and makes the same Rhomboidall.

In the squamous heads of *Scabious, Knapweed,* and the elegant *Jacea Pinea,* and in the Scaly composure of the *Oak-Rose,* which some years most aboundeth. After this order hath Nature planted the Leaves in the Head of the common and prickled Artichoak; wherein the black and shining Flies do shelter themselves, when they retire from the purple Flower about it; The same is also found in the pricks, sockets, and impressions of the seeds, in the pulp or bottome thereof; wherein do elegantly stick the Fathers of their Mother. To [2] omit the Quincunciall Specks on the top of the Miscle-berry, especially that which grows upon the *Tilia* or Lime-Tree. And the remarkable disposure of those yellow fringes about the purple Pestill of *Aaron,* and elegant clusters of Dragons, so peculiarly secured by nature, with an *umbrella* or skreening Leaf about them.

The Spongy leaves of some Sea-wracks, Fucus, Oaks, in **their severall kindes,** found about the Shoar, with eject-

ments of the Sea, are over-wrought with Net-work elegantly
containing this order, which plainly declareth the naturality
of this texture; And how the needle of nature delighteth to
work, even in low and doubtful vegetations.

The *Arbustetum* or Thicket on the head of the Teazell, may
be observed in this order: And he that considereth that fabrick so regularly palisadoed, and stemm'd with flowers of the
royall colour; in the house of the solitary maggot, may finde   3
the Seraglio of *Solomon*. And contemplating the calicular
shafts, and uncous disposure of their extremities, so accommodable unto the office of abstersion, not condemne as wholly
improbable the conceit of those who accept it for the herbe
Borith. Where by the way, we could with much inquiry never   4
discover any transfiguration in this abstemious insect, although we have kept them long in their proper houses, and
boxes. Where some wrapt up in their webbs, have lived upon
their own bowels, from September unto July.

In such a grove doe walke the little creepers about the
head of the burre. And such an order is observed in the acu-
leous prickly plantation, upon the heads of several common
thistles, remarkably in the notable palisados about the flower
of the milk-Thistle; and he that inquireth into the little bottome of the globe-thistle, may finde that gallant bush arise
from a scalpe of like disposure.

The white umbrella or medicall bush of Elder, is an
Epitome of this order: arising from five main stemms Quincuncially disposed, and tollerably maintained in their subdivisions. To omit the lower observations in the seminal spike
of Mercurie, weld, and Plantane.

Thus hath nature ranged the flowers of Santfoyne, and
French honey suckle; and somewhat after this manner hath
ordered the bush in *Jupiters* beard, or houseleek; which old
superstition set on the tops of houses, as a defensative against
lightening, and thunder. The like in Fenny Sengreen or the   †
water Souldier; which, though a militarie name from Greece,   5
makes out the Roman order.

A like ordination there is in the favaginous Sockets, and
Lozenge seeds of the noble flower of the Sunne. Wherein in

Lozenge figured boxes nature shuts up the seeds, and balsame which is about them.

But the Firre and Pinetree from their fruits doe naturally dictate this position. The Rhomboidall protuberances in Pineapples maintaining this Quincuncial order unto each other, and each Rhombus in it selfe. Thus are also disposed the triangular foliations, in the conicall fruit of the firre tree, orderly shadowing and protecting the winged seeds below them.

The like so often occurreth to the curiosity of observers, especially in spicated seeds and flowers, that we shall not need to take in the single Quincunx of Fuchsius in the grouth of the masle fearn, the seedie disposure of Gramen Ischemon, and the trunk or neat Reticulate work in the codde of the Sachell palme.

For even in very many round stalk plants, the leaves are set after a Quintuple ordination, the first leaf answering the fifth, in lateral disposition. Wherein the leaves successively rounding the stalke, in foure at the furthest the compass is absolved, and the fifth leafe or sprout, returns to the position of the other fift before it; as in accounting upward is often observable in furze, pellitorye, Ragweed, the sproutes of [6] Oaks, and thorns upon pollards, and very remarkably in the regular disposure of the rugged excrescencies in the yearly shoots of the Pine.

But in square stalked plants, the leaves stand respectively unto each other, either in crosse or decussation to those above or below them, arising at crosse positions; whereby they shadow not each other, and better resist the force of winds, which in a parallel situation, and upon square stalkes would more forcibly bear upon them.

And to omit, how leaves and sprouts which compasse not the stalk, are often set in a Rhomboides, and making long and short Diagonals, doe stand like the leggs of Quadrupeds when they goe: Nor to urge the thwart enclosure and furdling of flowers, and blossomes, before explication, as in the multiplyed leaves of Pionie; And the Chiasmus in five leaved flowers, while one lies wrapt about the staminous beards, the other foure obliquely shutting and closing upon each other;

and how even flowers which consist of foure leaves, stand not
ordinarily in three and one, but two and two, crossewise unto
the Stylus; even the Autumnal budds, which awaite the returne of the sun, doe after the winter solstice multiply their
calicular leaves, making little Rhombuses, and network figures, as in the Sycamore and Lilac.

The like is discoverable in the original production of plants,
which first putting forth two leaves, those which succeed bear
not over each other, but shoot obliquely or crossewise, untill
the stalke appeareth; which sendeth not forth its first leaves
without all order unto them; and he that from hence can discover in what position the two first leaves did arise, is no ordinary observator.

Where by the way, he that observeth the rudimental spring 7
of seeds, shall finde strict rule, although not after this order.
How little is required unto effectual generation, and in what
diminutives the plastick principle lodgeth, is exemplified in
seeds, wherein the greater mass affords so little comproduc-
tion. In Beanes the leaf and root sprout from the Germen, the
main sides split, and lye by, and in some pull'd up near the
time of blooming, we have found the pulpous sides intire or
little wasted. In Acorns the nebb dilating splitteth the two
sides, which sometimes lye whole, when the Oak is sprouted
two handfuls. In Lupins these pulpy sides do sometimes arise
with the stalk in a resemblance of two fat leaves. Wheat and
Rye will grow up, if after they have shot some tender Roots,
the adhering pulp be taken from them. Beanes will prosper
though a part be cut away, and so much set as sufficeth to
contain and keep the Germen close. From this superfluous
pulp in unkindely and wet years, may arise that multiplicity
of little insects, which infest the Roots and Sprouts of tender
Graines and pulses.

In the little nebbe or fructifying principle, the motion is
regular, and not transvertible, as to make that ever the leaf,
which nature intendeth the root; observable from their conversion, until they attain their right position, if seeds be set
inversedly.

In vain we expect the production of plants from different
parts of the seed; from the same *corculum* or little original

proceed both germinations; and in the power of this slender particle lye many Roots and sprouts, that though the same be pull'd away, the generative particle will renew them again, and proceed to a perfect plant; And malt may be observed to grow, though the Cummes be fallen from it.

The seminall nebbe hath a defined and single place, and not extended unto both extremes. And therefore many too vulgarly conceive that Barley and Oats grow at both ends; For they arise from one *punctilio* or generative nebbe, and the Speare sliding under the husk, first appeareth nigh the toppe. But in Wheat and Rye being bare the sprouts are seen together. If Barley unhulled would grow, both would appear at once. But in this and Oat-meal the nebbe is broken away, which makes them the milder food, and lesse apt to raise fermentation in Decoctions.

Men taking notice of what is outwardly visible, conceive a sensible priority in the Root. But as they begin from one part, so they seem to start and set out upon one signall of nature. In Beans yet soft, in Pease while they adhere unto the Cod, the rudimentall Leafe and Root are discoverable. In the seeds of Rocket and Mustard, sprouting in Glasses of water, when the one is manifest the other is also perceptible. In muddy waters apt to breed *duckweed,* and Periwinkles, if the first and rudimentall stroaks of Duckweed be observed, the Leaves and Root anticipate not each other. But in the Date-stone the first sprout is neither root nor leaf distinctly, but both together; For the Germination being to passe through the narrow Navell and hole about the midst of the stone, the generative germ is faine to enlengthen it self, and shooting out about an inch, at that distance divideth into the ascending and descending portion.

And though it be generally thought that Seeds will root at that end where they adhere to their Originals, and observable it is that the nebbe sets most often next the stalk, as in Grains, Pulses, and most small Seeds, yet is it hardly made out in many greater plants. For in Acornes, Almonds, Pistachios, Wallnuts, and accuminated shells, the germ puts forth at the remotest part of the pulp. And therefore to set Seeds in that posture, wherein the Leaf and Roots may shoot right without contortion, or forced circumvolution, which might render them strongly rooted, and straighter, were a Criticisme in Agriculture. And nature seems to have made some provision hereof in many from their figure, that as they fall from the tree they may lye in Positions agreeable to such advantages.

Beside the open and visible Testicles of plants, the seminall powers lie in great part invisible, while the Sun findes polypody in stone-wals, the little stinging Nettle and nightshade in barren sandy High-wayes, *Scurvy-grasse* in *Greeneland*, and unknown plants in earth brought from remote Countries. Beside the known longevity of some Trees, what is the most lasting herb, or seed, seems not easily determinable. Mandrakes upon known account have lived near an hundred yeares. Seeds found in Wilde-Fowls Gizards have sprouted in the earth. The Seeds of Marjorane and *Stramonium* carelesly kept, have grown after seven years. Even in Garden-plots long fallow, and digged up, the seeds of *Blattaria* and yellow henbane, after twelve years burial have produced themselves again.

That bodies are first spirits *Paracelsus* could affirm, which   8
in the maturation of Seeds and fruits, seems obscurely implied by *Aristotle,* when he delivereth, that the spirituous   9
parts are converted into water, and the water into earth, and attested by observation in the maturative progresse of Seeds, wherein at first may be discerned a flatuous distension of the husk, afterwards a thin liquor, which longer time digesteth into a pulp or kernell observable in Almonds and large Nuts. And some way answered in the progressionall perfection of animall semination, in its spermaticall maturation, from crude pubescency unto perfection. And even that seeds themselves in their rudimentall discoveries appear in foliaceous surcles, or sprouts within their coverings, in a diaphanous gellie, be-   †
fore deeper incrassation, is also visibly verified in Cherries, Acorns, Plums.

From seminall considerations, either in reference unto one   †
another, or distinction from animall production, the holy Scripture describeth the vegetable creation; And while it divideth plants but into Herb and Tree, though it seemeth to

make but an accidental division, from magnitude, it tacitely containeth the naturall distinction of vegetables, observed by Herbarists, and comprehending the four kinds. For since the 10 most naturall distinction is made from the production of leaf or stalk, and plants after the two first seminall leaves, do either proceed to send forth more leaves, or a stalk, and the folious and stalky emission distinguisheth herbs and trees, in a large acception it compriseth all Vegetables, for the frutex and suffrutex are under the progression of trees, and stand Authentically differenced but from the accidents of the stalk.

The Aequivocall production of things under undiscerned 11 principles makes a large part of generation, though they seem to hold a wide univocacy in their set and certain Originals, while almost every plant breeds its peculiar insect, most a Butterfly, moth or fly, wherein the Oak seems to contain the largest seminality, while the Julus, Oak-apple, pill, woolly †,12 tuft, foraminous roundles upon the leaf, and grapes under ground make a Fly with some difference. The great variety of Flyes lyes in the variety of their originals, in the seeds of Caterpillars or Cankers there lyeth not only a Butterfly or Moth, but if they be sterill or untimely cast, their production is often a Fly, which we have also observed from corrupted and mouldred Egges, both of Hens and Fishes; To omit the generation of Bees out of the bodies of dead Heifers, or what 13 is strange yet well attested, the production of Eeles in the backs of living Cods and Perches.

The exiguity and smallnesse of some seeds extending to large productions is one of the magnalities of nature, somewhat illustrating the work of the Creation, and vast production from nothing. The true seeds of Cypresse and Rampions 14 are indistinguishable by old eyes. Of the seeds of Tobacco a thousand make not one grain. The disputed seeds of Harts 15 tongue, and Maidenhair, require a greater number. From such undiscernable seminalities arise spontaneous productions. He that would discern the rudimentall stroak of a plant, may behold it in the Originall of Duckweed, at the bignesse of a pins point, from convenient water in glasses, wherein a watchfull eye may also discover the puncticular Originals of Periwincles and Gnats.

That seeds of some Plants are lesse then any animals, seems
of no clear decision; That the biggest of Vegetables exceedeth the biggest of Animals, in full bulk, and all dimensions,
admits exception in the Whale, which in length and above
ground measure, will also contend with tall Oakes. That the
richest odour of plants, surpasseth that of Animals, may seem
of some doubt, since animall-musk seems to excell the vegetable, and we finde so noble a sent in the Tulip-Fly, and   †
Goat-Beetle.   16

Now whether seminall nebbes hold any sure proportion
unto seminall enclosures; why the form of the germe doth
not answer the figure of the enclosing pulp; why the nebbe
is seated upon the solid, and not the channeld side of the seed
as in grains; why since we often meet with two yolks in one
shell, and sometimes one Egge within another, we do not
oftener meet with two nebbes in one distinct seed: why since
the Egges of a Hen laid at one course, do commonly out-
weigh the bird, and some moths coming out of their cases,
without assistance of food, will lay so many Egges as to out-
weigh their bodies, trees rarely bear their fruit in that gravity
or proportion: Whether in the germination of seeds according to *Hippocrates,* the lighter part ascendeth, and maketh
the sprout, the heaviest tending downward frameth the root;
Since we observe that the first shoot of seeds in water, will
sink or bow down at the upper and leafing end: Whether it
be not more rational Epicurisme to contrive whole dishes out
of the nebbes and spirited particles of plants, then from the
Gallatures and treddles of Egges; since that part is found to
hold no seminal share in Oval Generation; are quaeries which
might enlarge but must conclude this digression.   17

And though not in this order, yet how nature delighteth in
this number, and what consent and coordination there is in
the leaves and parts of flowers, it cannot escape our observation in no small number of plants. For the calicular or support-
ing and closing leaves, do answer the number of the flowers,
especially in such as exceed not the number of Swallows   18
Egges; as in Violets, [and] Stichwort, blossomes and flowers
of one leaf have often five divisions, answered by a like number of calicular leaves; as *Gentianella, Convolvulus,* Bell-

flowers. In many the flowers, blades, or staminous shootes and leaves are all equally five, as in cockle, mullein and *Blattaria;* Wherein the flowers before explication are pentagonally wrappcd up, with somc resemblance of the *blatta* or moth from whence it hath its name: But the contrivance of nature is singular in the opening and shutting of Bindeweeds, ʾperformed by five inflexures, distinguishable by pyramidicall figures, and also different colours.

The rose at first is thought to have been of five leaves, as it yet groweth wilde among us; but in the most luxuriant, the calicular leaves do still maintain that number. But nothing is more admired then the five Brethren of the Rose, and the [19] strange disposure of the Appendices or Beards, in the calicular leaves thereof, which in despair of resolution is tolerably salved from this contrivance, best ordered and suited for the free closure of them before explication. For those two which are smooth, and of no beard, are contrived to lye undermost, as without prominent parts, and fit to be smoothly covered; the other two which are beset with Beards on either side, stand outward and uncovered, but the fifth or half-bearded leaf is covered on the bare side but on the open side stands free, and bearded like the other.

Besides a large number of leaves have five divisions, and may be circumscribed by a *Pentagon* or figure of five Angles, made by right lines from the extremity of their leaves, as in Maple, Vine, Figge-Tree: But five-leaved flowers are commonly disposed circularly about the *Stylus;* according to the higher Geometry of nature, dividing a circle by five *radii,* which concurre not to make Diameters, as in Quadrilaterall and sexangular Intersections.

Now the number of five is remarkable in every circle, not [20] only as the first sphaerical number, but the measure of sphaerical motion. For sphaerical bodies move by fives, and every globular figure placed upon a plane, in direct volutation, returns to the first point of contaction in the fifth touch, accounting by the Axes of the Diameters or Cardinall points of the four quarters thereof. And before it arriveth unto the same point again, it maketh five circles equall unto it self, in each progresse from those quarters absolving an equall circle.

By the same number doth nature divide the circle of the
Sea-Starre, and in that order and number disposeth those elegant Semi-circles, or dentall sockets and egges in the Sea
Hedgehogge. And no mean Observations hereof there is in
the Mathematicks of the neatest Retiary Spider, which concluding in˚fourty four Circles, from five Semidiameters beginneth that elegant texture.

And after this manner doth lay the foundation of the circular branches of the Oak, which being five-cornered in the
tender annual sprouts, and manifesting upon incision the
signature of a Starre, is after made circular, and swel'd into a
round body: Which practice of nature is become a point of
art, and makes two Problemes in *Euclide.* But the Bramble   21
which sends forth shoots and prickles from its angles, maintains its pentagonall figure, and the unobserved signature of
a handsome porch within it. To omit the five small buttons
dividing the Circle of the Ivy-berry, and the five characters
in the Winter stalk of the Walnut, with many other Observables, which cannot escape the eyes of signal discerners; Such
as know where to finde *Ajax* his name in *Delphinium,* or   22
Aarons Mitre in Henbane.

. Quincuncial forms and ordinations, are also observable in
animal figurations. For to omit the hioides or throat bone of
animals, the *furcula* or *merry-thought* in birds, which supporteth the *scapulae,* affording a passage for the windepipe
and the gullet, the wings of Flyes, and disposure of their
legges in their first formation from maggots, and the position
of their horns, wings and legges, in their *Aurelian* cases and   23
swadling clouts: The back of the *Cimex Arboreus,* found often
upon Trees and lesser plants, doth elegantly discover the
Burgundian decussation; And the like is observable in the
belly of the *Notonecton,* or water-Beetle, which swimmeth
on its back, and the handsome Rhombusses of the Sea-poult,
or Weazell, on either side the Spine.

The sexangular Cels in the Honey-combs of Bees, are disposed after this order; much there is not of wonder in the
confused Houses of Pismires, though much in their busie life
and actions; more in the edificial Palaces of Bees and Monarchical spirits; who make their combs six-corner'd, declining   24

a circle, whereof many stand not close together, and compleatly fill the *area* of the place; But rather affecting a six-sided figure, whereby every cell affords a common side unto six more, and also a fit receptacle for the Bee it self, which gathering into a Cylindrical Figure, aptly enters its sexangular house, more nearly approaching a circular Figure, then either doth the Square or Triangle. And the Combes themselves so regularly contrived, that their mutual intersections make three Lozenges at the bottome of every Cell; which severally regarded make three Rows of neat Rhomboidall Figures, connected at the angles, and so continue three several chains throughout the whole comb.

As for the *Favago* found commonly on the sea shoar, though named from an honey-comb, it but rudely makes out the resemblance, and better agrees with the round Cels of humble Bees. He that would exactly discern the shop of a Bees mouth, needs observing eyes, and good augmenting glasses; wherein is discoverable one of the neatest peeces in nature; and must have a more piercing eye then mine, who findes out the shape of Buls heads, in the guts of Drones pressed out behinde, according to the experiment of *Gomesius;* [25] wherein notwithstanding there seemeth somewhat which might incline a pliant fancy to credulity of similitude.

A resemblance hereof there is in the orderly and rarely disposed Cels, made by Flyes and Insects, which we have often found fastened about small sprigs, and in those cottonary and woolly pillows, which sometimes we meet with fastened unto Leaves, there is included an elegant Net-work Texture, out of which come many small Flies. And some resemblance there is of this order in the Egges of some Butterflies and moths, as they stick upon leaves, and other substances; which being dropped from behinde, nor directed by the eye, doth neatly declare how nature Geometrizeth, and observeth order in all things.

A like correspondency in figure is found in the skins and outward teguments of animals, whereof a regardable part are beautiful by this texture. As the backs of several Snakes and Serpents, elegantly remarkable in the *Aspis,* and the Dart-snake, in the Chiasmus and larger decussations upon the back

of the Rattlesnake, and in the close and finer texture of the
Mater formicarum, or snake that delights in Ant-hils;
whereby upon approach of outward injuries, they can raise a
thicker Phalanx on their backs, and handsomely contrive
themselves into all kindes of flexures: Whereas their bellies
are commonly covered with smooth semicircular divisions, as
best accommodable unto their quick and gliding motion.

This way is followed by nature in the peculiar and remarkable tayl of the Bever, wherein the scaly particles are
disposed somewhat after this order, which is the plainest resolution of the wonder of *Bellonius,* while he saith, with incredible Artifice hath Nature framed the tayl or Oar of the Bever:
where by the way we cannot but wish a model of their
houses, so much extolled by some Describers: wherein since
they are so bold as to venture upon three stages, we might
examine their Artifice in the contignations, the rule and order
in the compartitions; or whether that magnified structure be
any more then a rude rectangular pyle or meer hovell-
building.

Thus works the hand of nature in the feathery plantation
about birds. Observable in the skins of the breast, legs and   26
Pinions of Turkies, Geese, and Ducks, and the Oars or finny
feet of Water-Fowl: And such a naturall Net is the scaly covering of Fishes, of Mullets, Carps, Tenches, &c. even in such
as are excoriable and consist of smaller scales, as Bretts,
Soals, and Flounders. The like Reticulate grain is observable
in some *Russia* Leather. To omit the ruder Figures of the
ostracion, the triangular or cunny fish, or the pricks of the
Sea-Porcupine.

The same is also observable in some part of the skin of man,
in habits of neat texture, and therefore not unaptly compared
unto a Net: We shall not affirm that from such grounds, the
Aegyptian Embalmers imitated this texture, yet in their linnen folds the same is still observable among their neatest
Mummies, in the figures of *Isis* and *Osyris,* and the Tutelary   27
spirits in the Bembine Table. Nor is it to be over-looked how
Orus, the Hieroglyphick of the world, is described in a Net-
work covering, from the shoulder to the foot. And (not to
enlarge upon the cruciated character of *Trismegistus,* or

handed crosses, so often occurring in the Needles of *Pharaoh*, [28]
and Obelisks of Antiquity) the *Statuae Isiacae*, Teraphims, [†,29]
and little Idols, found about the Mummies, do make a decussation or *Jacobs* Crosse with their armes, like that on the [30]
head of *Ephraim* and *Manasses*, and this *decussis* is also
graphically described between them.

This Reticulate or Net-work was also considerable in the
inward parts of man, not only from the first *subtegmen* or
warp of his formation, but in the netty *fibres* of the veins and
vessels of life; wherein according to common Anatomy the
right and transverse *fibres* are decussated, by the oblique
fibres; and so must frame a Reticulate and Quincunciall
Figure by their Obliquations, Emphatically extending that
Elegant expression of Scripture: Thou hast curiously embroy- [31]
dered me, thou hast wrought me up after the finest way of
texture, and as it were with a Needle.

Nor is the same observable only in some parts, but in the
whole body of man, which upon the extension of arms and
legges, doth make out a square, whose intersection is at the
genitals. To omit the phantastical Quincunx in *Plato* of the [32]
first Hermaphrodite or double man, united at the Loynes,
which *Jupiter* after divided.

A rudimentall resemblance hereof there is in the cruciated
and rugged folds of the *Reticulum*, or Net-like Ventricle of
ruminating horned animals, which is the second in order, and
culinarily called the Honey-comb. For many divisions there
are in the stomack of severall animals; what number they
maintain in the *Scarus* and ruminating Fish, common description, or our own experiment hath made no discovery. But in
the Ventricle of *Porpuses* there are three divisions. In many
Birds a crop, Gizard, and little receptacle before it; but in
Cornigerous animals, which chew the cudd, there are no less [33]
then four of distinct position and office.

The *Reticulum* by these crossed cels, makes a further digestion, in the dry and exuccous part of the Aliment received
from the first Ventricle. For at the bottome of the gullet there
is a double Orifice; What is first received at the mouth descendeth into the first and greater stomack, from whence it
is returned into the mouth again; and after a fuller mastica-

tion, and salivous mixture, what part thereof descendeth again, in a moist and succulent body, it slides down the softer and more permeable Orifice, into the Omasus or third stomack; and from thence conveyed into the fourth, receives its last digestion. The other dry and exuccous part after rumination by the larger and stronger orifice beareth into the first stomack, from thence into the *Reticulum,* and so progressively into the other divisions. And therefore in Calves newly calved, there is little or no use of the two first Ventricles, for the milk and liquid aliment slippeth down the softer Orifice, into the third stomack; where making little or no stay, it passeth into the fourth, the seat of the *Coagulum,* or Runnet, or that division of stomack which seems to bear the name of the whole, in the Greek translation of the Priests Fee, in the   34
Sacrifice of Peace-offerings.

As for those Rhomboidal Figures made by the Cartilagineous parts of the Wezon, in the Lungs of great Fishes, and other animals, as *Rondeletius* discovered, we have not found them so to answer our figure as to be drawn into illustration; Something we expected in the more discernable texture of the lungs of frogs, which notwithstanding being but two curious bladders not weighing above a grain, we found interwoven with veins not observing any just order. More orderly situated are those cretaceous and chalky concretions found sometimes in the bignesse of a small fetch on either side their spine; which being not agreeable unto our order, nor yet observed by any, we shall not here discourse on.

But had we found a better account and tolerable Anatomy, of that prominent jowle of the *Sperma Ceti* Whale, then questuary operation, or the stench of the last cast upon our shoar, permitted, we might have perhaps discovered some   35
handsome order in those Net-like seases and sockets, made like honey-combs, containing that medicall matter.

Lastly, The incession or locall motion of animals is made with analogy unto this figure, by decussative diametrals, Quincunciall Lines and angles. For to omit the enquiry how Butterflies and breezes move their four wings, how birds and   36
fishes in ayre and water move by joynt stroaks of opposite wings and Finnes, and how salient animals in jumping for-

ward seem to arise and fall upon a square base; As the station of most Quadrupeds, is made upon a long square, so in their motion they make a Rhomboides; their common progression being performed Diametrally, by decussation and crosse advancement of their legges, which not observed begot that remarkable absurdity in the position of the legges of [37] *Castors* horse in the Capitol. The Snake which moveth circularly makes his spires in like order, the convex and concave spirals answering each other at alternate distances; In the motion of man the armes and legges observe this thwarting position, but the legges alone do move Quincuncially by single angles with some resemblance of an V measured by successive advancement from each foot, and the angle of indenture great or lesse, according to the extent or brevity of the stride.

Studious Observators may discover more analogies in the orderly book of nature, and cannot escape the Elegancy of her hand in other correspondencies. The Figures of nails and crucifying appurtenances, are but precariously made out in the *Granadilla* or flower of Christs passion: And we despair to behold in these parts that handsome draught of crucifixion in the fruit of the *Barbado* Pine. The seminal Spike of *Pha-* [38] *laris*, or great shaking grasse, more nearly answers the tayl of a Rattle-Snake, then many resemblances in *Porta:* And if the man-*Orchis* of *Columna* be well made out, it excelleth all [39] analogies. In young Wallnuts cut athwart, it is not hard to apprehend strange characters; and in those of somewhat elder growth, handsome ornamental draughts about a plain crosse. In the root of *Osmond* or Water fern, every eye may discern the form of a Half Moon, Rain-bow, or half the character of Pisces. Some finde Hebrew, Arabick, Greek, and Latine Characters in Plants; In a common one among us we [40] seem to read *Aiaia, Viviu, Lilil.* [†]

Right lines and circles make out the bulk of plants; In the parts thereof we finde Helicall or spirall roundles, voluta's, conicall Sections, circular Pyramids, and frustums of *Archimedes;* And cannot overlook the orderly hand of nature, in the alternate succession of the flat and narrower sides in the tender shoots of the Ashe, or the regular inequality of big-

nesse in the five-leaved flowers of Henbane, and something
like in the calicular leaves of *Tutson*. How the spots of *Per-
sicaria* do manifest themselves between the sixt and tenth
ribbe. How the triangular capp in the stemme or *stylus* of
Tuleps doth constantly point at three outward leaves. That
spicated flowers do open first at the stalk. That white flowers
have yellow thrums or knops. That the nebbe of Beans and
Pease do all look downward, and so presse not upon each
other; And how the seeds of many pappous or downy flowers
lockt up in sockets after a gomphosis or *mortis*-articulation,
diffuse themselves circularly into branches of rare order, observable in *Tragopogon* or Goats-beard, conformable to the
Spiders web, and the *Radii* in like manner telarely interwoven.

And how in animall natures, even colours hold correspondencies, and mutuall correlations. That the colour of the Cater-
pillar will shew again in the Butterfly, with some latitude is
allowable. Though the regular spots in their wings seem but
a mealie adhesion, and such as may be wiped away, yet since
they come in this variety out of their cases, there must be
regular pores in those parts and membranes, defining such
Exudations.

That *Augustus* had native notes on his body and belly,   41
after the order and number in the Starres of *Charles wayne,*
will not seem strange unto astral Physiognomy, which accordingly considereth moles in the body of man, or Physicall
Observators, who from the position of moles in the face, reduce them to rule and correspondency in other parts.
Whether after the like method medicall conjecture may not
be raised upon parts inwardly affected; since parts about the
lips are the critical seats of Pustules discharged in Agues;
And scrophulous tumours about the neck do so often speak
the like about the Mesentery, may also be considered.

The russet neck in young Lambs seems but adventitious,
and may owe its tincture to some contaction in the womb;
But that if sheep have any black or deep russet in their faces,
they want not the same about their legges and feet; That
black Hounds have mealy mouths and feet; That black Cows
which have any white in their tayls, should not misse of some

in their bellies; and if all white in their bodies, yet if black-mouth'd, their ears and feet maintain the same colour; are correspondent tinctures not ordinarily failing in nature, which easily unites the accidents of extremities, since in some generations she transmutes the parts themselves, while in the *Aurelian Metamorphosis* the head of the canker becomes the Tayl of the Butterfly. Which is in some way not beyond the contrivance of Art, in submersions and Inlays, inverting the extremes of the plant, and fetching the root from the top, and also imitated in handsome columnary work, in the inversion of the extremes; wherein the Capitel, and the Base, hold such near correspondency.

In the motive parts of animals may be discovered mutuall proportions; not only in those of Quadrupeds, but in the thigh-bone, legge, foot-bone, and claws of Birds. The legs of Spiders are made after a sesqui-tertian proportion, and the long legs of some locusts, double unto some others. But the internodial parts of Vegetables, or spaces between the joints, are contrived with more uncertainty; though the joints themselves in many plants maintain a regular number.

In vegetable composure, the unition of prominent parts seems most to answer the *Apophyses* or processes of Animal bones, whereof they are the produced parts or prominent explantations. And though in the parts of plants which are not ordained for motion, we do not expect correspondent Articulations; yet in the setting on of some flowers, and seeds in their sockets, and the lineal commissure of the pulpe of severall seeds, may be observed some shadow of the Harmony; some show of the Gomphosis or *mortis*-articulation.

As for the Diarthrosis or motive Articulation, there is expected little Analogy, though long-stalked leaves doe move by long lines, and have observable motions, yet are they made by outward impulsion, like the motion of pendulous bodies, while the parts themselves are united by some kinde of *symphysis* unto the stock.

But standing vegetables, void of motive-Articulations, are not without many motions. For beside the motion of vegetation upward, and of radiation unto all quarters, that of contraction, dilatation, inclination, and contortion, is discov-

erable in many plants. To omit the rose of *Jericho,* the ear of
Rye, which moves with change of weather, and the Magical   42
spit, made of no rare plants, which windes before the fire,
and rosts the bird without turning.

Even Animals near the Classis of plants, seem to have the
most restlesse motions. The Summer-worm of Ponds and
plashes makes a long waving motion; the hair-worm seldome
lies still. He that would behold a very anomalous motion, may
observe it in the Tortile and tiring stroaks of Gnatworms.   43

Chapter IV

As for the delights, commodities, mysteries, with other concernments of this order, we are unwilling to fly them over, in
the short deliveries of *Virgil, Varro,* or others, and shall therefore enlarge with additionall ampliations.

By this position they had a just proportion of Earth, to supply an equality of nourishment. The distance being ordered,
thick or thin, according to the magnitude or vigorous attraction of the plant, the goodnesse, leannesse, or propriety of
the soyle, and therefore the rule of *Solon,* concerning the terri-   1
tory of *Athens,* not extendible unto all; allowing the distance
of six foot unto common Trees, and nine for the Figge and
Olive.

They had a due diffusion of their roots on all or both sides,
whereby they maintained some proportion to their height, in
Trees of large radication. For that they strictly make good
their profundeur or depth unto their height, according to
common conceit, and that expression of *Virgil,* though con-   2
firmable from the plane Tree in *Pliny,* and some few exam-   3
ples, is not to be expected from the generallitie of Trees
almost in any kinde, either of side-spreading, or tap-roots: Except we measure them by lateral and opposite diffusions; nor
commonly to be found in *minor* or hearby plants; If we except Sea-holly, Liquorish, Sea-rush, and some others.

They had a commodious radiation in their growth; and a
due expansion of their branches, for shadow or delight. For
trees thickly planted do runne up in height and branch with

no expansion, shooting unequally or short, and thinne upon the neighbouring side. And therefore Trees are inwardly bare, and spring and leaf from the outward and Sunny side of their branches.

Whereby they also avoided the perill of συνολεθρία or one tree perishing with another, as it happeneth ofttimes from the sick *effluviums* or entanglements of the roots, falling foul with each other. Observable in Elmes set in hedges, where if one dieth the neighbouring Tree prospereth not long after. †

In this situation divided into many intervals and open unto six passages, they had the advantage of a fair perflation from windes, brushing and cleansing their surfaces, relaxing and closing their pores unto due perspiration. For that they afford large *effluviums* perceptible from odours, diffused at great distances, is observable from Onyons out of the earth; which though dry, and kept until the spring, as they shoot forth large and many leaves, do notably abate of their weight. And mint growing in glasses of water, until it arriveth unto the weight of an ounce, in a shady place, will sometimes exhaust a pound of water.

And as they send forth much, so may they receive somewhat in: For beside the common way and road of reception by the root, there may be a refection and imbibition from without; For gentle showrs refresh plants, though they enter not their roots; And the good and bad *effluviums* of Vegetables promote or debilitate each other. So *Epithymum* and *Dodder*, rootlesse and out of the ground, maintain themselves upon Thyme, Savory, and plants, whereon they hang. And *Ivy* divided from the root, we have observed to live some years, by the cirrous parts commonly conceived but as tenacles and holdfasts unto it. The stalks of mint cropt from the root stripped from the leaves, and set in *glasses* with the root end upward, & out of the water, we have observed to send forth sprouts and leaves without the aid of roots, and *scordium* to grow in like manner, the leaves set downward in water. To omit severall Sea-plants, which grow on single roots from stones, although in very many there are side-shoots and *fibres*, beside the fastening root.

By this open position they were fairly exposed unto the

rayes of Moon and Sunne, so considerable in the growth of
Vegetables. For though Poplars, Willows, and severall Trees
be made to grow about the brinks of *Acharon,* and dark habitations of the dead; Though some plants are content to grow
in obscure Wells; wherein also old Elme pumps afford sometimes long bushy sprouts, not observable in any above-
ground: And large fields of Vegetables are able to maintain
their verdure at the bottome and shady part of the Sea; yet
the greatest number are not content without the actual rayes
of the Sunne, but bend, incline, and follow them; As large
lists of solisequious and Sun-following plants. And some observe the method of its motion in their owne growth and conversion, twining towards the West by the South, as Bryony,
Hops, Woodbine, and several kindes of Bindeweed, which we
shall more admire, when any can tell us they observe another
motion, and twist by the North at the *Antipodes.* The same
plants rooted against an erect North-wall full of holes, will
finde a way through them to look upon the Sunne. And in
tender plants from mustard-seed, sown in the winter, and in
a pot of earth in a chamber placed inwardly against a South-
window, the tender stalks of two leaves arose not erect, but
bending towards the window, nor looking much higher then
the Meridian Sun. And if the pot were turned they would
work themselves into their former declinations, making their
conversion by the East. That the Leaves of the Olive and
some other Trees solstitially turn, and precisely tell us, when
the Sun is entred *Cancer,* is scarce expectable in any Climate;
and *Theophrastus* warily observes it; Yet somewhat thereof
is observable in our own, in the leaves of Willows and Sal-
lows, some weeks after the Solstice. But the great *Convolvulus* or white-flower'd *Bindweed* observes both motions of
the Sunne: while the flower twists Aequinoctionally from the
left hand to the right, according to the daily revolution, the
stalk twineth ecliptically from the right to the left, according
to the annual conversion.

Some commend the exposure of these orders unto the
Western gales, as the most generative and fructifying breath
of heaven. But we applaud the Husbandry of *Solomon,*   4
whereto agreeth the doctrine of *Theophrastus.* Arise O North-   5

winde, and blow thou South upon my garden, that the spices thereof may flow out; For the North-winde closing the pores, and shutting up the *effluviums*, when the South doth after open and relax them, the Aromatical gummes do drop, and sweet odours fly actively from them. And if his garden had the same situation which mapps and charts afford it, on the East side of *Jerusalem*, and having the wall on the West; these were the windes, unto which it was well exposed.

By this way of plantation they encreased the number of their trees, which they lost in *Quaternio's*, and square-orders, which is a commodity insisted on by *Varro*, and one great intent of nature, in this position of flowers and seeds in the elegant formation of plants, and the former Rules observed in naturall and artificiall Figurations.

Whether in this order and one Tree in some measure breaking the cold and pinching gusts of windes from the other, trees will not better maintain their inward circles, and either escape or moderate their excentricities, may also be considered. For the circles in Trees are naturally concentricall, parallell unto the bark, and unto each other, till frost and piercing windes contract and close them on the weatherside, the opposite semicircle widely enlarging, and at a comely distance, which hindreth ofttimes the beauty and roundnesse of Trees, and makes the Timber lesse serviceable; whiles the ascending juyce not readily passing, settles in knots and inequalities. And therefore it is no new course of Agriculture, to observe the native position of Trees according to North and South in their transplantations.

The same is also observable underground in the circinations and sphaerical rounds of Onyons, wherein the circles of the Orbes are ofttimes larger, and the meridionall lines stand wider upon one side then the other. And where the largenesse will make up the number of planetical Orbes, that of *Luna* and the lower planets, excede the dimensions of *Saturne* and the higher: Whether the like be not verified in the Circles of the large roots of Briony and Mandrakes, or why in the knotts of Deale or Firre the Circles are often eccentricall, although not in a plane, but vertical and right position, deserves a further enquiry.

Whether there be not some irregularity of roundnesse in most plants according to their position? Whether some small compression of pores be not perceptible in parts which stand against the current of waters, as in Reeds, Bullrushes, and other vegetables toward the streaming quarter, may also be observed, and therefore such as are long and weak, are commonly contrived into a roundnesse of figure, whereby the water presseth lesse, and slippeth more smoothly from them, and even in flags of flat-figured leaves, the greater part obvert their sharper sides unto the current in ditches.

But whether plants which float upon the surface of the water be for the most part of cooling qualities, those which shoot above it of heating vertues, and why? whether *Sargasso* for many miles floating upon the Western Ocean, or Sea-lettuce, and Phasganium at the bottome of our Seas, make good the like qualities? Why Fenny waters afford the hottest and sweetest plants, as Calamus, Cyperus, and Crowfoot, and mudd cast out of ditches most naturally produceth Arsmart? Why plants so greedy of water so little regard oyl? Why since many seeds contain much oyle within them, they endure it not well without, either in their growth or production? Why since Seeds shoot commonly under ground, and out of the ayre, those which are let fall in shallow glasses, upon the surface of the water, will sooner sprout then those at the bottome? And if the water be covered with oyle, those at the bottome will hardly sprout at all, we have not room to conjecture.

Whether Ivy would not lesse offend the Trees in this clean ordination, and well kept paths, might perhaps deserve the question. But this were a quaery only unto some habitations, and little concerning *Cyrus* or the Babylonian territory; wherein by no industry *Harpalus* could make Ivy grow: And *Alexander* hardly found it about those parts to imitate the pomp of *Bacchus*. And though in these Northern Regions we are too much acquainted with one Ivy, we know too little of another, whereby we apprehend not the expressions of Antiquity, the Splenetick medicine of *Galen,* and the Emphasis of the Poet, in the beauty of the white Ivy.

The like concerning the growth of Misseltoe, which dependeth not only of the *species*, or kinde of Tree, but much also of the Soil. And therefore common in some places, not readily found in others, frequent in *France*, not so common in *Spain*, and scarce at all in the Territory of *Ferrara:* Nor easily to be found where it is most required upon Oaks, lesse on Trees continually verdant. Although in some places the Olive escapeth it not, requiting its detriment in the delightfull view of its red Berries; as *Clusius* observed in *Spain*, and *Bellonius* about *Hierusalem*. But this Parasiticall plant suffers nothing to grow upon it, by any way of art; nor could we ever make it grow where nature had not planted it; as we have in vain attempted by inocculation and incision, upon its native or forreign stock. And though there seem nothing improbable in the seed, it hath not succeeded by sation in any manner of ground, wherein we had no reason to despair, since we reade of vegetable horns, and how Rams horns will root about *Goa*.   10

But besides these rurall commodities, it cannot be meanly delectable in the variety of Figures, which these orders, open and closed, do make. Whilest every inclosure makes a *Rhombus*, the figures obliquely taken a Rhomboides, the intervals bounded with parallell lines, and each intersection built upon a square, affording two Triangles or Pyramids vertically conjoyned; which in the strict Quincunciall order doe oppositely make acute and blunt Angles.

And though therein we meet not with right angles, yet every Rhombus containing four Angles equall unto four right, it virtually contains four right. Nor is this strange unto such as observe the naturall lines of Trees, and parts disposed in them. For neither in the root doth nature affect this angle, which shooting downward for the stability of the plant, doth best effect the same by Figures of Inclination; Nor in the Branches and stalky leaves, which grow most at acute angles; as declining from their head the root, and diminishing their Angles with their altitude: Verified also in lesser Plants, whereby they better support themselves, and bear not so heavily upon the stalk: So that while near the root they often make an Angle of seventy parts, the sprouts near the top will often come short of thirty. Even in the nerves and master veins of the leaves the acute angle ruleth; the obtuse but seldome found, and in the backward part of the leaf, reflecting and arching about the stalk. But why ofttimes one side of the leaf is unequall unto the other, as in Hazell and Oaks, why on either side the master vein the lesser and derivative channels stand not directly opposite, nor at equall angles, respectively unto the adverse side, but those of one part do often exceed the other, as the Wallnut and many more, deserves another enquiry.

Now if for this order we affect coniferous and tapering Trees, particularly the Cypresse, which grows in a conicall figure; we have found a Tree not only of great Ornament, but in its Essentials of affinity unto this order. A solid Rhombus being made by the conversion of two Equicrurall Cones, as *Archimedes* hath defined. And these were the common Trees about *Babylon,* and the East, whereof the Ark was made; and *Alexander* found no Trees so accomodable to build his Navy; And this we rather think to be the Tree mentioned in the Canticles, which stricter Botanology [11] will hardly allow to be Camphire.

And if delight or ornamentall view invite a comely disposure by circular amputations, as is elegantly performed in Hawthorns; then will they answer the figures made by the conversion of a Rhombus, which maketh two concentricall Circles; the greater circumference being made by the lesser angles, the lesser by the greater.

The Cylindrical figure of Trees is virtually contained and latent in this order. A Cylinder or long round being made by the conversion or turning of a Parallelogram, and most handsomely by a long square, which makes an equall, strong, and lasting figure in Trees, agreeable unto the body and motive parts of animals, the greatest number of Plants, and almost all roots, though their stalks be angular, and of many corners, which seem not to follow the figure of their Seeds; Since many angular Seeds send forth round stalks, and sphaericall seeds arise from angular spindles, and many rather conform unto their Roots, as the round stalks of bulbous Roots, and in tuberous Roots stemmes of like figure. But why since the largest number of Plants maintain a circular Figure, there are so few with teretous or long round leaves; why coniferous

Trees are tenuifolious or narrowleafed; why Plants of few or no joynts have commonly round stalks; why the greatest number of hollow stalks are round stalks; or why in this variety of angular stalks the quadrangular most exceedeth, were too long a speculation; Mean while obvious experience may finde, that in Plants of divided leaves above, nature often beginneth circularly in the two first leaves below, while in the singular plant of Ivy, she exerciseth a contrary Geometry, and beginning with angular leaves below, rounds them in the upper branches.

Nor can the rows in this order want delight, as carrying an aspect answerable unto the *dipteros hypaethros,* or double order of columns open above; the opposite ranks of Trees standing like pillars in the *Cavedia* of the Courts of famous buildings, and the *Portico's* of the *Templa subdialia* of old; Somewhat imitating the *Peristylia* or Cloyster buildings, and the *Exedrae* of the Ancients, wherein men discoursed, walked and exercised; For that they derived the rule of Columnes from Trees, especially in their proportionall diminutions, is illustrated by *Vitruvius* from the shafts of [12] Firre and Pine. And though the inter-arborations do imitate the *Areostylos,* or thin order, not strictly answering the proportion of intercolumniations; yet in many Trees they will not exceed the intermission of the Columnes in the Court of the Tabernacle; which being an hundred cubits long, and made [13] up by twenty pillars, will afford no lesse then intervals of five cubits.

Beside, in this kinde of aspect the sight being not diffused but circumscribed between long parallels and the ἐπισκιάσμὸς and adumbration from the branches, it frameth a penthouse over the eye, and maketh a quiet vision: And therefore in diffused and open aspects, men hollow their hand above their eye, and make an artificiall brow, whereby they direct the dispersed rayes of sight, and by this shade preserve a moderate light in the chamber of the eye; keeping the *pupilla* plump and fair, and not contracted or shrunk as in light and vagrant vision.

And therefore providence hath arched and paved the great house of the world, with colours of mediocrity, that is, [14]

blew and green, above and below the sight, moderately
terminating the *acies* of the eye. For most plants, though
green above-ground, maintain their Originall white below it,
according to the candour of their seminall pulp, and the rudimental leaves do first appear in that colour; observable in
Seeds sprouting in water upon their first foliation. Green
seeming to be the first supervenient, or above-ground complexion of Vegetables, separable in many upon ligature or
inhumation, as Succory, Endive, Artichoaks, and which is also
lost upon fading in the Autumn.

And this is also agreeable unto water itself, the alimental
vehicle of plants, which first altereth into this colour; And
containing many vegetable seminalities, revealeth their
Seeds by greennesse; and therefore soonest expected in rain
or standing water, not easily found in distilled or water
strongly boiled; wherein the Seeds are extinguished by fire
and decoction, and therefore last long and pure without such
alteration, affording neither uliginous coats, gnatworms,
Acari, hair-worms, like crude and common water; And therefore most fit for wholsome beverage, and with malt makes
Ale and Beer without boyling. What large water-drinkers
some Plants are, the Canary-Tree and Birches in some
Northern Countries, drenching the Fields about them, do sufficiently demonstrate. How water it self is able to maintain
the growth of Vegetables, and without extinction of their
generative or medicall vertues; Beside the experiment of
Helmonts tree, we have found in some which have lived six   15
years in glasses. The seeds of Scurvy-grasse growing in wa-
terpots, have been fruitfull in the Land; And *Asarum* after
a years space, and once casting its leaves in water, in the
second leaves, hath handsomely performed its vomiting
operation.

Nor are only dark and green colors, but shades and shadows contrived through the great Volume of nature, and trees
ordained not only to protect and shadow others, but by their
shades and shadowing parts, to preserve and cherish themselves. The whole radiation or branchings shadowing the
stock and the root, the leaves, the branches and fruit, too
much exposed to the windes and scorching Sunne. The ca-

licular leaves inclose the tender flowers, and the flowers themselves lye wrapt about the seeds in their rudiment and first formations, which being advanced the flowers fall away; and are therefore contrived in a variety of figures, best satisfying the intention; Handsomely observable in hooded and gaping flowers, and the Butterfly bloomes of leguminous plants, the lower leaf closely involving the rudimental Cod, and the alary or wingy divisions embracing or hanging over it.

But Seeds themselves do lie in perpetual shades, either under the leaf, or shut up in coverings; And such as lye barest, have their husks, skins, and pulps about them, wherein the nebbe and generative particle lyeth moist and secured from the injury of Ayre and Sunne. Darknesse and light hold interchangeable dominions, and alternately rule the seminal state of things. Light unto *Pluto* is darknesse [16] unto *Jupiter*. Legions of seminall *Idaea's* lye in their second Chaos and *Orcus* of *Hippocrates;* till putting on the habits of their forms, they shew themselves upon the stage of the world, and open dominion of *Jove*. They that held the Stars [17] of heaven were but rayes and flashing glimpses of the Empyreall light, through holes and perforations of the upper heaven, took off the natural shadows of stars, while according to better discovery the poor Inhabitants of the Moone [18] have but a polary life, and must passe half their dayes in the shadow of that Luminary.

Light that makes things seen, makes some things invisible; were it not for darknesse and the shadow of the earth, the noblest part of the Creation had remained unseen, and the Stars in heaven as invisible as on the fourth day, when they were created above the Horizon, with the Sun, or there was not an eye to behold them. The greatest mystery of Re- [19] ligion is expressed by adumbration, and in the noblest part of Jewish Types, we finde the Cherubims shadowing the Mercy-seat: Life it self is but the shadow of death, and souls departed but the shadows of the living: All things fall under this name. The Sunne it self is but the dark *simulachrum,* and light but the shadow of God. [20]

Lastly, It is no wonder that this Quincunciall order was

first and [is] still affected as gratefull unto the Eye: For all
things are seen Quincuncially; For at the eye the Pyramidal   21
rayes from the object receive a decussation, and so strike a
second base upon the *Retina* or hinder coat, the proper organ
of Vision; wherein the pictures from objects are represented,
answerable to the paper, or wall in the dark chamber; after
the decussation of the rayes at the hole of the hornycoat, and
their refraction upon the Christalline humour, answering the
foramen of the window, and the *convex* or burning-glasses,
which refract the rayes that enter it. And if ancient Anatomy
would hold, a like disposure there was of the optick or visual
nerves in the brain, wherein Antiquity conceived a concurrence by decussation. And this not only observable in the
Laws of direct Vision, but in some part also verified in the
reflected rayes of sight. For making the angle of incidence
equal to that of reflexion, the visuall raye returneth Quincuncially, and after the form of a V, and the line of reflexion
being continued unto the place of vision, there ariseth a
semi-decussation, which makes the object seen in a perpendicular unto it self, and as farre below the reflectent, as it is
from it above; observable in the Sun and Moon beheld in
water.

   And this is also the law of reflexion in moved bodies and
sounds, which though not made by decussation, observe the
rule of equality between incidence and reflexion; whereby
whispering places are framed by Ellipticall arches laid side-
wise; where the voice being delivered at the *focus* of one
extremity, observing an equality unto the angle of incidence,
it will reflect unto the *focus* of the other end, and so escape
the ears of the standers in the middle.

   A like rule is observed in the reflection of the vocall and
sonorous line in Ecchoes, which cannot therefore be heard
in all stations. But happening in woody plantations, by waters, and able to return some words; if reacht by a pleasant
and well-dividing voice, there may be heard the softest notes
in nature.

   And this not only verified in the way of sence, but in
animall and intellectuall receptions. Things entring upon the
intellect by a Pyramid from without, and thence into the

memory by another from within, the common decussation being in the understanding, as is delivered by *Bovillus.* Whether the intellectual and phantastical lines be not thus rightly disposed, but magnified, diminished, distorted, and ill placed in the Mathematicks of some brains, whereby they have irregular apprehensions of things, perverted notions, conceptions, and incurable hallucinations, were no unpleasant speculation.

And if Aegyptian Philosophy may obtain, the scale of influences was thus disposed, and the geniall spirits of both worlds, do trace their way in ascending and descending Pyramids, mystically apprehended in the Letter X, and the open Bill and stradling Legges of a Stork, which was imitated by that Character. [22]

Of this Figure *Plato* made choice to illustrate the motion of the soul, both of the world and man; while he delivereth that God divided the whole conjunction length-wise, according to the figure of a Greek X, and then turning it about reflected it into a circle; By the circle implying the uniform motion of the first Orb, and by the right lines, the planetical and various motions within it. And this also with application unto the soul of man, which hath a double aspect, one right, whereby it beholdeth the body, and objects without; another circular and reciprocal, whereby it beholdeth it self. The circle declaring the motion of the indivisible soul, simple, according to the divinity of its nature, and returning into it self; the right lines respecting the motion pertaining unto sense, and vegetation, and the central decussation, the wondrous connexion of the severall faculties conjointly in one substance. And so conjoyned the unity and duality of the soul, and made out the three substances so much considered by him; That is, the indivisible or divine, the divisible or corporeal, and that third, which was the *Systasis* or harmony of those two, in the mystical decussation. [23]

And if that were clearly made out which *Justin Martyr* took for granted, this figure hath had the honour to characterize and notifie our blessed Saviour, as he delivereth in that borrowed expression from *Plato; Decussavit eum in universo,* the hint whereof he would have *Plato* derive from the figure of the brazen Serpent, and to have mistaken the Letter X for T, whereas it is not improbable, he learned these and other mystical expressions in his Learned Observations of Aegypt, where he might obviously behold the Mercurial characters, the handed crosses, and other mysteries not throughly understood in the sacred Letter X, which being derivative from the Stork, one of the ten sacred animals, might be originally Aegyptian, and brought into *Greece* by *Cadmus* of that Countrey.

CHAPTER V

To enlarge this contemplation unto all the mysteries and secrets accomodable unto this number, were inexcusable   1
Pythagorisme, yet cannot [we] omit the ancient conceit of
· · · five surnamed the number of justice; as justly di-   2
· · · viding between the digits, and hanging in the centre
· · · of Nine, described by square numeration, which angularly divided will make the decussated number; and so agreeable unto the Quincunciall Ordination, and rowes divided by Equality, and just *decorum,* in the whole complantation; And might be the Originall of that common game   3
among us, wherein the fifth place is Soveraigne, and carrieth the chief intention. The Ancients wisely instructing youth, even in their recreations, unto virtue, that is, early to drive at the middle point and Central Seat of justice.

Nor can we omit how agreeable unto this number an handsome division is made in Trees and Plants, since *Plutarch* and the Ancients have named it the Divisive Num-   4
ber, justly dividing the Entities of the world, many remarkable things in it, and also comprehending the generall   5
division of Vegetables. And he that considers how most blossomes of Trees, and greatest number of Flowers, consist of five leaves; and therein doth rest the setled rule of nature; So that in those which exceed there is often found, or easily made a variety; may readily discover how nature rests in this number, which is indeed the first rest and pause of numeration in the fingers, the naturall Organs thereof. Nor

in the division of the feet of perfect animals doth nature exceed this account. And even in the joints of feet, which in birds are most multiplied, surpasseth not this number; So progressionally making them out in many, that from five in the fore-claw she descendeth unto two in the hindemost; And so in fower feet makes up the number of joynts, in the five fingers or toes of man.

Not to omit the Quintuple Section of a Cone, of handsome practise in Ornamentall Garden-plots, and in some way discoverable in so many works of Nature; In the leaves, fruits, and seeds of Vegetables, and scales of some Fishes, so much considerable in glasses, and the optick doctrine; wherein the learned may consider the Crystalline humour of the eye in the cuttle fish and *Loligo*.

He that forgets not how Antiquity named this the Conjugall or wedding number, and made it the Embleme of the most remarkable conjunction, will conceive it duely appliable unto this handsome Oeconomy and vegetable combination; May hence apprehend the allegoricall sence of that obscure expression of *Hesiod,* and afford no improbable reason why *Plato* admitted his Nuptiall guests by fives, in the kindred of the married couple.

And though a sharper mystery might be implied in the Number of the five wise and foolish Virgins, which were to meet the Bridegroom, yet was the same agreeable unto the Conjugall Number, which ancient Numerists made out by two and three, the first parity and imparity, the active and passive digits, the materiall and formall principles in generative Societies. And not discordant even from the customes of the *Romans,* who admitted but five Torches in their Nuptiall solemnities. Whether there were any mystery or not implied, the most generative animals were created on this day, and had accordingly the largest benediction: And under a Quintuple consideration, wanton Antiquity considered the Circumstances of generation, while by this number of five they naturally divided the Nectar of the fifth Planet.

The same number in the Hebrew mysteries and Cabalistical accounts was the character of Generation; declared by the Letter *He,* the fifth in their Alphabet; According to

that Cabalisticall *Dogma,* If *Abram* had not had this Letter
added unto his Name, he had remained fruitlesse, and without the power of generation: Not onely because hereby the
number of his Name attained two hundred fourty eight, the
number of the affirmative precepts, but because as in created natures there is a male and female, so in divine and intelligent productions, the mother of Life and Fountain of
souls in Cabalisticall Technology is called *Binah;* whose Seal
and Character was *He.* So that being sterill before, he received the power of generation from that measure and mansion in the Archetype; and was made conformable unto
Binah. And upon such involved considerations, the ten of
Sarai was exchanged into five. If any shall look upon this as a
stable number, and fitly appropriable unto Trees, as Bodies
of Rest and Station, he hath herein a great Foundation in
nature, who observing much variety in legges and motive
Organs of Animals, as two, four, six, eight, twelve, fourteen,
and more, hath passed over five and ten, and assigned them
unto none. And for the stability of this Number, he shall not   12
want the sphericity of its nature, which multiplied in it self,
will return into its own denomination, and bring up the reare
of the account. Which is also one of the Numbers that makes
up the mysticall Name of God, which, consisting of Letters
denoting all the sphaericall Numbers, ten, five, and six, Emphatically sets forth the Notion of *Trismegistus,* and that   13
intelligible Sphere, which is the Nature of God.

Many Expressions by this Number occurre in Holy Scripture, perhaps unjustly laden with mysticall Expositions, and
little concerning our order. That the Israelites were forbidden
to eat the fruit of their new planted Trees, before the fifth
yeare, was very agreeable unto the naturall Rules of Husbandry: Fruits being unwholsome and lash before the fourth
or fifth Yeare. In the second day or Feminine part of five,
there was added no approbation. For in the third or masculine day, the same is twice repeated; and a double benediction inclosed both Creations, whereof the one in some part
was but an accomplishment of the other. That the Trespasser   14
was to pay a fifth part above the head or principall, makes
no secret in this Number, and implied no more then one

part above the principall; which being considered in four parts, the additionall forfeit must bear the Name of a fift. The five golden mice had plainly their determination from [15] the number of the Princes; That five should put to flight an [16] hundred might have nothing mystically implyed; considering a rank of Souldiers could scarce consist of a lesser number. Saint *Paul* had rather speak five words in a known [17] then ten thousand in an unknowne tongue: That is, as little as could well be spoken; A simple proposition consisting of three words and a complexed one not ordinarily short of five.

More considerable there are in this mysticall account, which we must not insist on. And therefore why the radicall [18] Letters in the Pentateuch should equall the number of the Souldiery of the Tribes; Why our Saviour in the Wildernesse fed five thousand persons with five Barley Loaves, and again, but four thousand with no lesse than seven of Wheat? Why *Joseph* designed five changes of Rayment unto *Benjamin?* and *David* took just five pibbles out of the Brook against the Pagan Champion? We leave it unto Arithmeticall Divinity, and Theologicall explanation.

Yet if any delight in new Problemes, or think it worth the enquiry, whether the Criticall Physician hath rightly hit the nominall notation of Quinque; Why the Ancients mixed five or three but not four parts of water unto their Wine: And *Hippocrates* observed a fifth proportion in the mixture of water with milk, as in *Dysenteries* and bloudy fluxes. Under what abstruse foundation Astrologers do Figure the good or bad Fate from our Children, in good Fortune, or the [19] fifth house of their Celestiall Schemes. Whether the Aegyptians described a Starre by a Figure of five points, with reference unto the five Capitall aspects whereby they transmit [20] their Influences, or abstruser Considerations? Why the Cabalisticall Doctors, who conceive the whole *Sephiroth* or divine emanations to have guided the ten-stringed Harp of *David,* whereby he pacified the evil spirit of *Saul,* in strict numeration doe begin with the Perihypate Meson, or si fa ut, and so place the Tiphereth answering C sol fa ut, upon the fifth string: Or whether this number be oftner applied unto bad things and ends then good in holy Scripture, and why? He may meet with abstrusities of no ready resolution.

If any shall question the rationality of that Magick, in the cure of the blind man by *Serapis*, commanded to place five fingers on his Altar, and then his hand on his Eyes? Why since the whole Comoedy is primarily and naturally comprised in four parts, and Antiquity permitted not so many persons to speak in one Scene, yet would not comprehend the same in more or lesse then five acts? Why amongst Seastarres nature chiefly delighteth in five points? And since there are found some of no fewer then twelve, and some of seven, and nine, there are few or none discovered of six or eight? If any shall enquire why, the Flowers of *Rue* properly consisting of four Leaves, the first and third Flower have five? Why since many Flowers have one leaf or none, as *Scaliger* will have it, diverse three, and the greatest number consist of five divided from their bottomes; there are yet so few of two: or why nature generally beginning or setting out with two opposite leaves at the Root, doth so seldome conclude with that order and number at the Flower? he shall not passe his hours in vulgar speculations.

If any shall further quaery why magneticall Philosophy excludeth decussations, and needles transversly placed do naturally distract their verticities? Why Geomancers do imitate the Quintuple Figure, in their Mother Characters of Acquisition and Amission, &c. somewhat answering the Figures in the Lady or speckled Beetle? With what Equity, Chiromantical conjecturers decry these decussations in the Lines and Mounts of the hand? What that decussated Figure intendeth in the medall of *Alexander* the Great? Why the Goddesses sit commonly crosse-legged in ancient draughts, since *Juno* is described in the same as a veneficial posture to hinder the birth of *Hercules*? If any shall doubt why at the Amphidromicall Feasts, on the fifth day after the Childe was born, presents were sent from friends, of *Polipusses*, and Cuttle-fishes? Why five must be only left in that Symbolicall mutiny among the men of *Cadmus*? Why *Proteus* in *Homer*, the Symbole of the first matter, before he setled himself in the midst of his Sea-monsters, doth place them out by fives?

21

22

23

Why the fifth years Oxe was acceptable Sacrifice unto
Jupiter? Or why the Noble *Antoninus* in some sence doth call   24
the soul it self a Rhombus? He shall not fall on trite or triviall
disquisitions. And these we invent and propose unto acuter
enquirers, nauseating crambe verities and questions over-
queried. Flat and flexible truths are beat out by every hammer; But *Vulcan* and his whole forge sweat to work out
Achilles his armour. A large field is yet left unto sharper
discerners to enlarge upon this order, to search out the
quaternio's and figured draughts of this nature, and moderat-   25
ing the study of names, and meer nomenclature of plants,
to erect generalities, disclose unobserved proprieties, not only
in the vegetable shop, but the whole volume of nature; affording delightful Truths, confirmable by sense and ocular
Observation, which seems to me the surest path, to trace the
Labyrinth of Truth. For though discursive enquiry and rationall conjecture may leave handsome gashes and flesh-
wounds, yet without conjunction of this expect no mortal or
dispatching blows unto errour.

But the Quincunx of Heaven runs low, and 'tis time to   26
close the five ports of knowledge; We are unwilling to spin
out our awaking thoughts into the phantasmes of sleep,
which too often continueth praecogitations; making Cables   †
of Cobwebbes and Wildernesses of handsome Groves. Beside, *Hippocrates* hath spoke so little, and the Oneirocriti-   27
call Masters have left such frigid Interpretations from plants,
that there is little encouragement to dream of Paradise it self.
Nor will the sweetest delight of Gardens afford much comfort in sleep; wherein the dulnesse of that sense shakes
hands with delectable odours; and though in the Bed of   28
Cleopatra, can hardly with any delight raise up the ghost of
a Rose.

Night which Pagan Theology could make the daughter of   29
Chaos, affords no advantage to the description of order: Although no lower then that Masse can we derive its Genealogy. All things began in order, so shall they end, and so shall
they begin again; according to the ordainer of order and
mystical Mathematicks of the City of Heaven.

Though *Somnus* in *Homer* be sent to rowse up *Agamem-*

non, I finde no such effects in the drowsy approaches of
sleep. To keep our eyes open longer were but to act our
Antipodes. The Huntsmen are up in *America,* and they are   30
already past their first sleep in *Persia.* But who can be
drowsie at that howr which freed us from everlasting sleep?
or have slumbring thoughts at that time, when sleep it self   31
must end, and as some conjecture all shall awake again?

FINIS.

A LETTER TO A FRIEND

A
LETTER
TO A
FRIEND,
Upon occasion of the
DEATH
OF HIS
Intimate Friend.

By the Learned

Sir *THOMAS BROWN*, Knight,

Doctor of Physick, late of *Norwich*.

LONDON:

Printed for *Charles Brome* at the *Gun* at the West-End
of S. *Paul's* Church-yard. 1 6 9 0.

TO A
FRIEND,
Upon occasion of the
Death of his Intimate Friend.

[Section numbers have been added by the editor.]

1. Give me leave to wonder that News of this nature should have such heavy Wings, that you should hear so little concerning your dearest Friend, and that I must make that unwilling Repetition to tell you, *Ad portam rigidos calces* [1] *extendit,* that he is Dead and Buried, and by this time no Puny among the mighty Nations of the Dead; for tho he left [2] this World not very many days past, yet every hour you know largely addeth unto that dark Society; and considering the incessant Mortality of Mankind, you cannot conceive there dieth in the whole Earth so few as a thousand an hour.

2. Altho at this distance you had no early Account or Particular of his Death; yet your Affection may cease to wonder that you had not some secret Sense or Intimation thereof by Dreams, thoughtful Whisperings, Mercurisms, Airy Nuncio's, or sympathetical Insinuations, which many seem to have had at the Death of their dearest Friends: for since we find in that famous Story, that Spirits themselves were fain [3] to tell their Fellows at a distance, that the great *Antonio* was dead; we have a sufficient Excuse for our Ignorance in such Particulars, and must rest content with the common Road and *Appian* way of Knowledge by Information. Tho the uncertainty of the End of this World hath confounded all Humane Predictions; yet they who shall live to see the Sun and Moon darkned, and the Stars to fall from Heaven, will [4] hardly be deceived in the Advent of the last Day; and therefore strange it is, that the common Fallacy of consumptive

Persons, who feel not themselves dying, and therefore still
hope to live, should also reach their Friends in perfect
Health and Judgment. That you should be so little acquainted with *Plautus's* sick Complexion, or that almost an   5
Hippocratical Face should not alarum you to higher fears, or   6
rather despair of his Continuation in such an emaciated
State, wherein medical Predictions fail not, as sometimes in
acute Diseases, and wherein 'tis as dangerous to be sentenced
by a Physician as a Judge.

3. Upon my first Visit I was bold to tell them who had not
let fall all hopes of his Recovery, That in my sad Opinion he
was not like to behold a Grashopper, much less to pluck   7
another Fig; and in no long time after seemed to discover
that odd mortal Symptom in him not mention'd by *Hippocrates,* that is, to lose his own Face and look like some of his
near Relations; for he maintained not his proper Countenance, but looked like his Uncle, the Lines of whose Face lay   8
deep and invisible in his healthful Visage before: for as from
our beginnings we run through variety of Looks, before we
come to consistent and settled Faces; so before our End, by
sick and languishing Alterations, we put on new Visages: and
in our Retreat to Earth, may fall upon such Looks which
from community of seminal Originals were before latent in
us.

4. He was fruitlesly put in hope of advantage by change of
Air, and imbibing the pure Aerial Nitre of these Parts;   9
and therefore being so far spent, he quickly found *Sardinia*   10
in *Tivoli,* and the most healthful Air of little effect, where
Death had set her Broad Arrow; for he lived not unto the   11
middle of *May,* and confirmed the Observation of *Hippocrates* of that mortal time of the Year when the Leaves of   12
the Fig-tree resemble a Daw's Claw. He is happily seated
who lives in Places whose Air, Earth, and Water, promote
not the Infirmities of his weaker Parts, or is early removed
into Regions that correct them. He that is tabidly inclined,
were unwise to pass his days in *Portugal:* Cholical Persons
will find little Comfort in *Austria* or *Vienna:* He that is
Weak-legg'd must not be in Love with *Rome,* nor an infirm

Head with *Venice* or *Paris.* Death hath not only particular
Stars in Heaven, but malevolent Places on Earth, which single out our Infirmities, and strike at our weaker Parts; in
which Concern, passager and migrant Birds have the great [13]
Advantages; who are naturally constituted for distant Habitations, whom no Seas nor Places limit, but in their appointed
Seasons will visit us from *Greenland* and Mount *Atlas,* and
as some think, even from the *Antipodes.*

5. Tho we could not have his Life, yet we missed not our
desires in his soft Departure, which was scarce an Expiration;
and his End not unlike his Beginning, when the salient Point [14]
scarce affords a sensible motion, and his Departure so like
unto Sleep, that he scarce needed the civil Ceremony of clos- [†]
ing his Eyes; contrary unto the common way wherein Death [15]
draws up, Sleep lets fall the Eye-lids. With what strift and [†]
pains we came into the World we know not; but 'tis commonly no easie matter to get out of it: yet if it could be made
out, that such who have easie Nativities have commonly hard
Deaths, and contrarily; his Departure was so easie, that we
might justly suspect his Birth was of another nature, and that
some *Juno* sat cross-legg'd at his Nativity. [16]

6. Besides his soft Death, the incurable state of his Disease
might somewhat extenuate your Sorrow, who know that Monsters but seldom happen, Miracles more rarely in Physick. [17]
Angelus Victorius gives a serious Account of a Consumptive, [18]
Hectical, Pthysical Woman, who was suddenly cured by the
Intercession of *Ignatius.* We read not of any in Scripture who
in this case applied unto our Saviour, tho some may be contained in that large Expression, That he went about *Galilee*
healing all manner of Sickness, and all manner of Diseases. [19]
Amulets, Spells, Sigils and Incantations, practised in other
Diseases, are seldom pretended in this; and we find no Sigil
in the Archidoxis of *Paracelsus* to cure an extreme Consump- [20]
tion or *Marasmus,* which if other Diseases fail, will put a
period unto long Livers, and at last make dust of all. And
therefore the *Stoicks* could not but think that the firy Principle would wear out all the rest, and at last make an end of
the World, which notwithstanding without such a lingring

period the Creator may effect at his Pleasure: and to make an
end of all things on Earth, and our Planetical System of the
World, he need but put out the Sun.

7. I was not so curious to entitle the Stars unto any concern
of his Death, yet could not but take notice that he died when
the Moon was in motion from the Meridian; at which time, an
old *Italian* long ago would persuade me, that the greatest
part of Men died: but herein I confess I could never satisfie
my Curiosity; altho from the time of Tides in Places upon or
near the Sea, there may be considerable Deductions; and
Pliny hath an odd and remarkable Passage concerning the   21
Death of Men and Animals upon the Recess or Ebb of the
Sea. However, certain it is he died in the dead and deep part
of the Night, when *Nox* might be most apprehensibly said to
be the Daughter of Chaos, the Mother of Sleep and Death,
according to old Genealogy; and so went out of this World   22
about that hour when our blessed Saviour entred it, and about 23
what time many conceive he will return again unto it. *Cardan* 24
hath a peculiar and no hard Observation from a Man's Hand,
to know whether he was born in the day or night, which I
confess holdeth in my own. And *Scaliger* to that purpose hath 25
another from the tip of the Ear. Most Men are begotten in the   †
Night, most Animals in the Day; but whether more Persons
have been born in the Night or the Day, were a Curiosity
undecidable, tho more have perished by violent Deaths in
the Day; yet in natural Dissolutions both Times may hold an
Indifferency, at least but contingent Inequality. The whole
course of Time runs out in the Nativity and Death of Things;
which whether they happen by Succession or Coincidence,
are best computed by the natural, not artificial Day.

8. That *Charles* the Fifth was Crowned upon the day of his   26
Nativity, it being in his own power so to order it, makes no
singular Animadversion; but that he should also take King
Francis Prisoner upon that day, was an unexpected Coincidence, which made the same remarkable. *Antipater* who had
an Anniversary Feaver every Year upon his Birth-day,   †
needed no Astrological Revolution to know what day he
should dye on. When the fixed Stars have made a Revolution   27

unto the points from whence they first set out, some of the Ancients thought the World would have an end; which was a kind of dying upon the day of its Nativity. Now the Disease prevailing and swiftly advancing about the time of his Nativity, some were of Opinion, that he would leave the World on the day he entred into it: but this being a lingring Disease, and creeping softly on, nothing critical was found or expected, and he died not before fifteen days after. Nothing is more common with Infants than to dye on the day of their Nativity, to behold the worldly Hours and but the Fractions thereof; and even to perish before their Nativity in the hidden World of the Womb, and before their good Angel is conceived to undertake them. But in Persons who out-live many Years, and when there are no less than three hundred sixty five days to determine their Lives in every Year; that the first day should make the last, that the Tail of the Snake should return into its Mouth precisely at that time, and they should wind up upon the day of their Nativity, is indeed a remarkable Coincidence, which tho Astrology hath taken witty pains to salve, yet hath it been very wary in making Predictions of it.

9. In this consumptive Condition and remarkable Extenuation he came to be almost half himself, and left a great part behind him which he carried not to the Grave. And tho that Story of Duke *John Ernestus Mansfield* be not so easily swallowed, that at his Death his Heart was found not to be so big as a Nut; yet if the Bones of a good Sceleton weigh little more than twenty pounds, his Inwards and Flesh remaining could make no Bouffage, but a light bit for the Grave. I never more lively beheld the starved Characters of *Dante* in any living Face; an Aruspex might have read a Lecture upon him without Extenteration, his Flesh being so consumed that he might, in a manner, have discerned his Bowels without opening of him: so that to be carried *sextâ cervice* to the Grave, was but a civil unnecessity; and the Complements of the Coffin might out-weigh the Subject of it.

10. *Omnibonus Ferrarius* in mortal Dysenteries of Children looks for a Spot behind the Ear; in consumptive Diseases

some eye the Complexion of Moals; *Cardan* eagerly views
the Nails, some the Lines of the Hand, the Thenar or Muscle
of the Thumb; some are so curious as to observe the depth of
the Throat-pit, how the proportion varieth of the Small of
the Legs unto the Calf, or the compass of the Neck unto the
Circumference of the Head: but all these, with many more,
were so drowned in a mortal Visage and last Face of *Hippocrates,* that a weak Physiognomist might say at first eye, This
was a Face of Earth, and that *Morta* had set her Hard-Seal   34
upon his Temples, easily perceiving what *Caricatura*   35
Draughts Death makes upon pined Faces, and unto what an
unknown degree a Man may live backward.

11. Tho the Beard be only made a distinction of Sex and
sign of masculine Heat by *Ulmus,* yet the Precocity and early   36
growth thereof in him, was not to be liked in reference unto
long Life. *Lewis,* that virtuous but unfortunate King of *Hun-*   37
gary, who lost his Life at the Battel of *Mohacz,* was said to
be born without a Skin, to have bearded at Fifteen, and to
have shewn some gray Hairs about Twenty; from whence the
Diviners conjectured, that he would be spoiled of his Kingdom, and have but a short Life: But Hairs make fallible Predictions, and many Temples early gray have out-lived the
Psalmist's Period. Hairs which have most amused me have   38,39
not been in the Face or Head but on the Back, and not in
Men but Children, as I long ago observed in that Endemial
Distemper of little Children in *Languedock,* called the *Mor-*
gellons, wherein they critically break out with harsh Hairs on   40
their Backs, which takes off the unquiet Symptoms of the Disease, and delivers them from Coughs and Convulsions.

12. The *Egyptian* Mummies that I have seen, have had their
Mouths open, and somewhat gaping, which affordeth a good
opportunity to view and observe their Teeth, wherein 'tis not
easie to find any wanting or decayed: and therefore in *Egypt,*
where one Man practised but one Operation, or the Diseases
but of single Parts, it must needs be a barren Profession to
confine unto that of drawing of Teeth, and little better than
to have been Tooth-drawer unto King *Pyrrhus,* who had but   41
two in his Head. How the *Bannyans* of *India* maintain the   42

Integrity of those Parts, I find not particularly observed; who notwithstanding have an Advantage of their Preservation by abstaining from all Flesh and employing their Teeth in such Food unto which they may seem at first framed, from their Figure and Conformation: but sharp and corroding Rheums had so early mouldred those Rocks and hardest parts of his Fabrick, that a Man might well conceive that his Years were never like to double or twice tell over his Teeth. Corruption [43] had dealt more severely with them, than sepulchral Fires and smart Flames with those of burnt Bodies of old; for in the burnt Fragments of Urns which I have enquired into, altho I seem to find few Incisors or Shearers, yet the Dog Teeth and Grinders do notably resist those Fires.

13. In the Years of his Childhood he had languished under the Disease of his Country, the Rickets; after which notwithstanding many I have seen become strong and active Men; [†] but whether any have attained unto very great Years the Disease is scarce so old as to afford good Observation. Whether the Children of the *English* Plantations be subject unto the same Infirmity, may be worth the observing. Whether Lameness and Halting do still encrease among the Inhabitants of *Rovigno* in *Istria,* I know not; yet scarce twenty Years ago Monsieur *du Loyr* observed, that a third part of [44] that People halted: but too certain it is, that the Rickets en- [45] creaseth among us; the Small-Pox grows more pernicious than the Great: the Kings Purse knows that the King's Evil grows [46] more common. *Quartan* Agues are become no Strangers in *Ireland;* more common and mortal in *England:* and tho the Ancients gave that Disease very good Words, yet now that [47] Bell makes no strange sound which rings out for the Effects thereof.

14. Some think there were few Consumptions in the Old World, when Men lived much upon Milk; and that the an- cient Inhabitants of this Island were less troubled with Coughs when they went naked, and slept in Caves and Woods, than Men now in Chambers and Feather-beds. *Plato* [48] will tell us, that there was no such Disease as a Catarrh in *Homer's* time, and that it was but new in *Greece* in his Age.

Polydore Virgil delivereth that Pleurisies were rare in *Eng-* 49
land, who lived but in the days of *Henry* the Eighth. Some
will allow no Diseases to be new, others think that many old
ones are ceased; and that such which are esteemed new, will
have but their time: However, the Mercy of God hath scattered the great heap of Diseases, and not loaded any one
Country with all: some may be new in one Country which
have been old in another. New Discoveries of the Earth
discover new Diseases: for besides the common swarm, there
are endemial and local Infirmities proper unto certain Regions, which in the whole Earth make no small number: and
if *Asia, Africa,* and *America* should bring in their List, *Pan-*
doras Box would swell, and there must be a strange Pa-
thology.

15. Most Men expected to find a consumed Kell, empty and
bladder-like Guts, livid and marbled Lungs, and a withered
Pericardium in this exuccous Corps: but some seemed too
much to wonder that two Lobes of his Lungs adhered unto
his side; for the like I had often found in Bodies of no sus- 50
pected Consumptions or difficulty of Respiration. And the
same more often happeneth in Men than other Animals; and
some think, in Women than in Men: but the most remarkable
I have met with, was in a Man, after a Cough of almost fifty 51
Years, in whom all the Lobes adhered unto the Pleura, and
each Lobe unto another; who having also been much troubled with the Gout, brake the Rule of *Cardan,* and died of 52
the Stone in the Bladder. *Aristotle* makes a Query, Why some 53
Animals cough as Man, some not, as Oxen. If coughing be
taken as it consisteth of a natural and voluntary motion,
including Expectoration and spitting out, it may be as proper
unto Man as bleeding at the Nose; otherwise we find that
Vegetius and Rural Writers have not left so many Medicines
in vain against the Coughs of Cattel; and Men who perish by
Coughs dye the Death of Sheep, Cats and Lyons: and tho
Birds have no Midriff, yet we meet with divers Remedies in
Arrianus against the Coughs of Hawks. And tho it might be 54
thought, that all Animals who have Lungs do cough; yet in
cetaceous Fishes, who have large and strong Lungs, the same

is not observed; nor yet in oviparous Quadrupeds: and in the greatest thereof, the Crocodile, altho we read much of their Tears, we find nothing of that motion.

16. From the Thoughts of Sleep, when the Soul was conceived nearest unto Divinity, the Ancients erected an Art of Divination, wherein while they too widely expatiated in loose and inconsequent Conjectures, *Hippocrates* wisely considered Dreams as they presaged Alterations in the Body, and so afforded hints toward the preservation of Health, and prevention of Diseases; and therein was so serious as to advise Alteration of Diet, Exercise, Sweating, Bathing, and Vomiting; and also so religious, as to order Prayers and Supplications unto respective Deities, in good Dreams unto *Sol, Jupiter caelestis, Jupiter opulentus, Minerva, Mercurius,* and *Apollo;* in bad unto *Tellus* and the Heroes.

17. And therefore I could not but take notice how his Female Friends were irrationally curious so strictly to examine his Dreams, and in this low state to hope for the Fantasms of Health. He was now past the healthful Dreams of the Sun, Moon, and Stars in their Clarity and proper Courses. 'Twas too late to dream of Flying, of Limpid Fountains, smooth Waters, white Vestments, and fruitful green Trees, which are the Visions of healthful Sleeps, and at good distance from the Grave.

18. And they were also too deeply dejected that he should dream of his dead Friends, inconsequently divining, that he would not be long from them; for strange it was not that he should sometimes dream of the dead whose Thoughts run always upon Death: beside, to dream of the dead, so they appear not in dark Habits, and take nothing away from us, in Hippocrates his Sense was of good signification: for we [55] live by the dead, and every thing is or must be so before it becomes our Nourishment. And *Cardan,* who dream'd that [56] he discoursed with his dead Father in the Moon, made thereof no mortal Interpretation: and even to dream that we are dead, was no condemnable Fantasm in old *Oneirocriticism,* as having a signification of Liberty, vacuity from Cares,

exemption and freedom from Troubles, unknown unto the dead.

19. Some Dreams I confess may admit of easie and feminine Exposition: he who dream'd that he could not see his right Shoulder, might easily fear to lose the sight of his right Eye; he that before a Journey dream'd that his Feet were cut off, had a plain warning not to undertake his intended Journey. But why to dream of Lettuce should presage some ensuing   57 Disease, why to eat Figs should signifie foolish Talk, why to eat Eggs great Trouble, and to dream of Blindness should be so highly commended, according to the *Oneirocritical* Verses of *Astrampsychus* and *Nicephorus*, I shall leave unto your Divination.

20. He was willing to quit the World alone and altogether, leaving no Earnest behind him for Corruption or Aftergrave, having small content in that common satisfaction to survive or live in another, but amply satisfied that his Disease should dye with himself, nor revive in a Posterity to puzzle Physick, and make sad *Memento's* of their Parent hereditary. Leprosie awakes not sometimes before Forty, the Gout and Stone often later; but consumptive and tabid Roots sprout more early, and at the fairest make seventeen Years of our Life doubtful before that Age. They that enter the World with original Diseases as well as Sin, have not only common Mortality but sick Traductions to destroy them, make commonly short Courses, and live not at length but in Figures; so that a sound *Caesarean* Nativity may out-last a natural Birth, and a Knife   58 may sometimes make way for a more lasting fruit than a Midwife; which makes so few Infants now able to endure the old Test of the River, and many to have feeble Children who   59 could scarce have been married at *Sparta,* and those provident States who studied strong and healthful Generations; which happen but contingently in mere *pecuniary* Matches, or Marriages made by the Candle, wherein notwithstanding   60 there is little redress to be hoped from an Astrologer or a Lawyer, and a good discerning Physician were like to prove the most successful Counsellor.

21. *Julius Scaliger,* who in a sleepless Fit of the Gout could make two hundred Verses in a Night, would have but five plain Words upon his Tomb, and this serious Person, tho no *minor* Wit, left the Poetry of his Epitaph unto others; either unwilling to commend himself, or to be judged by a Distich, and perhaps considering how unhappy great Poets have been in versifying their own Epitaphs; wherein *Petrarcha, Dante,* and *Ariosto,* have so unhappily failed, that if their Tombs should out-last their Works, Posterity would find so little of *Apollo* in them, as to mistake them for Ciceronian Poets. [61] [t,62] [63] [t,64]

22. In this deliberate and creeping progress unto the Grave, he was somewhat too young, and of too noble a mind, to fall upon that stupid Symptom observable in divers Persons near their Journeys end, and which may be reckoned among the mortal Symptoms of their last Disease; that is, to become more narrow minded, miserable and tenacious, unready to part with any thing when they are ready to part with all, and afraid to want when they have no time to spend; mean while Physicians, who know that many are mad but in a single depraved Imagination, and one prevalent Decipiency; and that beside and out of such single Deliriums a Man may meet with sober Actions and good Sense in *Bedlam;* cannot but smile to see the Heirs and concerned Relations, gratulating themselves in the sober departure of their Friends; and tho they behold such mad covetous Passages, content to think they dye in good Understanding, and in their sober Senses.

23. Avarice, which is not only Infidelity but Idolatry, either from covetous Progeny or questuary Education, had no Root in his Breast, who made good Works the Expression of his Faith, and was big with desires unto publick and lasting Charities; and surely where good Wishes and charitable Intentions exceed Abilities, Theorical Beneficency may be more than a Dream. They build not Castles in the Air who would build Churches on Earth; and tho they leave no such Structures here, may lay good Foundations in Heaven. In brief, his Life and Death were such, that I could not blame them who wished the like, and almost to have been himself; almost, I say; for tho we may wish the prosperous Appurtenances of

others, or to be an other in his happy Accidents; yet so intrinsecal is every Man unto himself, that some doubt may be made, whether any would exchange his Being, or substantially become another Man.

24. He had wisely seen the World at home and abroad, and thereby observed under what variety Men are deluded in the pursuit of that which is not here to be found. And altho he had no Opinion of reputed Felicities below, and apprehended Men widely out in the estimate of such Happiness; yet his sober contempt of the World wrought no *Democritism* or *Cynicism,* no laughing or snarling at it, as well †
understanding there are not [real] Felicities [enough] in this †
World to satisfie a serious Mind; and therefore to soften the stream of our Lives, we are fain to take in the reputed Contentations of this World, to unite with the Crowd in their Beatitudes, and to make our selves happy by Consortion, Opinion, or Co-existimation: for strictly to separate from received and customary Felicities, and to confine unto the rigor of Realities, were to contract the Consolation of our Beings unto too uncomfortable Circumscriptions.

25. Not to fear Death, nor desire it, was short of his Resolu-   65
tion: to be dissolved, and be with Christ, was his dying ditty. He conceived his Thred long, in no long course of Years, and when he had scarce out-lived the second Life of *Lazarus;*   66
esteeming it enough to approach the Years of his Saviour, who so ordered his own humane State, as not to be old upon Earth.

26. But to be content with Death may be better than to desire it: a miserable Life may make us wish for Death, but a virtuous one to rest in it; which is the Advantage of those resolved Christians, who looking on Death not only as the sting, but the period and end of Sin, the Horizon and Isthmus between this Life and a better, and the Death of this World but as a Nativity of another, do contentedly submit unto the common Necessity, and envy not *Enoch* or *Elias.*

27. Not to be content with Life is the unsatisfactory state of those which destroy themselves; who being afraid to live, run

blindly upon their own Death, which no Man fears by Experience: and the *Stoicks* had a notable Doctrine to take away the fear thereof; that is, In such Extremities to desire that which is not to be avoided, and wish what might be feared; [67] and so made Evils voluntary, and to suit with their own Desires, which took off the terror of them.

28. But the ancient Martyrs were not encouraged by such Fallacies; who, tho they feared not Death, were afraid to be their own Executioners; and therefore thought it more Wisdom to crucifie their Lusts than their Bodies, to circumcise than stab their Hearts, and to mortifie than kill themselves.

29. His willingness to leave this World about that Age when most Men think they may best enjoy it, tho paradoxical unto worldly Ears, was not strange unto mine, who have so often observed, that many, tho old, oft stick fast unto the World, and seem to be drawn like *Cacus's* Oxen, backward with [68] great strugling and reluctancy unto the Grave. The long habit of Living makes meer Men more hardly to part with Life, and all to be nothing, but what is to come. To live at the rate of the old World, when some could scarce remember themselves young, may afford no better digested Death than a more moderate period. Many would have thought it an Happiness to have had their lot of Life in some notable Conjunctures of Ages past; but the uncertainty of future Times hath tempted few to make a part in Ages to come. And surely he that hath taken the true Altitude of Things, and rightly calculated the degenerate state of this Age, is not like to envy those that shall live in the next, much less three or four hundred Years hence, when no Man can comfortably imagine what Face this World will carry: and therefore since every Age makes a step unto the end of all things, and the Scripture affords so hard a Character of the last Times; quiet Minds will be content with their Generations, and rather bless Ages past than be ambitious of those to come.

30. Tho Age had set no Seal upon his Face, yet a dim Eye might clearly discover Fifty in his Actions; and therefore since Wisdom is the gray Hair, and an unspotted Life old

Age; altho his Years came short, he might have been said to
have held up with longer Livers, and to have been *Solomon's*   69
Old Man. And surely if we deduct all those days of our Life
which we might wish unlived, and which abate the comfort
of those we now live; if we reckon up only those days which
God hath accepted of our Lives, a Life of good Years will
hardly be a span long: the Son in this sense may out-live the
Father, and none be climacterically old. He that early arriv-   †
eth unto the Parts and Prudence of Age, is happily old without the uncomfortable Attendants of it; and 'tis superfluous to
live unto gray Hairs, when in a precocious Temper we anticipate the Virtues of them. In brief, he cannot be accounted
young who out-liveth the old Man. He that hath early arrived   70
unto the measure of a perfect Stature in Christ, hath already
fulfilled the prime and longest Intention of his Being: and one
day lived after the perfect Rule of Piety, is to be preferred
before sinning Immortality.

31. Altho he attained not unto the Years of his Predecessors,   71
yet he wanted not those preserving Virtues which confirm the
thread of weaker Constitutions. Cautelous Chastity and
crafty Sobriety were far from him; those Jewels were Paragon, without Flaw, Hair, Ice, or Cloud in him: which affords   72
me an hint to proceed in these good Wishes and few *Memento's* unto you.

32. Tread softly and circumspectly in this funambulous Track
and narrow Path of Goodness: pursue Virtue virtuously; be
sober and temperate, not to preserve your Body in a sufficiency to wanton Ends; not to spare your Purse; not to be
free from the Infamy of common Transgressors that way, and
thereby to ballance or palliate obscure and closer Vices; nor
simply to enjoy Health: by all which you may leaven good
Actions, and render Virtues disputable: but in one Word,
that you may truly serve God; which every Sickness will
tell you, you cannot well do without Health. The sick mans
Sacrifice is but a lame Oblation. Pious Treasures laid up in
healthful days, excuse the defect of sick performances; with-   73
out which we must needs look back with Anxiety upon the
lost opportunities of Health; and may have cause rather to

envy than pity the Ends of penitent Malefactors, who go with clear parts unto the last Act of their Lives; and in the integrity of their Faculties return their Spirit unto God that gave it.

[As printed in 1690, *A Letter* had fifty sections; see also relevant section in the TEXTUAL NOTES.]

CHRISTIAN MORALS

To the Right HONOURABLE D A V I D
EARL OF BUCHAN Viscount AUCHTERHOUSE,
Lord CARDROSS and GLENDOVACHIE,
One of the LORDS COMMISSIONERS of POLICE,
and LORD LIEUTENANT of the Counties of
STIRLING and CLACKMANNAN
in NORTH BRITTAIN.

MY LORD, THE Honour you have done our Family Obligeth us to make all just Acknowledgments of it: and there is no Form of Acknowledgment in our power, more worthy of Your Lordship's Acceptance, than this Dedication of the Last Work of our Honoured and Learned Father. Encouraged hereunto by the Knowledge we have of Your Lordship's Judicious Relish of universal Learning, and sublime Virtue; we beg the Favour of Your Acceptance of it, which will very much Oblige our Family in general, and Her in particular, who is,

    My Lord,
        Your Lordship's
            most humble Servant,

                        ELIZABETH LITTELTON.

THE
PREFACE.

If any One, after he has read Religio Medici and the ensuing Discourse, can make Doubt, whether the same Person was the Author of them both, he may be Assured by the Testimony of Mrs. LITTELTON, Sr. THOMAS BROWN'S Daughter, who Lived with her Father, when it was composed by Him; and who, at the time, read it written by his own Hand: and also by the Testimony of Others, (of whom I am One) who read the MS. of the Author, immediately after his Death, and who have since Read the Same; from which it hath been faithfully and exactly Transcribed for the Press. The Reason why it was not Printed Sooner is, because it was unhappily Lost, by being Mislay'd among Other MSS for which Search was lately made in the Presence of the Lord Arch-Bishop of Canterbury, of which his Grace, by Letter, Informed Mrs. LIT-TELTON, when he sent the MS to Her. There is nothing printed in the Discourse, or in the short notes, but what is found in the Original MS of the Author, except only where an Oversight had made the Addition or Transposition of some words necessary.

JOHN JEFFERY
Arch-Deacon of Norwich.

PART I.

SECT. 1. Tread softly and circumspectly in this funambulatory Track and narrow Path of Goodness: Pursue Virtue virtuously: Leven not good Actions nor render Virtues disputable. Stain not fair Acts with foul Intentions: Maim not Uprightness by halting Concomitances, nor circumstantially deprave substantial Goodness.

Consider where about thou art in *Cebes's* Table, or that old Philosophical Pinax of the Life of Man: whether thou art 2 yet in the Road of uncertainties; whether thou hast yet entred the narrow Gate, got up the Hill and asperous way, which leadeth unto the House of Sanity, or taken that purifying Potion from the hand of sincere Erudition, which may send Thee clear and pure away unto a virtuous and happy Life.

In this virtuous Voyage of thy Life hull not about like the † Ark without the use of Rudder, Mast, or Sail, and bound for no Port. Let not Disappointment cause Despondency, nor difficulty despair. Think not that you are Sailing from *Lima* to *Manillia*, when you may fasten up the Rudder, and sleep before the Wind; but expect rough Seas, Flaws, and contrary Blasts, and 'tis well if by many cross Tacks and Veerings you arrive at the Port; for we sleep in Lyons Skins in our Progress unto Virtue, and we slide not, but climb unto it.

Sit not down in the popular Forms and common Level of Virtues. Offer not only Peace Offerings but Holocausts unto God: where all is due, make no reserve, and cut not a Cummin Seed with the Almighty: To serve Him singly to serve our selves were too partial a piece of Piety, not like to place us in the illustrious Mansions of Glory.

SECT. 2. Rest not in an Ovation*, but a Triumph over thy Passions. Let Anger walk hanging down the head: Let Malice

* Ovation a petty and minor Kind of Triumph.

go Manicled, and Envy fetter'd after thee. Behold within thee
the long train of thy Trophies, not without thee. Make the
quarrelling Lapithytes sleep, and Centaurs within lye quiet.
Chain up the unruly Legion of thy breast. Lead thine own
captivity captive, and be *Caesar* within thy self.

SECT. 3. He that is Chast and Continent not to impair his
strength, or honest for fear of Contagion, will hardly be He-
roically virtuous. Adjourn not this virtue untill that temper,
when *Cato* could lend out his Wife, and impotent Satyrs   3
write Satyrs upon Lust: But be chast in thy flaming Days,
when *Alexander* dar'd not trust his eyes upon the fair Sisters 4
of *Darius*, and when so many think there is no other way
but *Origen's**.

SECT. 4. Show thy Art in Honesty, and loose not thy Virtue
by the bad Managery of it. Be Temperate and Sober, not to
preserve your body in an ability for wanton ends, not to avoid
the infamy of common transgressors that way, and thereby
to hope to expiate or palliate obscure and closer vices, not
to spare your purse, nor simply to enjoy health; but in one
word that thereby you may truly serve God, which every
sickness will tell you you cannot well do without health.
The sick Man's Sacrifice is but a lame Oblation. Pious Treasures lay'd up in healthful days plead for sick non-
performances: without which we must needs look back with
anxiety upon the lost opportunities of health, and may have
cause rather to envy than pity the ends of penitent publick
Sufferers, who go with healthfull prayers unto the last Scene
of their lives, and in the Integrity of their faculties return
their Spirit unto God that gave it.

SECT. 5. Be Charitable before wealth make thee covetous,
and loose not the glory of the Mite. If Riches encrease, let
thy mind hold pace with them, and think it not enough to
be Liberal, but Munificent. Though a Cup of cold water from
some hand may not be without it's reward, yet stick not thou

* Who is said to have Castrated himself.

for Wine and Oyl for the Wounds of the Distressed, and treat
the poor, as our Saviour did the Multitude, to the reliques
of some baskets. Diffuse thy beneficence early, and while thy
Treasures call thee Master: there may be an Atropos of thy
Fortunes before that of thy Life, and thy wealth cut off before that hour, when all Men shall be poor; for the Justice of
Death looks equally upon the dead, and *Charon* expects no 5
more from *Alexander* than from *Irus*.

SECT. 6. Give not only unto seven, but also unto eight,° that
is unto more than many. Though to give unto every one that
asketh° may seem severe advice, yet give thou also before
asking, that is, where want is silently clamorous, and mens
Necessities not their Tongues do loudly call for thy Mercies.
For though sometimes necessitousness be dumb, or misery
speak not out, yet true Charity is sagacious, and will find out
hints for beneficence. Acquaint thy self with the Physiognomy of Want, and let the Dead colours and first lines of
necessity suffice to tell thee there is an object for thy bounty.
Spare not where thou canst not easily be prodigal, and fear
not to be undone by mercy. For since he who hath pity on
the poor lendeth unto the Almighty Rewarder, who observes
no Ides but every day for his payments; Charity becomes
pious Usury, Christian Liberality the most thriving industry,
and what we adventure in a Cockboat may return in a Car-
rack unto us. He who thus casts his bread upon the Water
shall surely find it again; for though it falleth to the bottom,
it sinks but like the Ax of the Prophet, to arise again unto 6
him.

SECT. 7. If Avarice be thy Vice, yet make it not thy Punishment. Miserable men commiserate not themselves, bowelless
unto others, and merciless unto their own bowels. Let the
fruition of things bless the possession of them, and think it
more satisfaction to live richly than dye rich. For since thy
good works, not thy goods, will follow thee; since wealth is
an appertinance of life, and no dead Man is Rich; to famish

° Ecclesiasticus [Ecclesiastes]. [11.2.]
° Luke [6.30.]

in Plenty, and live poorly to dye Rich, were a multiplying improvement in Madness, and use upon use in Folly.

SECT. 8. Trust not to the Omnipotency of Gold, and say not unto it Thou art my Confidence. Kiss not thy hand to that Terrestrial Sun, nor bore thy ear unto its servitude. A Slave   7 unto Mammon makes no servant unto God. Covetousness cracks the sinews of Faith; nummes the apprehension of any thing above sense, and only affected with the certainty of things present makes a peradventure of things to come; lives but unto one World, nor hopes but fears another; makes their own death sweet unto others, bitter unto themselves; brings formal sadness, scenical mourning, and no wet eyes at the grave.

SECT. 9. Persons lightly dipt, not grain'd in generous Honesty, are but pale in Goodness, and faint hued in Integrity. But be thou what thou vertuously art, and let not the Ocean wash away thy Tincture. Stand magnetically upon that Axis, where prudent simplicity hath fixt thee; and let no attrac-   †,† tion invert the Poles of thy Honesty. That Vice may be uneasy and even monstrous unto thee, let iterated good Acts and long confirmed habits make Virtue almost natural, or a second nature in thee. Since virtuous superstructions have commonly generous foundations, dive into thy inclinations, and early discover what nature bids thee to be, or tells thee thou may'st be. They who thus timely descend into themselves, and cultivate the good seeds which nature hath set in them, prove not shrubs but Cedars in their generation. And to be in the form of the best of the Bad, or the worst of the Good,* will be no satisfaction unto them.

SECT. 10. Make not the consequence of Virtue the ends thereof. Be not beneficent for a name or Cymbal of applause, nor exact and just in Commerce for the advantages of Trust and Credit, which attend the reputation of true and punctual dealing. For these Rewards, though unsought for, plain Vir-

* *Optimi malorum pessimi bonorum.*   8

tue will bring with her. To have other by-ends in good actions sowers Laudable performances, which must have deeper roots, motives, and instigations, to give them the stamp of Virtues.

SECT. 11. Let not the Law of thy Country be the non ultra of thy Honesty; nor think that always good enough which the Law will make good. Narrow not the Law of Charity, Equity, Mercy. Joyn Gospel Righteousness with Legal Right. Be not a mere *Gamaliel* in the Faith, but let the Sermon in the Mount be thy *Targum* unto the Law of *Sinah*.

SECT. 12. Live by old Ethicks and the classical Rules of Honesty. Put no new names or notions upon Authentick Virtues and Vices. Think not that Morality is Ambulatory; that Vices in one age are not Vices in another; or that Virtues which are under the everlasting Seal of right Reason, may be Stamped by Opinion. And therefore though vicious times invert the opinions of things, and set up a new Ethicks against Virtue, yet hold thou unto old Morality; and rather than follow a multitude to do evil, stand like *Pompey's* Pillar conspicuous by thy self, and single in Integrity. And since the worst of times afford imitable Examples of Virtue; since no Deluge of Vice is like to be so general, but more than eight will escape; Eye well those Heroes who have held their Heads above Water, who have touched Pitch, and not been defiled, and in the common Contagion have remained uncorrupted.

SECT. 13. Let Age not Envy draw wrinkles on thy cheeks; be content to be envy'd, but envy not. Emulation may be plausible and Indignation allowable, but admit no treaty with that passion which no circumstance can make good. A displacency at the good of others because they enjoy it, though not unworthy of it, is an absurd depravity, sticking fast unto corrupted nature, and often too hard for Humility and Charity, the great Suppressors of Envy. This surely is a Lyon not to be strangled but by *Hercules* himself, or the highest stress of our minds, and an Atom of that power which subdueth all things unto it self.

SECT. 14. Owe not thy Humility unto humiliation from adversity, but look humbly down in that State when others look upwards upon thee. Think not thy own shadow longer than that of others, nor delight to take the Altitude of thy self. Be patient in the age of Pride, when Men live by short intervals of Reason under the dominion of Humor and Passion, when it's in the Power of every one to transform thee out of thy self, and run thee into the short madness. If you cannot   11 imitate *Job*, yet come not short of *Socrates*, and those patient   12 Pagans who tired the Tongues of their Enemies, while they perceived they spit their malice at brazen Walls and Statues.

SECT. 15. Let not the Sun in Capricorn* go down upon thy wrath, but write thy wrongs in Ashes. Draw the Curtain of night upon injuries, shut them up in the Tower of Oblivion* and let them be as though they had not been. To forgive our Enemies, yet hope that God will punish them, is not to forgive enough. To forgive them our selves, and not to pray God to forgive them, is a partial piece of Charity. Forgive thine enemies totally, and without any reserve that however God will revenge thee.

SECT. 16. While thou so hotly disclaimest the Devil, be not guilty of Diabolism. Fall not into one name with that unclean   13 Spirit, nor act his nature whom thou so much abhorrest; that is to Accuse, Calumniate, Backbite, Whisper, Detract, or sinistrously interpret others. Degenerous depravities, and narrow minded vices! not only below St. *Paul's* noble Chris-   14 tian but *Aristotle's* true Gentleman.* Trust not with some   15 that the Epistle of St. *James* is Apocryphal, and so read with less fear that Stabbing Truth, that in company with this vice

---

* Even when the Days are shortest.
* Alluding unto the Tower of Oblivion mentioned by *Procopius,* which was the name of a Tower of Imprisonment among the *Persians;* whoever was put therein was as it were buried alive, and it was death for any but to name him.
* See *Aristotle's* Ethicks, chapter of Magnanimity. [4.5.]

thy Religion is in vain. *Moses* broke the Tables without breaking of the Law; but where Charity is broke, the Law it self
is shattered, which cannot be whole without Love, which is
the fulfilling of it. Look humbly upon thy Virtues, and though
thou art Rich in some, yet think thy self Poor and Naked
without that Crowning Grace, which thinketh no evil, which   16
envieth not, which beareth, hopeth, believeth, endureth all
things. With these sure Graces, while busy Tongues are crying out for a drop of cold Water, mutes may be in happiness
and sing the *Trisagion** in Heaven.

SECT. 17. However thy understanding may waver in the Theories of True and False, yet fasten the Rudder of thy Will,
steer strait unto good and fall not foul on evil. Imagination
is apt to rove and conjecture to keep no bounds. Some have
run out so far, as to fancy the Stars might be but the light of   17
the Crystalline Heaven shot through perforations on the
bodies of the Orbs. Others more Ingeniously doubt whether
there hath not been a vast tract of Land in the *Atlantick*   18
Ocean, which Earthquakes and violent causes have long ago
devoured. Speculative Misapprehensions may be innocuous,
but immorality pernicious; Theorical mistakes and Physical
Deviations may condemn our Judgments, not lead us into
Judgment. But perversity of Will, immoral and sinfull enormities walk with *Adraste* and *Nemesis* at their Backs, pursue   19
us unto Judgment, and leave us viciously miserable.

SECT. 18. Bid early defiance unto those Vices which are of
thine inward Family, and having a root in thy Temper plead
a right and propriety in thee. Raise timely batteries against
those strong holds built upon the Rock of Nature, and make
this a great part of the Militia of thy life. Delude not thy self
into iniquities from participation or community, which abate
the sense but not the obliquity of them. To conceive sins less,
or less of sins, because others also Transgress, were Morally to
commit that natural fallacy of Man, to take comfort from Society, and think adversities less, because others also suffer

* Holy, Holy, Holy.

them. The politick nature of Vice must be opposed by Policy. And therefore wiser Honesties project and plot against it. Wherein notwithstanding we are not to rest in generals, or the trite Stratagems of Art. That may succeed with one which may prove succesless with another: There is no community or commonweal of Virtue: Every man must study his own oeconomy, and adapt such rules unto the figure of himself.

SECT. 19. Be substantially great in thy self, and more than thou appearest unto others; and let the World be deceived in thee, as they are in the Lights of Heaven. Hang early plummets upon the heels of Pride, and let Ambition have but an Epicycle and narrow circuit in thee. Measure not thy self by thy morning shadow, but by the extent of thy grave, and Reckon thy self above the Earth by the line thou must be contented with under it. Spread not into boundless Expansions either of designs or desires. Think not that mankind liveth but for a few, and that the rest are born but to serve those Ambitions, which make but flies of Men and wildernesses of whole Nations. Swell not into vehement actions which imbroil and confound the Earth; but be one of those violent ones which force* the Kingdom of Heaven. If thou must needs Rule, be *Zeno's* King, and enjoy that Empire which every Man gives himself. He who is thus his own Monarch contentedly sways the Scepter of himself, not envying the Glory of Crowned Heads and Elohims of the Earth. Could the World unite in the practise of that despised train of Virtues, which the Divine Ethicks of our Saviour hath so inculcated unto us, the furious face of things must disappear, Eden would be yet to be found, and the Angels might look down not with pity, but Joy upon us.   20

SECT. 20. Though the Quickness of thine Ear were able to reach the noise of the Moon, which some think it maketh in its rapid revolution; though the number of thy Ears should equal *Argus* his Eyes; yet stop them all with the wise man's   21

* Matthew 11. [12.]

wax, and be deaf unto the suggestions of Talebearers, Ca-
lumniators, Pickthank or Malevolent Delators, who while
quiet Men sleep, sowing the Tares of discord and division,
distract the tranquillity of Charity and all friendly Society.
These are the Tongues that set the world on fire, cankers of
reputation, and like that of *Jonas* his Gourd, wither a good
name in a night. Evil Spirits may sit still while these Spirits
walk about, and perform the business of Hell. To speak more
strictly, our corrupted hearts are the Factories of the Devil,
which may be at work without his presence. For when that
circumventing Spirit hath drawn Malice, Envy, and all un-
righteousness unto well rooted habits in his disciples, iniquity
then goes on upon its own legs, and if the gate of Hell were
shut up for a time, Vice would still be fertile and produce the
fruits of Hell. Thus when God forsakes us, Satan also leaves
us. For such offenders he looks upon as sure and sealed up,
and his temptations then needless unto them.

SECT. 21. Annihilate not the Mercies of God by the Oblivion
of Ingratitude. For Oblivion is a kind of Annihilation, and for
things to be as though they had not been is like unto never
being. Make not thy Head a Grave, but a Repository of God's
mercies. Though thou hadst the Memory of *Seneca*, or *Simon-* 22
ides, and Conscience, the punctual Memorist within us, yet
trust not to thy Remembrance in things which need Phylacteries. Register not only strange but merciful occurrences: Let
Ephemerides not *Olympiads* give thee account of his mercies.
Let thy Diaries stand thick with dutiful Mementos and Asterisks of acknowledgment. And to be compleat and forget
nothing, date not his mercy from thy nativity, Look beyond
the World, and before the *Aera* of *Adam*.

SECT. 22. Paint not the Sepulcher of thy self, and strive not to
beautify thy corruption. Be not an Advocate for thy Vices, nor
call for many Hour-Glasses to justify thy imperfections. Think
not that always good which thou thinkest thou canst always
make good, nor that concealed which the Sun doth not behold. That which the Sun doth not now see will be visible
when the Sun is out, and the Stars are fallen from Heaven.

Mean while there is no darkness unto Conscience, which can see without Light, and in the deepest obscurity give a clear Draught of things which the Cloud of dissimulation hath conceal'd from all eyes. There is a natural standing Court within us, examining, acquitting, and condemning at the Tribunal of our selves, wherein iniquities have their natural Theta's, and no nocent is absolved by the verdict of himself. And therefore although our transgressions shall be tryed at the last bar, the process need not be long: for the Judge of all knoweth all, and every Man will nakedly know himself. And when so few are like to plead not Guilty, the Assize must soon have an end.

SECT. 23. Comply with some humors, bear with others, but serve none. Civil complacency consists with decent honesty: Flattery is a Juggler, and no Kin unto Sincerity. But while thou maintainest the plain path, and scornest to flatter others, fall not into self Adulation, and become not thine own Parasite. Be deaf unto thy self, and be not betrayed at home. Self-credulity, pride, and levity lead unto self-Idolatry. There is no *Damocles* like unto self opinion, nor any *Siren* to our own fawning Conceptions. To magnify our minor things, or hug our selves in our apparitions; to afford a credulous Ear unto the clawing suggestions of fancy; to pass our days in painted mistakes of our selves; and though we behold our own blood, to think our selves the Sons of *Jupiter**; are blandishments of self love, worse than outward delusion. By this Imposture Wise Men sometimes are Mistaken in their Elevation, and look above themselves. And Fools, which are Antipodes unto the Wise, conceive themselves to be but their *Perioeci,* and in the same parallel with them.

23

SECT. 24. Be not a *Hercules furens* abroad, and a Poltron within thy self. To chase our Enemies out of the Field, and be led captive by our Vices; to beat down our Foes, and fall down to our Concupiscences; are Solecisms in Moral Schools, and no Laurel attends them. To well manage our Affections,

* As *Alexander* the Great did.

and wild Horses of *Plato,* are the highest Circenses; and the [24]
noblest Digladiation is in the Theater of our selves: for
therein our inward Antagonists, not only like common Gladiators, with ordinary Weapons and down right Blows make at
us, but also like Retiary and Laqueary Combatants, with
Nets, Frauds, and Entanglements fall upon us. Weapons for [25]
such combats are not to be forged at *Lipara: Vulcan's* Art
doth nothing in this internal Militia: wherein not the Armour
of *Achilles,* but the Armature of St. *Paul,* gives the Glorious [26]
day, and Triumphs not Leading up into Capitols, but up into
the highest Heavens. And therefore while so many think it
the only valour to command and master others, study thou
the Dominion of thy self, and quiet thine own Commotions.
Let Right Reason be thy *Lycurgus,* and lift up thy hand unto
the Law of it; move by the Intelligences of the superiour Faculties, not by the Rapt of Passion, nor merely by that of
Temper and Constitution. They who are merely carried on
by the Wheel of such Inclinations, without the Hand and
Guidance of Sovereign Reason, are but the Automatous part
of mankind, rather lived than living, or at least underliving
themselves.

SECT. 25. Let not Fortune, which hath no name in Scripture,
have any in thy Divinity. Let Providence, not Chance, have
the honour of thy acknowledgments, and be thy *Oedipus* in
Contingences. Mark well the Paths and winding Ways
thereof; but be not too wise in the Construction, or sudden in
the Application. The Hand of Providence writes often by Ab-
breviatures, Hieroglyphicks or short Characters, which, like
the Laconism on the Wall, are not to be made out but by a [27]
Hint or Key from that Spirit which indited them. Leave future occurrences to their uncertainties, think that which is
present thy own; And since 'tis easier to foretell an Eclipse,
than a foul Day at some distance, look for little Regular below. Attend with patience the uncertainty of Things, and
what lieth yet unexerted in the Chaos of Futurity. The uncertainty and ignorance of Things to come makes the World
new unto us by unexpected Emergences, whereby we pass
not our days in the trite road of affairs affording no Novity;

for the novellizing Spirit of Man lives by variety, and the new Faces of Things.

SECT. 26. Though a contented Mind enlargeth the dimension of little things, and unto some 'tis Wealth enough not to be Poor, and others are well content, if they be but Rich enough to be Honest, and to give every Man his due: yet fall not into that obsolete Affectation of Bravery to throw away thy Money, and to reject all Honours or Honourable stations in this courtly and splendid World. Old Generosity is superannuated, and such contempt of the World out of date. No Man [28] is now like to refuse the favour of great ones, or be content to say unto Princes, stand out of my Sun. And if any there be of such antiquated Resolutions, they are not like to be tempted out of them by great ones; and 'tis fair if they escape the name of Hypocondriacks from the Genius of latter times, unto whom contempt of the World is the most contemptible opinion, and to be able, like *Bias*, to carry all they have about [29] them were to be the eighth Wise-man. However, the old tetrick Philosophers look'd always with Indignation upon such a Face of Things, and observing the unnatural current of Riches, Power, and Honour in the World, and withall the imperfection and demerit of persons often advanced unto them, were tempted unto angry Opinions, that Affairs were ordered more by Stars than Reason, and that things went on rather by Lottery, than Election.

SECT. 27. If thy Vessel be but small in the Ocean of this World, if Meanness of Possessions be thy allotment upon Earth, forget not those Virtues which the great disposer of all bids thee to entertain from thy Quality and Condition, that is, Submission, Humility, Content of mind, and Industry. Content may dwell in all Stations. To be low, but above contempt, may be high enough to be Happy. But many of low Degree may be higher than computed, and some Cubits above the common Commensuration; for in all States Virtue gives Qualifications and Allowances, which make out defects. Rough Diamonds are sometimes mistaken for Pebbles, and Meanness may be Rich in Accomplishments which Riches in vain desire. If our merits be above our Stations, if our intrinsecal Value be greater than what we go for, or our Value than our Valuation, and if we stand higher in God's, than in the Censor's Book; it may make some equitable balance in the inequalities of this World, and there may be no such vast Chasm or Gulph between disparities as common Measures determine. The Divine Eye looks upon high and low differently from that of Man. They who seem to stand upon *Olympus,* and high mounted unto our eyes, may be but in the Valleys, and low Ground unto his; for he looks upon those as highest who nearest approach his Divinity, and upon those as lowest, who are farthest from it.

SECT. 28. When thou lookest upon the Imperfections of others, allow one Eye for what is Laudable in them, and the balance they have from some excellency, which may render them considerable. While we look with fear or hatred upon the Teeth of the Viper, we may behold his Eye with love. In [30] venemous Natures something may be amiable: Poysons afford Antipoysons: nothing is totally, or altogether uselessly bad. Notable Virtues are sometimes dashed with notorious Vices, and in some vicious tempers have been found illustrious Acts of Virtue; which makes such observable worth in some actions of King *Demetrius, Antonius,* and *Ahab,* as are not to be [31] found in the same kind in *Aristides, Numa,* or *David.* Constancy, Generosity, Clemency, and Liberality have been highly conspicuous in some Persons not markt out in other concerns for Example or Imitation. But since Goodness is exemplary in all, if others have not our Virtues, let us not be wanting in theirs, nor scorning them for their Vices whereof we are free, be condemned by their Virtues, wherein we are deficient. There is Dross, Alloy, and Embasement in all human Temper; and he flieth without Wings, who thinks to find Ophyr or pure Metal in any. For perfection is not like Light center'd in any one Body, but like the dispersed Seminalities [32] of Vegetables at the Creation, scattered through the whole Mass of the Earth, no place producing all and almost all some. So that 'tis well, if a perfect Man can be made out of many Men, and to the perfect Eye of God even out of

Mankind. Time, which perfects some Things, imperfects also others. Could we intimately apprehend the Ideated Man, and as he stood in the intellect of God upon the first exertion by Creation, we might more narrowly comprehend our present Degeneration, and how widely we are fallen from the pure Exemplar and Idea of our Nature: for after this corruptive Elongation from a primitive and pure Creation, we are almost lost in Degeneration; and *Adam* hath not only fallen from his Creator, but we our selves from *Adam,* our Tycho and primary Generator.

SECT. 29. Quarrel not rashly with Adversities not yet understood; and overlook not the Mercies often bound up in them. For we consider not sufficiently the good of Evils, nor fairly compute the Mercies of Providence in things afflictive at first hand. The famous *Andreas Doria* being invited to a Feast by [33] *Aloysio Fieschi* with design to Kill him, just the night before, fell mercifully into a fit of the Gout and so escaped that mischief. When *Cato* intended to Kill himself, from a blow which he gave his servant, who would not reach his Sword unto him, his Hand so swell'd that he had much ado to Effect his design. Hereby any one but a resolved Stoick might have taken a fair hint of consideration, and that some mercifull Genius would have contrived his preservation. To be sagacious in such intercurrences is not Superstition, but wary and pious Discretion, and to contemn such hints were to be deaf unto the speaking hand of God, wherein *Socrates* and *Cardan* [34] would hardly have been mistaken.

SECT. 30. Break not open the gate of Destruction, and make no haste or bustle unto Ruin. Post not heedlesly on unto the *non ultra* of Folly, or precipice of Perdition. Let vicious ways have their Tropicks and Deflexions, and swim in the Waters [35] of Sin but as in the *Asphaltick* Lake, though smeared and defiled, not to sink to the bottom. If thou hast dipt thy foot in the Brink, yet venture not over *Rubicon.* Run not into Extremities from whence there is no regression. In the vicious ways of the World it mercifully falleth out that we become not extempore wicked, but it taketh some time and pains to undo our selves. We fall not from Virtue, like *Vulcan* from [36] Heaven, in a day. Bad Dispositions require some time to grow into bad Habits, bad Habits must undermine good, and often repeated acts make us habitually evil: so that by gradual depravations, and while we are but staggeringly evil, we are not left without Parentheses of considerations, thoughtful rebukes, and merciful interventions, to recal us unto our selves. For the Wisdom of God hath methodiz'd the course of things unto the best advantage of goodness, and thinking Considerators overlook not the tract thereof.

SECT. 31. Since Men and Women have their proper Virtues and Vices, and even Twins of different sexes have not only distinct coverings in the Womb, but differing qualities and Virtuous Habits after; transplace not their Proprieties and confound not their Distinctions. Let Masculine and feminine accomplishments shine in their proper Orbs, and adorn their Respective subjects. However unite not the Vices of both Sexes in one; be not Monstrous in Iniquity, nor Hermaphroditically Vitious.

SECT. 32. If generous Honesty, Valour, and plain Dealing, be the Cognisance of thy Family or Characteristick of thy Country, hold fast such inclinations suckt in with thy first Breath, and which lay in the Cradle with thee. Fall not into transforming degenerations, which under the old name create a new Nation. Be not an Alien in thine own Nation; bring not *Orontes* into *Tiber;* learn the Virtues not the Vices of thy [37] foreign Neighbours, and make thy imitation by discretion not contagion. Feel something of thy self in the noble Acts of thy Ancestors, and find in thine own Genius that of thy Predecessors. Rest not under the Expired merits of others, shine by those of thy own. Flame not like the central fire which enlightneth no Eyes, which no Man seeth, and most men think there's no such thing to be seen. Add one Ray unto the common Lustre; add not only to the Number but the Note of thy Generation; and prove not a Cloud but an Asterisk in thy Region.

SECT. 33. Since thou hast an Alarum in thy Breast, which tells
thee thou hast a Living Spirit in thee above two thousand
times in an hour; dull not away thy Days in sloathful supinity
and the tediousness of doing nothing. To strenuous Minds
there is an inquietude in overquietness, and no laboriousness
in labour; and to tread a mile after the slow pace of a Snail,
or the heavy measures of the Lazy of Brazilia, were a most
tiring Pennance, and worse than a Race of some furlongs at
the Olympicks. The rapid courses of the heavenly bodies are
rather imitable by our Thoughts than our corporeal Motions;
yet the solemn motions of our lives amount unto a greater   38
measure than is commonly apprehended. Some few men
have surrounded the Globe of the Earth; yet many in the set
Locomotions and movements of their days have measured
the circuit of it, and twenty thousand miles have been exceeded by them. Move circumspectly not meticulously, and
rather carefully sollicitous than anxiously sollicitudinous.
Think not there is a Lyon in the way, nor walk with Leaden   39,40
Sandals in the paths of Goodness; but in all Virtuous motions
let Prudence determine thy measures. Strive not to run like
Hercules a furlong in a breath: Festination may prove Pre-   41
cipitation: Deliberating delay may be wise cunctation, and
slowness no sloathfulness.

SECT. 34. Since Virtuous Actions have their own Trumpets,
and without any noise from thy self will have their resound
abroad; busy not thy best Member in the Encomium of thy
self. Praise is a debt we owe unto the Virtues of others, and
due unto our own from all, whom Malice hath not made
Mutes, or Envy struck Dumb. Fall not however into the common prevaricating way of self commendation and boasting,
by denoting the imperfections of others. He who discom-
mendeth others obliquely commendeth himself. He who
whispers their infirmities proclaims his own Exemption from
them, and consequently says, I am not as this Publican, or
Hic Niger,* whom I talk of. Open ostentation and loud vain-
glory is more tolerable than this obliquity, as but containing

* *Hic Niger est, hunc tu Romane caveto.* Horace. [*Sat.* 1.4.85.]   42

some Froath, no Ink; as but consisting of a personal piece of folly, nor complicated with uncharitableness. Superfluously we seek a precarious applause abroad: every good Man hath his plaudite within himself; and though his Tongue be silent, is not without loud Cymbals in his Breast. Conscience will become his Panegyrist, and never forget to crown and extol him unto himself.

SECT. 35. Bless not thy self only that thou wert born in *Athens;*° but among thy multiplyed acknowledgments lift up one hand unto Heaven, that thou wert born of Honest Parents, that Modesty, Humility, Patience, and Veracity lay in the same Egg, and came into the World with thee. From such foundations thou may'st be Happy in a Virtuous precocity, and make an early and long walk in Goodness; so may'st thou more naturally feel the contrariety of Vice unto Nature, and resist some by the Antidote of thy Temper. As Charity covers, so Modesty preventeth a multitude of sins; withholding from noon day Vices and brazen-brow'd Iniquities, from sinning on the house top, and painting our follies with the rays of the Sun. Where this Virtue reigneth, though Vice may show its Head, it cannot be in its Glory: where shame of sin sets, look not for Virtue to arise; for when Modesty taketh Wing, *Astraea*° goes soon after.

SECT. 36. The Heroical vein of Mankind runs much in the Souldiery, and couragious part of the World; and in that form we oftenest find Men above Men. History is full of the gallantry of that Tribe; and when we read their notable Acts, we easily find what a difference there is between a Life in *Plutarch* and in *Laërtius.* Where true Fortitude dwells, Loyalty, [43] Bounty, Friendship, and Fidelity, may be found. A man may confide in persons constituted for noble ends, who dare do and suffer, and who have a Hand to burn for their Country [44] and their Friend. Small and creeping things are the product of petty Souls. He is like to be mistaken, who makes choice of a covetous Man for a Friend, or relieth upon the Reed of

° As *Socrates* did. *Athens* a place of Learning and Civility.
° *Astrea* Goddess of Justice and consequently of all Virtue.

narrow and poltron Friendship. Pityful things are only to be found in the cottages of such Breasts; but bright Thoughts, clear Deeds, Constancy, Fidelity, Bounty, and generous Honesty are the Gems of noble Minds; wherein, to derogate from none, the true Heroick English Gentleman hath no Peer.

PART II.

SECT. 1. Punish not thy self with Pleasure; Glut not thy sense with palative Delights; nor revenge the contempt of Temperance by the penalty of Satiety. Were there an Age of delight or any pleasure durable, who would not honour *Volupia?* but the Race of Delight is short, and Pleasures have mutable faces. The pleasures of one age are not pleasures in another, and their Lives fall short of our own. Even in our sensual days the strength of delight is in its seldomness or rarity, and ¹ sting in its satiety: Mediocrity is its Life, and immoderacy its Confusion. The Luxurious Emperors of old inconsiderately satiated themselves with the Dainties of Sea and Land, till, wearied through all varieties, their refections became a study unto them, and they were fain to feed by Invention. Novices in true Epicurism! which by mediocrity, paucity, quick and healthful Appetite, makes delights smartly acceptable; whereby *Epicurus* himself found *Jupiter's* brain* in a piece of ² Cytheridian Cheese, and the Tongues of Nightingals in a dish of Onyons. Hereby healthful and temperate poverty hath the start of nauseating Luxury; unto whose clear and naked appetite every meal is a feast, and in one single dish the first course of *Metellus;** who are cheaply hungry, and never loose their hunger, or advantage of a craving appetite, because obvious food contents it; while *Nero** half famish'd could not feed upon a piece of Bread, and lingring after his snowed water, hardly got down an ordinary cup of Calda.* By such circumscriptions of pleasure the contemned Philosophers reserved unto themselves the secret of Delight, which the *Helluo's* of those days lost in their exorbitances. In vain

* *Cerebrum Jovis,* for a Delicious bit.
* *Metellus* his riotous Pontificial Supper, the great variety whereat is to be seen in *Macrobius.* [*Saturnalia,* 3.13.10.]
* *Nero* in his flight. *Sueton.* [*Nero,* 48.4.]
* *Caldae gelidaeque Minister.* [Juvenal, *Sat.* 5.63.]

we study Delight: It is at the command of every sober Mind,
and in every sense born with us: but Nature, who teacheth
us the rule of pleasure, instructeth us also in the bounds   †
thereof, and where its line expireth. And therefore Temperate Minds, not pressing their pleasures until the sting appeareth, enjoy their contentations contentedly, and without
regret, and so escape the folly of excess, to be pleased unto
displacency.

SECT. 2. Bring candid Eyes unto the perusal of mens works,
and let not *Zoilism* or Detraction blast well intended labours.
He that endureth no faults in mens writings must only read
his own, wherein for the most part all appeareth White. Quotation mistakes, inadvertency, expedition, and human Lapses
may make not only Moles but Warts in Learned Authors,
who notwithstanding being judged by the capital matter admit not of disparagement. I should unwillingly affirm that   3
Cicero was but slightly versed in *Homer,* because in his Work
de Gloria he ascribed those verses unto *Ajax,* which were delivered by *Hector.* What if *Plautus* in the account of *Hercules*   4
mistaketh nativity for conception? Who would have mean
thoughts of *Apollinaris Sidonius,* who seems to mistake the   5
River *Tigris* for *Euphrates;* and though a good Historian and
learned Bishop of *Auvergne,* had the misfortune to be out in
the Story of *David,* making mention of him when the Ark
was sent back by the *Philistins* upon a Cart; which was before his time. Though I have no great opinion of *Machiavel's*
Learning, yet I shall not presently say, that he was but a
Novice in Roman History, because he was mistaken in placing *Commodus* after the Emperour *Severus.* Capital Truths
are to be narrowly eyed, collateral Lapses and circumstantial
deliveries not to be too strictly sifted. And if the substantial
subject be well forged out, we need not examine the sparks
which irregularly fly from it.

SECT. 3. Let well weighed Considerations, not stiff and peremptory Assumptions, guide thy discourses, Pen, and Actions.
To begin or continue our works like *Trismegistus* of old,

verum certe verum atque verissimum est,* would sound arro-   6
gantly unto present Ears in this strict enquiring Age, wherein,
for the most part, Probably, and Perhaps, will hardly serve to
mollify the Spirit of captious Contradictors. If *Cardan* saith   7
that a Parrot is a beautiful Bird, *Scaliger* will set his Wits o'
work to prove it a deformed Animal. The Compage of all
Physical Truths is not so closely jointed, but opposition may
find intrusion, nor always so closely maintained, as not to
suffer attrition. Many Positions seem quodlibetically constituted, and like a *Delphian* Blade will cut on both sides. Some
Truths seem almost Falshoods, and some Falshoods almost
Truths; wherein Falshood and Truth seem almost aequilibri-
ously stated, and but a few grains of distinction to bear down
the ballance. Some have digged deep, yet glanced by the
Royal Vein; and a Man may come unto the *Pericardium,* but
not the Heart of Truth. Besides, many things are known, as
some are seen, that is by Parallaxis, or at some distance from
their true and proper beings, the superficial regard of things
having a different aspect from their true and central Natures.
And this moves sober Pens unto suspensory and timorous assertions, nor presently to obtrude them as *Sibyls* leaves,
which after considerations may find to be but folious appar-
ences, and not the central and vital interiours of Truth.

SECT. 4. Value the Judicious, and let not mere acquests in
minor parts of Learning gain thy preexistimation. 'Tis an
unjust way of compute to magnify a weak Head for some
Latin abilities, and to undervalue a solid Judgment, because
he knows not the genealogy of *Hector.* When that notable   8
King of *France** would have his Son to know but one sentence   9
in Latin, had it been a good one, perhaps it had been
enough. Natural parts and good Judgments rule the World.
States are not governed by Ergotisms. Many have Ruled
well who could not perhaps define a Commonwealth, and
they who understand not the Globe of the Earth command a
great part of it. Where natural Logick prevails not, Artificial
too often faileth. Where Nature fills the Sails, the Vessel goes

* *In Tabula Smaragdina.*
* Lewis the Eleventh. *Qui nescit dissimulare nescit Regnare.*

smoothly on, and when Judgment is the Pilot, the Ensurance
need not be high. When Industry builds upon Nature, we
may exspect Pyramids: where that foundation is wanting,
the structure must be low. They do most by Books, who
could do much without them, and he that chiefly ows himself unto himself is the substantial Man.

sect. 5. Let thy Studies be free as thy Thoughts and Con-   10
templations: but fly not only upon the wings of Imagination;
Joyn Sense unto Reason, and Experiment unto Speculation,
and so give life unto Embryon Truths, and Verities yet in
their Chaos. There is nothing more acceptable unto the Ingenious World, than this noble Eluctation of Truth; wherein,
against the tenacity of Prejudice and Prescription, this Century now prevaileth. What Libraries of new Volumes after-
times will behold, and in what a new World of Knowledge
the eyes of our Posterity may be happy, a few Ages may joy-
fully declare; and is but a cold thought unto those, who
cannot hope to behold this Exantlation of Truth, or that obscured Virgin half out of the Pit. Which might make some
content with a commutation of the time of their lives, and
to commend the Fancy of the *Pythagorean* metempsychosis;
whereby they might hope to enjoy this happiness in their
third or fourth selves, and behold that in *Pythagoras*, which
they now but foresee in *Euphorbus.** The World, which took   11
but six days to make, is like to take six thousand years to   †
make out: mean while old Truths voted down begin to resume their places, and new ones arise upon us; wherein there
is no comfort in the happiness of *Tully's* Elizium,* or any satisfaction from the Ghosts of the Ancients, who knew so little
of what is now well known. Men disparage not Antiquity,
who prudently exalt new Enquiries, and make not them the
Judges of Truth, who were but fellow Enquirers of it. Who
can but magnify the Endeavors of *Aristotle,* and the noble
start which Learning had under him; or less than pitty the

* *Ipse ego, nam memini, Trojani in tempore belli*
  Panthoides Euphorbus eram. [Ovid, *Metamorph.* 15.160–61.]
* Who comforted himself that he should there converse with the old Phi-
losophers. [*De Senectute,* 84.]

slender progression made upon such advantages? While many Centuries were lost in repetitions and transcriptions sealing up the Book of Knowledge. And therefore rather than to swell the leaves of Learning by fruitless Repetitions, to sing the same Song in all Ages, nor adventure at Essays beyond the attempt of others, many would be content that some would write like *Helmont* or *Paracelsus;* and be willing to endure the monstrosity of some opinions, for divers singular notions requiting such aberrations.

SECT. 6. Despise not the obliquities of younger ways, nor despair of better things whereof there is yet no prospect. Who would imagine that *Diogenes,* who in his younger days [12] was a falsifier of Money, should in the after course of his Life be so great a contemner of Metal? Some Negros, who believe the Resurrection, think that they shall Rise white.* Even in this life Regeneration may imitate Resurrection, our black and vitious tinctures may wear off, and goodness cloath us with candour. Good Admonitions Knock not always in vain. There will be signal Examples of God's mercy, and the Angels must not want their charitable Rejoyces for the conversion of lost Sinners. Figures of most Angles do nearest approach unto Circles, which have no Angles at all. Some may be near unto goodness, who are conceived far from it, and many things happen, not likely to ensue from any promises of Antecedencies. Culpable beginnings have found commendable conclusions, and infamous courses pious retractations. Detestable Sinners have proved exemplary Converts on Earth, and may be Glorious in the Apartment of *Mary Magdalen* in Heaven. Men are not the same through all divisions of their Ages. Time, Experience, self Reflexions, and God's mercies make in some well-temper'd minds a kind of translation before Death, and Men to differ from themselves as well as from other Persons. Hereof the old World afforded many Examples to the infamy of latter Ages, wherein Men too often live by the rule of their inclinations; so that, without any Astral prediction, the first day gives

* *Mandelslo.* [*Travels,* Eng. trans., 1662.]

the last,* Men are commonly as they were, or rather, as bad dispositions run into worser habits, the Evening doth not crown, but sowerly conclude the Day.

SECT. 7. If the Almighty will not spare us according to his merciful capitulation at *Sodom,* if his Goodness please not to pass over a great deal of Bad for a small pittance of Good, or to look upon us in the Lump, there is slender hope for Mercy, or sound presumption of fulfilling half his Will, either in Persons or Nations: they who excel in some Virtues being so often defective in others; few Men driving at the extent and amplitude of Goodness, but computing themselves by their best parts, and others by their worst, are content to rest in those Virtues, which others commonly want. Which makes this speckled Face of Honesty in the World; and which was the imperfection of the old Philosophers and great pretenders unto Virtue, who well declining the gaping Vices of Intemperance, Incontinency, Violence and Oppression, were yet blindly peccant in iniquities of closer faces, were envious, malicious, contemners, scoffers, censurers, and stufft with Vizard Vices, no less depraving the Ethereal particle and diviner portion of Man. For Envy, Malice, Hatred are the qualities of *Satan,* close and dark like himself; and where such brands smoak the Soul cannot be White. Vice may be had at all prices; expensive and costly iniquities, which make the noise, cannot be every Man's sins: but the soul may be foully inquinated at a very low rate, and a Man may be cheaply vitious, to the perdition of himself.

SECT. 8. Opinion rides upon the neck of Reason, and Men are Happy, Wise, or Learned, according as that Empress shall set them down in the Register of Reputation. However, weigh not thy self in the scales of thy own opinion, but let the Judgment of the Judicious be the Standard of thy Merit. Self-estimation is a flatterer too readily intitling us unto Knowledge and Abilities, which others sollicitously labour after, and doubtfully think they attain. Surely such confident

* *Primusque dies dedit extremum.* [Seneca, *Oedipus,* 988.]

tempers do pass their days in best tranquility, who, resting in the opinion of their own abilities, are happily gull'd by such contentation; wherein Pride, Self-conceit, Confidence, and Opiniatrity will hardly suffer any to complain of imperfection. To think themselves in the right, or all that right, or only that, which they do or think, is a fallacy of high content; though others laugh in their sleeves, and look upon them as in a deluded state of Judgment. Wherein notwithstanding 'twere but a civil piece of complacency to suffer them to sleep who would not wake, to let them rest in their securities, nor by dissent or opposition to stagger their contentments.

SECT. 9. Since the Brow speaks often true, since Eyes and [13] Noses have Tongues, and the countenance proclaims the Heart and inclinations; let observation so far instruct thee in Physiognomical lines, as to be some Rule for thy distinction, and Guide for thy affection unto such as look most like Men. Mankind, methinks, is comprehended in a few Faces, if we exclude all Visages which any way participate of Symmetries and Schemes of Look common unto other Animals. For as though Man were the extract of the World, in whom all were *in coagulato*, which in their forms were *in soluto* and at Extension; we often observe that Men do most act those Creatures, whose constitution, parts, and complexion do most predominate in their mixtures. This is a corner- [14] stone in Physiognomy, and holds some Truth not only in particular Persons but also in whole Nations. There are therefore Provincial Faces, National Lips and Noses, which testify not only the Natures of those Countries, but of those which have them elsewhere. Thus we may make *England* the whole Earth, dividing it not only into *Europe, Asia, Africa,* but the particular Regions thereof, and may in some latitude affirm, that there are *Aegyptians, Scythians, Indians* among us; who though born in *England,* yet carry the Faces and Air of those Countries, and are also agreeable and correspondent unto their Natures. Faces look uniformly unto our Eyes: How they appear unto some Animals of a more piercing or differing sight, who are able to discover the inequalities, rubbs, and hairiness of the Skin, is not without good doubt.

And therefore in reference unto Man, *Cupid* is said to be blind. Affection should not be too sharp-Eyed, and Love is not to be made by magnifying Glasses. If things were seen as they truly are, the beauty of bodies would be much abridged. And therefore the wise Contriver hath drawn the pictures and outsides of things softly and amiably unto the natural Edge of our Eyes, not leaving them able to discover those uncomely asperities, which make Oyster-shells in good Faces, and Hedghoggs even in *Venus's* moles.

SECT. 10. Court not Felicity too far, and weary not the favorable hand of Fortune. Glorious actions have their times, extent and *non ultra's*. To put no end unto Attempts were to make prescription of Successes, and to bespeak unhappiness at the last. For the Line of our Lives is drawn with white and black vicissitudes, wherein the extremes hold seldom one complexion. That *Pompey* should obtain the sirname of Great   15
at twenty five years, that Men in their young and active days should be fortunate and perform notable things, is no observation of deep wonder, they having the strength of their fates before them, nor yet acted their parts in the World, for which they were brought into it: whereas Men of years, matured for counsels and designs, seem to be beyond the vigour of their active fortunes, and high exploits of life, providentially ordained unto Ages best agreeable unto them. And therefore many brave men finding their fortune grow faint, and feeling its declination, have timely withdrawn themselves from great attempts, and so escaped the ends of mighty Men, disproportionable to their beginnings. But magnanimous Thoughts have so dimmed the Eyes of many, that forgetting the very essence of Fortune, and the vicissitude of good and evil, they apprehend no bottom in felicity; and so have been still tempted on unto mighty Actions, reserved for their destructions. For Fortune lays the Plot of our Adversities in the foundation of our Felicities, blessing us in the first quadrate, to blast us more sharply in the last. And since in the highest felicities there lieth a capacity of the lowest miseries, she hath this advantage from our happiness to make us truly miserable. For to become acutely miserable

we are to be first happy. Affliction smarts most in the most happy state, as having somewhat in it of *Bellisarius* at Beggers bush, or *Bajazet* in the grate. And this the fallen Angels severely understand, who having acted their first part in Heaven, are made sharply miserable by transition, and more afflictively feel the contrary state of Hell.

SECT. 11. Carry no careless Eye upon the unexpected scenes of things; but ponder the acts of Providence in the publick ends of great and notable Men, set out unto the view of all for no common *memorandums.* The Tragical Exits and unexpected periods of some eminent Persons cannot but amaze considerate Observators; wherein notwithstanding †
most Men seem to see by extramission, without reception or ¹⁶
self-reflexion, and conceive themselves unconcerned by the fallacy of their own Exemption: Whereas the Mercy of God hath singled out but few to be the signals of his Justice, leaving the generality of Mankind to the paedagogy of Example. But the inadvertency of our Natures not well apprehending this favorable method and merciful decimation, and that he sheweth in some what others also deserve; they entertain no sense of his Hand beyond the stroak of themselves. Whereupon the whole becomes necessarily punished, and the contracted Hand of God extended unto universal Judgments: from whence nevertheless the stupidity of our tempers receives but faint impressions, and in the most Tragical state of times holds but starts of good motions. So that to continue us in goodness there must be iterated returns of misery, and a circulation in afflictions is necessary. And since we cannot be wise by warnings, since Plagues are insignificant except we be personally plagued, since also we cannot be punish'd unto Amendment by proxy or commutation, nor by vicinity, but contaction; there is an unhappy necessity that we must smart in our own Skins, and the provoked arm of the Almighty must fall upon our selves. The capital sufferings of others are rather our monitions than acquitments. There is but one who dyed salvifically for us, and able to say unto Death, hitherto shalt thou go and no farther; only one enlivening Death, which makes Gardens of Graves, and that

which was sowed in Corruption to arise and flourish in
Glory: when Death it self shall dye, and living shall have no
Period, when the damned shall mourn at the funeral of
Death, when Life not Death shall be the wages of sin, when
the second Death shall prove a miserable Life, and destruc-   17
tion shall be courted.

SECT. 12. Although their Thoughts may seem too severe, who
think that few ill natur'd Men go to Heaven; yet it may be
acknowledged that good natur'd Persons are best founded
for that place; who enter the World with good Dispositions,
and natural Graces, more ready to be advanced by impressions from above, and christianized unto pieties; who carry
about them plain and down right dealing Minds, Humility,
Mercy, Charity, and Virtues acceptable unto God and Man.
But whatever success they may have as to Heaven, they are
the acceptable Men on Earth, and happy is he who hath his
quiver full of them for his Friends. These are not the Dens
wherein Falshood lurks, and Hypocrisy hides its Head,
wherein Frowardness makes its Nest, or where Malice,
Hardheartedness, and Oppression love to dwell; not those
by whom the Poor get little, and the Rich some times loose
all; Men not of retracted Looks, but who carry their Hearts
in their Faces, and need not to be look'd upon with perspectives; not sordidly or mischievously ingrateful; who cannot
learn to ride upon the neck of the afflicted, nor load the heavy
laden, but who keep the Temple of *Janus* shut by peaceable
and quiet tempers; who make not only the best Friends, but
the best Enemies, as easier to forgive than offend, and ready
to pass by the second offence before they avenge the first;
who make natural Royalists, obedient Subjects, kind and
merciful Princes, verified in our own, one of the best natur'd   18
Kings of this Throne. Of the old Roman Emperours the best
were the best natur'd; though they made but a small number, and might be writ in a Ring. Many of the rest were as
bad Men as Princes; Humorists rather than of good humors,
and of good natural parts, rather than of good natures: which
did but arm their bad inclinations, and make them wittily
wicked.

SECT. 13. With what strift and pains we come into the World [19,†]
we remember not; but 'tis commonly found no easy matter to
get out of it. Many have studied to exasperate the ways of
Death, but fewer hours have been spent to soften that necessity. That the smoothest way unto the grave is made by
bleeding, as common opinion presumeth, beside the sick and
fainting Languors which accompany that effusion, the experiment in *Lucan* and *Seneca* will make us doubt; under   [20]
which the noble Stoick so deeply laboured, that to conceal
his affliction, he was fain to retire from the sight of his Wife,
and not ashamed to implore the merciful hand of his Physician to shorten his misery therein. *Ovid* the old Heroes,
and the Stoicks, who were so afraid of drowning, as dreading
thereby the extinction of their Soul, which they conceived to
be Fire, stood probably in fear of an easier way of Death;   [†]
wherein the Water, entring the possessions of Air, makes a
temperate suffocation, and kills as it were without a Fever.
Surely many who have had the Spirit to destroy themselves,
have not been ingenious in the contrivance thereof. 'Twas a
dull way practised by *Themistocles* to overwhelm himself   [21]
with Bulls-blood, who, being an *Athenian,* might have held
an easier Theory of Death from the state potion of his Country; from which *Socrates* in *Plato* seemed not to suffer much   [22]
more than from the fit of an Ague. *Cato* is much to be pitied,
who mangled himself with poyniards; And *Hannibal* seems
more subtle, who carried his delivery not in the point, but
the pummel* of his Sword.   [23]

The *Egyptians* were merciful contrivers, who destroyed
their malefactors by Asps, charming their senses into an invincible sleep, and killing as it were with *Hermes* his Rod.   [24]
The Turkish Emperour, odious for other Cruelty, was herein
a remarkable Master of Mercy, killing his Favorite in his
sleep, and sending him from the shade into the house of
darkness. He who had been thus destroyed would hardly

---

* *Demito naufragium, mors mihi munus erit.* [*Trist.* 1.2.52.]
* *Plutarch.*
* Pummel, wherein he is said to have carried something, whereby upon a
struggle or despair he might deliver himself from all misfortunes.
* *Solyman* [in] Turkish History. [R. Knolles.]

have bled at the presence of his destroyer; when Men are already dead by metaphor, and pass but from one sleep unto another, wanting herein the eminent part of severity, to feel themselves to dye, and escaping the sharpest attendant of Death, the lively apprehension thereof. But to learn to dye is better than to study the ways of dying. Death will find some ways to unty or cut the most Gordian Knots of Life, and make men's miseries as mortal as themselves: whereas evil Spirits, as undying Substances, are unseparable from their calamities; and therefore they everlastingly struggle under their *Angustia's,* and bound up with immortality can never get out of themselves.

PART III.

SECT. 1. 'Tis hard to find a whole Age to imitate, or what Century to propose for Example. Some have been far more approveable than others: but Virtue and Vice, Panegyricks and Satyrs, scatteringly to be found in all. History sets down not only things laudable, but abominable; things which should never have been, or never have been known: So that noble patterns must be fetched here and there from single Persons, rather than whole Nations, and from all Nations, rather than any one. The World was early bad, and the first sin the most deplorable of any. The younger World afforded the oldest Men, and perhaps the Best and the Worst, when length of days made virtuous habits Heroical and immoveable, vitious, inveterate and irreclaimable. And since 'tis said ¹ that the imaginations of their hearts were evil, only evil, and continually evil; it may be feared that their sins held pace with their lives; and their Longevity swelling their Impieties, the Longanimity of God would no longer endure such vivacious abominations. Their Impieties were surely of a deep dye, which required the whole Element of Water to wash them away, and overwhelmed their memories with themselves; and so shut up the first Windows of Time, leaving no Histories of those longevous generations, when Men might have been properly Historians, when *Adam* might have read ² long Lectures unto *Methuselah,* and *Methuselah* unto *Noah.* For had we been happy in just Historical accounts of that unparallel'd World, we might have been acquainted with Wonders, and have understood not a little of the Acts and undertakings of *Moses* and his mighty Men, and Men of renown of old; which might have enlarged our Thoughts, and made the World older unto us. For the unknown part of time shortens the estimation, if not the compute of it. What hath escaped our Knowledge falls not under our Consideration, and what is and will be latent is little better than non existent.

SECT. 2. Some things are dictated for our Instruction, some acted for our Imitation, wherein 'tis best to ascend unto the highest conformity, and to the honour of the Exemplar. He honours God who imitates him. For what we virtuously imitate we approve and Admire; and since we delight not to imitate Inferiors, we aggrandize and magnify those we imitate; since also we are most apt to imitate those we love, we testify our affection in our imitation of the Inimitable. To affect to be like may be no imitation. To act, and not to be what we pretend to imitate, is but a mimical conformation, and carrieth no Virtue in it. *Lucifer* imitated not God, when he said he would be like the Highest, and he imitated not *Jupiter,* who counterfeited Thunder. Where Imitation can go ³ no farther, let Admiration step on, whereof there is no end in the wisest form of Men. Even Angels and Spirits have enough to admire in their sublimer Natures, Admiration being the act of the Creature and not of God, who doth not Admire himself. Created Natures allow of swelling Hyperboles; nothing can be said Hyperbolically of God, nor will his Attributes admit of expressions above their own Exuperances. *Trismegistus* his Circle, whose center is every where, and circumference no where, was no Hyperbole. Words cannot exceed, where they cannot express enough. Even the most winged Thoughts fall at the setting out, and reach not the portal of Divinity.

SECT. 3. In Bivious Theorems and *Janus*-faced Doctrines let Virtuous considerations state the determination. Look upon Opinions as thou doest upon the Moon, and chuse not the dark hemisphere for thy contemplation. Embrace not the opacous and blind side of Opinions, but that which looks most Luciferously or influentially unto Goodness. 'Tis better to think that there are Guardian Spirits, than that there are no Spirits to Guard us; that vicious Persons are Slaves, than that there is any servitude in Virtue; that times past have been better than times present, than that times were always bad, and that to be Men it suffiseth to be no better than Men in all Ages, and so promiscuously to swim down the turbid stream, and make up the grand confusion. Sow not thy understanding with Opinions, which make nothing of Iniquities, and fallaciously extenuate Transgressions. Look upon Vices and vicious Objects with Hyperbolical Eyes, and rather enlarge their dimensions, that their unseen Deformities may not escape thy sense, and their Poysonous parts and stings may appear massy and monstrous unto thee; for the undiscerned Particles and Atoms of Evil deceive us, and we are undone by the Invisibles of seeming Goodness. We are only deceived in what is not discerned, and to Err is but to be Blind or Dim-sighted as to some Perceptions.

SECT. 4. To be Honest in a right Line,* and Virtuous by Epitome, be firm unto such Principles of Goodness, as carry in them Volumes of instruction and may abridge thy Labour. And since instructions are many, hold close unto those, whereon the rest depend. So may we have all in a few, and the Law and the Prophets in a Rule, the Sacred Writ in Stenography, and the Scripture in a Nut-Shell. To pursue the osseous and solid part of Goodness, which gives Stability and Rectitude to all the rest; To settle on fundamental Virtues, and bid early defiance unto Mother-vices, which carry in their Bowels the seminals of other Iniquities, makes a short cut in Goodness, and strikes not off an Head but the whole Neck of *Hydra*. For we are carried into the dark Lake, like [5] the *Aegyptian* River into the Sea, by seven principal Ostiaries. [6] The Mother-Sins of that number are the Deadly engins of Evil Spirits that undo us, and even evil Spirits themselves, and he who is under the Chains thereof is not without a possession. *Mary Magdalene* had more than seven Devils, if these with their Imps were in her, and he who is thus possessed may literally be named *Legion*. Where such Plants grow and prosper, look for no Champion or Region void of

* *Linea Recta brevissima.*

Thorns, but productions like the Tree of *Goa,** and For-   ⁷
rests of abomination.

SECT. 5. Guide not the Hand of God, nor order the Finger of
the Almighty, unto thy will and pleasure; but sit quiet in the
soft showers of Providence, and Favorable distributions in
this World, either to thy self or others. And since not only
Judgments have their Errands, but Mercies their Commis-
sions; snatch not at every Favour, nor think thy self passed
by, if they fall upon thy Neighbour. Rake not up envious dis-
placences at things successful unto others, which the wise
Disposer of all thinks not fit for thy self. Reconcile the events
of things unto both beings, that is, of this World and the next:
So will there not seem so many Riddles in Providence, nor
various inequalities in the dispensation of things below. If
thou doest not anoint thy Face, yet put not on sackcloth at
the felicities of others. Repining at the Good draws on rejoic-
ing at the evils of others, and so falls into that inhumane   ⁸
Vice,* for which so few Languages have a name. The blessed
Spirits above rejoice at our happiness below; but to be glad
at the evils of one another is beyond the malignity of Hell,
and falls not on evil Spirits, who, though they rejoice at our
unhappiness, take no pleasure at the afflictions of their own
Society or of their fellow Natures. Degenerous Heads! who
must be fain to learn from such Examples, and to be Taught
from the School of Hell.

SECT. 6. Grain not thy vicious stains, nor deepen those swart
Tinctures, which Temper, Infirmity, or ill habits have set
upon thee; and fix not by iterated depravations what time
might Efface, or Virtuous washes expunge. He who thus still
advanceth in Iniquity deepneth his deformed hue, turns a
Shadow into Night, and makes himself a *Negro* in the
black Jaundice; and so becomes one of those Lost ones, the
disproportionate pores of whose Brains afford no entrance

---

* *Arbor Goa de Ruyz* or *ficus Indica,* whose branches send down shoots
which root in the ground, from whence there successively rise others, till one
Tree becomes a wood.

* Ἐπικαιρεκακία.

unto good Motions, but reflect and frustrate all Counsels, Deaf unto the Thunder of the Laws, and Rocks unto the Cries of charitable Commiserators. He who hath had the Patience of *Diogenes,* to make Orations unto Statues, may more sensibly apprehend how all Words fall to the Ground, spent upon such a surd and Earless Generation of Men, stupid unto all Instruction, and rather requiring an Exorcist, than an Orator for their Conversion.

SECT. 7. Burden not the back of *Aries, Leo,* or *Taurus,* with thy faults, nor make *Saturn, Mars,* or *Venus,* guilty of thy Follies. Think not to fasten thy imperfections on the Stars, and so despairingly conceive thy self under a fatality of being evil. Calculate thy self within, seek not thy self in the Moon, but in thine own Orb or Microcosmical Circumference. Let celestial aspects admonish and advertise, not conclude and determine thy ways. For since good and bad Stars moralize not our Actions, and neither excuse or commend, acquit or condemn our Good or Bad Deeds at the present or last Bar; since some are Astrologically well disposed who are morally highly vicious; not Celestial Figures, but Virtuous Schemes must denominate and state our Actions. If we rightly understood the Names whereby God calleth the Stars, if we knew his Name for the Dog-Star, or by what appellation *Jupiter, Mars,* and *Saturn* obey his Will, it might be a welcome accession unto Astrology, which speaks great things, and is fain to make use of appellations from Greek and Barbarick Systems. Whatever Influences, Impulsions, or Inclinations there be from the Lights above, it were a piece of wisdom to make one of those Wise men who overrule their Stars,* and with their own Militia contend with the Host of Heaven. Unto which attempt there want not Auxiliaries from the whole strength of Morality, supplies from Christian Ethicks, influences also and illuminations from above, more powerfull than the Lights of Heaven.

SECT. 8. Confound not the distinctions of thy Life which Nature hath divided: that is, Youth, Adolescence, Manhood,

* *Sapiens dominabitur Astris.*

and old Age, nor in these divided Periods, wherein thou art in a manner Four, conceive thy self but One. Let every division be happy in its proper Virtues, nor one Vice run through all. Let each distinction have its salutary transition, and critically deliver thee from the imperfections of the former, so ordering the whole, that Prudence and Virtue may have the largest Section. Do as a Child but when thou art a Child, and ride not on a Reed at twenty. He who hath not taken leave of the follies of his Youth, and in his maturer state scarce got out of that division, disproportionately divideth his Days, crowds up the latter part of his Life, and leaves too narrow a corner for the Age of Wisdom, and so hath room to be a Man scarce longer than he hath been a Youth. Rather than to make this confusion, anticipate the Virtues of Age, and live long without the infirmities of it. So may'st thou count up thy Days as some do *Adams,*° that is, by anticipation; so may'st thou be coetaneous unto thy Elders, and a Father unto thy contemporaries.

SECT. 9. While others are curious in the choice of good Air, and chiefly sollicitous for healthful habitations, Study thou Conversation, and be critical in thy Consortion. The aspects, conjunctions, and configurations of the Stars, which mutually diversify, intend, or qualify their influences, are but the varieties of their nearer or farther conversation with one another, and like the Consortion of Men, whereby they become better or worse, and even Exchange their Natures. Since Men live by Examples, and will be imitating something; order thy imitation to thy Improvement, not thy Ruin. Look not for Roses in *Attalus*° his Garden, or wholsome Flowers in a venemous   10 Plantation. And since there is scarce any one bad, but some others are the worse for him; tempt not Contagion by proximity, and hazard not thy self in the shadow of Corruption. He who hath not early suffered this Shipwrack, and in his Younger Days escaped this *Charybdis,* may make a happy Voyage, and not come in with black Sails into the port. Self   11 conversation, or to be alone, is better than such Consortion.

° *Adam* thought to be created in the State of Man, about thirty years Old.
° *Attalus* made a Garden which contained only venemous Plants.

Some School-men tell us, that he is properly alone, with whom in the same place there is no other of the same Species. *Nabuchodonozor* was alone, though among the Beasts of the Field, and a Wise Man may be tolerably said to be alone though with a Rabble of People little better than Beasts about him. Unthinking Heads, who have not learn'd to be alone, are in a Prison to themselves, if they be not also with others: Whereas on the contrary, they whose thoughts are in a fair and hurry within, are sometimes fain to retire into Company, to be out of the crowd of themselves. He who must needs have Company, must needs have sometimes bad Company. Be able to be alone. Loose not the advantage of Solitude, and the Society of thy self, nor be only content, but delight to be alone and single with Omnipresency. He who is thus prepared, the Day is not uneasy nor the Night black unto him. Darkness may bound his Eyes, not his Imagination. In his Bed he may ly, like *Pompey* and his Sons,* in all quarters of the Earth, may speculate the Universe, and enjoy the whole World in the Hermitage of himself. Thus the old *Ascetick* Christians found a Paradise in a Desert, and with little converse on Earth held a conversation in Heaven; thus they Astronomiz'd in Caves, and though they beheld not the Stars, had the Glory of Heaven before them.

SECT. 10. Let the Characters of good things stand indelibly in thy Mind, and thy Thoughts be active on them. Trust not too much unto suggestions from Reminiscential amulets, or Artificial *Memorandums*. Let the mortifying *Janus* of *Covarrubias** be in thy daily Thoughts, not only on thy Hand and Signets. Rely not alone upon silent and dumb remembrances. Behold not Death's Heads till thou doest not see them, nor look upon mortifying Objects till thou overlook'st them. Forget not how assuefaction unto any thing minorates the pas-

---

* *Pompeios Juvenes Asia atque Europa, sed ipsum*
   Terra tegit Libyes. [Martial, 5.74.1–2.]

* *Don Sebastian de Covarrubias* writ 3 Centuries of moral Emblems in *Spanish*. In the 88*th* of the second Century he sets down two Faces averse, and conjoined *Janus*-like, the one a Gallant Beautiful Face, the other a Death's Head Face, with this Motto out of *Ovid*'s *Metamorphosis* [11.551.], *Quid fuerim quid simque vide.*

sion from it, how constant Objects loose their hints, and steal
an inadvertisement upon us. There is no excuse to forget
what every thing prompts unto us. To thoughtful Observators
the whole World is a Phylactery, and every thing we see an
Item of the Wisdom, Power, or Goodness of God. Happy are
they who verify their Amulets, and make their Phylacteries
speak in their Lives and Actions. To run on in despight of the
Revulsions and Pul-backs of such Remora's aggravates our
transgressions. When Death's Heads on our Hands have no   15
influence upon our Heads, and fleshless Cadavers abate not
the exorbitances of the Flesh; when Crucifixes upon Mens
Hearts suppress not their bad commotions, and his Image
who was murdered for us with-holds not from Blood and
Murder; Phylacteries prove but formalities, and their despised hints sharpen our condemnations.

SECT. 11. Look not for *Whales* in the *Euxine* Sea, or expect
great matters where they are not to be found. Seek not for
Profundity in Shallowness, or Fertility in a Wilderness. Place
not the expectation of great Happiness here below, or think
to find Heaven on Earth; wherein we must be content with
Embryon-felicities, and fruition of doubtful Faces. For the
Circle of our felicities makes but short Arches. In every clime
we are in a periscian state, and with our Light our Shadow
and Darkness walk about us: Our Contentments stand upon
the tops of Pyramids ready to fall off, and the insecurity of
their enjoyments abrupteth our Tranquilities. What we magnify is Magnificent, but like to the *Colossus*, noble without,   16
stuft with rubbidge and coarse Metal within. Even the Sun,   †
whose Glorious outside we behold, may have dark and
smoaky Entrails. In vain we admire the Lustre of any thing
seen: that which is truly glorious is invisible. *Paradise* was
but a part of the Earth, lost not only to our Fruition but our
Knowledge. And if, according to old Dictates, no Man can be
said to be happy before Death, the happiness of this Life
goes for nothing before it be over, and while we think our
selves happy we do but usurp that Name. Certainly true
Beatitude groweth not on Earth, nor hath this World in it the
Expectations we have of it. He Swims in Oyl, and can hardly

avoid sinking, who hath such light Foundations to support him. 'Tis therefore happy that we have two Worlds to hold on. To enjoy true happiness we must travel into a very far Countrey, and even out of our selves; for the Pearl we seek for is not to be found in the *Indian,* but in the *Empyrean* Ocean.

SECT. 12. Answer not the Spur of Fury, and be not prodigal or prodigious in Revenge. Make not one in the *Historia Hor-* [17] *ribilis;*° Flay not thy Servant for a broken Glass, nor pound [18,19] him in a Mortar who offendeth thee; supererogate not in the worst sense, and overdo not the necessities of evil; humour not the injustice of Revenge. Be not Stoically mistaken in the equality of sins, nor commutatively iniquous in the valuation of transgressions; but weigh them in the Scales of Heaven, and by the weights of righteous Reason. Think that Revenge too high, which is but level with the offence. Let thy Arrows of Revenge fly short, or be aimed like those of *Jonathan,* to [20] fall beside the mark. Too many there be to whom a Dead [21] Enemy smells well, and who find Musk and Amber in Revenge. The ferity of such minds holds no rule in Retaliations, requiring too often a Head for a Tooth, and the Supreme revenge for trespasses, which a night's rest should obliterate. But patient Meekness takes injuries like Pills, not chewing but swallowing them down, laconically suffering, and silently passing them over, while angred Pride makes a noise, like *Homerican Mars,*° at every scratch of offences. Since Women [23] do most delight in Revenge, it may seem but feminine manhood to be vindicative. If thou must needs have thy Revenge of thine Enemy, with a soft Tongue break his Bones,° heap Coals of Fire on his Head, forgive him, and enjoy it. To forgive our Enemies is a charming way of Revenge, and a short *Caesarian* Conquest overcoming without a blow; laying our Enemies at our Feet, under sorrow, shame, and repentance; leaving our Foes our Friends, and solicitously inclined to

---

° A Book so entituled wherein are sundry horrid accounts.
° *Tu tamen exclamas ut Stentora vincere possis*
   Vel saltem quantum Gradivus Homericus. [22]
            Juvenal. [*Sat.* 13.112–13., (not quite accurately)]
° A soft Tongue breaketh the bones. *Proverbs* 25.15.

grateful Retaliations. Thus to Return upon our Adversaries is a healing way of Revenge, and to do good for evil a soft and melting ultion, a method Taught from Heaven to keep all smooth on Earth. Common forceable ways make not an end of Evil, but leave Hatred and Malice behind them. An Enemy thus reconciled is little to be trusted, as wanting the foundation of Love and Charity, and but for a time restrained by disadvantage or inability. If thou hast not Mercy for others, yet be not Cruel unto thy self. To ruminate upon evils, to make critical notes upon injuries, and be too acute in their apprehensions, is to add unto our own Tortures, to feather the Arrows of our Enemies, to lash our selves with the Scorpions of our Foes, and to resolve to sleep no more. For injuries long dreamt on take away at last all rest; and he sleeps but like *Regulus*, who busieth his Head about them.   24

SECT. 13. Amuse not thy self about the Riddles of future things. Study Prophecies when they are become Histories, and past hovering in their causes. Eye well things past and present, and let conjectural sagacity suffice for things to come. There is a sober Latitude for prescience in contingences of discoverable Tempers, whereby discerning Heads see sometimes beyond their Eyes, and Wise Men become Prophetical. Leave Cloudy predictions to their Periods, and let appointed Seasons have the lot of their accomplishments. 'Tis too early to study such Prophecies before they have been long made, before some train of their causes have already taken Fire, laying open in part what lay obscure and before buryed unto us. For the voice of Prophecies is like that of Whispering-places: They who are near or at a little distance hear nothing, those at the farthest extremity will understand all. But a Retrograde cognition of times past, and things which have already been, is more satisfactory than a suspended Knowledge of what is yet unexistent. And the Greatest part of time being already wrapt up in things behind us; it's now somewhat late to bait after things before us; for futurity still shortens, and time present sucks in time to come. What is Prophetical in one Age proves Historical in another, and so must hold on unto the last of time; when there will be

no room for Prediction, when *Janus* shall loose one Face, and
the long beard of time shall look like those of *David's* Serv- 25
ants, shorn away upon one side, and when, if the expected
Elias should appear, he might say much of what is past, not
much of what's to come.

SECT. 14. Live unto the Dignity of thy Nature, and leave it
not disputable at last, whether thou hast been a Man, or since
thou art a composition of Man and Beast, how thou hast pre-
dominantly passed thy days, to state the denomination. Un-
man not therefore thy self by a Beastial transformation, nor
realize old Fables. Expose not thy self by four-footed manners
unto monstrous draughts, and *Caricatura* representations. 26
Think not after the old *Pythagorean* conceit, what Beast thou
may'st be after death. Be not under any Brutal *metempsychosis* while thou livest, and walkest about erectly under the
scheme of Man. In thine own circumference, as in that of the
Earth, let the Rational Horizon be larger than the sensible,
and the Circle of Reason than of Sense. Let the Divine part
be upward, and the Region of Beast below. Otherwise, 'tis
but to live invertedly, and with thy Head unto the Heels of
thy *Antipodes*. Desert not thy title to a Divine particle and 27
union with invisibles. Let true Knowledge and Virtue tell the
lower World thou art a part of the higher. Let thy Thoughts
be of things which have not entred into the Hearts of Beasts:
Think of things long past, and long to come: Acquaint thy
self with the *Choragium* of the Stars, and consider the vast
expansion beyond them. Let Intellectual Tubes give thee a
glance of things, which visive Organs reach not. Have a
glimpse of incomprehensibles, and Thoughts of things, which
Thoughts but tenderly touch. Lodge immaterials in thy
Head: ascend unto invisibles: fill thy Spirit with Spirituals,
with the mysteries of Faith, the magnalities of Religion, and
thy Life with the Honour of God; without which, though
Giants in Wealth and Dignity, we are but Dwarfs and Pygmies in Humanity, and may hold a pitiful rank in that triple
division of mankind into Heroes, Men, and Beasts. For
though human Souls are said to be equal, yet is there no small
inequality in their operations; some maintain the allowable

Station of Men; many are far below it; and some have been
so divine, as to approach the *Apogeum* of their Natures, and
to be in the *Confinium* of Spirits.

SECT. 15. Behold thy self by inward Opticks and the Crystalline of thy Soul. Strange it is that in the most perfect sense
there should be so many fallacies, that we are fain to make a
doctrine, and often to see by Art. But the greatest imperfection is in our inward sight, that is, to be Ghosts unto our
own Eyes, and while we are so sharp-sighted as to look
thorough others, to be invisible unto our selves; for the inward Eyes are more fallacious than the outward. The Vices
we scoff at in others laugh at us within our selves. Avarice,
Pride, Falshood lye undiscerned and blindly in us, even to
the Age of blindness: and therefore, to see our selves interi-
ourly, we are fain to borrow other Mens Eyes; wherein true
Friends are good Informers, and Censurers no bad Friends.
Conscience only, that can see without Light, sits in the
Areopagy and dark Tribunal of our Hearts, surveying our
Thoughts and condemning their obliquities. Happy is that
state of vision that can see without Light, though all should
look as before the Creation, when there was not an Eye to
see, or Light to actuate a Vision: wherein notwithstanding
obscurity is only imaginable respectively unto Eyes; for unto
God there was none, Eternal Light was ever, created Light
was for the creation, not himself, and as he saw before the
Sun, may still also see without it. In the City of the new
Jerusalem there is neither Sun nor Moon; where glorifyed   28
Eyes must see by the *Archetypal* Sun, or the Light of God,
able to illuminate Intellectual Eyes, and make unknown Visions. Intuitive perceptions in Spiritual beings may perhaps
hold some Analogy unto Vision: but yet how they see us, or
one another, what Eye, what Light, or what perception is
required unto their intuition, is yet dark unto our apprehension; and even how they see God, or how unto our glorified
Eyes the Beatifical Vision will be celebrated, another World
must tell us, when perceptions will be new, and we may hope
to behold invisibles.

SECT. 16. When all looks fair about, and thou seest not a cloud so big as a Hand to threaten thee, forget not the Wheel ²⁹ of things: Think of sullen vicissitudes, but beat not thy brains to fore-know them. Be armed against such obscurities rather by submission than fore-knowledge. The Knowledge of future evils mortifies present felicities, and there is more content in the uncertainty or ignorance of them. This favour our Saviour vouchsafed unto *Peter,* when he fore-told not his ³⁰ Death in plain terms, and so by an ambiguous and cloudy delivery dampt not the Spirit of his Disciples. But in the assured fore-knowledge of the Deluge *Noah* lived many Years under the affliction of a Flood, and *Jerusalem* was taken unto *Jeremy* before it was besieged. And therefore the ³¹ Wisdom of Astrologers, who speak of future things, hath wisely softned the severity of their Doctrines; and even in their sad predictions, while they tell us of inclination not coaction from the Stars, they Kill us not with *Stygian* Oaths and merciless necessity, but leave us hopes of evasion.

SECT. 17. If thou hast the brow to endure the Name of Traytor, Perjur'd, or Oppressor, yet cover thy Face when Ingratitude is thrown at thee. If that degenerous Vice possess thee, hide thy self in the shadow of thy shame, and pollute not noble society. Grateful Ingenuities are content to be obliged within some compass of Retribution, and being depressed by the weight of iterated favours may so labour under the inabilities of Requital, as to abate the content from Kindnesses. But narrow self-ended Souls make prescription of good Offices, and obliged by often favours think others still due unto them: whereas, if they but once fail, they prove so perversely ungrateful, as to make nothing of former courtesies, and to bury all that's past. Such tempers pervert the generous course of things; for they discourage the inclinations of noble minds, and make Beneficency cool unto acts of obligation, whereby the grateful World should subsist, and have their consolation. Common gratitude must be kept alive by the additionary fewel of new courtesies: but generous Gratitudes, though but once well obliged, without quickening repetitions or expectation of new Favours, have thankful minds for ever; for they write not their obligations in sandy but marble memories, which wear not out but with themselves.

SECT. 18. Think not Silence the wisdom of Fools, but, if rightly timed, the honour of Wise Men, who have not the Infirmity, but the Virtue of Taciturnity, and speak not out of the abundance, but the well weighed thoughts of their Hearts. Such Silence may be Eloquence, and speak thy worth above the power of Words. Make such a one thy friend, in whom Princes may be happy, and great Councels successful. Let him have the Key of thy Heart, who hath the Lock of his own, which no Temptation can open; where thy Secrets may lastingly ly, like the Lamp in *Olybius* his Urn,* alive, and   **32** light, but close and invisible.

SECT. 19. Let thy Oaths be sacred and Promises be made upon the Altar of thy Heart. Call not *Jove** to witness with   **33** a Stone in one Hand, and a Straw in another, and so make Chaff and Stubble of thy Vows. Worldly Spirits, whose interest is their belief, make Cobwebs of Obligations, and, if they can find ways to elude the Urn of the *Praetor,* will trust the   **34** Thunderbolt of *Jupiter:* And therefore if they should as deeply swear as *Osman** to *Bethlem Gabor;* yet whether   **35** they would be bound by those chains, and not find ways to cut such *Gordian* Knots, we could have no just assurance. But Honest Mens Words are *Stygian* Oaths, and Promises inviolable. These are not the Men for whom the fetters of Law were first forged: they needed not the solemness of Oaths; by keeping their Faith they swear,* and evacuate such confirmations.

SECT. 20. Though the World be Histrionical, and most Men live Ironically, yet be thou what thou singly art, and personate only thy self. Swim smoothly in the stream of thy Na-

---

* Which after many hundred years was found burning under ground, and went out as soon as the air came to it.
* *Jovem lapidem jurare.*
* See the Oath of *Sultan Osman* in his life, in the addition to *Knolles* his Turkish history. [1638 ed., p. 1383.]
* *Colendo fidem jurant.* Curtius. [*Hist.* 7.8.29.]

ture, and live but one Man. To single Hearts doubling is dis-
cruciating: such tempers must swear to dissemble, and prove
but hypocritical Hypocrites. Simulation must be short: Men
do not easily continue a counterfeiting Life, or dissemble
unto Death. He who counterfeiteth, acts a part, and is as it
were out of himself: which, if long, proves so irksome, that
Men are glad to pull off their Vizards, and resume themselves again; no practice being able to naturalize such un-
naturals, or make a Man rest content not to be himself. And
therefore since Sincerity is thy Temper, let veracity be thy
Virtue in Words, Manners, and Actions. To offer at iniquities,
which have so little foundations in thee, were to be vitious up
hill, and strain for thy condemnation. Persons vitiously inclined want no Wheels to make them actively vitious, as having the Elater and Spring of their own Natures to facilitate
their Iniquities. And therefore so many, who are sinistrous
unto Good Actions, are Ambi-dexterous unto bad, and *Vulcans* in virtuous Paths, *Achilleses* in vitious motions.   36

SECT. 21. Rest not in the high strain'd Paradoxes of old Phi-   37
losophy supported by naked Reason, and the reward of mortal Felicity, but labour in the Ethicks of Faith, built upon
Heavenly assistance, and the happiness of both beings. Understand the Rules, but swear not unto the Doctrines of *Zeno*
or *Epicurus*. Look beyond *Antoninus*, and terminate not thy
Morals in *Seneca* or *Epictetus*. Let not the twelve, but the
two Tables be thy Law: Let *Pythagoras* be thy Remem-
brancer, not thy textuary and final Instructer; and learn the
Vanity of the World rather from *Solomon* than *Phocylides*.
Sleep not in the Dogma's of the *Peripatus*, Academy, or *Porticus*. Be a moralist of the Mount, an *Epictetus* in the Faith,
and christianize thy Notions.

SECT. 22. In seventy or eighty years a Man may have a deep
Gust of the World, Know what it is, what it can afford, and
what 'tis to have been a Man. Such a latitude of years may
hold a considerable corner in the general Map of Time; and
a Man may have a curt Epitome of the whole course thereof
in the days of his own Life, may clearly see he hath but acted

over his Fore-fathers, what it was to live in Ages past, and
what living will be in all ages to come.

He is like to be the best judge of Time who hath lived to   38
see about the sixtieth part thereof. Persons of short times
may Know what 'tis to live, but not the life of Man, who, having little behind them, are but *Januses* of one Face, and
Know not singularities enough to raise Axioms of this World:
but such a compass of Years will show new Examples of old
Things, Parallelisms of occurrences through the whole course
of Time, and nothing be monstrous unto him; who may in
that time understand not only the varieties of Men, but the
variation of himself, and how many Men he hath been in
that extent of time.

He may have a close apprehension what it is to be forgotten, while he hath lived to find none who could remember
his Father, or scarce the friends of his youth, and may sensibly see with what a face in no long time oblivion will look
upon himself. His Progeny may never be his Posterity; he
may go out of the World less related than he came into it,
and considering the frequent mortality in Friends and Relations in such a Term of Time, he may pass away divers years
in sorrow and black habits, and leave none to mourn for
himself; Orbity may be his inheritance, and Riches his Repentance.

In such a thred of Time, and long observation of Men, he
may acquire a *Physiognomical* intuitive Knowledge, judge
the interiors by the outside, and raise conjectures at first
sight; and knowing what Men have been, what they are,
what Children probably will be, may in the present Age behold a good part, and the temper of the next; and since so
many live by the Rules of Constitution, and so few overcome
their temperamental Inclinations, make no improbable predictions.

Such a portion of Time will afford a large prospect backward, and Authentick Reflections how far he hath performed
the great intention of his Being, in the Honour of his Maker;
whether he hath made good the Principles of his Nature and
what he was made to be; what Characteristick and special
Mark he hath left, to be observable in his Generation;

whether he hath Lived to purpose or in vain, and what he hath added, acted, or performed, that might considerably speak him a Man.

In such an Age Delights will be undelightful and Pleasures grow stale unto him; Antiquated Theorems will revive, and *Solomon's* Maxims be Demonstrations unto him; Hopes or presumptions be over, and despair grow up of any satisfaction below. And having been long tossed in the Ocean of this World, he will by that time feel the In-draught of another, unto which this seems but preparatory, and without it of no high value. He will experimentally find the Emptiness of all things, and the nothing of what is past; and wisely grounding upon true Christian Expectations, finding so much past, will wholly fix upon what is to come. He will long for Perpetuity, and live as though he made haste to be happy. The last may prove the prime part of his Life, and those his best days which he lived nearest Heaven. **39**

SECT. 23. Live happy in the *Elizium* of a virtuously composed Mind, and let Intellectual Contents exceed the Delights wherein mere Pleasurists place their Paradise. Bear not too slack reins upon Pleasure, nor let complexion or contagion betray thee unto the exorbitancy of Delight. Make Pleasure thy Recreation or intermissive Relaxation, not thy *Diana*, Life and Profession. Voluptuousness is as insatiable as Covetousness. Tranquility is better than Jollity, and to appease pain than to invent pleasure. Our hard entrance into the World, our miserable going out of it, our sicknesses, disturbances, and sad Rencounters in it, do clamorously tell us we come not into the World to run a Race of Delight, but to perform the sober Acts and serious purposes of Man; which to omit were foully to miscarry in the advantage of humanity, to play away an uniterable Life, and to have lived in vain. Forget not the capital end, and frustrate not the opportunity of once Living. Dream not of any kind of *Metempsychosis* or transanimation, but into thine own body, and that after a long time, and then also unto wail or bliss, according to thy first and fundamental Life. Upon a curricle in this World depends a long course of the next, and upon a narrow Scene **40**

here an endless expansion hereafter. In vain some think to
have an end of their Beings with their Lives. Things cannot
get out of their natures, or be or not be in despite of their constitutions. Rational existences in Heaven perish not at all,
and but partially on Earth: That which is thus once will in
some way be always: The first Living human Soul is still
alive, and all *Adam* hath found no Period.

SECT. 24. Since the Stars of Heaven do differ in Glory; since
it hath pleased the Almighty hand to honour the North Pole
with Lights above the South; since there are some Stars so
bright, that they can hardly be looked on, some so dim that
they can scarce be seen, and vast numbers not to be seen at
all even by Artificial Eyes; Read thou the Earth in Heaven,
and things below from above. Look contentedly upon the
scattered difference of things, and expect not equality in lustre, dignity, or perfection, in Regions or Persons below;
where numerous numbers must be content to stand like
Lacteous or *Nebulous* Stars, little taken notice of, or dim in
their generations. All which may be contentedly allowable in
the affairs and ends of this World, and in suspension unto
what will be in the order of things hereafter, and the new
Systeme of Mankind which will be in the World to come;
when the last may be the first and the first the last; when
Lazarus may sit above *Caesar,* and the just obscure on Earth
shall shine like the Sun in Heaven; when personations shall
cease, and Histrionism of happiness be over; when Reality
shall rule, and all shall be as they shall be for ever.

SECT. 25. When the *Stoick* said that life would not be accepted, if it were offered unto such as knew it,* he spoke too
meanly of that state of being which placeth us in the form of
Men. It more depreciates the value of this life, that Men
would not live it over again; for although they would still live
on, yet few or none can endure to think of being twice the
same Men upon Earth, and some had rather never have lived
than to tread over their days once more. *Cicero* in a prosper-

_____

* *Vitam nemo acciperet si daretur scientibus.* Seneca. [*Consol. ad*   41
Marc. 22.3.]

ous state had not the patience to think of beginning in a [42]
cradle again. *Job* would not only curse the day of his Nativity,
but also of his Renascency, if he were to act over his Disasters, and the miseries of the Dunghil. But the greatest under-
weening of this Life is to undervalue that, unto which this is
but Exordial or a Passage leading unto it. The great advantage of this mean life is thereby to stand in a capacity of a
better; for the Colonies of Heaven must be drawn from Earth,
and the Sons of the first *Adam* are only heirs unto the second.
Thus *Adam* came into this World with the power also of another, nor only to replenish the Earth, but the everlasting
Mansions of Heaven. Where we were when the foundations
of the Earth were lay'd, when the morning Stars sang together* and all the Sons of God shouted for Joy, He must
answer who asked it; who understands Entities of preordina-
tion, and beings yet unbeing; who hath in his Intellect the
Ideal Existences of things, and Entities before their Extances.
Though it looks but like an imaginary kind of existency to be
before we are; yet since we are under the decree or prescience of a sure and Omnipotent Power, it may be somewhat more than a non-entity to be in that mind, unto which
all things are present.

SECT. 26. If the end of the World shall have the same fore-
going Signs, as the period of Empires, States, and Dominions
in it, that is, Corruption of Manners, inhuman degenerations,
and deluge of iniquities; it may be doubted whether that
final time be so far of, of whose day and hour there can be
no prescience. But while all men doubt and none can determine how long the World shall last, some may wonder that it
hath spun out so long and unto our days. For if the Almighty
had not determin'd a fixed duration unto it, according to his
mighty and merciful designments in it, if he had not said unto
it, as he did unto a part of it, hitherto shalt thou go and no
farther; if we consider the incessant and cutting provocations
from the Earth, it is not without amazement how his patience
hath permitted so long a continuance unto it; how he, who

* Job 38.

cursed the Earth in the first days of the first Man, and
drowned it in the tenth Generation after, should thus lastingly contend with Flesh and yet defer the last flames. For
since he is sharply provoked every moment, yet punisheth to
pardon, and forgives to forgive again; what patience could
be content to act over such vicissitudes, or accept of repent-
ances which must have after penitences, his goodness can
only tell us. And surely if the patience of Heaven were not
proportionable unto the provocations from Earth; there
needed an Intercessor not only for the sins, but the duration
of this World, and to lead it up unto the present computation.
Without such a merciful Longanimity, the Heavens would
never be so aged as to grow old like a Garment; it were in   43
vain to infer from the Doctrine of the Sphere, that the time   44
might come when *Capella,* a noble Northern Star, would have
its motion in the *Aequator,* that the Northern *Zodiacal* Signs
would at length be the Southern, the Southern the Northern,
and *Capricorn* become our *Cancer.* However therefore the
Wisdom of the Creator hath ordered the duration of the   .
World, yet since the end thereof brings the accomplishment
of our happiness, since some would be content that it should
have no end, since Evil Men and Spirits do fear it may be
too short, since Good Men hope it may not be too long; the
prayer of the Saints under the Altar will be the supplication   45
of the Righteous World: That his mercy would abridge their
languishing Expectation and hasten the accomplishment of
their happy state to come.

SECT. 27. Though Good Men are often taken away from the
Evil to come, though some in evil days have been glad that
they were old, nor long to behold the iniquities of a wicked
World, or Judgments threatened by them; yet is it no small
satisfaction unto honest minds to leave the World in virtuous
well temper'd times, under a prospect of good to come, and
continuation of worthy ways acceptable unto God and Man.
Men who dye in deplorable days, which they regretfully behold, have not their Eyes closed with the like content; while
they cannot avoid the thoughts of proceeding or growing
enormities, displeasing unto that Spirit unto whom they are

then going, whose honour they desire in all times and throughout all generations. If *Lucifer* could be freed from his dismal place, he would little care though the rest were left behind. Too many there may be of *Nero's* mind, who, if their [46] own turn were served, would not regard what became of others, and, when they dye themselves, care not if all perish. But good Mens wishes extend beyond their lives, for the happiness of times to come, and never to be known unto them. And therefore while so many question prayers for the dead, they charitably pray for those who are not yet alive; they are not so enviously ambitious to go to Heaven by themselves; they cannot but humbly wish, that the little Flock might be [47] greater, the narrow Gate wider, and that, as many are called, so not a few might be chosen.

SECT. 28. That a greater number of Angels remained in [48] Heaven, than fell from it, the School-men will tell us; that the number of blessed Souls will not come short of that vast number of fallen Spirits, we have the favorable calculation of others. What Age or Century hath sent most Souls unto Heaven, he can tell who vouchsafeth that honour unto them. Though the Number of the blessed must be compleat before the World can pass away, yet since the World it self seems in the wane, and we have no such comfortable prognosticks of Latter times; since a greater part of time is spun than is to come, and the blessed Roll already much replenished; happy are those pieties, which solicitously look about, and hasten to make one of that already much filled and abbreviated List to come.

SECT. 29. Think not thy time short in this World since the World it self is not long. The created World is but a small *Parenthesis* in Eternity, and a short interposition for a time between such a state of duration, as was before it and may be after it. And if we should allow of the old Tradition that the World should last Six Thousand years, it could scarce have the name of old, since the first Man lived near a sixth part thereof, and seven *Methusela's* would exceed its whole duration. However to palliate the shortness of our Lives, and

somewhat to compensate our brief term in this World, it's
good to know as much as we can of it, and also so far as
possibly in us lieth to hold such a *Theory* of times past, as
though we had seen the same. He who hath thus considered
the World, as also how therein things long past have been
answered by things present, how matters in one Age have
been acted over in another, and how there is nothing new
under the Sun, may conceive himself in some manner to have
lived from the beginning, and to be as old as the World;
and if he should still live on 'twould be but the same thing.

SECT. 30. Lastly, if length of Days be thy Portion, make it not
thy Expectation. Reckon not upon long Life: think every day   40
the last, and live always beyond thy account. He that so often
surviveth his Expectation lives many Lives, and will scarce
complain of the shortness of his days. Time past is gone like
a Shadow; make time to come present. Approximate thy latter times by present apprehensions of them: be like a neighbour unto the Grave, and think there is but little to come.
And since there is something of us that will still live on, join
both lives together, and live in one but for the other. He who
thus ordereth the purposes of this Life will never be far from
the next, and is in some manner already in it, by a happy
conformity, and close apprehension of it. And if, as we have
elsewhere declared, any have been so happy as personally to   50
understand Christian Annihilation, Extasy, Exolution, Transformation, the Kiss of the Spouse, and Ingression into the
Divine Shadow, according to Mystical Theology, they have
already had an handsome Anticipation of Heaven; the World
is in a manner over, and the Earth in Ashes unto them.

FINIS

MISCELLANY TRACTS
Printed from autograph MS versions

Of Languages, and Particularly of the Saxon Tongue

Of the Answers of the Oracle of Apollo at Delphos
to Croesus King of Lydia

A Prophecy
Writt upon occasion of an old prophecie sent
mee from a freind to read

[Of Languages, and Particularly of the Saxon Tongue]   †

The late discours wee had of the Saxon tongue, recalled †
into my mind some dormant thoughts or forgotten considerations, both of that and other Languadges. If the earth were
widely peopled before the flood, as most conjecture, yet in †
the space of above fifteen hundred yeares and a large disper- †
sion withall; whether they strictly maintained their originall
and Adamicall speech, and did not runne into different
words, so as to alter though not diversifie their Languadge,
some question might be made. And though the progenie of
Noah before the miraculous confusion at Babel, might justly ¹
bee sayd to have been of one Lippe; yet if they had been
very long permitted unto themselves their humors, inventions, necessities and new objects, in long tract of time they
could hardly have escaped such varietie in their languadge as
almost to have made it another thing.

If America were peopled of old by one nation, some Ora- †,²
cle must tell us, how their great varietie of Languadges did
arise in that separated part of the earth. And if by diverse
nations, as is most probably conjectured, yet doth the number
of different planting nations no waye answer the multiplicity
of the present distinct and diverse languadges. Even in the
northerne nations and uncommunicating angles thereof,
where they may bee best conceaved to have most single originalls, their Languages are widely different. A native interpreter brought from California proved of litle use unto the †
Spanyards upon the neibour coasts. From Chiapa to Guati-
mala, St. Salvador and Honduras there are at least *eighteen ³
languages, which are also so numerous both in the Mexican
and Peruvian provinces, that great princes are fayne to have

* Gage.

one common language; which beside their vernaculous and mother tongue, may serve for commerce between them.

And since the confusion of tongues at first fell only upon those of the new world which were present at the work of Babel in Sinaar, where the primitive languadge is conceaved to have been preserved in the family of Heber; whether the same were not also retained in many others which were not at that building; whether all came down to Sinaar, and many were not left behind in the first plantations, about those parts where the Arke rested and Noah became an Husbandman; whether in that space of an hundred and fiftie yeares, according to common compute, before the conduct of Nimrod, many might not expatiate northward eastward or southward; and many of the posteritie of Noah might not disperse themselves before the great migration unto Sinaar, and many also afterward, is not unreasonably doubted.

And this would become more probable from the Septuagint and Greeck cronologie not long ago asserted by the learned [†] Isaac Vossius.* For accounting above four hundred yeares [†,4] from the deluge unto the dayes of Peleg, there ariseth a fayre latitude for such a numerous multiplication; and a more probable dispersion of many into other parts before the descent of that great body, which accompanied Nimrod from the East. And so beside what the severall languadges might retaine thereof in their first confusion, the primitive tongue, [5] conceaved to bee Hebrewe, might in time branch out into severall parts of the world where Nimrod came not; and the Hebrewe, which seemes to have ingresse into so many languages, might have more large originalls and wayes of its communication and traduction then from the familie of Abraham, the land of Canaan, and words contained in the Scripture, which comes short of the full of that Languadge.

Religious obligation unto the Hebrewe Languadge hath so [†] notably continued the same, that it might still be understood by Abraham, whereas by the Mazorite poynts and Chaldie [6] character, the old letter stands so transformed, that if Moses were alive, hee must be tought to read his owne Lawe.

---

* [In his *dissertatio de vera mundi aetate*. MS Sloane 1827.]

Though this languadge bee duly magnified and allwayes of   †
high esteeme; yet if with Goropius Becanus wee admitt that   7
tongue to bee most perfect, which is most copious or expressive, most delucide and cleare unto the understanding, most
short or soone delivered, and best pronounced with most ease
unto the organs of speech, the Hebrewe now knowne unto
us will hardly obtaine the first place; since it consisteth of
fewer words then many others, and words beginne not with
vowells, since it is so full of homonymies, and words which
signifie many things, and so ambiguous, that translations so
litle agree. And since though the Radixes consist butt of three
Letters, yet they make two syllables in speaking, and since
the pronunciation is such as St. Jerome, who was borne in a
barbarous country, thought the words anhelant, strident, and
of very harsh sound.

The Chineses who live at the borders of the earth, who   †
have admitted of litle communication and suffered successive
conquests and incursions from one nation, may probably give
an account of a very ancient languadge. Butt now consisting
of many tongues and nations, confusion, admixtion, and corruption must probably have so farre crept in, as without the
help of a common character and letter of things, they could
never make out the strange memorialls which they pretend,
while they still make use of the workes of their magnified   †
Confutius many hundred yeares before Christ, and in an his-   8
toricall series ascend as high as Poncuus, who is conceaved
to bee Noah.

The present Welch and remnants of the old Britains retaine
so much of that ancient Languadge, that they make a shift to
understand the poemes of Merlin, Enerin, and Telesin, after   †
a thousand yeares. Whereas the Herulian *pater noster* set   9
down by *Wolfgangus Lazius is not without much criticisme
made out by present times, and that also butt in some words.
And the present Parisians cannot without much difficultie
cleave out those fewe lines of the League between Charles
and Lewis, the sonnes of Ludovicus Pius, yet remaining in   10
old French.

* Lazius *de migratione gentium.*

The Spanyards in their Romance and corruptive traduction from the Latin, have so happily retained the feminine   †
terminations of the Latin, that notwithstanding the Gothick
and Moorish intrusion of words, they are able to frame a discourse compleatly consisting of grammaticall Latin and Spanish, which to effect, the Italians and French will be very much
to seeke.

The many mother tongues spoake in divers corners of Europe and quite different from onanother, are not recon-
cileable to any one common originall; whereas the great
languages of Spayne France and Italie are derivative from
the Latin, that of Grecia and its Islands from the old Greeck,
the rest are of the familie of the Duch or Schlavonian. As for
the *Lingua Fullana* spoaken in part of Friuli, and the *Lingua
Curvallica* in Rhaetia, they are corruptians of the Italian, as
that of Sardinia is also of the Spanish.

Even the Latin itself, which hath embroyled so many lan-   †
guages of Europe, if it had been the speech of one countrey
and not continued by writers and the consent and studie of
all ages since, it had found the same fate and been swallowed
like other Languages; since in its ancient state one age
could scarce understand another, and that of some generations before must be read by a dictionarie by a fewe successions after, as beside the famous pillar of Duillius, may bee   †,11
illustrated in these fewe lines.

*Endo omnibus honestitudo praeterbitanda nenu escit. Quianam
itaque istuc effexis hauscio, Temperi et topper tutemet tam
hibus insegne, quod ningulus potestur aut ruspare nevolt. Sap-
sam saperdae seneciones sardare nequinont, cuoi siemps et-so-
cienum quipis specit?*   12

Some derive the bulk of Europaean languages from the   †
Scythian and the Greeck. If wee had as good a Knowledge of
the old Scythian as of the Greeck much more might be sayd
thereon. The learned Dr. Casaubone conceaveth that a dia-   13
logue might bee composed in Saxon only of such words as are
derivable from the Greeck, which surely might bee performed and so as the learned might make it out. Verstegan   14
makes no doubt that hee could contrive a Letter that might

bee understood by the English Duch and East Frislander,
which as the confusion now standeth, might prove no very
cleare or easie peece. Yet so much of the Saxon remaineth still
in our English as may afford an orderly discourse, and series
of good sense, such as not only the present English but Alfric,
Beda, and Alured might understand, after so many hundred   15
yeares. As for that languadge as it now stands in reference   †
unto the present English, I find many words thereof totally
lost, divers of harsh sound disused or refined in the pronunciation, and many words now of common use not to bee found in
that tongue nor venially derivable from any other from which
wee have largely borrowed; and yet so much of the Saxon
still remaineth with us as to make the grosse of our Language.

Nations that live promiscuously under the power and
lawes of conquest, do seldom escape the losse of their Language with their Liberties. Wherin the Romans were so
strict that the Grecians were fayne to conforme and make
use of Latin in their Judiciall processes. This made the He-
brewes loose more in seventie yeares dispersion in the provinces of Babylon then in many hundred in their distinct
habitation in Aegypt. And the English which dwelt promiscuously with the natives to loose their language in Ireland,
whereas there are still more tollerable remaines thereof in
that part of the countrey called Fingall, where they were   16
closely and almost solely planted. And the Moores which
were most huddled together and united about Granada, have
yet left their *Arviraga* among the Granadian Spanyards.   17

Butt shut up in Angles and lesse accessible corners divided
by lawes and manners, nations often continue their languadge
long and with litle mixture: which hath afforded that lasting
life unto the Cantabrian and British tongues, wherein the   18
Britaines are very remarkable, who though they lived about
four hundred yeares together with the Romans, yet retained
so much of the British as made a distinct Languadge; which
having resolutely maintained in their long cohabitation with
them in Britaine, they more easily preserved it when they
afterwards fled from the Saxons into Wales and countries litle
or less acquainted with the Roman conversation.

Butt probably no Languages have been so straytly lockt

up as not to admitt of commixture. The Irish hath entertained   †
diuers Latin and English words. In the Welsh are found
many words from Latin, some from Greeck and Saxon. Under
what commixture and paritie the Languadge of that people
stood which were casually discovered in the heart of Spayne
between the mountaines of Castile, no longer ago then in the
dayes of the famous Duke D'Alva, wee have not met with a
neerer account, then that their words were Basquish or Cantabrian. Butt the present Basquensa, one of the minor mother   19
tongues of Europe, is not without commixture of Latin and
Castillian; while wee meet with *Sanctifica, tentationeten,
gloria, puissança,* and four more words in the short forme of
the Lords prayer sett downe by Paulus Merula.* Neverthelesse, though in this breif prayer wee find such commixture,
yet the bulk of that Language seemes more distant, consisting
of words of no affinitie unto those of other tongues, of numeralls totally different, and of differing grammaticall rules;
as may bee observed in the dictionary and short Basquença
grammer composed by Raphael Nicoleta, a priest of Bilbao.   †

And since they have in their language the auxiliary verbes
of *Equin* and *ysan,* to have and to bee, answerable unto
Haver and *Ser* in the Spanish, which formes came in with   †
the northerne nations into Italian Spanish and French; and
if they crept not into the Basquish from imitation of their
Spanish neibours, butt were in use before such commixture,
they may declare some ancient northern originall and traduction, or else must seeme somewhat strange, for the southerne countries used not these formes, and some doubt may
bee made whether any such mode of speech bee used in the
Languages of America.

The Romans who made such great alteration in Languages,
brought the same to effect not only by their owne tongue butt
also by those of their military forces employed in severall
provinces; as holding a standing militia in conquerd countries and commonly of strange nations. So while the cohorts
of British forces were quartered in Aegypt, Armenia, Spayne,
Illyria etc, the Stablaesian and Dalmatian in Britaine, the

* In his geographie. [i.e. *Cosmography.*]

Gauls, Spanyards, and Germans in other countries, and other nations in theirs, they could not butt leave many words behind them, and carry away many with them. From whence it may come to passe that in many words of very distant nations there may bee some communitie; and many words also remaine of very unknowne or doubtfull genealogie.

The Saxons and Saxon nations settling over all England maintained one Language diversified in dialects idiomes and smaller differences, accordinge to their different nations which came in unto the common conquest; which may yet occasion some variation in the speech and words in severall parts of England, where different nations most abode or settled. And having expulsed the Britains they had litle cause of alteration in their Languadge, their warres being cheifly among themselves, and having litle action with forreign nations untill the union of the Heptarchie under Egbert. After which time although the Danes greatly infested this land, and scarce left any part free; yet their incursions made more havock in buildings, churches, and townes, then in the Languadge of the country; because it was in the maine the same, and such whereby they might make a shift to be understood by onanother.

And if the Normans which conquered Neustria or Normandie under Rollo had preserved their Languadge in their new acquists, the succeeding conquest of England by Duke William, one of his race, had not begott among us such notable alteration. Butt having in a manner lost their Languadge during their abode in Normandie, they confused the English with their French and made the grand mutation. Which was successively encreased by our possessions in Normandie Guien and Aquitaine, as also by our long warres in France, by frequent resort of the French into England, who to the number of some thousands came over with Isabell Queen to Edward the second, and the severall ma[t]ches of England and France before and since that time.

Butt this commixture though able to confuse, proved not sufficient to abolish the Saxon words. From the French wee have borrowed many substantives, adjectives, and some verbes, butt the great body of numeralls, auxiliarie verbes,

Articles, pronouns, adverbes, conjunctions, and prepositions, which are the distinguishing and lasting parts of a Languadge, remaine with us from the Saxon. Which having suffered no great Alteration for many hundred yeares, may probably still remaine: though the Languadge swell with the inmates of French Italian and Latin, which with some allowance may bee exemplified in this following illustration.   20

The first and formost steppe to all good workes is the dread and feare of the Lord of heaven and earth, which thorough the holy ghost enlighteneth the blindnesse of our synfull hearts to tred the wayes of wisedome, and then leades our feet into the land of blessing.

The erst and fyrmost staep to eal gode weorka is the draed and fehrt of the Lavord of heofan and eorth, whilc thurh the heilig gast onlihtneth the blindnysse of ure synfull heorta to traed the waeg of wisdome and thone laed ure fet into the land of blessung.

For to forgett his Lawe is the doore, the gate and key to lett in all unrighteousnesse making our eyes eares and mouths to answeare the lust of sinne, our braines dull to good thoughts, our lippes dumb to his prayse, our eares deaf to his gospell, and our eyes dim to behold his wonders. Which witnesse agaynst us that wee have not well learned the word of god, that wee are the children of wrath unworthy of the love and manifold gifts of god, greedily following after the wayes of the devell and wi[t]chcraft of the world, doing nothing to free and keepe our soules from the burning fyre of hell till wee be buried in synne and swallowed in death not to rise agayne in any hope of Christs Kingdome.

For to fuorgyt his lag is the dure the gat and caeg to let in eal unrihtwisnysse, makend ure eyge eore and muth to andsware the Lust of sinne, ure braegan dole to gode theoht, ure lippan dumb to his preys, ure earen deaf to his gospell, and ure eyg dim to behealden his wundra. Whilc gewitnysse ongen us that we aef noht wel gelaered the weord of god, that we are the cilda of ured unwyrthe of the Lufe and maenigfeald gift of god, grediglice felygend aefter the waegen of the deoful and wiccraft of the weorld, doend nething to fry and caep our saula from the brynend fyr of hell til we be geburied in synne and swolgen in death not to arise ygen in aenig hope of Christes Kynedome.

Which drawe from above the bitter dome of the Almightie of hunger, sword, sicknesse, and brings more sad plagues then those of hayle, stormes, thunder, blood, frogs, swarms of gnats, and grasshoppers which eat the corne, grasse, and leaves of the trees in Aegypt.

Whilc drag from buf the bitter dome of the Almagan of hunger, sweord, seoknesse, and bring mere sad plag thone they of hagal, storme, thunnor, blode, frog, swearme of gnaet and graeshupper whilc eatan the gaers and leaf of the treowen in Aegypt.

If wee reade his booke and holy writ these among many other wee shall find to bee the tokens of his hate, which gathered together might mind us of his will and teach us when his wrath beginneth; which sometime comes in open strength and full sayle, oft steales like a theif in the night, like shafts shot from a bowe at midnight before wee thinck upon them.

Gyf we raed his boc and heilig gewrit, these gemong maenig othern we sceall findan the tacna of his hate, whilc gegathered together miht gemind us of his willan and taec us whone his ured onginneth, whilc sometime come in open strength and fyll seyle, oft stael gelyc a theof in the niht, gelyc sceaft scoten fram a boge at midneoht beforan wee thinck uppan them.

And though they were a deale lesse, and rather short then beyond our sinnes, yet doe wee not a whit withstand or forbeare them; we are wedded to not wearie of our misdeeds, wee seldome looke upward and are not ashamed under synne. Wee cleanse not our selves from the blacknesse and deepe hue of our guilt, wee want teares and sorrowe, wee weepe not, fast not, wee crave not forgivenesse from the mildnesse, sweetnesse, and goodnesse of God, and with all lively hood and stedfastnesse to our uttermost will hunt after the evel of guile, pride, cursing, swearing, drunckennesse, overeating, uncleanesse, and all idle lusts of the flesh, yes many uncouth and namelesse sinnes hid in our inmost breast and bosomes which stand betwixt our forgivenesse and keep god and man asunder.

And theow they waere a dael lesse and reither scort thone beyond our sinnan, yet do we naht a whit withstond and forbeare them; we eare bewudded to, noht wearig of ure agen misdeed, we seldon loc upweard and ear not ofschaemod under sinne. We cleans naht ure selvan from the blacnesse and daep hue of ure guilt, we wan teare and sara, we weope noht, faest noht, we craf noht foregyfnesse from the mildnesse, swetenesse, and godenesse of God, and mit eal lifelyhood and stedfastnesse to ure uttermost will hunt aefter the ufel of guile, pryde, cursung, swearung, druncenesse, overeat, unclaennesse and eal idle lust of the flaesc, yis maenig uncuth and nameleas sinnan hid in ure inmaest brist and bosome, whilc stand betwixt ure foregyfnesse, and caep god and man asynder.

Thus are we far beneath and also worse then the rest of gods works; for the Sun and Moon, the King and Queen of Starres, snowe, Ice, rayne, frost, dewe, mist, wind; four-footed and creeping things, fish and fethered birds and faules ether of sea or land do all hold the lawe of his will.

Thus eare we far beneoth and ealso wyrse thone the rest of gods weorka, for the sun and mone, the Cyng and Cquen of stearran, snaw, Ise, ren, frost, deaw, mist, wind, feower fet and crypend dinga, fix, gefetherod brid and fulen auther in sae or land do eal heold the Lag of his willan.

Thus have you sawe in fewe words how neer the Saxon and English meet.

I am your true freind T B.

Thus aef eow gesawon in feaw weord hu naer the Saxon and Anglisc maet.

Ic eom eour treow freond T B.

Now of this account the French will be able to make nothing; the modern Danes and Germans allthough from severall words, they may conjecture at the meaning, yet may they bee to seeke in the orderly sense and continued construction thereof. Whether the Danes can continue a series of sense made up of their present Languadge and the old Runick, as [21] to bee intelligible both unto the present and ancient times, some doubt may well be made. And if the present French should attempt a discourse in words common unto their present tongue and the old *Romana Rustica* knowne to elder times; or in the old languadge of the Francks which came to bee in use some successions after Pharamond, it might prove a buisinesse of some trouble to effect.

It were not impossible to make an originall reduction of many words of no great generall reception in England, but of common use in Norfolk or peculiar unto the East Angle countries: As Bawnd, mauther, enemmis, Thurk, sammodithy, Fangast, strafft, fest, dere, nonere, Thepes, Gosgood, Fasgon, Sibritt, Sap, Cothish, Thokish, bideowe, paxwax, etc. Of these and some others of no readie origination when time will permit the resolution may bee attempted; whereto the Danish Languadge later and more ancient may probably prove some advantage, for upon agreement the Danes remained fiftie yeares in these parts and left many families descended from them. And surely the speech of these countries had suffered a greater commixture if the fleet of Hugo de Boves had not been cast away; for therin three score thousand souldiers out of Flanders and Bretaigne were to bee wafted over, and by the appoyntment of King John were to have a settled habitation in the countries of Norfolk and Suffolk.

Butt beside some endeavours of yours in the Saxon, you are not like to repent of your studies in the moderne and westerne Languages of Europe, for therin are delivered many excellent historicall morall and philosophical discourses, wherin men meerely versed in the learned tongues are often at a losse. And though you are alreadie so well acquainted with the French, yet surely you will not conceave that you understand all the Languadges in France; for to omit the Briton, Britonant or old British, yet retained in some parts of Britaigne, I shall only propose this following unto your construction. Chavalisco, chez acho, perche faizes commachodochi, chau vol treboula lou cap con taulas caussos. Ero nesci, qui voluiget bouta saun tens ambe aquelles: yeu ay ies de plazer d'ausir la mitat de paraullos din lou mounde. Anin. Aprep abé prou rambouillat l'armo ambe otros afas, yeou resoulbegui

In the right margin, the following reference markers appear:

22

†

†,23

24

25

†,26

saber guicom de la lengo moundino, et pertant soun aro ben-
gut aci en aqueste bilo. Certadieromen las paraullasos de las
fennos soun pla agradiboulos, et passen lou garganto dousso-
men. Tabes yeu trobi las dounzelos moundinetos jantios et
coutinados. Talomen que creze belomen parla daban nadal.
Adissiats. Moussur de vostre rebelencio d'enquios al clot.

Serbitou

TB

Apres avoir asses embrouillé l'ame environ autres affaires j'ay
resolu scavoir quelque chose de la langue Tholosaine etc.

These are the dialects spoaken about Montpellier and
Thoulouze, and a part of that speech which Scaliger termeth
Idiotismus Tectosagicus or *Langue d'oc* in contradistinction   27
unto the *Idi[o]tismus Francicus* or *Langue d'ouy;* understood
not in a petty corner or between a few mountaines butt in
parts of early civilitie, in Prouence, Languedock, part of Gascoigne, and Catalonia, which putt together will make no small   †
countrie.

Without some knowledge herin you cannot well read the   †
works of Goudelin, or exactly apprehend that notable peece   28
of Rablais. By some help from this the French are fayne to
make out some old preserved writings, and by the help hereof
severall bookes written in the Catalonian tongue may bee
tolerably understood; as may be observed in that tract of   29
Falconrie writ by Theodosius and Symmachus and published
in the Catalonian translation. In this Languadge of southerne   †
France is yet preserved the poem of Vilhuardin concerning   30
the French expedition in the eastern warre and the taking of
Constantinople, and among the works of Marius Aequicola   31
an Italian poet you may find in this Languadge a pleasant
dialogue of Love; and the people in these parts being very   †
poeticall I was often delighted with their songs and poems in
that speech while I lived in their country. This above an hundred yeares ago was in great esteeme when many flocked
into Prouence, and the famous Petrarcha wrote many of his
poems at Vaucluse in that countrie.

Now having wearied you with old Languages or litle under-   †
stood, I shall putt an end unto your trouble in moderne   32

French, by a short letter composed by mee for your sake, though not concerning yourself; wherin though the words bee playne and genuine, yet the sense may afford some trouble.

Monsieur,

Ne vous laisses plus manger la laine sur le dors. Regardes bien ce gros magot, [et malitorne de maigre mince] lequel   †
vous voyes de si bon oeil. Assurement il fait le mitou. Monsieur vous chausses les Lunettes de travers, ne voyant poynt comme il practique vos dependants. Il s'est desia gueri de mal St. Francois et bride sa mule a vostre despens: croyes moi, il ne s'amusera a la moustarde; mais vous ayant miné, et massacré vos affaires, au dernier coup il vous rendra monsieur sans queue.

Mais pour l'autre goulafre, et beuveur a tire larigau, qui a vous a si rognement fait la barbe, l'envoyes vous a Pampelune. Mais auparavant a mon advis, il auroit a miserere jusques a vitulos, et je le ferois un moutton de Berry. En le traittant bellement et de bon conseil, vous assayes de rompre un anguille sur les genoux; ne lui fies poynt, il ne rabbaissera le menton, et mourra dans sa peau. Il scait bien que les belles parolles n'eschorchent pas la gueule, lesquelles il payera a septmaine de deux Jeudies. Chasses le de chez vous a bonne heure, car il a esté a Naples sans passer les monts, et ancore qui parle en Maistre, est patient de Sainct Cosme.

Soucies vous aussi de la garconiere chez vous, q'elle n'ayst   †
le mal de neuf mois. Assurement elle a le nez tourné a la friandise, et les talons bien courts. Elle jouera voluntiers a l'Hom[m]e; et si le hault ne defend le bas, avant la venue des cicoignes, lui s'enlevera la juppe.

Mais pour le petit Gymnosophiste chez vous, caresses le vous au bras ouverts. Voyes vous pas comme a toutes les menaces de fortune il branle comme la Bastille? Vrayment il est Stoic a vingt quatre carrats, et de mesme calibre avec les vieus Ascetiques. Alloran* lui vault autant que l'isle de

* Alloran, Allusana or insula erroris, a small desolate barren Island whereon nothing liveth butt coneys, in the Mediterranean Sea between Carthagena and Calo di tres furcas in Barbarie.

France, et la tour de Cordan* lui revint le mesure avec la Louvre.

Serviteur tres humble

T B.

* Cordan, a small island or Rock in the mouth of the river Garonne, with one tower in it where a man liveth to take care of lights for such as go to or come from Bourdeaux.

[Of the Answers of the Oracle of Apollo
at Delphos to Croesus King of Lydia] [†]

Men looke upon ancient Oracles as naturall, Artificiall, [†]
Demonicall or all. They conceaved somewhat naturall in
them, as being in places affording exhalations which were
found to operate upon the braynes of persons unto raptures,
strange utterances, and divinations; which being observed
and admired by the people, an advantage was taken thereof
and an artificiall contrivance made by subtle and craftie
persons confederating to carry on a practise of divination pretending some power of divinitie therin. Butt because they
sometimes made very strange predictions and above the
power of human reason, men were inclined to believe some
demonicall cooperation, and that some evell spirit ruled the
whole scene; having so fayre an opportunity to delude mankind and to advance his owne worshippe, and were thought
to proceed from the spirit of Apollo or other heathen deitie;
so that these oracles were not only apprehended to bee naturall, human, or artificiall, but also demoniacall, according to
common opinion and also of learned men, as Vossius* hath ¹
declared: *Constitere quidem oracula fraudibus vatum, sed
non solis, solertia humana, sed saepe etiam diabolica, cum
multa predixerint, ad quae nulla ratione humanae mentis
acumen pertigisset in natura humana non est subsistendum,
sed assurgendum ad causas superioris naturae quales sunt
daemones.* According unto which sense and opinion wee shall
enlarge upon this following oricle of Delphos.

Among the oraculous answers of Apollo there are none
more remarkable then those delivered unto Croesus King of
Lydia; who seemes of all men to have held the greatest dependence on them. Butt most considerable are his playne and

---

* *Vossii Idol. Lib.* 1.

intelligible Replies made unto the same King; when after his overthrowe by Cyrus, hee sent his chaines of captivity unto Delphos; with sad expostulations, why the oracle encouraged him unto that fatall warre, why at least he prevented not that infelicity of his beneficent and devoted servant; and whether it were fayre and honorable for the Gods of Greece to bee ungratefull. Which being answered at Delphos with plaine and open replies, and scarce to bee paralleled in any ancient storie, may well deserve your further consideration. The account thereof is extant in the first booke of Herodotus.

The first Apologie or excuse of the Oracle was this. *Sortem*   †
fato destinatam defugere deo quoque est impossibile. This was   2
an open confession that it was not in his power to prevent or hinder the misfortune of Croesus, as being decreed in the booke of fate and beyond his power to resist. A generall evasion for any falsifying promise or prediction; and widely discovering the folly of all persons which repayre unto him about future events; which according to this rule, must go on as fate hath ordered, beyond his power to avoyd: and consequently inferring, that his oracles had only this use, to render men more miserable by foreknowing their misfortunes. And hereof Croesus had found sensible experience in his verie familie, from that demoniacall dreame concerning his eldest sonne, wherin hee was warned, that hee should bee killed by a speare; which after all care and caution hee found inevitably to befall him.

His second Reply was *crimen quintae retro aetatis id est*   3
tritavi fuit. That Croesus suffered not upon his owne account, but payd the transgression of his praedecessor Gyges, who killed his master Candaules, and usurped the crowne, where-   4
unto hee had no title. Now whether Croesus suffered upon this account or not, as hee would make him beleeve, yet in this answer hee plainly acknowledged the inevitable justice of God, that although divine vengeance might bee long dormant, yet would it not allwayes sleep; and so confessing the just hand of the Allmightie, punishing unto the fourth generation nor suffering such iniquities for ever unrevenged. The   †
Devill who sees how things of this nature go on in Kingdomes, nations, and families, is able to saye much in this

poynt. Whereas wee that understand not the reserved judgments of God, or the due time of their executions, are fayne
to bee doubtfully silent; which makes Riddles unto us in the
tragicall ends of many noble persons and families. In this Answer hee also obliquely discovered his knowledge of Croesus
his affliction; for knowing that wicked act lay yet unpun- 5
ished, hee might justly expect that some of Gyges his posteritie would smart for it; and finding that his successors, Argis, †
Sardiattes, and Halyates had escaped, hee might reasonably 6
concludo that Croesus must bee the man; and knowing also
from other conjectures, that Croesus was like to bee the last
of that race; might justly conclude his infelicitie upon him.
And lastly, in this reply to extenuate his miseries he flatter-
ingly southed him up in the opinion of his owne merits, as
only suffering for the transgression of other persons; meanewhile concealing and passing over the pride of Croesus, his
vaynglorie, elation and secure conceit of his unparalleled
felicity, together with the vanities, pride, and Luxurie of the
Lydian nation; which the spirit of Delphos knewe well to be
ripe and readie for destruction.

In his third Apologie hee endeavours to testifie his gratitude unto Croesus; assuring him that he had labourd to transferre this evell fate and to passe it upon his children; and did
however procrastinate his infelicitie, by deferring the destruction of Sardis and his owne captivitie for three yeares
longer then was fatally determined. Butt herin while hee
wipes of the stayne of Ingratitude, hee cleareth not his power
concerning the things pretended; for whether hee that could
not transferre the fate of Croesus, was able to deferre his
captivity and the taking of his capitall citty Sardis; or whether
at least, it bee in his power to deferre such signall events
whereon the fate of whole nations do depend, hee leaveth
no small doubt.

And whether hee really intended or laboured to bring
about that which hee pretended, some question might bee
made, for to attempt or thinck to translate his infelicitie upon
his sonnes it could not consist with his judgement; which at-
tempteth not impossibles, or things beyond his power. Nor
was it agreable unto his foreknowledge of future things and

the fate of succeeding generations: for hee understood that
monarchie was to expire in Croesus, could foretell the infelicitie of his sonnes, and also make remote predictions
unto others concerning the fortunes of many succeeding
descents, as clearely appeares in his answer unto Attalus: 7

> Bee of good courage Attalus thou shalt Raygne,
> And thy sonnes sonnes, butt not their sonnes agayne.

As also in that oracle unto Cypselus King of Corinth:

> Happy is the man who at my Altar stands
> Great Cypselus, who Corinth now commands,
> Happy is hee, his sonnes shall happy bee,
> Butt for their sonnes, unhappy dayes they'l see.

Now being able to have so long a prospect of future things,
and the fortunes of many generations, it may well be conceaved that hee was not ignorant of the fate of Croesus his
sonnes, and well understood it was in vayne to attempt the
translation of his infelicity upon them.

In his fourth reply he still cleares himself of ingratitude   †
(which Hell itself will not heare of). Therin alledging that
hee had saved Croesus his life when hee was condemned
and ready to bee burnt, by sending a mightie shower of
Raine in a fayre and clowdelesse day to quench the fire al-
readied kindled; which all the servants of Cyrus could not
do. Now though such contrivances are not beyond his power,
when countenanced by divine permission or decree, yet
whether this were his Act or not of better spirits, by whom
God sometimes showeth pitty upon pagans, rewarding some
eminent virtues in them by extraordinary temporall mercies
in the unexpected hitts of this nature; it is no cleare poynt.
And so whether contingency or any other hand were the
Author of those fewe fayre minutes which in an extreme
showrie day afforded only time enough for the burning of
the body of Sylla* [Sulla], no man can fully determine.   8
In the fift and last excuse the oracle divolveth the mis-   †,9
cariadge of the buisinesse upon Croesus*; playnly affirming

---

* See Plutarch in the life of Sylla.

* Κροῖσος Ἅλυν διαβὰς μεγάλην ἀρχὴν καταλύσει

that hee had deceaved himself by an inconsiderate miscon-
struction of the oracle; that if hee had doubted, hee should
have consulted agayne for an exposition of the same; that
hee had neither discussed nor well perpended his former
oracle concerning Cyrus, whereby he might have been fore-
warned not to engage agaynst him. Wherin to speake indifferently the deception and miscariadge seemes cheifly to lye
at Croesus his doore, who if not infatuated by confident se-
curitie, might have well doubted the construction; beside
hee had receaved two oracles before which clearly hinted
an unhappy time unto him. The first was that concerning
Cyrus:

> Whenever a Mule shall 'ore the Medians raygne
> Staye not, butt unto Hermus flye amayne.

Now herin though hee understood not the Median Mule
[to be] Cyrus, who was of a mixed descent from Assyrian
and Median parents; yet hee could not butt apprehend some
misfortune from that quarter.

Though this prediction concerning Cyrus seemed a notable
peece of divination yet did it not so highly declare his naturall sagacity and prescience of future events as might bee
conceaved upon first thoughts, for herin hee might have
no small assistance from the prophecie of Daniel concerning
the Persian monarchie; as also the prophecies of Jeremie
and Esaiah, wherin hee might find the name of Cyrus; who
should restore the captivitie of Judaia, and was therefore to
bee the monarch and great Lord of all those nations.

A great infelicitie had also been foretold him when hee
enquired of Apollo if ever hee should heare his dumb sonne
speake:

> O foolish Croesus who hath made this choyce
> To knowe when thou shalt heare thy dumb sonnes voyce,
> Better hee still were mute, could nothing saye,   †
> When hee first speakes, looke for a dismall daye.

This, if hee contrived not the time and meanes for the re-
coverie of Croesus his sonnes speach and hearing at the
decisive battail, was no ordinarie divination. Butt how to

make out the veritie of the storie in all poynts some doubts
may remaine; for though the causes of deafnesse and dumb-
nesse were removed, so that he suddenly spoake; yet since
words are attained by hearing, and men speake not without
instruction; how the sonne of Croesus should immediately
bee able to utter such apt and apposite words as *O homo ne
occides Croesum* O man kill not Croesus, it cannot escape
some doubt: since the story also delivers that hee was deaf
and dumb, that hee then first began to speake and spoake all
his life after.

Now notwithstanding this plausible apologie and evasion,
if Croesus had consulted agayne for a clearer exposition of
what was doubtfully delivered, whether the oracle would
have spoake out the second time, or afforded a clearer answer, some doubt may bee made from examples of his practise upon the like enquiries.

So when the Spartans had often fought with ill successe
agaynst the Tegeates, they consulted the oracle what god
they should appease, to become victorious over them. The
answer was, that they should remove the bones of Orestes.
Though the words were playne yet the thing was obscure
and like finding the body of Moses; and therefore they once
more demanded in what place they should find those bones;
unto which hee returned this answer

> When in the Tegean playnes a place thou findst,
> Where blasts are made by two impetuous winds,
> When that which strikes is struck, blowes follow blowes,
> There doth the earth Orestes bones enclose.

Which obscure reply the wisest of Sparta could not make
out, and was casually unriddled by one talking with a smith,
who had found large bones of a man buried about his howse;
the oracle implying no more then a smiths forge, expressed
by a double bellows, the hammer and anville therin.

Now why the oracle should place such consideration upon
the bones of Orestes, a mad man and a murtherer, or why
in a buisinesse so clearly in his knowledge, hee should affect
so obscure expressions, if not to maintaine the warie and
evasive method of his answers, it may well be wondred; for

10

speaking obscurely in things clearly within his knowledge, hee might when hee pleased, bee more tolerably dark in matters beyond his prescience.

In vayne wee looke for open sense in oracles, there was † not only obscuritie in the recesse butt in the outside of Delphos; and the two letters EI set over the entrance of it 11 have puzzled learned conjectures to expound the meaning of them. And to speake in generall of Oracles and Gentile divinations, there was no uniformitie in their deliveries; they being sometimes made with that obscuritie as argued a fearefull prophecy; sometimes so plainly as might conclude a spirit of divinity; sometimes morally, deterring from vice and villany; another time vitiously, and in the spirit of blood and crueltie; observably modest in that civill Enigma and periphrasis of that part which old Numa would playnely name † when hee advised Aegeus not to drawe out his foot* before, 12 untill hee arrived on the Athenian ground; whereas another time the oracle seemed too literall in that unseemely 13 epithite* unto Cyanus [Cinyrus] King of Cyprus; and putt † a beastly trouble upon Aegypt to find out the urine of a true 14 virgin to cure the kings eyes.

Sometimes more beholding unto memorie then invention, † hee delighted to expresse himself in the bare verses of Homer; but that hee principally affected poetrie, and the preists not only nor allwayes composed his prosall deliveries into verse, seemes plaine from his necromanticall prophecyes. The dead head in Phlegon* delivers a long prediction in 15 verse, and at the raysing of the ghost of Commodus* unto 16 Caracalla, when none of his ancestors would speake, the divining spirit versified his infelicitie; herin complying unto the apprehension of elder times, which conceaved not only a majestie, butt something of divinitie in poetrie; and wherin the old Theologians delivered their inventions.

Criticall considerators might looke for rare poetrie, and

* Drawe not thy foot out of the bagge before,
   Until thou comest on the Athenian shoare.

* Κυάνος βασιλεῦς Ἀνδρων δασυπρώκτων. *Rex hominum hirsuti natium.*
* Phlegon.
* Dion.

expect in his oraculous verses a more then ordinarie strayne
and high spirit of Apollo; nor bee content to find that spirits   17
make verses like men, beating upon filling epithites, nor
omitting the licence of Dialects and lower helpes common
unto human poetrie; wherin since Scaliger, who hath scarce
spared any of the Greek poets, hath thought it wisdome to
bee silent, wee shall make no animadversion.

Others may wonder how the curiositie of elder times having this opportunitie of his oracles omitted natural questions:
or why old magitians discoursed no more philosophie, and
if they had the assistance of spirits, could rest content with
the common hoties or trite notions of things, without addition by such discoveries; which unwarrantable beginnings
time long ere this might have confirmed, and made an innocent part of our knowledge. Some divines conceave a   †
Reality in the acts of the magitians of Aegypt, and that their   †
great performances before Pharaoh were not mere delusions.   18
Rightly to understand how they contrived Serpents out of
Rods, froggs and blood of water, were worth half Porta's
magick.

Hermolaus Barbarus was scarce in his right witts who upon   19
conference with a spirit would propose no other question
then an explication of Aristotles Entelecheia. Appion the   20
Grammarian, that would raise the Ghost of Homer, to decide the controversie about his countrey, made a frivolous
and pedantick use of Necromancy; and Philostratus did as   21
litle who called up the ghost of Achilles, for a particular of
the warre of Troye. Smarter curiosities would have been at
the great Elixir, the flux and reflux of the Sea, with such
noble obscurities in nature; butt yet probably all in vayne.
In matters cognoscible and framed for our disquisition, In-
dustrie must bee our Oracle, and Reason our Apollo.

Not to knowe things beyond the Arch of our intellectualls,
or what spirits apprehend, is the imperfection of our nature
not our Knowledge, and rather Inscience then Ignorance in
man. Revelation might render a great part of the creation
easie which now seemes beyond the stre[t]ch of human indagation; and welcome no doubt from good hands might
bee a true Almagest or great celestial construction: A cleare

systeme of the planeticall bodyes; of the invisible and seeming uselesse starres unto us; of the many sunnes in the eigth spheare, what they are, what they contrive, and unto what those stupendous bodies are more immediately serviceable. Butt this being not hinted in the Authentick Revelation and written booke of God, nor yet knowne how farre their discoveries are stinted; if the same should come unto us from the mouth of evell spirits, the belief thereof might bee as unsafe as the enquiries, and how farre to credit the father of darknesse and great obscurer of truth, might bee yet obscure unto us.

[This is a copious Subject; but having exceeded the bounds of a Letter, I will not now pursue it farther. I am

Yours, etc.]

[A Prophecy]
Writt upon occasion of an old prophecie
sent mee from a freind to read.

   I take no pleasure in prophecies hardly intelligible poynting at future things from the single and groundlesse spirit of
divination: of which sort this seemes to bee, which came unto
your hand, and you sent unto mee. And therefore for your
easier apprehension, divertisement, and consideration, I present you with a very different kind of prediction, not positively or peremptorily telling what shall come to passe, yet
poynting at things, not without some reason or rationall
probability of their events. †

     When newe England shall terrifie newe Spayne, †
     When Jamaica shall bee Lady of the Isles and the Maine.
     When Spayne shall bee in America hid,
     And Mexico shall prove a Madrid.
     When Mahomets shipps in the Baltick shall ride, †
     When we shall have ports on the Pacifick side. †
     [And Turks shall labour to have ports on that side.] †
     When Africa shall no more sell out their Blacks,
     Butt slaves must bee had from Incognita tracts. †
     [To make Slaves and Drudges to the American Tracts.]
     When Batavia the old shall bee contemned by the newe,
     When a newe drove of Tartars shall China subdue.
     When America shall cease to send forth its treasure
     Butt employe it at home for American pleasure. †
     When the newe world shall the old invade,
     Nor count them their Lords, butt their fellowes in trade.
     When men shall almost passe to Venice by Land
     Nor in deepe waters, butt from sand to sand.
     When Nova Zembla shall be no staye
     Unto those which passe to or from Cathaye.
     Then thinck strange things are come to Light
     Whereof fewe eyes have had a foresight.

When New England shall terrifie newe Spayne,

When that Thriving Colonie, which hath so well encreased in our dayes, and in the space of about fiftie yeares,   2
that they can allreadie rayse twentie or thirtie thousand men,   †,3
shall in processe of time bee so advanced, as to send forth
their fleets or shipps so as to bee a terrour unto the American   †
Spanish ports and dominions; which they are not unlike to   †
attempt as abounding in the materialls of shipping, oake
and firre. And when time shall so far encrease that industrious people, that the neighbour Lands shall not containe   †
them; they will bee able to sett forth great Armies and seeke
for new possessions. Wherin it is not like that they will range
northward butt toward the southern and richer countries
which are either in the dominion or frontiers of the Span-
yard; and may not improbably erect great Kingdomes in   †
places not as yett thought of, and yet for many yeares beyond their power or Ambition.   †

When Jamaica shall bee Lady of the Isles and the Maine.

When that advantageous Island shall bee well peopled, it
may become so strong and potent as to overpower the nei-
bouring Isles of Hispaniola, Cuba and the rest, and also a good
part of the adjacent mayneland, especially the maritime
parts, they having alreadie in their infancy given testimony
of their power in their bold attempts upon Campeche and   4
Santa Martha: and been able to make their way as farre as   †
Panama on the westerne side of America. Especially this
Island being sufficiently large to containe a numerous
people and of a northern and warlike descent addicted to
martiall affayres both by sea and Land; and advantageously
seated to infest and invade their neibours, both of the Isles
and the continent.   †

When Spayne shall bee in America hid,

When Spayne, either by disasters or by continued emissions of people into America, which hath allreadie thinned
the countrey, shall be farther exhausted at home or when
their colonies shall growe more ample then their originalls;
then Mexico may prove more considerable then Madrid, in   †,†

wealth and splendour; and that place is alreadie so well advanced, that accounts scarce credible are given thereof; and   5
so commodiously seated that by Acapulco and other ports on
the south side, they may maintain communication and trade
with the Indian Isles and territories, and with China and
Japan; and on this side, by Porto Bello and others, have commerce with Europe and Africa.

When Mahomets shipps in the Baltick shall ride,

This may well be feared; for if the Turk should make him-   †
self master of Poland, hee would soon be at this sea. And
from the odde constitution of the Polish gover[n]ment, the
divisions among themselves, jealousies between their Kingdom and Republick, vicinity of the Tartars, and the method of
Turkish policie to have peace with the Emperour when hee is
at warre with the Poles; there may be cause to conjecture that
this may come to passe. And then hee would earnestly endeavour to have ports upon this sea, as not wanting materialls for shipping; and having a new acquist of stout and
warlike men, may bee a terrour unto the confiners on that
sea and nations which conceave themselves secure and safe
from any approach of the Turk.

When we shall have ports on the Pacifick side.   †

On the Pacifick side or west side of America upon the *mare
pacificum* or south sea. Which may come to passe hereafter
upon the enlargement of trade and industrious navigation,
when the strayghts of Magellan, fretum Le Maire or more
southerly passages bee well knowne and frequently navi-
gated.

When Africa shall no more sell out their Blacks,

When African countries shall no longer make it a common
trade to sell away their people to serve in the drudgerie of
American plantations. Which may come to passe when they   †
are civellised, converted unto Christianitie or especially
unto Mahometisme; for then they will not sell those of that
religion to bee slaves unto Christians. Then slaves must bee
sought for in other tracts not yett well knowne or perhaps

from some parts of Terra incognita whenever hereafter they shall be discovered and conquered, or else when that trade shall be left, and slaves bee made from captives and from malefactors of their respective countries.

When Batavia the old shall be contemned by the newe,

When the Holland plantations of new Batavia and other places, shall by their conquests become so powerfull in the Indian territories that their originall country of Holland will be contemned by them. And they are in a way unto it from their severall plantations and new acquists; and have also discovered a part of the southerne continent, where they can want no place to derive their colonies when time hath encreased them unto such necessitie.

When a new drove of Tartars shall China subdue.

Which is no strange thing if wee consult the histories of China, for that Countrie hath been often overcome by Tartars, as every two, three, or four hundred yeares. When the invaders in processe of time have degenerated into the effeminacy and softnesse of the Chineses, then they have suffered a new Tartarian inundation; and this hath happened from times beyond our histories, for according to their owne account the famous China wall was built one hundred and fifteen yeares before Christ.

When America shall cease to send forth its treasure

When America shall bee generally civillised and divided between great princes they will no longer send out their treasure of sylver and gold to maintaine the Luxurie of Europe and other parts: butt employe it to their owne advantages in great exployts, works, noble structures, warres or expeditions of their owne.

When the newe world shall the old invade,

When America shall bee so well peopled, civillised and divided into Kingdoms independent of Europe, they shall have so litle regard unto their originalls, as to acknowledg no subjection unto them: they may have distinct commerce between themselves or butt independently with Europe,

and may hostily and pyratically assault and invade them, as
the colonies of Greecks and Romans sometimes dealt with
their originary countries.   †

When men shall almost passe to Venice by land

When in long processe of time the silt and sands shall
choake and shallowe the sea in and about it. And this hath
very considerably come to passe within these fourscore
yeares, and is like still to encrease, from severall causes, especially by the turning of the river Brenta, as the learned   7
Castelli hath declared.

When Nova Zembla shall be no staye

When that often sought for northeast passage unto China
and Japan shall bee discovered, the hinderance whereof was
imputed to Nova Zembla: which was conceaved to shoot out
so farre northward that it discouraged all navigation about
it; and therefore adventurers tooke in at the southerne part
thereof, at a strayght by Weygatz next the Tartarian shoare,
and so sayling forward, thay found that sea frozen and full of
ice, that they could not advance, and so gave over the attempt. Butt of late times and by the enquirie of the Mus-
covites, a better discoverie is made of these parts and a
mappe or cart made of them. Thereby Nova Zembla is found   †
to bee no Island extending very farre northward, butt winding eastward joyneth to the Tartarian continent and so
makes a peninsula; and the sea between it which they first
entred, at Weygatz, is found to bee a large bay, apt to bee
frozen by reason of the great river Oby, and other sweet
rivers which enter into it; whereas the mayne sea doth not
freez upon the north of Zembla except neere unto shoares.
So that if the Muschovites were skillfull navigators, they
might with lesse difficultie discover this passage unto China;
butt however the English Duch and Danes are now like
agayne to attempt it.

[Butt this is Conjecture, and not Prophecy: and so (I
know) you will take it. I am,

Sir, etc.]

ESSAYS AND OBSERVATIONS FROM NOTEBOOKS

On Dreams

The Search for Truth

Circumscriptions of Pleasure

The Line of our Lives

Ways of Dying

Aggregation and Coacervation

Intention, Imitation, Coincidence

Guardian Angels

A Letter to a Friend

[On Dreams]

Half our dayes wee passe in the shadowe of the earth, and the brother of death exacteth a third part of our lives. A good part of our sleepes is peeced out with visions, and phantasticall objects wherin wee are confessedly deceaved. The day supplyeth us with truths, the night with fictions and falshoods; which unconfortably divide the naturall account of our beings. And therefore having passed the day in sober labours and rationall enquiries of truth, wee are fayne to betake ourselves unto such a state of being, wherin the soberest heads have acted all the monstrosities of melancholy, and which unto open eyes are no better then folly and madnesse. [1]

Happy are they that go to bed with grand music like Pythagoras, or have wayes to compose the phantasticall spirit whose unrulie wanderings takes of inward sleepe, filling our heads with St. Antonies visions, and the dreames of Lipara*, in the sober chambers of rest.

Virtuous thoughts of the day laye up good treasors for the night. Whereby the impressions of imaginarie formes arise into sober similitudes; acceptable unto our slumbering selves, and preparatory unto divine impressions. Hereby Solomons sleepe was happy; thus prepared Jacob might well dreame of Angells upon a pillow of stone, and the first sleepe of Adam might bee the best of any after. [2] [3]

That there should bee divine dreames seemes unreasonably doubted by Aristotle. That there are demonicall dreames wee have litle reason to doubt. Why may there not bee Angelicall? If there bee Guardian spirits, they may not bee unactively about us in sleepe, butt may sometimes order our dreames; and many strange hints, instigations, or

---

* *Somnia Liparitana*, turbulent dreames, as men were observed to have in the Isle of Lipara, abounding in sulphureus and minerall exhalations, sounds, smoakes and fires.

discoveries which are so amazing unto us, may arise from such foundations.

Butt the phantasmes of sleepe do commonly walk in the great roade of naturall and animal dreames; wherin the thoughts or actions of the day are acted over and ecchoed in the night. Who can therefore wonder that Chrysostome should dreame of St. Paul who dayly read his epistles; or that Cardan whose head was so taken up about the starres should dreame that his soule was in the moone! Even pious persons whose thoughts are dayly buisied about heaven, and the blessed state thereof, can hardly escape the nightly phantasmes of it; which though sometimes taken for illuminations or divine dreames, yet rightly perpended may prove butt animal visions and naturall night scenes of their waking contemplations.

Many dreames are made out by sagacious exposition and from the signature of their subjects: carrying their interpretation in their fundamentall sense and mysterie of similitude; whereby hee that understands upon what naturall fundamentall, every notionall dependeth, may by symbolicall adaptation hold a readie way to read the characters of Morpheus. In dreames of such a nature, Artemidorus, Achmet, and Astrampsychius, from Greeck, Aegyptian, and Arabian oneirocriticisme, may hint some interpretation; who while wee read of a Ladder in Jacobs dreame will tell us, that Ladders and scalarie ascents signifie preferment, and while wee consider the dreame of Pharaoh, do teach us, that rivers overflowing speake plentie, leane oxen famine and scarcitie. And therefore it was butt reasonable in Pharaoh to demand the interpretation from his magitians, who being Aegyptians, should have been well versed in symbols and the hieroglyphicall notions of things. The greatest tyrant in such divinations was Nabuchodonosor, while beside the interpretation hee demanded the dreame itself; which being probably determined by divine immission, might escape the common roade of phantasmes, that might have been traced by Satan.

When Alexander going to beseidge Tyre dreamt of a Satyre, it was no hard exposition for a Grecian to say, Tyre

will be thine.* Hee that dreamed that hee sawe his father
washed by Jupiter and annoynted by the sunne, had cause
to feare that he might be crucified, whereby his body would
bee washed by the rayne and drop by the heate of the sunne.
The dreame of Vespasian was of harder exposition, as also   10
that of the Emperour Mauritius concerning his successor
Phocas; and a man might have been hard putt to it to interpret the languadge of Aesculapius, when to a consumptive
person hee held forth his fingers, implying therefore that his
cure laye in dates; from the homonomie of the Greeck,*
which signifies dates and fingers.

Wee owe unto dreames that Galen was a physitian, Dion   11,12
an historian, and that the world hath seen some notable
peeces of Cardan. Yet hee that should order his affayres by
dreames, or make the night a rule unto the day, might be
ridiculously deluded. Wherin Cicero is much to bee pittied;   13
who having excellently discoursed of the vanitie of dreames,
was yet undone by the flatterie of his owne, which urged him
to apply himself unto Augustus.

However dreames may be fallacious concerning outward
events, yet may they bee truly significant at home, and
whereby wee may more sensibly understand our selves. Men
act in sleepe with some conformity unto their awaked senses,
and consolations or discouragements may bee drawne from
dreames, which intimately tell us our selves. Luther was not   14
like to feare a spiritt in the night when such an apparition
would not terrifie him in the daye. Alexander would hardly
have runne away in the sharpest combates of sleepe, nor
Demosthenes have stood stoutly to it, who was scarce able
to do it in his prepared senses. Persons of radicall integritie
will not easily be persuaded in their dreames, nor noble
minds do pitifully things in sleepe. Crassus would have   15
hardly been bountifull in a dreame, whose fist was so close
awake; butt a man might have lived all his life upon the
sleeping hand of Antonius.

There is an Art to make dreames, as well as their interpretations, and physitians will tell us that some food makes

* σάτυρος
* Dactylus.   9

turbulent, some gives quiet dreames. Cato who doated
upon cabbadge might find the crude effects thereof in his
sleepe, wherin the Aegyptians might find some advantage
by their superstitious abstinence from onyons. Pythagoras   16
might have more calmer sleepes if hee totally abstained from
beanes. Even Daniel that great interpreter of dreames, in his   17
leguminous dyet seemes to have chosen no advantageous
food for quiet sleepes according to Graecian physick.

To adde unto the delusions of dreames, the phantasticall
objects seeme greater then they are and being beheld in the
vaporous state of sleepe, enlarge their diameters unto us,
whereby it may prove more easie to dreame of Gyants then
pygmies; Democritus might seldome dreame of Atomes who
so often thought of them; Helmont might dreame himself a
bubble extending unto the eigth sphere. A litle water makes
a sea, a small puff of wind a Tempest, a graine of sulphur
kindled in the blood may make a flame like Aetna, and a
small spark in the bowells of Olympias a lightning over all   18
the chamber. Butt beside these innocent delusions there is
a sinfull state of dreames; death alone not sleepe is able to
putt an end unto sinne and there may bee a night booke of
our Iniquities, for beside the transgressions of the day,
casuists will tell us of mortall sinnes in dreames arising
from evill precogitations; meanewhile human lawe regards
not noctambulo's, and if a night walker should breake his
neck or kill a man, takes no notice of it.

Dionysius was absurdly tyrannicall to kill a man for dream-   19
ing that he had killed him, and really to take away his life
who had butt phantastically taken away his. Lamia* was   20
ridiculously unjust to sue a yong man for a reward, who had
confessed that pleasure from her in a dreame, which shee
had denyed unto his awaking senses, conceaving that shee
had merited somewhat from his phantasticall fruition and
shadowe of herself. If there bee such debts, wee owe deeply
unto sympathies, butt the common spirit of the world must
bee judg in such arrearages.

If some have swounded they may have also dyed in

* Plutarch.

dreames, since death is butt a confirmed swounding. Whether Plato dyed in a dreame* as some deliver hee must rise agayne to informe us; that some have never dreamed is as improbable as that some have never laughed. That children dreame not the first half yeare, that men dreame not in some Countries, with many more, are unto mee mere sick mens dreames, dreames out of the Ivorie gate,* and visions before midnight.

* Tertullian. [*De Anima*, 52,3.]

* Sunt geminae somni portae; the Ivory and the horny gate, false dreames out of the ivory gate, true out of the horny. [Virgil, *Aeneid*, 6, 893–98.]

[The Search for Truth]   †

There is nothing more acceptable unto the Ingenuous
world then this noble eluctation of truth, wherin agaynst
the tenacitie of prejudice custome and prescription this cen-
turie now prevayleth. What Vaticans of new works after
ages will behold, and in what a new world of knowledge the
eyes of our posteritie may bee happy, were half a resurrection to behold, and is a cold thought unto those, who cannot
hope to see this exantlation of truth, or that obscured virgin
half out of the pitt. Which might make some desire a commutation of time in their beings, or rest content with a
metempsuchosis whereby they might hope for this happinesse in their third or fourth selves, and behold that in
Pythagoras which they now foresee in Euphorbus.*
The world which tooke six days to make will take above
six thousand yeares to make out; meanetime old truths voted
downe beginne to take their places, and new ones arise upon
us, wherin there is no confort in the happines of Tullies
Elizium, and cold satisfaction to bee had from the ghosts of
Aristotle or the ancients. Men disparage not Antiquitie who
wisely exalt new enquiries, and make not them the judges of
truth butt fellowe enquirers of it. Who can butt honour the
endeavors of Aristotle and the noble start which Learning
and Arts had under him, or lesse then pitty the slender
progression thereof upon that notable advantage? While
many centuries were lost in repetitions and transcriptions
sealing up the booke of knowledge. And therefore rather then
to continue such tautologie in writing and merely to swell
the leaves of knowledge by trite and fruitlesse repetition,
to cuckoe out the same note in all ages, nor adventure at
essayes beyond the leaves of others, some had rather men   †
would write like Helmont or Paracelsus, and would en-

* *Ipse ego nam memini Troiani in tempore belli Panthoides Euphorbus eram.*

dure the monstrosities of some opinions, for divers singular notions requiting such aberrancies.

And therefore also to judge of mens works which were written at distant times of their lives, to make them out as genuine or spurious according as they containe repugnant or congruent conceptions, and to expect a constancy of opinions in former and after writings, is to forget the difference of men and students allowable for their successive enquiries; to presume in improveing heads an early stand in knowledge; nor to commend but disparage good Authors, whom they suppose in their yonger or middle yeares to have sett up their *non ultra* in knowledge. A constant tenour of discourse or strict uniformitie of sense and notions from the same elder and junior penns is only expectable from improficient heads; wherin supinitie, credulity, obstinacy, or self conceit affordeth no accretion.

The many men that every man is by the great varietie of tempers, inclinations, opinions, and apprehensions unto the age of man, makes a kind of metempsychosis before death, and makes good that Pythagoricall opinion in one generation and the same habitation of flesh. Time brings not only frequent repentancie in actions butt iterated resipiscency in opinions thoughts and notions. Even of what I now apprehend I have no settled assurance. These are my present thoughts this night in England; what they will prove tomorrow when I arise toward China,* I may bee yet to determine. †,21

[See also *Christian Morals,* 11.5]

* Which may bee sayd in some latitude upon the diurnall motion of the earth from west to east.

[Circumscriptions of Pleasure] †

Were there an Age of delight or any pleasure perpetuall, who would not bee an Epicure? Butt the race of delight is short and pleasures have mutable faces. The pleasures of our youthfull dayes draw sowre faces on our elder browes: and even in our most sensuall yeares the strength of pleasure is placed in its raritie and sting in its satietie; mediocrity is its life and immoderacy its destruction.

The old Luxurious emperours inconsiderately satiated themselves with the dainties of Sea and Land; till wearied through all their varieties their refections became a study unto them, and they were driven to feed by invention; and nauseating phaysants and partridges, they were fayne to descend unto despised dishes, and prove tasters unto common palates of the flesh of colts and Asses.

Novices in true Epicurisme, which by paucitie, raritie, and heal[th]ful appetite makes delights smartly acceptable; whereby old Epicurus found Jupiters brayne* in a peece of Cytheridian cheese, and in a dish of onyons the braynes of nightingales and peacocks.

Hereby healthfull povertie hath the start of satiated Luxurie, unto whose cleere and naked appetite, every meale is a feast, and in each common dish the first course of Metellus*: while Nero* half famisht could not deale with a peece of bread, and lingring after his snowed water, butt coldly gott downe an ordinarie cuppe of calda.

By such circumscriptions of pleasure, the contemned philosophers, in every sense reserved unto themselves the secret of delight, which the Helluo's of those times quite lost

* *Cerebrum Jovis* for a delightfull bitt.
* Metellus his riotous pontificiall supper the great varietie whereof to be seen in Macrobius.
* Nero in his flight. v. Sueton.

by their exorbitancies. In vayne wee study delight: it is at the command of every sober mind, and in every sense borne with us. Butt nature which teacheth us the rule of pleasure instructeth us also in the circumference and where the line thereof expireth. And therefore temperate minds not pressing their pleasures untill the sting appeareth, enjoy their contentations contentedly and without regret, which is one of the necessarie rewards of virtue, as the naturall punishment of excesse, to bee pleased unto displacency.

[See also *Christian Morals*, 11.1.]

The line of our lives is drawne with white and black vicissitudes, wherin the extremities hold seldome one complexion. That yong men are fortunate and performe notable actions is no observation of deepe wonder they having the strength of their fates before them, nor yet acted their parts in the world for which they were cheifly brought into it; whereas men of yeares seeme to bee beyond the vigour of their fortunes, and the high designes of the world providentially disposed unto ages best agreable unto them. And therefore many brave men discovering that their fates grew faynt, or feeling their declination, have timely withdrawn themselves from great attempts, and escaped the ends of mightie men dispropoportionable to their beginnings; wisely stopping about the meridian of their felicities, and unwilling to hazard the favours of the descending wheele, or to fight downwards in the setting arch of fortune.

Butt magnanimous and high flowne thoughts have so dimmed the eyes of many, that forgetting the very essence of fortune and vicissitude of good and evell, they conceave no bottome in felicitie, and so are tempted into mightie actions reserved for their destructions. Whereof I that have not seen the sixtieth part of time have beheld great examples.

Fortune layes the plot of our adversities on the foundation of our felicities; blessing us in the first quadrate to blast us more sharpely in the last: and since in the highest felicities there lyeth the capacitie of the lowest miseries, shee hath this advantage of our precedent happinesse, to make us truly miserable. And this is the observable cours not only in this visible stage of things butt may bee feared in our second beings and everlasting selves: wherin the good things past are seconded by the bad to come, and many unto whom the embraces of fortune are open heere may find Abrahams armes shutt unto them hereafter. Which makes serious considerators not so much to pittie as envy some mens infelicities, wherin considering the circle of both our beings and the succession of good unto evell, Tyranny may sometime prove courteous, and malice mercifully cruell.

By this method of providence the divell himself is deluded, who maligning us at all poynts, and beating felicitie from us even in this earthly being; hee becomes assistant unto our future happinesse, and blessed vicissitude of the next. And this is also the unhappinesse of himself: who having acted his first part in heaven is made sharpely miserable by transition, and more afflictively feeles the contrarie state of Hell.

[See also *Christian Morals,* 11.10 and 111.22.]

Many have studied to exasperate the wayes of death, butt
fewe howers have been spent to soften the last necessitie.
That the smoothest waye unto the grave is made by Bleeding,
as common opinion presumeth, the experiment in Lucan and
Seneca will make us doubt; under which the noble Stoick
so deepely labourd, that hee was fayne to retire from the
sight of his wife, to conceale the affliction thereof: and was
not ashamed to implore the mercifull hand of his physitian,
to shorten his miserie therin. Nor will they readily bee of
that beleif who behold the sick and fainting Languors which
accompany the effusion of blood, when it proceedeth unto
death.

Ovid,* the old Heroes, and the Stoicks who were so afrayd
of drowning, as dreadinge thereby the extinction of their
Soules, which they conceaved to bee fire, stood surely in
feare of an easier way of death wherin the water entring the
possessions of ayer makes a temperate suffocation, and kills
as it were without a fever.

Surely many who have had the spirit to destroy themselves, have not bee ingenious in the contrivance. Twas a
dull way practised by Themistocles to overwhelme himself
with Bulls blood, who being an Athenian might have held
an easier Theorie of death from the authentick and state
potion of his country; from which Socrates seemed not to
suffer more then from the fitt of an Ague. Cato is much to
bee pittied who mangled himself with poyniards; and Hannibal seemes more subtle, who caryed his deliverie, not in
the poynt, butt the pummell* of his sword.

The Aegyptians were mercifull contrivers, who destroyed

* *Demito naufragium, mors mihi munus erit.*
* Wherin hee is sayd to have caryed a something that might upon a straight
despach and deliver him from all misfortunes.

their malefactors by Aspes, charming their senses into an irrecoverable sleep, and killing as it were with Hermes his rod. The Turkish Emperour odious for other crueltie was herin a remarkable master of mercy; killing his favourite in his sleepe, and sending him from the shade into the howse of darknesse. Hee that had been thus destroyed, would hardly have bled at the presence of his destroyer, where men are alreadie dead by metaphor, and passe butt from one sleepe unto another; wanting herin the eminent part of severitie to bee made to feele themselves dye: and escaping the sharpest attendant of death, the lively apprehension thereof.

[See also *Christian Morals*, 11.13.]

The virtuous parts or eccelencies both of men and nations are allowable by aggregation and must bee considered by coacervation as well as single merit. The Romans performed much of their conquest by the conquered; and the valour of all nations made up the glorie of Rome. So the poets which writ in Latin built up the credit of Latium, and passed for Roman witts. Whereas if Carthage deducted Terence, Aegypt Claudian, if Marseilles should call home Petronius, if the Senecas, Lucan, Martial and Statius should be restored unto Spayne, it would much abridge the glory of pure Italian phancy. And even in Italy it self if the Cisalpine Gauls should take away their share, if Verona and Mantua should challenge Virgil and Catullus, if in other parts out of Campagnia di Roma the Venusine Apulians should call away their Horace, the Umbrians their Plautus, the Aquinations Juvenal, the Volaterians Persius, and the Pelignians of Abruzzo their Ovid, the rest of Rome or Latium would make no large volume.

[Intention, Imitation, Coincidence]

Many things are casually or favorably superadded unto the best Authors and the Lines of many made to containe that advantageous sense and exposition which was never intended by them. In that flattering expression of Lucan concerning Nero—

Aetheris immensi spatium si presseris altrum sentiet axis onus   22

—some would have it, and the inward sense will beare it, to have been a close jeere at Neros fatt and swaggy belly. It was handsomely said by Virgil *una dolo Divum si foemina*   23 *capta duorum* and probably intended by him that in every word there should be a considerable emphasis. Nor is it unlikely that in another consisting of slowe and heavy spondays,° hee intended to humour the heaving stroakes of the gigantick forgers. Butt that another verse° should beare such a numerous transposition of words as may bee observed in it: that a second should prove a retrograde verse,° and a third° from the numerall disposition of its vowells should afford a ground for that handsome trick at cards (now in use and well knowne) of singling out Turks from Christians, it may rather bee ascribed to after invention and casuallie, then unto the first intention.

Conceats and expressions are sometimes common unto divers Authors and of different countries and ages, and that not by imitation butt coincidence and concurrence of imagination upon some harmony of production. Different men have had the same dreames, and divers plants have been thought to bee peculiar unto some one country, yet upon better discoverie the same have been found in distant regions

° *illi inter sese magna vi brachia tollunt.*   24
° *Tot tibi sunt dotes virgo quot sydera caelo.*   25
° *Musa mihi causas memora quo numine laeso.*   26
° *populeam virgam mater regina ferebat.*   27

and under all communitie of parts. Scaliger* observes how
one Italian poet fell upon the same verse with another, and
that a man who had never read Martiall made a verse which
was to bee found in him. Thus it is lesse strange that Homer
should sometimes Hebraize and that many sentences in human Authors seeme to have had their originall in Scripture.
In a peece of myne* published long ago the Learned and   †,†
civill Annotator hath paralleld many passages with others in
Mountaignes Essayes, whereas, to deale cleerely, when I
penned that peece I had scarce read six leaves in that Author, and scarce so much ever since.

* Scaliger in *Quaestionibus familiaribus. Extra fortunam est quicquid*   28
donatur amicis.
  * *Rel. Med.*

[Guardian Angels]

The learned Gaspar Schottus dedicates his *Thaumaturgus Mathematicus* unto his tutelary or Guardian Angell, in which epistle he useth these words; *cui post deum conditorem* [29] *deique magnam matrem mariam omnia debo.* Now though wee must not loose God in good Angells or, because their presence is allwayes supposed about us, hold lesse memorie of the omnipresency of God in our prayers and addresses for his care and protection over us: yett they who do assert such spirits do find something out of Scripture and Antiquitie for them. Butt whether the Angel which wrasled with Jacob [30] were Esaus good angel; whether our Saviour on earth had one deputed unto him, or whether that was his good Angel which appeared and strengthened him before his passion; whether Anti-christ shall have any, whether all men have one, some more; whether these Angells do guard successively and distinctly unto one person after another or whether butt once and singly butt one person at all; whether wee are under the care of our mothers good Angell in the womb or whether that spirit undertakes us when the starres are thought to concerne us, that is at our nativities, men have a libertie and latitude to opinion.

[A Letter to a Friend]   †

[Section numbers added by editor.]

S^r   †

1. I am sorry you vnderstood so litle concerning that
worthy gentleman your deare freind & that I must also performe that vnwelcome office to tell you Ad portam rigidos
calces extendit, hee is dead & buried & by this time no
punie in the famous nations of the dead. For though he left
this world not many dayes ago, yet euery hower largely
addeth vnto that dark societie. & considering the incessant
mortallity of mankind you cannot well conceaue there dyeth
in the whole world fewer then a thousand an hower.

2. Though at this distance you had no particular information of his death yet your affection may cease to wonder you
had nott some sense or intimation thereof by dreames,
visions, sympathicall communications or thoughtfull whisperings which diuers seeme to haue had at the death of their
dearest freinds. For since wee read in that famous story
that spirits themselues were fayne to tell their fellowes at a
distance that the great Antonio was comming; wee haue sufficient excuse for our ignorance in such poynts, nor can wee
well looke for such secret insinuations but must rest content
in the vsuall way of knowledge by information.

3. Though the incertainty of the worlds end hath confounded all human prediction yet they wch shall liue to see
the sunne & moone darkened & the starres to fall from heauen
will hardly be deceaued in the approach of the last daye.
And therefore somewhat strange it is that the common fallacy of consumptiue persons who feele not themselues to

dye & therefore still hope for life should also reach their freinds in perfect health & iudgement; that you should bee so litle acquainted with Plautus sick complexion or that an Hippocraticall face could not alarum you vnto higher feares or rather despayre of his continuance among vs vnder such languishing emaciations, wherin medicall predictions fayle not as sometimes in acute diseases, and wherin tis as dangerous to bee condemned by a physitian as a Iudge.

4. Hee was fruitlesly putt in hope of aduantage by change of ayre and therefore being so farre spent hee quickly found Sardinia in Tibur & the most healthfull ayre of litle effect where death had set his broad arrowe, for he liued not vnto the middle of May & confirmed the obseruation of Hippocrates of that mortall time of the yeare when the figge tree putts forth his leaf like vnto a choughs clawe. ✕   †

5. Angelus Victorius* giues a serious account of a consumptiue tabid hecticall & phthysicall woeman who was suddenly cured by the intercession of Ignatius: wee read not of any in Scripture who in this case applyed vnto our Sauiour, though some might bee contained in that expression, that hee went about Galilie* healing all manner of sicknesse and all manner of disease. Amulets, spells sigills & incantations commended in other diseases are seldom or neuer pretended agaynst this, and wee find no Sigill in the Archidoxis of Paracelsus to cure a consumption or marasmus. which if other diseases fayle must make an end of the longest liuers & putt a period euen vnto oaks and cedars: so that the stoicks could not butt think the firy principle would weare out all the rest and at last make an end of the world. which without such a lingring period the creatour may do at his pleasure and to make an end of all things on earth & the planeticall systeme of the world hee need not butt putt out the sunne.

6. At my first visit of him I was bold to tell his freinds who had not lett fall all hope of his recouery that in my sad opin-

* Angeli Victorii consultationes.
* Mathewe 4/23.

ion he was not like to behold a grassehopper agayne much
lesse to tast another figge. and though it bee not vsual with
mee to forgett the face of freinds yet to knowe him without
doubt I was fayne to looke twice vpon him & withall I seemd
to discouer in him that odde mortall symptome not mentioned by Hippocrates. for hee maintained not his owne
countenance butt looked like his grandmother the lines of
whose face lay deep & inuisibly in his healthfull face before.

7. In this consumptiue condition & remarkable emaciation
hee came to bee almost half himself and left a great part
behind him which hee caryed not to the graue: And though
it bee not easie to giue a full assent vnto the account (story)
of Count Ernestus Mansfeild that after his death his heart
was found to bee no bigger then a wallnutt, yet if the bones
of a good sceleton waigheth litle more then twentie pounds,
surely his bowells & flesh remaining could make butt a light
course & a short bitt for corruption in St. Innocents church-
yard. I neuer more liuely beheld the starued characters of
Dante in any liuing face. an Aruspex might haue read a lecture upon him without exenturation. so that to bee caryed
sexta ceruice to the graue was butt a ciuill vnnecessity; and
the complements of the coffin might outwaygh the subiect of
it.

8. Though wee could not haue his life yet wee had our desires in his soft departure, which was scarce an expiration.
with what strift and paynes wee come into the world wee
knowe not and tis commonly no easie matter to get out of it.
butt if it could bee made out, that such as haue an easie
natiuity haue commonly a hard death, and contrarily; his departure was so easie, that wee might iustly suspect his birth
was of another nature and that some Iuno satt crosse legd at
his natiuity.

9. I was not so curious to intitle the fixed starres to any concerne in his death yet could not butt obserue that hee dyed
when the moone was descending from the meridian at which
time an old Italian long ago would persuade mee that the
greatest part of men dyed. butt herin I confesse I could neuer

satisfie my curiositie. allthough from the time of tides in places upon or neere the sea there may bee considerable deductions.

10. In the yeares of his childhood hee had languished vnder the disease of his country the Rickets. after which notwithstanding I haue seen many to haue become strong & actiue men. butt whether any who haue had the same haue attained vnto very great yeares, the disease is not yet so old as to afford good obseruation. Whether Lameness & halting still encreaseth among the inhabitants of Rouigno in Istria I do not vnderstand, yet not twentie yeares ago Monsr de Loyre obserued upon the place that a third part of the inhabitants halted. butt to[o] certaine it is that the Rickets encreaseth among us, the small pox growes more pernicious then the great, the Kings purse knoweth that the Kings euell growes more common: and though the ancients giue that disease good words*, it is not now rare to heare the bell ring out for such as dye of Quartans. Yet the sound of a bell is not strange that rings out for a Quartan ague.   †

11. Some I obserued to wonder how in this tabid con-   †
sumptiue state his hayre held on so well without that considerable defluuium which is one of the last symptomes in such diseases: butt they took not notice of a mark in his face which if hee had liued was a probable security agaynst baldnesse if the obseruation of Aristotle will hold that persons are lesse apt to be bald who are double chinnd;* nor of the   31
varices or knotted veynes in his legge which they that haue, in the same authors assertion are lesse disposed to baldnesse.

12. Though the beard bee only made a distinction of sex and signe of masculine heat by Vlmus yet the precocitie & early comming thereof in him was not to bee liked in reference vnto long life. Lewis that virtuous butt butt vnhappy King of Hungary who was lost at the battail of Mohacz was sayd to bee borne without a skinne, to haue bearded at fifteen

---

* Ἀσφαλέστατος και ῥήιστος Febrium securissima et facillima. Hippocrates.
* According as Theodorus Gaza renders it though Scaliger reades the text otherwise.

& to haue begunne to showe some graye hayres about
twentie, whereby the Diuiners coniectured that hee should
be spoyled of his kingdom, and haue butt a short life. butt
many persons wee haue knowne early graye who haue out-
liued Dauids period. Though hayres afford butt fallible   †
coniectures yet wee cannot butt take notice of them. They
growe not equally in bodyes after death. Woemens sculls
afford mosse as well as mens. and the best I haue seen was
upon a woemans scull taken up and layd in a roome after 25
yeares buriall. Though the skinne bee made the place of
hayres, yet sometimes they are found on the heart and inward parts. The plica or elues locks happen vnto both sexes
& being cutt of will come agayne. butt they are wary in cutting the same, for feare of headach & other diseases. Hayres
which most amused mee were those in the Morgellons an
endemicall disease of litle children in Languedoc which
some times in sharp distempers breake out with harsh hayres
on their backs wch takes of the vnquiet symptomes of the
disease & preserues from conuulsions & coughs.

   13. That Charles the fift was crowned upon the daye of his
natiuity, it being in his power to order it so makes no singular animaduersion; butt that hee should also take king Francis
prisoner upon that day was a notable coincidence that made
the same obseruable. King Antipater who had an anniuersary
feuer euery yeare on his birthday and dyed at last on the
same day needed not an Astrologicall reuelation to knowe
what daye hee should dye on. When the fixed starres haue
made a reuolution vnto the place from whence they first sett
out, some of the Antients thought the world would haue an
end, which was a kind of dying upon the daye of its natiuity.
Now the disease preuayling about the time of his birth many
were of the opinion that hee would leaue the world on the
daye hee entred into it. butt this being a lingring disease and
creeping softly on, nothing criticall was expected or found on
that daye, and hee dyed fifteen dayes after. To dye upon the
day and euen hower of their natiuity is ordinarie in many
ephemerous children and such as see butt one day. butt in
those who outliue many yeares and when there are 3 hundred

sixtie fiue dayes to determine our liues in euery yeare; that
the first day should make the last, that the tayle of the snake
should returne into its mouth precisely at that time and wee
should wind up upon the day of our birth is indeed a remarkable coincidence and such which though Astrologie hath
taken witty paynes to resolue, yet hath it been very warie in
making predictions of it.

14. Affection had so blinded some of his neerest relations   †
as to retaine some hope of a postliminious life and that hee
might come to life agayne and therefore would not haue had
him coffind before the third daye. Some such Virbiusses I   32
confesse wee find in story and one or two I remember my
self butt they liued not long after. Such contingent reuiuic-
tions are to bee hoped in diseases wherin the lamp of life is
butt puft out or seemingly choaked, & not where the oyle is
quite spent & exhausted. Though Nonnus will haue it a feuer,
yet what disease Lazarus first dyed of is vncertaine from the
text as his second death from good Authentick history, but
since some persons conceaued to bee dead do sometimes return agayne vnto evidence of life, that miracle was wisely
managed by our Sauiour. for had hee not been dead 4 dayes
& vnder corruption, there had not wanted enough who would
haue cauilled the same. which the scripture now putts out
of doubt & tradition also confirmeth. That hee liued thirtie
yeares after and being pursued by the Iewes came by sea
into Prouence by Marseilles with Marie Magdalen Maximinus
& others where remarkable places carry their names or memories vnto this daye. butt to arise from the graue to returne
agayne vnto it is but an vnconfortable reuiuiction; few men
would be content to cradle it once agayne. Except a man   †
could lead his second life better then the first a man may be
doubly condemned for liuing euelly twice. which were butt to
make the second death in Scripture the third and to accumu-
late in the punishment of 2 bad liues at the last daye. To   †
haue performed the duty of corruption in the graue, to liue
agayne as farre from sinne as death and arise like our sauiour
for euer, are the only satisfactions of well wayghed expectations.

15. In this deliberate & creeping progresse vnto his end, hee was somewhat to[o] yong and of to[o] noble a mind to fall into that stupid accident (symptome) obseruable in diuers neere their iourneys end & proues a mortall symptome (signe) in their last sicknesse: that is to bee narrowe minded parsimonious miserable & tenacious, vnready to part with anything when they are ready to part with all and afrayd to want when they haue butt a few dayes or howers of life to spend anything they haue when they haue no time to spend. †

Meanewhile physitians who knowe that many are mad but in a single depraued imagination and one preualent dicipiencie and that out of this single delirium, a man may meet with sober actions & good sense in Bedlam, cannot butt smile to see the heirs & concerned relations to gratulate themselues in the sober departure of their freinds, and though they behold such couetous & mad passages are content to think they dye in good vnderstanding & in their sober senses. Auarice which is not only Idolatrie butt infidelity, ether from couetous progenie or questuary education, had no root in his brest who made good works the expression of his fayth and was bigge with desires to publick & lasting charities. & surely where good wishes and charitable intentions exceed abillities, theoricall beneficency may bee more then a dreame. They build not castles in the ayre who would build churches upon earth & though they leaue no such structures here may lay good foundations in heauen.

16. Iulius Scaliger who in a sleeplesse fitt of the gout could make 2 hundred verses in a night would haue butt fiue plaine words upon his tomb.* and this serious person though no minor poet left the poetrie of his epitaph vnto others ether vnwilling to commend himself, or to bee iudged by a distich. and perhaps considering how vnhappy great poets haue been in versifying their own epitaphs. wherein Petrarcha Dante & Ariosto haue so vnhappily fayled that if their tombs should outlast their works posterity would find so litle of Apollo in them as to mistake them butt for Ciceronian poets.

* Iulii Ca'saris Scaligeri quod fuit.

17. Nether to feare death nor desire it was not his resolution, to bee dissolued & bee with Christ was his sick dittie.
Though his yeares were not many yet would he often com-
playne nimio de stamine and thought he had liued to[o] long   33
to see on earth one Lustre more then his Sauiour. his life
and death were such that I would not blame them who
wished to [be] like him and almost to haue been himself. al-   †
most I say; for though wee may wish the prosperous appurtenances of others, or to bee another, in his happy accidents,
yet so intrinsecall is cuory man vnto himself, that some doubt
may bee made whether any one would exchange his being or
substantially become another man.

18. Hee had wisely seen the world at home and abroad and
therin obserued vnder what varietie men are madly deluded
in the pursuit of that which is not heare to bee found. And
though he had no opinion of reputed felicities belowe &
thought men were widely out in the estimate of such happinesse, yet his sober contempt of the world wrought no De-
mocritisme or cynicisme no laughing or snarling at it. There
are not reall felicities enough in nature to satisfie a serious
mind. and therefore to soften the streame of our liues, wee are
fayne to take in the receaued contentations of the world, to
vnite with the crowd in their beatitudes, & so make ourselues
happy by consortion, opinion, & coimagination: for strictly to
separate from reputed and customarie felicities and to confine
vnto the rigour of reallities were to contract the consolation
of our beings vnto confortlesse circumscriptions.

19. Though age had not set his seale of yeares vpon his face
yet a dimme eye (sight) might haue cleerely discouered
three score in his Actions & so although his yeares were not
many hee might bee sayd to haue equalld the dayes of longer
liuers, since in the compute of Solomon° wisedome is the gray
hayre vnto men and an vnspotted life is old age. And certainly if wee deduct all those dayes which wee might wish
vnliued, & which take away the confort of those wee now
liue: if wee reckon only those dayes wch god hath accepted

° Wisedome 4.

of our liues, the thred of our dayes at fourscore will hardly
bee a spanne long, the sonne in this sence may bee elder then
the father, and none bee climacterically old. Hee that early
arriueth vnto the parts and prudence of age is happily old
without the vnconfortable marks of it. tis superfluous to liue
vnto graye hayres when in a timely (precocious) complexion
wee anticipate the virtues of them. hee cannot bee accounted
yong who outliueth the old man. hee that hath early arriued
vnto the measure of a perfect stature in Christ hath fulfilled
the best & longest intention of his being. and one day liued
after the perfect rule of piety is to bee preferred before peccant (sinning) immortallity.

20. Lastly though hee attained not vnto the yeares of his †
predecessors yet hee wanted not those preseruing virtues
which confirmes & strengthens the thred of doubtfull constitutions. Cautelous chastitie & cunning sobrietie were far from
him. These virtues were paragon without hayre Ice spot or
blemish in him, which affords me a hint to conclude in these
good wishes vnto you. Tread softly and circumspectly in this
funambulatory tract and narrow path of goodnesse. pursue
virtue virtuously. bee sober and temperat, not to preserue
your body in a sufficiency for wanton ends, not to spare your
purse, not to bee out of the obliquie of common transgressors
that way, or thereby to balance or palliat obscure and closer
vices, nor simply to enioy health. by all which you may leuen
good actions and render virtues disputable; butt in one word
that you may truly serue god, which euery sicknesse will tell
you (you) cannot well do without health; the sick mans sacrifice is butt a leane (lame) offering. treasures of pietie layd
up in healthfull dayes excuse the defect and impotency of sick
performances; without which wee must needs looke back
with anxietie upon the lost opportunities of health and may
haue cause rather to enuy then pitty the ends of paenitent
malefactors, who come with cleare parts vnto their last act,
and in the integrity of their faculties returne their spirit vnto
god that gaue it.

LETTERS

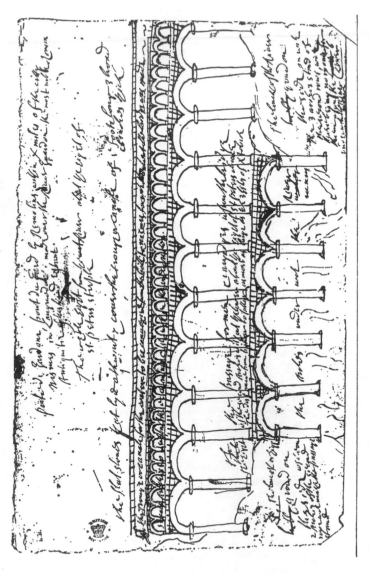

Reproduction of a drawing by Sir Thomas Browne of the Pont du Gard, called "the most noble Roman Antiquitie of this kind extant." From BM Add. MS 5233, folio 58, by courtesy of the British Museum.

Dec: 22, Norwich, [1660].

[To Thomas Browne]

Honest Tom,

I hope by Gods assistance you have been some weeks in Boardeaux. I was yesterday at Yarmouth, where I spoke with yr Unckle Charles Mileham, who told me Mr. Dade would accomodate you with what moneys wore fitting for defray of yr Charges in any kind & therefore would not have mee at Present send you any bill to receive any perticuler summ, but however when I hear from you I will take care for such a bill to be sent to Mr. Dade to whom in the mean time present my true respects & service & be sure to be observant of what he shall advice you; be as good a husband as Possible and enter not upon any course of superfluous expences, be not dejected and malencholy because you can yet have litle Comfort in Conversation, & all things will seem strange unto you. Remember the Camells back & be not troubled for anything that other ways would trouble yr Patience here, be courteous and Civil to all, but [put] on a decent boldness and avoid pudor Rusticus, not much known in France, hold firm to the Protestant Religion and be diligent in goeing to Church when you have any Litle Knowledge of the Language. God will accept of yr desires to serve him in his Publick worship, tho you cannot make it out to yr desires, be constant not negligent in yr dayly private prayers & habituate yr heart in yr tender days unto the fear and reverence of God. It were good you had a map of France that you might not be unacquainted with the severall parts & to resort unto upon occation for yr information; view & understand all notable buildings and places in Bourdeaux or near it, & take a draught thereof, as also the ruind Amphitheatre, but these at yr leisure. There is I think a book in French cal'd le[s] Monuments or les Antiquites de Bourdea[u]x, enquire of the same; read some books of French and Latin, for I would by no means yu should loose yr Latin but rather gain more.

Ned comes not home this Xtmas. I shall God willing re-   3
member yr New Years gift, give me an account of yr voyage
by sea as Perticuler as you Can, for I doubt you had a rough
Passage; be temperate in dyet and wary to overheat yr self;
remember to Comprimere et non Extendere labra; to Gods   4
Providence I commit you.

Vostre tres Chere Pere,
Tho Browne

I have sent a litle box by this ship.

Aprill the 22, Norwich, [1661]

[To Thomas Browne]   †
Honest Tom,
    I hope by this time thou art got some what beyond plaist
il, and ouy Monsieur, & durst ask a question & give an Answer
in French, & therefore now I hope you goe to the Protestant
Church, to which you must not be backward, for tho there
Church order & discipline be different from ours, yet they
agree with us in doctrine and the main of Religion; endeavor
to write French, that will teach you to understand it well; you
should have signified the Apotica[r]y[s] name with whom
you dwell; in such a place you may see the drugs and remember them all yr life. I received yr letter and like yr discription of the Place, both the Romans & English have Lived
there; the name of Santonna, now Xaintes, is in the geographie of Ptolomie, who lived under Antoninus, as also Porto
Santonicus where Rochell stands, and Promontorium San-
tonicum where now Bloys. My coynes are encreased since you
went, I had 60 coynes of King Stephen found in a grave before Christmas, 60 Roman silver coyns I bought a month agoe,
& Sr Robart Paston will send me his box of Saxon & Roman   5
coyns next week wch are about thirtie, so that I would not
beg any there except some few Choice ones wch I have not
already, but you doe very well to see all such things; some
likely have Collections wch they will in Courtesie show, as
also urns & Lachrimatories, any freind will help you to a sight
thereof, for they are not nice in such things. I should be con-

tent you should see Rochell, & the Isle of Rhee salt works
are not far from you, for the sommer will be too hot to travail
and I would have you wary to expose yr self then to heats,
but to keep quiet and in shades; write some times to Mr Dade
Civel Letters with my service. I send at this time by Rochell
whither the ships will be passing from Yarmouth for Salt;
point yr Letters hereafter, I mean the ends of Sentences.
Christ Church is in a good condition, much freqented, and [6]
they have a sweet Organ; on Tuesday next is the Coronation
day when Mr. Bradford Preacheth, it will be observed with
great solemnity Especially at London; a new Parliment on
the 8th of May and there is a very good Choice almost in all
places. Cory the Recorder and Mr Jay, 2 Royallists gaind it
here against all opposition that could possibly bee made, the
voices in this number, Jay 1070, Corie 1001, Barnham 562,
Church 436.

My Lord Richardson and Sr Ralph Hare caryed it in the
County without opposition. Lent was observed this year wch
made Yarmouth and fishermen rejoyce; the Militia is setled in
good hands through all England, besides volunteer troops of
hors; in this Citty Collonel Sr Joseph Pain, Lieutenant Coll:
Jay, Major Bendish, Captain Wiss, Brigs, Scottow, 2 volunteer
troops in the Country under Mr Knivet, and Sr Horace Town-
send, who is made a Lord. Good boy doe not trouble thy self
to send us any thing either wine or Bacon. I would have sent
money by Exchange, but Charles Mileham would not have
me send any Certain sum, but what you spend shall be made
good by him. I wish some Person would direct you for a while
for the true Pronounsation & writeing of French; by noe means [7]
forget to encrease yr Latin, be Patient Civel & debonair unto
all, be Temperate and stir litle in the hot season; by the books
sent, you may understand most that has pasd since yr departure, & you may now read the French Gazets wch come out
weekly. Yesterday the Dean Preachd and red the Liturgie or
Common Prayer, & had a Comunion at Yarmouth as haveing
a right to doe so some times, both at St Marys, the great
Church at Lynn, & St Nicholas Church at Yarmouth, as he is
dean; it is thought by degrees most will come to Conformitie;

there are great preparations against tomorrow the Coronation
day, the County hors came hither to joyn the Regiment of
foot of this Citty, a feast at the new hall, generall contribu-
tions for a feast for the Poor, wch they say will be in the Market Place, long & solemn service at Christ Church beginning
at 8 a clock & with a sermon ending at twelve, masts of ships
and long stageing Poles already set up for becon bon fires,
speeches and a litle play by the schollers in the Market Place,
an other by young Cittyzens at Timber hill on a stage, Cromwell hangd and burnt evrywhere, whose head is now upon   8
Westminster hall, together with Ireton & Bradshows. Have
the love and fear of God ever before thine eyes, God Confirm
yr faith in Christ and that you may live accordingly, Je vous
recommende a dieu. If you meet with any Pretty insects of
an[y] kind keep them in a box, if you can send les Antiquites de Bourdeaux by any ship, it may come safe.

                                                          [July, 1663]
    [To Edward and Thomas Browne]   †
Ned & Tom god blesse you,
    I am glad thou hast performed thy exercises with credit   9
though they have proved very chargeable. Tom bensley is
much satisfied with his Journey. I am going out of towne & I
doubt returne not till Monday, & so I must bee breif & have
only time to present my service to all freinds Mr Bridge Mr
Nurse & Mr Craven. Our Assises begin not till August. Take
notice of the extraordinarie overthrowe given to the Span-   10
iards by the Portugues.
    Honest Tom bee of good heart & followe thy buisinesse. I
doubt not butt thou wilt doe well. God hath given thee parts
to enable thee. If you practise to write you will have a good
pen & style. It were not amisse to take the draught of the col-
leg or part thereof if you have time, butt however omitt
no opportunitie in your studie. You shall not want while I
have it.
                        Your Loving father Tho Browne.

[February, 1667]

For Mr Thomas Browne Lieutenant of his Majesties Shippe
the Marie Rose riding in Plimmouth Sound †

I receaved yours & would not deferre to send unto you
before you sayled, wch I hope will come unto you; for in this
wind, nether can Reare Admirall Kempthorne come to you,
nor you beginne your voyage. I am glad you like Lucan so
well; I wish more military men could read him. In this passage 11
you mention there are noble straynes & such as may well affect generous minds. Butt I hope you are more taken with
the verses then the subject, and rather embrace the expression then the example. And this I the rather hint unto you,
because the like, though in another waye, is sometimes practised in the Kings shipps; when in desperate cases they blowe
up the same. For though I know you are sober & considerative,
yet knowing you also to bee of great resolution; & having also
heard from ocular testimonies with what undaunted & persevering courage you have demeaned yourself in great difficulties, & knowing your Captaine to bee a stout & resolute man,
& withall the cordiall freindshippe that is between you: I cannot omitt my earnest prayers unto god to deliver you from
such a temptation. Hee that goes to warre, must patiently
submitt unto the various accidents thereof. To bee made a
prisoner by an unequal and overruling power, after a due
resistance, is no disparagement; butt upon a carelesse sur-
prizall or faynt opposition, and you have so good a memory
that you cannot forgett many examples thereof, even of the
worthiest commanders in your beloved Plutark. God hath
given you a stout, but a generous and mercifull heart withall,
& in all your life you could never behold any person in miserie
butt with compassion & relief; wch hath been notable in you
from a child. So have you layd up a good foundation for Gods
mercy, & if such a disaster should happen hee will without
doubt mercifully remember you. However let god that
brought you into the world in his owne good time lead you
thorough it, & in his own season bring you out of it, & without
such wayes as are displeasing unto him. When you are at
Cales, see if you can get a box of the Jesuitts powder at easie 12,13

rate & bring it in the bark, not in powder. I am glad you have receaved the bill of exchange for Cales, if you should find occasion to make use thereof. Enquire farther at Tangier of the minerall water you told mee wch was neere the toune & whereof many made use. Take notice of such plants as you meet with ether upon the Spanish or African coast & if you knowe them not, putt some leaves into a booke, though care-lessely, and not with that neatenesse as in your booke at Norwich.

Enquire after any one who hath been at Fez, and learne what you can of the present state of that place, wch hath been so famous in the discription of Leo & others. The merci- ¹⁴ full providence of god go with you. Impellant animae lintea ¹⁵ Thraciae.

Your Loving father
Thomas Browne.

Febr. 25 [1676?]

[To Edward Browne]   †
D. S.

My neibour Mr Bickerdike going towards London to mor-rowe I would not deny him a Letter, and I have sent by him Lucretius his six bookes de rerum natura, because you lately sent mee a quotation out of that Author, that you might have one by you to find out quotations wch shall considerably offer themselves at any time. Otherwise I do not much recommend the reading or studying of it, there being divers impieties in it, and tis no credit to bee to[o] punctually versed in it[;] it containeth the epicurean naturall philosophie. Mr Tenison ¹⁶ I told you had written a good poem, contra hujus saeculi Lucretianos, illustrating Gods wisdome & providence from Anatomie, & the rubrick and use of parts in a manuscript dedicated to mee & Dr Lawson in Latin after Lucretius his ¹⁷ style. With it goes along a very litle Tullies offices, which was either yours or your brothers. Tis as remarkable for the litle sise as the good matter contained in it, and the authentick and classicall Latin. I hope you do not forgett to carry a Greeke Testament allwayes to church; you have also the

Greek or septuagint translation of the other parts of Scripture. In reading those bookes a man learnes 2 good things together & profiteth doubly, in the languadge, and the subject. You may at the beginning of Lucretius read his life prefixed by Peter Crinitus, a learned philologer or Humanist, & that hee [18] proved mad & dyed by a philtrum or poculum amoris given him by his wife Lucillia. Mr Tho Peck and his good wife are dead; shee dyed in child bed some 8 or X moneths past. Hee left this life about a moneth agoe. Hee found obstacles that hee could not come to Skickford without compounding with the widdowe in possession for a thousand pound, though his father Mr James Peck parted with his owne share upon tolerable termes unto Mr Thomas. Hee lived in Norwich, was growne very fatt, & dranck much; they saye hee dranck dayly a quart bottle of clarett before dinner one at dinner and one at night. If any company came to him which was seldome hee might exceed that quantitie. However hee made an end of that proportion by himself; hee dyed suddenly none being with him. His daughter finding him indisposed asked whether shee should send for mee, hee putt it of, & soon after was found dead. Hee had litle or no money in his howse, his father James sent ten pounds for his buryall which served the turne. Surely if hee had lived a litle longer hee would have utterly spoyled his brayne & been lost unto all conversation. Happy is the temperate man, God send all my freinds that virtue. God blesse my daughter Fairfax my daughter Browne & the litle ones.

YLFTB.

April 25 [1679].

[To Edward Browne]

D S

I have litle to write butt because I have not writt this weeke before, I would not omitt a fewe Lines. I have had a great cough wch tooke mee about a moneth since & in a weeke the Rheume grewe ripe butt of a sudden grewe thinne agayne & proved of exceeding molestation day & night & the wether all the while was very sharpe & wind at north east

butt God be thancked, it is well abated & butt seldome trou-
blesome. My daughter Betty who is very seldome out of
health though shee sitts often in cold wether 5 or 6 howers
together in her closett reading & praying, & in all wethers &
seasons never omitts to go to church, sundayes & weekedayes
to sermons & prayers in our parish fell into a very extreme
waye, whereof God bee thancked shee is now newly recov-
ered. I presume your time of Reading will bee about a fort-   19
night hence; bee therefore provided & have your speec[h]es
memoriter, & pronounce them not fast butt distinctly & like
an orator, with their due pauses & words with their proper
emphases. Most of our gentlemen & witnesses concerning the
election are ether returned or returne tomorrowe. The day of
election for a newe choyce of the Knights for Norfolk will
bee on Monday come sevenight. Sr John Hobart Sr Christopher Calthorp & Sr Neville Catelyn stand agayne, & also Mr
Windham of Felbrigge. There is like to bee very great en-
deavoring for the places, wch will still keepe open divisions
wch were to wide before, & make it a countrey of Guelphs &   20
Ghibellines. I am sorry to find my Lord of Aylesbury left out   21
of the list of the privie counsellors, hee being so worthy &
able a person & so well qualified for the publick good. Tom
presents his duty. My love & blessing unto you all.

                                        Y L F T B.

                                              April 28 [1679].
    [To Edward Browne]   †
    D. S:
    A Norwich man in London sent a letter hither to a freind
to this effect, that being at a Coffie howse hee sawe Mr Rob.
Bendish in a high distraction breaking windowes and doing
outrageous things so that they were fayne to laye hold of him;
what become of him afterwards hee sayth nothing. This came
to his fathers eare who is much troubled at it, butt can do
very litle for him having been at great charges for him before.
Now if you heare of any such distraction or what is become
of him you may give a touch thereof in any of your Letters,
butt I would not urge you to be buisine therein, butt I heare

my brother Bendish hath allreadie writt to a freind to informe
him of the truth thereof, wch is like to bee done before you
can say anything in a Letter from London. These are the sad
ends of many dissolute & governelesse persons, who, if they
bee of a sheepish temper runne into melancholy or fatuity
and if proud haughtie & obstinate into maniacall madnesse. I
am glad you left Madame Cropley better. You had the opportunity to see the shipps and forts upon the river. I am glad
there is so strong a shippe built at Wolleige & a large shippe
of a second rate. I wish wee had half a dosen of them. The
bill agaynst popery is intended to be very severe, butt the ²²
howse of Lords will moderate it, and whether the King will
allowe of it, it is yet uncertaine; or what execution there will
bee of it may bee as doubtfull. The deferring of the triall of
our election may much incommodate the gentlemen who
went up for witnesses & also encrease the charge & how matters will bee determined wee are but uncertaine. Monday is
the day appoynted, butt whether it will not be putt of to a
day farther wee are in doubt. Litle Tom comes loaded from
the fayre this day & wishes his sister had some of them. God
blesse you all. I rest,

Y L F.
T B.

Take notice of the sea horse skinne.

May 7, [1679]. †

[To Edward Browne]
D. S.
   It is not well contrived by the Chirurgeons that you are at
such uncertainties about your Lectures, and it will bee very
inconvenient to beginne the Lectures on Saturday, by reason
of Sunday intervening; & the hard keeping of the body in
this warme and moyst wether, butt I remember you read so
once before, butt with some inconveniency. Our election was
the last Monday. The competitors were the former elected Sr
Christopher Calthorp & Sr Neville Catelyn & Sr John Hobart
and Mr Windham. I never observed so great a number of
people who came to give there voyces, butt all was civilly

caryed at the hill, & I do not heare of any rude or unhansome
caryadge: the competitors having the weeke before sett
downe rules and agreed upon articles for their regular and
quiet proceeding. They came not downe from the hill until
eleven a clock at night. Sr John Hobart & Sr Neville Catelyn
caryed it, and were caryed in chayres about the markett place
after eleven a clock, with trumpets & torches, candles being
lighted at windows, & the markett place full of people. Dr
Brady was with mee that day, who presents his service, &
speakes well of you, & sayth hee was your constant Auditor,
& sayth yours are very good lectures & proper to the intention, as being very good & profitable, wch they have rarely
been formerly. He came with Sr Tho. Hare of Stowe Sr Ralph
Hares sonne & not long of age. Sr Tho. was of Caius Colledge
and brought, they say, four hundred for Sr Neville & Sr Christopher, & Dr Brady brought 18 or 19 from Cambridg, schollars
who were freeholders in Norfolk. These were the number of
the voyces

> Sr John Hobart 3417
> Sr Neville Catelyn 3310
> Sr Ch. Calthorp 3174
> Mr Windham 2898

I do not remember such a great poll. I could not butt observe
the great number of horses which were in the towne, & conceave there might have been 5 or 6 thousand, which in time
of need might serve for dragoone horses, beside a great number of coach horses & very good sadle horses of the better
sort. Wine wee had none butt sack & Rhenish, except some
made provision thereof before hand, butt there was a strange
consumption of beere and bread & cakes, abundance of people slept in the markett place and laye like flocks of sheep in
and about the crosse. My wife sent the receit for orenge cakes
and they are confortable to the stomach especially in winter
butt they must bee eaten moderately for otherwise thay may
heartburne as I have sometimes found especially riding upon
them. Tom presents his duty. God bless you all.

                                                    YLFTB

May 18, [1679].

[To Edward Browne]   †
D. S.

Mr Alderman Wisse being to go for London to morrowe, I
tooke the opportunity to send you an East India drugge
called sebets or zebets, given mee some yeares agoe by Mr
Peirce, who lived in the Indies & hath a stock I thinck yet
going in the company. I shall God willing write a litle more
of it to morrowe by the post. Mr Wisse is a meticulous doubting man of a good nature & unwilling to offend God or man,
& seldome without thoughts to perplex himself & [make] his   †
life the more unconfortable. I perceaved his head to [be]
buisie 5 or 6 dayes ago so hee was lett blood & tooke his usuall
purge of Cassia which hee takes often of himself & sometimes
sene [senna] & liquor of prunes & sometimes Infusion of sene;
hee is a good sleeper, yet 4 nights ago hee tooke Laud. gr.1
& I have given him formerly gr.1 fs and gr.2 in febribus. Hee
is doubtfull whether his head will not bee more unquiet &
[came] to mee to take his leave this evening of Sunday, and
if there should bee occasion sayd hee would consult you and
therefore I would not omitt to give you this notice & short
information. Hee hath dranck Epsam waters 20 yeares since
as being hypochondriacall & spleneticall; if hee had stayd I
should have advised him to have bled agayne, & so I told
him, & to have taken a potion; he hath a Tumor in scroto   23
which I never sawe, butt Mr Crop wished him to lett it alone,
& hee is not willing to make it one, though it is now so bigge
that it can not easily bee concealed; perhaps hee will not bee
unwilling to lett you see, who have had often sight of the like;
encourage him in those disturbed thoughts. I am fayne to
compose him sometimes by good counsell & rationall argument; the truth is hee is a very honest inoffensive person &
his owne foe most, butt hee is very temperate & sober, & I
wish him health & wellfare.

Your loving father,
T. Browne

Nov. 28, [1679].

[To Edward Browne]   †

D.s.,

I receaved yours. I am glad to heare wee have so many shipps launched, & hope there may bee more before the spring. God send faythfull, valiant & sober commanders, well experienced and carefull, above all, if places bee sould or given by favor only, such virtues will concurre butt contingently. The French are a sober, diligent & active nation, and the Duch, though a drincking nation, yet managed their warre [more] carefully and advantageously then the English, who thought it sufficient to fight upon any termes, & carry to[o] many gentlemen & great persons to bee killed upon the deck, & so encreaseth the number of the slayne & blott their victories. Pray present my service to Sr John Hinton when you   24 see him; tis a long time agoe since I had the honour to knowe him beyond sea. Mr Nortone maryed Sr Edm. Bacons daughter, who was [a] very good lady and dyed last summer, and I thinck hee was a member of the last parliament. Performe your buisinesse with the best ease you can, yet giving every one sufficient content. I believe my Lady O'Bryon is by this time in better health & safetie; though hypochond. & splenitick persons are not long from complayning, yet they may bee good patients & may bee borne withall, especially if they bee good natur'd. A bill is enclosed; Espargnez nous autant que vous pourres, car je suis agé et aye beaucoup d'anxiete et peine de sustenir ma famille. God send my L. Bruce well in France & well to returne; surely travelling with so many attendants it must bee a great charge unto him. Dr Briggs wrote a letter to mee concerning the bronchocele of his sister who was touched. Your mother & sisters remember to you, & Tom presents his duty. God blesse you all.

YLFTB.

Dec. 9, [1679].

[To Edward Browne]   †
D. S.,

Wee are all glad to understand that the bill of mortallity   25
decreased so much the Last weeke, for people were fearefull
that there might bee somewhat pestilentiall in the disease.
The sentences of Catilines conspiracy were I beleeve much
taken notice of & were very apposite to our present affayres.
Pray write mee word in your next the best speciall remedies
are commend[ed] or practised in London in Acrimonia
urinae, dysuria or stranguria. Wee understand the King hath
issued out a proclamation for all papists or so reputed to depart from London ten miles which makes men conjecture that
the parliament will sitt at the prefixed time. I sawe the last
transactions or philosophicall collections of the R.S. Here are   26
some things remarkable as Lewenhoecks finding such a vast   27
number of litle animals in the melt of a cod or the liquor wch
runnes from it as also in a pike a hare a cock & computeth
that they much exceed the number of men upon the whole
earth at one time, though hee computes that there may bee
thirteen thousand millions of men upon the whole earth,
which is very many. It may bee worth your reading: as also
of the vast inundation which was last yeare in Gascoigne, by
the irruption of the waters out of the Pyrenians mountaines,
as also of a flying man and a shippe to sayle in the ayro,
wherin there are some ingeneous discourses. Likewise the
damps in coale mines, & Lorenzini, a Florentine, concerning
the Torpedo, beside some other Astronomicall observations.
God blesse you all Your mother & sisters send their Respects
& Tom his duty.

YLFTB.

[Sept. 15, 1681.]

[To Elizabeth (Browne) Lyttelton]   †
Deare Betty,

Tho it were noe wonder this very Tempestious and stormy
winter, yet I am sorry you had such an unComfortable sight

as to behold a ship cast away, so neer you; this is noe strange
tho unwelcome sight at Yarmouth, Cromer, Winterton & sea
Towns; tho you Could not save them I hope they were the
better for yr Prayers, both those that Perishd and those that
scapd. Some wear away in Calmes, some are Caried away in
storms, we Come into the World one way, there are many
gates to goe out of it. God give us grace to fit and prepare
our selves for that Necessity, & to be ready to leave all when
& how so ever he shall call. The Prayers of health are most
like to be acceptable, sickness may Choak our devotions, &
we are accepted rather by our life then our death; we have a
rule how to lead the one, the other is uncertain & may Come
in a moment. God I hope will spare you to serve him long,
who didst begin early to serve him. There dyed 36 last week
in Norwich, the small pox very common, & we must refer·it
to Gods mercy when he pleaseth to abate or Cease it, for the
last run of the small Pox lasted much longer then this has yet
dun.

   Yr Brother Thomas went once from Yarmouth in the evening and arrived at the Isle of White the next day at one a
Clock in the afternoon, but it was with such a wind, that he
was never so sick at sea as at that time. I came once from
Dublin to Chester at Michaelmas & was so tossed, that noth-   28
ing but milk & Possets would goe down with me 2 or 3 days
after. Yr self is not impatient, you will have no Cause to be
sad, give noe way unto Malencholy, wch is purely sadnes
without a reasonable cause. You shall never want our dayly
Prayers & also our frequent Letters. God bless you both. I rest,

                                        Yr Loveing father,
                                        Tho. Browne

                                        April 29, 1653. [?]
[To Henry Power?]   †.29
   Εκ βιβλίου κυβερνῆτα [i.e. to steer from the book] is grown
into a proverb; and no less ridiculous are they, who think out
of Books to become Physicians. I shall therefore mention such
as tend less to ostentation,than use, for the directing a novice
to observation and experience, without which, you cannot

expect to be other than ἐκ βιβλίου κυβερνῆτης. Galen and Hippocrates must be had as fathers and fountains of the faculty. And indeed Hippocrates's *Aphorisms* should be conned for the frequent use, which may be made of them. Lay your foundation in Anatomy, wherein αὐτοψία must be your *fidus Achates*. The help that books can afford, you may expect, besides what is delivered *sparsim* from Galen and Hippocrates, Vesalius, Spigelius, and Bartholinus. And be sure you make yourself master of Dr Harvey's Piece *De Circul. Sang.* which discovery I prefer to that of Columbus. The knowledge of Plants, Animals, and Minerals, (whence are fetch'd the *Materia Medicamentorum*) may be your πάρεργον; and so far as concerns Physic, is attainable in gardens, fields, Apothecaries and Druggists shops. Read Theophrastus, Dioscorides, Matthiolus, Dodonaeus, and our English Herbalists; Spigelius's *Isagoge in rem herbariam* will be of use. Wecker's *Antidotarium speciale,* Renodaeus for composition and preparation of medicaments. See what Apothecaries do. Read *Morelli Formulas medicas, Bauderoni Pharmacopaea, Pharmacopaea Augustana.* See Chymical Operations in hospitals, private houses. Read Fallopius, Aquapendente, Paraeus, Vigo, etc. Be not a stranger to the useful part of Chymistry. See what Chymistators do in their officines. Begin with *Tirocinium Chymicum,* Crollius, Hartmannus, and so by degrees march on. *Materia Medicamentorum,* Surgery, and Chymistry, may be your diversions and recreations; Physic is your business. Having therefore gained perfection in Anatomy, betake yourself to Sennertus's *Institutions,* which read with care and diligence two or three times over, and assure yourself that when you are a perfect master of these institutes, you will seldom meet with any point in Physic to which you will not be able to speak like a man. This done, see how institutes are applicable to practise, by reading upon diseases in Sennertus, Fernelius, Mercatus, Hollerius, Riverius, in particular Treatises, in Counsells, and Consultations; all which are of singular benefit. But in reading upon diseases, satisfy your self not so much with the remedies set down (altho' I would not have these altogether neglected) as with the true understanding the nature of the disease, its causes, and proper indications for cure. For by this knowledge, and that of the instruments you are to work by, the *Materia Medicamentorum,* you will often conquer with ease those difficulties, thro' which Books will not be able to bring you. *Secretum medicorum est judicium.* Thus have I briefly pointed out the way which, closely pursued, will lead to the highest pitch of the art you aim at. Altho' I mention but a few Books (which well digested will be *instar omnium*) yet it is not my intent to confine you. If at one view you would see who hath written, and upon what diseases, by way of counsel and observation, look upon Moronus's *Directorium Medico-practicum.* You may look upon all, but dwell upon few. I need not tell you the great use of the Greek Tongue is of [*sic*] in Physic; without it nothing can be done to perfection. The words of art you may learn from Gorraeus's *Definitiones Medicae.* This and many good wishes from your loving friend,

T.B.

NOTES

Textual Notes

Notes and Commentary

Selected Bibliography

Glossary

TEXTUAL NOTES

Save for the MS version of *A Letter*, which is printed practically verbatim (punctuation and alternative readings excepted), the texts in this
volume have been minimally modernized—"u" for "v", "i" for "j", etc.—
but it has not been thought necessary to change the spelling. In the matter of punctuation, it is impossible to achieve consistency with texts published over so long a period of years, and from such different kinds of
copy. A large amount of autograph MS is still extant in the British Museum and the Bodleian, and some of this is careful fair copy. Even in
the latter, however, Browne's usual rather hurried, casual and on the
whole somewhat indiscriminate use of the period makes one realize the
alternatives that were open to his printers, and compels editorial decisions which must sometimes be arbitrary when applied to "sections" or
paragraphs made up of linked clauses joined by "and" or, even worse,
by gaggles of "whethers". Browne's first printers did not react uniformly;
in texts printed after his death there was clearly a good deal of change.

Turned letters and simple misprints have been silently corrected, ligatures disregarded. The many errors noted in the *errata* of original editions have also been silently corrected. In *Hydriotaphia* and *The Garden
of Cyrus* Browne's own MS corrections of the text (in author-corrected
copies of the volume still extant) have been noted from Mr. Carter's editions *only when not included in the errata*.[1] Presumably Browne expected
printers of his authorized works to italicize foreign quotations, titles,
etc., but this was done with great inconsistency.

For an edition such as this the problem of what to do about Browne's
notes is formidable. When he wrote *Religio Medici* he was, so he said,
out of the reach of "any good booke"; we may be grateful. But accompanying *Hydriotaphia* and *The Garden of Cyrus* there are (counting
both the octavo and quarto editions of 1658) nearly 250 marginal notes.
A good many are in Greek or Latin, and a very large number are mere
verifications of title or author. The proportion of original notes per page,
and their general character, is almost the same in *A Letter*. Printed in
the margin, as in the original editions, they provide an immediate visual
evidence of Browne's range of reading, even if one is sensibly lazy in

[1] I have examined the author-corrected copies in the Osler Library, the British Museum, Columbia University, and Yale University.

pursuit; occasionally they give us so quick an indication of the relation between learning and imagination that this becomes part of even our first perusal. They are given here in full, on the text pages, for *Religio Medici, Pseudodoxia, Christian Morals,* and the selections from MS. A selection of those in other works is to be found in the Notes. In recent years Professor J-J. Denonain, Dr. Vittoria Sanna, and Professor L. C. Martin have provided critical texts of *Religio Medici* of primary importance, the latter also of other works (see Selected Bibliography). There is no annotated or critical edition of *Pseudodoxia* or *Certain Miscellany Tracts;* of some of the latter there is no satisfactory text.

RELIGIO MEDICI

Eight 17th-century MSS of *Religio* are extant; none are autograph, and all have numerous textual corruptions; one is very incomplete. The following abbreviations are used: Pembroke College (Oxford) MS, *P;* British Museum Lansdowne MS 489, *L;* St. John's College (Cambridge) MS, *J;* Norwich Public Library, MS Wilkin 1, *W;* Norwich Public Library, MS Wilkin 2, *N;* Bodley MS Rawlinson D 162, *R;* McGill University, Osler Library MS 44170, *O;* Lehigh University Library, Honeyman Collection MS, *H.*[2] Two pirated editions were printed in 1642, the first of 190 pages (*42*[a]), the second of 159 pages (*42*[b]); *42* indicates agreement in these two texts. In 1643 Browne published an authorized text (*43*). The numerous subsequent 17th-century editions have no substantial textual importance.

The 1643 text, which must be the basic copy text for a modern editor,[3] was a correction of the inaccurate 1642 text, not one printed directly from the author's MS. There were also, however, additions and modifications intended to make certain expressions less personal, less positive, or more suitable for public consumption. It seems pretty clear that Browne's very imperfect editing led him to leave unchanged a number of corrupt as well as inferior readings, and the punctuation of *43* seems to me again and again not only not-modern, which one could not take exception to, but so mechanical as to make intelligent first reading impossible. In addition to the general modernizations referred to above, the spelling has been altered on a very few occasions to avoid annoyance or disruption ("limbe" to "limn," "on" to "one," "there" to "their," "toure" to "towre," "aunts" to "ants," "set" to "sit").

Passages in square brackets in the text are those found in the MSS

[2] For the relationships among the MSS see especially Denonain and Sanna.
[3] The present text is based on photographic copies of this edition in the British Museum and the Osler Library, McGill University.

and 1642 but eliminated in 1643. *Passages added in 1643,* and also variations which show real modification of sentiment or tone, *have been marked with this symbol* (§) in the Textual Notes, not in the text itself. A few important passages found only in the Pembroke MS have also been added and noted, with the same intention of showing the development and modification of the text.

To the reader] *added in 43.*

The First Part, Section 1

ardour and contention] ardour of contention *42/MSS except L. Flyleaf of R opposite Sect. 1 (but in different hand) has the lines*

> Quousque patiere bone Jesu!
> Judaei te semel, Ego Saepius Crucifixi
> Illi in Asia, Ego in Europa,
> Illi in Judaea, Ego in Britania
> Gallia Germania
> Bone Jesu Miserere mei, et
> Judaeorum

(How long dost thou suffer, good Jesus! The Jews crucified thee once, but I often; they in Asia, I in Europe, they in Judaea, I in England, France, Germany. Good Jesus have pity on me and on the Jews.)

Section 2

Prelates] *PL;* Presbyters *other MSS/42.*
begets] *MSS;* beget *42/43.*

Section 3

Church] church-window *42/MSS, with variations in sentence, such as* loose my arme, cut off my arme rather then violate a church windowe.
§ but rather pity] *added in 43.*
accesse] excesse *42b/P L J W H;* extasie (*or* exstasy) *N O R.*

Section 5

no man . . . a Canon more] *42/MSS* (rech *and* retch *in 42a and 42b*) *with misprint* wreath (*or* reath) *for* reach *in L P J.*
nor disapproving] *most MSS;* or disproving *W 42/43.*
to whom] *MSS/42;* whom *43.*

SECTION 6

§ love to] *added in 43.*
§ I hope] *added in 43.*

SECTION 7

Origen] the Origenists or (and) Chiliasts *P L;* the Chiliasts *other MSS;*
the Chiliast *42.*

from some charitable inducements . . .] whereunto I was enclined by
an excesse of charitie; whereby I thought the number of the living too
small an object of devotion; *42/MSS (text of 42).*

SECTION 8

§ *Section 8 added in 43.*

SECTION 9

o *altitudo*] *most MSS;* Oh altitudo *W 42/43.*
difficultest points] *MSS;* difficultest point *42/43.*

SECTION 10

to know we know nothing] *P L;* to know we knew nothing *W 42/43;*
to know *other MSS.*

That allegorical description of . . .] That Rhetoricall definition of
Hermes pleaseth mee beyond all the metaphysicall descriptions of
Divines *P L.*

Deus est] *H J W.*
sit downe] *MSS;* set downe *42/43.*
effects] *MSS;* effect *42/43.*
where God] *MSS;* when God *42/43.*

SECTION 11

blast of his will] placet of his will *P L.*
Saint Peter] St. Paul *MSS.*
spake . . . said] *MSS;* speakes . . . saith *42/43.*
instants] *MSS;* instances *42/43.*
a thousand] *MSS/42;* thousand *43.*

SECTION 13

§ Wisedome is his most . . . stood in feare to know him] *added in 43.*
even in Angels] there is noe threed or line to guide us in this labyrinth
addit. phrase in P L; text that of P.

impressions . . . on] *MSS;* expressions . . . in *42/43.*

§ small honour] no honour *MSS/42.*

§ highly magnifie] only magnifie *MSS/42.*

§ Therefore . . . resurrection] *Verses and remainder of section added
in 43.*

SECTION 14

the Sunne] *MSS/42;* Sunne *43.*
profound] propound *MSS/42.*
§ sometimes, and in some things] *added in 43.*

SECTION 15

sets forth] *O W 42;* set forth *several MSS/43.*
pieces of wonder] *MSS;* pieces of wonders *42/43.*

SECTION 16

effects of nature] *MSS;* effect of nature *42/43.*
sweetned . . . preserved] *MSS;* sweetneth . . . preserveth *42/43.*

SECTION 17

dispenseth her favour] *MSS except W;* disposeth her favour *W. 42/43.*
which must] *P L;* and must *W 42/43;* and they must *other MSS.*

SECTION 18

Those that held] *MSS;* those that hold *42/43.*
operations] *MSS;* operation *42/43.*

SECTION 19

both unto Faith] *P;* both unto Reason *some MSS, 42/43; lacuna in
R O.*

There are, as in philosophy] *MSS except W;* there is as in philosophy
W 42/43.
§ For our endeavours . . .] *to end of section added in 43.*

SECTION 20

§ or any other] *added in 43.*

SECTION 21

testimony] *MSS except W;* testimonies *W 42/43.*
fables] *MSS;* fable *42/43.*
§ that she was edified . . . Resurrection.] *added in 43.*
successively] *MSS/42;* successive *43.*

SECTION 22

very foesible] very forcible *P;* difficile *other MSS* (difficill *R*); difficult *42.*
a Horse?] *MSS/42, Sanna;* a horse, is very strange *43.*
That Judas . . . land of *Shinar*] *Instead of this P reads* That Judas
hanged himselfe, tis an absurdity and an affirmative that is not expressed
in the text but quite contrarie to the words and their external construction; with this paradoxe I remember I netled an angrie Jesuite who had
that day let this fall in his sermon, who afterwards upon a serious perusall of the text, confessed my opinion, and prooved a courteous friend
to mee, a stranger, and noe enemy.
to instance . . . in England] *MSS/42, text of P. Following this in P
alone is another example:* To inferre the obedient respect of wives to
their husbands from the example of Sarah, who usually called her husband Lord, which if you examine you shall finde to be noe more then
Seignior, or Mounsieur, which are the ordinarie languages all civill nations use in their familiar compellations, not to their superiors or equalls
but to their inferiors allso and persons of Lower condition.
that is, might some say] that is (say I) *P.*
doubtfull Families] doubtful Famulus *Denonain 1953;* doubtful
Famulies *Denonain 1955;* simple servants *P.*

SECTION 23

Learning. That *or* Learning, That] *MSS;* Learning, that *42/43.*

SECTION 24

three great inventions] *marg. note in* H J W; Gunnes, Printing, the
Marriners Compasse (*text of* J).

desire] *MSS;* desires *42/43.*

differences] *MSS;* difference *42/43.*

SECTION 25

amazed] *MSS except* W; ashamed W *42/43.*

Interpretations] *MSS;* interpretation *42/43.*

descend] *MSS;* condescend *42/43.*

commendation] P J N W O H *Denonain;* condemnation R *42/43 and
most editors.*

SECTION 26

§ He must needs offend . . . sayes] Is it false divinity if I say *MSS/42
with variants.*

miserable Bishop] marginal note in H J W: Virgilius.

exposing his living] exposing his life *42/MSS.*

§ there are not many] there is not a man *MSS/42.*

respect] *MSS;* respects *42/43.*

Politick point] *MSS;* politick points *42/43.*

SECTION 27

effects] *MSS;* effect *42/43.*

SECTION 28

§ *Section 28 added in 43.*

SECTION 29

even Pagans] *MSS;* every Pagan *42/43.*

Megasthenes] Magasthenes *43.*

§ as some will have it] *added in 43.*

SECTION 30

detection] *MSS;* defection *42/43.*

Maid of Germany] *marg. note in H J W:* That lived without meate upon the Smell of a Rose.

SECTION 31

derived] divined (*or* devined) *several MSS.*

from one to another] *P;* to one another *43;* to another *MSS/42.*

the honour of] *MSS except W;* discovery of *W 42/43.*

SECTION 32

life and radicall heat] *marg. note in H J W:* Spiritus Domini incubabat aquis Gen. 1.

verses] After line 12 the MSS and 42 have addit. couplet found in the evening hymn of Part 2, Sect. 12 (lines 5–6).

SECTION 33

§ an old one] *added in 43.*

first definition of Porphyry] *marg. note in H J W:* essentia rationalis immortalis.

specificall differences] *MSS;* specificall difference *42/43.*

§ those in] *added in 43.*

SECTION 34

one world] *MSS;* one *42/43.*

have left noe description] *P, Sanna;* have left description *H J W N 42/43;* have least description *R O.*

in controversie] *marg. note H J W:* The element of fire.

SECTION 35

affections of time] *MSS except W;* affection of time *W 42/43.*

§ and herein is Divinity . . .] *to end of section added in 43.*

SECTION 36

Antimetathesis of Augustine] antanaclassis of Augustine *MSS/42, note in H J W:* a figure in Rhetorick where one word is inverted upon another.

§ and in all acceptions] *added in 43.*

§ and this is a sensible . . . receive it] *added in 43.*

SECTION 38

of a spirit] a spirit *W/42.*

never dye] *MSS/42;* ever die *43.*

desire death] *MSS/42;* defie death *43.*

The passage in square brackets is in all MSS, but not in 42, perhaps by oversight, since it was omitted in W (though added in margin in later hand), the MS nearest to 42. Text from P.

§ highly] *added in 43.*

SECTION 39

addit. passage from P] hermeticall *is spelled* hermitical *in P.*

SECTION 41

in his name] *most MSS;* his name *43; whole phrase rather than . . . earth missing in 42 and W, where it is added in another hand.*

on earth] *P;* in the earth *other MSS/43.*

nearest] *MSS/42;* neatest *43.*

shaken] *MSS/42;* shaked *43.*

SECTION 42

It is not I confesse . . . went before it] *missing in P which goes from* severer contemplations *to passage quoted below.*

precedes in] proceeds into *MSS/42.*

And though I thinke] *Instead of this and what follows, to the end of the section, MSS/42 have a less closely related sentence:* The course and order of my life would be a very death to others; I use my selfe to all dyets, humours, ayres, hunger, thirst, cold, heate, want, plenty, necessity, dangers, hazards; when I am cold, I cure not my selfe by heate; when sicke, not by physicke; those that know how I live, may justly say, I regard not life, nor stand in fear of death.

SECTION 43

§ *Section 43 added in 43.*

SECTION 44

§ Men that looke no further . . .] *to end of section added in 43.*

SECTION 45

creation was a work] *MSS except W;* the worke of creation was
W 42/43.
fire] *MSS except W;* force *W 42/43.*
§ some beleeve] I believe *MSS/42.*
that great] *MSS;* the great *42/43.*
in the intellect] *MSS;* of the intellect *42/43.*

SECTION 46

authors of new] *P adds* these prognastickes of Scripture are obscure.
I knowe not how to construe them.
In those dayes . . . warres] *in square brackets in 42/43 to indicate
quotation.*
speake freely] *following this MSS read* omitting those ridiculous
Anagrams, *H J W have a marginal note* "whereby men labour to prove
the Pope Antichrist from there names making up the number of the
Beast."
of opinion] of Paracelsus opinion and thinke *MSS.*
§ hardly any man] no man *MSS/42.*

SECTION 47

Ipsa sui] MSS/42; wrongly "corrected" *to* ipsa suae *in Er. 43.*
and inbred] *MSS/42;* an inbred *43.*
fruits] *MSS;* fruit *42/43.*

SECTION 48

What is made . . . immortall] *in MSS and 42, but with variant readings; text from P.*
to] PRJNH; into *W 42/43.*
a thousand] *MSS/42;* thousand *43.*

sensible Artist] subtile (suttle) Artist *H W/42.*

§ This is made good . . . which can] this I make good . . . and can *MSS/42.*

revivifie] *P J N H;* lacuna in *R O;* revive *W 42/43.*

SECTION 49

insatiable] *MSS;* unsatiable *42/43.*

SECTION 50

either prey upon, or purifie] *MSS except W;* Neither prey upon nor purifie *W/42;* either . . . nor *43.*

§ admire] adore *MSS/42.*

"annihilation"] *in square brackets in 43 to indicate quotation.*

they doe] *P;* it doth other *MSS 42/43.*

SECTION 51

§ Surely though . . .] *to end of section added in 43.*

SECTION 52

§ vertuous] Godly *MSS/42.*
§ can hardly thinke] cannot thinke *MSS/42.*

SECTION 53

should onely ordaine a Fine] *Er 43;* should say, only ordaine a Fine *42/43.* Should only ordaine a box of the eare *P; lacuna in other MSS,* whipping *in diff. hand in margin of N.*

SECTION 54

they that derive] *MSS/42;* they derive *43.*

SECTION 55

confuted themselves] *P O R;* confute themselves *other MSS 42/43.*

casting therein] *MSS;* casting thereinto *42; omitted 43.*

lye at close ward (or guard) . . . lye not open] *MSS except W;* lye not at . . . lye open *42;* lye at . . . lye open *43.*

vennie] avenues *P; absent in other MSS.*

SECTION 56

§ *Section 56 added in 43.*

SECTION 57

§ can hardly divine] cannot divine *MSS/42.*

SECTION 58

hath much] *MSS;* have much *42/43.*

SECTION 59

how little wee stand in need] how much we stand in need *P H 42;*
little *"corrected"* to much *in W.*
§ and thus was I dead . . . *Cain]* *added in 43.*

SECTION 60

§ onely upon] on *MSS/42.*
merit] *MSS;* merits *42/43.*

THE SECOND PART, SECTION 1

French, Italian] Flemmish, Italian W/42.
to bee framed] *P;* for to be framed *43; various corruptions of* for to
bee *in MSS and 42 (e.g.* forty, framed; forty beframed).
§ any essence but] *added in 43.*
him] *72;* them *MSS 42/43.*

SECTION 2

give no almes to] give no almes only to *78/82.*
politick kind of charity] *in P an added phrase:* buy out of God a facultie
to bee exempted from it.

SECTION 3

acts] *MSS except W;* act *W 42/43.*
pecuniary] *P;* the pecuniary *MSS 42/43.*

remaine not many] remaines not one *MSS/42*; remaines not many *43*.

How many Synods . . . maribus] *text from P.*

the shock] shock *P;* the stroke *42/MSS except P.*

SECTION 4

his owne] *MSS/42;* his *43.*

SECTION 5

§ I thinke] *added in 43.*

Impostors] *MSS except W;* impostures *W 42/43.*

runnes] *P;* runne *other MSS 42/43.*

Achilles and *Patroclus*] *in P an addit. pair: Nysus* and *Euryalus.*

hold] *MSS;* held *42/43.*

§ mee thinkes upon some grounds] *added in 43.*

§ if I conceive I may love] if I confesse I love *MSS/42.*

From hence . . . the love of God] *Instead of this P reads:* These individual Sympathies are stronger, and from a more powerful hand then those specificall unions.

SECTION 6

like our owne selves] *H J W 42;* like our owne *P 43;* like our selves *N O R.*

our affection makes] *P;* our affections makes *42/43;* our affections make *most MSS.*

procure. And further] *Editor;* procure, and further *MSS 42/43.*

§ contentedly] *added in 43.*

SECTION 7

§ can hold] can *added in 43.*

or generall absolution] generall *added in Er 43.*

§ For there are certaine tempers . . . any of these] *added in 43.*

that I detest . . . selfe] *text from 42.*

there goes indignation, anger, contempt and hatred] *MSS except W;* . . . indignation, anger, sorrow, hatred *W 42/43.*

SECTION 8

§ constellations] starres *MSS/42.*

§ most of] almost all *MSS/42.*

unteach us] *P;* teach us *other MSS;* teach *42;* unteach *43.*
all sects] *MSS;* all sorts *42/43.*

<h2 style="text-align:center">Section 9</h2>

§ commend their resolutions . . . twice] am resolved never to be married twice *MSS/42.*
§ some times and] *added in 43.*
woman] *all MSS except W;* world *W 42/43.*
the rib] the rib onely *MSS/42.*
§ be content] wish *MSS/42.*
Whosoever is harmonically composed] *all MSS except W;* whatsoever is . . . *W 42/43.*
§ all Church musicke] our church musick *MSS/42.*
§ my obedience] my Catholicke obedience *MSS/42.*
§ I doe embrace] I am obliged to maintaine *MSS/42.*
strikes mee into] *MSS;* strikes in mee *42/43.*
§ Composer] my maker *MSS/42.*
It unties . . . Heaven] *MSS/42, text from P.*
in Lawe] *MSS;* in laws *42/43.*
reason of Man] *MSS except W;* reasons of man *W 42/43.*
the opinions of his predecessours] the fourth figure *MSS/42.*

<h2 style="text-align:center">Section 10</h2>

is the poesie (*or* posy)] *MSS;* it is the posie *42/43.*
in nature] *MSS;* in natures *42/43.*

<h2 style="text-align:center">Section 11</h2>

Atlas his shoulders] *P adds:* and though I seeme on earth to stand, on tiptoe in heaven.
§ The earth is a point . . . Alphabet of man] *added in 43.*
I am as happy as any] The happiest man alive *variant in MSS/42, followed by passage in square brackets from P.*
with this I can bee a King . . .] *variants in MSS and 42, text from P.*
conceits of the day] *MSS;* conceit *42/43.*
watery signe] *Er 43;* earthly *or* earthy signe *MSS 42/43.*
§ me thinkes] *added in 43.*
§Thus it is observed that men sometimes] thus I observe that men often times *MSS/42.*

SECTION 12

§ 'Tis indeed a part . . . Seneca did not discover it] *added in 43.*
and truly . . . an Orizon] *text from P; variants (and errors) in MSS.*

SECTION 13

§ I thinke] *added in 43.*
conclusions] *MSS; conclusion 42/43.*
no *delirium* . . . Atheist] *punctuation of 42/43 and some MSS very faulty.*
that which] *P; that other MSS 42/43.*
§ surely poore men . . . Cathedralls] I can justly boast I am as charitable as some who have built hospitalls, or erected Cathedralls *MSS/42; text 42.*
when I am reduc'd . . . poore] *text from P.*
acts of vertue] *MSS/42; act 43.*

SECTION 14

noble friends] *Er 43/P; loving friends other MSS 42/43.*
the love of our parents] *P; the loves of . . . other MSS and Er 43; the lives of . . . 42/43.*
our affection] *MSS except H R; our affections H R 42/43.*

SECTION 15

a story out of Pliny] a tale of *Boccace* or *Malizspini added 1678.*
§ thy selfe and my dearest friends] thy selfe and *added in 43;* friend *not* friends *in MSS.*
§ wisedome] justice *MSS/42.*
§ undoing] damnation *P W H/42; sentence missing in other MSS.*

PSEUDODOXIA EPIDEMICA

The text of these selections is based on the 2d edition, 1650 (*50*), collated with copies of the first edition of 1646 (*46*) from which it was printed, and the editions of 1658 (*58*), or, if different in folio and quarto, *58*[a] and *58*[b]), 1672 (*72*), 1686 (*86*) (*Works*).[1]

[1] My copies, collated with others in the University of Toronto library.

I do not fully subscribe to the view of Sir Geoffrey Keynes that "the first edition of 1646 was very accurately printed" while the revision of 1650 was only "almost as good," and have printed from 50 for a number of reasons. There are a great many authorial changes and "improvements" of phrase and word; there are many corrections of misprints, and there are additions. The punctuation of 50, though heavier than that of 46, is also, in my opinion, better. Certainly it does not rely so much on the all-purpose comma and is much less mechanical; sometimes, at least, the alteration of punctuation must be authorial. There are of course errors and corruptions in 50, and the spelling, like the punctuation, is sometimes not that of Browne; but 46 has also much non-Brownean spelling and punctuation.

In the textual notes I have attempted to indicate changes of attitude or knowledge in successive editions, this being of special interest and importance in a work like *Pseudodoxia*. Save when there might be doubt about the reading, slight changes of phrase, interrogatives turned into statements, stylistic substitution of one word for another, correction of misprints, corrections noted in the *errata*—but not always corrected subsequently—are not indicated in the Textual Notes. Marginal notes added in 50 are not distinguished from those of 46, but those added later are noted. The summarizing marginal notes added in 50 "by some strange hand" (according to "N.N", half apologetically) and continued in subsequent editions have here been omitted. The authorial (but rather erratic) process of transferring some references from the text to the margin is not recorded beyond 50. There are a few modernizations of spelling ("Jubilee" for "Jubile," "Phoenix" for "Phaenix"—Browne's habitual spelling—"wicks" for "weeks," "roll" for "roale") and I have on a few occasions italicized titles when there was confusing inconsistency in the same passage.

To the Reader

reviewing judgements] renewing judgements *46*.
swinge] swindge *46;* swing *58–*.
Acorns in our younger brows] twigges in our younger dayes *46*.
Scipio Mercurii . . . our Doctrine] *added in 50*.
footnote to Andreas] *added in 50*.
friendliest] friendiest *46–72*.
Fallaciously] Elenchically *46*.
and yet desiderated] at least, desiderated *46*.
Thomas Browne] T.B. *46*.

The First Book, Chapter 1

to a beast] unto a beast of the field *46.*
mendacities] mendacites *46.*
uncivilly] unmannerly *46.*
especially . . . tasted of it] *added in 50.*

Chapter 3

Fable, *footnote to* Apologue] *added in 50.*
the creation] his creation *46.*
Julian, *footnote to* Apostate Christian] *added in 50.*
footnote to quotation about Orestes] *added in 50.*
all professions and ages] all professions whatsoever *46.*
Theudas an Impostor] *46;* Theudas an imposture *50* (*but spelling interchangeable*).
For thus] for thus, what is scarce imaginable *46.*
Physitians . . .] *new paragraph 50.*
and running . . . easier questions] *added in 50.*
Pont Neuf] Ponte Neufe *46; footnote added in 50.*
considering the independencie] besides the independency *46.*
without illumination] without infusion *46.*
lest the name] The reason hereof was superstitions, lest the name *46.*
Deceptions, *footnote to* ingannations] *added in 50.*

Chapter 4

χεῖρας] *86;* χεῖρες *46–72.*
the same Elench] this Elench *46;* Elench *omitted 58–86.*
ye shall not incurre] shee shall not incurre *46.*
De Haeresibus *footnote to* Epiphanius, *etc.*] *added in 58.*
ye shall eat thereof] *58[b];* shee shall eat thereof *46 58[a].*
he disproveth] he denyeth and disproveth *46.*
worshipped as the body] worshipped for the body *46.*

Chapter 5

copulation] conjunction *46.*
surely that man . . . for those, who] surely it had been happy he had been born in Antycera, and is only fit to converse with their melancholies who *46.*

Anticyra] *86;* Antycera *46;* Anticera *50–72.*

rather beleeving, then] rather beleeving, as we say, then *46.*

endowments] and such as will accuse the omissions of perfection *added clause in 46.*

attain to any measure of it] attain to any perfection in it *46.*

CHAPTER 6

dictates of Antiquity] dictates of Antiquities *46.*

years agoe] *72;* yeare ago *46–58.*

Thirdly . . .] *new paragraph in 50.*

Juments] *Greek original from Aristotle in 46.*

why man alone hath gray haires] *Latin and Greek phrase for* "why man alone" *in 46.*

And though . . . and lead] *added in 50.*

Thus hath Justine borrowed] *new paragraph in 72.*

Eudorus] Edorus *46.*

de Nilo] de Milo *46.*

to omit . . . Parthenius Chius] *added in 50.*

Trojan horse] Trojan horses *46.*

Scribonius] Scriboneus *46.*

Nor did . . . take notice] *added in 72.*

Tricarinia] *46–86, but* Trinacria *(in Greek) three heads or promontories, i.e. Sicily, is perhaps the right reading.*

In like manner . . . signification] *added in 50.*

no extraordinaries] no such rarities *46.*

severall others] several other *46.*

many more] divers other *46.*

CHAPTER 7

For first . . .] *new paragraph in 50.*

Secondly . . .] *new paragraph in 50.*

scientificall] scientificiall *46.*

supported by solid reasons] supported by solid reason *46.*

In Morality . . .] *new paragraph in 50.*

a legall testimony] legitimum testimonium or a legall testimony *46.*

Tract] tract in Dutch *46.*

Christian Religion] *added phrase in 46:* and hath since contracted the same into six bookes in Latin.

tenth] *46;* truth *50 58.*

Rhabarbe] Rhubarbe 72 86.
Ars longa] in text not margin in 46.

CHAPTER 8

latter Century] 46; later century 50 58.

In his Indian relations] in his Indiary relations 46, *and very confused punctuation.*

with former ages] *addit. phrase in 46:* and made him contemptible unto most.

some succeeding Writers] Most succeeding writers 46.

Liège] 72; Leige 46–58ᵇ.

Phlegon Trallianus] Plegon Trallianus 46–86.

good Antiquity and use] good Antiquity and better use 46.

Aetius] 58; Acius 46; Aecius 50.

by his writings] by the number of his writings 46.

his naturall History] his natural Historie comprised in 36 bookes 46.

writes but as he reades] writes himselfe by hearesay 46.

Casaubone *twice*] 58; Causabone 46 50.

footnote to Epick Poets] *added in 50.*

twenty books] 25 bookes 46.

out of Harpocration] of Harpocration 46.

Alexis Pedimontanus] Alexis, Pedimontanus 50; Alexis Pedimont 46.

although he hath delivered many strange relations in his *Phytognomonica*] although he have delivered many Strange relations in other peices, as his Phytognomy *46; Phytognomica Er 50, misspelled; Phytognomia 50–72.*

CHAPTER 9

the simile] the smile 46.

matters of undeniable truth] matters, though not of consequence, yet undeniable truths 46.

yet doth it notoriously . . . truth] Yet are the effects thereof unwarrantable, in as much as they strengthen common errors, and confirme as veritable, those conceits which verity cannot allow 46.

Phoenix] 58–; Phaenix 46 50.

in Latine published by Hoschelius] *omitted 72 86.*

But no man . . . Kircherus] *added in 58.*

Harpies] 58; Harpes 46 50.

CHAPTER 10

an accesse in Religion] an excesse in Religion 46.
Demonstrative, *footnote to* Apodicticall] *added in* 50.
Abrahams bosome; that] 46; *punctuation in* 50–86 *faulty.*
Divination by the dead *footnote to* Necromancy] *added in* 50.
Croesus] 86; *Craesus* 46–72.
footnotes to Hipericon, pentangle, Tetragrammaton] *added in* 50.
Saturns mouth] 46, 58–72; Satans mouth 50 86.
Nor hath he only] *new paragraph in* 50.
Eutyches] Eutichus 46.

THE SECOND BOOK, CHAPTER 2

Now whether . . . gyration] 46 *only.*
footnote to apparencies] *added in* 50.
This polarity from] This polarity Iron 46.
footnote to Fern] *added in* 50.
And therefore those Irons . . . Aldrovandus] *added in* 50.
stand without deflection] stand parallel, and deflecteth neither 46.
a long Steel wire, equilibrated] a long steele, wires equilibrated 46.
intersect the horizontall circumference] interest the horizontall circumference 46.
unto which with alacrity] unto which alacrity 46.
Cosmographically] geographically 46.
answerable Tract] *Er* 50; almost answerable tract 46–86.
Unto this . . . variation over the place] *added in* 50.
Phoenician] 58–; Phaenician 46 50.
And therefore . . . good question] *added in* 50.

CHAPTER 3

Consonant . . . Kircherus] *added in* 50.
Nor is it . . . in any other] *added in* 50.
And that duly . . . years agoe] *added in* 50.
Pyramidographia, *footnote to* M. Graves] *added in* 58.
True it is . . . attractive quality] *instead of this* 46 *reads:* Beside, vitrification is the last or utmost fusion of a body vitrifiable, and is performed by a strong and violent fire, which keeps the melted glass red hot. Now certain it is, and we have shewed it before, that the loadstone will not attract even steele itself that is candent, much less the incanger-

ous body of glass being fired. For fire destroys the Loadstone, and therefore it declines in its own defence, and seekes no union with it.

pieces of Loadstone] pieces of magnet or perhaps manganese 72 86. or perhaps manganes] *added in 72.*

But that the Magnete attracteth] *new paragraph in 50.*

It attracteth the Smyris] It seems to attract the Smyris 58–86.

King Cheops in his tomb] *added in 50.*

and delight to sleep meridionally] *added in 50.*

or rather falsity] *46 only.*

and untrue] *46 only.*

a work of leasurable hours] *58;* his work, of leasurable hours *50;* in the title of his Worke, *Hora Subsecivae,* or leasurable howres *46.*

Pantarbes] Panturbes *46.*

Isle of Ilva] Isle of Flua *46.*

and thus must be interpreted Fracastorius] *46 only.*

and thus is to be understood Gilbertus] *46 only.*

Wherein notwithstanding . . . loveth Iron] *added in 50.*

To this minerall condition] *new paragraph in 50.*

many Physicians] many ages and Physitians *46.*

de Cultrivoro Prussiaco] *58; de cultivoro 50.*

Wherein to speak compendiously] *new paragraph in 50.*

operations] conditions *46.*

though we disavow not these plaisters] though we affirm not these plaisters wholly ineffectual *46.*

Tzetzes] Tzetzes in his Chiliads *46 only (reference probably intended for margin in 50, and entirely omitted 50–86).*

boundaries, or Sphere] boundaryes, or as we terme it Sphere *46.*

insision] *58 86;* incision *46 50 72.*

De curtorum chyrurgia, footnote to Taliacotus] *58; title in text 46, omitted 50.*

the Art of Pythagoras] the lost Art of Pythagoras *58.*

Nuncius inanimatus] written of late years by Dr. Godwin Bishop of Herford *in text 46.*

fields of Medicines] fields of medicine sufficient *46.*

Many other Magnetismes] *new paragraph added in 50.*

THE THIRD BOOK, CHAPTER 1

latter times] *46;* later times *50–86.*

Jointlike parts, *footnote to* arthriticall analogies] *added in 50.*

Trees found joints] trees found legs *46.*

all pedestrious animals] all pedestrious animalls whatsoever *46.*

wherein although it seem] *new paragraph 72.*
Now various parts . . . extension] *added in 50.*
They forget . . . leggs] *added in 50.*
well suppressed] reasonably well suppressed *46.*
some strings] the strings *46.*
fore legs] *46;* four legs *50;* former legs *58–86.*
Other concernments] *new paragraph in 50.*
Cyneget, footnote to Oppianus] *added in 50.*
Since also . . . great doubt] *added in 50.*

CHAPTER 5

Diagonion, *footnote to* Diagoniall] *added in 50.*

CHAPTER 18

Of Molls] *46/50;* Of Moles *58;* Of Moles or Molls *72.*
as in the judgement of Heinsius] *added in 50.*
slow-Wormes] *Caeciliae* or slow-worms *72.*
Other concerns . . . them both] *added in 72.*
ossa Jugalia] *Ossa Fugalia 72 86.*

CHAPTER 20

That Snailes have two eyes . . . if approached unto their roots.] *Instead of these 2 paragraphs, 72 reads:* Whether snayles have eyes some learned men have doubted. For *Scaliger* terms them but imitations of eyes; and Aristotle upon consequence denyeth them when he affirms that *Testaceous* Animals have no eyes. But this now seems sufficiently asserted by the help of exquisite Glasses, which discover those black and atramentous spots or globales [globules *86*] to be their eyes.

That they have two eyes is the common opinion, but if they have two eyes, we may grant them to have no less than four, that is, two in the larger extensions above, and two in the shorter and lesser horns below, and this number may be allowed in these inferior and exanguious animals; since we may observe the articulate and latticed eyes in Flies, and nine in some spiders: And in the great *Phalangium* Spider of *America,* we plainly number eight.

But in sanguineous animals, quadrupeds, bipeds, or man, no such number can be regularly verified, or multiplicity of eyes confirmed. (*See Notes and Commentary*)

the two lesser below] the two lesser below, as is evident unto any *46.*
into their beings] beyond their beings *46.*

CHAPTER 21

footnote to Bellonius] *added in* 58.

whereto we might . . . Meal-worms] *added in* 58.

So when . . . of a Tortoise] *deleted in* 72 86.

do not urine at all] do not urine properly 58.

Tortoys] Tortoys beyond any other 46.

as fishes . . . with the other] *deleted in* 72 86.

exact delineation] the exact delineation of Aldrovand 46.

mucous and slymy] spongy and mucous 46.

resemblance with a Camell] *addit. passage in* 46: for this derivation offendeth the rules of Etymology, wherein indeed the notation of names should be Orthographicall, not exchanging diphthongs for vowells, or converting consonants into each other.

corpulency] compulcency 46.

And so when it is said by the same Author . . . identity unto it] *deleted in* 72, *and the following substituted:* And though the air so entreth the Lungs, that by its nitrous Spirit, [it] doth affect the heart, and several ways qualifie the blood; and though it be also admitted into other parts, even by the meat we chew, yet that it affordeth a proper nutriment alone, is not easily made out.

Again, Some are so farre] *new paragraph added in* 50.

we doubt that] we doubt the common conceit, which affirmeth that 46.

for then Diamonds] for then Diamonds and glasse 46.

better then] as well as 46.

Although, I confess . . . frosts] *added in* 50.

Libavius] Zibavius 58–86; Libonius 50.

but especially in Sentortoises] 72.

for so to argue is fallacious] that is, *A Minori ad majus, a Dicto secundum quid ad dictum simpliciter* 46.

Which not with standing . . . miracle] *added in* 50.

CHAPTER 22

Oestridge] 46–58 (*Browne's spelling*); Ostrich 72 86.

given them] given them in paste 46.

And whether . . . considered] *added in* 58.

That therefore an Oestridge . . . doubted] *paragraph added in* 50.

CHAPTER 27

Chap. 27 of 50 is an addition to 46, as is also Chap. 25. In 58 another
chapter was added, thus Chap. 27 of 50 becomes Chap. 28 of 58 and
subsequent editions.

with some ancient Philosophers the people still opinion] was the opinion of some ancient philosophers 58.

an umbilicall] 58; one umbillical 50.

Aquapendente and stricter enquiry] Aquapendente 72.

for at the blunter end] as the blunter end 72.

But these at last . . . solid reason] *added in 58.*

Why there is also a little grando or tred at the lesser end] *omitted 58–.*

Why some eggs . . . Buzzards?] *added in 58.*

THE FOURTH BOOK, CHAPTER 1

it may admit of question] it must not be strictly taken 46.

footnote to Anser Magellanicus] added in 50.

footnote to Zoographers] added in 50.

Provence] *spelled* Province *until 86.*

And for the accomplishment . . . otherwise] *new paragraph added in*
50.

as Galen thus delivers] as Galen plainly delivers, the effect of whose
words is this 46.

such as have their bones] such as have the Apophyses of their spine
46.

in their upper eyelid] and in that they move not their upper eyelid
46.

THE FIFTH BOOK, CHAPTER 1

Zoographers] 46 86; zodiographers 50–72.

upon another consideration . . .] upon another story, that is from
earnestly protecting 46.

black] brown 72.

for therein] for therein (as Aristotle, Aelian, and Bellonius since
averreth) 46.

A possibility . . . with blood] *added in 72.*

CHAPTER 5

Now the Navell] now the navell or vessells whereof it is constituted] *46.*

They who hold the egge . . . part remaining] *added in 50.*

CHAPTER 22

Chap. 22 added in 50, but a few questions transferred to it from Chap. 21 of 46; in 72 another chapter added, so that Chap. 22 becomes Chap. 23.

in Athenaeus] *72.*

wicks] weeks *50–72 (Browne's spelling);* wicks *86.*

We are unwilling to enlarge . . . misconjectures] *paragraph amplified by addit. examples and transferred to become final paragraph (item 9) in 72;* philosophers *substituted for* Selden, Philologers *misprinted* philosophers; *again revised in 86, when* Philologers *disappears (in error?).*

footnote, Gaffarel] *86;* Iaffarel *50–72.*

THE SIXTH BOOK, CHAPTER 5

convincingly] convinsively *46.*

Valesius, *footnote to* Spanish Physitian] *added in 50,* but Valesius (F. Valles) *misprinted* Valerius *50–86.*

approacheth nearest our Zenith or verticall point] approacheth nearest to us *46.*

enlighten the other] enlighted the other *46.*

which from his artifice is so effected] which is prudently affected *72.*

received] *72.*

CHAPTER 10

no man hath yet beheld] few or none have yet beheld *72.*

The Chymists . . . causes] The Chymists have laudably reduced their causes *72.*

yet Salt may have a strong cooperation] and Salt may carry a strong concurrence therein *46.*

CHAPTER 11

we shall Benegroe] we shall denigrate *58–*.
his race] this race *58–*.
Hivites] Hevites *46*.
Happy, and Stony; possessions] Happy and Stony possessions *58–*.
Nor did the curse . . . discovery] *added in 50.*
were a slippery designation] were very dangerous *46*.
with all] unto all *46*.

THE SEVENTH BOOK, CHAPTER 18

at least as improbable truths have been received] as improbable truths
do stand rejected *46*.
That Archimedes . . . impregnated] *paragraphs 3 and 4 added in 50.*
would from hence confute] would perhaps from hence confute *46*.

HYDRIOTAPHIA OR URNE BURIALL
AND THE GARDEN OF CYRUS

Hydriotaphia and *The Garden of Cyrus* were first published in a small
octavo in 1658 (*58*) prefaced by the two dedicatory letters which are
so integral to them. They were republished in quarto (*58²*) in the same
year (with a list of additional marginal notes) in company with the 4th
edition of *Pseudodoxia,* and there were subsequent editions in 1659,
1669, and 1686 (*Works*).[1] By his investigation of Browne's corrections
in a considerable number of copies of *58*, Mr. John Carter (*C*) has in
recent years contributed most to the establishment of better texts of both
works, Professor Martin most to their elucidation. In the Osler copy
Browne has written "The Epistle to the first Booke" and "The Epistle unto the second Booke" above the dedicatory letters, as if he might have
wished that they had not been printed together, as they were, but placed
before each work, and leading into each. At all events, they have been
so placed here. The quincunx figure has been placed at the appropriate
place in the text itself.

MS drafts or versions of a number of sentences or paragraphs in
Hydriotaphia and *The Garden of Cyrus* (some of considerable length)
have been printed as supplementary material by several editors. A few

[1] The present text is based on a photocopy of the first edition in the library
of Yale University, collated with the author-corrected copies in the British Museum, Columbia University, and the Osler Library, McGill University.

of these passages were probably written as discrete little essays. Commenting on one such passage printed by Wilkin and others from MS Sloane 1848 as supplementary to *Hydriotaphia*, Professor Martin suggests that it belongs rather to *Christian Morals* and prints it (but from a version in the Bodleian) in his notes to the latter. I should doubt if it really "belongs" to either work. (See comments on *Christian Morals*.)

HYDRIOTAPHIA

giving the Law] *C;* giving the laws 58.
Nor] *C;* not 58.
contrived] *C and other editors;* continued 58.
Attica] *St. John from Pausanias ref.;* Africa 58.
no injustice] *C;* not injustice 58.
For since] *C;* and since 58.
And unlike] *Er;* nor unlike 58.
Pluto] 58²; Plato 58.

THE GARDEN OF CYRUS

Laertes] Laertas 58.
fix to] 86; fix 58.
picturers] *C;* pictures 58.
Narses] *C;* Nasses 58; nurses *Er* 58².
Fenny Sengreen] *C;* Fenny Seagreen 58.
diaphanous] 58²; diaphonous 58.
one another] 58²; mother 58.
Oak-apple] *C;* oak, apple 58.
sent] *C;* scent 58.
Isiacae] 58²; *Isiicae* 58.
needs] 69; need 58, 86.
Aiaia] *C; Acaia* 58²; Aiain *Er* 58².
συνολεθρία] *C;* συνολεφρισμὸς 58.
too often] *C (improvement rather than correction);* often 58.

A LETTER TO A FRIEND

A Letter to a Friend Upon Occasion of the Death of his Intimate Friend was published as a handsome folio pamphlet in 1690 (90), eight years after Browne's death. In 1686 however, the *Term Catalogues* had advertised a reprint of the *Works* (a project not carried out) "To which

is added, A Letter to a Friend, never before published. Folio." An earlier
and shorter version, obviously regarded as complete at the time it was
transcribed by Browne into MS Sloane 1862 (*Sl. 1862*) and which has
been used for notes by various editors, was first published by Professor
Martin in 1964, and is to be found in the present volume (with slight
differences of transcription) among other pieces from the Notebooks.
A Letter was also published in *Posthumous Works*, 1712 (*1712*). To
both versions of *A Letter* section numbers, as found in the original editions of *Religio* and *Christian Morals*, have here been added to simplify
reference. The text of *90* is from photocopies of two copies in the Osler
Library, McGill University, collated with a copy in the British Museum.

Part of section 32, and sections 33 to 49 of the 1690 text are also found
in part one of *Christian Morals*, though sometimes revised and in a different order (see Joan Bennett, *Sir Thomas Browne*, 1962). Section 50,
the last section of *90*, beginning "Lastly," became part of the final section
of Part Three of *Christian Morals*. The text printed in this volume ends
with section 32 of *90*. This no doubt invites criticism. But the somber
finality of section 32 (which is also the conclusion, with a "Lastly" inserted above the line, of the version in MS Sloane 1862) with its concluding phrase "and in the integrity of their Faculties return their Spirit unto
God that gave it" is lost in the entirely new beginning of "Consider
whereabout thou art in Cebes his table." As I have suggested elsewhere
at greater length (UTQ), in its MS form *A Letter* has a well proportioned,
not to say traditionally rhetorical, structure of introduction, narrative, and
eulogy. This structure Browne at a later stage or stages amended, ex-
panded, and in the final "mementos" so overdeveloped that one can
sensibly believe that he must finally have realized what had happened
to his "good wishes" and "few mementos." At the very least, surely, he
would never have countenanced a duplicate publication. In 1716, when
Christian Morals was published, he had been dead for thirty-four years.

As stated in the introduction to the textual notes, Browne's own footnotes have been omitted, although a number of them, sometimes abbreviated and translated, are to be found in the Notes and Commentary.

SECTION 5

Sleep] Sheep *90*.
Sleep lets] Sheep lets *90; Sheep let fall their Eye-lids *1712*.

SECTION 7

tip of the Ear. Most] tip of the Ear, most *90*.

SECTION 8

Feaver] *Wilkin, from MS Notebooks;* Feast 90.

SECTION 10

Omnibonus Ferrarius] *1712;* Omnibonus Terrarius 90.

SECTION 13

many I have seen become] *Sl. 1862;* many have been become 90.

SECTION 21

Tomb, and] *Ed.;* Tomb. And 90.
Apollo in them] *Sl. 1862;* Apollo on them 90.

SECTION 24

Democritism] *Wilkin;* Democratism 90.
real . . . enough] *added from Sl. 1862.*

SECTION 30

climacterically] climaterically 90.

CHRISTIAN MORALS

First published in 1716, *Christian Morals* is typographically, in its spelling, lavish capitalization, and punctuation an 18th-century text, and therefore in these details uncharacteristic of its author. Whether the title is Browne's one may also doubt. As editors from Wilkin to the present have realized, several Sloane MSS in the British Museum and MS Rawlinson D.109 in the Bodleian contain sentences and paragraphs found, in revised form, in *Christian Morals,* and others closely related.

Without for a moment impugning the sincerity or truthfulness of either Elizabeth Lyttelton (Browne's daughter) or John Jeffery in his Preface, one can say that their statements need not be taken at their face value as to the date of composition, because *Christian Morals* is so clearly in

parts an arrangement of observations and reflections of the most varied
character, some no doubt written long before the late 1670s. MS Sloane
1879 especially—described on the cover in Browne's hand as "Obseruations upon seucral subiects"—illustrates precisely and interestingly the
way he added a preliminary and final admonitory sentence or two and
thus "applied" reflections which were not originally hortatory, and which
he might better have developed into little essays like that "On Dreams"
found also (and only) in this MS. Part 2 of *Christian Morals*, in particular, seems to be in large part a collection of unused passages from
the notebooks. Sections 5 and 9 are good examples, and the former in
its MS form, printed, I think, for the first time in this volume, has a much
greater personal flavour.

The longish passage on "Ways to sweeten death" (2.13) was at one
stage incorporated into *A Letter*, and to precede it, presumably again
at a later date, Browne wrote another passage on death and consumptions which did not find its way into either *A Letter* or *Christian Morals*,
and has survived (as "by T.B. M.D.") only in a transcription by Elizabeth
Lyttelton (*Works*, ed. Keynes, 1964, I, 120–21). The present text is from
a photocopy of the first edition in the University of Toronto Library,
collated with one in the Osler Library, McGill University. As elsewhere
the spelling of a few words has been modernized ("to" to "too," "dye"
to "die"—i.e. singular of dice, "haches" to "hatches"). Abbreviations:
ed. of 1716, *16*, of 1756, *56*. The latter is prefaced by Dr. Johnson's
life of Browne, and has notes, some of which certainly read like Johnson.

PART 1. SECTION 1

hull not about] *56;* hall not about *16*.

SECTION 9

where prudent simplicity] *90;* when prudent simplicity *16*.
fixt thee] *90;* fixt there *16*.

PART 2. SECTION 1

instructeth us] *MSS Sl. 1879 and 1885;* instructeth *16*.

SECTION 5

six thousand years] *MS Sl. 1879;* six thousand *16*.

SECTION 11

amaze] *MSS Sl. 1862, 1885, 1879;* amuse *16* (*but* amuse *also means puzzle, amaze, as in A Letter*).

SECTION 13

strift] *90;* shift *16.*
fire] *MSS Sl 1885, 1879;* a fire *16.*

PART 3. SECTION 11

coarse] course *16* (*spelled either way until 18th century*).

MISCELLANY TRACTS

The learned or informative letters published in 1683, shortly after Browne's death, as *Certain Miscellany Tracts (MT)*, were prepared for the press by Thomas Tenison, a friend though not an intimate one, and from 1694, Archbishop of Canterbury. Tenison selected the texts, according to his preface, "out of many disordered Papers, and dispos'd them into such a method as They seem'd capable of," Browne characteristically "having given no charge [to his son or wife] either for the suppressing or the publishing of them." The letters ("occasional Essaies" Tenison also called them) had been composed at different times over a number of years, and were often related to previous conversations or queries, but Tenison said he could not learn the names of those to whom they had been addressed. John Evelyn noted in his own copy that most were addressed to Nicholas Bacon, to whom *The Garden of Cyrus* was dedicated, but that one ("Of Garlands") was addressed to him, and another ("Of Artificial Hills") to the distinguished antiquary, Sir William Dugdale.

The remark of Browne's old friend, Whitefoot, that Browne's writings were "often transcribed, and corrected by his own Hand, after the fashion of Great and Curious Wits" is amply borne out by extant MSS. The habit of revision was incurable, sometimes even after he had written out fair copy, as may be seen by comparing MS Sloane 1827 with MS Sloane 1839. It is not surprising if Tenison did not always print from the best copy.

The texts of the three pieces included here have been printed from MS, collated with *MT*. The first two are certainly more accurate and

satisfactory than the earlier versions in *MT*, where there are a few considerably jumbled effects. Of the third I should only say that it is in details nearer to what Browne wrote.

OF LANGUAGES

A collation of the texts of *Of Languages* shows that the version in MS
Sloane 1839 (39) is a revision of the text in MS Sloane 1827 (27), though
the latter is fair copy in folio. The Text in *MT*, the only one up to the
present printed as a whole, is earlier and in various ways less satisfactory textually, but the differences in both structure and phrasing are so
numerous that it would be impossible to indicate them without complex
parallels. I have noted only a number of readings which show Browne's
habit of qualifying first statements, others which correct the received
text of *MT*, and some additions. The notes must therefore be regarded
as illustrative only. The two pages in *MT* on "Dread" in the royal title
"Dread Sovereign" are not found in either 39 or 27, and were perhaps
dropped as too much an appendix. A blank space of more than a folio
page was left for the Saxon and English parallels in 27; in 39 only the
first sentence was copied out. They are given here from the Rawlinson
MS indicated, but the text is virtually identical with that in *MT*. There
is a somewhat different fragment of Saxon in MS Sloane 1848 (folio
200) also ending "Ic eom euer treaw freond T.B.", and perhaps other
tentatives in other MSS. *MT* has only one footnote, the reference to
Spelman's *Concilia* in the pages on "Dread."

*Title from MT (Tract viii); text from Brit. Mus. MS Sloane 1839,
folios 27–44, but the illustration of Saxon from Bodley MS Rawlinson
Letters, 58, folios 36–37.*
late discours] last discourse *MT*.
as most conjecture] as many learned men conceive *MT*.
of above fifteen hundred yeares] of about 16 hundred years 27; of
sixteen hundred years *MT*.
If America were peopled] *new paragraph in 27 and 39 with many
changes showing succession of texts.*
proved of litle use] proved uselesse 27; proved of no use *MT*.
not long ago asserted by the learned Isaac Vossius] lately asserted
by . . . 27; strenuously asserted by Vossius *MT*.
above four hundred yeares] about five hundred years 27; five hundred years *MT*.
Religious obligation] The religious obligation *MT*.

Though this languadge . . . harsh sound] *whole section absent in 27 and MT.*

Chineses] Chinois *MT.*

their magnified Confutius] their great Confutius *MT.*

Merlin, Enerin, and Telesin, after a thousand yeares] *Merlin, Enerin, Telesin, a thousand years ago MT.*

feminine terminations of the Latin] terminations of the Latin *MT.*

even the Latin itself . . . *to end of illustration*] *absent in MT; first paragraph only in 27.*

Duillius] Quillius *Wilkin, Keynes; other differences in transcription.*

Some derive . . . more might be sayd thereon] *not in MT, which has, further on, more explicit reference to Scythian and Buxhornius, absent in 27 and 39.*

As for that languadge . . . the grosse of our Language] *absent in MT.*

The Irish hath entertained . . .] The Irish, although they retain a kind of Saxon character *added phrase in MT.*

Nicoleta] *See Notes and Commentary.*

Haver and *Ser*] Hazer and Ser *MT.*

paxwax, etc.] *In MS Sl. 1827 (folio 35) the words* Bunny, seele, Kedg, clever, nicked, stingy *are added. In MS Rawl. Lett. 58 (torn)* kamp *and* strindgie *are new. In MT the list is as in Sl. 1827 with* Fasgon *missing and* kamp *added.*

Hugo de Boves] *misprinted* Hugo de Bones *in MT and all subsequent editions (Browne wrote* Boues).

examples of Provençal] *shorter and different example in MT; in 27 textual variations, signature TB missing, first paragraph given also in French.*

no small countrie] little less than England *MT.*

cannot well read the works of Goudelin] *absent in MT.*

In this Languadge of southerne France . . .] *whole passage very confused in MT.*

and the people in these parts . . . lived in their country] *absent in MT.*

Now having wearied you *to end of letter*] *absent in MT. which ends with discussion of "Dread."*

et malitorne de maigre mince] *27.*

garconiere] garcionaire *27, 39.*

OF THE ANSWERS OF THE ORACLE OF APOLLO

As with "Of Languages," the text of MS Sloane 1839 is a revision of Sloane 1827 which in its turn is later than the text of *MT.* Wilkin commented on Browne's mistake in describing the second reply of the Oracle as the first; it will be noticed that this has here been corrected by the author. I have modernized "Craesus" to "Croesus," but (like "Phaenix" in *PE*) the former is Browne's habitual spelling. The notes are, again, illustrative.

Title from MT (Tract xi), *text from Brit. Mus. Sloane 1839, folios 1–17.*
Men looke upon . . . oricle of Delphos] *opening section not in MT.*
The first Apologie] (*wrongly*) *given as second apology in MT.*
The Devill who sees . . . and families] *inserted into text of 27; developed at greater length in Sl. 1862 and CM 2.11.*
Argis, Sardiattes, and Halyates] *so in both 27 and 39, but presumably mistake for Ardis, Sadyattes and Alyattes* (*Herodotus 1.15–16*); *passage not in MT.*
In his fourth reply] In the Fourth part of his reply *MT.*
In the fift and last excuse] *MT gives more in Greek and Latin in first section* (*of MT version*) *of letter.*
could nothing saye] would nothing say *MT.*
In vayne wee looke for open sense in oracles] *absent in MT.*
which old Numa would playnely name] *MT adds and Medea would not understand. Footnote ref. absent in MT; ref. to Plutarch's life of Theseus absent in 27 and 39.*
Cyanus King of Cyprus] *so also in 27 and MT, but read Cinyras; see Notes. The marg. ref.* (*V. Herod.*) *in MT should be attached to oracle about king's eyes.*
Sometimes more beholding] *not new paragraph in MT.*
Some divines] divers divines *27; many wise Divines MT.*
their great performances] those *magnalia* which they performed *MT and 27.*

A Prophecy

The text of this piece in *MT* is a revision of what is here printed from MS, with very slight amplification, so that the process indicated in the notes is in the opposite direction from that noted for the two previous letters. But the MS is nearer to Browne in punctuation and spelling. Omissions, additions, and modifications are noted, not slight stylistic changes. In the MS the separate lines are not fully written out for the exposition, nor italicized.

Title from MT (Tract xii); *text from Bodley MS Rawl. Lett. 58, folios 19–18, and Brit. Mus. Sloane 1849, folio 12, a leaf separated from Rawl. Lett. 58.*

probability of their events] of *perhaps crossed out for* at. *MT adds* not built upon fatal decrees, or inevitable designations, but upon conjecturall foundations, whereby things wished may be promoted, and such as are feared, may more probably be prevented.

terrifie] trouble *MT*.

in the Baltick] on the Baltick *MT*.

When we shall have ports on the Pacifick side] *omitted MT*.

And Turks . . . that side] *substituted line in MT*.

Butt slaves . . . Incognita tracts] To make Slaves and Drudges to the American Tracts *substituted line in MT*.

for American] in American *MT*.

that they can allreadie] *MT adds* That is *to each exposition*.

that they can allreadie] that they can, as they report *MT*.

bee a terrour unto] infest *MT*.

ports and dominions] *MT adds* by depradations or assaults.

containe them] *MT adds* they will range still farther and be able in time.

great Kingdomes] new Dominions *MT*.

their power] and courage *added MT*.

been able . . . Panama] *MT reads instead* in that notable attempt upon Panama.

and the continent] *MT adds* and like to be a receptacle for colonies of the same originals from Barbadoes and the neighbour Isles.

more considerable] as considerable *MT*.

in wealth and splendour] in people, wealth and splendour *MT*.

This may well be feared] of this we cannot be out of all fear *MT*.

When we shall have ports on the Pacifick side] *for* ports *MS reads* (*by error*) shipps; *passage crossed through, omitted MT*.

when they are civellised . . . countries] *instead of the rest of this section MT reads* and acquainted with Arts and Affairs sufficient to employ people in their countries; if also they should be converted to Christianity, but especially unto Mahometanism; for then they would never sell those of their religion to be Slaves unto Christians.

And they are in a way unto it] And they seem to be in a way unto it at present *MT*.

have also discovered] have lately discovered *MT*.

When a new drove] and a new drove *MS and MT*.

they will no longer send out] it may come to pass that *added in MT*.

originary countries] Original Countries *MT;* originall *altered to* originary *in MS*.

mappe or cart] Map or Chart *MT;* Chart *altered to* cart *in MS*.

ESSAYS AND OBSERVATIONS FROM NOTEBOOKS

The essay on dreams with which MS Sloane 1879 begins is not pagi-
nated; to me it seems to be in a considerably earlier hand than what
follows. Following it, the leaves are consecutively numbered by the author from 1 to 48, and can be described as fair copy, though not in the
folio form of MS Sloane 1827. I have already referred sufficiently to
Browne's habit of revision; reflections that deeply touched his imagination and therefore challenged his virtuosity may still be read in successive order. There are, for instance, four extant versions of the passage
on ways of dying, three in Sloane MSS, one in the Bodleian. A passage
rather similar in verbal structure on the moral good fortune that human
nature is incapable of "longevitie in voluptuousness" [Circumscriptions
of Pleasure] may be followed through similar rewritings. Sir Geoffrey
Keynes prints many interesting and sometimes odd fragments from the
Notebooks (*Works*, III) including scientific observations; most of these
are also in Wilkin, in less satisfactory form. With one or two exceptions
I have not attempted to indicate where fragments or versions of these
little essays or observations are to be found in other MSS, nor give alternative readings. The headings in square brackets are editorial.

[ON DREAMS]

MS Sloane 1879, folios 2–10.

[THE SEARCH FOR TRUTH]

MS Sloane 1879, folios 44–46.
some had rather] I had rather men would write *MS Sloane 1885*
(some *above line*); many would be content that some would write *CM*.
tomorrow when I arise] *MS Sloane 1848 (folio 142) has what appears
to be a draft of this sentence in which the parallel phrase is* about 6
hours hence when I am in America.

[CIRCUMSCRIPTIONS OF PLEASURE]

MS Sloane 1879, folios 11–13.

[THE LINE OF OUR LIVES]

MS Sloane 1879, folios 17v–20.

[WAYS OF DYING]

MS Sloane 1879, folios 21–23.
Above this is an insertion by Browne: This is in the epistle give me leave to wonder, *the first sentence of A Letter, in the text of 90.*

[AGGREGATION AND COACERVATION]

MS Sloane 1879, folios 25–26.

[INTENTION, IMITATION, COINCIDENCE]

MS Sloane 1879, folios 26–28.

In a peece of myne (*i.e. Religio Medici*)] MSS Sl. 1885 and Sl. 1879 *first read* never read three leave . . . scarce any more; never *changed to scarce in Sl. 1879 and* any more *to* so much. *Sloane 1869 has another version in which Browne began to write* two leaves *and changed to* three.

and civill] *later insertion above line.*

[GUARDIAN ANGELS]

MS Sloane 1879, folios 56–57.

[A LETTER TO A FRIEND]

For illustrations of the textual relationships of this version and that of the printed text (90) see Martin's edition, where many erasures are also indicated, and also an article by the present editor in *UTQ* 36 (1966), 68–86. A diagonal line across the first leaf seems to indicate, here and often elsewhere, that another transcription has been made. At the top of the blank leaf opposite, Browne has written "this Letter may bee added to the Letters in the folio with red leaues"; this would seem to be a reference to at least some of the letters published in 1683 as *Miscellany Tracts.*

MS Sloane 1862 folios 8–25; title from 1690 text; section numbers added.
Sr.] *inserted.*

SECTION 4

choughs clawe] *large X in illustration.*

SECTION 10

Quartan ague] *undecipherable alternative* or *added phrase here in MS.*

SECTION 11

not in 90.

SECTION 12

Though hayres . . . other diseases] *not in* 90.

SECTION 14

not in 90.

agayne] *undecipherable insertion beginning with* unto *and ending* and death.

2 bad lives] *perhaps* two bad liuers.

SECTION 15

when they haue no time to spend] *perhaps alternative, not additional phrase.*

SECTION 17

to [be] like him] *erasures; possible reading* the like.

SECTION 20

Lastly] *inserted.*

LETTERS

The bulk of Browne's correspondence was printed by Simon Wilkin in the first volume of his edition of the *Works,* 1836. Wilkin also printed letters and journals by Browne's sons Edward and Thomas, and some miscellaneous correspondence. A better text and additional letters (also some letters to Browne, but not those of Edward and Thomas) are to be found in vol. 4 of the *Works,* ed. Keynes, 1964. The spelling in letters transcribed by Browne's daughter Elizabeth Lyttelton, must sometimes be regarded as hers, not her father's. The text of letters printed here is taken from the originals; some punctuation, however, has been added.

To Thomas Browne, Dec. 22] *Bod. MS Rawl. D 391, folio 8. Copy by Elizabeth Browne (Mrs Lyttelton), Browne's daughter.*

To Thomas Browne, April 22] *MS Rawl. D 391, folio 82. Copy by Elizabeth Browne.*

To Edward and Thomas Browne, July] *Brit. Mus. MS Sloane 1848, folio 267.*

To Thomas Browne, Lieutenant, *etc.* February] *MS Sloane 1745, folio 11.* Copy by Browne himself.

To Edward Browne, Febr. 25] *MS Sloane 1847, folio 186.*

To Edward Browne, April 25] *MS Sloane 1847, folio 115.*

To Edward Browne, April 28] *MS Sloane 1847, folio 111.*

To Edward Browne, May 7] *MS Rawl. D 108, folio 90.*

To Edward Browne, May 18] *MS Sloane 1847, folio 219.* make] *MS* making.

To Edward Browne, Nov. 28] *MS Sloane 1847, folio 207.*

To Edward Browne, Dec. 9] *MS Sloane 1847, folio 127.*

To Elizabeth Lyttelton, Sept. 15] *MS Rawl. D 391, folio 87. Copy by Elizabeth Lyttelton.*

To Henry Power?] *MS not known to be extant;* text from *A General Dictionary, Historical and Critical . . . 3,* 1735 612–613. It is described as having been communicated to the editors, or Thomas Birch, author of the notice of Browne, by Richard Middleton Massey, and written from Bury. (See also Notes and Commentary)

NOTES AND COMMENTARY

Full details of books and articles cited or referred to will be found in the Selected Bibliography.

Titles and editions found in the auction *Sale Catalogue* (*SC*) are given in part as source references, but more especially to indicate something of the extent and variety of Browne's personal library. Modern literature, as distinct from learning, he seems to have bought and read very sparingly. Curiously, there is, as far as I know, no volume from his large collection with either his signature or his annotations. He gave a few books to what is now the Norwich Public Library, among them a copy of *Pseudodoxia*. The Glossary following the *Notes and Commentary* provides biographical identification of some (but by no means all) of the authors cited by Browne as well as the meaning of many words and phrases.

RELIGIO MEDICI

Reference is made in the Selected Bibliography to the notes in the editions of Wilkin, Greenhill, Murison, Sanna, and Martin. The annotations of Thomas Keck (*Religio Medici*, 1656, but written ten years before), the *Observations* of Sir Kenelm Digby (1643), and even the voluminous enormity of the annotations of L.N.M.E.M. (L. L. von Moltke) in the 5th Latin edition (Strasbourg, 1652), are useful as illustration of contemporary interests, the still scholastic character of theological thought, and for classical references. In 1645 Alexander Ross, a violent Protestant and crusading Aristotelian, issued his *Medicus Medicatus: or the Physicians Religion Cured* . . . . Dr. Sanna's belief that Browne used Burton's *Anatomy of Melancholy* extensively is not to me plausible, but the parallels are interesting. It is odd, in view of the great popularity of the *Anatomy* at Oxford in the sixteen twenties, that Browne seems never to have referred to Burton, unless obliquely in the remark that *Pseudodoxia* was not a work that could be performed "standing on one leg," Burton having said, not so much earlier (in his preface "Democritus to the Reader") that he had composed his "Cento", or patchwork, in that way. But probably both Browne and Burton are independently quoting a well known tag from Horace.

To the Reader

1. *greedy of life:* a paraphrase of two lines from Seneca's *Thyestes,* 883–84.

2. *incapable of affronts:* too unimportant to be affronted.

3. *private exercise:* On March 3, 1643, having heard that Sir Kenelm Digby had written some Animadversions on *RM* (in its pirated form) for the Earl of Dorset, and that they were "in the Presse," Browne wrote to Digby about the corruptions in the text of *42* and the circumstances of composition and printing. His letter and Digby's reply are included in some copies of *43*. The text, Browne wrote, "past from my hand under a broken and imperfect Copy, by frequent transcription it still run forward in corruption." It was also "pend many years past and (what cannot escape your apprehension) with no intention for the Presse . . . contrived in my private Study, and as an exercise unto my self . . . ."

4. *in such a place:* The places proposed, Halifax, or Oxfordshire, do not seem entirely convincing in relation to this statement. Browne must already have owned quite a few books.

The First Part

5. *generall scandall:* originating in a mediaeval suspicion of men whose study, as Chaucer said of his doctor of physic, was "but litel on the Bible." Keck quotes a Latin tag that where there are three doctors, two are atheists, but adds that this is a common speech "only among the unlearned sort."

6. *naturall course:* scientific nature.

7. *the name:* Protestant, a negative or combative word.

8. *Prelates:* the reading Presbyters (see Textual Notes) need not be attributed to Browne.

9. *the person:* Luther, whose father was a miner.

10. *shaken hands:* said good-by to.

11. *desperate Resolutions:* i.e. unyielding Roman Catholics.

12. *solemne Procession:* e.g. at Montpellier where he studied and where there were Protestant students.

13. *another Article:* Greenhill points out that objections to two heresies Browne later mentions are referred to in the original 42 articles, but were dropped from the later 39 Articles. Milton shared the heresy of "the Arabians."

14. *Councell of Trent:* Roman Catholic council held at Trent from 1545 to 1563 to examine and redefine points of doctrine.

15. *Synod of Dort:* held at Dordrecht in 1618–19, to which English observers were sent, to resolve the arguments of Calvinists and Arminians about predestination and free will.

16. *State of Venice:* when excommunicated in 1606, by Pope Paul V, threatened to secede from the Roman Church.

17. *Oedipus:* who delivered Thebes by solving the riddle of the Sphinx.

18. *prayer for the dead:* not at the time an Anglican heresy or formally condemned. In *Christian Morals* (3.27) Browne says "while so many question prayers for the dead."

19. *prophecy of Christ:* Matt. 24.11.

20. *o altitudo:* Romans 11.33 in words of Vulgate: "O the depth of the riches both of the wisdom and knowledge of God."

21. *Certum est . . . :* It is certain because it is impossible [to reason]; said of Christ's resurrection.

22. *the Apostle:* Paul, in Ephes. 6.16.

23. *allegorical description:* The phrase quoted (God is a circle whose center is everywhere, circumference nowhere) has not been exactly located, but became a popular expression in the later Middle Ages and Renaissance. It is referred to, for instance, by Rabelais and Montaigne, and on other occasions by Browne. Here he declares for a "Platonick description" as against an Aristotelian definition, in part for temperamental reasons, but also because he thinks the Aristotelian words from the *De Anima* do not really define. *Entelecheia* is that by virtue of which a thing is what it is, e.g. the soul is the *entelecheia* of the body; *actus perspicui* is variously translated as "the act of clarity," "actual transparency," "visible movement." "Platonic" or Hermetic (see also 1.32 n. 87) phrases like "the soul is man's angel," "light is the shadow of God" please the imagination ("humour the fancy") in a symbolic image or representation of a mystery. In his essay on the oracle of Delphi, Browne speaks of the Italian scholar Hermolaus Barbarus (Almoro Barbaro) wanting to conjure up Aristotle to ask him the meaning of *entelecheia;* Cicero's interpretation of the word was discussed at great length in the Renaissance.

24. *plants of the field:* Browne perhaps misunderstood the verses in Genesis.

25. *which God ordained:* Deut. 22.13–17.

26. *Neque enim . . . :* nor even in my hours of relaxation can I forget myself; from Horace *Satires* 1.4.133–34.

27. *Saint Pauls Sanctuary:* another reference to Romans 11.33.

28. *world eternall:* as against Christian theology of creation from noth-

ing. In the *De Anima,* speaking of the vegetative, sensitive, and rational souls, Aristotle says a square implies the triangle.

29. *mysticall way of Pythagoras:* that the world could be interpreted as a mathematical system.

30. *Beware of Philosophy:* St. Paul in Coloss. 2.8.

31. *severe Schooles:* Aristotelian as opposed to "Platonic," with reference to Plato's view that physical objects are a shadow of reality, which is Idea (see also 1.32 n. 87).

32. *the Devill . . . at Delphos:* The motto "know thyself" over the gate of the temple of Apollo at Delphi. Like most Christians of his own time as well as earlier times Browne associates oracles and pagan deities with the devil.

33. *Moses Eye:* Exod. 33.23.

34. *first cause:* God. The four secondary causes according to Aristotle, are the efficient (the agency by which the thing is produced), the formal (the pattern or form of the thing produced), the material (the matter itself), the final (the end for which it is produced).

35. *Galen . . . Suarez:* Galen's "On the Uses of the Parts" is put with the metaphysics of Suarez (16th-century Thomistic philosopher) because Galen is so emphatic about design in nature.

36. *Natura nihil agit frustra:* nature does nothing to no purpose, an axiom of Aristotle and later science, and contrary to what is sometimes stated, no great obstacle to the advancement of experimental science in the 17th century. Robert Boyle, the distinguished chemist, "remembered" Harvey telling him that he was led to the discovery of the circulation of the blood by thinking that "so provident a Cause as Nature had not plac'd so many valves without Design." (Quoted by J. Needham, *History of Embryology,* rev. ed., London, 1959, p. 59.)

37. *the most imperfect creatures:* It was traditionally held that worms, insects, and other small creatures (e.g. mice) were spontaneously generated by the action of the sun, and consequently did not take up space either in the Ark or the first creation. Not until some time after the microscopic discoveries of the sixteen-sixties and seventies was this idea abandoned. Though doubtful about mice, Browne did not change his references to spontaneous generation (as a question of enquiry) in successive editions of *PE,* 1650–1672.

38. *two soules:* according to scholastic doctrine the cedar has only a vegetative soul; the fly a vegetative and sensitive soul; man a rational soul, containing the faculties of the other two.

39. *generall pieces of wonder:* and of much discussion, as indicated by Browne's treatment in *PE.*

40. *principle of motion and rest:* as defined by Aristotle in the *Physics* 2.1.

41. *sweetned the water:* Exod. 15.25.

42. *God is like a skilfull Geometrician:* not found in Plato, but attributed to him by Plutarch.

43. *single Essences:* individual beings.

44. *the letter:* a letter delivered to Lord Mounteagle by which the Gunpowder Plot of 1605 was discovered.

45. *victory of 88:* over the Spanish Armada (in 1588).

46. *Grand Seignieur:* Turkish Emperor.

47. *Epithets: i.e.* for Fortune.

48. *judiciall Astrology:* is astrology that forecasts the future, as compared to the more acceptable astrology that indicates the influence of the stars.

49. *Homers chaine:* linking man with Zeus (*Iliad* 8.18–26).

50. *Archidoxis:* the *Archidoxis Magica* of Paracelsus, a potpourri of cures and "secrets" operating by occult sympathies.

51. *Brazen Serpent:* Num. 21.9.

52. *miracle in Elias:* 1 Kings 18.35.

53. *three Impostors:* In the 16th and 17th centuries various writers were named as having written an anonymous book of this title, describing Moses, Christ, and Mahomet as impostors, but the book is thought imaginary. The legend may go back to a similar accusation leveled at the Emperor Frederick II (1194–1250), generally regarded as very libertine in his thinking.

54. *three lines of Seneca:* After death there is nothing; death itself is nothing. Death is the destruction of the body; there is no question of a soul. We die wholly and no part whatever remains (*Troades* 397, 401–2).

55. *whether the world was created:* see A. Williams, *The Common Expositor* for description of Renaissance commentaries on this and other problems (e.g. the size of the Ark, below) involving Genesis; also note 4, "of Languages."

56. *Pantagruels Library:* in Rabelais, (*Pantagruel,* 7) is a library of imaginary books, to which Browne paid tribute in his *Musaeum Clausum*, a catalogue of imaginary pictures, rarities and books, and Donne in his *Courtier's Library.* Pierre Tartaret, a butt of Rabelaisian satire, wrote commentaries on Aristotle, but not this imaginary book on evacuation.

57. *honest Father:* St. Augustine (*Of the City of God* 15.8).

58. *That Judas perished:* since the accounts in Matt. 27.3–5, and Acts 1.16–18 seem contradictory, and the Greek word in Matthew may mean hanging or suffocation. Keck quotes various early Fathers.

59. _Angel_ . . . _Messenger:_ the Greek may mean either.

60. _doubtfull Families:_ P reads "simple servant," and in his 1953 edition of RM Denonain read "famulus." But the servant was Rhoda. Martin gives, from the _OED,_ the obsolete sense "the servants of a house," but the plural seems awkward.

61. _answered: i.e._ was replying in a formal disputation.

62. _the Alcoran:_ It has been pointed out that Browne's statements about the Koran, here and elsewhere, do not come from the book itself but rather from writings about the Turks; they are however closely paralleled in books by contemporary scholars. Browne (or, less probably his son Edward) owned a copy of the Koran in Arabic.

63. _That_ . . . _this:_ the Koran . . . the Bible.

64. _combustion of the Library of Alexandria:_ burned at the siege of Alexandria by Caesar.

65. _the Vatican:_ i.e. the library of.

66. _leaves of Solomon:_ 1 Kings 4.32–33.

67. _Enochs Pillars_ . . . _Josephus:_ "the story is, that Enoch or his father Seth having been informed by Adam that the world was to perish once by water and a second time by fire, did cause two Pillars to be erected, the one of Stone against the water, and another of Brick against the fire, and that upon these Pillars was engraven all such learning as had been delivered to, or invented by mankinde." (Keck from Josephus, who said he saw the surviving pillar).

68. _three great inventions:_ from PE 2.2 it would seem that printing, gunpowder, and the mariner's compass are meant, but the contemporary opinion of Digby, Keck, and Moltke is for clocks rather than the compass.

69. _foure members of Religion:_ pagans, Jews, Mohammedans, Christians.

70. _commendation:_ (not condemnation) is the reading of P and other MSS save R, but not of editors other than Denonain; it seems to me much more like Browne, i.e. they are so brave that _even_ their enemies must praise them.

71. _Aristotle requires: Nicomachean Ethics_ 3.6–9.

72. _Councell of Constance_ . . . _John Husse:_ John Huss, a Bohemian reformer, was burnt at the stake in 1415, and his doctrines condemned at the Council of Constance (1414–1418).

73. _Unity of God:_ Although this accusation (of monotheism) was not, according to Plato, the charge for which Socrates was condemned to death, Plutarch emphasizes this as the belief of Plato and Socrates, and Keck quotes various Fathers (e.g. Tertullian and Lactantius) who in anti-pagan polemics speak of Socrates in this way.

74. *miserable Bishop*: Virgilius, 8th-century bishop of Salzburg, asserted that the earth was round and was accused of heresy. Browne seems to have changed "life" (MSS and *42*) to "living" in *43* to indicate that he lost his bishopric, not his life.

75. *Jesuites of their Miracles*: in various relations of missions.

76. *Esdras*: Apocrypha, 2 Esdras 4.5.

77. *Helena*: mother of Emperor Constantine, reputed to have found Christ's cross in the Holy Land in 326.

78. *cessation of Oracles*: more fully discussed in *PE* 7.12. *Cf.* Milton's *Nativity Ode*, 145–52.

79. *Joshua*: Josh. 19.13.

80. *the Eclipse*: at the Crucifixion (Matt. 27.45).

81. *Oracle to Augustus*: having a supposed reference to Christ. In *PE* (7.12) given and translated.

82. *a piece of Justine*: for Justin see Glossary; the reference is to Deut. 28.27.

83. *Spirits and witches*: Browne's attitude to witchcraft, and his part in a witch trial at Bury St. Edmunds in 1664 (when two unfortunate women were condemned to death) have been much commented on, sometimes without historical knowledge or accuracy. For general background, W. Notestein's *History of Witchcraft in England, 1558–1718*, and the twenty "theses" at the end of G. L. Kittredge's *Witchcraft in New England* are recommended, and for Browne's insignificant part in the trial, Dorothy Tyler, *Anglia* (1930) 179–95, or W. P. Dunn, *Sir Thomas Browne*, pp. 24–30. The great majority of educated men in the seventeenth century, and many in the eighteenth, believed in witchcraft; the distinguished judge in 1664, Sir Matthew Hale, vehemently supported his belief by reference to the Bible. Yet it may be noted that Keck, commenting on this passage, wrote firmly: "But for the opinion that there are Witches which cooperate with the Devil, there are Divines of great note and far from any suspicion of being irreligious, that oppose it."

84. *Maid of Germany*: Eva Flegen who in 1597 supposedly gave up eating, but by 1628 had been exposed and imprisoned for fraud.

85. *Paracelsus*: Aureolus Philippus Theophrastus Bombast of Hohenheim, 1493–1541, was a Swiss physician, alchemist, and natural philosopher of an Hermetic (see n. 87) and mystical-magical cast of mind. The names he gave himself—Paracelsus ("beyond Celsus," the greatest Roman writer on medicine), Theophrastus (from the great Greek botanist), Aureolus (golden)—suggest his notorious boastfulness, and he has been much written about and differently valued. "Whatever may be thought of himself or his doctrines, Paracelsus will endure as one of the greatest

forces of the 16th century. He revolutionized medicine" (J. Ferguson *Bibliotheca Chemica*, 2.171). For Browne's general attitude to his extravagance and also his value see *CM* 2.5.

86. *Ascendens constellatum:* a rising constellation reveals much to those who search out the great works of nature, i.e. the works of God.

87. *universall and common Spirit* . . . : the *anima mundi* or soul of the world of Plato's *Timaeus*, the Neoplatonists, and occult later writers. In the reference to Genesis further on in this section (there is a marginal quotation from the Vulgate in some MSS) Browne contrasts this acceptable but unauthoritative speculation with belief based on Scripture, but uses the language of alchemy in various phrases. Hermetic literature, that is, writings supposedly composed by and around Hermes Trismegistus (Hermes thrice-great) is a literature of rhapsodic rather than philosophic content on God, man, and nature. The core of it was thought in the Renaissance to have been composed in great antiquity by the Egyptian god Thoth—identified with Hermes Trismegistus. It is now known to have been written in the 2d and 3d centuries at Alexandria by men familiar with Platonic and Stoic thought as well as with gnosticism and Egyptian mysticism and demonology. It is a blend of cosmic mysticism (with a great deal of Pythagorean emphasis on purity of life and thought) in which there are pantheistic and even polytheistic, as well as monotheistic and Christian elements, number mysticism, etc. The microcosmic idea (*RM* 1.34 and elsewhere) in general has roots in Plato but Hermetic writers think of the whole cosmos as a vast harmony (or "tye of bodies" in Henry Vaughan's phrase) with influences—sympathies and antipathies—raying out from the macrocosm to the microcosm. For a similar (but more extravagant) linking together of Pythagoras, Plato, Trismegistus, Moses, etc. (Sect. 34) see Canto 1, stanza 4 of the *Psychozoia* of the Cambridge Platonist Henry More, published in the same year (1642) as *RM*. Kenelm Digby, however, calls this talk of a universal spirit a "wilde fancie."

88. *negative way:* i.e. what God is not, rather than what he is.

89. *or in a comparative:* or by comparing them to man and other creatures.

90. *definition of Porphyry* . . . : In this section Browne attempts to make, from St. Augustine and Neoplatonic and scholastic sources, a conception of the nature and position of angels in the chain of being, especially how angels "know" and how they move the bodies they assume. He doubts whether "Let there be light," the work of the first day in Genesis, means the creation of angels, though in *The City of God* (11, 9–10) St. Augustine guardedly suggests this, but scholastically attempts to

"conceive" immaterial or angelic substance as light invisible, perhaps from a phrase of St. Augustine (?) about the soul, "anima lux invisibilis," quoted in a notebook.

91. *Habbakuk:* Apocrypha, Bel and the Dragon 33–39.

92. *Philip:* Acts 8.39–40.

93. *best part of nothing:* since the whole Creation was from nothing.

94. *Moses . . . noe description:* this essential correction of the text (adding "noc" from *P*) made by Denonain and Sanna.

95. *the other:* the visible.

96. *beyond their first matter:* matter without form.

97. *hee hath sworne:* Gen. 9.11.

98. *that the world was eternall:* i.e. was not created out of nothing, has always existed, and is imperishable. (*De Caelo* 1.12.)

99. *blast of his mouth:* Gen. 1.24.

100. *as the text:* Gen. 2.7.

101. *as make:* Gen. 2.19, an apparent contradiction much discussed.

102. *Plato:* in the *Phaedrus* 245c.

103. *Aristotle:* in the *De Anima* 2.2–4.

104. *without conjunction:* i.e. in a test tube.

105. *Creando infunditur . . . :* Apparently (Greenhill) from one of Peter Lombard's *Sentences* expositing St. Augustine on Grace: in the act of creating it is poured, in the act of pouring creation takes place. An argument for infusion, not traduction (see Glossary).

106. *our study of Anatomy . . . Heathens to Divinitie:* probably a reference to Galen; Browne's view is echoed by Lord Herbert of Cherbury in his *Autobiography:* "I must no less commend the study of anatomy which whosoever considers I believe will never be an atheist . . . the greatest miracle in nature" (Quoted by C. E. Raven, *English Naturalists . . .* , 232–33).

107. *Lot's wife:* turned into a pillar of salt (Gen. 19.26).

108. *Nabuchodonosor:* "his hairs grew like eagles' feathers and nails like birds' claws and he ate grass" (Dan. 4.33).

109. *frequent Cemiteries:* Plato (and Kenelm Digby in his *Observations*) think it is because they are souls which still retain a longing for material objects.

110. *Adam quid fecisti:* Adam what hast thou done; Vulgate, Apocrypha, 2 Esdras 7.48.

111. *not yet without:* i.e. not still without, though they are not fully operative.

112. *that ineffable place:* paradise, where spirits dwell (2 Corinth. 12.4).

113. *Philosophers stone:* elixir or secret substance of alchemists which would transmute base metals into gold. By analogy the only important transmutation, from the base metal of the body to the gold of immortality, needs more than the philosopher's stone for "exaltation" or sublimation.

114. *mysticall transmigrations:* because a traditional emblem of the soul's escape from the body.

115. *I have therefore forsaken:* Ordinary medical definitions of death are followed by the alchemically phrased "final transformation by which the noble extract of the microcosm is perfected." "Digestion" is slow purification by gentle heat.

116. *in a tempest:* perhaps on the Irish Sea in 1629.

117. *quantum mutatus ab illo:* how changed from that [Hector he was]. Aeneas about the shade of Hector in Hades (*Aeneid* 2.274).

118. *courage:* here, confidence.

119. *Lucan: Pharsalia* 7.89.

120. *Crowes and Dawes:* their supposed longevity is discussed (sceptically) in *PE* 3.9.

121. *one revolution:* Saturn completes a revolution every twenty-nine and a half years.

122. *excepting one:* Christian IV of Denmark.

123. *left underground:* Martin names the persons intended and suggests that though Leo XI died six months before Browne was actually born, the beginning of Sect. 39 and a passage in *PE* justify Browne on his own terms! Kenelm Digby (*Observations,* 1643) becomes very ironic about Browne's vanity in making great princes the landmarks in his own chronology and thinks these personal details and "private thoughts" "cannot much conduce to any man's betterment."

124. *Cicero's ground:* in *De Senectute* 23.24.

125. *six thousand:* commonly thought to be the term of the world's existence from the Creation; again and again referred to by Browne.

126. *Lucan: Pharsalia* 4.519–20.

127. *Curtius, Scevola, or Codrus:* three famous examples of Stoical contempt for pain and death.

128. *Emori nolo:* quoted in Latin as from a Greek poet, Epicharmus, by Cicero, *Tusculan Questions,* 18.

129. *Memento mori:* remember that you must die.

130. *quatuor novissima:* the four last things.

131. *Lucan: Pharsalia* 7.814.

132. *growes neare its end:* In the 6000 years' chronological scheme, Browne was living in the sixteen hundreds of the last 2000 years. Like Hakewill in his *Apology* (1627) and unlike Donne (who was using, if

not believing, the idea) in the *Devotions* (1624), Browne rejects the idea of the decay and senility of the world.

133. *Some beleeve:* changed from the "I beleeve" of the MSS and 42 probably because a little unorthodox.

134. *communicated to a Rabbi:* i.e. part of Talmudic tradition.

135. *denyed unto his Angels:* Matt. 24.36.

136. *In those dayes:* Matt. 24.6; following refs. also from New Testament.

137. *halfe of opinion:* MSS read "half of Paracelsus opinion."

138. *Quousque, Domine:* Rev. 6.9–10.

139. *Ipsa sui . . . sibi:* a Stoic proverb.

140. *honest artifice of Seneca:* Keck quotes passage from Seneca *Epistles* 11, but 25 is more appropriate.

141. *that great resolution:* Seneca *Epist.* 113.

142. *those impieties:* disrespect for the gods in Euripides; in Lucian and Julian the Apostate, satire of, or attacks on, Christianity.

143. *This is made good by experience:* The MSS and 42 read "This I make good by experience" (i.e. experiment). On reading this section Browne's young friend Henry Power (see Letters, n. 29) wrote for advice, but no reply is extant. For illustrations of the frequency of both the notion and the experiment in the 17th century, see L. Thorndike, *A History of Magic and Experimental Science*, vols. 7 and 8, Index; there are over 20 entries. But Digby and von Moltke are doubtful.

144. *these more perfect and sensible structures:* human bodies.

145. *as Ezekiel:* in his vision of the valley of dry bones (Ezek. 37.5–10).

146. *elegant Apostle:* Paul in 1 Corinth. 2.9; "elegant" seems to mean "chosen."

147. *Saint Johns description:* Rev. 21.19–21.

148. *the Parable:* Luke 16.19–25.

149. *Aristotles Philosophy:* in *De Anima* 2.7.

150. *flames . . . in the Scriptures:* Rev. 21.8.

151. *Legion:* in Mark 5.9 the "unclean Spirit" says "my name is Legion, for we are many."

152. *Anaxagoras conceited* [i.e. fancied] *worlds:* Cicero credits this view to Anaximander.

153. *Magdalen:* Luke 8.2.

154. *those soules in Hell:* as "divinity" demands; they are in the outermost circle in Dante's *Inferno*. Digby (like Lactantius, as Keck points out) rejects this theological logic.

155. *one Limbo left:* like the limbo (region) on the borders of hell for unbaptized infants, and another for patriarchs who lived before Christ.

156. *the Philosopher:* identified variously as Antisthenes, Aristippus, Crates; most probably Aristippus, from Diogenes Laertius' *Lives of the Philosophers.*

157. *the bridge:* Matt. 7.14: "strait is the gate, and narrow is the way."

158. *Atomist:* member of 17th century sect founded by a Mrs. Atomy; *Familist:* member of a sect called the Family of Love, instituted about 1575.

159. *little Flocke:* Luke 12.32, and a favorite phrase with the Puritans.

160. *Hierarchies amongst the Angels:* three divisions, each with three orders, according to accepted angelology.

161. *decry good workes:* a feature of Lutheranism and Calvinism, and debated very fiercely in Browne's time.

162. *decreed by God:* in Judges 7.4–7.

The Second Part

1. *one man placed . . . below:* as the 2 of 2789 means more than 789; "below" as in contemporary enumeration tables (Martin).

2. *counterfeit Egyptians:* gypsies.

3. *24 Letters:* not 26 because "i" and "j," "u" and "v" were interchangeable.

4. *Parenthesis on the party:* digression on a part.

5. Βατραχομυομαχία: battle of the frogs and mice, a mock-epic poem attributed (wrongly) to Homer.

6. *S. and T. in Lucian:* In a piece by Lucian the letter *sigma* complains to the vowels, as judges, of the conduct of the letter *tau.*

7. *Propria quae maribus:* The general rules of gender in Lily's much-used school *Grammar* began with these words.

8. *Priscian:* Priscian (c.500–530) was so famous a grammarian that the expression "to break Priscian's head" meant to break the rules.

9. *Si foret . . . :* How Democritus would laugh if he were alive (Horace, *Epistles* 2.1.194).

10. *Actius his razor:* as the result of a challenge by Tarquinius Priscus (5th king of Rome) the chief augur Actius cut a whetstone in two with a razor (Livy 1.36).

11. *there goes:* i.e. a great deal of conscience should be employed.

12. *no reproach to:* no reproach like.

13. *Le mutin Anglois . . . :* these lines have been derived (by H. G. Ward) from sonnet 68 of Du Bellay's *Les Regrets*—Browne owned a 1569 edition of Du Bellay's French works—but the differences are striking; "bougre" means "buggering."

14. *Saint Paul:* in Titus 1.12, quoting the ancient Cretan prophet Epimenides.

15. *as Neroes was:* Keck raised the question (discussed by editors) whether Browne was referring to a cruel speech of Nero (quoted) or whether, by a slip of memory, to Caligula's notorious wish that the people of Rome had but one neck so that he could destroy them all at one blow. (Suetonius *Nero* 38 or *Caligula* 50; references in *PE* and *CM* (3.27) support Nero.)

16. *trajection of a sensible species:* mental image of the appearance of an object.

17. *Non occides:* thou shalt not kill.

18. *I thinke . . . mee thinkes:* these and many other qualifying words and additions of 43 in the following sections (see Textual Notes) illustrate Browne's claim that *RM* was a private exercise, and his embarrassment at its publication.

19. *Heroick examples:* of friendship; Damon and Pythias under the Tyrant Dionysius; Patrocles and Achilles in Homer; Nisus and Euryalus (in *P* alone) in Virgil.

20. *I doe not finde in my selfe:* Browne lost his father at the age of eight, and within seven months his mother married a decidedly robustious soldier and courtier Sir Thomas Dutton, who died from a blow in a quarrel in 1634, the year before *RM* was written (see also 2.9).

21. *I never yet cast:* written in 1635; Browne married in 1641.

22. *to procure. And further:* the punctuation of original texts and all editors "procure, and further" does not seem to me to make good sense.

23. *the Italian:* who, according to a popular story, was promised his life if he would disclaim his faith, and having done so was immediately stabbed to forestall the penitence necessary for divine forgiveness.

24. *that Lecher:* a story concerning a young man and a statue by Praxiteles told by Lucian and Pliny (Keck).

25. *Spintrian recreations:* sexual perversions observed by the Emperor Tiberius, as reported by Suetonius.

26. *Pride:* this passage has, from the time of publication, roused comment. Alexander Ross (*Medicus Medicatus,* 1645 p. 74) commented tartly: "And have you not pride, in thinking you have no pride. [St.] Bernard makes twelve degrees of pride, of which bragging is one." The bragging granted, Browne was presumably thinking of pride in the more "deadly" sense—the pride of a Lucifer or Faustus.

27. *construction:* construing, or explaining and analyzing.

28. *Babel:* Gen. 11.9.

29. *Poynters:* the two stars of the Dipper or Great Bear, which point to the Pole Star.

30. *Simpled . . . Cheapside:* gathered herbs in the market at Cheapside near which Browne lived as a boy in the parish of St. Michael.

31. *the riddle of the Fisherman:* Fisherman should be plural, as in *PE* 7.13. Having caught no fish they were delousing themselves and their riddle was "what they had taken they had left behind them, and what they had not taken they had with them"; a story from Herodotus and Plutarch.

32. *flux and reflux of Euripus:* See *PE* 7.13.

33. *Peripateticks, Stoicks, or Academicks:* Aristotelian, Stoic, or Platonic.

34. *accessory of our glorification:* a consequence of being in heaven.

35. *commend their resolutions:* the original reading was much stronger (see Textual Notes).

36. *odde and unworthy piece of folly:* Browne's intellectualism has been often pointed at, but Keck refers to a passage in Hippocrates and quotes a long parallel from Montaigne. (*Essays,* 3.5.)

37. *all Church musicke:* the original "our church music" is more revelatory of contemporary Puritan attacks.

38. *Plato . . . Harmony:* especially in *Timaeus* 47d.

39. *Tacitus . . . Cicero:* in *Annals* 1.1, and *Pro Archia* 1.1.

40. *three Noble professions:* medicine, law, divinity.

41. *the sinne against the Holy Ghost:* Matt. 12.31 and Mark 3.29; an unpardonable sin, but not named, and hence much debated.

42. *Magnae virtutes . . . . :* great were his virtues and his faults no less. Plutarch (*Demetrius,* 1) quotes this as a saying of Plato.

43. *the greatest Balsames:* a common medical and alchemical belief.

44. *the man without a Navell:* Adam, created not born. See also *PE* 5.5.

45. *Nunquam minus solus . . . :* never less alone than when I am solitary (Cicero *De Officiis* 3.1).

46. *more invulnerable then Achilles:* referring to Achilles' heel, not dipped in the river Styx.

47. *Ruat coelum . . . :* thy will be done though the heavens fall.

48. *Planetary hour of Saturne:* in a letter Browne said he was born on November 19, 1605, but this horoscope reference seems to describe October. To be born under Saturn (the leaden planet) to a Renaissance Platonist did not necessarily imply sullen melancholy, but rather solitary meditative thoughtfulness, as in Milton's *Il Penseroso.*

49. *Themistocles therefore:* the story is apparently told of various classical worthies; Themistocles may be an error.

50. *Lucan and Seneca:* commanded by Nero to commit suicide, but with choice of the means.

51. *Hellebore:* a supposed cure for madness.

52. *that Snow is blacke:* a view attributed to Anaxagoras.

53. *that the earth moves:* the Copernican hypothesis was still not generally accepted; Browne is not equating these various opinions as folly, but saying that they are "philosophy", i.e. speculation. Aristotle (*De Anima* 1.2) refers to the three views of the soul and their proponents.

54. *subterraneous Idoll:* Mammon.

55. *Aristotle is too severe:* a not entirely accurate comment on Aristotle's remarks about munificence and liberality in *Nic. Ethics.*

56. *He that giveth . . . :* Prov. 19.17.

57. *prophecy of Christ:* Although the texts in the New Testament do not use the future tense, the marginal gloss in three MSS, "the poor ye shall have always with you," indicates how the texts were understood. Martin refers also to Deut. 15.11 where the tense is future.

58. *summum bonum:* i.e. Aristotle's greatest good (from *Nic. Ethics*) is as much an abstraction as Plato's Ideas.

59. *story out of Pliny:* who has many tall stories, as Browne notes in *PE* 1.8, and elsewhere.

60. *thy selfe* [God] *and:* this insertion in *43* may have been caused by Digby's strictures (in the *Observations* of 1643) on the intensity of Browne's praise of friendship. Ross (*Medicus Medicatus,* 1645) was also very critical. In the sixteen seventies Browne jotted down in a notebook (MS Sloane 1843, f. 14) "I cannot fancy unto my selfe a more acceptable representation or state of things then if I could see all my best friends and worthy acquaintance of fortie yeares last past upon the stage of the world at one time."

61. *my owne undoing:* "my own damnation" of *42,* and those MSS which contain this sentence, must have seemed to Browne too predestinarian in 1643.

PSEUDODOXIA EPIDEMICA
(VULGAR ERRORS)

For some comments on a reasonably historical approach to Browne's learning, objectives, and sources in *Pseudodoxia Epidemica,* see the Introduction.

To the Reader; The First Book

1. *cooperating advancers:* a reference to the need for societies of the learned, as advocated also by Bacon, and exemplified a little later in the Royal Society for the Advancement of Science.

2. *performed upon one legge:* i.e. extemporaneously; from Horace *Satires* 1.4.10.

3. *smell of oyle:* should suggest laborious study by lamplight (a taunt spoken against Demosthenes by Pytheas).

4. *Dr. Primrose: De Vulgi Erroribus in Medicinae* (1639), translated into French and English (1651).

5. *Scipio Mercurii* (i.e. Girolamo Mercurio): *Degli Errori Popolari d'Italia* (1603); ed. of 1645 in *SC;* concerned with medical errors.

6. *Laurentius Joubertus* (Joubert): His *Erreures Populaires et Propos Vulgaires touchant la Médicine* (1579 and many subsequent editions) is an extraordinary jumble of old wives' tales and popular beliefs, treated quite uncritically.

7. *Andreas:* this work on pseudo-truths, etc. is known only from the reference in Athenaeus.

8. *desired . . . desiderated:* the distinction seems to be between what is wanting and what is desirable.

9. *wounds of constitution:* i.e. from the original sin of Adam.

10. *hear a Serpent speak:* See Gen. 3 for Browne's various references and quotations.

11. *fertility of his sleep:* Eve.

12. *as some affirm . . . as others have conceived:* to appreciate the contemporary interest in this and similar questions see A. Williams, *The Common Expositor,* a book on Renaissance Commentaries on Genesis.

13. *St. John:* 1 John 2.16.

14. *integrity:* i.e. before original sin had damaged him.

15. *perswaded by fire:* even being burned at the stake for heresy has not made them recant a literal interpretation.

16. *manuall expressions:* described in human bodily terms.

17. *Mahomet:* for this and also remarks in *PE* 1.4 and 1.5 see note on Koran, *RM* 1.23, n. 62.

18. *Galen . . . Moses:* presumably with reference to Galen's contrast between the conception of a creation from nothing, and the Greek views of Epicurus and Plato (*De Usu Partium,* 11.14).

19. *Orestes* (and footnote): Some of the legends make a good deal of the madness of Orestes when haunted by the Erinyes after the murder of his mother Clytemnestra. In his essay on the oracle of Apollo, Browne also refers to Orestes as a madman.

20. *Lystrian rabble:* Acts 14.11–20.

21. *tumult of Demetrius:* Acts 19.23–29.

22. *stolen ear-rings:* Exod. 3.22 and 12.35–36. A misreading of the text in the Authorized translation.

23. *Peter:* John 18.10.

24. *that Aphorisme:* vox populi vox dei, "quoted as a saying by Alcuin, c. A.D. 800", and proverbial.

25. *adorement of Cats, Lizards and Beetles:* by the Egyptians.

26. *Theudas an Impostor:* a Jewish impostor of the first century B.C. whose acts are described by early Christian historians.

27. *David George:* a glazier of Leyden or Ghent who proclaimed himself a Messiah in 1525. Called "the Father of the Familists" (the "Family of Love").

28. *Arden:* not identified.

29. *Aarons brest-plate:* which had four rows of three jewels set in gold, each bearing the name of one of the twelve tribes, and to which special supernatural powers were ascribed in divination.

30. *devil of Delphos:* oracle of Apollo at Delphi, as in *RM* 1.13.

31. *Were Aesop alive:* "alluding, probably, to Aesop's fable of 'the Astrologer and the Traveller'" (Wilkin).

32. *Cujus alterum nomen . . . :* to use this name at the ceremonies of the mysteries was held to be criminal (Pliny *Natural History* 3.5.65). The now accepted text is amended to read "except at the ceremonies."

33. *Councell of the bean:* the council chosen by lot (the bean being used in drawing lots) as distinguished from the Areopagus (Thucydides 8.66).

34. *Empedocles:* this mysterious Pythagorean commandment from the taboos of Empedocles is literally "wretched men withhold your hands from beans," but has had much annotation. Browne's interpretative translation has, as he claims, classical support.

35. *Brutus . . . Tarquine:* Lucius Junius (Brutus) nephew of Tarquinius Superbus, last king of Rome (who had killed Tarquinius' brother) accompanied the two sons of Tarquinius to Delphi to consult the oracle. The two princes asked the oracle who should succeed to the throne and the answer was "The one who first kisses his mother." Brutus pretended to stumble and kissed the earth (in another version the earth of Italy, on return).

36. *Athenians . . . wooden walls:* the Athenians were advised by the oracle to take refuge from Xerxes within a wooden wall. On the persuasion of Themistocles they misinterpreted this to mean their fleet.

37. *doubled the Altar:* a command of the Delian, not the Delphic, oracle.

38. *Epiphanius, Austin, or Prateolus:* Epiphanius and St. Augustine wrote against heresies in the 4th and 5th centuries, Prateolus (Gabriel de Préau) in the 16th; the *Panarion* of Epiphanius is a "medicine chest" naming eighty heresies, Origen being the principal heretic.

39. *Belus:* Hellenization of Ba'al, Bel, one of the first kings of Babylon.

40. *assault of Pompey:* according to Josephus, made on Jewish sabbath.

41. *Saint Paul . . . beware of philosophy:* Coloss. 2.8.

42. *last medicine:* latest medicine.

43. *Geber, Avicenna and Almanzor:* This invention about the Koran seems to have come from the *Observations* of Pierre Belon (Bellonius) to whom Browne often refers. See B. Moran, *Notes and Queries* 197 (1952), 380–82, 406–8, for this and what follows. Geber, Avicenna, Almanzor are perhaps named as distinguished Arabs.

44. *hoc tantum scio . . . :* I know [only] so much as to know that I know nothing.

45. *like Zeno:* Zeno of Elea; pupil and friend of Parmenides (born c.490 B.C.) and famous for his dialectical propositions about motion (especially Achilles and the tortoise, and the proposition that before a moving body can reach the end of a line, it must reach the middle point, before this the middle point again and so on. Therefore it can never start at all).

46. *in sudore . . . :* Gen. 3.19, in the sweat of thy brow.

47. *Magis extra . . . :* rather without vices than with virtues.

48. *Ultimus bonorum:* the last of the good.

49. *Nos numerus sumus:* Horace *Epist.* 1.2.27, we are a mere cipher.

50. *Lanthorn . . . Athens:* referring to the story of Diogenes with his lantern in the daytime, looking for an honest man.

51. *Hippocrates . . . Galen . . . Aristotle:* justifiably remained three great names among the new experimental scientists who were concerned with biology and medicine rather than physics. Referring in the 1660's or 1670's to the general attacks on Aristotle, to a book by Jean de Launay on Aristotle's academic reputation in France (*SC* 1656), and to the fact that Aristotle was "almost at the point of death" among the moderns, Browne suggested (? to his son Edward): "while hardly touching the Physics and reading the Metaphysics superficially, make much of all the rest" (Keynes, III.206, tr. by W. R. Le Fanu).

52. *Aristotle . . . Problemes:* Aristotle's *Problems* is now considered largely spurious, and to have been composed in the 5th or 6th centuries and later. See Browne's notes on more of them in Keynes III, 206–17.

53. *aiunt, ferunt, fortasse:* so they say, they assert, perhaps.

54. *the Greeks and Latines each other:* A judgment on the reasonableness of most of these rather literal-minded observations could only be attempted by a bored classical scholar. While Browne had read, or read in, all these texts, his comments were not very original. Charges of plagiarism were frequent even among Greek writers, and almost an occupation of Alexandrian criticism, to say nothing of some scholars of the Renaissance.

55. *Lucius:* a shorter version of Apuleius' novel, *The Golden Ass,* called *Lucius,* was attributed to Lucian. It is thought that both versions may derive from a work by Lucius of Pratas.

56. *wittiest peece of Ovid:* his *Metamorphoses.*

57. *mendacity of Greece:* Browne seems singularly unwilling or unable to distinguish legendary (mythikon) from lying.

58. *Palaephatus:* A Greek writer of the 4th century B.C., who, with Euhemerus of Sicily (also 4th–3d century B.C.), rationalized Greek mythology as based on real incidents in human history. Browne is clearly much influenced; *cf.* Bacon's scientific rationalization in *The Wisedome of the Ancients.*

59. *Gerion [Geryon]:* a monster with three heads, with a two-headed dog.

60. *Cerberus:* a dog of Pluto with three heads who guarded the descent to Hades against the living. Orpheus drugged him with music, Hercules dragged him out.

61. *Tricarinia:* Wilkin quotes Wren "read Trinacria," i.e. Sicily, with three heads, or promontories.

62. *an hundred hands:* the meaning in Greek of the city named.

63. *Diomedes:* to capture the man-eating horses of King Diomedes was the eighth labor of Hercules.

64. *Minotaure:* a creature half man, half bull, the offspring of Pasiphae, wife of King Minos, and a bull sent out of the sea by Poseidon to be sacrificed. It was hidden in a maze constructed by Daedalus.

65. *Domitian:* as narrated by Dio Cassius, *Roman History,* 67.

66. *Nosce teipsum . . . Nosce tempus . . . Nihil nimis:* know thyself; know the right time; nothing beyond measure.

67. *Laertius* [Diogenes Laertius] . . . *Lycosthenes* [Conrad Wolfhart, Graecized into Lycosthenes, 1518–1561] . . . *Macrobius* [fl.c.400]: respective authors of the *Lives of the Philosophers, Apothegmata* (1555 and many subsequent editions), *Saturnalia* (a collection of supposed table talk on many subjects).

68. *salts of Cicero:* witty saying of Cicero.

69. *Augustus:* J. O. Augustus, *De Imperio Romano* (1548) has a section of epigrams.

70. *Erasmus:* whose *Adages* went into dozens of editions and was read at most schools.

71. *Nemo mortalium . . . :* no mortal man is at all hours wise; than virtue nothing is more excellent or beautiful; love conquers all; truth is something splendid.

72. *Contra negantem principia . . . :* [there is no arguing with a person who] denies first principles; for he himself has said it; you must believe.

73. *assertions of Philosophy:* see parallel statement in *RM* 2.13, where, however, the revolution of the earth is included.

74. *the sea . . . sweat of the earth:* This phrase of Empedocles may be merely poetical (as Aristotle said) but has been related to Empedocles' idea that the earth was first mixed with water and the water pressed out by the velocity of the earth's revolution.

75. *Then was Aristotle injurious:* in the *Physics* (1.2) and *De Caelo,* and in a separate attack on Melissus; Aristotle calls his arguments contentious, gross, and ridiculous.

76. *Aristotle affirming . . . :* Aulus Gellius (c.123–c.165) in his *Attic Nights* (3.16) has a long discussion of authorities, and refers to Hadrian. Rabelais satirically makes Gargantua an eleventh month child and cites the whole clutch of authorities given in A. Gellius.

77. *Dove si possa . . . :* where the North Star may be seen.

78. *Alciats Emblems:* moral verses in Latin by Andrea Alciati with illustrative pictures; first published in 1531 and much imitated and translated. *Avem Philomelam . . .* That the nightingale lacks a tongue I am able to affirm, positively (a literal application of the story of Philomela).

79. *remedy of Sammonicus:* Sammonicus was the 2d- or 3d-century author of a medical (text) book in verse; put the 4th book of Homer's Iliads under one shaking with quartan fever (Sect. 49).

80. *Kiranides:* see *PE* 1.8.12.

81. *the Chymistes:* referring to some of the chemical cure-alls in Paracelsus and his more extravagant followers.

82. *the father Poet:* Homer.

83. *Ego quae fando . . . :* setting down what I have learned I feel obliged to put down everything; but I am not obliged to believe it all true.

84. *Equidem facilius . . . :* One could more easily believe Hesiod and Homer or the tragic poets than Ctesias, Herodotus, Hellanicus, and others of this kind (Strabo 11.6.3). *Scripsit Ctesias:* Ctesias wrote about India and things there that he had not seen himself nor heard from reliable report (*A True History* 1).

85. *lately performed:* 2 vols. folio 1629 (*SC*).

86. *Deipnosophista:* learned banquet or "symposium"; for further evidence of the kind of pleasure Browne got from Athenaeus see "Some Notes from a Reading of Athenaeus" Keynes, III, 170, tr. by Le Fanu.

87. *Nicander:* the works referred to are didactic poems on antidotes for poisonous snake bites and other poisons.

88. *annuall mutation . . . Hyaena:* many of these "errors" are discussed in *PE.*

89. *Antoninus:* the Emperor Caracalla, 188–217.

90. *Chiliads de Varia Historia:* the title indicates that there are thousands of verses (like "centuries" in *Centuries of Meditations*). The author, of the 12th century, has been described as "a copious, careless, quarrelsome Byzantine polymath."

91. *Cardanus:* Cardan's *Works*, 10 vols. folio (1663) are in *SC*.

92. *Salamander, Pelican, Basilisk . . . Pliny:* for the pelican see *PE* 5.1 (in this volume); the other fables referred to below are that the Salamander can live in the fire; that the basilisk can kill at a distance through the eye; that the bear licks its cubs into shape; that young vipers bite their way out through the mother's body. By Browne's time some of them had become literary rather than literal beliefs, but they are all disposed of in *PE*.

93. *Pierius:* his *Hieroglyphica* (ed. of 1631 in *SC*) gives a good visual impression of this material.

94. *Kircherus* [Kircher]: is added in 1658 for the material in his *Oedipus Aegyptiacus* (1652, *SC*).

95. *Galens study:* i.e. library, supposedly part of the great library of Pergamum, which, transported to Alexandria, was burned by the Saracens in 642.

96. *Socrates only suffered:* see *RM* 1.26, n. 73.

97. *Minervas:* Minerva was born of Jupiter's brain without a mother.

98. *play a solemne prize:* Exod. 9.17–18.

99. *the old Serpent:* Satan.

100. *Pythia Philippised:* in 339 B.C. Demosthenes used this phrase about the oracle of Apollo at Delphi (Pythia) to persuade the Athenians not to consult it, because it had become so favorable to Philip of Macedon, their enemy.

101. *Croesus:* for Browne's attitude see his essay on the oracle of Delphi, in this volume.

102. *fuga Daemonis:* i.e. with power to put the devil to flight.

103. *Tobias . . . Asmodeus:* Apocrypha, Tobit 6–8.

104. *Parthian flights:* tactical flights, so called from the skill of the Parthians in shooting their arrows behind them while galloping in retreat.

105. *Brutus, Cassius:* in Plutarch (*Brutus*. 36–37) a spirit appears and says "I am thy evil spirit Brutus." Cassius, as an Epicurean sceptical about spirits, explains it away.

106. *the unbelief of witches:* not believing in witches.

107. *Valentinus, Arrius* [Arius], *Marcion:* and other writers mentioned below expressed views (gnostic, Arian, Manichee, anti-Trinitarian) condemned as heretical in the 2d and 3d centuries.

108. *Julian, Maximinus, Dioclesian:* Roman emperors, Julian an apostate, Maximinus and Diocletian zealous persecutors of Christians in the early 4th century.

109. *Saturns mouth:* Saturn (Kronos) devoured his sons as they were born, having promised his brother Titan that he would not bring up children to succeed him.

110. *Melchisedech:* the king-priest of Salem (Gen. 14), in traditional biblical exegesis the "type" of Christ.

THE SECOND BOOK

1. *Concerning the Loadstone:* for general discussion of this chapter see G. K. Chalmers, "The Loadstone and the Understanding of Science in the Seventeenth Century."

2. *the earth . . . a Magneticall body:* the influence of Gilbert's *De Magnete* (1600, tr. Mottelay, 1893 and 1958) may be seen throughout this chapter; Browne's phrase "the Father Philosopher" of magnetism shows his respect. Gilbert was a strong supporter of what he called the Greek and Copernican hypothesis of the rotation of the earth.

3. *Psal. 93.1 . . . Job 38:* these and similar texts were frequently quarreled over in debates about the new astronomy.

4. *Now whether the earth stand still:* the omission of this paragraph from all but the first edition of *PE* seems to indicate Browne's reluctance to commit himself. To judge from a remark in MS Sloane 1879 (printed in this volume) by the 1660s or 1670s Browne seems to have been either a Copernican or a follower of Tycho Brahe.

5. *effluxions . . . effluviums:* see articles by Chalmers referred to in the Selected Bibliography. Gilbert speaks (in Aristotelian language) of "the immaterial act of the form" and its "incorporeal going forth," "entelecheia not ergon." Bacon is quoted by Chalmers from the *Novum Organum:* "this may be an instance of divorce between corporeal nature and natural action" and "a proof furnished by merely human philosophy of the existence of essences and substances separated from matter and incorporeal." Browne's prophetic paragraph about "the doctrine of effluxions" is quoted in full in the *Experimental Philosophy* (1664, p. 58) of Henry Power.

6. *species of visible objects:* a supposed emanation from outward things forming the direct object of cognition for the various senses or for the understanding (OED).

7. *Renatus des Cartes:* in *Principia Philosophiae* (1644), 4. art. 146.

8. *Sir Kenelme Digby:* in *Of Bodies,* 1644.

9. *Aldrovandus:* the 1648 edition of Aldrovandus' *Musaeum Metallicum* listed in SC suggests that Browne had just been reading this.

10. *Ridley:* Mark Ridley (1560–1624) for some time physician to the Czar Boris Godunov, and a great admirer of Gilbert, published a *Short Treatise of Magnetical Bodies* in 1613.

11. *Brigs:* Henry Briggs (1561–1630) was first professor of geometry at Gresham College and Savilian professor of astronomy at Oxford; in a letter to his son Edward, Browne speaks of having as an undergraduate talked geometry and geography with him at Oxford.

12. *Kircherus:* the 1654 folio edition of *Magnes sive de Arte Magnetica* is in SC but Browne added this passage in 50; the first (shorter) edition of *Magnes* appeared in 1641.

13. *Hic ventus . . .* : this is now a good wind, about ship (or tack); not quite literally from Plautus *Mercator*, 875.

14. *Salomon . . . Aristotle:* Solomon's "universality of knowledge" was considered by John Smith, M.D., (in a book noticed in the Transactions of the Royal Society, 1665) to have extended to acquaintance with the circulation of the blood (Thorndike, VII, 579).

15. *Candish:* Cavendish.

16. *Catalogue of Laertius:* Diogenes Laertius gives lists of works in his *Lives of the Philosophers.*

17. *Praeterea magnes . . .* : the magnet attracts the iron, or rather the magnet and the iron come together unless something prevents them (*Principia Philosophiae*, 4. art. 171).

18. *nec magnes . . .* : neither the magnet attracts of itself the iron, nor does the iron draw the magnet to itself, but both by equal effort come together.

19. *doctrine of Gilbertus:* these technical terms from Gilbert are annotated on pp. 110–11 of Mottelay's translation (1958).

20. *Helmontus, Kircherus, and Licetus:* these additions in 50 and 58 show Browne's interest and also a certain fondness for "authorities," even when not accepted, and unnecessary; SC lists the 1653 folio edition of Fortunio Liceto's book on stones and gems, in which the loadstone is discussed.

21. *most violent termes of their language:* instead of the stone which "seizes" iron, as in Augustine and Hippocrates, Galen suggested "pulls," and Aristotle "moves."

22. *Magnes Carneus:* see Thorndike (VII, Index) for this and similar magnetic beliefs; also, below for the widespread belief in garlic as preventative of magnetic force.

23. *and many more:* well into the 17th century.

24. *Homers Moly:* a magic herb given to Ulysses by Hermes to protect him from Circe; "and" equals "or" in this and other similar sentences.

25. *Adamas dissidet . . . :* The diamond has an aversion to the magnet, so that when placed close to the iron it prevents the iron from being attracted from itself; or, if the magnet is moved toward the iron and seizes it, the diamond snatches the iron and takes it off (Pliny *Nat. Hist.* 37.15).

26. *Pyramidographia* [*1646*]: by John Greaves (1602–1652), mathematician and traveler, Gresham professor of geometry, London, 1630, Savilian professor of astronomy, 1643, but ejected by parliament in 1648.

27. *King Cheops:* so described by Greaves, in his account of the great pyramid of Cheops.

28. *the verity hereof:* the added phrase in 46 clearly dropped in order not to spoil the joke, not from intellectual timidity; similarly with "and untrue," below.

29. *Michael Sundevogius* [*usually Sendivogius*]: Polish alchemist, c.1550–1640, famous for his supposed transmutations, as in 1605 at the court of Rudolph II at Prague. This tract published in 1616.

30. *Pantarbes:* a magical stone of the Brahmans, described by Apollonius of Tyana, in the life by Philostratus.

31. *Franciscus Rueus:* a Discourse of gems mentioned in the Apocalypse seems extravagant, but SC lists quite a number of separate 17th-century books on flora and fauna in the Bible: animals (Bochart and also Franzius), reptiles (Bustamente), medical and physiognomical matters (Vecchi), "physics" (De Mey). The longest piece in Browne's *Miscellany Tracts* is on "Plants mentioned in Scripture."

32. *generally beleeved:* must mean popularly, but G. T. Vossius, also a Scholar, discusses it in his *Theologia Gentili* (1641).

33. *the way of Baptista Porta:* Book 7 of Porta's very popular *Natural Magick*, 1558 (Eng. ed., 1658; facsimile, Basic Books, New York, 1957) is about the loadstone and includes various magnetical parlour games.

34. *Garcias ab Horto* [*Garcia da Orta*]: the blend of experience, good sense, and superstition in his *Colloquies on the Simples and Drugs of India* (1563) is illustrated by Thorndike, V, 476.

35. *the Art of Taliacotius:* Tagliacozzi of Bologna (1546–1599) was a plastic surgeon of considerable repute, and his *De Curtorum Chirurgia per Insitionem* (1597) was widely read. Van Helmont and others tell a pleasant story of the difficulties of "insition" and "permutation" about a man of Brussels who lost his nose in a quarrel and by the skill of Tagliacozzi got a new one from a porter's arm. A year later the nose grew cold and then rotted and it was found that just at the same instant that the nose grew cold, the porter at Bologna died.

36. *unguentum Armarium . . . Magneticum:* weapon salve, an oint-
ment (common ingredients skull moss and bear's grease) which cured
wounds at a distance by occult power, as the result of anointing the
weapon, or a bandage taken from the wound, not the wound itself. In
1658, according to his own account, Sir Kenelm Digby lectured with
great distinction on the subject at Montpellier. His *Discourse* on the
weapon salve (1658) had a great success in numerous editions in English, French, German, Dutch, and Latin.

37. *fields of Medicines:* i.e. fields full of medicinal herbs.

38. *flux and reflux . . . Magnetisme from the Moon: Selenographia* by
Hevelius (Johann Hevel), the first important book on the geography of
the moon, with chapters on the astronomical telescope, was published in
1647. Browne refers to it admiringly in a chapter added in 50 to Book 6
of *PE* (6.14). Kircher's work was published in 1646, also too late for
the first edition of *PE*.

THE THIRD BOOK

1. *Ixion, Sisiphus, Titius, Tantalus:* Ixion was tied to a wheel in perpetual motion; Sisiphus was condemned to roll a huge stone to the top
of a mountain; Titius (a giant) was spread on the Caucasus while vultures tore at his liver; Tantalus was placed up to his chin in a pool of
water which ran out when he tried to drink.

2. *Indus qui Elephantem . . . :* the Indian who was leading the animal believed that he (Porus) was getting down, and as usual made the
animal kneel (Curtius *History of Alexander,* 8.14, 39).

3. *Pontificem ter genibus . . . :* which three times with bent knees
and lowered head reverently saluted the pontiff.

4. *memorable shew of Germanicus:* this spritely scene is to be found
in Pliny *Nat. Hist.* 8.2.

5. Greek footnote: i.e. knee from angle.

6. *à dicto secundum . . . :* to infer an absolute truth from a qualified
premiss.

7. *assented unto by most:* it is hard to believe this, either as a fact or
as a joke, but harder to doubt Browne's truthfulness or imagine him
humorless.

8. *Talpa Caecior:* blinder than a mole; *caecitas* blindness.

9. *humorem nigrum:* black liquid.

10. *oblaesos:* maimed, imperfect.

11. *I am not satisfied:* "And therefore, though the learned Doctor
Brown (my ever honoured friend) hath ranked this conceit of the Eyes

of a Snail (and especially their quadruplicity) amongst the Vulgar Errours of the Multitude; yet through a good Microscope he may easily
see his own errour . . ." (Henry Power, *Experimental Philosophy*, 1664,
p. 36). The effect of this may be seen in the changes in the 1672 edition
of *PE*. The two large tentacles of the snail have eyes, one on each, but
the black spots on the pair of mouth tentacles are not eyes.

12. *Commento in Ocellus Lucanus:* SC lists an edition of 1596 with
notes.

13. *Pulmo contrarium* . . . : the lungs draw a nutrition which is the
opposite of that of the body; all the other parts draw the same (*"Of
Nutrition"* 29).

14. *Why some lamps:* on numerous unextinguishable lamps, etc. see
Thorndike (VIII, Index). Fortunius Licetus (*De Lucernis Antiquorum
reconditis* (1653 SC) discusses the subject, and a paper by Robert Plot
was published in the transactions of the Royal Society in 1684 (*v.* 14).
The lamp of Olibius was unearthed about 1500.

15. *Creusa and Alexanders boy:* As Creusa was going to marry Jason,
who had divorced Medea, she put on a poisoned garment which set her
body on fire. Plutarch (*Alexander* 25.3–6) tells the story about "Alexander's boy" and says "some who wish to bring fable into conformity with
truth" say Medea used naptha on Creusa.

16. *reall plant of Cornerius:* not identified.

17. *Libavius [Andreas Libavius, 1540–1616]:* whose *Alchymia* was
first published in 1597.

18. *Mares in Spain:* a story found in Aristotle, Pliny (*Nat. Hist.* 8.67),
and succeeding centuries. *Rabican* (Rabicano) is a horse (born of a
mother impregnated by the wind) in Ariosto's *Orlando Innamorato* and
Orlando Furioso.

19. *that famous battell:* see RM 2.3, n. 5.

20. *Rhintace, Canis Levis, Manucodiata:* mythical creatures, or with
mythical habits; the manucodiata, or bird of paradise, for instance, was
said to have sinews instead of feet, with which it attached itself to trees;
there is a handsome picture in the *Ornithologia* of Aldrovandi (SC
1610). In *PE* 3.12 Browne says some think the Rhintace is the Phoenix.

21. *excellent Tract:* of creatures which live without food (SC 1612);
there is a good deal about the chameleon.

22. *outfasted Elias:* who fasted 40 days (1 Kings 19.8).

23. *with an horshoe:* there is a fine example in Wither's *Emblemes*,
1635 (Book 1, illustration 36).

24. *opportunity of its experiment:* In 1681 Edward Browne gave his
ostrich a piece of iron weighing 2½ ounces. When later it died of cold,
the iron was found unchanged, as Edward informed his father.

25. *Surdum ac simplex* . . . : it is a stupid animal and whatever it finds, from the agreeable to iron, it devours.

26. *De abditis rerum causis:* on the secret causes of things.

27. *seven hundred:* does the *we* include cook and kitchen maid?

28. *That a Chicken is formed:* for comment on the ideas in this chapter see E. S. Merton, "Sir Thomas Browne's embryological theory," JHM 5 (1950), 416–21.

29. *Dr. Harvey . . . discourse of Generation:* this was first published in 1651, that is, after the first two editions of *PE.* See Browne's encomium of it and Harvey in Keynes, III, 196–99 (tr. by Le Fanu).

THE FOURTH BOOK

1. *the Poet:* Ovid. And while other animals look down to earth, he gave man a lofty face and commanded him to lift his eyes to heaven and see the stars. (*Metamorphoses* 1.84–86.)

THE FIFTH BOOK

1. *Sed quod Pelicanum* . . . : But that the Pelican (as is believed by many) opens its breast with its bill so that it may nourish its young with its own blood, is far from the Egyptians' accounts, for they have the tradition that the vulture does this. (*Hieroglyphica,* Book 17); SC 1631.

2. *Sanctius* [F. Sanchez, 1523–1601] *delivers:* presumably in a comment on the pelican in Alciati's *Emblems,* on which he wrote a long commentary. But I have not found it.

3. *Urbin, Angelo:* i.e. Raphael (of Urbino) and Michelangelo; here Browne is presumably referring to engravings.

4. *suddenly framed:* Butler's Sir Hudibras (*Hudibras* 1. 177) could unriddle "What Adam dreamt of, when his Bride, / Came from her Closet in his Side."

5. *They who hold:* it is perhaps worth noting that a chapter which begins with a scholastic inquiry ends with personal observations on tadpoles and the maggots of flies.

6. *Cheiromancy,* [and later] *Palmistrie, Rhabdomancy, Belomancy:* There are illustrations (and explanations) of these in G. de Givry's *Witchcraft and Alchemy,* tr. by J. C. Locke. (See Glossary.)

7. *the primitive language:* This question was raised by Herodotus and the discussion was still going on in the 17th century, in various languages. "Whether the Devil tempted her / By a High-Dutch interpreter" in

Hudibras (like Jonson's satire in *The Alchemist*) may be aimed at Goropius Becanus whom Browne quotes in his essay on languages and about whose patriotic views on the ancientness of German there is evidence and anecdote in R. Verstegan's *Restitution of Decayed Intelligence,* 1605. In one of his Latin pieces Browne says the learned count 72 tongues since the confusion of Babel.

8. *Aruspices* . . . : the soothsayers consider coral a powerful amulet for warding off dangers, and branches bound about infants are believed to be protective (an abridgement of a passage in Pliny *Nat. Hist.* 32.11).

9. *Moses, Aaron:* Exod. 8.8–13.

10. *Tu regere* . . . : Remember, Roman, to rule the nations with thy sway (*Aeneid* 6.851).

11. *Ostendunt terris* . . . : The fates shall but show him to the earth, nor suffer him longer to live (*Aeneid* 6.869), referring to Marcellus, who was adopted by Augustus and chosen as his successor, but died at twenty-five. Gordianus was reluctantly Emperor for a few weeks at the age of eighty and committed suicide in the year 236.

12. *our learned Selden:* in his comparative study of folklore and mythology Selden (1584–1654) was a remarkable scholar for his time.

13. *triangles . . . by this order* [*and footnote*]: the *Unheard of Curiosities Concerning the Horoscope of the Patriarkes* by Jaques Gaffarel (tr. E. Chilmead, 1650) has large folding plates of this celestial Jewish alphabet.

14. *Disce, sed ira* . . . : Listen, but drop that anger and those wrinkled sneers from your nose while I pluck these old wives' fables from your breast (Persius *Satires* 5.91–92).

The Sixth Book

1. *some of late . . . spots in the Sunne:* Galileo's famous letters on spots in the sun were published in 1613, and were followed by further observations and much controversy.

2. *Sal, Sulphur, Mercury:* in alchemy the supposed ultimate elements or principles of all material substances.

3. *Arabia, the Happy, and Stony:* by ancient historians, Arabia was divided into three parts: Arabia Felix, Petraea, Deserta.

4. *the Text:* Gen. 9.25.

5. *Thersites and Paris:* beauty and monstrosity, but in reverse order, Thersites being the most deformed of the Greeks besieging Troy.

6. *Canticles:* Song of Solomon.

7. *when it is said:* Song of Solomon 5.11.

8. *evil odor of the Jews:* which Browne denies in *PE* 4.10, one of his arguments being a personal "this offensive odor is in no way discoverable in their Synagogues."

9. *the other:* falling back on occult qualities.

THE SEVENTH BOOK

1. *Behold, he drinketh:* Job 40.23.

2. *Mercurialis . . . representeth:* i.e. there is a picture in the *De Arte Gymnastica* (1573 and later eds.).

3. *Grandgousiers feast:* a menu is given beginning with 16 oxen, 32 calves, 6000 pullets, etc. (*Pantagruel,* 1. 37).

4. *some men critically disposed:* Even this extravagant humor has contemporary relevance: "another ancient objection persisted for a century. If the earth is in motion, why does it not leave the air behind and cause bodies to fall far from the vertical. . . . The objection seemed fatal to Tycho Brahe, the next [after Copernicus] of the great triumvirate of planetary theory, who accordingly always denied that the earth could be in motion, and professed himself anti-Copernican" (H. T. Pledge, *Science Since 1500,* 1939, p. 38).

5. *Lactantius:* the first step toward wisdom is to recognize the false. The choice of an Epigraph from a Church Father is not inadvertent, and perhaps illustrates the sometimes uneasy relation of religion and science.

HYDRIOTAPHIA or URNE BURIALL

In the Introduction, reference is made to Browne's use of source material. In addition to Kirchmann and Perucci, mentioned there, one should add L. G. Giraldi's *De Sepulchris* (1539), A. Bosio's very handsome *Roma Sotteranea* (a folio, of which Browne owned both the Italian edition of 1632 and the Latin edition of 1659), and Ole Worm's *Danicorum Monumentum libri sex* (1643), also handsome. The crude but vivid engravings in Perucci, and the extraordinarily fine illustrations in Bosio of "Scripture Stories," "Cypresse, Palmes, and Olive," "mystical Figures of Peacocks, Doves, and Cocks" certainly caught Browne's attention, which was always appreciative of visual illustration and dramatic anecdote in the books he read.

I do not think any editor needs to point to particular sources for translation of *siste viator* ("Epitaphs were fain to stay and look") or the placing of an obolus in the mouth of the dead as passage money for Charon. And other details, for example, Pliny's charming description of the burial of a raven, or Tacitus' account of Poppaea being embalmed after the Eastern manner with spices, were pretty familiar items of historical gossip.

For learned elucidation and annotation of the text and Browne's notes, see the editions of St. John (1838), Greenhill, and Martin. Quite a number of Browne's own notes are given here (sometimes translated or abbreviated) to show the character and range of material on which *Hydriotaphia* rests, or from which it rises, but I cannot hope that the choice will be entirely satisfactory to any reader, or that it will even seem very consistent. Browne himself, of course, is in this respect not very consistent. I have not differentiated between those found in the first octavo edition and those listed as to be added, in the second, quarto, edition.

Dedicatory Letter and Chapter One

1. *Thomas le Gros:* son of Sir Charles le Gros, of Crostwick Hall, near Norwich.

2. *ruines of Pompeys:* see *CM* 3.9; *ruines* from the last line of Martial's epigram (5.74): "in one spot so vast a ruin could not lie."

3. *known Earth:* because Crostwick Hall was only about twenty miles from the sea.

4. *seen again:* brought back again by Cimon. Plutarch (Browne).

5. *Hippodrome Urnes:* conceived to resound the voices of people at their shows (Browne), but he apparently misread Vitruvius (*SC* 1641) who refers to urns amplifying the actors' voices.

6. *noblest pyle:* Raynham Hall, built by Inigo Jones, and belonging to a friend, Sir Horatio Townshend, later Baron Townshend and Lord Lieutenant of Norfolk.

7. *Imperiall faces:* on Roman coins.

8. *the greater number:* abiit ad plures (Browne) a common euphemism (as in Greek) for the dead.

9. *Aegyptian account:* which makes the world so many years old (Browne).

10. *new Britannia:* Browne's first published piece was a Latin poem (in *Camdeni Insegni,* 1624) in praise of William Camden, author of *Britannia* (1586 and enlarged later eds.). A marginal note on *industrious heads* refers to the important antiquarian studies of Browne's friend Sir William Dugdale.

11. *one handsome Venus:* Greenhill suggests that Venus is a mistake for Helen and that the reference is to a story about Zeuxis in Cicero.

12. *bones of King Arthur:* in the time of Henry the Second. *Cambden* (Browne).

13. *pretend relation:* since Browne mistakenly thought they were Roman.

14. *pisse not:* Horace *Ars Poetica* 471; but quoted by Camden (*Remains*) and Weever *Funeral Monuments* (Greenhill).

15. *Gemme of the Old Rock:* a phrase about certain Indian diamonds quoted in Latin by Browne.

16. *Potosi:* the rich mountain of Peru (Browne).

17. *extract of the Earth:* i.e. out of earth from the four quarters of the earth, as some expositors argued.

18. *buried but one:* Moses: Deut. 34.6; the *hot contest* referred to is from Jude 9.

19. *from Hercules:* i.e. from cremation of Argeus by Hercules, as Kirchmann argues in *de Funeribus*.

20. *Patroclus, and Achilles:* as described in *Iliad* 23 and *Odyssey* 24; *Hector* (below) in *Iliad* 24.

21. *Table Laws:* i.e. laws found in the XII Tables of ancient Roman law.

22. *even Crows:* the cremation of a very popular talking raven (killed by a jealous rival of its owner, a shoemaker) is described by Pliny (*Natural History* 10.60). The draped bier was carried by two Aethiopians, and the procession, with all kinds of wreaths, went all the way to the pyre on the Appian Way.

23. *Poppaea:* Tacitus *Annales* 16.6.

24. *this practise:* i.e. burning rather than burying.

25. *Ajax Oileus* [not the more famous Ajax]: was drowned by Poseidon for an impious speech; Browne refers to *Odyssey* 4.511, in a version of the line justifying *totall destruction*.

26. *some have suffered:* a marginal note refers to Bishop Martialis, from the *Letters* of Cyprian (Church Father, martyred in 258).

27. *black and white Angels:* Browne probably took this from the *Travels* of G. Sandys (various editions) who gives the names of the angels.

28. *Saul:* 1 Sam. 31.12.

29. *their friends:* Amos 6.10.

30. *Jehoram:* 2 Chron. 21.19.

31. *Sedechias:* Jer. 34.5.

32. *pyre of Asa:* 2 Chron. 16.14.

33. *the Jews lamenting:* Suetonius in the life of Julius Caesar (Browne).

34. *their own Nation:* as that magnificent sepulchral Monument erected by Simon Mach. (Browne); Apocrypha, Maccabees 1.13.

35. *the Prophecy:* various biblical passages are referred to in what follows: Psalms 16.10; Acts 2.31; John 19.36; 1 Kings 1.52.

36. *types:* prefigurations of Christ's resurrection.

37. *Absalom:* O Absalom, Absalom, Absalom. Sam. 2.18. (Browne).

38. *triple valediction:* referred to in Chap. 4.

39. *examples of sepulture:* the examples are drawn from the natural histories of Aelian and Pliny, where other examples are also found; Pliny is very good on the "sorrowful buzzing" of bees as they "keep gazing" at the lifeless body of their "king" (*Nat. Hist.* 11.20).

Chapter Two

1. *solemnly delivered:* i.e. customarily delivered (see OED); if *disparage* seems too unreal, see the range of commendatory pieces in prose and verse by 17th-century scholars which prefaced Kirchmann.

2. *Opale:* In one sent to me by my worthy friend Dr. Thomas Witherley of Walsingham (Browne); described as blue a little further on, and by Douglas (1838) and Sir John Evans as probably a glass or crystal bead. The other objects are apparently characteristically Saxon.

3. *Arae and Altars:* one is an altar for a hero or demigod; the other for a supreme god (for *manes* see Glossary).

4. *Burnham:* Although respectable by contemporary standards, Browne's etymological derivation is incorrect, as also about the Iceni and some of the places referred to as on the Roman road to London.

5. *this Countrey:* i.e. this county (as commonly in 17th century).

6. *Count of the Saxon shore:* a translation from Latin; the history is from Tacitus and others.

7. *if the Iceni:* for the introduction of Gammadims (from Ezek. 27.11) and Phoenician inhabitants of Ancona, see Wilkin, Greenhill, and Martin, and authors cited by them.

8. *expression of Caesar:* "infinita multitudo" quoted from Caesar by Browne.

9. *Seventy Thousand:* from Tacitus *Ann.* 14.33.

10. *Buxton:* In the ground of my worthy Friend Rob. Jegon Esq. wherein some things contained were preserved by the most worthy Sir William Paston Bt. (Browne).

11. *the two Casters:* most at *Caster* by *Yarmouth,* found in a place called *East-bloudy-burgh furlong* [!] belonging to Mr. Thomas Wood . . . from whom we have received divers Silver and Copper Coynes. (Browne).

12. *Brancaster:* Belonging to that Noble Gentleman and true example of worth Sir *Ralph Hare,* Baronet, my honoured Friend. (Browne).

13. *silver peeces:* one of these pieces, attributed on hearsay to the reign of Matilda in a note by Browne, has been described as a reckoning counter of a much later date, but Browne was knowledgeable about coins and had a large number. (See John Evelyn's account of a visit to Norwich, and letters in Keynes [III, 8 and 387]).

14. *Spartans:* Plutarch in the Life of Lycurgus [9] (Browne).

15. *a great obscurity:* and a clear demonstration that they were not Roman (Douglas in *1838*).

16. *Spittle Fields:* Stowes Survey of London (Browne).

17. *in his dayes:* i.e. in the 5th century.

18. *magnificent burning . . . Severus:* referred to again in Chap. 3, with a note from Dio Cassius about the choice of urns.

19. *double Sepulture:* Gen. 23.9.

20. *the Gemme:* The fire had eaten away even the beryl ring on her finger (Propertius *Elegies* 4.7.9).

21. *Cardinall Farnese:* Browne gives a reference to the description of the contents of this urn in Vigenère's edition of Livy (1617).

22. *Childerick the first* [c. 437–481]: a marginal ref. to J. J. Chifflet's *Anastasis Childerici . . .* (1655 SC) helps to date the composition of *Hydriotaphia,* since the tomb was discovered in 1653.

23. *Septuagint expression:* i.e. the detail is in the Septuagint not the Authorized version (Josh. 24.30).

24. *that Letter . . . or the account:* these two lost or imaginary works are again referred to in Browne's *Musaeum Clausum,* a *jeu d'esprit* of scarce or never seen books, rarities, etc.

25. *that frugall Bit:* Browne gives a reference for this early example of concentrated food from Dio Cassius on the Emperor Severus (*Roman History* 72.12).

26. *Saxo and Olaus:* Saxo Grammaticus (c. 1150–c. 1206) and Olaus Magnus (1490–1558), famous for their histories of Denmark and Scandinavia.

27. *Rollrich stones:* in Oxfordshire, Cambden (Browne). From Rollo, Camden suggests, but they are now thought pre-Celtic.

28. *Ashburie . . . Massingham . . . Anglesea:* Browne has apparently blended two finds mentioned in a marginal note (Martin).

Chapter Three

1. *the righteous:* Matt. 23.29; apparently the tombs were annually whitewashed because touching brought pollution (Num. 19.16).

2. *Ulysses in Hecuba:* by Euripides (317–20).

3. *nether part:* Psalm 63.

4. *Pliny: Nat. Hist.* 35.49.

5. *Pythagoras . . . Varro:* Pliny *Nat. Hist.* 35.45.

6. *Patroclus: Iliad* 33.254; there is a note in *1838* questioning Browne's learning or memory about the details.

7. *retaining a Vinosity:* Lazius (Browne).

8. *fatall periods of Kingdomes:* About five hundred years, *Plato* (Browne); presumably derived (heaven knows how) from the strange arithmetic of *Republic* 8.546, which is certainly about fatal periods of kingdoms but not "great conjunctions."

9. *Opimian Wine:* wine one hundred years old. Petronius (Browne); at Trimalchio's feast, *Satyricon* 34. Opimius was consul in 121 B.C. Pliny (*Nat. Hist.* 14.6.55) speaks of Opimian wine by then nearly two hundred years old and "reduced to the consistency of honey."

10. *gold . . . fasten their teeth:* from 11th law of 12 Table Laws (Browne).

11. *Epithete:* in Pliny 50.16 (Browne).

12. *Cypresse . . . Diana:* Pliny *Nat. Hist.* 16.215.

13. *North-East position:* Browne refers to a chapter [3] in Goropius Becanus, *Origines Antwerpianae* (*SC* 1569).

14. *Coals found fresh:* marginal note referring to Biringuccio's *Pirotechnia* (*SC* 1559).

15. *Urne of Philopaemen:* from Plutarch *Philopaemen* (21.3).

16. *Democritus . . . honey:* from Varro via Kirchmann. Herodotus and Pliny both refer to honey as preservative and the body of Achilles (*Odyssey* 24) is lapped with spices and honey before being burned.

17. *Plato:* in the *Laws* 958e.

18. *Judas:* Matt. 27.5–8.

19. *contrived upon Tiberius:* the MS emendation "contriued" for *continued* in one copy of *58* (not in Browne's hand) seems to be more satisfactory, and was made by St. John (*1838*). The account in Suetonius (*Tiberius* 75) might support *continued*. The affronts began with saying that his body ought to be thrown into the Tiber, continued with other threats, and climaxed in many crying out that it ought to be half burned in the amphitheatre for farces.

20. *Nero:* Suetonius *Nero* 49.

21. *Domitian:* Suetonius *Domitian* 17.

22. *Achilles: Odyssey* 24.76–77.

23. *family Urnes:* See the most learned and worthy Mr. Casaubon upon *Antoninus* (Browne); Méric Casaubon, in a translation of the *Meditations,* 1635.

24. *mirth from Anatomies:* a reference, supported by a marginal quotation, to an incident of Trimalchio's feast (Petronius *Satyricon* 34) when a slave puts on the table a silver skeleton with movable limbs and spine, and Trimalchio becomes sentimentally and mournfully poetical.

25. *hanging was plaied:* A barbarous pastime at Feasts, when men stood upon a rolling globe, with their necks in a Rope, fastned to a beame, and a knife in their hands, ready to cut it when the stone was rolled away, wherein if they failed, they lost their lives to the laughter of the spectators. *Athenaeus* [4.155] (Browne).

26. *D.M.: Diis Manibus [Sacrum]*, sacred to the spirits of the dead, a common grave inscription.

27. *Jewish Hypogaeum:* the statements and pictures referred to are from *Roma Sotteranea*, as a marginal note suggests. There are fine illustrations of these *Scripture Stories*, etc., on pages 239, 373, 381, 547 of the ed. of 1632.

28. *empty grave:* the practice took its rise in Greece, where, if a great man fell abroad, and his ashes could not be obtained, an empty tomb (cenotaph) was erected to his memory (St. John *1838*).

29. *golden Urne:* the emperor Trajan (Browne).

30. *civill Rhetorick:* a marginal note paraphrases from Cassiodorus on the commissioners of Theodoric the Goth.

31. *this Island:* Great Britain; the comparison is from Pliny *Nat. Hist.* 30.

32. *Plato's historian: Republic* 10.614b.

33. *Pyrrhus his toe:* which could not be burnt (Browne); Pliny *Nat. Hist.* 7.2, and a favourite fancy with Browne, as in *PE* 3.14 and MS. Sloane 1843 ff. 49–50, where there are six lines of verse on "one in the gout" wishing for this toe "which laye unburnt when all the rest burnt out" . . . And the most powerfull blast the gout could blowe / Prove butt an Ignis Lambens to that toe" (Keynes, IV, 280–81).

34. *lamp of Galvanus:* see footnote on such lamps in *CM* 3.18, and *PE* 3.21, n. 14.

35. *Metropolis of humidity:* the brain. Hippocrates (Browne).

36. *King of Edom:* Amos 2.1.

37. *drink of the ashes:* As Artemisia of her husband Mausolus (Browne); from Valerius Maximus, 4.6 (Martin).

38. *stay and look: siste viator.*

39. *first thus buried:* Cuthbert, Archbishop of Canterbury, in 758 (Greenhill).

40. *crosses found by Helena:* see *RM* 1.28, n. 77.

41. *gnaw'd:* Martin suggests that the misprint "knav'd" in 58 (corrected in errata of 58²) may have risen from a spelling "knawd"—recorded in

OED; in author-corrected copies it is spelled *gnaw'd*. Browne's own skull (surreptitiously removed when his coffin was accidentally broken into) was for over fifty years, from 1847, exhibited in the Norfolk and Norwich Hospital Museum. It was again buried in 1922. A vivid picture of some of these *abominations* among the Scythians is given by Herodotus.

42. *large lumps of fat:* later "discovered" by Fourcroy in "St. Innocents Churchyard" in Paris, and then named Adipocere (from Wilkin).

43. *found uncorrupted:* Browne gives a long note about this; buried 1538, exhumed 1608, described 1622 (Burton, *Description of Leicestershire*).

44. *Ortelius:* in his picture of Russia (Browne); in the extreme east of the map in *Theatrum Orbis Terrarum* there is a picture of a tribe of natives turned into stone (Wilkin plus Greenhill).

45. *Cariola:* that part in the Skeleton of an Horse, which is made by the hanch-bones (Browne).

46. *Negro's sculls:* for their extraordinary thicknesse (Browne).

47. *Dantes Characters:* The Poet *Dante* in his view of Purgatory, found gluttons so meagre, and extenuated, that he conceited them to have been in the Siege of *Jerusalem*, and that it was easie to have discovered *Homo* or *Omo* in their faces: M being made by the two lines of their cheeks, arching over the Eye brows to the nose, and their sunk eyes making OO which makes up *Omo*.

> Parean l'occhiaie anella senza gemme
> Che nel viso de gli huomini legge huomo
> Ben'hauria quivi conosciuto l'emme.
> *Purgatorio,* 23.31–33 (Browne)

This "conceit" is referred to again in *A Letter*, sect. 9.

48. *Ezechiels vision:* Ezek. 37, the famous valley of dry bones; *Jehosaphat:* Joel 3.2, with a marginal reference giving the source of "as some will have it."

CHAPTER FOUR

1. *to all distinctions:* on all points of difference.

2. *Greek devotion:* in the ritual of burial; *pathetically:* moving the emotions.

3. *Pliny:* in *Nat. Hist.* 7.55.

4. *Lucretius:* 2.999–1000: What was before from earth returns to earth (Browne in Latin), compared to Eccles. 12.7: "Then shall the dust return to the earth as it was."

5. *soul had wings: Odyssey* 11.222.

6. *Socrates:* Plato in *Phaedo* (Browne); the conclusion.

7. *Diogenes:* see footnote on Diogenes, *RM* 1.41.

8. *tedious term:* see footnote on Plato's Year in *RM* 1.6.

9. *last valediction:* vale, vale, nos te ordine quo natura permittet se-quemur. (Browne): Farewell, farewell, whither in turn we shall follow when nature allows it.

10. *traced by antiquity:* Martin refers to Macrobius on the *Dream of Scipio,* and Renaissance "Platonic" expositions of this.

11. *disturbed their ghosts:* tu manes ne laede meos (Browne): do not thou hurt my spirit (Tibullus *Elegies* 1.1.67).

12. *And unlike:* Martin leaves the text unaltered from "Nor unlike" but suggests a confusion from the fact that Browne may have intended to write "and unlike" or "nor like."

13. *some Christians:* Russians etc. (Browne).

14. *not inconsonant unto reason:* virtually a quotation from Pliny *Nat. Hist.* 7.8.

15. *The Archimime:* St. John (*1838*) refers especially to the description of the funeral of Vespasian in Suetonius (10.19).

16. *the Elysian Ferriman:* Charon ferried the dead over the Styx and Acheron for an obol, placed in the mouths of the dead.

17. *Tartara's:* a double plural; 58² reads "Tartarus."

18. *Perianders Wife:* the story is told in some detail in Herodotus 5.92.

19. *Female Ghosts:* This, and the series of underworld references which follow, come largely from the unforgettable scene in *Odyssey* 11 and from *Aeneid* 6; there is also a probable reference to Dante (*Inferno* 10) in the statement about departed spirits, and two references to Lucian's *Dialogues of the Dead.*

20. *Hercules . . . Simulachrum:* simulacrum (image) is a common Latin word for ghost, like the word eidolon in Greek. In *Odyssey* 11 Odysseus says he recognized Hercules, and adds "I mean his shade, his soul being with the immortal gods."

21. *Platoes denne:* the famous cave metaphor of images, and shadows of images, and their relation to reality, at the beginning of Book 7 of the *Republic.*

22. *Pythagoras escapes in . . . Dante:* i.e. is not found in *Inferno,* canto 4, to which Browne refers; *Cato* is in *Purgatorio* canto 1, *Epicurus* in canto 10.

23. *Were the happiness:* To judge from the character of passages in MSS, this conclusion of Chap. 4 (which runs without a single marginal note) seems to have been incorporated into *Hydriotaphia,* slightly revised, from two "observations" or little essays not written with *Hydriotaphia* in mind.

24. *Machiavel, that Christianity: Discourses* (on the history of Livy) 2.2.

25. *Socrates:* again from the conclusion of Plato's *Phaedo,* referred to as "the immortality of Plato" in Browne's reference to Cato (which is from Plutarch *Cato of Utica* 68.70).

CHAPTER FIVE

1. *three conquests:* Saxon, Danish, Norman.

2. *Sic ego . . . :* So should I wish to be laid to rest when I am bones (Tibullus *Elegies* 3.2.26).

3. *some old Philosophers:* Browne refers to and quotes a book on Chaldee wisdom.

4. *Moses his man:* in the Psalme of Moses (Browne). Psalm 90 is subtitled "A Prayer of Moses the Man of God"; verse 10 contains "The days of our years are threescore and ten."

5. *one little finger:* According to the ancient Arithmetick of the hand, wherein the little finger of the right hand contracted, signified an hundred (Browne); with a reference to the *Hieroglyphics* of Pierius (*SC* 1595).

6. *When Avarice:* see *A Letter,* sect. 23.

7. *even David:* probably 1 Kings 2.5–9; *and Solomon:* 1 Kings 11.4.

8. *Alcmenas nights:* one night as long as 3 (Browne); the night of Hercules' conception.

9. *What Song:* The puzzling questions of Tiberius. *Marcel. Donatus in Suet.* (Browne). Suetonius (*Tiberius* 70) refers to these "silly" questions as examples of the vanity of Tiberius about his mythological knowledge; Homer has a try at the first question in *Odyssey* 12.184–91.

10. *famous Nations:* Browne quotes *Odyssey* 10.526.

11. *and slept:* Job [3.13–15] (Browne).

12. *Provinciall . . . or tutellary:* i.e. guardian spirits over districts or over particular persons, as in MS Sloane 1848 (folio 174): "Whether the lower order of Angels guard perticular persons, the higher, regions and countries."

13. *Elias:* That the world may last but 6000 years (Browne).

14. *Hector:* Hector's fame lasting above two lives of Methusaleh before that famous prince was born (Browne). Charles V was born in 1500, and the third period of 2000 years (of the total 6000) was thought to begin about the time of Christ; this explains *are acted* and *setting part of time* in next paragraph.

15. *mortall . . . circle:* Theta, the character of death (Browne); the first letter of thanatos, death.

16. *scarce fourty years:* old ones being taken up, and other bodies laid under (Browne).

17. *Mummies:* which men show in several countries, giving them what names they please; and unto some the Names of the old Aegyptian Kings out of Herodotus (Browne).

18. *Cardan:* Browne refers in a note to a passage in Cardan's *Autobiography.*

19. *Hippocrates Patients:* lists of them survive.

20. *Achilles horses: Iliad* 16.149.

21. *Canaanitish woman . . . Herodias:* one gave water to Christ (Matt. 15.22–28), the other asked for the head of John the Baptist (Matt. 14.8).

22. *almost lost:* The temple of Diana was one of the Seven Wonders of the World; Pliny (*Nat. Hist.* 36.21) names the architect (Chersiphon). It was burned by Herostratus (Eratostratus) on the night of Alexander's birth.

23. *Adrians* [Hadrian's] *horse:* The Emperor Hadrian raised a monument with an epitaph to his favorite horse Borysthenes.

24. *Twenty seven Names:* Before the flood (Browne).

25. *one living Century:* one hundred living at one time.

26. *even Pagans:* Euripides (Browne); a fragment of Euripides quoted by Plato in the *Gorgias* (Martin).

27. *longest Sunne:* at the summer solstice we have the longest sun and the highest arch; even the longest human life is only a winter day.

28. *light in ashes:* according to the custom of the Jewes, who place a lighted wax-candle in a pot of ashes by the corps. *Leo* (Browne); Leo is Leo Modena.

29. *weep into stones:* like Niobe.

30. *feeding the winde:* Browne refers to a book of biblical annotations on "all is vanity" in Eccles. 1.14.

31. *Mummie:* or mumia, a medicinal-magical preparation, supposedly (at least at first) the substance of mummies, and in Browne's time still commonly regarded by some as a universal panacea; see many references in L. Thorndike, *A History of Magic and Experimental Science,* vols. V–VIII.

32. *Mizraim:* a son of Ham, the supposed ancestor of the Egyptians.

33. *Nimrod is lost:* i.e. Orion had been called Nimrod.

34. *incorruption in the heavens:* a fiercely argued tenet of the old astronomy. Galileo's discovery of, and observations on, sunspots (1613) had raised a great deal of discussion and had an important bearing on various aspects of the new astronomy as telescopes (*perspectives*) began to *tell tales.*

35. *which is the peculiar:* i.e. only God has the power to destroy, but he cannot destroy himself.

36. *quality of either state:* i.e. condition in either heaven or hell.

37. *burn like Sardanapalus:* last king of Assyria in Greek story, who, after a long and desperate siege, burned himself with his wives, concubines, and treasures in his great palace at Nineveh.

38. *funerall Laws:* as in earlier reference.

39. *wherein few . . . Urne:* some Latin verses from Gruter's *Inscriptions* (SC 1603) are given in 58[2] as to be added as marginal illustration. Even the word *mean* in Browne leaves us at an imaginative remove from the paid woman mourner and the bought jar of Gruter's inscription.

40. *Gordianus:* In Greek, Latine, Hebrew, Aegyptian, Arabick, defaced by *Licinius* the Emperor (Browne).

41. *man of God:* Moses.

42. *Enoch:* Heb. 11.5.

43. *Elias:* 2 Kings 2.11.

44. *received translation:* 1 Cor. 15.51.

45. *coverings of Mountaines:* Rev. 6.16.

46. *Alaricus:* Alaric the Goth; Browne gives a reference to a history of the Goths.

47. *Isaiah:* Isa. 14.4–17.

48. *Angles of contingency: Angulus contingentiae,* the least of Angles (Browne).

49. *Chaos of pre-ordination:* See *RM* 1.39 (and Psalm 139.15–16).

50. *as truly to understand:* the terms following are used in mystical theology to express union with God. Browne repeats this sentence, revised, at the end of *CM;* see Glossary for some of the words.

51. *praedicament of Chymera's:* see Glossary.

52. *S[t]. Innocents Church-yard:* In Paris where bodies soon consume (Browne).

53. *Moles of Adrianus* [Hadrianus]: A stately *Mausoleum* or sepulchral pyle . . . where now standeth the Castle of St. *Angelo* (Browne).

54. *Tabesne . . . :* whether bodies decompose or are burned on the pyre is of no importance (Lucan *Pharsalia* 7.809–10).

THE GARDEN OF CYRUS

The Garden of Cyrus, like *Hydriotaphia,* was plentifully supplied with marginal notes by its author (who even added more, almost immediately, for the second edition) and most of the books and writers—and their annotators—are used, cited, or referred to elsewhere in Browne's works. The Bible is probably met with most frequently. Plato, Plutarch, Hippocrates, Aristotle, Pliny, Homer, Virgil make several appearances and other classical writers less frequently. And of course there is a wide representation of 16th- and 17th-century scholars, e.g. Scaliger, Salmasius, Gruter, Cabeo, Plempius, Bosio, della Porta. Vitruvius* and Bauhinus (J. Bauhin) have particular importance in certain sections. If the two books from which Browne took most, the *Villa* of della Porta (SC 1592) and the *Horti* (SC 1560) of Curtius (see Introduction) were not very new, the great *Historia Plantarum Universalis* of Bauhinus (SC 3 vols. folio 1650), described by John Ray as "the greatest book yet published on the subject" (C. E. Raven, *John Ray*, 1943, p. 78) certainly was.

In addition to the editions of Martin (whose annotations are indispensable for full understanding of some passages), Greenhill, and Wilkin (the latter with two important letters from and to Henry Power about seeds and "plastic nature"), and omitting literary criticism, special reference may be made to E. S. Merton's "The Botany of Sir Thomas Browne" and G. K. Chalmers, "Hieroglyphs and Sir Thomas Browne." Thomas Stanley's *History of Philosophy* (1655, 1656, 1660, 1687) is interesting, in its chapters on Pythagoras (Part 9.8–9), as contemporary criticism by a very respectable classical scholar. Professor F. L. Huntley, in his *Sir Thomas Browne* (1962) compares *Hydriotaphia* and *The Garden of Cyrus* as intimately connected companion pieces in relation to subject matter, structure, and style. It might be noted that whereas one marginal reference in *Hydriotaphia* (to Chifflet's *Anastasis Childerici* (SC 1655) would seem to definitely date its writing (or at least final putting together) as 1656, marginal references in *The Garden of Cyrus* take it up to 1658; there is in fact one reference to the third edition of *Pseudodoxia*, itself published in 1658. Both works were licensed on March 9, 1658; the dedicatory letters are both dated May 1; the reference to the constellation of the Hyades at the end of *The Garden of Cyrus* implies March.

The engraving on p. 297 is found with the quotation from Quintilian in both Porta and Curtius (see introductory comments).

DEDICATORY LETTER AND CHAPTER ONE

1. *Nicholas Bacon:* Born 1623; grandson of Sir Nicholas Bacon, the half-brother of Francis Bacon; created baronet in 1661; died 1666. In

---

* It is interesting to note that Browne was enough of a "virtuoso" to have in his library, in Norwich, copies of Vitruvius (Ital. ed. of *de Architectura*), Scamozzi, (*Idea della Architettura Universale*), Leonardo da Vinci (*Trattato della Pittura*), and Dürer (Ital. tr. of the *Four Books of Human Proportion*).

the Life prefixed to *Posthumous Works,* 1712 (A₂, in its cancel state) Sir
Nicholas and Sir Charles Le Gros are given as two of the three men who
persuaded Browne to settle in Norwich; but in 1637–38 Nicholas Bacon
would have been fourteen or fifteen years old. The uncancelled state of
the leaf speaks only of Dr. Thomas Lushington, Browne's tutor, and
among other things author of an unpublished piece on Proclus in the
British Museum. Nicholas Bacon was a man of letters and learning.

2. *Purblinde: Plempius, Cabeus* etc. (Browne).

3. *without issue:* D. *Harvy* (Browne); Harvey's *De Generatione
Animalium* appeared in 1651 (*SC*), the Eng. ed. in 1653.

4. *the massiest:* marginal reference to the herbal of Besler, 1613
(Browne).

5. *three Folio's:* By an odd slip, apparently, Browne refers in a marginal note to J. Bauhinus' 3 vol. *Historia Plantarum* (*SC* 1650) as
Theatrum Botanicum; the latter, by Parkinson, a huge folio of over
seventeen hundred double-column pages, appeared in 1640.

6. *and old:* My worthy friend Mr. *Goodier* an ancient and learned
Botanist (Browne).

7. *Wherein England:* As in *London* and divers parts, whereof we
mention none, lest we seem to omit any (Browne).

8. *and Hippocrates:* the attempt to credit the Greeks with "modern"
discoveries in medicine and astronomy is very common in the 16th and
17th centuries.

9. *great example:* marginal reference to Hippocrates (Browne).

10. *Scaliger:* in commentaries on Aristotle and Theophrastus.

11. *true use:* i.e. in medicine, of which botany was still a part.

12. *venemous Vegetables:* the garden of Attalus, referred to again in
Chap. 1, and also in *CM* 3.9 (from Plutarch *Demetrius* 20).

13. *Cato . . . Cabbadge:* "Cato sings marvellous praises of the head
of cabbage"; Pliny *Natural History* 19.41.

14. *hard language:* "Tulipomania," Browne notes, by P. Hondius.

15. *sown in corruption:* 1 Cor. 15.42.

16. *Nullum sine venia . . . :* no eloquence would please without indulgence. Seneca *Epistles* 114.12 (from Martin).

17. *Apelles:* Pliny *Nat. Hist.* 35.36.

18. *Noble Family:* Of the most worthy Sir Edmund Bacon, prime
baronet, my true and noble friend (Browne).

19. *That Vulcan:* for comment on this, and some other passages, see
J. S. Finch, "Early Drafts of *The Garden of Cyrus.*" In some instances
at least, observations seem to have been written without thought of *GC,*
and additional passages are quoted in Wilkin's edition.

20. *divine Philosopher: Plato* in *Timaeus* (Browne).

21. *three words:* fronde tegi silvas (the woods to be covered with leaves) Ovid *Metamorphoses* 1.44.

22. *Chirurgery:* In a marginal note, Browne quotes the Greek for opening up, taking out, closing up; he repeated the fancy in his "Plants in Scripture."

23. *much controversie:* For some there is, from the ambiguity of the word *Mikedem,* whether *ab oriente* [from the east] or *a principio* [from the beginning] (Browne).

24. *Zoroaster:* perhaps a reference to Pliny *Nat. Hist.* 18.55, where Zoroaster is quoted about times for sowing.

25. *However:* The details which follow are largely from Curtius, who took them from the usual authors for this kind of material.

26. *melancholy metamorphosis:* Dan. 4.33.

27. *the Countrey:* the details are from the Book of Esther.

28. *Xenophon: Anabasis.*

29. *Laertes:* father of Ulysses; *Odyssey* 24.223–31.

30. *live in . . . Vegetables:* e.g. *Artemisia arborescens, Andromeda polifolia.*

31. *Xenophon:* In *Oeconomica* [4.21] (Browne); *arbores pari intervalls . . . :* the trees planted at equal intervals in straight rows and all very beautifully in the straight lines of a quincunx.

32. *most elegant: Cicero in Cat. Major* [17] (Browne).

33. *Emphaticall:* i.e. best example of.

34. *Tuscan Pedestall:* pillar base in the simplest of the five classical orders of architecture.

35. *pattern in the Sky:* Constantine saw a cross in the sky when marching against Byzantium. For pictures and history of crosses, *Labarum,* etc., see good encyclopaedia under CROSS. Martin has illustrations of some of the hieroglyphic crosses referred to. The *character of Venus,* is the astronomical symbol (♀) for Venus.

36. *Ulysses: Odyssey* 24.341–42.

37. *Aristotle:* marginal reference to *Politics* (Browne).

38. *handsome Description:* Browne quotes *Georgics* 2.277–78.

39. *Saturn . . . Noah:* Greenhill refers to Bochart, *Geographica Sacra* (*SC* 1646).

40. *first sinne:* drunkenness (Gen. 9.21).

41. *own description:* Eccles. 2. (Browne).

42. *Learned Abramas:* Browne refers to a Latin "Guide" or "Lamp" to the Holy Scriptures [1648] by N. Abram.

43. *Statua of Janus:* which King Numa set up with his fingers so disposed that they numerically denoted 365. Pliny [*Nat. Hist.* 34.16] (Browne).

CHAPTER TWO

1. *sculpture draughts:* engraved drawings; Laureat draughts: laurel patterns.

2. *founded upon fives:* Of a structure five parts, *Fundamentum, parietes, Aperturae, Compartitio, tectum.* Leo Alberti. Five Columes, *Tuscan, Dorick, Ionick, Corinthian, Compound.* Five different intercolumniations, *Pycnostylos, dystolos, Systylos, Areostylos, Eustylos.* Vitruvius (Browne). See Martin's note, however, on careless reading of Alberti.

3. *That of Charles* [i.e. Charlemagne]: described by J. J. Chifflet in *Anastasis Childerici* (*SC* 1655)—obscure marginal note verified by Martin.

4. *common picture:* i.e. in illustrated Bibles.

5. *two Crowns:* Macc. 1.11 [Apocrypha] (Browne).

6. *Blancanus:* There is a marginal note here, and further references later, to a book of selections from Aristotle by Blancanus (*SC* 1615); with pictures.

7. *medallions:* the larger sort of Medals (Browne).

8. *Canticles:* Song of Solomon 2–9; it was assumed to be about Christ.

9. *Craticula or grate:* Exod. 27.4.

10. *Reticulum Jecoris:* Leviticus (Browne); Lev. 3.4, about sacrifices; from Vulgate.

11. *unextinguishable laugh:* Browne quotes this phrase (from *Odyssey* 8.326), describing the laughter of the gods when they saw Venus and Mars trapped in bed.

12. *no vulgar mythologie:* Greenhill notes that this is discussed by Leo the Jew in his *Dialogi d'Amore,* 2.

13. *nettle Minerva:* as in the contention between *Minerva* and *Arachne* (Browne); she challenged Minerva, was defeated, tried to hang herself, was turned into a spider.

14. *played at Penelope:* In Eustathius his Comment upon Homer [*Odyssey* 1.401] (Browne).

15. *as High as Hermes: Plato* (Browne); *Phaedrus* 274c–d; Theuth is Thoth, who is Hermes Trismegistus. Plato speaks of Theuth inventing draughts.

16. *Roman Batalia:* Browne refers to works by Salmasius, one of which, *de re militari Romanorum,* containing the diagram in Browne's text, was apparently first published in 1657.

17. *the quadrate of Virgil:* i.e. the "handsome description" referred to earlier.

18. *Apocalyps:* Rev. 21.16.

19. *pillars of Seth:* see *RM*, 1.24. n. 67.

20. *six score thousand Infants:* Jonah 4.11.

21. *monument of Ninus:* given a grandiose description in Diodorus Siculus, 2.7.

22. *Agostino:* Antonio Agostino delle medaglie (Browne); (*SC* 1625).

23. *Ark . . . table . . . stone:* as described in Genesis and Exodus.

24. *as some pictures:* Browne's literalism about pictures illustrating Scripture runs through a good many chapters of *PE*. 5.

25. *Og:* Deut. 3.11.

CHAPTER THREE

1. *Gaffarell:* the strange cryptography of Gaffarel's *Unheard of Curiosities . . .* (Fr. 1629, Eng. 1650) is a rabbinical statement that the stars are ranged in the Heavens in the form of letters and that it is possible to predict from them. The book was condemned by the Sorbonne in 1629.

2. *Fathers . . . Mother:* referring to lines of an epigram in the Greek Anthology (quoted).

3. *solitary maggot:* From there being a single maggot almost in every head (Browne); Solomon had seven hundred wives and three hundred concubines.

4. *Borith:* Jer. 2.22 (Browne).

5. *water Souldier: Stratiotes* (Browne).

6. *sproutes:* i.e. upon pollard oaks and thorns.

7. *he that observeth:* For complementary observations see also notes on plants and natural history, from Notebooks, in Keynes, IV 374–400. Wilkin quotes letters to and from Browne, in which the "plastic principle" is discussed. For notes on birds and fishes, and letters to Christopher Merrett, partly on plants, see *Notes and Letters on the Natural History of Norfolk, from the MSS of Sir Thomas Browne M.D.,* ed. Thomas Southwell, F.Z.S., 1902.

8. *Paracelsus:* Martin gives the reference from the *Opera* (1605, 10.23) of Paracelsus.

9. *Aristotle:* marginal reference by Browne to *Meteorologica* with notes by Cabeus (1646).

10. *four kinds:* given later (in Latin) in a note by Browne: trees, shrubs, sub-shrubs, herbs.

11. *Aequivocall production:* see Glossary.

12. *Oak-apple:* These and more are to be found upon our Oaks; not well described by any till the Edition of *Theatrum Botanicum* (Browne) [by Parkinson, 1640].

13. *Bees* . . . *Eeles:* for eels (actually entozoa) Browne quotes from *Ichthyologia* (SC 1624) by Schonevelde; the other is one of the commonplaces of "aequivocall" or "spontaneous" production.

14. *true seeds:* Browne refers to *Horticultura* (1632) of "the most learned" [W.] Lauremberg.

15. *disputed seeds:* i.e. botanists still argued as to whether they had seeds.

16. *Goat-Beetle:* The long and tender *Capricornus* rarely found, we could never meet with but two (Browne).

17. *this digression:* beginning with "He that observeth," and continuing for 11 pages of 58, has had nothing to do with fives, but much with Browne's interest in botany.

18. *Swallows Egges:* which exceed not five (Browne).

19. *five Brethren* . . . *Rose:* five leaves of the calyx; Wilkin quotes a pretty "rustic rhyme."

20. *number of five:* This incomprehensible paragraph is nevertheless explained by Martin, with the help of diagrams and references to books by Bovillus and Kircher (both in SC).

21. *Euclide: Elem.* Bk 4 (Browne).

22. *Ajax* . . . *Delphinium:* Ovid (*Metamorphoses* 10.206–19 and 13.394–98) speaks of a purple flower, with AI AI (for Ajax) on it, springing up from the blood of the latter; henbane, resembling *Aaron's* mitre, is from Josephus, 3.7.6 (Greenhill).

23. *Aurelian:* i.e. chrysalis, from Lat. *aurelia.*

24. *Monarchical spirits:* on the assumption that the queen bee was a king.

25. *Gomesius:* marginal reference to a book by Gomesius (in SC) with this "experiment."

26. *the skins:* Elegantly conspicuous on the inside of the stripped skins of Dive-Fowl, of the Cormorant, Goshonder, Weasell, Loon, *etc.* (Browne).

27. *Mummies* . . . *Bembine Table* . . . *Orus:* As Martin points out there are illustrations in Kircher's handsome *Oedipus Aegyptiacus* (SC 2 vols. folio 1652).

28. *handed crosses: cruces ansatae,* being held by a finger in the circle (Browne); see earlier reference.

29. *Statuae Isiacae, Teraphims:* statues of Isis; little household idols.

30. *Jacobs Crosse:* Gen. 48.13–14 (*and* commentaries).

31. *curiously embroydered:* Psalm 139.15. A.V. reads "wrought" for Heb. "embroidered"; "curiously" is skillfully.

32. *in Plato:* the extravagant fancy and "discourse of love" of Aristophanes (*Symposium* 189–93). Aristophanes says the primitive man "was

round and had four hands and four feet, back and sides forming a circle, one head with two faces looking opposite ways."

33. *no less then four:* marginal reference to, and quotation from Gaza's translation of Aristotle, "On the Parts of Animals."

34. *Greek translation . . . Priests Fee:* A learned comment on the Septuagint version of a word in Lev. 7.29.

35. *cast upon our shoar:* 1652, [i.e. in 1652] described in our *Pseud. Epidem.* Edit. 3. (Browne) (*PE* 1658.3.26).

36. *breezes:* gad-flies; Edith Sitwell, apparently not aware of the meaning of "breeze," has a poem starting with this phrase.

37. *remarkable absurdity:* Browne objects to the fact that both left feet, only, are on the ground. The statues of Castor and Pollux are late imperial, discovered in the 16th century.

38. *Barbado Pine:* Martin quotes R. Ligon's *A true history of the Barbadoes* (SC 1653), but Browne read carelessly.

39. *man-Orchis:* marginal reference to Fabius Columna (Fabio Colonna, Italian naturalist [SC 1616]); from orchis, testicle.

40. *a common one:* Henry Power wrote to Browne for the identification of the plant; no answer is extant.

41. *Augustus:* Browne refers to Suetonius (*Augustus* 30).

42. *Magical spit:* In Porta's *Natural Magick*, 14.10 (1658, p. 323) under the heading "A Bird to rost himself" there is a description (from Albertus Magnus) of how to roast a wren on a spit of hazelwood, which will twist and turn.

43. *Gnatworms:* Found often in some form of red maggot in the standing waters of Cisterns in the Summer (Browne).

CHAPTER FOUR

1. *rule of Solon:* Plutarch *Solon* 23, but Plutarch says five and nine.

2. *Virgil:* Browne quotes the *Aeneid* 4.445–6: "As far as it lifts its head to heaven, so far it strikes its roots toward Tartarus."

3. *Pliny:* speaks of a plane tree with roots fifty feet long, wider than its branches (*Nat. Hist.* 12.5).

4. *of Solomon:* Song of Solomon 4.16.

5. *doctrine of Theophrastus:* when he discusses the influence of various winds on growth.

6. *But whether:* These are questions raised by both experience and herbal theory.

7. *little concerning Cyrus:* a desperate effort to get back to the title!

8. *Harpalus:* Pliny *Nat. Hist.* 16.62, with a reference to Theophrastus; Plutarch *Alexander* 35.

9. *the Poet:* marginal reference to Virgil *Eclogue* 7.38, where Corydon describes Galatea as "lovelier than pale ivy."

10. *Rams horns:* marginal reference "Linschoten"; his much read account of voyages to the East Indies was first published in 1598. "Vegetable horns" were investigated by Sir Philiberto Vernatti, Resident in Batavia, at the report of the Royal Society, according to Sprat's *History of the Royal Society*, 1667, (p. 161).

11. *Canticles:* Song of Solomon 1.14 and 4.13; the margins of the A.V., and the Vulgate, have "cypress" (Greenhill).

12. *Vitruvius: De Architectura* 5.1.

13. *Tabernacle:* Exod. 27.9–11.

14. *colours of mediocrity:* between white and black, which were called extreme colors (from Greenhill).

15. *Helmonts tree:* referring to a well-known experiment by Van Helmont in which he demonstrated how much water a willow tree absorbed over a period of five years.

16. *Light unto Pluto:* Browne quotes (in Latin tr.) from Hippocrates on changes in nature, light and darkness. For "forms" see Glossary.

17. *They that held:* a view attributed to Anaximander.

18. *better discovery:* marginal reference to *Selenographia* by J. Hevelius (*SC* 1647).

19. *greatest mystery . . . adumbration:* i.e. the Incarnation; Luke 1.35 reads (in A.V.) "overshadow," "obumbrabit" in Vulgate.

20. *light but:* quoted in Latin form in *RM* 1.10.

21. *Pyramidal rayes:* For the optical observations following, see the diagrams and notes in Martin.

22. *Aegyptian Philosophy:* what follows is drawn from, and illustrated in, Kircher's *Obiliscus Pamphilus* (*SC* folio 1650).

23. *Plato . . . Justin Martyr:* Browne is referring to *Timaeus* 36 (and 35), a notoriously complicated mathematical (Pythagorean) description of the making of the soul of the universe. The part of Plato about which Browne quotes Justin Martyr (*First Apology*) on the letter X begins: "This entire compound he divided lengthwise into two parts, which he joined to one another at the centre like the figure of a X and bent them into circular form. . . ." The letter Tau was used as a symbol for the cross and the brazen serpent of Num. 21.9: "And Moses made a serpent of brass, and put it upon a pole, and it came to pass that if a serpent [i.e. Satan] had bitten any man, when he beheld the serpent of brass [i.e. Christ] he lived." Browne also used the books of Kircher already mentioned for their exposition of hieroglyphics, and probably other similar material (see some specific references in Martin). For Plato, Moses, Egypt, etc. see also *RM* 1.32, n. 87.

CHAPTER FIVE

1. *inexcusable Pythagorisme:* i.e. mystical mathematics.

2. *number of justice:* the number of justice was sometimes 4 or 8, as well as five, but Browne's marginal note shows that he had some authority. In the original edition there is a marginal illustration of nine asterisks in threes.

3. *that common game:* ninepins.

4. *Plutarch:* quoting Empedocles.

5. *generall division of Vegetables:* a marginal note in Greek and Latin refers to four divisions, mentioned earlier, and a fifth of *fungi* and *tubera.*

6. *in many:* As Herons, Bitterns, and long claw'd Fowls (Browne).

7. *Cone:* Elleipsis, parabola, Hyperbole, Circulus, Triangulum (Browne).

8. *wedding number . . . five Torches:* Plutarch *Moralia* "Roman Questions" 2, and "Of EI at Delphi." In Holland's translation of the former, "Now among al odde numbers it seemeth that Cinque is most nuptial, and best beseming mariage, for that Trey is the first odde number, and Deuz the first even; of which twaine, five is compounded, as of the male and female." On this, *and the respect for Greek wisdom,* F. B. Jevons (*The Romane Questions,* Nutt 1892) remarks that to say in modern English that "five is the odd number most connected with marriage" would be to expose the Pythagorean doctrine of numbers to modern ridicule, but "even the irreverent modern cannot fail to feel that Cinque was an eminently respectable character whose views were strictly honourable and a bright example to other odde numbers."

9. *Hesiod . . . Plato:* in a footnote Browne quotes from Hesiod's *Works and Days* (802: avoid fifth days; they are unkindly and terrible) and refers to Plato's *Laws* (775a) where it is said that the guests for the wedding feast should be invited in fives.

10. *Nectar . . . fifth Planet:* marginal quotation from Horace, *Odes* 1.13.15–16; the fifth planet is Venus.

11. *Cabalistical accounts:* See quotations and annotations in Martin for what follows.

12. *unto none:* "or very few," marginal note (Browne), quoting his authorities and referring to the description of a spider with ten legs in De Laet's *Description of America* (SC 1633), "if perfectly described."

13. *Notion of Trismegistus:* i.e., again, that God is a circle.

14. *the Trespasser:* Lev. 6.5.

15. *five golden mice:* 1 Sam. 6.4 and 18.

16. *five . . . an hundred:* Lev. 26.8.

17. *Saint Paul . . . five words:* 1 Cor. 14.19.

18. *radicall Letters:* consonants in roots of Hebrew words.

19. *good Fortune:* . . . the name of the fifth house (Browne); celestial space is divided into twelve houses.

20. *five Capitall aspects:* Conjunct, opposite, sextile, trigonal, tetragonal (Browne). Aspect is the relative position of the planets as seen from earth at a given time.

21. *four parts:* protasis, epistasis, katastasis, catastrophe (Browne); not more than three actors in a scene.

22. *as Scaliger:* on Cardan, but apparently a mistake on Browne's part.

23. *Geomancers:* Browne could have got his "figures" (or pictures) from Fludd (*Microcosmi Historia*) or Cornelius Agrippa (*De Occulta Philosophia* 2.48), both of which he knew.

24. *Antoninus in some sence:* in his *Meditations* 11.12.

25. *quaternio's:* the tetraktus of Pythagorean number mysticism, i.e. $1 + 2 + 3 + 4 = 10 =$ all sorts of things.

26. *Quincunx of Heaven:* Hyades near the Horizon about midnight at that time (Browne); this is true in March. *GC* was licensed March 9, 1658, the dedicatory letter is dated May 1.

27. *Hippocrates: De Insomniis* (Browne); he names Artemodorus and Apomazar as "Oneirocriticall Masters," i.e. masters of dream interpretation.

28. *Bed of Cleopatra:* Strewed with Roses (Browne).

29. *Pagan Theology:* Hesiod *Theognis* 123 (Greenhill).

30. *Huntsmen are up:* this delighted Coleridge, but (as a slip) has puzzled editors; see for contrast ("tomorrow . . . China") passage from MS Sloane 1879 ("The Search for Truth") in this volume.

31. *that time:* midnight.

A LETTER TO A FRIEND

I have expressed my views on some aspects of the structure and literary character of *A Letter,* and the relationship between the printed text of 1690 (90) and the much shorter, and earlier MS version in MS Sloane 1862, in *UTQ* 36 (1966) 68–86. Although 90 is an amplified version of the whole, the MS has interesting additions in sections 11 and 13, and a long and personal passage which Wilkin placed after section 12 in his notes. As with *Hydriotaphia* and *The Garden of Cyrus,* Browne's very numerous marginal notes are only represented.

1. *Ad portam* . . . : stretches his stiff heels toward the door; Persius *Satire* 2.105, in an (inappropriately) ugly description of a sudden death by illness, not really very appropriate to Browne's subject.

2. *Nations of the Dead* . . . *dark Society:* both these phrases are very classical in tone, the latter reminiscent of Homer and Virgil, the former of the *abiit ad plures* quoted in the dedication to *Hydriotaphia.*

3. *that famous Story:* a story from the *Travels* of George Sandys (several editions) about an English merchant who with some sailors ascended the volcano at Stromboli (popularly called the jaws of Hell) and heard a spirit voice say "Dispatch, the rich Antonio is coming." On returning to Palermo and enquiring they found that Antonio had died.

4. *Sun* . . . *Moon* . . . *Stars:* Matt. 24.29.

5. *Plautus's:* a (not very appropriate) description of a sharp face in the *Captivi* 647–48.

6. *Hippocratical Face:* a very famous description of a dying man's appearance in the *Prognostics* of Hippocrates.

7. *Grashopper* . . . *Fig:* used symbolically for *summer* and *autumn*, an allusion perhaps to Juvenal *Satires* 9.69 and Horace *Epistles* 1.7.5 (Greenhill).

8. *like his Uncle:* MS version, "like his grandmother."

9. *pure Aerial Nitre:* Browne's Letters and the SC show that as a progressive doctor he was much interested, in the late 1660s and 70s, in discussions of this "nitrous spirit of the air" and how it "affects the heart" and "qualifies the blood." In late 1668 he wrote twice to Edward Browne about Mayow's *De Respiratione* (1668); the SC lists Clarke's *Natural History of Nitre* (1670) and Ent's *Animadversions* (1670); to the 1672 ed. of *PE* Browne added a paragraph on the matter in the section on the chameleon (3.21). *these Parts* is Norfolk.

10. *Sardinia in Tivoli:* There is a marginal quotation from Martial's *Epigrams* (4.60.56) "when death comes, even in the middle of Tibur [Tivoli] it is Sardinia," the latter being as notorious for its climate as the other famous.

11. *Broad Arrow:* In the King's Forests they set the figure of a broad Arrow upon Trees that are to be cut down (Browne).

12. *Hippocrates* . . . *Daw's Claw:* marginal reference to Hippocrates (*Epidemics* 6.7.9) and in MS version a large X.

13. *passager and migrant Birds:* marginal note, misplaced, to Bellonius (P. Belon) *de Avibus* (SC Fr. ed. 1555). Belon does not give the details which follow, details in which Browne was much interested. The migratory habits of birds were not known until much later.

14. *salient Point: punctum saliens,* "the heart as first seen in embryos."

15. *Death draws up:* also referred to in a series of MS (notebook) queries about the pseudo-Aristotelian *Problems* (Keynes III, 208).

16. *Juno:* was the goddess of childbirth; in Ovid (*Metamorphoses* 4.298–300) Alcmena tells how Juno delayed the birth of Hercules.

17. *Monsters:* marginal quotation and paraphrase from Hippocrates: Strange and rare escapes there happen sometimes in medicine (Browne).

18. *Angelus Victorius:* marginal reference to the *Consultationes* (*SC* 1640).

19. *Diseases:* Matt. 4.25 (Browne).

20. *Archidoxis of Paracelsus:* in which there are some very exotic and occult talismans and charms.

21. *Pliny:* long marginal quotation from Pliny on Aristotle (*Natural History* 2.101).

22. *old Genealogy:* as in Hesiod *Theognis* 212.

23. *about that hour:* midnight, as in last sentence of *GC*.

24. *Cardan:* Martin has a long note on this.

25. *Scaliger:* long marginal quotation by Browne from a commentary on Aristotle by Scaliger.

26. *Charles the Fifth:* In MS version of this passage Browne has marginal note "St. Mathias," which is February 24. The dates are February 24, 1500, 1525, and 1530. Antipater is from Pliny *Nat. Hist.* 7.52.

27. *When the fixed Stars:* See *RM* 1.6 and notes.

28. *good Angel:* See *RM* 1.31. In MS Sloane 1869 (Keynes, III, 289) Browne says we are free to "opinion" whether, if we have a guardian angel, its watch begins at birth or earlier.

29. *Tail . . . Mouth:* According to the Egyptian Hieroglyphick (Browne), no doubt referring to Pierius. There is a fine engraving in Wither's *Emblemes* (1633), Book 3, Illust. 23.

30. *Duke John Ernestus Mansfield: Turkish History* (Browne) (by R. Knolles). Two characters (who died within a few days of each other in 1626) seem to be here telescoped, but in a note-book entry (Keynes, III, 328) Count Mansfield and Duke John Ernestus are correctly referred to.

31. *Dante:* In the Poet Dante his Description (Browne); the lines are quoted in *Hydriotaphia* 3, n. 47.

32. *sextâ cervice:* carried by six (Juvenal, *Satires* 1.64).

33. *Omnibonus Ferrarius: De morbis Puerorum* (Browne) (*SC* title, *De Arte Medica Infantium,* 1577).

34. *Morta:* the Deity of Death or Fate (Browne).

35. *Caricatura:* When Mens Faces are drawn with resemblances to some other Animals, the Italians call it, to be drawn in *Caricatura* (Browne).

36. *Ulmus: Ulmus de usu barbae humanae* (Browne).

37. *Lewis:* King of Hungary (1506–1526). *Mohacz* was a disastrous battle in which the Turks annihilated a Hungarian army of about 25,000 men. For the details about skin and beard, Martin refers to *The Historie of the Troubles of Hungarie* (*SC* 1600).

38. *Psalmist's Period:* The life of a Man is Threescore and Ten (Browne).

39. *amused:* here, engaged the attention of.

40. *Morgellons*] See G.E. Kellett (Annals of Med Hist 7 [1935] 467–79) for an account of this disease, associated with Languedoc and referred to under various names, as "masquelous," "masclous," etc.

41. *King Pyrrhus . . . but two:* His upper and lower Jaw being solid, and without distinct rows of teeth (Browne). Browne seems to have taken such a fancy to the teeth and toe of Pyrrhus (for the latter see *Hydriotaphia* 3, and the rhyme given in note 33) as to read Plutarch carelessly or lightheartedly; Plutarch says the upper row was solid, with "rifts," as North puts it.

42. *Bannyans:* Hindus.

43. *Teeth:* Twice tell over his Teeth, never live to threescore years (Browne).

44. *du Loyr: Voyages* (*SC* 1654). The phrase *scarce twenty Years ago* runs "not twentie years ago" in the MS version, and to *PE* 1672 (7.13) the same information is added as of "about twenty years ago."

45. *Rickets:* called "Morbus Anglicus" and, according to F. Glisson, *De Rachitide* (*SC* 1650), known in East Anglia for about thirty years only. "Country" probably here means "county."

46. *Kings Purse . . . King's Evil:* When persons were touched for the King's Evil (scrofula) a little gold medal was hung around their necks. In John Brown's *Adenochoiradelogia* (a treatise on the King's Evil), 1684, statistics show that thousands were touched, the figures rising steadily in 1672, 1673, and 1674.

47. *that Bell:* the bell rarely sounds for a quartan ague (Browne in Latin, unidentified).

48. *Plato: Republic* 3.405d.

49. *Polydore Virgil: Historia Anglica,* (1570), 26 (Martin).

50. *often found:* Autopsies were becoming increasingly common.

51. *a Man:* So A.J. (Browne). A.J. is Sir Arthur Jenny, as noted in MSS Sloane 1879 (folio 47ᵛ) and 1866 (folio 73ᵛ); the date is given as May 26, 1668. "A.J." is misprinted "A.F." in 90.

52. *Rule of Cardan:* Cardan in his *Encomium Podagrae* (Praise of Gout) reckoneth this among the *Dona Podagrae* (Gifts of Gout) that they are delivered thereby from the Pthysis and Stone in the Bladder (Browne).

53. *Aristotle:* in the pseudo-Aristotelian *Problems* (10.1); this is another of the problems put down by Browne in a notebook (Keynes III, 209) and quoted as a glaring error in *PE* 1.6.

54. *Arrianus:* Martin suggests Aldrovandus (*SC Ornithologia* 1610) since Arrian did not write about hawks but hunting and dogs, and Aldrovandus did, and also about the coughs of hawks. In his own tract on hawks Browne refers to quite a number of writers but to neither Aldrovandus nor Arrian.

55. *Hippocrates: Hippoc. de Insomniis* (Browne); the details which follow (but not the rhythms of Sect. 16) are from this work. Tellus is the Roman name for the ancient earth-goddess.

56. *Cardan:* the Autobiography (*de Vita Propria*) 37; see also Browne's essay "On Dreams."

57. *why to dream:* These puzzles are found in the authors cited.

58. *Caesarean Nativity:* A sound Child cut out of the Body of the Mother (Browne).

59. *the River:* marginal quotation from *Aeneid* 9.603–4: We first bring our new born sons to the river and harden them with the water's cruel cold.

60. *Marriages . . . Candle:* as in auction-sales by an inch of candle, when goods were knocked down to the last bidder before the candle went out (Greenhill).

61. *five plain Words:* marginal quotation from Joseph Scaliger's life of his father: Julii Caesaris Scaligeri quod fuit. But see J. Ferguson (*Bibliotheca Chemica* 2.235) for the very boastful lines of verse Scaliger wrote for himself.

62. *this serious* [i.e. weighty] *Person:* J. C. Scaliger, in my view, although the syntax is peculiar, save for Browne. In MS version "no *minor wit*" is "no minor poet." Scaliger's output of Latin poetry (about 1000 pages in *Poemata, SC* 1591) would justify Browne's phrase in Renaissance terms.

63. *Petrarcha, Dante, Ariosto:* these are given in Paulus Jovius (Jovio), *Elogia doctorum virorum* (*SC* 1571).

64. *Ciceronian Poets:* cf. *RM* 2.9, where Cicero is called "the worst of Poets."

65. *Not to fear . . . desire it:* marginal reference to Martial *Epigrams* 10.47.13, of which this is a translation.

66. *Lazarus:* Who upon some Accounts, and Tradition, is said to have lived 30 years after he was raised by our Saviour. Baronius (Browne). The MS version reads "one Lustre more then his Sauiour," i.e. 35 not 30.

67. *not to be avoided:* In the Speech of *Vulteius in Lucan* [*Pharsalia* 4.486–87] animating his Souldiers in a great struggle to kill one another . . . [lines quoted] All fear is over, do but resolve to dye, and make your Desires meet Necessity (Browne). See also Browne's letter to his son Tom (Feb. 1667) in this volume, and note.

68. *Cacus's Oxen:* Cacus (*Aeneid* 8.209) dragged his stolen oxen backward by their tails into his cave.

69. *Solomon's Old Man:* Wisdom 4 [Apocrypha] (Browne).

70. *the old Man:* as in Rom. 6.6 or Ephes. 4.22, etc. unregenerate human nature; *cf.* the "old Adam."

71. *Altho:* In the MS version "Lastly" was inserted before "Though."

72. *Paragon:* a diamond without flaw.

73. *sick performances:* "sick non-performances" of *CM* makes the sense clearer.

CHRISTIAN MORALS

For comment on some aspects of structure and relation to passages in MSS, see Textual Notes. The title page of the second edition of 1756 (*1756*) reads "WITH / A LIFE OF THE AUTHOR. / BY / SAMUEL JOHNSON; AND / EXPLANATORY NOTES." This leaves open the authorship of the notes. Yet some of them seem to suggest Johnson.

DEDICATION, PREFACE, PART ONE

1. *David, Earl of Buchan:* in 1697 married Frances Fairfax, daughter of Sir Thomas Browne's daughter Anne and Henry Fairfax. Frances died in 1719, and the earl remarried.

2. *whether thou art yet:* what follows is largely free paraphrase of sentences in *Cebes's Table,* 12.

3. *Cato:* Plutarch *Cato of Utica* 25.52.

4. *Sisters of Darius:* a mistake for "daughters of Darius," the reading in *A Letter,* 1690, sect. 33. From Justin *Historiarum Philippicarum* 11.9 (Greenhill).

5. *Charon expects no more:* See *Hydriotaphia* 4, n. 16.

6. *the Ax of the Prophet:* 2 Kings 6.5–7.

7. *bore thy ear:* Exod. 21.6: "Then his master shall bring him to the

judges . . . and his master shall bore his ear through with an aul; and he shall serve him forever."

8. *Optimi malorum* . . . : the best of the bad, the worst of the good.

9. *follow a multitude:* Exod. 23.2.

10. *more than eight:* Noah, his wife, three sons and their wives.

11. *the short madness:* anger is a short madness (Horace *Epistles*, 1.2.62).

12. *imitate Job* . . . *Socrates:* the patience of Job is proverbial; Aelian (*Varia Historia* 11.13, Greenhill) speaks of the patience or indifference of Socrates when Aristophanes mocked him on the stage.

13. *Diabolism:* from Greek for calumny; in Vulgate, Diabolus sometimes word for the devil.

14. *St. Paul's noble Christian:* presumably Rom. 13.7–14.

15. *Trust not with some:* from the time of Eusebius and Jerome doubts were expressed about the Epistle of St. James; the reference is presumably to James 4.11.

16. *that Crowning Grace:* Charity, as described in 1 Cor. 13.

17. *as to fancy the Stars:* a view attributed to Anaximander, and referred to also again in *GC*.

18. *a vast tract of Land:* this speculation about Atlantis had its origin in Plato's *Timaeus*.

19. *Adraste and Nemesis:* are synonymous, the first being a name for Nemesis from an altar erected to her by Adrastus. Browne sometimes uses "and" for "or" and vice versa.

20. *Zeno's King:* The ideal wise man is described by Zeno, founder of the Stoic school, as the true king.

21. *the wise man's wax:* in the famous story of Ulysses and the Sirens (*Odyssey* 12.173); Ulysses was tied to the mast, the ears of the crew were filled with wax.

22. *Simonides:* a lyrical poet (c. 556–486 B.C.) whose technique for memorizing is referred to by Cicero in his *De Oratore*.

23. *behold our own blood:* i.e. and realize we are only human.

24. *wild Horses of Plato: Phaedrus* 246, 253; a myth of the soul in a metaphor of two winged horses, one black and one white, and a charioteer. As Martin remarks, only one horse is wild.

25. *Weapons* . . . *Vulcan's Art:* Vulcan's forge was on one of the Lipari islands; Homer has a description of Vulcan forging a shield for Achilles, Virgil of one forged for Aeneas.

26. *Armature of St. Paul:* Ephes. 6.13–17.

27. *Laconism on the Wall:* the cryptic words written on the wall at Belshazzar's feast. Dan. 5.25–28.

28. *No Man . . . say unto Princes:* the reply of Diogenes, when Alexander the Great asked him what he had to request.

29. *Bias:* one of the seven wise men of Greece, who, when asked in a crisis why he was not carrying off his valuable possessions like others, replied that he carried all he had with him—i.e. in his head.

30. *his [the viper's] Eye with love:* The viper has an elliptical cat-like pupil. John Aubrey describes Bacon as having "a delicate lively hazel eie; Dr Harvey told me it was like the eie of a viper," (Aubrey, *Brief Lives* ed. Andrew Clark, I. 72).

31. *Demetrius, Antonius . . . Aristides, Numa or David:* see Plutarch's *Lives* (Demetrius and Antony are formally compared). But Ahab (in 1 Kings 16.30 described as having done evil beyond all that were before him) seems of quite a different order of "vicious temper" than Demetrius and Antony, and David's virtue was not of the consistent kind attributed to Numa and Aristides.

32. *dispersed Seminalities:* at the Creation nature was endowed with a "plastic" power to form matter into various organisms.

33. *Andreas Doria:* famous Genoese admiral (1466–1560); the story comes from the end of Cardan's "Praise of the Gout" to which Browne also refers in *A Letter* sect. 15; see n. 52.

34. *Socrates and Cardan:* Plato (*Apology* 37) speaks of Socrates' belief in his guardian spirit (genius), and Cardan is emphatic about his in his autobiography (*De vita propria,* 17).

35. *Tropicks and Deflexions:* turning back and turning aside.

36. *Vulcan from Heaven:* he was hurled from heaven by Jupiter (*Iliad* 1.592).

37. *Orontes into Tiber:* "Syrian Orontes has long since poured into Tiber," from Juvenal's *Satires* (3.62), in a passage ridiculing the influx of foreign fashions.

38. *solemn:* here (from Latin), customary.

39. *a Lyon in the way:* Prov. 22.13: "the slothful man saith, There is a lion without, I shall be slain in the streets."

40. *Leaden Sandals:* the word *Sandals* leads Greenhill plausibly to a reference in Hippocrates about a leaden surgical sandal, but the proverb is still common.

41. *Hercules:* in his pursuit of the hind of Ceryneia (the fourth of the twelve Labors).

42. *Hic Niger est . . . :* This man is black, Roman be on guard.

43. *Plutarch . . . Laërtius:* i.e. Plutarch wrote lives of captains and statesmen, Diogenes Laertius, lives of philosophers.

44. *a Hand to burn:* like M. Scaevola, as related by Livy; see *RM* 1.44, n. 127.

PART TWO

1. *delight . . . rarity: 1756* refers to the final line in Juvenal's *Satire* 11, much of which is about gluttony.

2. *Jupiter's brain:* and the references to delicacies which follow are, respectively, from Athenaeus, Diogenes Laertius, and (Martin) Lampridius on the Emperor Heliogabalus. Browne wrote an amusing piece in Latin on classical delicacies, etc. (Keynes, III, 178–81, tr. by Le Fanu).

3. *I should unwillingly affirm:* the errors that follow are in some degree drawn from commentators. There is a longer list in MS Sloane 1879 folios 47–48.

4. *Hercules:* in the *Amphitruo* of Plautus.

5. *Apollinaris Sidonius:* lived c.430–c.488; the two passages of verse referred to (from the *Carmina*) are given in marginal notes in MS Sloane 1879.

6. *verum certe . . . :* true, certainly true, and most true.

7. *Cardan . . . Scaliger:* the first in his *de Subtilitate,* the other in his critical examination (*Exercitationes*) of Cardan. Scaliger is quoted by Greenhill to show how he set his wits to work.

8. *the genealogy of Hector:* with "What Song the *Syrens* sang" (*Hydriotaphia* 5, n. 9) one of the questions Tiberius asked the grammarians (Suetonius *Tiberius* 70).

9. *but one sentence in Latin:* he who does not know how to dissimulate does not know how to reign.

10. *Sect. 5:* See also version of this section as found in MS Sloane 1879; printed in this volume.

11. *Euphorbus:* a Trojan who wounded Hector and was killed by Menelaus. Pythagoras claimed that he had been Euphorbus in a previous existence and could remember incidents of the Trojan War.

12. *Diogenes . . . falsifier of Money:* as related by Diogenes Laertius in his *Lives of the Philosophers* (6.20–21).

13. *Sect. 9:* "This is a very fanciful and indefensible section" (1756— by Johnson?).

14. *corner-stone in Physiognomy:* and illustrated in various books on physiognomy, e.g. in G. B. della Porta, whose *de humana physiognomia* (1586) went through a great many editions in Latin and translation for many years.

15. *Pompey . . . Great:* from Plutarch *Pompey.*

16. *extramission . . . self reflexion:* Martin quotes *PE* (3.7 on Basilisk) on Aristotle and others "who hold that sight is made by Reception and

not by Extramission; by receiving the rayes of the object into the eye, and not by sending any out."

17. *the second Death:* Rev. 20.14: "And death and hell were cast into the lake of fire. This is the second death."

18. *our own:* Charles II; even his most severe critics called him good-natured.

19. *Sect. 13:* at some stage intended by Browne for *A Letter to a Friend.*

20. *Lucan and Seneca:* see RM 2.12, n. 50.

21. *a dull way . . . Themistocles:* Plutarch (*Themistocles* 31) says bull's blood or poison; in his *Hannibal* he calls the bull's blood story a false report.

22. *Socrates in Plato:* as told in the conclusion of the *Phaedo.*

23. *pummel:* Martin gives the probable source of this in Thomas Ross, whose *Continuation* (1661) of the huge epic on the Punic Wars by Silius Italicus is in SC. Plutarch speaks of bull's blood or poison.

24. *Hermes his Rod:* Caduceus, one touch of which awakened or put to sleep. (e.g. *Odyssey* 5.47–48)

PART THREE

1. *since 'tis said:* in Gen. 6.5; a favorite Calvinist text.

2. *Adam . . . Methusaleh . . . Noah:* their lives overlapped, since Methusaleh lived for 969 years.

3. *counterfeited Thunder:* Salmoneus. *Aeneid* 6.585–86 (Gardiner).

4. *Trismegistus his Circle:* see RM 1.10, n. 23.

5. *dark Lake:* presumably Styx, as in *Aeneid* 6.134.

6. *seven principal Ostiaries:* i.e. Seven Deadly Sins.

7. *Tree of Goa* [and footnote]: This description of the Banyan tree has its distant origin in Pliny (*Natural History* 12.11), where one tree encloses a circle sixty yards across. It is the tree of *Paradise Lost* 9.1101–12.

8. *that inhumane Vice* [and footnote]: malignant joy over some one's badness or cowardice (Aristotle *Nicomachean Ethics* 2.6, 2.7).

9. *Sapiens dominabitur Astris:* this saying, translated in text, was apparently proverbial.

10. *Attalus his Garden:* see GC 1, n. 12.

11. *black Sails:* On his return from conquering the Minotaur in Crete, Theseus forgot to change the black sails with which he had sailed; in despair his father Aegeus threw himself off a cliff (Plutarch *Theseus* 17).

12. *Pompeios Juvenes . . . :* Asia and Europe cover the sons of Pompey, but Lybia, Pompey himself.

13. *Reminiscential amulets:* anything worn on the hand or body by way of monition or remembrance (*1756*).

14. *Quid fuerim . . . .* : consider what I was and what I now am.

15. *on our Hands:* i.e. in rings.

16. *the Colossus:* the Colossus of Rhodes as described by Pliny (*Nat. Hist.*, 34.18).

17. *Historia Horribilis:* the short title of a book on dreadful crimes and dreadful punishments published in 1597 and again in 1656 (from Greenhill).

18. *Flay not thy Servant:* when Augustus supped with one of the Roman senators, a slave happened to break a glass, for which his master ordered him to be thrown into a pond to feed his lampreys. Augustus to punish his cruelty ordered all the glasses in the house to be broken (*1756;* from Seneca *de Ira*).

19. *nor pound him in a Mortar:* Anaxarchus, pounded in a mortar by a tyrant (from Diogenes Laertius *Lives* 9.10).

20. *Jonathan:* 1 Sam. 20.20.

21. *a Dead Enemy smells well:* Suetonius (*Vitellius* 10) quotes this as an "abominable remark" of the Emperor Vitellius.

22. *tu tamen . . .* : but you may shout so as to outdo Stentor, or at least as loudly as Homer's Mars. *Gradivus* was a surname of Mars; the reference is to *Iliad* 5.785.

23. *Since Women:* referred to Juvenal [13.191–92], with quotation, in *1756*.

24. *Regulus:* Roman consul and general tortured by the Carthaginians by keeping him awake.

25. *David's Servants:* 2 Sam. 10.14.

26. *Caricatura:* see Browne's note on the word in *A Letter*, sect. 10, n. 35.

27. *Divine particle:* referred to Horace *Satires* 2.2.79 by Martin: "and ties to earth the divine particle."

28. *neither Sun nor Moon:* Rev. 21.23.

29. *cloud so big as a Hand:* 1 Kings 18.44.

30. *vouchsafed unto Peter:* John 21.18–19.

31. *taken unto Jeremy:* i.e. since Jeremiah had prophesied that it would happen.

32. *Olybius his Urn:* see note on this in *PE* 3.21, n. 14.

33. *Call not Jove* [and footnote]: the oath-maker swore on a stone and then, throwing it from him, wished to be also thrown away if the oath were broken.

34. *Urn of the Praetor:* the magistrate's urn for votes for condemnation or acquittal.

35. *deeply swear as Osman:* on p. 1383 of the 1638 ed. of Knolles; picturesque, and quoted in full by Martin.

36. *Vulcans:* Vulcan was lame, from having been thrown from heaven by Jupiter.

37. *Rest not in . . . old Philosophy:* the general contrast is of course between even the best examples of pagan moral philosophy (or law) and the *Ethicks of faith* culminating in the Sermon on the Mount. The twelve tables is a collection of the principal rules of the oldest Roman law, the two tables those given to Moses. Phocylides was a 6th-century B.C. gnomic moralizing poet. Peripatus, Academy, Porticus stand for Aristotelianism, Platonism, and Stoicism.

38. *best judge of Time:* The important word is "best." A deep taste of the world may be had in seventy or eighty years (previous paragraph) but a much better understanding if a man were able to live one hundred years, the sixtieth part of time in the commonly accepted chronology of the world's duration to which Browne so often refers. Plato (*Republic* 10.615) uses the phrase "the hundred years which are reckoned as the life of man."

39. *Solomon's Maxims:* that all is vanity (Eccles. 1.2).

40. *not thy Diana:* Acts 19.24–25, about silversmiths of Ephesus who made shrines for Diana and objected to the practical effect on their craft of Paul's preaching about Gods made with hands. (Ref. from Martin.)

41. *Vitam nemo . . . :* translated in text.

42. *beginning in a cradle:* Cicero *de Senectute* 23; referred to again by Browne in *A Letter.*

43. *grow old like a Garment:* presumably from Isa. 51.6, where it is said "the earth shall wax old like a garment" and the heavens vanish like smoke.

44. *the Doctrine of the Sphere:* the argument about Capella and changing declinations of stars because they "move upon the Poles of the Ecliptick, distant 23 degrees and an half from the poles of the Aequator, and describe circles parallel not unto the Aequator, but the Ecliptick . . ." is expounded in *PE* 4.13.

45. *prayer . . . under the Altar:* Rev. 6.9–10; quoted in *RM* 1.46.

46. *Nero's mind:* "a certain person upon a time, spoke in his hearing these words when I am dead let Earth be mingled with Fire. Whereunto the Emperor uttered these words yea whilst I live." Keck (who quotes the Greek) on the similar reference in *RM* 2.4; (Suetonius *Nero* 38).

47. *little Flock:* see *RM* 1.58, n. 158.

48. *greater number . . . vast number:* Each of the nine orders was thought to have 6666 legions, each legion 6666 members. It was proposed

that either 1 or 3 orders fell; that is, either 133,306,668 or 44,435,566.

49. *think every day the last:* Horace *Epistles,* 1.4.13; quoted in *1756*.

50. *elsewhere declared:* in the last paragraph but one of *Hydriotaphia;* see Glossary for some words.

MISCELLANY TRACTS

Of Languages

The range of Browne's interest in languages can be seen in the large number of books which he cites, quotes, and owned. He begins his discussion with the Bible, Babel (the source of confusion), and the supposed original language, but his curiosity extends to recent discussion. He is not a pioneer philologist, rather a learned virtuoso, yet even this essay (in part written for amusement) is not unremarkable, with its pastiches of pre-classical Latin, "Saxon," Provençal, Rabelais, its knowledgeable curiosity about Basque, its Norfolk dialect words. One has only to read some of the other contemporary discussions to realize with what intelligence and good sense, when he is serious, Browne presents his material. For some background material see the Selected Bibliography.

1. *confusion at Babel:* for Babel, Sinar, Heber, etc. see Gen. 11.

2. *If America were peopled:* This was much discussed, e.g. by scholars like J. De Laet and Hugo Grotius in 1643 and 1644. De Laet thought the Scythians furnished the basic population, Grotius disagreed violently. E. Brerewood, in *Enquiries Touching the Diversity of Languages and Religions* . . . 1614 proposes Tartars (from Israelites, with some ingenious etymology). *Cf.* also H. L'Estrange, *Americans No Jews (SC* 1652).

3. *eighteen languages:* from Thomas Gage, *A New Survey* . . . *or the English American his Travail of Sea and Land (SC* 2d ed. 1655), p. 213.

4. *Isaac Vossius:* His *Dissertatio de vera aetate mundi (SC* 1649) is a very firm assertion of a chronology with precise dates. The last sentence gives the precise date of writing as 7048. D. Petavius (Petau) in the two large folio volumes of his *De Doctrina Temporum (SC* 1629) is even more precise. The world was created in the autumn (Oct. 26), the flood lasted from January to October, 1655 years after the creation, etc.

5. *primitive tongue:* still a subject of serious as well as facetious comment, and the almost inevitable beginning of cosmographies and books concerned with different languages and the migrations of peoples. Among authors Browne refers to are R. Verstegan, *A Restitution of Decayed Intelligence* (1605 and several later eds.), C. Crinesius, *De Con-*

fusione Linguarum . . . (SC 1629), Meric Casaubon, *De Quatuor Linguis . . . (SC* 1650). The *ingresse* of Hebrew is sometimes illustrated by extraordinary etymological examples.

6. *Mazorite* [Massorite] *poynts:* are dots used to indicate the vowels in the authoritative text of the Old Testament as established between the 6th and 8th centuries.

7. *Goropius Becanus:* says this, more amply, in his *Origines Antwerpianae (SC* 1569), pp. 538–40.

8. *many hundred yeares:* Confucius was born in 550 or 551 B.C.; *Poncuus:* the mythical Chinese ancestral figure P'an-Ku.

9. *Herulian pater noster:* This is set down, with a translation, on pp. 787–88 of the *De Migratione Gentium (SC* 1557). The practice of putting down parallel examples of the Pater Noster is also found copiously in the *Cosmography* of P. Merula (*SC* 6 vols. 1636). *Herulians* are "Goths." Lazius says some words are corrupted Latin, others are of Teutonic origin.

10. *League . . . Charles and Lewis:* a division of territories between Louis and Charles, grandsons of Charlemagne, made at Strasbourg in 842; given in Merula, 3 (Gallia), p. 83.

11. *pillar of Duillius* [incorrectly "Quillius" in all editions of Browne]: the Columna Rostrata, or column decked with beaks (rostra) of ships, erected in honor of G. Duilius (consul 260 B.C.) after his defeat of the Carthaginian fleet; with an inscription which survives in what is now described as a copy or restoration of Imperial times. Brerewood gives the inscription with a later Latin translation, and comments on it. Merula says there is "nothing more ancient."

12. *Endo omnibus . . . :* Reading *ruspari* for *ruspare, siremps* for *siemps,* my colleague Professor Niall Rudd translates: "In all matters honour should not be neglected. And so I do not know why you have done this. In good time and with all despatch, you yourself, however, tell these people what no one is able, or else is unwilling, to search out. Clever old men are unable to understand their own affairs. In what light does a citizen regard an ally?" The last sentence is very tentative. In Festus (De *Significatione Verborum,* which Browne must have used) "sardare" is "intellegere", but since "saperda" and "sarda" are saltfish, I suspect that there must be a pun, and that perhaps old wiseacres rather than clever old men is intended. The MS is fair copy.

13. *Casaubone conceaveth:* Meric Casaubon goes through the Greek alphabet finding related words. The statement referred to is put even more strongly (on p. 378) where Casaubon says he thinks that (excepting those words which have a Latin origin) little that is truly English cannot—with proper care and diligence—be traced to roots in Greek.

14. *Verstegan: Restitution* . . . (1605), p. 198, not quite literally quoted.

15. *Alured: Cf.* R. Powell, *The Life of Alfred or Alured* (*SC* 1634): "Alfred, or as some name him Aelfred, or Alured, the 23 King of the West-Saxons and the first Monarch of England."

16. *Fingall:* (from "white foreigners," i.e. Norsemen) the district north of Dublin; the English plantations of this district began in the 12th century under Henry II.

17. *Arviraga:* a word from Scaliger to describe the dialect of the district.

18. *Cantabrian and British:* Cantabrian is the language of the Pyrenees, into which the original inhabitants retreated from the Romans; British is Gaelic. In the maps in Merula, Brittany is still labeled "Britannia, vulgo La Duché de Bretaigne" (from the ancient "Britannia major" and "Britannia minor"). Merula gives a Pater Noster of the "Cambro-britani."

19. *the present Basquensa:* The Lord's Prayer referred to is in vol. 2 of Merula (Spain), pp. 69–70; Merula picks out these words and *six* more. For comment on the important MS Basque dictionary and grammar (c.1653) of Nicoleta (or Micoleta) which Browne owned see *TLS* 1962, p. 645, and references there.

20. *this following illustration:* Eleanor Adams (see Selected Bibliography) remarks that Browne's examples "are more properly Middle English, but the early scholars did not recognize the difference between the successive stages of the language." Professor Norman Garmonsway has been kind enough to look at these illustrations and indeed rendered the first sentence into Anglo-Saxon idiom. After remarking on the justness of Dr. Johnson's comment that the words are Saxon but the phraseology modern, Professor Garmonsway notes that "Apart from substituting noun for noun Browne makes no attempt to adapt the sentence structure to the rules of Anglo-Saxon syntax, or to give the correct inflexional forms. . . . He has, however, skilfully weighted his argument by using passages composed of words the majority of which occur in A.S." The passage certainly has suggestions of 14th- or 15th-century homiletic prose, and Professor Garmonsway speaks of "a pleasant echo of Boethius" in the last paragraph but one. MS Rawlinson 390 (see also Wilkin *Works*, IV, 466–76) lists a number of Middle English MSS which were in Browne's library, e.g. the present MSS Sloane 1825, 1859, 1888.

21. *old Runick:* Ole Worm's handsome folio on Danish antiquities, *Danicorum Monumentum libri sex* (*SC* 1643), gives Runick inscriptions.

22. *common use in Norfolk:* Most of the Norfolk words are copiously annotated by Wilkin (*Works*, IV, 205–9), who was an East Anglian, and (with the exception of *Fasgon, Gosgood, kamp*) are in Wright's *Dialect*

Dictionary, sometimes only with reference to Browne or derivatively from him.

23. *Hugo de Boves:* A fleet under Hugh de Boves, a mercenary coming to the aid of King John, was wrecked on the Norfolk coast in 1215. He and his followers had been promised large grants of land in Norfolk and Suffolk.

24. *some endeavours of yours:* The recipient of this letter has not been identified.

25. *Britaigne:* i.e. Brittany.

26. *Chavalisco:* There are variations in the vocabulary in Sloane 1827 (e.g. aquestes for *taulas, sin* for *soun, de paraullas en el mon* for *din lou mounde*) and some rearrangement. *MT* has a shorter example, and Sl. 1827 a French translation of the first example: "Chavalisque, qu'estecy, pourquoi faites vous a cette manière. Che veut trouble sa teste avec cettes choses. Il esloyt fol qui voudroyt employer son temps anuiron celles. Je nay poynt plaisir ouyr la moitié de paroles au monde. Allons." The "etc." at the end of the beginning of Browne's translation of the second example implies that he had written this out in another MS. The rest of the passage may be translated "and for that reason have come to this city. Certainly the speeches of the women are very agreeable and flow sweetly from their throats. Also I have found the girls of Toulouse charming and pretty; so much so that I believe I shall speak well before Christmas. Adieu. Monsieur, I am yours with great respect, from now to the grave.

Your servant

T.B."

Browne may have made a mistake about the word "paraullasos", which seems to mean tedious or even improper speeches.

27. *Idiotismus:* vulgar, uneducated speech.

28. *Goudelin* [1579–1649]: was regarded as the most important Toulousian Provençal poet of his time (*SC Obros,* 1647). Goudelin and another Provençal poet, Daniel Sage of Montpellier (1567–1642) whose poems Browne also owned, were local celebrities when Browne was a student at Montpellier.

29. *tract of Falconrie:* not identified.

30. *poem of Vilhuardin: The Conquest of Constantinople,* by Geoffroi de Villehardouin (c.1160–c.1215) is not a poem but a prose chronicle, although the style is sometimes "poetic." It is not written in the language of southern France, but Browne possibly made this statement on the authority of Joseph Scaliger, who mistakenly said that Villehardouin wrote in the language of Touraine, not Paris (*Scaligeriana,* 1668, p.

358). The chronicle was first published (with a French translation) in 1585; there were later editions in 1601 and 1657.

31. *Marius Aequicola* [1470–1525]: apparently another error. Dennis Rhodes (*TLS* 1962, p. 679) points out that Browne was mistaken about Equicola being a poet (*SC* lists *Libro di Natura d'amore*, 1560). In his *Chronica di Mantua* Equicola refers to Sordello as having written excellent poetry on love; Sordello lived in Provençe for some years.

32. *in moderne French:* Browne knew Rabelais well and also owned Cotgrave's *Dictionary*, which, according to Professor Huntington Brown, provides almost a complete gloss to Rabelais. A puzzle piece should be puzzled over, but some explanations follow, for the most part from Cotgrave, and in the order of the passage: *manger la laine sur le dors:* eat the cloth off a man's back; *magot:* baboon; *pappelarde:* one who pretends to be pious; *fait le mitou:* played the hippocrite (*mitou* a great cat); *chausses les lunettes a travers:* mistake exceedingly; *mal St François:* want of money; *bride sa mule a vostre despens:* furnish yourself at another's expense; *s'amuse a la moustarde:* hold one busied about trifles while passing over great matters; *monsieur sans queue:* a master without any additions, a single-soled gentleman; *goulafre* (gouliafre): glutton; *beuveur a tire larigau:* drink till his throat cracke; *fait la barbe:* deceived; *Pampelune:* Pamplona in Spain; also the name of a dance in *Pantagruel* 5.33 *bis; a miserere jusques a vitulos* (from the beginning and end of one of the seven penitential psalms): one that's to be whipped extremely or a long time; *moutton de Berry:* he hath gotten a rap over the nose, whereon the shepherds of Berry marke their sheepe; *rompre un anguille:* attempt an impossible matter (i.e. break an eel); *rabaisser le menton:* humble, pluck down; *mourra dans sa peau* (from *le loup moura en sa peau*): a knave will die in a knave's skin; *A Naples sans passer les monts:* he has syphilis (*mal de Naples*) without passing the Alps; *patient de Sainct Cosme:* deceived (from one of Gargantua's games); *garconière:* a lascivious queane; *mal de neuf mois:* pregnant; *le nez tourné a la friandise:* said of a light housewife; *talons bien courts;* i.e. can be easily made to fall on her back; *Gymnosophiste:* Brahman; *branle comme le Bastille:* i.e. not shake at all; *Stoic a vingt quatre carrats:* the finest gold is 24 carats, but perhaps from *fol a vingt-cinque carats,* "an egregious foole."

Of the Answers of the Oracle

Browne's interest in the Greek oracles and what had been said about them by classical, early Christian, and Renaissance writers may be variously illustrated from *RM* onward. *PE* 4.12 is on the cessation of the oracles, taking off from Plutarch's essay on the subject in the *Moralia,* and in *PE* 1.4 Browne easily passes from Satan's success in Paradise to his efforts in "Oracles through all the world." But it is also characteristic of him to preface his discussion (though the quotation is not found in the earlier versions of the essay, i.e. MS Sloane 1827 and *Certain Miscellany Tracts* [*MT*]) with a comprehensive statement of different views abridged from the *de theologia Gentili . . . sive de origine et progressu Idolatriae* of G. J. Vossius (*SC* 2 vols. 1641), a huge compilation of about twenty-four hundred quarto pages covering a vast range of non-Christian belief and also various other matters. Browne's basic source is the *History* of Herodotus, books one (many references), two, and five; detailed reference is here omitted. Other references, although not always accurate, show, as one would expect, that he was familiar with a wide range of classical commentary.

1. *as Vossius:* in *de theologia Gentili* 1.6, 43–44. Browne has abridged and abbreviated but not changed the sense of Vossius: oracles consisted in the frauds of soothsayers, but not only that; in human skill but also demoniacal. When much they foretold could not be arrived at by any calculation and acumen of the human mind, we must not stop at human nature, but rise to causes of a higher nature, such as demons.

2. *Sortem fato . . . :* It is not in the power of God to hinder the Decree of Fate (Browne in *MT*).

3. *crimen quintae . . . :* Croesus "payd the transgression of his [fifth] predecessor."

4. *Candaules:* was not only in love with his own wife, as Herodotus says, but thought her the fairest woman in the world. To prove this he persuaded Gyges, much against his judgment, to see her naked. The queen saw Gyges leaving and, outraged, offered him the choice of his own death or that of Candaules.

5. *yet unpunished:* The Pythian priestess had prophesied vengeance in the fifth generation.

6. *Argis, Sardiattes, and Halyates:* ordinarily Ardis, Sadyates, Alyattes.

7. *answer unto Attalus:* from Diodorus Siculus 35.13.

8. *Sylla* [Sulla]: of whose brutality and cruelty Plutarch gives a full account.

9. *fift and last:* perhaps the most notoriously ambiguous of all the oracular replies (given by Browne in Greek): that if Croesus went to war against the Persians he would destroy a great empire. This of course happened when he was himself defeated by Cyrus.

10. *Orestes:* In some of the legends a good deal is made of the madness of Orestes when pursued by the Erinyes after the murder of his mother Clytemnestra. Browne speaks of Orestes in the same way in *PE* 1.3.

11. *two letters EI:* In Plutarch's essay on this subject (*Moralia*) there are a number of ingenious possible explanations centering on the fact that EI (a diphthong used in Plutarch's time for E) can mean both "if," "thou art," and "five," E being both the fifth letter of the alphabet and also a number with esoteric meanings.

12. *Aegeus:* was (by a trick) the father of Theseus; see Plutarch *Theseus* 3.5. An added phrase about Medea in the MT version shows that Browne was also thinking of the *Medea* of Euripides. His translation slightly disguises the ambiguous impropriety.

13. *unseemely epithite:* given by Browne in Greek and Latin—"hairy-bottomed." But Cyanus should be Cinyras, and the oracle comes from Athenaeus, *Deipnosophistae* 456 a. (I owe the reference to Mr. D. D. Russell, fellow of St. John's College, Oxford.)

14. *beastly trouble:* a slightly altered version of the story of Pharos, son of Sesostres, mythical king of Egypt, who went blind when he hurled a spear into a river.

15. *dead head in Phlegon:* This monstrous story, with a long oracular utterance, occupies chap. 2 of the book of strange happenings of Phlegon of Tralles (*SC, Historiarum mirabilium* . . . ed. Meursius, 1622, pp. 19–32).

16. *ghost of Commodus:* Dio Cassius *Roman History* 78. The Emperor Caracalla called up the ghost of the Emperor Commodus for help in getting rid of hallucinations that his brothers and father were pursuing him with drawn swords, but the ghost only increased his fears.

17. *spirits make verses:* For the style of the Delphic oracles see H. W. Parke and D. E. W. Wormell, *The Delphic Oracle,* 2 vols., Blackwell, Oxford, 1956, II, xxix–xxxiii.

18. *great performances:* Exod. 7 and 8.

19. *Hermolaus Barbarus:* See *RM* 1.10, n. 23.

20. *Appion the Grammarian:* In some remarks about magic, Pliny (*Natural History* 30.2) refers to having heard Appion say that he had conjured up spirits to ask Homer where he was born.

21. *Philostratus:* or rather Apollonius of Tyana as told (dramatically) by Philostratus. The ghost of Achilles answered five questions about the war of Troy and then departed with a little flash of lightning as the cocks began to crow.

A PROPHECY

Browne's curiosity about the new world was not much less than his interest in the old. It is to be hoped that his daughter Elizabeth shared this curiosity in view of the long list of folio volumes of history and travels (many thousands of pages) she read out at nights "till she read them all out" (Keynes, III, 331–32). Having been loaned, and asked for his opinion on some prophecies, perhaps of the kind written by Nostradamus (or possibly even the French-English version of Nostradamus published in 1672),[1] Browne replied in similar verses about things which he felt were at least not without some historical probability, the present situation weighed. His friend of nearly forty years, John Whitefoot, put on record his respect for Browne's "Sagacity and Knowledge of all History, Ancient and Modern" and his power of shrewd conjecture. But the approach to Browne has apparently been so conditioned by his phrase (in *Religio Medici*) about "loving a mystery" that even a modern critic (and one who has written illuminatingly about *Pseudodoxia*) can say that *A Prophecy* "exemplifies rather Browne's *mystical* [my italics] penchant for extravagant prophecies than any well-reasoned conjectures about future states." It is a slight literary and historical amusement, no doubt, but not a failed ecstasy. Various references in the text suggest that *A Prophecy* may have been written in the early or middle seventies.

1. *a freind:* not identified.

2. *about fiftie yeares:* presumably from the Charter of 1620.

3. *twentie or thirtie thousand:* Figures are given in various vols. of the *Calendar of State Papers, Colonial Series,* e.g. for 1661–1668, No. 1660 (? 1667), 30,000 fighting men; for 1669–1674, No. 1159 (1673), 50,000. L. K. Mathews (*Expansion of New England,* Houghton, Mifflin, Boston, 1909, p. 56) suggests 16,000 by 1675.

4. *Campeche and Santa Martha . . . Panama:* The English edition of Esquemeling, *The Buccaneers of America,* was not published until 1684, but the exploits of the buccaneers received great publicity, especially Henry Morgan's sack of Panama in 1671.

5. *accounts scarce credible:* Thomas Gage in his *Travels* (*SC* 1655, p. 56) said that it was "a most credible report" that there were above 15,000 coaches in Mexico City.

6. *histories of China:* Among the books read aloud at nights by Elizabeth Browne were A. Semmedo's *History of China* (1655), and F. Mendes Pinto's *Voyages . . . and Travels . . . in China, Tartaria etc.* (1653, 1663, etc.). The *SC* also lists Kircher's *China Illustrata* (1667).

7. *the learned Castelli:* Italian mathematician and defender of Galileo. His "Considerations concerning the Lake of Venice" (and the river

[1] But the French quatrains are translated into a curious doggerel prose.

Brenta) were written in 1641 and published in translation in T. Salusbury's *Mathematical Collections and Translations* (SC 1661).

ESSAYS AND OBSERVATIONS FROM NOTEBOOKS

[On Dreams]

In this essay on dreams, and in A *Letter*, Browne cites many of the more important writers on dreams, beginning with a treatise attributed to Hippocrates, and illustrates from the usual range of ancients and moderns. Martin refers to *Oneirocritica*, 1603, for some of the puzzles in A *Letter*, sect. 19; it was also, no doubt, used for this essay and the SC lists separate commentaries on Hippocrates by J. C. Scaliger (1610) and J. Collis (1628). Aristotle's views were also commented on at length in Browne's editions of Aristotle. E. G. Merton discusses the psychology of dreams and their relation to the soul in a very interesting article on Browne.

1. *brother of death:* sleep (*Iliad* 14.231).
2. *Solomons sleepe:* Prov. 3.24.
3. *Jacob:* Gen. 28.11–12.
4. *naturall and animal dreames:* Classical and Renaissance writers on dreams commonly made three categories: divine (infused into the mind supernaturally); natural (proceeding from dominant humors or distemperature); animal (arising from the daily affairs with which men are occupied).
5. *Chrysostome:* wrote perhaps two hundred and fifty homilies on St. Paul.
6. *Cardan:* In chap. 38 of his *Autobiography* Cardan tells this dream at considerable length.
7. *dreame of Pharaoh:* Gen. 41.
8. *Nabuchodonosor:* Dan. 2.3–5.
9. *Tyre . . . thine:* The Soothsayers punningly interpreted "saturos" in this way (Plutarch *Alexander* 24.5).
10. *Vespasian . . . Mauritius:* Vespasian dreamed that he saw a balance (scales) in one pan of which stood Claudius and Nero, in the other himself and his sons (Suetonius *Vespasian* 25). Claudius and Nero together reigned as long as Vespasian and his sons Titus and Domitian.
11. *Galen:* says so in his commentary on Hippocrates "On the Humours" (2.2).

12. *Dion: Roman History* 72. His literary career began with a small book on the portents and dreams that indicated that Severus would ascend the throne. Dreams also encouraged him to continue as an historian.

13. *Cicero:* fully related in Plutarch's *Cicero,* 44. Augustus Caesar sacrificed Cicero at the persuasion of Antony.

14. *Luther:* Luther's *Table Talk* records frequent lively and coarse encounters with the devil, but the most popular story (of his throwing his ink stand at the devil) is apparently apocryphal.

15. *Crassus . . . Antonius:* The reputation of Crassus for wealth and avariciousness was matched by that of Antony for liberality.

16. *Pythagoras . . . beanes:* See *PE* 1. n. 34.

17. *Daniel:* Dan. 1.12–16.

18. *bowells of Olympias:* Olympias, the mother of Alexander the Great, dreamed on her wedding night that "lightning fell into her belly and that withall there was a great light fire that dispersed it self about in divers flames" (Plutarch *Alexander* 2.2; North's translation).

19. *Dionysius:* the elder, Tyrant of Syracuse, killed his Captain Marsias for telling him this dream (Plutarch *Dion* 9).

20. *Lamia:* a famous courtesan; Plutarch did not say this of Lamia, but of another less famous courtesan who lost her suit; unjustly, in Lamia's view (*Demetrius* 27).

[The Search for Truth]

See also notes on *CM* 2.5.

21. *tomorrow when I arise:* MS Sloane 1848 (folio 142) has what appears to be a draft of this sentence in which the parallel phrase runs "about 6 hours hence when I am in America."

[Circumscriptions of Pleasure]

See notes on *CM* 2.1.

[The Line of Our Lives]

See notes on *CM* 2.10 and 3.22.

[Ways of Dying]

See notes on *CM* 2.13.

[Intention, Imitation, Coincidence]

22. *Aetheris immensi* . . . : If you lean on any one part of boundless space, the axis will be weighed down (Lucan *Civil War* 1.56–57, slightly misquoted).

23. *una dolo* . . . : if one woman is carried off by the wiles of two gods—an ironic remark by Saturnia to Venus (*Aeneid* 4.95).

24. *illi inter sese* . . . : they alternately lift their arms with great force (*Georgics* 4.174).

25. *Tot tibi* . . . : thou hast, virgin, as many joys as there are stars in heaven. By the Jesuit Bernard van Bauhuysen, and hyperbolically praised by Ericius Putianus in 1617 because (as he illustrated) the words could be arranged, in hexameters, in 1022 ways (M. Praz, *Studies in Seventeenth Century Imagery*, 2nd ed. 1964, p. 20), Bernouilli apparently increased the permutations to 3312.

26. *Musa mihi* . . . : tell me O Muse, the causes, in what thwarted will (*Aeneid* 1.8); a retrograde verse is one which can be metrically reversed, i.e. *Laeso numine quo memora causas mihi musa*.

27. *populeam virgam* . . . : mother and queen of heaven she bore me, rod of poplar (Professor Szövèrffy, *virga* being the rod of Jesse). Browne took this line, and also perhaps the line *musa mihi*, from [Etienne Tabourot] *Les Bigarrures du Seigneur des Accords* (SC 1595) 1583 and many subsequent editions. It is there given (1583, folio 126r) as a line of "nos anciens", and there is a long description of how to play an elaborate game on a draughts board with pieces placed according to the numerical order of the vowels in the line. In Tabourot it is called a game of Christians and Jews.

28. *Extra fortunam* . . . : what is given to one's friends is beyond the reach of fortune (Martial, *Epigrams*, 5.42.7).

[Guardian Angels]

29. *cui post* . . . : to whom, after my maker God and his great mother Mary, I owe everything.

30. *the Angel* . . . *Jacob:* Gen. 32.24–30.

[A Letter to a Friend]

For passages in both MS and 90 see notes on the latter.

31. *double chinnd*, [and footnote]: Scaliger corrects Gaza to read *not* double chinned (from Martin).

32. *Virbiusses:* Virbius was the name given to Hippolytus after he had been brought back to life by Aesculapius (from Ovid *Metamorphoses* 15.544).

33. *nimio de stamine:* a too-long thread (of life) (Juvenal *Satires* 10.252).

LETTERS

With one exception the letters printed here show Browne in his family life, as a Norwich doctor and citizen, and as an observer of persons and events. Anyone who doubts his dry sense of humor should look at the reflections on Alderman Wisse (letter to Edward Browne, May 18, 1679). If space had permitted, sentimentality would certainly have prevailed to include illustrations of his amused affection for his grandson Tommy and his activities, as illustrated in such a postscript as "Tom holds well, though hee toyles and moyles at all sorts of play and after schoole. Wee take all care wee can to make him sit still [he was five] and spare himself and to bee a litle more composed and attentive to instructions and learne, and do all wee can to have sober stayd litle girls for his playfellowes that hee maie imitate them. God blesse you all."

The letter on medical studies, which was dated 1647 by Wilkin, and described on very plausible grounds as addressed to Henry Power, was first published in *A General Dictionary, Historical and Critical* . . . 3,1735,612–13. It is there described as having been communicated to the editors (or to Thomas Birch, F.R.S., F.S.A., who wrote the notice of Browne and was for many years, later, secretary of the Royal Society) by "the learned and ingenious Richard Middleton Massey, M.D. and F.R.S.," and as "dated at Bury, April the 29th, 1653." It was reprinted in *Biographia Britannica* (2,1748,998–999, without the date), again in French in Chauffepié's *Nouveau Dictionnaire* . . . (2,1750,452, with the date), and in the second edition of *Biographia Britannica* ed. Kippis (2,1780,633, without the date). Wilkin, followed by Keynes, refers only to the latter text. If the date 1653 is accepted, the letter is not, presumably, addressed to Power. (I am indebted to Dr. René Graziani for directing my attention to *A General Dictionary* . . .). An historian of medicine might annotate the books mentioned. The respectful character of the references to Hippocrates and Galen would not, at the time, negate the emphasis on autopsy, and chemistry, or the praise of Daniel Sennert (1572–1637), Spigelius (A. Van Spieghel, 1578–1625), and William Harvey (1578–1657).

1. *Honest Tom:* At this date, though traveling abroad by himself, Thomas Browne was only about fourteen years of age; a boy of great promise and talent, he unexpectedly went into the navy, served with distinction in several engagements, but seems to have died in 1667, at the

age of twenty-one. One of his letters to his father (Wilkin, I, 131–34) has vivid and sympathetic comments on the ill-treatment of ordinary sailors and his concern for a wounded shipboy. He also speaks of a gunner who "understands and speakes Latin, French, Italian, Spanish, high Duch, Polish and the vulgar Greeke!" with whom he practices his Latin and French and intends to work at Italian.

2. *pudor Rusticus:* countrified shyness.

3. *Ned:* Edward Browne, at Trinity College, Cambridge.

4. *Comprimere et non Extendere labra:* keep your mouth shut, not open.

5. *Sr Robart Paston:* second baronet and later Earl of Yarmouth (1631–1683), a Norfolk neighbor and friend.

6. *Christ Church:* Norwich Cathedral.

7. *Pronounsation:* Elizabeth Browne's spelling.

8. *Cromwell, Ireton, Bradshows:* as regicides, responsible for the execution of Charles I. Charles II was crowned on April 23, 1661.

9. *exercises:* Edward Browne had taken his M.B.

10. *extraordinarie overthrowe:* On June 8, 1663, the Portuguese army, reinforced by British, French, and German troops decisively defeated Don John of Austria.

11. *this passage you mention:* The passage from Lucan, Vulteius' speech to his soldiers urging them to kill each other rather than surrender, is given and translated by Browne in *A Letter* (sect. 27). Wilkin points out that in a naval action of 1666 the Duke of Albermarle, as commander-in-chief, "confessed his intent rather to blow up his ship and perish gloriously, than yield to the enemy." Captain Archibald Douglas refused to retire before de Ruyter's ships in the Medway in 1667 and died in the burning of his ship. Hence Browne's extreme anxiety.

12. *Cales:* Cadiz.

13. *Jesuitts powder:* an old name for powdered Peruvian bark (quinine).

14. *Leo* [Africanus]: a geographer (c. 1494–1552) known for his description of Africa.

15. *Impellant animae . . . :* Thracian Zephyrs swell the sails (Horace *Odes* 4.12.2).

16. *Mr Tenison:* Thomas Tenison, editor of the posthumously published *Miscellany Tracts* of Browne (1683) and Archbishop of Canterbury, 1694–1715. The poem "against the Epicureans of this age," and obviously appropriate to views expressed in *Religio Medici* (see 1.36, n. 106), was not, apparently, published.

17. *Dr Lawson:* Fellow of the Royal College of Physicians, 1673, Censor, 1676; also an accomplished scholar and linguist.

18. *Peter Crinitus* [Pietro Crinito 1465–c.1504, Florentine poet and humanist]: in an edition of Lucretius. The legend about madness and the love philter or aphrodisiac was widely known through reference to it by St. Jerome.

19. *time of Reading:* i.e. lecturing before the Royal College of Physicians.

20. *Guelphs & Ghibellines:* the two violently opposed factions in mediaeval Italian politics (one imperial, the other papal).

21. *my Lord of Aylesbury:* Robert Bruce, created Earl of Aylesbury in 1664, Lord Lieutenant of Bedfordshire, 1667.

22. *The bill agaynst popery:* In 1678 Titus Oates had deposed (with perjured evidence) that there was a Popish Plot to murder Charles II and establish Roman Catholicism, with the help of foreign arms. Fifteen of the accused were later executed and the next three years were years of violent controversy centering on an attempt to exclude the king's brother James, Duke of York (an avowed Roman Catholic) from succession to the throne. The bill to which Browne refers was read for the first time on March 27, 1679.

23. *Mr Crop:* a Norwich surgeon.

24. *Sr John Hinton* (1603?–1682): physician to the king and queen; like Browne he had studied at Leiden "long agoe," in fact fifty years ago.

25. *bill of mortallity:* an official return, published periodically, of the number of deaths in a certain district.

26. *R.S.:* Royal Society.

27. *Lewenhoecks . . . litle animals:* Leeuwenhoek's microscopical observations of protozoa and bacteria had been known to the members of the Royal Society from 1674 and had excited enormous interest. In 1677 he discovered spermatozoa and his discoveries were published, in 1679, in the Society's Transactions. (For the arithmetic of numbers, etc. see C. Dobell, *Antony van Leeuwenhoek and His "Little Animals,"* Russell & Russell, New York, and Heffer, Cambridge, 1958, pp. 188–204.)

28. *Dublin to Chester:* Elizabeth copied out some verses Browne wrote about this tempest, which probably occurred in September 1629; *Works,* ed. Keynes, III, 236–37.

29. *Henry Power:* Henry Power of Halifax (1623–1668) was the son of one of Browne's early friends and in 1663 became a Fellow of the Royal Society. His *Experimental Philosophy . . .* , 1664, was the first work on microscopy published in England (see *RM* 1.48, n. 143 and *PE* 2.2, n. 5).

SELECTED BIBLIOGRAPHY

The following standard abbreviations of periodicals are used:

JEGP Journal of English and Germanic Philology
JHI   Journal of the History of Ideas
JHM   Journal of the History of Medicine
MP   Modern Philology
PMLA Publications of the Modern Language Association of America
PS   Philosophy of Science
RES   Review of English Studies
SP   Studies in Philology
TLS   Times Literary Supplement
UTQ   University of Toronto Quarterly
VQR   Virginia Quarterly Review

1. Bibliography

Keynes, G. *A Bibliography of Sir Thomas Browne*, 1924. (Also contains books and articles about Browne; a mistake about the order of the two pirated editions of *Religio Medici*, 1642, was later recognized by the editor.)

Leroy, O. *A French Bibliography of Sir Thomas Browne*, Harrap, London, 1931.

Bush, J. D. *English Literature in the Earlier Seventeenth Century*, 2d rev. ed., Oxford University Press, 1962. (Criticism and bibliography)

2. Works

For original editions, including the collected *Works* of 1686, and editions up to the date of the bibliography, see Keynes, above.

Works, ed. S. Wilkin, 4 vols., 1835–36. Vol. 1 contains Johnson's "Life," a long supplementary memoir by Wilkin, and journals of Edward and Thomas Browne, as well as Sir Thomas Browne's letters and some letters to him. Also issued in 3 vols. (Bohn's Antiquarian Library) with some material omitted.

Works, ed. C. Sayle, 3 vols., 1904–7. Does not contain material from MSS, letters, etc.

Works, ed. G. Keynes, 4 vols., University of Chicago Press, and Faber, London 1964. The most complete edition (a revision of the 6 vol. ed. of 1928–31); with Latin pieces tr. by W. R. Le Fanu.

Religio Medici and Other Works, ed. L. C. Martin, Oxford University Press, 1964. Contains *Religio Medici, Hydriotaphia, The Garden of Cyrus, A Letter to a Friend* (both versions), *Christian Morals.* With full annotations and textual notes.

The critical editions of *Religio Medici* by J.-J. Denonain, Cambridge University Press, 1953, and Vittoria Sanna, 2 vols., Università di Cagliari, Sardinia 1958 (with Italian translation and annotations) are of primary importance, as is the text of John Carter's edition of *Urne Buriall* and *The Garden of Cyrus,* Cambridge University Press, 1958 (Browne's marginal notes are omitted). The editions of *Religio Medici, Christian Morals, A Letter to a Friend,* 1881 (Golden Treasury Series, often reprinted) and *Hydriotaphia* and *The Garden of Cyrus,* 1896 (also Golden Treasury Series) ed. by W. A. Greenhill have valuable notes (especially the former) as do the editions of *Religio Medici, Hydriotaphia,* and *The Garden of Cyrus* ed. by W. Murison, 1922 (Pitt Press Series).

3. *Biography and Criticism*

(A) BOOKS

Bennett, Joan. *Sir Thomas Browne,* Cambridge University Press, 1962.

Cawley, R. R., and G. Yost. *Studies in Sir Thomas Browne,* 1965. (Cawley, "The Timeliness of *Pseudodoxia Epidemica*" and "Sir Thomas Browne and his Reading"; Yost, "Sir Thomas Browne and Aristotle."

Dunn, W. P. *Sir Thomas Browne: a Study in Religious Philosophy,* University of Minnesota Press, 3d. ed., 1958.

Finch, J. S. *Sir Thomas Browne: a Doctor's Life of Science and Faith,* Schuman, New York, 1950; paper, Collier Books, New York; Longmans Green, London, 1962.

Green, P. *Sir Thomas Browne,* 1959. (Booklet)

Huntley, F. L. *Sir Thomas Browne: a Biographical and Critical Study,* University of Michigan Press, 1962.

Leroy, O. *Le Chevalier Thomas Browne,* chateauroux, chez l'auteur, 1931.

Merton, E. S. *Science and Imagination in Sir Thomas Browne,* Columbia University Press and Oxford University Press, 1949.

Nathanson, L. *The Strategy of Truth: A Study of Sir Thomas Browne,* Chicago University Press, 1967.

Ziegler, D. K. *In Divided and Distinguished Worlds, Religion and Rhetoric in the Writings of Sir Thomas Browne,* published by the author, Boston, 1943.

(B) ARTICLES IN JOURNALS (see abbreviations above) AND CHAPTERS
OF BOOKS.

Chalmers, G. K. "Hieroglyphs and Sir Thomas Browne." *VQR* 11 (1935),
547–60.

———. "The Loadstone and the Understanding of Science in the Seventeenth Century." *PS* 4 (1937), 75–95.

———. "Sir Thomas Browne, True Scientist." *Osiris* 2 (1936), 28–79.

———. "Three Terms of Corpuscularian Philosophy." *MP* 33 (1936),
243–60.

Cline, J. M. "Sir Thomas Browne's *Hydriotaphia*," in *Five Studies in Literature*, ed. B. H. Bronson, University of California Press, 1940.

Coleridge, S. T. In *Miscellaneous Criticism*, ed. T. M. Raysor, Harvard
University Press, 1936.

Endicott, N. J. "Sir Thomas Browne's *A Letter to a Friend.*" *UTQ* 36
(1966), 68–86.

———. "Some Aspects of Self-Revelation and Self-Portraiture in *Religio
Medici*," in *Essays in English Literature . . . Presented to A. S. P.
Woodhouse*, ed. M. MacLure and F. W. Watt, University of Toronto
Press, 1964.

Finch, J. S. "Sir Thomas Browne and the Quincunx." *SP* 37 (1940),
274–300.

———. "Early Drafts of *The Garden of Cyrus.*" *PMLA* 55 (1940), 742–47.

Heidemann, M. A. "*Hydriotaphia* and *The Garden of Cyrus:* a Paradox
and a Cosmic Vision." *UTQ* 19 (1950), 235–66.

Howell, A. C. "A Note on Sir Thomas Browne's Knowledge of Languages." *SP* 22 (1925), 412–17.

Huntley, F. L. "The Occasion and Date of Sir Thomas Browne's *Letter
to a Friend.*" *MP* 48 (1952), 157–71.

———. "Sir Thomas Browne, M.D., William Harvey, and the Metaphor of
the Circle." *Bulletin of the History of Medicine* 24 (1951), 236–47.

Johnson, S. "Life," in *Christian Morals*, 1756.

Merton, E. S. "The Botany of Sir Thomas Browne." *Isis* 47 (1956) 161–
71.

———. "Sir Thomas Browne as a Zoologist." *Osiris* 9 (1950) 413–34.

———. "Sir Thomas Browne's Scientific Quest." *JHM* 3 (1948), 214–28.

Moloney, M. F. "Metre and Cursus in Sir Thomas Browne's Prose."
JEGP 58 (1959), 60–67.

Parker, E. L. "The Cursus and Sir Thomas Browne." *PMLA* 52–53
(1938), 1037–53.

Pater, W. "Sir Thomas Browne," in *Appreciations*, 1889.

Strachey, L. "Sir Thomas Browne," in *Books and Characters, French and
English*, Harcourt, Brace, New York, 1922.

Warren, A. "The Style of Sir Thomas Browne." *Kenyon Review* 13 (1952), 674–87.

Wiley, M. L. "Sir Thomas Browne and the Genesis of Paradox." *JHI* 9 (1948), 303–22.

4. *Background Material*

(General books of literary criticism, and books and articles on 17th-century style—e.g. the concept of baroque—have been omitted.)

Allen, D. C. "The Legend of Noah: Renaissance Rationalism in Art, Science, and Letters." In *Illinois Studies in Language and Literature,* vol. 33, nos. 3, 4, (1949).

Allen, Phyllis. "Medical Education in Seventeenth Century England." *JHM* 1 (1946), 115–46.

Hunt, J. *Religious Thought in England from the Reformation to the End of the Eighteenth Century,* 3 vols., 1870.

Hunter, W. B. "The Seventeenth Century Doctrine of Plastic Nature." *Harvard Theological Review* 43 (1950), 197–213.

Johnson, F. R. *Astronomical Thought in Renaissance England,* Johns Hopkins Press, and Oxford University Press, 1937.

Kittredge, G. L. *Witchcraft in Old and New England,* Harvard University Press, and Oxford University Press, 1929. (For general treatment and especially "theses" at end)

Needham, J. *A History of Embryology,* rev. 2d ed., Abelard-Schuman, New York, and Cambridge University Press, 1959. (Chap. 3, sect. 3, is on Browne.)

Notestein, W. *A History of Witchcraft in England from 1558 to 1718,* 1911, reprinted by Russell & Russell, New York, 1965.

Osler, W. *Bibliotheca Osleriana,* Oxford University Press, 1929, (ed. by W. W. Francis, R. H. Hill and A. Malloch, with many biographical and bibliographical notes by Sir William Osler).

Pagel, W. "William Harvey and the Purpose of Circulation." *Isis* 42 (1951), 22–38.

Raven, C. E. *English Naturalists from Neckham to Ray: a Study of the Making of the Modern World,* Macmillan, New York, and Cambridge University Press, 1947. (Chap. 18, Epilogue, on Browne)

Thorndike, L. *A History of Magic and Experimental Science,* 8 vols., Columbia University Press, and Oxford University Press, 1923–58. (Especially vols. 5–8)

Webber, J. *The Eloquent I: Style and Self in Seventeenth-Century Prose,* University of Wisconsin Press, 1968.

Wiley, M. L. *The Subtle Knot: Creative Scepticism in Seventeenth-Century England,* Harvard University Press and G. Allen, London, 1952.

Willey, B. *The Seventeenth Century Background,* Chatto & Windus, London, 1934; paper, Doubleday Anchor, New York, 1953. (Some specific discussion of Browne)

Williams, A. *The Common Expositor,* University of North Carolina Press, and Oxford University Press, 1945. (Interpretation of scripture, and hence problems of reason and faith)

Wilson, F. P. *Seventeenth Century Prose,* University of California Press, 1960.

The library of Sir Thomas Browne (with some additions made by his son Edward Browne) was sold in London at an auction beginning on Jan. 8, 1711. Copies of the *Sale Catalogue* are extremely rare but many libraries have a photographic reproduction. About three thousand volumes are listed.

GLOSSARY OF WORDS AND PERSONS

"... it is but attending a little longer, and wee shall enjoy that by instinct and infusion which we endeavour at here by labour and inquisition." *RM* 2.8

The Glossary should be used with the Notes and Commentary. It does not contain technical terms (e.g. in botany, architecture, music) nor for the most part words which may be found in a good desk dictionary. Since different spellings are found in different works, they have here been modernized. The biographical information is only for identification, but sometimes books referred to are those most relevant to Browne. Some words are used by him in an ordinary as well as Latinized sense.

Abraham's bosom: among the blessed (Luke 16.22)
abstersion: cleansing, scouring
absumption: a consuming
accension: kindling of fire
access: excess
accident: attribute, a property or quality not essential to our conception of a substance
acies: the glance, vision of the eye
admiration: wonder (sometimes wonder mingled with reverence); also surprise, astonishment .
Adraste and Nemesis: the powers of vengeance (Adraste is another name for Nemesis)
adumbration: foreshadowing
Aegineta: Roman physician of the 5th (?) or 6th century who wrote on medicine
Aelian, Claudius, c.170–235: Roman rhetorician and author of moralizing anecdotes about animals
aequicrural: isosceles
aequivocal (production or generation): spontaneous generation, i.e. supposed generation of animals without parents
Aesculapius: god of medicine, son of Apollo

Aeson's bath: a magic bath by which Medea renewed the youth of Aeson, Jason's father

Aetius: 6th-century Greek author of a medical miscellany

affection: attribute, influence

Ahasuerus: ancient king of Persia

Alberti, Leone, 1404–1472: musician and architect, famous for book on architecture, *de re Aedificatoria*

Albertus [surnamed] *Magnus,* 1194?–1280: scholastic philosopher and expositor of Aristotle. Works by him on a great range of subjects (secret causes, animals, vegetables, minerals) were widely read in the 15th and 16th centuries

Aldrovandus (Ulisse Aldrovandi), 1522–1605: Italian naturalist and scholar whose collected works are in 14 vols., folio, published (revised, etc.) after his death. He himself published 4 vols. of ornithology

alliciency: attraction

Almagest: Claudius Ptolemy's great astronomical treatise; also other books of astronomy and alchemy

Almanzor (Al Mansur, Caliph of Bagdad) 754–775: made Bagdad a centre of learning without regard to religious views

Alpinus (Prospero Alpini), 1553–1617: Venetian physician and botanist, best known for books on Egyptian plants and medicine

Amatus Lusitanus (Juan Ruderigo), 1511–1568: Spanish Jewish physician and author of "centuries" of medical case histories

amazed: perplexed, filled with panic

Amazonian tomb: various grave-mounds, monuments, etc. were identified as Amazonian (Browne ref. from Plutarch)

Ambrose: 4th-century Archbishop of Milan and Church Father

ambulatory: shifting, changeable

amission: loss

amphibology: equivocation; ambiguous wording

amphidromical: relating to the Amphidromia, an Attic festival at the naming of a child

amuse: puzzle, arrest the attention

Anaxagoras, c. 500–428 B.C.: Greek philosopher

Anaximander, b. 610 B.C.: Greek philosopher

anhelant: (much) aspirated

animosity: courage, spiritedness

anticipatively: prematurely

Anticyra: had a reputation for the presence of hellebore, supposed cure for madness

antimetathesis: inversion of the parts of an antithesis

Antipater: Jewish ruler of Palestine who was made a Roman citizen by Julius Caesar; father of Herod the Great

antipathy: natural contrariety, often on occult grounds

antiperistasis: contrast

antipodes: those who live directly opposite to each other on the globe; figurative, exact opposite

apogeum: meridional altitude of the sun on the longest day, hence the highest point from earth

apologue: moral fable

apparency: appearance

appetible: desirable

Appian Way: the principal highway from Rome to the south (from Appius Caecus, censor in 312 B.C.)

Appollonius Thyaneus (Apollonius of Tyana): Neopythagorean sage, magician, and traveler of the 1st century

apprehension: understanding

Apuleius: Latin author of 2d century, known for his novel *The Golden Ass*

Aratus, c.315–240 B.C.: Greek poet known for his astronomical poem, the *Phaenomena,* and author of many short poems now lost

arcana, arcane: secret

arefaction: process of drying

areopagy: secret tribunal

Argus: had one hundred eyes, of which only two were asleep at one time

Arians: followers of Arius, 4th-century Alexandrian presbyter who denied that Christ was consubstantial with God

Arrianus, Flavius: 2d-century Greek author, known for a history of Alexander the Great and an account of India

ariolation: divination, soothsaying

Ariston: 2d century B.C. Greek explorer who explored the coast of Arabia for Ptolemy II

Artaxerxes (Longimanus): king of Persia in 464 B.C.

Artaxerxes II (Mnemon): king of Persia, 404 B.C.; called Mnemon because of his extensive memory

artist: man of science or studied skill

aruspex (haruspex): diviner by inspection of entrails

asarum: plant used as emetic

ascendant: just above the horizon

aspect: (astrology) position of the planets at a given time

asperous: rough, uneven

Asphaltick lake: the lake of Sodom (the Dead Sea)

assuefaction: habituation

asterisk: little star

Athenaeus: 2d-century Greek scholar, author of *Deipnosophista* (a learned banquet) of extracts from more than 1500 works (mostly lost) over a wide range of subjects

Atropos: the third of the Fates, who cuts the thread of life

auditory: lecture-room, audience

augurial: divination from the behavior of birds

Aurum potabile: gold held in a state of minute subdivision in some volatile oil, and taken as a cordial

Australize: turn to the south

authentic: accepted, authoritative

Avicenna, 980–1037: Arabian scholar and physician whose *Canon of Medicine* became one of the oracles of medicine in the Middle Ages

Aristoxenus: Greek philosopher and musical theorist of the 4th century B.C., who wrote lives of Pythagoras, Plato, and others

avolation: flying off

away with: tolerate, put up with

balsome, radical: a healthful preservative essence, thought (esp. in Paracelsan medicine) to exist in all organic bodies

barbara: a scholastic mnemonic term designating the first mood of the first syllogistic figure

Basil: 4th-century bishop of Caesarea and Church Father

Beda, 672–735: commonly called the Venerable Bede, English historian and theologian; his ecclesiastical history was composed in 731

Bellonius (Pierre Belon), 1517–1564: French physician and naturalist who wrote scientific studies of birds and fishes

Bembus (Pietro Bembo), 1470–1547: Italian cardinal and scholar

beneplacit: good pleasure

Bevis of Hampton: hero of 14th-century romance of knight errantry

Bezo las manos: kiss the hands (in thanks)

bittor: bittern

bivious: having or offering two ways

blast of his will: assertion, literally a trumpeting

Boccace (Giovanni Boccaccio), 1313–1375: humanist and author of the *Decameron*

bolary: of the nature of bole, several kinds of unctuous earth

borith: a cleansing herb

bouffage: satisfying meal

bottom: a clew on which to wind thread

bought: bend

Bovillus (Carlo Bovillo), c.1470–1553: Italian philosopher and mathematician *bowelless:* pitiless

bravery: display

breeze: gad-fly

burden: refrain

bush: signboard of tavern, from custom of hanging up a bunch of ivy for a vintner's

cabala: the (secret) Rabbinical tradition of Old Testament interpretation; by derivation any secret tradition of interpretation

Cabeus (Niccolo Cabeo), 1585–1650: Italian Jesuit, professor of mathematics and moral philosophy; *Philosophica Magnetica* pub. 1629

Cadmus: in mythology Cadmus introduced writing into Greece, and Palamedes completed the alphabet

caitif: mean-spirited

calcined: burned to powder

calda: warm water

Calvin, John, 1509–1564: French reformer and theologian; from 1536 at Geneva

Camerarius, Joachim, 1500–1574: German classical scholar and translator

candour: whiteness

canicular: days of great heat, here used metaphorically for early manhood

canton: corner

card (the card): chart

Cardanus (Cardano, Girolamo), 1501–1576: Italian scholar, physician, mathematician; *Works,* 10 vols., folio, 1663

carnalled: had sexual intercourse with

carnified: made flesh

Casaubon, Isaac, 1559–1614: distinguished scholar and commentator; naturalized Englishman in 1611

Casaubon, Meric, 1599–1671: son of Isaac Casaubon, scholar and prebend of Canterbury

castle-soap: Castile soap

castrensiall mansions: camp quarters

catastrophe: conclusion

Catholicon: panacea, drug of universal effectiveness

Cato, Marcus Porcius, "the Censor," 234–149 B.C.: Roman statesman with reputation for severity and uprightness

Cato the Younger, "of Utica," 95–46 B.C.: Roman general, Stoic, and republican opponent of Caesar, great grandson of Cato "the Censor"

causes: in Aristotle, material, formal, efficient, final (see *RM* 1. n. 34)

cautelous: cautious, crafty

cavedia: the inner courts of Roman houses

Cebes Table: allegorical representation or picture (table) of human life in a dialogue attrib. to Cebes, pupil of Socrates

cecity: blindness

cecutiency: partial blindness

cenotaph: sepulchral monument

censor's book: census or register of citizens for purposes of taxation

cento: patched garment, patchwork

central fire: in Pythagorean theory a central fire around which circle the celestial bodies

chetmat: checkmate, in chess

chiasmus: an X or intersection from Greek *chi*

Chiliast: a believer in the doctrine of the millennium, Christ's reign on earth for a thousand years

Chimaera: fire-breathing monster killed by Bellerophon, hence wild fancy

chiromancy: palmistry, reading of character and prophesying, from the hand

Chiron: a centaur, half man and half horse

cholical: bilious

choragium: dancing ground of Greek chorus

chorography: description on a map of particular regions

circenses: the public contests in the Roman circus

cirrous (cirrus): tendril

civilian: one whose study is the law

civility: social order

clamations: invocations, cries

climacter: critical periods (every seven or nine years) in life, the grand climacter being the sixty-third year

climacterically: referring to the sixty-third year, the grand climacter

climate: belt between two latitudes, the eighth including southern England

coacervation: accumulation

coherencies: logical connections

Columella: 1st-century Roman (Spanish) writer on agriculture (*de Re Rustica*)

compage: the whole made up of the parts

commutative justice: an exchange for an equivalent, hence in arithmetical proportion (see also *distributive justice*)

competent: suitable, proper

complexionally: temperamentally

conceit: fancy, notion, figure; verb: to conceive, imagine

concitation: excitement

conclusions [practiced]: practical outcomes

concourse [of God]: concurrence, co-operation

confinium: border-ground

conservatory: public building

consist: stand firm

Constantine the Great, 274?–337: Roman emperor converted to Christianity by a vision of a cross in the sky which he used afterward as his device; founder of Constantinople (Byzantium)

constellated: literally predisposed by position of planets at birth; predisposed by nature and disposition

consultation: deliberation

contempor: mingle together, moderate

contentation: satisfaction

contignation: joining-together

conversation: way of life, behavior

convincible: of convincing power; capable of proof

copel (*cupel*): porous cup usually made of bone-ash, for assaying gold, etc.

Copernicus (Nicolaus Koppernigk), 1473–1543: his hypothesis of a heliocentric universe was still much debated in the 17th century

corpulency: material substance

country: (sometimes) county

courage: confidence (as well as ordinary meaning)

cramb: hackneyed repetition (from Latin, cabbage served up again)

crasis: combination of humors in the body

criticism: nice point, distinction

Ctesias: late 5th-century Greek physician to Artaxerxes Mnemon and author of a Persian history and a work on India

cubit: forearm

cummin seed: a very small seed, hence (Greek) to split a cummin seed, to be extremely miserly

cunctation: hesitation

curious: intricate, delicate

curricle: short course (running)

Curtius (Quintus Curtius Rufus): 1st-century Roman historian (life of Alexander the Great)

cynegeticks: hunting

Cyrus, the Elder, 559–529 B.C.: founder of the Achaemenid Persian empire

Cyrus II, c. 400 B.C.: in whose army Xenophon had enlisted and who was killed by his brother Artaxerxes

Dalecampus (D'Alechamps, Jaques), 1513–1588: physician, scholar, botanist

Damocles: courtier of the tyrant Dionysius I who overpraised the latter's happiness and was symbolically feasted with a sword hanging by a hair over his head

dastard: verb, intimidate, challenge

decipiency (*desipiency*): madness

decumbence: lying down

decussation: intersection so as to form a figure like an X

defluvium: falling off

delator: secret informer

Delphian blade: like oracles of Delphi capable of different interpretations (cut both ways)

Delphos, the devil of: the oracle of Apollo at Delphi, presumed to be the work of Satan

Democritus, c. 460–c. 370 B.C.: Greek philosopher, founder of atomic theory; sometimes called "the laughing philosopher"

Demosthenes, 384–322 B.C.: Athenian orator and opponent of Philip of Macedon and Alexander the Great

deopilation (*deoppilation*): removal of obstructions

Descartes, René, 1596–1650: French philosopher

Deucalion: son of Prometheus, in whose reign the earth was inundated; Deucalion built a ship and saved himself

deuteroscopy: second view, i.e. ulterior meaning

desumed: borrowed

diameter, in: directly opposite

Didymus, c. 80–10 B.C.: Alexandrian scholar of immense learning

die: singular of dice

difference: verb, differentiate

Digby, Sir Kenelm, 1603–1665: English author, diplomatist, amateur philosopher and scientist; fellow of Royal Society

digladiation: fighting with swords

dignotion: distinguishing sign

Diodorus Siculus: 1st century B.C. author and compiler of a Greek world history to 54 B.C.

Diogenes, c. 400–325 B.C.: Greek philosopher, celebrated in innumerable stories for his repartee and churlish independence

Diogenes Laertius: Greek writer of the 3d century whose *Lives of the Philosophers* is full of sayings and anecdotes

Diomedes: companion of Ulysses

Dion (Dio Cassius): Roman historian of the 2d and 3d centuries

Dioscorides: Greek physician of the 1st century; his *Materia Medica* was the standard work in pharmacology for many centuries

dipteros hypaethros: building with two wings of uncovered columns

discuss: disperse, drive away

displacency: dissatisfaction

dissentaneous: contrary to

distributive justice: concerned with rewards not as a matter of strict payment but perhaps double or treble—hence geometrical proportion (see also *commutative justice*)

diuturnity: lastingness

divulsion: biting off

donative: gift

dorado: wealthy man (from a golden Spanish fish)

doubtful conceit of: doubt concerning

eagle-stone: aetites, fabled to be found in the eagle's nest and possessing rare qualities

elator: moving power

election: (theology) the exercise of God's sovereign will in preferring some of his creatures, esp. to eternal life; deliberate choice

elegant ("elegant apostle"): ? chosen; (ordinarily) polished, appropriate

elemental composition: i.e. composed of the four elements

elench: syllogism in refutation of a syllogistic conclusion; hence more widely a sophistical argument, a fallacy

elevation: devout exaltation of feeling

elixir: (alchemy) a preparation to change baser metals to gold; sometimes means philosopher's stone

Elohims: gods, from Hebrew for God or gods

eluctation: struggling forth

embezzle (*Hydriotaphia* 3): diminish, waste

Empedocles: 5th century B.C. philosopher and poet

empirick: one who practices medicine without scientific knowledge; a quack

empyreal: of the highest (tenth) heaven, the empyrean, sometimes called the abode of God

entelechia: see *RM* 1.10, n. 23

enthymeme: argument based on probable premises as distinguished from a demonstration

entreat: handle

ephemerides: diary, journal; astronomical almanac

Epicurus, 341–270 B.C.: Greek philosopher

epicycle: in astronomy a circle having its center on the circumference of another circle

Eratosthenes, c. 275–194 B.C.: Greek scholar, the first systematic geographer

ergotism: logical argument

ethnic: pagan

Eudorus of Alexandria, c. 25 B.C.: Greek eclectic philosopher whose works are now lost

Eusebius: c.260–340 bishop, scholar, and church historian

Eustathius: 12th-century Byzantine archbishop, classical scholar and commentator

evacuate: make void, nullify

eviction: establishment by argument

exaltation: (alchemy) to refine, raise to higher degree

exantlation: drawing out, as from a well

exasperate: to sharpen

exedra: semicircular extension of colonnade in *gymnasium*

exenteration: evisceration

exility: slenderness

existent: in being

exolution: setting free of the spirit

expatiate: wander freely

experiment: derived from experience; also in modern sense

expilator: plunderer

explication: (botany) freeing from folds

exsiccated: thoroughly dried

exsucous: without juice, sapless

extance: emergence

extenuate: thin out, lessen in size

extradictionary: (of fallacies) not consisting in expression; real

exuperance (exsuperance): excess

factories: establishments of merchants in foreign countries

faculties: powers of the mind, e.g. the will, the reason, etc.

faculty: power

Familist: member of the sect called the Family of Love, instituted about 1575

fasciations: bandages

favaginous: resembling a honeycomb

feretra: biers, litters

ferity: savagery

Fernelius (Jean Fernel), 1497–1558: French physician, author of an authoritative book on medicine, 1554 *ferous:* carrying away

festination: speed

fictile: pottery

fly: any winged insect (not just Browne's weakness in rhyming)

form: in scholastic philosophy the essential determinant principle; essence as opposed to matter

fougade: small charge of gunpowder

fulciment: fulcrum

funambulous, funambulatory: pertaining to rope-walking

fungous: sudden growth

furdling: furling, folding

fusil: (heraldry) "bearing" in form of elongated lozenge

Gaffarel, Jaques, 1601–1681: learned Rabbinical writer and librarian of Cardinal Richelieu; partial to occult astrology

Galen (Claudius Galenus), 129?–199: the most authoritative physician, after Hippocrates, in antiquity, and also up to the 17th century

gallature: germ in an egg

galliardise: gaiety, revelry

Gargantua: the giant of *Gargantua and Pantagruel* by Rabelais

Geber: Arabian alchemist of obscure origin and date, whose alchemical writings appeared in a number of editions from the end of the 15th century

Gellius, Aulus, c. 123–165: Roman writer whose miscellany, *Noctes Atticae,* continued to be valuable for its extensive use of Greek and Roman writers

genial: natural disposition

geomancer: diviner by lines and figures

Giges' (Gyges') ring: a brazen ring that made Gyges, king of Lydia, invisible

Gilbertus (William Gilbert), 1540–1603: English physician and scientist (*De Magnete,* 1600)

Giraldus Cambrensis, 1146?–1220: mediaeval English historian

Glanvill, Bartholomew, known as Bartholomew of England, fl. 1230–1250: his *Of the Properties of Things* was one of the two great encyclopedias of the Middle Ages; in late 16th century in England read in version of Stephen Batman

glome: ball or clue of yarn

Gordian knot: an intricate knot which Alexander the Great cut to fulfil the oracle that Asia would fall to the man who could unloose it

Gordianus I, Marcus Antonius: Roman emperor for a few weeks in 238

grate: cage

Gregorius Turonensis (Gregory of Tours), 538–594: author of *Historia Francorum*

Grotius, Hugo (Huig van Groot), 1563–1645: Dutch scholar, writer, and statesman, best known for work on international law

Gruter, Jan, 1560–1627: Dutch-English scholar who published in 1603 an important collection of ancient inscriptions

Gulielmus de Conchis (William of Conches): scholastic philosopher and encyclopaedist of the 12th century

gustation: taste

haggard: untamed hawk

halieuticks: fishing

helix: spiral

harmony: (surgery) the union of two bones by simple opposition of their surfaces

helluo: glutton

hellebore: plant of great repute for healing madness

Helmontius (J. B. van Helmont), 1577–1664: Belgian chemist, physiologist, and physician; at once experimental and extravagantly occult

Heraclitus, fl. c. 500 B.C.: Greek philosopher

Hercules furens: boisterously mad (from plays of this title by Seneca and Euripides about Hercules' madness as result of Juno's enmity

Hermes his rod: one touch of which awakened or put to sleep (Homer)

Hermes Trismegistus: see *RM* 1.32, n. 87

hermeticall: concerned with occult philosophy, esp. alchemy (from Hermes Trismegistus)

Herodotus: Greek historian of the 5th century B.C.

Hesiod: Greek descriptive and didactic poet, contemporary with, or little later than Homer; best known for his *Works and Days* and his *Theogony* on the Greek gods

Hippocrates: 5th century B.C. Greek physician and father of "scientific" medicine

Horapollo: supposedly an Egyptian writer of the 4th or 5th century A.D. whose *Hieroglyphics* (in a later Greek version) is both a fanciful explanation of Egyptian symbols and a collection of fables from Galen, Aelian, etc.

hospital: hostel or inn

hoties: assertion

hough: part behind the knee joint

humble bee: bumble bee

humorist: a person swayed by one of the four humors

humors: blood, phlegm, choler, and black choler, the proportions of which determine the temperament

Hydra: a many-headed monster, whose heads, cut off, grew again double

hypogeum: underground chamber, vault

hypostasis: (theology) person; in metaphysics, substance

Ides, observe no: days for repaying debts (Roman calendar)

illation: deduction or conclusion

imbecillity: weakness

immaterial: incorporeal, spiritual

impassible: not subject to pain or injury

impatible: see *impassible*

improperation: taunt

inartificial: not according to the art of logic, but derived from testimony or authority

incantatory: magical

incession: progression

in coagulato: in a congealed mass; *in soluto:* in a state of expansion and separation

indagation: investigation

indifferency: impartiality; *indifferently:* impartially

indigitate: point out

inflexure: bend, curve

inform: to give "form" to, animate

infusion: pouring into the mind, inspiration; see also *traduction* for another sense

ingenuities: generous and high-minded people (also in modern sense)

ingenuous: generous, high-minded

iniquity [Hydriotaphia 5]: inequity, unfairness

innitency: leaning

inoculation: engrafting

inquinated: corrupted

insensible: imperceptible by senses

insition: grafting

Intelligences: spirits supposed to guide the spheres

irony, ironical: figure of speech in which intended meaning is opposite of that expressed by words used; hence, sometimes, dissembling

Irus: a beggar in the *Odyssey*

Isidor, Bishop of Seville, c. 560–636: Spanish encyclopaedist and historian

item: intimation

Janus: a god of beginnings, represented by a double-faced head, looking in opposite directions

Josephus: Jewish historian of the 1st century

Julian the Apostate, 332–363: Roman emperor 360–363, educated and baptized as Christian, reverted to paganism

julus (iulus): catkin, or downy part of many plants

jument: beast of burden

Justin Martyr, c. 100–163 or 167: Christian apologist and theologian, a
   converted Jew

Justin (Justinus): Latin historian who composed (probably in the 3d century) an abstract of the universal history of Pompeius Trogus, author
   of the first Roman general history, c. 50 B.C.

Juvenal: Latin satiric poet of 1st century

King's evil: scrofula, supposed to be curable by the king's or queen's
   touch

Kircherus (Athanasius Kircher), 1602–1680: German Jesuit mathematician of great general learning and almost equal credulity

knabble: nibble, gnaw

knop: bud

lacrymatory: vase to hold tears

Lactantius: a Latin Church Father of the 4th century

Lais: courtesan of the 5th century B.C., mistress of Alcibiades, admired
   by Diogenes, and famously expensive

lash: soft, watery

laqueary: gladiator who fought with a noose

Lapithytes: i.e. unruly passions, from famous battle of Centaurs and
   Lapithae

last: most unlikely

latitancy, latitant: lying hid, hibernation

lazy of Brazilia: the sloth

lecture: reading, discourse

Lemnius, Levinus (Ludwig Lemmens): 16th-century Dutch physician
   and writer, whose totally uncritical book on the occult miracles of
   nature, 1559, went into many editions and translations in the next
   hundred years

Leo Africanus, c.1494–1552: a geographer known for his description of
   Africa

Leo the Jew (Judah Abrabanel) c.1465–c.1535: whose "neoplatonic"
   Dialogi d'Amore (1535) was much read

Lepanto: a naval battle between Christians and Turks in 1571, of great
   importance in checking the Turkish threat to Europe

Libavius, Andreas, 1550–1616: German scholar and chemist (*Alchymia,*
   1597)

Licetus, Fortunius (Fortunio Liceto): 17th-century Italian philosopher,
   physician, and miscellaneous writer

ligation: binding

limbo: a region on the border of Hell, abode of the just who died before Christ's coming, and of unbaptized infants

Lipsius, Justus (Joest Lips), 1547–1606: Belgian scholar, editor of Seneca and Tacitus

livery: clothing and food given to servants, hence "without livery," without reward

loadstone, armed: with an iron cap at the pole to increase and preserve the magnetic power

longanimity: long-suffering

Lucian: 2d-century Greek writer famous for his satiric dialogues and the *True History*

Lucina: goddess of childbirth

lustre: period of five years

lions skins: i.e. military readiness

Machiavelli, Niccolo, 1469–1527: best known for *The Prince* and *Discourses on Livy*

Macrobius, fl. c. 400: Latin writer best known for his *Saturnalia,* a symposium in seven books on many subjects, and his neoplatonic commentaries on Cicero's *Somnium Scipionis*

magdaleon: cylindrical roll of dough

magisterial: supreme, works of a master

magnalities: wonders

Malizspini, Celio, 1531–1609: writer of *novelle*

manes: spirits of the dead; also in singular

maniple: handful; numbered subdivision of Roman cohort

Marcellus Empiricus, c. 410, of Bordeaux: wrote a compilation of medical remedies

mascle: (heraldry) "charge" in form of a lozenge

mechanic: manual laborer

mediocrity: moderation

Megasthenes, fl. 300 B.C.: Greek writer on topography and the religion and customs of India

mercurism: message (from Mercury, messenger of the gods)

Mercurialis (Gerolamo Mercuriale): 16th-century Italian physician and author of *De Arte Gymnastica* (1572)

meridian: halfway point

meteors: all atmospheric phenomena, winds being airy meteors, dew and rain watery meteors, etc.

meticulously: timidly

Minerva: invoked by every artist, and especially by those who worked in embroidery, wool, etc.

miscreant: infidel, as well as villainous, etc.

morbosity: ill-health, disease

mortified: (alchemy) to mortify is to destroy the outward form

motive: moving

mystery: trade guild (*RM* 1.24)

natural magic: bringing something into operation through what were regarded as occult principles, but without recourse to spirits; since actually brought about by now known laws of causation, much "natural magic" is now just "natural"

Nicephorus: Byzantine historian of the early 9th century

Nierembergius (Juan Nieremberg), 1595–1658: Jesuit author of spiritual exercises, and of a book of occult philosophy (1643)

nocent: criminal

noctambulo: sleepwalker

Nonnus: 5th-century Greek poet, author of a paraphrase of St. John's gospel and of an epic poem on Dionysius

numerical: particular, individual

nuncio: messenger

object (verb): place before the mind

obliquation: slanting, oblique lined

occult qualities: qualities or attributes which were supposed to lie hid in bodies and be the causes of evident effects

Oedipus: delivered Thebes by solving the riddle of the Sphinx

Og, the bed of: nine cubits (Deut. 3.11)

Olympiad: period of four years

oneirocriticism: the art of interpreting dreams

opprobrious disease: presumably syphilis

orbity: to be deprived of parents and children

Oribasius: 4th-century physician to Julian the Apostate who abridged the works of Galen and other medical writers

Origen: Greek Christian writer of the 2d century

ostiary: entrance, mouth

Palamades: see *Cadmus*

Pancirollus (Guido Panciroli): 16th-century Italian jurist and scholar, author of a book of memorable things (including inventions)

pancratical man: most accomplished athlete (from Greek contests)

pantalone (*pantaloon*): stage fool, from type character of Italian comedy

Paracelsus, 1493–1541: Swiss physician and writer on medicine and alchemy; see *RM* 1.31, n. 85

parallaxis: difference in apparent position of heavenly body caused by difference of position of point of observation

paralogical: illogical, fallacious

parcells: particles

Parthenius: Greek poet and writer of the 1st century B.C.; his poetry was well known in antiquity, but only fragments remain

party: part, division

patronal: guardian, tutelary

Paulus Venetus (Paul of Venice), d. 1429: scholar and theologian

penates: household gods

Peregrinus, Petrus (Peter the Pilgrim): 13th-century scholar whose letter describing his experiments with the loadstone was first printed in 1558

perioeci: living in the same latitude but opposite meridians

periscian: like the periscii, "those who dwell within the polar circles, whose shadows revolve around them on a summer day"

perpend: ponder

perspectives: magnifying glasses, especially telescopes

Persius: Latin satiric poet of 1st century

Phalaris: Sicilian tyrant of 6th century B.C. who roasted his victims in a brazen bull

Philo Judaeus, c. 30 B.C.–A.D. 45: Alexandrian Jewish neoplatonic writer

philosopher's stone: (alchemy) reputed substance supposed to have power to change base metals into gold or silver

phylactery: small leather box containing texts of Scripture worn by Jews during prayers; hence, a religious reminder

phytognomy: vegetable physiognomy, inferring properties from appearance

Pia Mater: innermost membrane investing the brain

piae fraudes: see *pious frauds*

pickthank: flatterer, sycophant

Pierius: see *Valerianus*

pinax: picture

pious frauds: deceptions intended to strengthen faith or religious feeling

Pisander (Peisander): Greek epic poet of the 6th or 7th century B.C.

piscation: fishing

plash: marshy pool

Plato's year: see Browne's note in *RM* 1.6

plaudite: customary appeal for applause by Roman actors

Plempius (V. F. Plemp), 1601–1671: Dutch scholar and physician (*Opthalmographia,* 1648)

Pliny the Elder, 23–79: famous for his *Natural History,* compiled from observation and hundreds of authors of every kind

politicians: people concerned with the state; also in modern sense

Polybius: Greek historian of 2d century B.C.

Pompeius Trogus: see *Justin*

Pompeys pillar: a pillar celebrating the capture of Alexandria

Pomponius Mela: 1st century Roman geographer

Porta, Giambattista Della, 1545–1615: Italian scholar who wrote on plants, mathematics, "natural magic," etc. etc.

pose: puzzle

posse, in: in potentiality (contrasted to *in esse,* in being)

pourtract: image, likeness

praedicament: category, class

predestination: (theology) the action of God in fore-ordaining certain of mankind through grace to salvation or eternal life

preferred: raised, advanced in status

prescious: foreknowing

primum mobile: first moving thing, i.e. the outermost sphere of "Ptolemaic" astronomy, supposed to revolve around the earth in twenty-four hours; added to Ptolemy in Middle Ages

profound (verb): penetrate deeply

Procopius: Byzantine historian of the 6th century

proper: peculiar to oneself

Propertius, Sextus: 1st-century Roman elegiac poet

property: quality belonging to a thing or person

proprieties: properties

Ptolemy Philadelphus, 308–246 B.C.: Ptolemy II, king of Egypt, patron of scholars, and famous for building up great library at Alexandria

Ptolemy (Claudius Ptolemaeus): 2d century geographer and astronomer whose *Almagest* was authoritative until the time of the "new" astronomy

puny: junior

Pythagoras: 6th century B.C. philosopher, referred to by Browne in relation to transmigration of souls, number as the explanation of the harmony of the universe, and for his moral sayings

quadrate: to square with; (astronomy) one of the two points in space or time at which the moon is 90° distant from the sun

quartan ague: paroxysm of fever every fourth day

questuary: profit-seeking; also investigating

Quintilian: 1st-century Latin writer and rhetorician, whose *Institutes of Oratory* had an enormous Renaissance reputation

quodlibetical: of a disputation, determinable on either side

racemation: cluster

ragione di stato: reasons of state (often used in relation to the pragmatic approach of Machiavelli)

rampier: rampart

rapt: force, sweep

Regiomontanus (Johann Müller) *of Konigsberg:* was supposed to have made an iron fly and a wooden eagle, the fly being naturally more intricate

relentment: dissolution

remora: a small fish believed to stay the course of any ship to which it attached itself; hence a serious obstacle

remotion: removal

reprobated: (theology) rejected of God; in Calvinist doctrine ordained by God to eternal misery

resipiscency: repentance

retiary: gladiator who fought with a net to entangle his opponent; (of spider) net-making

reverberated: as in a kiln or reverberatory furnace

rhabarb: rhubarb

rhabdomancy: divination by a rod

Rhadamanth: in mythology one of the judges in the lower world

rhapsodist: one who strings together, collector

rhapsody: medley

right (GC): vertical, without crosspiece

rodomontado: boasting, from boastful Saracen in Ariosto's *Orlando Furioso*

Rondeletus (Guillaume Rondelet), 1507–1556: French physician and naturalist, author of important book on marine fishes

rorid: dewy

royal vein: the *vena basilica* of the arm, one of veins opened in bloodletting (Greenhill)

Rubicon: to cross the Rubicon is to take a decisive step—by crossing it Caesar declared war on Pompey

rubbes: in game of bowls, impediments diverting the bowl from its course

salamander's wool: asbestos

Salmasius (Claude Saumaise), 1588–1653: French classical scholar

saltimbanco: quack

saltyr: (heraldry) an "ordinary" in form of St. Andrew's cross

salve: resolve by presenting an hypothesis to account for difficulties

salvifically: for our salvation

sapor: taste

sation: planting

scale and roundle: ladder and rung

Scaliger, J. C., 1484–1558: classical scholar and man of letters; everywhere recognized for his very great erudition

scenical: theatrical, fictitious

Schools, the: Schoolmen, scholastic philosophers and theologians collectively (from about 9th to 14th centuries)

Scribonius Largus: Roman physician who went to Britain with the Emperor Claudius in 43

sculptor: engraver, as well as in modern sense

Sebund, Raymond (Raymond of Sabunde): 15th-century Spanish scholar, physician, and theologian. His *Natural Theology* was translated by Montaigne

Sectaries: English Protestant dissenters

secutores: light-armed (pursuing) gladiators

Semiramis, c. 800 B.C.: Queen of Assyria to whose exertions Babylon owed its magnificence

sensible: perceptible by the senses as opposed to intelligible by reason; *sensible structures:* human beings

septentrionate: turn to the north

Servius: 4th-century grammarian famous for commentary on Virgil

sesqui-tertian: relation of one and one third to one, i.e. 4 to 3

Severus, Septimius, 145–211: Roman emperor

sharp: to fight at sharp is to duel with unbated swords

shop (*chop*): jaw

Sibyll: one of various women in classical fable and history thought to possess prophetic powers

Sibyll's leaves: a reference (from *Aeneid* 3.444–52) to the Sibyll of Cumae writing her prophecies on leaves

Sidonius Apollinaris: 4th-century Roman Christian author

sigil: seal supposed to have occult power

signality: meaning

signature: distinguishing mark, peculiarity in form or coloring on a plant or natural object supposed to indicate its qualities, especially for medicine

simples: herbs used medicinally

Sinah (Sinai), *law of:* the Ten Commandments

sinister: left-handed

sinistrously: maliciously, unfairly; also left-handedly

smallage: celery or parsley

smartly: vigorously

snast: the burning wick of a candle

Solinus: 3d-century Roman writer author of a collection (*Memorabilia* or *Polyhistor*) mostly taken from Pliny's *Natural History*

solisequious: following the sun

sorites: series of propositions in logic in which the predicate of each is the subject of the next

sortilegie: casting by lots
species: outward form
specifical: i.e. by the species
specious (Hydriotaphia 5): beautiful, handsome
speculate: ponder on
sphere: one of the concentric hollow globes which in Ptolemaic astronomy revolve around the earth
spruce: neat, lively
Spruceland: Prussia
stained: in glass or wood
station: condition of standing still
statist: statesman
steganography: secret writing, cipher
Stephanus (Henri Estienne), 1531–1598: French scholar and publisher
stiver: Dutch coin worth about a penny
Strabo: 1st-century Greek geographer whose *Geographia* is the principal geographical work of ancient times; he compared the then-known habitable world to a cloak
strift: striving
Stygian oaths: unbreakable oaths, sworn on the river Styx by the gods
Suarez, F., 1548–1617: Spanish Jesuit theologian and Thomist
subject (Hydriotaphia 1): substance
subventaneous: by snuffing the wind
sulphur: (alchemy) one of the supposed ultimate elements of all material substances
superstruction: higher rank
surd: irrational
swinge (or *swindge*): impetus, motion
sympathetical: depending on or effected by a real or supposed affinity, occult influence
Synesius, c. 373–414: bishop of Ptolemais, Neoplatonic philosopher and writer
tabidly: consumptively
Thargum or Targum: Aramaic or Chaldee paraphrases of Hebrew scriptures
telarely: like a web
telesm: talisman
temperament: constitution formed by the four humors
templa subdialia: temple with open galleries
tergiversation: retreat
terra damnata: residue after burning, etc. in alchemy or chemistry
terella: spherical loadstone or natural magnet

Tertullian: 3d-century Church Father

tetrick: morose, sour

Thales, 640–546 B.C.: regarded as the father of Greek science and philosophy

Theocritus, fl. 276 B.C.: Greek pastoral poet

Theophrastus, c. 370–286 B.C.: Greek philosopher, known especially for his enquiry into plants and his "characters"

Thersites: the most deformed and malicious of the Greeks in the Trojan war

theta: initial letter of Greek word for death, as inscribed on judge's ballot as death sentence

thrum: shaggy top

Thucydides, c. 460–400 B.C.: Greek historian

thwart: transverse

Timon: a type misanthrope, from Timon of Athens, a semi-legendary figure of the 5th century B.C.

Timotheus, c. 450–c. 360 B.C.: Greek poet, author of *The Persae,* known only in fragments

tincture: color; also (alchemy) quintessence or essential spiritual substance

topical: pertaining to topic or general maxim, hence not demonstrable

tortile: coiling

Tostatus (A. Tostato): 15th-century Spanish commentator on Genesis

tract: track; also in modern sense

traduction: transmission by generation to offspring as opposed to *infusion,* the doctrine of divine emanation after conception

transcorporating: referring to Pythagorean doctrine of transmigration of souls

treaty: treatise

treddle: albuminous cord, uniting yolk to white

Tricassus (P. Tricasso): 16th-century chiromancer and physiognomist

trepudiary: divination especially from sacred chickens

tropical: metaphorical; tropology: use of metaphor

tropics and defluxions: greatest height and curve downward (from astronomy)

tubes: telescopic tubes

Tycho: maker (from Greek)

types, mystical: prefigurations in interpretation of the Bible, as Melchisedec is a type of Christ

U finita: rule without exception, from rule of Latin prosody that last syllable of every word ending in *u* is long

uliginous: oozy

Ulmus (Giovanni Olmo): late 16th-century Italian physician and medical writer

uncous: hooked

undoing ("undoing fires"): ruinous since expensive

ultion: revenge

uniterable: unrepeatable

univocacy: normal generation or production (see *aequivocal production*)

utinam: would that, if only

vair: (heraldry) fur represented by bells or cup-shaped spaces

Valerianus (Piero Valeriano), 1477–1558: his *Hieroglyphica* first published in 1556, and thereafter in many editions and translations

Varro, M. T., 116–127 B.C.: Latin scholar and writer on agriculture

Vegetius (F. V. Renatus): 4th-century Latin writer on military matters

velleity: low degree of volition (i.e. not leading to action)

venation: hunting

veneficial: the result of malignant magic

vennie (venue): thrust in fencing

vernish: varnish (and so pronounced)

verticity: faculty of turning toward a pole, especially as shown in magnetic needle; polar strength

Verulam, Lord of: Francis Bacon

vespillo: man who carried out the dead at night

Vincentius Bellvacensis (Vincent of Beauvais), c. 1190–c. 1264: scholar and encyclopedist whose vast *Speculum Naturale* is a compendium of natural (and unnatural) history

Virgil, Polydore, c. 1470–1555: English historian of Italian extraction

visitation: inspection

Vitruvius (M. Vitruvius Pollio): 1st-century Roman architect and engineer whose *De Architectura* was rediscovered and published in 1486 and became the bible of classical architecture

vivacious: long-lived

Volupia: goddess of sensual pleasure

voluta: spiral twist or turn

Vossius, G. J. (G. J. Voss), 1577–1649: distinguished Dutch scholar and theologian

Vossius, Isaac, 1618–1689: son of G. J., scholar, canon of Windsor

vulgar translation: the Vulgate, or Latin version of the Bible made by St. Jerome; the authorized version for Roman Catholics

waster: wooden foil used in sword exercise

winded: bent

worm'd out: got rid of

Wormius (Ole Worm), 1588–1654: Danish scholar and antiquarian

Xenophon, c. 430 B.C.: Greek general, philosopher, historian

Zeno of Elea, c. 490 B.C.: Greek philosopher, called inventor of dialectic

Zeno, 335–263 B.C.: Greek philosopher, founder of the Stoic school

Zibethum occidentale: treated human excrement (Paracelsus)

Zoilism: carping criticism, from Zoilus, a grammarian and critic of Homer

Zoroaster (also known as Zarathustra): the first of the semimythical Magi, and reformer of religion; dates uncertain, pre-500 B.C.

THE NORTON LIBRARY
SEVENTEENTH-CENTURY SERIES

J. MAX PATRICK, *General Editor*